ROUTLEDGE HANDBOOK ON TURKISH LITERATURE

This *Handbook* provides a comprehensive overview of Turkish literature within both a local and global context.

Across eight thematic sections a collection of subject experts use close readings of literature materials to provide a critical survey of the main issues and topics within the literature. The chapters provide analysis on a wide range of genres and text types, including novels, poetry, religious texts, and drama, with works studied ranging from the fourteenth century right up to the present day. Using such a historic scope allows the volume to be read across cultures and time, while simultaneously contextualizing and investigating how modern Turkish literature interacts with world literature, and finds its place within it. Collectively, the authors challenge the national literary historiography by replacing the Ottoman Turkish literature in the Anatolian civilizations with its plurality of cultures. They also seek to overcome the institutional and theoretical shortcomings within current study of such works, suggesting new approaches and methods for the study of Turkish literature.

The *Routledge Handbook on Turkish Literature* marks a new departure in the reading and studying of Turkish literature. It will be a vital resource for those studying literature, Middle East studies, Turkish and Ottoman history, social sciences, and political science.

Didem Havlioğlu is a literary historian working on women and gender in the Ottoman intellectual culture. She has published several articles both in Turkish and English. Her book *Mihrî Hatun: Performance, Gender-Bending, and Subversion in Early Modern Ottoman Intellectual History* (2017) introduces Mihrî Hatun (ca. 1460–1515), the first woman writer in Ottoman history whose work survived in manuscript copies, and contextualizes her work in the early modern intellectual culture. She is currently an associate professor of the practice, teaching in the Department of Asian and Middle Eastern Studies at Duke University.

Zeynep Uysal is an associate professor of modern Turkish literature at Boğaziçi University. As a visiting scholar, she taught modern Turkish literature and gave public lectures in the Oriental Institute at the University of Oxford between 2001 and 2003. She published a book titled *Olağanüstü Masaldan Çağdaş Anlatıya: Muhayyelât-ı Aziz Efendi* [From Marvelous Tales to Modern Narratives: Aziz Efendi's Imaginations] in 2006. She edited a book, titled *Edebiyatın Omzundaki Melek: Edebiyatın Tarihle İlişkisi Üzerine Yazılar*, about the relationship between history and literature in 2011. Her recent book, *Metruk Ev*, on the leading modern Turkish writer Halit Ziya Uşaklıgil, was published in 2014. She has also written extensively on various issues in modern Turkish literature, including the relationship between literature and space, literature and history, and literature and nationalism in leading academic journals.

ROUTLEDGE HANDBOOK ON TURKISH LITERATURE

Edited by
Didem Havlioğlu and Zeynep Uysal

LONDON AND NEW YORK

Designed cover image: Murat Gülsoy

First published 2023
by Routledge
4 Park Square, Milton Park, Abingdon, Oxon OX14 4RN

and by Routledge
605 Third Avenue, New York, NY 10158

Routledge is an imprint of the Taylor & Francis Group, an informa business

© 2023 selection and editorial matter, Didem Havlioğlu and Zeynep Uysal; individual chapters, the contributors

The right of Didem Havlioğlu and Zeynep Uysal to be identified as the authors of the editorial material, and of the authors for their individual chapters, has been asserted in accordance with sections 77 and 78 of the Copyright, Designs and Patents Act 1988.

All rights reserved. No part of this book may be reprinted or reproduced or utilised in any form or by any electronic, mechanical, or other means, now known or hereafter invented, including photocopying and recording, or in any information storage or retrieval system, without permission in writing from the publishers.

Trademark notice: Product or corporate names may be trademarks or registered trademarks, and are used only for identification and explanation without intent to infringe.

British Library Cataloguing-in-Publication Data
A catalogue record for this book is available from the British Library

Library of Congress Cataloging-in-Publication Data
A catalog record for this book has been requested

ISBN: 978-0-367-23318-1 (hbk)
ISBN: 978-1-032-43186-4 (pbk)
ISBN: 978-0-429-27927-0 (ebk)

DOI: 10.4324/9780429279270

Typeset in Bembo
by Apex CoVantage, LLC

In memory of Walter G. Andrews

CONTENTS

Endorsements	*xi*
Acknowledgments	*xii*
Advisory Board	*xiv*
Contributor Biographies	*xv*

Introduction   1
Didem Havlioğlu and Zeynep Uysal

SECTION I
Mystical Genesis   17

1   It All Starts With a Dream: The Motif of Dream in Turkish Literature   19
    Özgen Felek

2   *Aşık* Literature in Historical Context   29
    Ali Aydın Karamustafa

3   Selfhood and Mystical Language in the Poetry of Yunus Emre   40
    Zeynep Oktay

SECTION II
Ottoman Poetics   57

4   Words That Are Daggers: Reassessing the Historical Dimensions
    of the Ottoman *Kaside*   59
    Oscar Aguirre-Mandujano

Contents

5 Gazel as Genre Among the Ottoman Ruling Elite
Selim S. Kuru — 70

6 Towards a Theory of Ottoman Allegory: Allegorical Narratives From
Ḥüsn ü Dil to *Ḥüsn ü 'Aşq*
Berat Açıl — 82

7 Human Voice Echoing in the Silence of God: Tevfik Fikret
and Modern Ottoman Poetry
Deniz Aktan Küçük — 93

SECTION III
Cultures of Reading — **103**

8 Reading and Writing Practices in the Ottoman Empire
İrvin Cemil Schick — 105

9 Rewriting as an Ottoman Translation Practice: Two *Bīh-i Çīnī*
Translations by Sixteenth-Century Poets
Gülşah Taşkın — 116

10 Narrative as the Literary Public: Reader and Author Figures in
Modern Ottoman Turkish Literature (1866–1896)
Fatih Altuğ — 127

SECTION IV
Women and Gender — **137**

11 Methodological Challenges in Late Ottoman and Turkish Literary
Scholarship: Gender, Aesthetics, and Sociopolitical Contexts
Hülya Adak — 139

12 Gender in Islamicate Ottoman Poetry
Didem Havlioğlu — 149

13 Gendered Narratives of Ottoman Prose Fiction: The "Wiles
of Women" Stories
N. İpek Hüner Cora — 160

14 Towards a Gynocritical Study of Turkish Fiction: Contemporary
Turkish Women's Literature (1950–1970)
Olcay Akyıldız — 169

Contents

SECTION V
Linguistic Diversity   **185**

15 Karamanlidika Literary Production in the Mid-nineteenth Century   187
   Şehnaz Şişmanoğlu Şimşek

16 Comparative Glimpse of the Early Steps of Novelistic Imagination in
   Turkish: Armeno-Turkish Novels of the 1850s and 1860s   198
   Murat Cankara

17 Making the "Other" Your Own: The Challenge of Modern Kurdish
   Literature Regarding Kurdish Voices in Turkish   209
   Suat Baran and Ömer Faruk Yekdeş

SECTION VI
National Identity   **221**

18 National Literary Historiography in Turkey: Mehmet Fuat Köprülü
   and His Legacy   223
   Halim Kara

19 Theatre as a Propaganda Tool From the Late Ottoman Empire
   to the 1930s   235
   Esra Dicle

20 Imagining the Nation From the Street: Nationalism, Daily Life,
   and Emotions in the Short Stories of Ömer Seyfettin   246
   Erol Köroğlu

21 Translated Humanism and the Making of Modern Turkey   256
   Fırat Oruç

SECTION VII
Literary Modernisms   **269**

22 Envisioning the Modern Individual in Late Nineteenth-Century
   Ottoman-Turkish Fiction   271
   Zeynep Uysal

23 "We, Too, Are Eastern": Nâzım Hikmet's Futurist and Anti-colonial
   Modernity   285
   Kenan Behzat Sharpe

Contents

24 The Emergence and the End of an Endemic Genre in Turkish
    Literature: The Case of the Village Novel in a Comparative Context   298
    Erkan Irmak

25 Poetic Urbanism in Turkish Modernist Poetry: Dramatic Monologue
    in the Second New Wave   309
    Veysel Öztürk

26 Laughter in the Dark: The Modernist Avant-Garde Path in
    Turkish Literature   321
    Murat Gülsoy

SECTION VIII
Political Turmoils and Traumas   **331**

27 The *Aufhebung* of Traumatic Memory: Literary Responses to
    Military Coups in Turkey and Çetin Altan's *Büyük Gözaltı*   333
    Çimen Günay-Erkol

28 Intelligentsia Narratives of the 1970s Turkish Novel   343
    Burcu Alkan

29 The Grammar of Conspiracy in Orhan Pamuk's *Snow*   354
    Erdağ Göknar

Timeline   *367*
Index   *449*

ENDORSEMENTS

A reasonable and balanced general survey of Turkish literature that is engaging and fun to read.
Orhan Pamuk

Rather than answer the question, What is Turkish literature?, this Handbook of Turkish Literature raises this very question in order to reveal the fictional basis of any such geopolitical and cultural historical category of literature. This is the gift of Havlioglu and Uysal's remarkable collection: To offer a model of a national tradition of literature that stretches the full seven centuries of print literature relatively untethered to a place, a people, or even a national vernacular—it travels, it absorbs and is absorbed by other literatures, it undergoes multiple translation. Such a model, in short, demonstrates just how our modern national literatures have always been global.
Nancy Armstrong

This comprehensive handbook of Turkish literature introduces readers to a hitherto obscured republic of letters. Stretching from the 14th century to today, the 29 authors cover all literary genres from the perspective of writers and readers alike. Sensitive to issues of gender, linguistic and ethnic diversity, performance, religion, politics and trauma, the volume provides a roadmap to over six centuries of fascinating history beginning with the formation of the long-lived Islamic Ottoman Empire to its revolutionary transformation into a secular nation-state. Bringing together leading scholars of Turkish literature, the editors have offered up an aesthetic feast that will delight specialists and general readers alike.

Miriam Cooke

This volume treats genres, developments, aspects of content, social function, ideology, and form, as well as the reception and conceptualization of Ottoman and Republican Turkish literature with remarkable breadth and outstanding depth. It will be an indispensable guide for both students and scholars to navigate through the unfathomable depths and the perilous shoals of the adventurous and exciting ocean of Turkish literature.

Julian Rentzsch

A comprehensive and indispensable guide to the study of Turkish literature.   *Robert Dankoff*

ACKNOWLEDGMENTS

When this project began in 2018, Walter Andrews was one of the central contributors. While fighting a terminal disease, he was also writing his chapter for this volume, titled "The Big Picture." As he wrote there, he was "looking back at the big picture of Ottoman (literary) history and pull[ing] together some things [he had] learned and written about over the past more than 50 years." Andrews devoted his career to deciphering Ottoman poetry for all of us and insisted on its relevance to everything we try to understand about the Ottomans. As he wrote in his draft,

> there is copious evidence that poetry was extremely important to the Ottomans. . . Poets gathered their poems in compilations called "divans," which contained many hundreds and even thousands of poems. Nearly all social events and ceremonies featured poetry. The *meclis* [medjlis], a salon or gathering with friends, poems, music, and cultured conversation was *a*—and perhaps *the*—prime venue for social networking. Powerful individuals, the equivalents of cabinet ministers, supreme court justices, theologians, and even sultans wrote poetry.

Unfortunately, he was unable to complete his final chapter. Many of us who contributed to this volume worked closely with Walter, either as his students or colleagues. He was instrumental in most of our careers and his work shaped the way we consider premodern Ottoman Turkish literature. Therefore, it is only appropriate to dedicate this volume to his memory.

This book would not be possible without the diligent work of the contributing writers. They did not give up even during the COVID-19 pandemic, which put tremendous pressure on the health and well-being of ourselves, our loved ones, and our communities. We are tremendously grateful to have worked with such scholars who deliver even during the hardest times.

Apart from the writers, we have been very lucky to receive intellectual support from our Advisory Board, which consists of both pioneers and younger generation of scholars such as Robert Dankoff, Hatice Aynur, Murat Belge, Nüket Esen, Erdağ Göknar, E. Efe Khayyat, Selim S. Kuru, Sibel Irzık, Jale Parla, İrvin Cemil Schick, and Halim Kara. We are grateful to all members of the board for meticulously reviewing the articles. Based on their judgment, we trust that the book provides the latest approaches to Turkish literature.

Acknowledgments

We have received generous funds from the Duke University Trent Grant and the Arts and Sciences Council Committee on Faculty Research (ASC-CFR). Thanks to their support, we were able to hold an editorial meeting at Duke University in February 2019 and hire our assistant editor Kenan Behzat Sharpe. Kenan was instrumental in making the 29 chapters consistent in language and style. His attention to detail and diligent care allowed the book to flow across chapters. The timeline at the end of the book emerged thanks to the meticulous work of Oltan Baran, a student at the Turkish Language and Literature Department of Boğaziçi University, with the support of its Nâzım Hikmet Culture and Art Research Center.

This book started as an initiative of Joe Whiting, the commissioning editor for Middle East, Islamic and Jewish studies at Routledge, who reached out to us four years ago with the idea of publishing a handbook on Turkish literature. We are thankful for his insight and trust in us to deliver it as a needed contribution in our field.

The cover image is a photograph taken by one of our contributors, Murat Gülsoy. The composition of the image reflects the arguments and discussions made in this volume. Gülsoy captured this image—especially thinking about the cover of this book—last summer in front of a park in Çanakkale's Ayvacık, an Aegean town in Turkey. We are thankful for his keen eye and willingness to share it as the face of the book.

ADVISORY BOARD

Hatice Aynur
Murat Belge
Robert Dankoff
Nüket Esen
Erdağ Göknar
Sibel Irzık
Halim Kara
E.Efe Khayyat
Selim S. Kuru
Jale Parla
Irvin Cemil Schick

CONTRIBUTOR BIOGRAPHIES

Berat Açıl received his PhD in Turkish language and literature from Boğaziçi University in 2010. He has taught at Istanbul Bilgi University (2007–2009) and Istanbul Şehir University (2010–2020). He is now a faculty member at Marmara University, where he teaches Ottoman literature. He is interested in the fields of Ottoman literature, allegory, narratology, literary theory, book culture, and manuscript studies. His most recent works focus on critical-edition studies on Ottoman literary texts and different aspects of Ottoman book culture. Some of his published books include *Klasik Türk Edebiyatında Alegori* (2018), *Osmanlı Kitap Kültürü: Cârullah Efendi Kütüphanesi ve Derkenar Notları* (2020), and *On Altıncı Yüzyılın Tanıklarından Cûşî ve Dîvânı* (2016).

Hülya Adak is the Director of SU Gender and holds a visiting scholar position at the Margherita von Brentano Zentrum at the Freie Universität Berlin. Since 2018, she has served as Professor of Ottoman and Turkish Studies at the Freie Universität Berlin. At Sabancı University, she cofounded the Cultural Studies BA and MA programs and Gender Studies PhD Programs. She is the recipient of the Alexander von Humboldt Fellowship for Experienced Researchers and Newton Grant (British Academy). Her articles in the fields of gender studies, memory and trauma studies, empire studies and nationalism, the history of human rights, literature, theater, and film studies have been published in prominent journals. Her recent works include *Mapping Gender: What's New and What's Ahead in Ottoman and Turkish Studies* (2022, with Richard Wittmann); *Gewalt, Diktaturen und Menschenrechte: Halide Edib in der Zwischenkriegszeit* (forthcoming); *Critical Perspectives on Genocide: History, Politics and Aesthetics of 1915* (forthcoming, with Müge Göçek and Ron Suny). She is currently working on the forthcoming book *Afterlives of Archives* (with Melanie Tanielian and Erdağ Göknar).

Oscar Aguirre-Mandujano is Assistant Professor of History at the University of Pennsylvania. His research focuses on the intellectual and cultural history of the early modern Ottoman Empire. He is currently working on his first monograph, which examines the relation between literary composition and the transformation of political thought in the early modern Islamic world.

Deniz Aktan Küçük received her BA in philosophy (2003) and both her MA (2007) and PhD (2014) in Turkish language and literature from Boğaziçi University. She worked as a research assistant at the Turkish Language and Literature Department there and has taught modern Turkish culture, literature, and language courses at Bahçeşehir University, Istanbul Şehir University, and Boğaziçi University. She has published various articles and book chapters, edited books on modern Ottoman/Turkish literature, and worked on the TÜBİTAK-supported research project, "Servet-i Fünun Journal in Ottoman Cultural History." Her research interests include nineteenth-century Ottoman literature and print culture, modern Turkish literature, and literary criticism.

Olcay Akyıldız received her PhD from the Comparative Literature Department of Tübingen University, Germany. Since 2001 she has been teaching at the Turkish Language and Literature Department at Boğaziçi University. She has edited a book on autobiographical genres and a book on travel writing. She is a member of the editorial board of the journals *Toplum ve Bilim* and *Metafor* and a member of the executive board of Boğaziçi University Nâzım Hikmet Culture and Art Research Center. She directs a project on the personal archive of the Turkish author Leylâ Erbil. She edited a book with Murat Gülsoy on Nâzım Hikmet, which was published as *Şiir Dünyadan İbaret: Nâzım Hikmet Üzerine Yeni Çalışmalar.*

Burcu Alkan is a research fellow at the Europe in the Middle East / The Middle East in Europe program of the Forum Transregionale Studien, Berlin. She is also an honorary research fellow at the English, American Studies and Creative Writing program of the University of Manchester. She received her PhD at the same department in Manchester in 2009, and her doctoral dissertation was later published in Germany as *Promethean Encounters: Representation of the Intellectual in the Modern Turkish Novel of the 1970s* (2018). She is also the co-editor (with Çimen Günay-Erkol) of a two-volume reference work: *Dictionary of Literary Biography: Turkish Novelists Since 1960* (2013, 2016). Her latest book is co-edited collection (also with Çimen Günay-Erkol) titled *Turkish Literature as World Literature* (2021). She is currently working within the field of medical humanities with a focus on the relationship between literature and psychiatry.

Fatih Altuğ is an assistant professor in the Turkish Language and Literature Department of Boğaziçi University, where he also earned his PhD. His work focuses mostly on representations of subjectivity, agency, and gender in modern Ottoman-Turkish literature. His current research explores literary networks of women writers in the late Ottoman period. He recently published *Kapalı İktisat Açık Metin* (Closed Economy Open Text) in 2018. His articles on writers such as Namık Kemal, Fuad Köprülü, Sevgi Soysal, and Onat Kutlar have appeared in journals and essay collections in Turkey.

Suat Baran has studied modern Greek language and English language teaching for his BA degrees and cultural studies in the MA program at Istanbul Bilgi University. He is currently a PhD student at the Turkish Language and Literature Department at Boğaziçi University. His fields of interest include identity, silence, children studies, and Balkan and Middle Eastern literatures in a world literature context.

Murat Cankara majored in drama in Ankara University (2001). He received his PhD, in Turkish literature, from Bilkent University with a dissertation titled "Empire and Novel: Placing Armeno-Turkish Novels in Ottoman/Turkish Literary Historiography" (2011) where he focused on the novels written by Ottoman Armenians in the Turkish language using the Armenian script between 1850 and 1870. He was a fulbright visiting fellow at Harvard University, in the departments of Comparative Literature and Near Eastern Languages and Civilizations, in the academic years 2007–2008 and 2012–2013 Manoogian Simone Foundation Post-Doctoral Fellow in the Armenian Studies Program at the University of Michigan, Ann Arbor, where he gave a course on Armeno-Turkish texts. He is currently a member of the Faculty of Social Sciences and Humanities at the Social Sciences University of Ankara and is particularly interested in the historiography of Ottoman/Turkish theatre and popular performances, the nineteenth-century literary culture of the Ottoman Empire, encounters between Armenians and Turks, as well as modern Ottoman/Turkish literature and the social history of Turkish language. He edited *Ankara Vukuatı: Menfilik Hatıralarım* [The Ankara Incident: My Memoir of Exile by Simon Arakelian], an Armeno-Turkish testimony which was originally published in 1921 (Aras Publishing, 2017) and *Boşboğaz Bir Âdem* [A Garrulous Person by Hovsep Vartanian], a satirical piece which was printed in Istanbul in 1852 (Koç University Press, 2017). He also published extracts from the late Ottoman Empire Armenian press for the journal *Toplumsal Tarih* between 2018 and 2021 and wrote monthly book reviews for the *Agos* newspaper between 2014 and 2020.

Esra Dicle has been an instructor in Turkish courses at Boğaziçi University since 2005. She received her MA and PhD in Turkish language and literature from Boğaziçi University. Her PhD thesis, "Official Ideology Is on the Stage: The Effect of the People's Houses Period Theater Plays on the Construction of Kemalist Ideology") was published in Turkish in 2013. Her second book, *Ben Yüz Çiçekten Yanayım: Nâzım Hikmet Tiyatrosunda Metinler-Türler-Söylemler*" (I Am for Hundred Flowers: Texts, Genres, Discourses in Nâzım Hikmet's Theatre) was published in 2020. She lectures on Turkish language, literature, modern theatre, adaptation theory, and theatricality at Boğaziçi University.

Özgen Felek is a lecturer of Ottoman Turkish at Yale University. Her research interests include early modern Ottoman literature, gender, and Sufism. In addition to several articles, she published a collection of Walter G. Andrews' nonacademic work, *Walter G. Andrews: Writer, Poet, Playwright, Unitarian Universalist* (2021), and a diplomatic edition of Ottoman Sultan Murad III's dream letters, *Kitābü'l-Menāmāt Sultan III. Murad'ın Rüya Mektupları* (2014). She is also co-editor of *Dreams and Visions in Islamic Societies* (2012) with Alexander Knysh, and *Victoria Rowe Holbrook'a Armağan* (2006) with Walter G. Andrews.

Erdağ Göknar is Associate Professor of Turkish Studies in the Department of Asian and Middle Eastern Studies at Duke University and former director of the Duke Middle East Studies Center. He is a scholar of literary and cultural studies and an award-winning translator whose research focuses on late Ottoman legacies in contemporary Turkish fiction, historiography, and popular culture. His books include *Orhan Pamuk, Secularism and Blasphemy: The Politics of the Turkish Novel* (2013); the co-edited volume *Mediterranean Passages: Readings from Dido to Derrida* (2008); and English-language translations of Ahmet Hamdi Tanpınar's *A Mind at Peace* (2011), Orhan Pamuk's *My Name Is Red* (2001; 2010), and Atiq Rahimi's *Earth and Ashes* (2002).

Murat Gülsoy, engineer, academician, writer, started his literary career as a publisher and a writer of the bimonthly magazine *Hayalet Gemi* (Ghost Ship) in 1992. He has published short stories, novels, and literary essays since then, and his works have been translated into many languages. He is the recipient of some of the most prestigious Turkish literary awards. He was the chairperson of the editorial board of Boğaziçi University Press from 2003 to 2021.

Çimen Günay-Erkol works on Cold War anxieties, masculinity, and trauma. Currently, she is associate professor of Turkish literature at Özyeğin University. She co-edited *Turkish*

Literature as World Literature (2020) and two volumes of the *Dictionary of Literary Biography*, consisting of bio-bibliographical essays on writers of Turkey, with Burcu Alkan. Her book *Broken Masculinities* (2016) focuses on the Turkish 1968 movements and her recent project targets neo-patriarchal discourses advocated by state-supported nongovernmental organizations.

Didem Havlioğlu is a literary historian working on women and gender in the Ottoman intellectual culture. She has published several articles both in Turkish and English. Her book *Mihrî Hatun: Performance, Gender-Bending, and Subversion in Ottoman Intellectual History* (2017), introduces Mihrî Hatun (ca. 1460–1515), the first woman writer in Ottoman history whose work survived in manuscript copies and contextualizes her work in the early modern intellectual culture. Havlioğlu is currently an Associate Professor of the Practice, teaching in the Department of Asian and Middle Eastern Studies at Duke University.

N. İpek Hüner Cora received her PhD from the Department of Near Eastern Languages and Civilizations at the University of Chicago. She is currently an assistant professor in the Turkish Language and Literature Department at Boğaziçi University. Her research interests include the history of Ottoman literature in the early modern period, gender, and sexuality. She is especially interested in tracing stories and their versions featuring women across centuries and geographies. Among her publications is " 'Isn't She a Woman?': The 'Widow of Ephesus' in the Ottoman Empire," which appeared in the *Journal of Near Eastern Studies* in 2020.

Erkan Irmak was born in 1983 in Istanbul. He completed his undergraduate, graduate and doctorate degrees at Boğaziçi University, Department of Turkish Language and Literature. In addition to his two books on Nâzım Hikmet and village novels, he continues to publish articles on Turkish and world literatures. His main areas of interest are late-Ottoman literature, early-Republican period, genre studies, nationalism and leftist literature. He still teaches Turkish language and literature at Sabancı University.

Halim Kara teaches modern Turkish literature in the Department of Turkish Language and Literature at Boğaziçi University, Istanbul, Turkey. He was a visiting scholar in the Department of Oriental Studies at the University of Oxford for the 2003–2004 and 2004–2005 academic years and in the Department of Near Eastern Languages and Civilizations at the University of Chicago for the 2016–2017 academic year. He has published articles in English and Turkish on various literary and cultural issues in modern Turkish and contemporary Central Asian Turkic literatures. His books include (co-edited with Olcay Akyıldız and Börte Sagaster) Autobiographical *Themes in Turkish Literature* (Würzburg: Ergon Verlag, 2007) and *Osmanlı'yı Tahayyül Etmek: Tarihsel Romanda Fatih Temsilleri* (Boğaziçi University Press in 2017). Kara's forthcoming book projects will examine modern literary historiography in Turkish literature and the 1940s novelistic turn in Turkish fiction.

Ali Aydın Karamustafa is a historian of the Ottoman and Safavid worlds. His research focuses on oral and written traditions concerning origins, conquest, legitimacy, and rebellion which were produced and circulated by political communities from the fourteenth to the eighteenth centuries. He received his PhD from Stanford in 2020 and is currently a postdoctoral researcher at the University of Ca' Foscari in Venice, in the Department of Asian and North African Studies.

Erol Köroğlu is Associate Professor of Modern Turkish Literature at Boğaziçi University's Turkish Language and Literature Department. His dissertation was published both in Turkish

Contributor Biographies

(in 2004 as *Türk Edebiyatı ve Birinci Dünya Savaşı (1914–1918): Propagandadan Millî Kimlik İnşasına*) and in English (in 2007 as *Ottoman Propaganda and Turkish Identity: Turkish Literature during World War I*). The Turkish version was awarded the Afet Inan History Award of the History Foundation in 2004. He has published many articles and book chapters in English and Turkish. He also studies the emergence of the novel in Turkish, Turkish nationalist movements, and narrative theory.

Selim S. Kuru is Associate Professor of Ottoman and Turkish Language and Literature in the Department of Middle Eastern Languages and Cultures at the University of Washington. His current research focuses on the development and function of literature among the male elite circles of Istanbul at the turn of the sixteenth-century Ottoman Empire.

Zeynep Oktay completed her PhD in Islamic civilization at Sorbonne University École Pratique des Hautes Études in Paris, France. She currently works as an assistant professor at the Turkish Language and Literature Department at Boğaziçi University, where she teaches courses on Sufism, folklore, and the emergence of Turkish literature. Oktay is the author of *Mesnevî-i Baba Kaygusuz* (Harvard University Department of Near Eastern Languages and Literatures, 2013), as well as articles published in journals such as *BJMES, JOTSA*, and *Turcica*. Oktay's forthcoming monograph, titled *Kaygusuz Abdal and His Book of Prattle*, focuses on the literature produced by antinomian Sufi groups (*abdals*) in Anatolia and the Balkans.

Fırat Oruç is Associate Professor of Comparative Literature at Georgetown University's School of Foreign Service in Qatar. His scholarship has appeared in a range of peer-reviewed journals, including *English Language Notes, Criticism, Postcolonial Text, Journal of World Literature, Comparative Literature*, and *Film History*. He is also the editor of *Sites of Pluralism: Community Politics in the Middle East* (2019), which examines which examines state and community relations in the Middle East. He is currently working on two book projects: one on world literature and the making of modern Turkey, and the other on the cultural and political history of film in the Arabian Peninsula.

Veysel Öztürk is an assistant professor in the Department of Turkish Language and Literature at Boğaziçi University, Istanbul. He received his BA and MA degrees from the same university. He received his PhD in 2010 with his dissertation entitled "The Rise of Romantic Subjectivity in Turkish Poetry". His research interests are early modern Turkish poetry, nineteenth century Turkish periodicals, Ottoman-Turkish literary modernization.

İrvin Cemil Schick holds a PhD from MIT and has taught at Harvard University, MIT, and Istanbul Şehir University. He is the author, editor, or co-editor of 12 books including *The Erotic Margin: Sexuality and Spatiality in Alteritist Discourse* and *Writing the Body, Society, and the Universe: On Islam, Gender, and Culture* (in Turkish). His research interests include the Islamic arts of the book; gender, sexuality, spatiality, and the body in Islam; occult practices in Islam; and animals and the environment in Islam. He is currently working on a second doctorate at École des Hautes Etudes en Sciences Sociales (EHESS, Paris).

Kenan Behzat Sharpe received his PhD in 2019 from the Literature Department of the University of California, Santa Cruz. His research focuses on twentieth-century Turkish literature and history, modernism, aesthetics and politics, popular music, the cultural production of protest movements, and Greek-Turkish connections. His work has appeared in the *Journal* *of Ottoman and Turkish Studies, Dibur Literary Journal,* and *Turkish Historical Review.* During the 2022–2023 academic year, he is a postdoctoral research fellow with the American Research Institute in Turkey for his project "Rockers and Radicals in Anatolia: Turkish Psychedelic Music and the Global 1960s."

Şehnaz Şişmanoğlu Şimşek is an assistant professor at Kadir Has University in Istanbul, where she coordinates the Turkish courses. She received her PhD from the Turkish Language and Literature Department at Boğaziçi University with a doctoral thesis on Karamanlidika literature (Turkish in Greek script) in the nineteenth century. Her research interests also include nineteenth-century Ottoman-Greek culture and literature, Ottoman minority literatures, the serial novel, rewriting, intertextuality, and gender studies. Currently she is a postdoctoral fellow in the European Research Council's Starting Grants Program with the project "Staging National Abjection: Theatre and Politics in Turkey and Its Diasporas."

Gülşah Taşkın is an assistant professor in the Turkish Language and Literature Department at Boğaziçi University. She received her MA in classical Ottoman literature from Boğaziçi University and her PhD in 2009 from Marmara University with a dissertation titled "A Divan by Zarifi from Çorlu: Textual Analysis and Critical Edition." During 2016–2017 she conducted her postdoctoral studies on autobiographical texts in Ottoman literature at the University of Washington, Seattle. In addition, she is the Project Manager and Editor of the Baki Project at the University of Washington. Her fields of interest include Ottoman Turkish, Ottoman paleography, classical Ottoman poetry, autobiographical texts in Ottoman literature, Ottoman textual studies, and digital humanities.

Zeynep Uysal is an associate professor of modern Turkish literature at Boğaziçi University. As a visiting scholar, she taught modern Turkish literature and gave public lectures in the Oriental Institute at the University of Oxford between 2001 and 2003. In 2006, she published *Olağanüstü Masaldan Çağdaş Anlatıya: Muhayyelât-ı Aziz Efendi* [From Marvelous Tales to Modern Narratives: *Aziz Efendi's Imaginations*]. In 2011, she edited *Edebiyatın Omzundaki Melek: Edebiyatın Tarihle İlişkisi Üzerine Yazılar* about the relationship between history and literature. Her recent book, *Metruk Ev*, on the leading modern Turkish writer Halit Ziya Uşaklıgil, was published in 2014. She has also written extensively on various issues in modern Turkish literature, including the relationship between literature and space, literature and history, and literature and nationalism in leading academic journals.

Ömer Faruk Yekdeş studied theology in Ankara University in 2001 and then received his MA in Turkish literature from Bilkent University, Ankara, in 2008 with the dissertation "The Ideology of Nâzım Hikmet and Cegerxwîn's Love Poetry." He is continuing his graduate studies as a PhD student at the Department of Turkish Language and Literature at Boğaziçi University. His main fields of interest include literary theory, cultural history, postcolonial studies, and comparative literature.

INTRODUCTION

Didem Havlioğlu and Zeynep Uysal

The Routledge Handbook of Turkish Literature is a product of recent studies in Turkish literature and seeks to provide an overview to assist the reading and studying of Turkish literature today. Although it covers literary production in Anatolia and the Balkans from the fourteenth century to the present, it is not a chronological history of Turkish literature. Rather, it is a broad critical survey, organized around thematic sections, with chapters written by leading literary specialists. These chapters represent the growing interest in, new approaches to, and overall state of the field.

Inspired by David Damrosh's concept of the "glocal"—a term defined as "think globally, act locally" by the nongovernmental agencies of the 1990s—this volume presents Turkish literature as world literature.[1] Damrosh explains his appropriation of the term for literary studies for thinking about local issues while considering global readership. Damrosh refers to Orhan Pamuk, who received the 2006 Nobel Prize in Literature, and points to his novels as good examples of glocal authors and literature. This award marked a significant moment not only for Pamuk but also Turkish literature more broadly being accepted as a part of world literature. Growing interest allowed translations from the original Turkish to languages including primarily but not limited to English. However, from the 2000s onwards, "glocality" as a concept became insufficient for explaining the multiplicity and diversity of Turkish literature. Whether or not their work is translated into other languages, contemporary writers in Turkish have been engaging with global issues. While they are unapologetically local, they have the potential to belong to anywhere and everywhere. In our era of the Anthropocene, the climate crisis, and the digital and cyber worlds, more and more texts are written in Turkey that think transnationally, transculturally, and in terms of the post–human.

As a contribution to the growing interest in reading Turkish literature as world literature in the contemporary period, this volume showcases earlier periods and their literary productions also as part of world literature.[2] To do so, we switch the focus from the author's intention to the methods of reading or studying literature. In other words, for the earlier periods, we see a developing interest in contextualizing Turkish literature in a global context. For instance, recent studies on Islamic genres such as the *gazel* or *kaside* within the context of Arab, Persian, Ottoman, or Urdu literatures allow for readings across cultures and time.[3] Similarly, the mystical foundations of Ottoman Turkish literature have been discussed within the larger context of Neoplatonic ideals from Europe and Asia to North Africa.[4]

DOI: 10.4324/9780429279270-1

Introduction

For this handbook on Turkish literature in English, we organized the contributions around global issues such as gender, mysticism, and the poetics of literary practice, while the individual chapters make arguments based on close readings of the local materials. Our hope is that this organizational schema will allow readers to make comparisons to other world literatures through specific themes. We would like to encourage further research in the areas that inevitably surfaced throughout the process of compiling this volume. Each thematic section is relevant to both global and local contexts, including cases from different periods in Turkish literature. This makes it possible to trace continuities, transitions, and deviations from the norm. Although the discussions we have compiled around particular themes represent the variety of interests in the field today, it does not include everything the way an encyclopedia or literary history would. Instead, this volume represents contemporary interests and methods of reading Turkish literature in the broader global context.

This volume intends to challenge the established study of Turkish literature, which is still influenced by the scholarship produced by the nationalist ideals of the twentieth century. For instance, based on the principles of national literary historiography, even today, studies in Turkish are mainly divided into two periodizing categories: the Old (premodern) literature and the New (modern) literature. This volume seeks to address the institutional and theoretical shortcomings of this binary division. Moreover, we scrutinize the concept of "Turkishness" as a pure linguistic or ethnic origin for Turkish literature. Instead of following national literary historiography, we focus on alternative dimensions that highlight the literary and linguistic diversities that constitute what we call "Turkish literature" today.

Covering more than 600 years of a literary tradition, from its multilingual and multicultural imperial roots to the secular nation-state, is an arduous task and requires deliberate choices. Rather than repeating what can be found in existing literary histories, anthologies, and/or encyclopedias of Turkish literature, our goal is to ask critical questions about conceptual frameworks that allow us to better read across historical periods and expand our understanding of what Turkish literature entails.

Defining literary traditions through a single language as a static entity is a modern phenomenon and was determined by the political ideologies of the nineteenth and twentieth centuries. The Turkish case is no different. Before the rise of the nationalist movements in the region, literatures were defined by celebrated authors who wrote their works in multiple languages and were invited to join royal courts, such as that of the Safavids or the Ottomans, regardless of their linguistic or ethnic origin. The organic relationship between Islamic languages and cultures— such as Qur'anic influence, the hadith tradition, or Persianate court etiquette—is still visible in Turkish literature. Even though it occurred sporadically, it was not uncommon for European poets or artists to also visit Ottoman courts.

From the nineteenth century onward, however, European works, in particular by French writers, began to influence both the language and genres used in literary circles. Students of Turkish literature are aware of the drastic changes in language from one period to another, reflecting the shifting cultural and political landscape. Recent studies have paid attention to the diverse linguistic and religious backdrop of Turkish literature, in addition to Turkish and Islamic roots. Besides the expected linguistic influences of Persian, Arabic, or French, for instance, recent studies discuss the languages of Anatolia (such as Greek, Armenian, and Kurdish) that interacted with Turkish and Anatolian culture.

Our purpose in this volume is to unravel the modern construction of Turkish language and literature. After the collapse of the Ottoman Empire in the wake of World War I, and the foundation of the Turkish Republic in 1923, creating a modern Turkish language was one of the major concerns of the new nation-state. A series of language reforms were undertaken

Introduction

to transform Ottoman Turkish into modern Turkish, whether by changing the script from Arabic to Latin or by engineering the "cleansing" of Arabic of Persian loanwords.[5] The language reform project was conducted by a state-sponsored organization, the Türk Dil Kurumu (Turkish Language Association). In the same vein, the literary histories of the period formed a modern Turkish national identity in this period by searching for linguistic purity in the Central Asian roots of Turks and their language. This intervention sought to effect a clear break from the Ottoman past, but it also resulted in the exclusion of ethnic and linguistic minorities from mainstream histories. The exclusionary process began in the late nineteenth century and continued in the Republican period, during which the nation-state was founded on an ideology of Turkishness as imagined by Republican elites who sought also to nationalize the country's literature. National literary historiography sought and discovered its Turkish origins in Central Asia at the expense of imperial cultural sources. The attempts to "purify" it from other Islamic literatures and languages, such as Persian and Arabic, did not mean that the project was open to the inclusion of the minority languages of Anatolia such as Greek or Armenian.

In the Republican period, the study of Turkish literature took an unprecedented turn spearheaded by leading literary historian and ideologue Mehmed Fuad Köprülü, when he claimed a pre-Islamic existence for the Turkish language and its literary productions.[6] Apart from language, the religion of this literature was rediscovered as a form of specifically Anatolian Islam, mystical and humanist and therefore thought to be compatible with the secular nature of the new nation-state. This form of mystical Islam, however, has been part of Islamic history since its inception and appears in various languages, cultures, and geographies.[7]

Although the Turkish scholarship has primarily focused on Muslim Turkish texts in the Ottoman period, this volume includes the work of researchers studying the Kurdish (Muslim but not Turkish) or Jewish, Greek, and Armenian sources of Ottoman literature. Our intention is to examine the construction of Ottoman imperial identity through its diversity of literary texts, languages, and genres. In terms of the cultural and religious legacies of Ottoman Turkish literature, particularly before the nineteenth century, the ties to the Islamic world are clear. Ottoman poetry was primarily influenced by Islamic literatures, and its actors positioned themselves vis-à-vis the great poets of the Muslim world.

Encountering European modernity in the nineteenth century, however, the Ottoman Empire embarked on a social, cultural, and political project of modernization. Accordingly, a modern literature began to appear in literary and cultural productions of all communities in the empire, including Armenian Ottomans who published the first Turkish novel in the Armenian alphabet.[8] This volume examines the major turning points of late nineteenth-century Ottoman and early Republican literature in response to this new encounter with European modernity with all its sociopolitical consequences. In this period, literary texts begin to problematize modernity and the modern subject within a broader global framework. The quest for a new identity played out through a struggle between westernization, a revival of pan-Islamism, and imperial ideals. All of this renders the axis of East-West and modern-traditional pivotal for understanding the literary movements of the period. This was the period when literary texts dealt with the questions of the individual and national identities, the invention of a new literature, cultural modernity, linguistic diversity, and gender. They explored the construction of the new Ottoman individual, the literary tools and genres employed in this construction, the role of the novel as a new literary genre, and the transformation of poetry in relation to fin-de-siècle literary movements around the world.

As we mentioned, this volume investigates how modern Turkish literature interacts with world literature, exposing the coincidences and intersections between thematic and narrative structures. Pushing against early Republican literature as an isolated and self-centered literature until

Introduction

the 1940s, the end of the 1940s saw literary movements open themselves up to encounters with world literatures and global literary developments. Literary texts began to probe cross-cultural issues. The country's foundational poetic doxas began to lose their dominance as the official authoritarian discourse was increasingly challenged by oppositional discourses and increasing narrative/thematic diversity. This was also the start of the period, lasting into our contemporary moment, in which consecutive military coups attempted to maintain the political and social status quo by suppressing and brutally destroying social diversity and political opposition. Yet, diversity and critical thinking have been maintained in literature precisely through narrative and thematic tools enriched by transcultural encounters. Given the drastic movement away from nationalist ideals in the contemporary literary scene, this volume investigates how modern Turkish literature interacts with world literature, searching it out and finding its place within it.

A Brief History of Turkish Literature in English

Even though this volume is not a history of Turkish literature, it will be useful to briefly survey the major literary histories produced so far in order to situate this book in the existing scholarship, particularly in Anglophone academia. The first attempt to present a concise overview of Turkish literature was in the fifteenth century with the production of *tezkire*s, or biographical dictionaries. These were compiled to preserve the names of poets from various provinces in certain periods.[9] They were commissioned by various rulers and intended to claim space for an Ottoman literature while still recognizing the great Persian poets. It is worth noting that at this point, the Ottomans still produced work using Arabic and Persian genres, such as the *tezkire* itself, as the most common form of literary history. This was also a period of mass translations from both languages into Ottoman Turkish, such as the interlinear interpretations of the Qur'an, hadith collections, and classical Persian poems.

In the twentieth century, the *tezkire*s were replaced by encyclopedias and anthologies as modern versions employing a similar methodology. One of the major sources of Turkish literature and history in English is the *Encyclopedia of Islam*[10] or its Turkish version, *İslam Ansiklopedisi*,[11] produced by the Türkiye Diyanet Vakfı. It follows the method of *tezkire*s in listing major authors and their works. The general survey entries written about Turkish literature in resources such as the *Encyclopedia Britannica* or the *Encyclopedia of Islam* are usually organized around the literary-historical classifications and periodization of national literary historiography produced using the Republican approach. In particular, these encyclopedic articles seek to introduce Turkish literary production in all genres and periods starting from the eighth-century Orkhon Inscriptions in Central Asia as the representative of the earliest extant writing in Turkish.

Literary modernity in the nineteenth century altered the understanding of premodern literary history present in the *tezkire*s. It was in the early twentieth century that Fuat Köprülü systematically developed national literary historiography. From then on, his literary periodization and classification in particular has dominated Turkish literary historiography.

The first literary history of Ottoman Turkish literature in English was E.G.W. Gibb's six-volume work published between 1900 and 1909. It is a massive compilation of Ottoman poets from the fifteenth to nineteenth centuries directly translated from the *tezkire*s.[12] Nearly a century later, Louis Mitler produced bibliographical dictionaries that followed a similar format for later periods, with one covering the Republican period[13] and another following developments into the 1980s.[14] The prolific Turkish poet, translator, and academic Talât Halman published numerous books and articles in English on Turkish literature. He also completed several Turkish literary histories consisting of essays or chapters categorized according to literary-historical periodization or thematic issues. The last such work by Halman was *A Millennium of Turkish*

4

Literature: A Concise History, which reintroduced the Central Asian roots in an incredibly concise overview of Turkish literary history spanning fewer than 200 pages.[15] His *Rapture and Revolution: Essays on Turkish Literature* presents literary history from another perspective with a collection of essays and articles on Turkish literary tradition in different genres and periods.[16] Similarly, several multiauthor volumes that have been published consist of essays that offer a broader perspective by focusing on different aspects of literature. These individual chapters on Turkish literature provide some of the most concise introductions to anyone interested in the subject.[17]

There are also a number of influential English-language anthologies that used a similar chronological method and offered translations of literary works accompanied by relatively detailed introductions. These anthologies introduced English speakers to Turkish authors and their works. *Ottoman Lyric Poetry* was the first collection of translations of Ottoman poetry that included explanations of literary terms and concepts in detail.[18] Another compilation by Kemal Silay that included the twentieth century still presents a concise overview of literary works in Turkish across different periods and genres.[19] Apart from anthologies, there are a number of book-length translations in English from earlier periods to the present day.[20] Talât Halman was one of the pioneers in this area with his many translations of ancient and contemporary literary works.[21]

As for monographs in English based on critical research, Walter Andrews' first book, *Poetry's Voice, Society's Song*,[22] and his final book-length contribution with co-author Mehmet Kalpaklı both offer unprecedented ways of reading Ottoman poetry and poetic culture in the early modern era.[23] These works have changed the way Ottoman poetry is studied and offer discussions on sociopolitical issues such as gender in the literary cultures of Ottoman history. Some additional monographs follow a similar critical approach to the study of Ottoman poetry in English. Victoria Holbrook's work on Şeyh Galip and his magnum opus *Beauty and Love* introduced an alternative methodology for studying Ottoman literary culture. More recent welcome contributions include Didem Havlioğlu's work on Mihrî Hatun, the first Ottoman woman poet whose poetry has survived in manuscript form, and Sooyong Kim's study of another celebrated early modern Ottoman poet, Zatî.[24]

There have also been noteworthy monographs published on the novel and contemporary Islamic literature in Turkey.[25] Until the 2000s, the scholarship in English mainly sought to introduce Turkish literature to foreign readers, in particular English-speaking students outside Turkey, while offering source material to instructors teaching Turkish language and culture. These works paved the way for later contextualizations of Turkish literature as part of world literature and allowed Turkish literary studies to be included in transnational and transcultural academia. Recent contributions in this vein include Azade Seyhan's study of the modern Turkish novel, Erdağ Göknar's work on Orhan Pamuk, and Nergis Ertürk's reading of Turkish modernity in a theoretical framework. These all represent particular analytical perspectives treating modern Turkish literary history within a global context.[26]

Thematic Sections

The first thematic section of this book, "Mystical Genesis," covers the early establishment of Turkish literature in Anatolia starting in the fourteenth century. This first section lays the groundwork for the following chapters, primarily in the next two sections, as mysticism will come up time and again in discussions of Ottoman poetics and gender. "Mystical Genesis" opens with Özgen Felek's overview of one of the most popular literary devices in Turkish literature: dreams. As Felek writes in her chapter, fittingly titled "It All Starts With a Dream," dreams are one of the most frequently recurring motives in Turkish literature, whether the dream that marked the genesis of the Ottoman Empire or the one at the beginning of Evliya Çelebi's monumental travelogue that covers almost the entirety of Ottoman geographies, ethnicities, and languages. Dreams appear in almost all genres—such as histories, biographical dictionaries, and poetry collections—and in a genre of its own, dream compilations. Felek discusses the function of dreams as a literary tool in various genres across different periods as she masterfully brings examples from pre-Islamic and Central Asian contexts and merges them with the example of Ottoman Islamic literature.

Ali Aydın Karamustafa presents the early formulations of literature through his discussion of *aşık*s, or minstrels who traveled around and sang songs in syllabic meter. Like Felek, Karamustafa does not remain limited to Anatolia but connects the tradition to both the pre-Islamic Oghuz Turkish past and a vast geography. More accurately, he suggests that the region for *aşık* performance was Eurasia (the Balkans, Anatolia, the Caucasus, and Iran). However, in the specifically Turkish Anatolian context, he highlights the diffusion of the Turkish language in the colloquial Turkish that *aşık*s used. Karamustafa suggests that *aşık*s contributed to the period's literature more broadly in various genres such as letter writing and also left their mark on elite literature. Moreover, *aşık*s composed in different languages, such as Armenian, and in different public spaces, such as Sufi lodges, coffee houses, and private homes.

Just as Karamustafa introduces mystical poetry through *aşık* literature, Zeynep Oktay discusses Yunus Emre, the father of Anatolian Turkish mystical poetry. She argues that Yunus' reception transformed based on certain historical and political pressures. She focuses specifically on the Republican period, when Yunus was embraced as the quintessential Turkish poet, and on Islamist movements after the 1990s, which transformed him into a Muslim. As Oktay deftly addresses the intersections among mystical poetry, selfhood, language, and meaning, she also showcases how to read mystical poetry, both in terms of close readings and literary style but also in the larger context spanning historical temporalities. Like Karamustafa, Oktay highlights the significance of language in the formation of Turkish literature in Anatolia.

The second section, titled "Ottoman Poetics," theorizes the development of a performative courtly practice and changes in the later periods while introducing readers to three major genres of Ottoman literature: the *kaside, gazel*, and *mesnevi*. All three genres were inherited from Arabic and Persian literatures. These chapters contextualize them not only within the larger context and history of Ottoman literature but also in comparison with their Arabic and Persian predecessors. Each chapter elaborates on how Ottomans used Islamic genres for their own purposes from the premodern period to the nineteenth century. Selim S. Kuru marks the date 1453, when the Ottomans conquered Constantinople and began building a Muslim Istanbul, as the turning point when Ottoman literature started to become a literature of its own.

Unlike traditional readings of the *kaside* based on its basic function of praising the ruler—which has caused the genre to be dismissed as artificial and pretentious—Oscar Aguirre-Mandujano theorizes it as directly related to the power through the patronage of rulers and administrators. He reads a classical poem by Necatî, one of the most celebrated Ottoman poets, and maps out the sections and subgenres of the poem. Putting the practice of patronage at center stage, he carefully points out the importance of understanding the influence of various kinds of patrons, not only the sultan or his grand vizier. Aguirre-Mandujano argues that the *kaside* should be understood as a communal activity and/or economic tool; while they may seem to be little more than praise poems, they include satirical twists that transform them into subversive interventions. He adds that a *kaside* is more meaningful when it is read intertextually within the historical context of a corpus of texts.

If *kaside*s were the way to attract a patron's attention and secure economic resources, *gazel*s were a more everyday literary practice. There are no Ottoman poets who did not compose *gazel*s. In his chapter, Selim S. Kuru explains the Arabic and Persian origins of the poetic form

Introduction

but focuses on the Ottoman *gazel* in particular, defining it as part of an overarching Anatolian or "*Rumi*" culture. In the light of his close reading of one of Necatî's *gazel*s, he argues that, in the context of courtly love, the *gazel* "evolved in the form of a competitive game and reformulated Islamicate cosmology." The *gazel* provided intricate details and a puzzle-like structure that engulfed multiple layers of meaning. Both the poet and audience were involved in an interactive game to produce the meaning of the poem. The oral nature of *gazel*s made them more popular and appropriate for the culture of the *meclis*—entertainment circles where poetry was produced, performed, and enjoyed. Kuru presents the *gazel*, a genre that has been traditionally dismissed for being the same poem over and over again, as a kind of role-play between lover and beloved, ruler and subject (*kul*), masculine and feminine.

The next chapter in "Ottoman Poetics" turns instead to the modernizing turn and secularization of an Ottoman poetic genre. The third genre in this trilogy is the *mesnevi*, or narrative poem. Unlike the *gazel* and *kaside, mesnevi* are only loosely related to *meclis* culture due to their lengthy structures. They were more reading material than performance pieces. Berat Açıl focuses on an aspect of *mesnevi*s previously overlooked. He contextualizes the genre through an important literary device: allegory. Most *mesnevi*s were written as allegories, and Açıl presents them in the larger context of allegory in both European and Islamic literature. What makes Ottoman allegories different, he argues, is that they employ all three characteristics of allegory.

The final chapter of this section on Ottoman poetry focuses on the poetics of a representative figure in modern, nineteenth-century Ottoman literature. Deniz Aktan Küçük develops a reading of Tevfik Fikret's poetry as a manifestation of the modern worldview that centers on the human subject instead of God. Accordingly, her chapter argues that Fikret's poetics reveals how Ottoman literature relates to modernity and makes visible the social and cultural consequences of modernity on Ottoman poetry and its intellectual environment. Aktan Küçük argues that "the gradual retreat of God and the human subject's assignment as the substitute" engender a new conceptualization of the subject and the world in Fikret's poetry, even though he uses Ottoman and western poetic traditions side by side in his early work. The elimination of God and the melancholy of being alone in a godless world leaves its place to the dominance of the human subject with a strong embrace of science—in particular, the theory of evolution.

In the next section, "Cultures of Reading," we delve into the essential question of literacy. Most of the earlier chapters, even those focusing on the nineteenth century, discuss literary practices as oral performances. The *meclis*, be it at the royal palace or a coffee house, was the primary space for the consumption of literature. Poets composed their work to perform at these gatherings. Collective readings were also common, primarily popular books like Yazıcıoğlu Mehmed's *Muhammediyye*. As İrvin Cemil Schick explains in his chapter here, until the end of the nineteenth century literacy was rare in the Ottoman Empire, and even after the printing press became more common, books remained extremely expensive. Schick contextualizes reading in a larger context of Islamic culture and situates it as a revered practice. For instance, the custom of engraving citations from the Qur'an onto architecture or valuable objects meant that even though people could not read them completely, they could recognize the writing based on a few known words. Accordingly, calligraphy was and still is one of the most valuable artistic expressions in the Islamic world. Schick discusses the gendered nature of reading as well, by emphasizing the male-dominated nature of *meclis*es. Although we don't know much about women's collective reading spaces, we can make educated guesses that they also read in homosocial gatherings.

Apart from reading and writing in Turkish or Arabic (for religious texts), translation has also been a common practice throughout literary history. As Gülşah Taşkın discusses, from the fourteenth to nineteenth century translation was one of the most notable literary practices. Following

Introduction

the frameworks of Lefevere and Saliha Paker, Taşkın argues that any translation is essentially a rewriting, something that Ottoman writers took the liberty to do. To demonstrate the variety of translations, Taşkın focuses on translations of a treatise on herbal medicine by two different translators. She close reads and compares the two texts to discuss the concepts of rewriting, poetics, and patronage. In this way, she highlights one important aspect of translation: competition among translators and their patrons. This approach enriches our understanding of the practice.

In his chapter, Fatih Altuğ discusses authorship and readership within the context of the nineteenth-century literary public. Focusing on five different writers, he discusses how modern texts constructed the modern Ottoman subject. Namık Kemal's reflections on early modern morality books and his attempt to differentiate novels as a more open-ended and fun alternative situates storytelling at the center even of modern literature. Moreover, Ahmet Mithat's engagement with female sexuality and its relation to reading novels, or his comparison of writing fiction to constructing buildings, demonstrate how these late Ottoman authors helped define not only the new writer but also the new reader. Storytelling techniques in this period's novels—which imagine dialogue among the author, the characters, and the imagined reader—present an experience of collective reading both quite different from and strikingly similar to the collective readings in an early modern *meclis*. Altuğ reviews the first women novelists in the Ottoman Empire and describes how male authors such as Ahmet Mithat encouraged women to be active in the literary scene.

Women and issues of gender are further scrutinized in the next thematic section of this book, "Women and Gender." The question of gender and sexuality appears briefly in previous chapters, but this fourth section specifically includes chapters focusing on women, the construction of gender, ideas of masculinity and femininity, and homosociality from the early modern period to modern times. This section opens with Hülya Adak's chapter reviewing the European and American scholarship on gender studies and argues that such studies for Ottoman Turkish literature are extremely scarce. Adak argues that although there are a few full-length studies both in Turkish and English—she does not include scholarly articles or edited volumes in her discussion—there are not enough critical biographies that situate women writers within their aesthetic, political, sociological, and historical contexts. She mentions that the abundant critical editions of women writers' novels from the nineteenth century onwards are not very useful for the classroom because they lack the criteria of critical editions: editorial commentary, publication history, or historical background. She compares publication houses in Turkey to Norton and Macmillan, which have produced several modernized versions of canonical writers like James Joyce and Shakespeare to make them accessible for K-12 classrooms. Adak's article may inspire students of Turkish literature with ideas for future research.

The following three articles by Didem Havlioğlu, N. İpek Hüner Cora, and Olcay Akyıldız discuss women's literature and gender in literary history in different time periods and various genres. However, they all present similar patterns of women writers' resistance and endurance. Havlioğlu writes about the construction of gender in Ottoman Turkish poetry from the sixteenth to nineteenth centuries. She discusses valuable recent publications focusing on the early modern period, during which Ottoman literary circles were defined as homosocial, male-dominated aesthetic and cultural spaces. In a gender-fluid male world, both masculinity and femininity were values that could be claimed by men. Although multi-sexuality among men implied transgressive opportunities, it did not transform the misogynistic view of the female. Havlioğlu argues that women tried to carve a space out for themselves in the poetic male-dominant world not only to claim masculinity but also to redefine the negative notions of femaleness.

While Havlioğlu focuses on women poets and poetry, N. İpek Hüner Cora discusses gender construction in prose fiction from the early modern to modern periods. Both women as

Introduction

trickster figures and the "wiles of women" stories, which were told by and for men, reveal a prose representation of womanhood similar to that of poetry, which defined it as devilish, wily, and dangerous. Cora reviews the most common stories and discusses their place in the larger context of Ottoman literature. She also goes a step further and asks whether or not these stories have a place in women's literature. Following in Najmabadi's footsteps, Cora makes an effort to understand whether it is possible for the female reader to enjoy misogynistic stories. She concludes that women's negative representation in prose fiction goes along with the general gender structure of Ottoman literature and the mainstream understandings of a positive masculinity and negative femininity.

Olcay Akyıldız moves the discussion to the modern period and investigates approaches to contemporary female writers by male-dominated socialist realist criticism. Through the feminist concept of gynocriticism, Akyıldız examines four modernist female writers who, according to her, generate a new way of writing, in particular with female characters reflecting on their inner conflicts, the female body, and sexuality. These were aspects of their work that were overlooked by the male-dominated socialist realism. An interesting overlap between the earlier chapters in this section and Akyıldız's discussion is that they all agree that women writers did not try to challenge male-centered narratives. Instead, they offered a new angle, especially in presenting the female perspective that was otherwise missing from mainstream, male-dominated narratives. Moreover, like earlier chapters, Akyıldız suggests that women writers—whether in poetry, short story, or the novel—opened up new horizons in Turkish literature.

The fifth section, "Linguistic Diversity," explores literary texts dealing with the multilingual nature of the late Ottoman and modern Republican periods. As we mentioned earlier, Turkish literature interacted with all communities of the empire, more precisely with the languages spoken and written in Anatolia. The diverse linguistic structure of the empire was decisive in the production of these complex literary texts. The chapters in this section attempt to challenge the " 'Turkish-only' approach dominating Ottoman/Turkish literary historiography," as Murat Cankara emphasizes in line with the pioneering attempts of Altuğ and Uslu to acknowledge how the multilingual nature of Anatolia was reflected in literary production, especially in the nineteenth century.[27]

Accordingly, in her chapter, Şehnaz Şişmanoğlu Şimşek discusses the literary activities of the Turcophone Orthodox Christians of Anatolia who produced texts in Turkish using Greek script, known as Karamanlidika. Şişmanoğlu Şimşek reveals their literary production, mainly published in local journals, and discusses how their literary output paralleled that of the other communities that made up modern Ottoman Turkish literature. In the eighteenth and nineteenth centuries, Turcophone Greeks published religious texts to teach "the doctrine of the Orthodox Church [to those] not able to read in Greek." In the second half of the nineteenth century, secular book printing began and the Karamanlidika press, namely newspapers and periodicals, introduced the reading public to a new genre: the novel. Şişmanoğlu Şimşek offers a general survey of the Karamanlidika press, focusing in particular on the newspaper *Anatoli* run by Evangelinos Misailidis (1820–1890). Also, Misailidis' novelistic adaptation *Temaşa-i Dünya ve Cefakâr u Cefakeş* (1871–1872) was one of the first Turkish novels, though it was neglected in national Turkish literary historiography. The work illuminates the final period of the empire's multilingual, multiethnic, and multicultural world.

In a similar manner, Murat Cankara continues the discussion by showing the multilingual character of nineteenth-century literary production in the Ottoman Empire. He introduces and contextualizes the first novels in Armeno-Turkish (or Turkish in Armenian script) in the period: *Akabi Hikâyesi* by Hovsep Vartanyan [The Story of Akabi, 1851]; *Karnig, Gülünya ve Dikran'in Dehşetlü Vefatleri* by Hovhannes H. Balıkçıyan [Karnig, Gülünya and Dikran's Horrible Deaths,

9

Introduction

1863)]; and *Bir Sefil Zevce* by Hovsep Maruş [A Miserable Wife, 1868]. Cankara discusses how the Ottomans encountered the novel as a new genre, emphasizing that "all three texts, written by Ottoman Armenians in the Turkish language using the Armenian script, were printed before the publication of the 'first Turkish novel' modern Turkish literary scholarship has hitherto acknowledged." He looks for the answer to how the Turkish language met the novel and compares these pioneering examples with subsequent novels written by Muslim Turkish authors.

The last chapter in this section is by Suat Baran and Ömer Faruk Yekdeş, who discuss Kurdish influence in Turkish literature. Since the population of non-Muslim minorities drastically decreased due to nationalist policies during the collapse of the Ottoman Empire and the building of the nation-state, "the most populous and autochthonous non-Turkic population of the Turkish Republic" has been the Kurds. Baran and Yekdeş examine modern Kurdish literature and Kurdish writers using Turkish in a comparative perspective. Kurdish literature in general has developed in a fragmented way because of both legal and communicational obstacles. Until the rise of modern Kurdish literature, most of those born in Kurdish-speaking environments adopted the dominant languages of the country they lived in as their literary language. Baran and Yekdeş study the literary history of Kurds in parallel with Turkish literature and its readership.

The sixth section of the book, "National Identity," concentrates on authors and texts that reflect the rise of nationalist movements since the beginning of the twentieth century. To put it more accurately, they deal with how literature imagines Turkish national identity or the role literature played in the construction of national identity in the late Ottoman and early Republican periods. The category of "national literature" and "homeland literature," covering 1911–1950 in national literary historiography, has become a literary norm within the framework of the nationalist paradigm. The chapters reconsider the complex nature of nationalist literary trends in Turkey through examinations of fictional works, comprehensive literary histories, translation activities, and plays produced in the period when the nationalist paradigm dominated the literary sphere.

Accordingly, the first chapter by Halim Kara discusses how national literary historiography developed alongside the nation-building process. He investigates the prominent role of Fuat Köprülü as the leading literary historian of the period who worked for "the institutionalization of the concept of national literary historiography" in Turkey. Kara first examines the creation of the first modern narrative (literary) histories based on "the idea of historical progress and a conceptualization of time as linear" in the nineteenth century, which replaced the *tezkires*, or biographical collections produced during the Ottoman Empire. Kara then shows the gradual transformation of these histories into national literary histories under Köprülü, who formulated the basic premises of national literary historiography which linked literature and society to connect the Turkish literature of past, present, and future.

In the second chapter in this section, Esra Dicle argues for the central role of theatre as a propaganda tool from the late nineteenth century to the 1930s. Dicle first shows the process of institutionalization and nationalization of theatre during the period of Ottoman-Turkish modernizing reforms. She then discusses how Kemalist modernization used theatre to propagate its ideology to the public and generate a new concept of Turkish citizenship based on both modern and national values. Focusing on the plays of Yakup Kadri, Nâzım Hikmet, and Halide Edip written in the 1930s, she reveals the tension and conflict between the dominant ideology and oppositional tendencies fed by different political positions.

The third chapter in this section on national identity is by Erol Köroğlu, who examines the role of Ömer Seyfettin as a leading figure of the National Literature movement who constructed national identity through his short stories. Köroğlu first discusses the process of nation-building and nationalization of society before arguing that national movement intellectuals engaged in

Introduction

"patriotic propaganda" to nationalize society in line with the period's requirements. Writers such as Refik Halit Karay and Ömer Seyfettin display a specific realism compatible with their nationalism, especially in their literary works focusing on people's daily lives. Köroğlu shows how Ömer Seyfettin differed from other realist writers before him due to the narratological tools he used and his concept of humor.

The last chapter in this section is by Fırat Oruç. He discusses the role of the translated humanist canon in constructing a new national culture as a part of the modernization project "reconciling nationalism and Westernism." Oruç describes how translation projects reflected the tensions between nationalism and transnationalism, universalism and particularism, religious and secular, and modern and traditional in the making of modern Turkey. Oruç shows that Kemalist ideologues "believed that by translating and re-creating the humanistic corpus of Western thought and literature not simply in form but in spirit, understanding, and worldview, Turkey would find its true cultural identity." Turkish intellectuals of the time who supported the Kemalist reforms tried to find sources for the new national culture. Their solution was to turn to the European humanist canon.

"Literary Modernisms," the seventh section, deals with the work of writers and poets who engaged with modernity and modernist literature in different ways during various periods and who paved the way for the opening of new paths in modern Turkish literature. While the first chapter focuses on the radical changes in late-nineteenth-century Ottoman literature, the other five chapters deal with milestones of Republican literature.

Zeynep Uysal deals with the paradigm shift of 1890s literature centered around the magazine *Servet-i Fünun*. Unlike the first modernizers, who instrumentalized literature to address social and political issues, this generation of literati sought to create an autonomous literature. Uysal explores how this autonomous space was engendered by studying both *Servet-i Fünun* and the novels of Halit Ziya Uşaklıgil, who was the leading writer of the period. Based on the discursive world of magazines and novels, Uysal also shows how this generation appropriated modernity to envision a new, modern individual.

The second chapter in this section also deals with the experiences of modernity but through a focus on Nâzım Hikmet, the world-famous communist poet who left his mark on the first half of the twentieth century. Kenan Behzat Sharpe investigates how Nâzım Hikmet reformulated what it meant to be modern and, in doing so, challenged the pro-western orientation of the Turkish state. Sharpe also discusses how the poetry appropriated the experience of modernity in the Turkish context and how the poet, as both a futurist and a communist, optimistically embraced modern urban life and technology, unlike conservative modernists. As Sharpe argues, "In the internationalist vision of Nâzım's early poetry, Turkey will be truly modern when it aligns itself with the east against European capitalism and colonialism." Emphasizing the close connection between Marshall Berman's conceptualization of the "modernism of underdevelopment" and Nâzım's modernism, Sharpe close reads some of the poet's early, unpublished work and underlines the "fantastic character" of his modernism.

Nâzım Hikmet's vision of modernity helped to create another alternative in socialist realist novels of the 1950s, in particular village novels. These had an ambivalent relation to the state, unlike explicitly communist writers like Nâzım. In his chapter, Erkan Irmak examines the village novel as subgenre and defines its main characteristics and position within the cultural and political environment of Turkey's mid-century. He questions the typical and quite limited definition of the village novel as one in which the "events take place in the village." After discussing the differences among subgenres such as the regional novel, rural/rustic novel, and pastoral novel, he explores the village novels that appeared in other world regions. Arguing that the connection between the village and the nationalization process is the common factor, Irmak points out that the emergence of the village novel in Turkey is a consequence of steps taken to solve the "village problem" in the early Republican era. He explores the Köy Enstitüleri (Village Institutes) as a unique experience that sheds light on the genre and its authors, the majority of whom were educated at the institutes. Last, he reveals how this genre came to an end and lost its identity when it tried to merge with socialist realist literature.

Though socialist realist literature dominated until the 1980s, a parallel path was also visible in Turkish literature between 1940 and 1980. This modernist path, which includes avant-garde works in both poetry and fiction, would come to shape the structure, forms, and ground of postmodernist literature after 1980. The last two chapters of this section deal with prominent examples of modernist poetry and fiction.

Veysel Öztürk focuses on the influential poetics of the Second New Wave, which was a vanguard poetry movement in the 1950s. After emphasizing the period's modernist turn with poems uncovering new themes and forms of expression, Öztürk underlines the role of urbanism in creating new forms of writing. He also discusses how dramatic poetry became instrumental in representing the modern experiences of alienation and the isolation of the fractured self. In this way, the dramatic poems of Second New Wave poets like Edip Cansever and Turgut Uyar were representative of the "poetics of urbanism."

In the last chapter of this section on literary modernisms, Murat Gülsoy discusses modernist authors who were not typically accepted as modernists in their own lifetimes, as the writers Nâzım Hikmet, Ahmet Hamdi Tanpınar, Haldun Taner, and Leyla Erbil were all categorized within different literary schools and genres. Gülsoy aims to show their contribution to modernist Turkish literature, particularly their influence on contemporary literary production. The quest for new narrative forms and fictional strategies in their literary production completely distinguishes these writers from their literary environment, in which a realist understanding prevailed. Gülsoy draws a line between all these unique writers, starting with Nâzım Hikmet and leading to Orhan Pamuk. Describing "the link between experimenting with new ways of crafting fiction and redefining existing ideological engagements," Gülsoy uncovers the modernist kinship among them.

The final section of this book is "Political Turmoils and Traumas." It comprises three chapters focusing on the literary production that accompanied the traumatic experiences and upheavals of Turkey's political history in the twentieth and twenty-first centuries. In a country where democracy has been interrupted by coups d'état since the foundation of the Republic, literary texts, especially novels, are one of the few mediums where traumatic experiences can be expressed.

Within this framework, Çimen Günay-Erkol discusses literary responses to military coups in Turkey by focusing on testimonial novels. She explains that after military coups, voices and demands from below were suppressed by tight security measures and violence against the opposition. Novels that revolve around memories of the military coups (May 27, 1960; March 12, 1971; September 12, 1980; and February 28, 1997) contain fictional histories rich in social, cultural, and political details of Turkey's struggles for democratization. Günay-Erkol offers a summary of the history of coups and an overview of post-coup novels before closely examining one of these novels in particular: Çetin Altan's *Büyük Gözaltı* (Extreme Surveillance, 1972). To understand this novel, she draws on trauma theory and the Hegelian concept of *Aufhebung* as detailed by Eric Kliegerman. She evaluates Altan's novel as "a side product of the 1971 military coup, in which a traumatic post-coup prison experience is claimed and transformed into a creative moment of *Aufhebung*." Günay-Erkol's chapter also lays the groundwork for the next chapters, which take us into the present day.

Introduction

Burcu Alkan focuses on the depictions of intellectuals in the novels of writers who were themselves politically engaged intellectuals in the 1970s under the shadow of military interventions and political turmoil. After showing that the decade of the 1970s was the most political period of the Turkish novel, Alkan describes how these novels present a complex picture of the "conflicting ideologies" and the "competing ideals" of the different but interlinked intellectual types of the time. This renders the works distinctive as self-reflexive literary artifacts. She draws on the concept of "intelligentsia narratives" from Andrew Kahn, who used the term to explain literary texts based on "the intelligentsia self-consciously thinking about its own mission and history" in Russian literature. Using the examples of 1970s novels, Alkan explores intellectual characters who endeavor for social change as portrayed by novelists who also desired to transform society.

The final chapter of this section and the volume is by Erdağ Göknar, who focuses on Nobel laureate Orhan Pamuk's parodic conspiracy novel *Snow*, which engages with contemporary politics in Turkey from the 1980s onward. The chapter starts with a question: "Could a Turkish novel about conspiracism help us better understand Turkey's political transition from the 1997 soft coup to the 2016 failed coup?" Göknar first shows the relationship between conspiracies and literature in Turkey, analyzing the striking way that contemporary Turkish literature engages with "the logic of conspiracy as a [plot] device." Göknar then analyzes the grammar of conspiracy that "functions on the level of form and content" in *Snow*. With its characters related to "ideologically 'constructed' truths" and its dominant tropes of coup and conspiracy, *Snow* functions as "a vehicle of political critique." The chapter also argues that the novel's discursive practice juxtaposing the political power and culture of conspiracy offers a forecast for the future Turkish politics and, in particular, the AKP era's conspiracism as a political melodrama with authoritarian turns.

As seen in these thematically and conceptually categorized sections, across 29 unique chapters we have sought to reveal the nerve endings of Turkish literature as they overlap with Turkey's sociopolitical and cultural development. Though this volume does not claim to encompass all topics or literary-historical periods in Turkish literature, it does offer a roadmap that reveals the turning points and complex strands of this literary tradition lasting more than 600 years.

Accordingly, instead of requesting very limited and specific periods and topics from our authors, we gave them the opportunity to write and make connections between periods and themes according to their areas of specialization. As mentioned above, the book is not a chronological history of Turkish literary history. Nevertheless, to help our readers who are interested in seeing certain authors and works in relation to their time, we provide a timeline at the end of the book.

Finally, we made editorial choices for translation, transliteration, and transcriptions in the articles to establish consistency. We use common modern Turkish transliteration for Turkish words. For Arabic and Persian words, we rely on the guide suggested by the *International Journal of Middle East Studies*. Unfortunately, due to space limitations, we could not include originals of the quotations. However, interested readers will be able to find them in the relevant bibliographies. For frequently used Ottoman Turkish words and terms, we provide translations right after its first italic occurrence in each chapter.

Notes

1 David Damrosh, *How to Read World Literature* (Hoboken: John Wiley & Sons, 2008).
2 Burcu Alkan and Çimen Günay-Erkol have edited a volume contextualizing the concept of Turkish literature as world literature focusing in the modern period. See Burcu Alkan and Çimen Günay-Erkol, eds., *Turkish Literature as World Literature* (London: Bloomsbury, 2021).

Introduction

3 See Stefan Sperl and Christopher Shackle, eds., *Qasida Poetry in Islamic Asia and Africa*, vol. 2 (Leiden: Brill, 1996); Angelika Neuwirth, Michael Hess, Judith Pfeiffer, and Boerte Sagaster, eds., *Ghazal as World Literature*, vol. 2 (Beirut: Beiruter Texte und Studien, 2006).

4 See Stefan Sperl and Yorgos Dedes, eds., *Faces of the Infinite: Neoplatonism and Poetics at the Confluence of Africa, Asia and Europe* (Oxford: Oxford University Press, 2022).

5 For a detailed discussion of the language reform, see Geoffrey Lewis, *The Turkish Language Reform: A Catastrophic Success* (Oxford: Oxford University Press, 1999).

6 Fuad Köprülü and his works are still considered milestones of Turkish literature. See *Türk Edebiyatında İlk Mutasavvıflar* (Ankara: Akçağ, 2003); *Türk Edebiyatı Tarihi* (Ankara: Akçağ, 2004). For an English translation, see *Early Mystics in Turkish Literature*, trans. Gary Leiser and Robert Dankoff (London: Routledge, 2006).

7 A pioneering work on the subject is by Annemarie Schimmel, *Mystical Dimensions of Islam* (Chapel Hill: University of North Carolina Press, 1975).

8 For more discussion on the subject, see Fatih Altuğ and Mehmet Fatih Uslu, eds., *Tanzimat ve Edebiyat: Osmanlı İstanbulu'nda Modern Edebi Kültür* (Istanbul: İş Bankası Kültür Yayınları, 2014).

9 The first tezkire in Ottoman Turkish is by Sehî Bey (d. 1548), *Heşt Bihişt* [Eight Heavens], which was followed by Latîfî (d. 1582) and Âşık Çelebi (1519–1571). Ibnülemin Mahmut Kemal İnal (1871–1957) transformed the genre and produced the first major encyclopedia, *Son Asır Türk Şairleri*, which was published between 1930 and 1941.

10 *Encyclopedia of Islam* (Leiden: Brill, 1913), https://referenceworks.brillonline.com/browse/encyclopaedia-of-islam-1.

11 *İslam Ansiklopedisi*, vol. 15 (Istanbul: Diyanet, 1988), https://islamansiklopedisi.org.tr/.

12 E.G.W. Gibb, *A History of Ottoman Poetry*, vol. 6 (London: Luzac, 1900–1909).

13 Louis Mitler, *Contemporary Turkish Writers: A Critical Bio-bibliography of Leading Writers in the Turkish Republican Period up to 1980* (Abingdon-on-Thames: Routledge, 1997).

14 Louis Mitler, *Ottoman Turkish Writers: A Bibliographical Dictionary of Significant Figures in Pre Republican Turkish Literature* (Bern: Peter Lang Inc., 1988).

15 Talât Halman, *A Millennium of Turkish Literature* (New York: Syracuse, 2011).

16 Talât Halman, *Rapture and Revolution: Essays on Turkish Literature* (New York: Syracuse, 2007).

17 "Ottoman Literature" is a comprehensive article by Hatice Aynur in *The Cambridge History of Turkey*, vol. 3, ed. Soraiya Faroqhi (Cambridge: Cambridge University Press, 2006), 481–520. Erdağ Göknar's "The Novel in Turkish: Narrative Tradition to Nobel Prize," another comprehensive overview focusing on the novel and its contextualization in Turkish literary history, appears in *The Cambridge History of Turkey*, vol. 4, ed. Reşat Kasaba (Cambridge: Cambridge University Press, 2008), 472–503.

18 Walter Andrews, Najaat Black, and Mehmet Kalpaklı, *Ottoman Lyric Poetry: An Anthology* (Austin: University of Texas Press, 1997).

19 Kemal Silay, *An Anthology of Turkish Literature* (Bloomington: Indiana University Press, 1996).

20 For translations from earlier periods, see Victoria Holbrook's translation of Şeyh Galip's *Beauty and Love* (New York: MLA, 2005); Geoffrey Lewis' translation of *The Book of Dede Korkut* (New York: Penguin, 1974); Bill Hickman's translation of *The Story of Joseph: A Fourteenth Century Turkish Morality Play by Sheyyad Hamza* (New York: Syracuse University Press, 2014); Robert Dankoff's translation of Yusuf Khass Hajib's *Wisdom of Royal Glory: A Turco-Islamic Mirror for Princes* (Chicago: University of Chicago Press, 1983). For later periods, see Mutlu Konuk's translation of Nâzım Hikmet's *Life's Good, Brother: A Novel* (New York: Persea, 2013); Erdağ Göknar's translation of Orhan Pamuk's *My Name Is Red* (New York: Vintage, 2002); Maureen Freely's translations of many novels by Orhan Pamuk such as *The Black Book* (London: Faber and Faber, 2015).

21 Among Talât Halman's works, see *A Brave New Quest: 100 Modern Turkish Poems* (Syracuse, NY: Syracuse University Press, 2006); *The Humanist Poetry of Yunus Emre* (Istanbul: Istanbul Matbaası, 1972); *Listening to İstanbul: Selected Poems of Orhan Veli Kanık* (New York: Autumn Press, 2002); *A Dot on the Map: Selected Stories and Poems of Sait Faik* (Bloomington: Indiana University Press, 1995); *Living Poets of Turkey: An Anthology of Modern Poems* (Ann Arbor: University of Michigan, 1989); *Contemporary Turkish Literature: Fiction and Poetry* (East Brunswick, NJ: Fairleigh University Press, 1982).

22 See Walter G. Andrews, *Poetry's Voice, Society's Song: Ottoman Lyric Poetry* (Seattle: University of Washington Press, 1985); Victoria Holbrook, *The Unreadable Shores of Love: Turkish Modernity and Mystic Romance* (Austin: University of Texas Press, 1994).

23 Walter Andrews and Mehmet Kalpaklı, *The Age of Beloveds: Love and the Beloved in Early-Modern Ottoman and European Culture and Society* (Durham, NC: Duke University Press, 2005).

Introduction

24 Didem Havlioğlu, *Mihrî Hatun: Performance, Gender-Bending, and Subversion in Ottoman Intellectual History* (Syracuse, NY: Syracuse University Press, 2017); Sooyong Kim, *The Last of an Age: The Making and Unmaking of a Sixteenth Century Ottoman Poet* (Abingdon-on-Thames: Routledge, 2018).

25 Among the monographic contributions on modern Turkish literature and the earlier period of the Turkish novel, see Robert Finn, *The Early Turkish Novel: 1872–1900* (Istanbul: Isis Press, 1984); Ahmet Evin, *Origins and Development of The Turkish Novel* (Minneapolis: Bibliotheca Islamica, 1983). For Islamist fiction since the 1980s, see Kenan Çayır, *Islamic Literature in Contemporary Turkey: From Epic to Novel* (London: Palgrave, 2017).

26 Azade Seyhan, *Tales of Crossed Destinies: The Modern Turkish Novel in a Comparative Context* (New York: MLA, 2008); Erdağ Göknar, *Orhan Pamuk, Secularism and Blasphemy: The Politics of the Turkish Novel* (Abingdon-on-Thames: Routledge, 2013); Mushirul Hasan, *Between Modernity and Nationalism: Halide Edip's Encounter with Gandhi's India* (Oxford: Oxford University Press, 2009); Nergis Ertürk, *Grammatology and Literary Modernity in Turkey* (Oxford: Oxford University Press, 2011).

27 Altuğ and Uslu, *Tanzimat ve Edebiyat*.

References

Altuğ, Fatih, and Mehmet Fatih Uslu, eds. *Tanzimat ve Edebiyat: Osmanlı İstanbulu'nda Modern Edebi Kültür.* Istanbul: İş Bankası Kültür Yayınları, 2014.

Andrews, Walter G. *Poetry's Voice, Society's Song: Ottoman Lyric Poetry.* Seattle: University of Washington Press, 1985.

Andrews, Walter G., Najaat Black, and Mehmet Kalpaklı, eds. *Ottoman Lyric Poetry: An Anthology.* Austin: University of Texas, 1997.

Andrews, Walter G., and Mehmet Kalpaklı. *The Age of Beloveds: Love and the Beloved in Early-Modern Ottoman and European Culture and Society.* Durham, NC: Duke University Press, 2005.

Çayır, Kenan. *Islamic Literature in Contemporary Turkey: From Epic to Novel.* London: Palgrave, 2017.

Damrosch, David. *How to Read World Literature.* Hoboken: Wiley Blackwell, 2009.

Dankoff, Robert, trans. *Wisdom of Royal Glory: A Turco-Islamic Mirror for Princes.* Chicago: University of Chicago Press, 1983.

Encyclopedia of Islam. Leiden: Brill, 1913. https://referenceworks.brillonline.com/browse/encyclopaedia-of-islam-1.

Erkol, Çimen, and Burcu Alkan, eds. *Turkish Literature as World Literature.* London: Bloomsbury, 2021.

Ertürk, Nergis. *Grammatology and Literary Modernity in Turkey.* Oxford: Oxford University Press, 2011.

Evin, Ahmet. *Origins and Development of the Turkish Novel.* Beirut: Bibliotheca Islamica, 1983.

Faroqhi, Soraiya, and Reşat Kasaba, eds. *The Cambridge History of Turkey*, vols. 3–4. Cambridge: Cambridge University Press, 2006–2008.

Finn, Robert. *The Early Turkish Novel: 1872–1900.* Istanbul: Isis Press, 1984.

Freely, Maureen, trans. *The Black Book.* London: Faber and Faber, 2015.

Gibb, E.G.W. *A History of Ottoman Poetry*, vol. 6. London: Luzac, 1900–1909.

Göknar, Erdağ, trans. *My Name Is Red.* New York: Vintage, 2002.

———. *Orhan Pamuk, Secularism and Blasphemy: The Politics of the Turkish Novel.* Abingdon-on-Thames: Routledge, 2013.

Halman, Talât. *The Humanist Poetry of Yunus Emre.* Istanbul: İstanbul Matbaası, 1972.

———. *Contemporary Turkish Literature: Fiction and Poetry.* East Brunswick, NJ: Fairleigh University Press, 1982.

———. *Living Poets of Turkey: An Anthology of Modern Poems.* Ann Arbor: University of Michigan, 1989.

———. *A Dot On the Map: Selected Stories and Poems of Sait Faik.* Bloomington: Indiana University Press, 1995.

———. *Listening to İstanbul: Selected Poems of Orhan Veli Kanık.* New York: Autumn Press, 2002.

———. *A Brave New Quest: 100 Modern Turkish Poems.* Syracuse, NY: Syracuse University Press, 2006.

———. *Rapture and Revolution: Essays in Turkish Literature.* Syracuse, NY: Syracuse University Press, 2007.

———. *A Millennium of Turkish Literature.* Syracuse, NY: Syracuse University Press, 2011.

Hasan, Mushirul. *Between Modernity and Nationalism: Halide Edip's Encounter with Gandhi's India.* Oxford: Oxford University Press, 2009.

Havlioğlu, Didem. *Mihrî Hatun: Performance, Gender-Bending, and Subversion in Ottoman Intellectual History.* Syracuse, NY: Syracuse University Press, 2017.

Introduction

Hickman, Bill, trans. *The Story of Joseph: A Fourteenth Century Turkish Morality Play by Sheyyad Hamza*. Syracuse, NY: Syracuse University Press, 2014.

Holbrook, Virginia. *The Unreadable Shores of Love: Turkish Modernity and Mystic Romance*. Austin: University of Texas Press, 1994.

İslam Ansiklopedisi, vol. 15. Istanbul: Diyanet, 1988. https://islamansiklopedisi.org.tr/.

Kim, Sooyong. *The Last of an Age: The Making and Unmaking of a Sixteenth Century Ottoman Poet*. Abingdon-on-Thames: Routledge, 2018.

Konuk, Mutlu, trans. *Life's Good, Brother: A Novel*. New York: Persea, 2013.

Köprülü, Fuad. *Türk Edebiyatında İlk Mutasavvıflar*. Ankara: Akçağ, 2003.

———. *Türk Edebiyatı Tarihi*. Ankara: Akçağ, 2004.

———. *Early Mystics in Turkish Literature*. Translated by Gary Leiser and Robert Dankoff. Abingdon-on-Thames: Routledge, 2006.

Lewis, Geoffrey. *The Turkish Language Reform: A Catastrophic Success*. Oxford: Oxford University Press, 1999.

———, trans. *The Book of Dede Korkut*. New York: Penguin, 1974.

Mitler, Louis. *Ottoman Turkish Writers: A Bibliographical Dictionary of Significant Figures in Pre Republican Turkish Literature*. Bern: Peter Lang Inc., 1988.

———. *Contemporary Turkish Writers: A Critical Bio-bibliography of Leading Writers in the Turkish Republican Period up to 1980*. Abingdon-on-Thames: Routledge, 1997.

Neuwirth, Angelika, Michael Hess, Judith Pfeiffer, and Boerte Sagaster, eds. *Ghazal as World Literature*, vol. 2. Beirut: Beiruter Texte und Studien, 2006.

Schimmel, Annemarie. *Mystical Dimensions of Islam*. Chapel Hill: University of North Carolina Press, 1975.

Seyhan, Azade. *Tales of Crossed Destinies: The Modern Turkish Novel in a Comparative Context*. New York: MLA, 2008.

Silay, Kemal. *An Anthology of Turkish Literature*. Bloomington: Indiana University Press, 1996.

Sperl, Stefan, and Yorgos Dedes, eds. *Faces of the Infinite: Neoplatonism and Poetics at the Confluence of Africa, Asia and Europe*. Oxford: Oxford University Press, 2022.

Sperl, Stefan, and Christopher Shackle, eds. *Qasida Poetry in Islamic Asia and Africa*, vol. 2. Leiden: Brill, 1996.

SECTION I

Mystical Genesis

1

IT ALL STARTS WITH A DREAM

The Motif of Dream in Turkish Literature

Özgen Felek

In the *Epic of Oğuz Kağan*, an account of the mythical origin of the Oghuz, the vizier Uluğ Türük dreams of a golden bow and three silver arrows. The golden bow stretches from the East to the West, while the three silver arrows point North. As he narrates his dream to Oğuz Kağan, Uluğ Türük prays "May the Sky-God make my dream come true. May He grant all the earth to your descendants."[1] Very much pleased with Uluğ Türk's dream, Oğuz Kağan summons his six sons and asks them to follow Uluğ Türk's advice to go hunting. He sends Kün, Ay, and Yulduz (Sun, Moon, and Star) to the East; Kök, Tağ, and Tengiz (Sky, Mountain, and Sea) to the West. After hunting for a long time, Kün, Ay, and Yulduz find a golden bow and bring it to their father. Oğuz Kağan happily breaks the golden bow into three pieces and advises his sons to be like a bow and shoot their arrows towards the sky. Meanwhile, Kök, Tağ, and Tengiz find three silver arrows as they return from hunting. Like their brothers, they also bring their discovery to their father. Oğuz Kağan divides the arrows between them, saying that just as the bow shoots the arrows, they should act like arrows and spread in all directions. To Oğuz Kağan, Uluğ Türük's dream is a good omen that his descendants will conquer the world.

This dream anecdote is not the only symbolic dream in Turkish folk literature. Such symbolic dreams, seen as good omens for newly established states or as warnings of disasters to come, also appear in other Turkish epics such as the epics of *Göç, Türeyiş*, and *Manas*. Another, much later auspicious dream is attributed to 'Osmān, Oğuz Kağan's descendant and the founder of the Ottoman Empire in 1299. 'Osmān's dream comes to him while he is staying at the house of a spiritual figure, Sheikh Edebalı, he is given a room to spend the night. 'Osmān notices that there is a Qur'an in the room, out of respect to the Qur'an, he does not lie down and spends the night as sitting. Towards the morning, a dream comes to him:

> When 'Osmān Ġāzī slept he saw in his dream how from the chest of this saint a moon rose, and came towards him and entered his ['Osmān's] chest. The moment that the moon entered his chest a tree sprang up from his navel, and its shadow covered the earth. There were mountains in the shadow, and water sprang from the foothills of the mountains. Some people drank from these waters, and others watered their gardens, and yet others caused fountains to flow. Then he woke up.[2]

DOI: 10.4324/9780429279270-3

'Osmān later recounts his dream to the sheikh. Much like Oğuz Kağan's interpretation of Uluğ Türük's dream, Sheikh Edebalı's response to 'Osmān's dream portends greatness: "Good tidings to you: God Most High has given sovereignty to you and your descendants. May it be blessed."[3]

Both of these dreams function to establish the newly founded state on the basis of spiritual power by offering good news regarding the future and guiding the protagonists through difficult situations. Furthermore, they demonstrate how Islam influenced Turkish culture and subsequently Turkish dream culture as well. Although both dreams were spiritual-legalistic tools for their respective reigns, in certain elements 'Osmān's dream (i.e., respect for the Qur'an) denote the Islamic religion as a significant addition to Turkish dream culture. In contrast to the first dream mentioned above, this dream demonstrates the continued significance of dreams and dream interpretations in Turkish culture even after the Turks' conversion to Islam in the eighth century.

Although the study of dreams in the Ottoman and greater Islamic worlds is still in its early emergent stages, the broader study of dreams in world literature offers a tremendous and diverse range of research on the universal experience of dreaming. Ottoman dream culture is of particular interest, given the significant contribution of Ottoman Sufis to the history and development of Sufi teachings and practices for more than 600 years. The present chapter examines the role and function of dreams in different genres of early modern Turkish literature. Following a brief introduction to the perception of dreams in Islam and Islamic mysticism which had a great influence on Turkish/Ottoman people, dream compilations and dream interpretations produced in Ottoman Turkish literature will be discussed. This will contextualize how Turkish dream culture was reshaped under the influence of Islam and how this change was reflected in Turkish literature in the premodern Ottoman world.

Dreams in Islam

The 12th chapter of the Qur'an narrates one of the most well-known stories in the Hebrew Bible and the Qur'an: that of Joseph/Yūsuf. In both post-biblical and post-Qur'anic literatures, the story has been rewritten using a variety of narrative features that pay particular attention to the passion that Züleyḫā (the name given in Muslim tradition to the biblical figure of Potiphar's wife) had for Joseph. Joseph's story starts with his dream, in which 11 stars, the sun, and the moon prostrate themselves to him. To Joseph's father Jacob, Joseph's dream is the initial sign that he will become a ruler by the story's end.[4]

Another well-known Islamic dream involves the Prophet Abraham, who is asked in his dream to sacrifice his son Ishmael. When Abraham conveys his dream to Ishmael, who is also a named prophet in the Qur'an, the latter willingly submits himself to his father to be sacrificed. This was revealed to be in fact a test for both of them, and in response to their submission to Divine Will, God "ransomed him with a momentous sacrifice."[5] Islamic tradition interprets this sacrifice as a ram and commemorates this great self-sacrifice through the annual sacrificing of a ram, or an equivalent animal during the 'Īd al-Aḍḥā, one of the two major holy days in the Islamic tradition. Abraham's dream was widely relayed by storytellers both in oral traditions and literary texts like the Ḳıṣaṣu'l-enbiyā ("Stories of the Prophets").

Dreams also maintained their significance with Prophet Muhammad. Islamic tradition holds that Prophet Muhammad received his first revelations as true dreams. Furthermore, not only his own dreams, but also those of his companions seem to have been important to the Prophet.[6] In Islamic dream lore, most dreams are identified by a set of prophetic traditions known as rü'yā-yı ṣādıḳ or aḥkām which are tidings (mübeşşirāt) from God, and ḥulm or aḍġāṣü aḥlām which are confused dreams reflecting images and situations from the dreamer's daily activities and encounters.[7] The third type is identified as frightening or baseless dreams that are influenced by the devil. While true dreams are seen as the most significant and require interpretation, bad dreams lead a pious Muslim astray. The Prophet stated that the prophecy came to end with him, meaning that there will be no further messengers or prophets after him. However, the tidings revealed through dreams to the righteous men are considered to be one of the 46 parts of prophecy.[8]

Dreams and dream interpretations gained additional functions and roles with the development of mystic movements in the Islamic world beginning in the eighth century. To the Sufis, dreams were symbolic messages that arose from the knowledge hidden in the center of being and prominent Sufis sought out to understand the real meaning of dreams.[9] Indeed, one of the foremost contributions of mysticism to Islamic dream culture is the idea of *'ālem-i miṣāl*, "the world of dream-imagination in which the mysteries of God and his creation, otherwise impenetrable to the human intellect and sense perceptions, are unveiled."[10] This theory of *'ālem-i miṣāl* suggests the existence of a third universe that lies between the divine world and the real world.[11]

Sufi literature also used dreams for completely functional and practical purposes. Although "mission and prophecy have come to an end," Sufis understood good tidings within Islamic dream lore, and claimed to have communicated with the Prophet and the Divine through dreams and waking visions. Dreams thus provided a legitimization tool for the Sufis, who defined themselves as friends of God. Medieval and early modern Islamic hagiographical texts harbor a voluminous dream literature that vividly encapsulates the central role of dreams, not only in the relationships between the Sufis and their disciples, but also in daily life.

By the twelfth century, Sufi orders (*ṭarīḳat*) became major social organizations and, by the fifteenth century, enjoyed great popularity. With the development of the spiritual guide (*mürşīd*) and disciple (*mürīd*) relationship, Sufis attributed a variety of functions to dreams and waking visions. This includes being a mechanism for identifying Sufis' mystical states, with the expectation that dreams will provide personal guidance during their spiritual journeys. Disciples were thus required to share every dream they had with their masters. In some instances, their geographical/physical distance meant that this sharing took place in the form of letters, which stimulated an epistolary correspondence in Sufi circles that has produced a rich body of literature.

Dreams in Turkish Literature and Culture

The word for dream in Turkish is *düş* or *tüş*, as defined in the *Ḳutadġu Bilig* ("Wisdom of Royal Glory"), one of the first Turkish-Islamic books composed by Yūsuf Ḥās Ḥācib in 1069–1070, and the *Dīvānü Lüġati't-Türk* ("Dictionary of Turkish Dialects") by Mahmud Kashgari in 1072–1074. Arabic and Persian words (e.g., in Arabic, *rü'yā, rü'yet, vāḳı'a, menām, seyr, seyrān*, and *ḥulm*; and in Persian, *ḫʷāb*) also have been used in Turkish dialect. In addition to these "foreign" words for dream, stories based on dream narratives in Arabic and Persian literatures have also entered the Turkish canon. The influence of their respective literary products demonstrates that many dreams attributed to historical and religious figures can be found in different genres of Ottoman literature.

Perhaps the most unique genre of dreams in Turkish culture is the usage of dreams in oral traditions by Turkish minstrels (*'āşıḳ*). Indeed, having a dream was (and still is) necessary to become a minstrel. However, seeing just any dream is not sufficient. Instead, the dreams recounted in folk tales all have specific characteristics. First, they appear to the protagonist at the age of puberty. The dreamer, who is soon to become a troubadour, is given a glass of wine *bāde* (wine) by a beautiful girl, an old man, or a saintly figure near a mosque, cemetery, or fountain in his dream. Once he wakes from his dream, he has a fever or remains in a daze for about a week. Eventually an old woman starts to play a long-necked lute (*saz*) and he wakes up upon hearing the music. As soon as he awakes, the young man starts to recite his own poems. A common trope found in most folk tales about the life stories of minstrels begins with a young man who falls in love with a beautiful girl who appears in his dream; he then embarks on a journey to find the girl. Dreaming about sacred beings during an initiation is another common motif in folktales about the Turkish bards.[12]

Another genre was heroic epics. *The Epic of Oğuz Kağan*, which opened the present volume, is the earliest Turkic heroic epic. While its main structure has remained the same over the centuries, Islamic influence can be seen in the dream narrations in later versions, as with other Turkish epics. In post-Islamic heroic epics, Islamic figures, such as the Prophet Muhammad, Rightly Guided Caliphs (Ebū Bekir, ʿÖmer, ʿOsmān, and ʿAlī), and the Prophet's grandsons Ḥasan and Ḥüseyin, take important roles as helpers of the protagonist. Dreams also function not only to herald a future event or situation, such as the birth of a hero (e.g., *The Epic of Köroğlı*) or the conquest of Rum (e.g., *The Epic of Baṭṭāl Ġāzī*), but also to warn the hero against enemies (e.g., *The Epic of Dānişmend-nāme*). One of the more striking motifs in the post-Islamic epic narratives is that of conversations to Islam through dreams, in which the Prophet Muhammad or saints appear to non-Muslims in their dreams and ask them to convert to Islam.

Another popular genre where one can find dreams is the romance genre of lengthy narrative poems (*mesnevī*). The dream of Odgurmış in *Wisdom of Royal Glory*, Yusuf Has Hacib's eleventh-century didactic work, appears to have been the earliest dream account in Turkish narrative poetry tradition. Odgurmış' dream in which he claims to see a staircase to the sky has symbolic implications with extraordinary features as interpreted by his vizier Ögdülmiş.[13] Starting in the thirteenth century, the dreams of preeminent religious, historical, and hagiographical figures appear in romances as significant narrative tools that assist the poets in creating and developing their plots. One striking example is Aḥmedī's (d. 1413) didactic work *İskender-nāme* ("Book of Alexander"), in which dreams bring news about the future in order to warn the protagonist and thus shape the story's plot.[14]

In the romances titled *Yūsuf u Züleyḫā,* dreams attributed to Joseph became popular both in oral and written literature. From the thirteenth to the nineteenth centuries, many *Yūsuf u Züleyḫā* romances were penned. Although the main story is about Züleyḫā's obsession with Joseph, each romance re-narrated Joseph's dreams with explicit details meant to touch the reader's heart. Mystic poets, on the other hand, focused on dreams as a means of spiritual guidance for novices. In his well-known *Mesnevī*, Celāle'd-dīn Rūmī (d. 1273), one of the most influential Sufi masters and poets in the Ottoman world, not only articulates his theories on dreams but also relates the dream narrations attributed to different figures, such as a concubine who falls in love with the Sultan or a philosopher.

Dreams appear in poetry collections as well. For example, in the lyrics of prominent Turkish poets Ḳāḍī Burhāne'd-dīn (d. 1398), Nesīmī (d. 1418?), and Aḥmedī (d. 1413), dreams both serve as narrative devices to describe mystical issues and function as tools through which poets can discover the world of images (*ʿālem-i misāl*). Ottoman poets also often offer some thoughts about the essence of dreams and the conditions of the dreamers and interpreters in their poetry. Not surprisingly, their understanding of dreams usually does not differ from the depictions found in the hadith tradition.

Some poets used dreams as rhetorical and political devices. The genres called *Ḫvāb-nāme* or *ḫvābiyye* ("Book of Sleep"), or *vāḳıʿa-nāme* ("Book of Dreams") are dream narratives that allow poets to express their concerns and criticisms of political, religious, or other relevant conditions. Among several *ḫvāb-nāmes*, the most renowned example of the genre is Veysi's *Ḫvāb-nāme*, known as *Vāḳıʿāt* or *Vāḳıʿa-nāme*. It is a story in the form of a dream narrative in which Sultan Ahmed I (r. 1603–1617) meets Alexander the Great. Although a concise excerpt from Islamic history, "[D]reams' authoritative power" provides a venue in which Veysi can express his political

It All Starts With a Dream

criticisms and give advice to Sultan Aḥmed I through the words of Alexander the Great.[15] The increasing numbers of *ḫʷāb-nāmes* circa the nineteenth century is a clear indicator of the utility of dream narratives during a time of strict political and social oppression.[16]

Dreams were highly valued and often recorded in various prose forms as well. A common custom among early modern Ottomans was to recount dreams at gatherings and meetings. Ottoman biographers likewise participated in this dream sharing by incorporating the dreams they heard about into biographical dictionaries dedicated to different professional and/or intellectual groups. Prominent biographers discovered the appeal of using narrative dreams to explain junctures in life and to demonstrate their subjects' career choices, appointments, and social networks. For them, dreams were "rhetorical tools to comment on their contemporaneous situation." They used dreams not only to justify the high positions of their subjects, but also to criticize those of whom they did not approve.[17] In his *Meşā'irü'ş-şu'arā* ("Gatherings of Poets"), ʿĀşık Çelebi, for example, uses dreams as mirrors both to reveal hidden aspects of the lives of Ottoman poets requiring explanation and to relate news—good or bad—regarding their future.[18] Likewise, the sixteenth-century biographer Laṭīfī, the author of the *Tezkiretü'ş-şu'arā* ("Biographical Dictionaries of Poets"), relates the contemporary poet Nihānī's nightmare upon which Nihānī quits his job as a judge.[19] Niyazioğlu calls these dreams "career dreams" as well, since they point to "important stages in a Sufi's career: initiation, appointment, and a succession."[20] The biographers thus mostly focused on "career dreams" to explain why their subjects chose their jobs, or why one left his Sufi lodge and joined another.

Hagiographical literature dedicated to the biographies of preeminent Sufis also often employs dreams and waking visions of Sufis alongside their saintly miracles in order to establish them as accomplished Sufis. Hagiographers verify their protagonists' sainthood not only through the Sufis' dreams, but also through their access to their disciples' dreams. One distinguishing example is Mehmed Muhyiddin-i Gülşeni's *Menāḳıb-ı İbrāhīm-i Gülşenī* ("Hagiographical Biography of İbrāhīm-i Gülşenī"), dedicated to İbrāhīm-i Gülşenī (d. 940/1534), the founder of the Halveti-Gülşeni Sufi order. İbrāhīm-i Gülşenī, for example, has access to the contents of his disciples' dreams even if they do not relate.[21] Dreams served to justify the dreamer's earlier actions, affirm his spiritual or intellectual status, alert him to some issues of ritual purity, or serve as signs for the future. Although Ottoman biographers and hagiographers took their subjects' dreams seriously, they were in fact quite selective in their choice of which of their subjects' dreams to include or exclude: the dreams had to support the shape of their biography project.

Likewise, Ottoman chroniclers occasionally narrated the dreams of sultans or bureaucrats as real historical events; this historiographical device helped them to explain or clarify actions and decisions. Using a selection of dream accounts found in Ottoman chronicles from the fifteenth through seventeenth centuries, Gottfried Hagen discusses Ottoman chroniclers' perception of dreams as actual historical events that offer "high explanatory value" and clarification of seemingly senseless events and catastrophes. As Hagen writes, dreams were "taken for real by the actors in the narrative, by [the] author of the account, and, finally, by his audience."[22]

Furthermore, dreams appear in Ottoman chronicles as motivational calls to action, whether for an event or conversion (for non-Muslims). One vivid example concerns the conversion of Köse Miḥal, the Greek Byzantine governor of Chirmenkia, to Islam, which purportedly was instigated by a dream. Mehmed II was likewise divinely inspired by a dream to order the fleet to be hauled over the hills from the Bosporus into the Golden Horn during the siege of Constantinople. Perhaps one of the most common motifs in dreams is the prediction of future glory and conquest. The Ottoman chroniclers write, for example, that Sultan Murād III learned of his future ascension to the throne through a dream.[23] Chroniclers also reported the dreams of Sufi masters and even some bureaucrats, who hoped that the contents of their dreams would be taken seriously and believed them to be significant enough to warrant being shared with the palace.

One can also find dreams in travel accounts. One of the most celebrated dream accounts in Turkish culture belongs to Dervīş Meḥmed Żıllī (d. 1682), known as Evliyā Çelebi, a seventeenth-century Ottoman author who journeyed through the Ottoman Empire and adjacent lands. In writing about his travels in his lengthy travel narrative, *Seyāḥatnāme* ("The Book of Travels"), he narrates a dream as the inciting factor for his 40-year journey. In this dream, he relates that his overexcitement upon seeing the Prophet Muhammad caused him to misspeak and beg for travel (*seyāḥat*) instead of intercession (*şefāʿat*). As a response, the Prophet granted Evliya not only travel and intercession, but also a visit to the holy tombs of the prophets and saintly figures.[24] Evliyā Çelebi narrates numerous dreams along with his own interpretations throughout his *Seyāḥatnāme*. Unsurprisingly, he classifies his dreams as true or strange, and those interpreted as true eventually become reality. It is through the true dreams that Evliyā is informed about the near future events, such as the conquest of a castle, or the reasoning behind the construction of a shrine. As he documents the history of the places he visits, he is also sure to relate the dreams of legendary figures in the area.[25] His great attention to the dreams of and about his patron Melek Aḥmed Pasha is a great demonstration of the significance of dreams in his life and writing.[26]

In fact, Evliyā Çelebi is not alone in using his dream as a means of literary inspiration. Several Ottoman poets and authors proclaim that it is within dreams that they were advised or encouraged to pen their books. Among several examples, Yazıcıoğlu Meḥmed's *Kitāb-ı Muḥammediyye* ("Book of Muhammad") begins with a dream narrative that is the starting point of this highly popular text.[27] Such dreams are considered valuable additions that only strengthen the validity of those books.

Dream Compilations

Thus far, we have briefly touched on the functions and roles of dreams as they appear in different genres. Although not many, a collection of dream letters belonging to various Sufis survives as well. Of them, two collections in particular are noteworthy: the dream letters of Sultan Murād III (r. 1574–1595) and of Āsiye Ḥātūn of Skopje.

Murād III is reported to have shared his dreams with his sheikh on a regular basis in the form of letters. The letters were subsequently compiled in 1595 under the title the *Kitāb-ı menāmāt* ("Book of Dreams"). As a unique collection of letters from a disciple to his spiritual master, the *Kitāb-ı menāmāt* is significant not only as an extremely rich, lengthy sample of such Sufi epistolary forms, but also as a window into the private life and intimate social relations of an Ottoman Sultan.[28] Another significant Ottoman collection contains the dream letters of Āsiye Ḥātūn, a seventeenth-century woman dervish of the Halveti order. Like Sultan Murād, Āsiye Ḥātūn sent her dreams in letter forms to her sheikh between 1641/42 and 1643/44.[29] Āsiye Ḥātūn's dream letters verify that female disciples also shared their dreams with their (male) Sufi masters.

Other dream accounts and hagiographical stories provide dream narratives and interpretations by several Sufi figures, namely Niyāzī-i Mısrī (d. 1694), the founder of Halvetiyye's Mısriyye branch, and ʿAzīz Maḥmūd Hüdā'ī (d. 1628), the founder of the Celvetiyye order, who also shared his dreams for three years with his Sufi master to request the latter's interpretations.[30] The dream letters of Ḥüseyin Vaṣṣāf who recorded between 1923 and 1927 demonstrate that the practice of writing dreams to one's spiritual guide continued until the early twentieth century.

Dreams were penned not only to be shared with one's Sufi master. An eighteenth-century *cönk*, a personal anthology and diary that gathered favorite poems, daily notes, significant dates, and notes regarding credit and debits by the *cönk* keeper, shows that non-Sufis also recorded their dreams for themselves. Ḳulaḳzāde Maḥmūd Pasha, an administrative authority of Avlonya sanjak in Albania, recorded his dreams between 1730 and 1735 under the title *Düş-nāme* ("Book of Dream"), which indicates both his concerns and hopes about his career as well as his daily worries.[31]

This great attention to dreams, not surprisingly, fostered the production of numerous manuals of dream interpretations.

Dream Interpretations

The science of interpreting dreams (Oneirocriticism/Oneirocritica) is called *'ilm-i ta'bīr, ta'bīr el-ru'yā* (or *rüyā tā'bīri* in Turkish) in Islamic literature. After adopting dream interpretations from Greek and Roman thought, Muslims produced numerous dream interpretations of their own for centuries.[32] The earliest examples of dream interpretation in Turkish appear in the aforementioned *Ḳutadġu Bilig* ("Wisdom of Royal Glory").[33] While the earliest full dream interpretations were translations from Arabic, new Turkish interpretations began to be penned in the fourteenth century. The existence of hundreds of manuscripts on dream interpretations from the fourteenth to the late nineteenth centuries in manuscript libraries in and outside of Turkey shows the significant level of interest that early modern Ottoman dreamers gave to dreams and their implications.[34]

Dream interpretations were primarily penned in prose, either as separate texts or chapters and notes in the margins of Sufi manuals and compilations. There are a few surviving examples of dream interpretations composed in poetic form. The written correspondences between the Sufi masters and their disciples, and the interpretation of dreams through letters, also influenced the physical form of dream interpretations.[35] Good examples of this are the letters of Meḥmed Nāşūhī Efendi, who interpreted his disciple İbrāhīm Aġa's dreams through letters.[36]

Dream interpretation manuals provide important clues regarding daily life. Furthermore, we can trace early modern Ottoman perceptions of gender and sexuality through dream interpreters' eyes.[37]

Conclusion

Dreams have long played a significant role in Turkish culture. With the Turks' conversion to Islam, and later with the rise of mystic teachings, dreams gained new roles and functions in Ottoman society. Since we have only limited access to pre-Islamic Turkish literature, it is difficult to provide a detailed comparative analysis. Yet, looking at what is available, one can argue that dreams maintained their significance in Turkish culture and functioned in different roles and through different genres.

This chapter has attempted to display the scope of changes and differences in Turkish dream culture between ancient epics to early modern literature of the Ottoman world. Dreams appeared in folk tales, legends, epics, and narrative poetry as tools to serve as significant turning points in the protagonists' lives, thus shaping the plot. They also helped Ottoman biographers and hagiographers to support the shape of their biography projects but became particularly meaningful and practical in the hagiographical literature, as Sufis valued their dreams as a venue through which they interacted with the Divine. In particular, dreams functioned as a communication tool between spiritual masters and their disciples. Insights thus gained from the study of dreams provide visions of the world of images and the lived experience of Ottoman men and women.

Özgen Felek

Acknowledgment

I am grateful to Robert Dankoff for his careful review and valuable comments on the earlier version of this chapter.

Notes

1 W. Bang and G. R. Rahmeti, eds., *Oğuz Kağan Destanı* (Istanbul: Burhaneddin Basımevi, 1936), 29–31.

2 Aşıkpaşaoğlu Ahmed Âşıkî, *Tevārīḫ-i Āl-i Oṣmān'dan Āşıkpaşazāde Tārīḫi* (Istanbul: Matba'a-i Amire, 1332), 6. I borrow the English translation of the passage by Gottfried Hagen in "Dreaming 'Osmans of History and Meaning,'" in *Dreams and Visions in Islamic Societies*, ed. Ozgen Felek and Alexander D. Knysh (Albany: SUNY Press, 2011), 104.

3 Aşıkpaşaoğlu Ahmed Âşıkî, *Tevārīḫ-i Āl-i Oṣmān*, 105.

4 Qur'an 12:4–6; Qur'an 12:43–49.

5 Qur'an, 37:102–7.

6 Bukhari 1979: 1:2–3, 6:450–4, 9:91; Tirmidhi 2007: 2:619; Bukhari 2:468; Muhammad.

7 See Al-Qushayri, *Al-Qushayri's Epistle on Sufism: Al-Risala al-qushayriyyafi 'ilm al-tasawwuf*, trans. Alexander D. Knysh (Reading: Garnet, 2007), 392–93. On the prophetic traditions regarding dreams, see also John Lamoreaux, *The Early Muslim Tradition of Dream Interpretation* (Albany: SUNY Press, 2002), 117–18.

8 Different hadith accounts give different numbers. For a brief discussion, see Fareeha Khan, "Sometimes a Dream Is Just a Dream," in *Dreams and Visions in Islamic Societies*, ed. Ozgen Felek and Alexander D. Knysh (Albany: SUNY Press, 2011), 127.

9 Regarding the significance of dreams in Islamic mysticism, see Jonathan Katz, "Dreams and Their Interpretation in Sufi Thought and Practice," in *Dreams and Visions in Islamic Societies*, ed. Ozgen Felek and Alexander D. Knysh (Albany: SUNY Press, 2011), 181–97; Leah Kinberg, *Morality in the Guise of Dreams: A Critical Edition of Kitab Al-Manam Islamic Philosophy, Theology, and Science* (Leiden: E.J. Brill, 1994); Nile Green, "The Religious and Cultural Roles of Dreams and Visions in Islam," *Journal of the Royal Asiatic Society* 3, no. 13 (2003): 287–313; Louise Marlow, *Dreaming Across Boundaries: The Interpretation of Dreams in Islamic Lands* (Washington, DC: Ilex Foundation, Center for Hellenic Studies, 2008); Henry Corbin, "The Visionary Dream in Islamic Spirituality," in *The Dream and Human Societies*, ed. G. E. Von Grunebaum and Roger Caillois (Berkeley: University of California Press, 1966), 381–408.

10 Alexander Knysh, "Introduction," in *Dreams and Visions in Islamic Societies*, ed. Ozgen Felek and Alexander D. Knysh (Albany: SUNY Press, 2011), 1.

11 Fazlur Rahman, "Dream, Imagination, and a'lam al-mithāl," in *The Dream and Human Societies*, ed. G. E. Von Grunebaum and Roger Caillois (Berkeley: University of California Press, 1966), 409–19; Dror Ze'evi, "Dream Interpretation and Unconsciousness," in *Producing Desire Changing Sexual Discourse in the Ottoman Middle East, 1500–1900* (Berkeley: University of California Press, 2006), 102.

12 İlhan Başgöz, "Dream Motif in Turkish Folk Stories and Shamanistic Initiation," in *Turkish Folklore and Oral Literature: Selected Essays of İlhan Başgöz*, ed. Kemal Sılay (Bloomington: Indiana University Turkish Studies, 1998). On dreams in the folk poetic tradition, see Umay Günay, *Türkiye'de Âşık Tarzı Şiir Geleneği ve Rüya Motifi* (Ankara: Akçağ Yayınları, 2005).

13 Yūsuf Khāṣṣ Ḥājib, *Wisdom of Royal Glory (Kutadgu Bilig): A Turko-Islamic Mirror for Princes, Translated, with an Introduction and Notes by Robert Dankoff* (Chicago: University of Chicago Press, 1983), 233–38, 182.

14 Gülçiçek Akçay, "Mesnevilerde Rüya Teorisi," *Türkbilig* 36 (2018): 213–34.

15 Ahmet Tunç Şen, "A Mirror for Princes, a Fiction for Readers: The Habname of Veysi and Dream Narratives in Ottoman Turkish Literature," *Journal of Turkish Literature, Bilkent University Center for Turkish Literature* 8 (2011): 41–65.

16 Metin Kayahan Özgül, *Türk Edebiyatında Siyasi Rüyalar* (Ankara: Akçağ, 1989), 12–20.

17 Aslı Niyazioğlu, *Dreams and Lives in Ottoman Istanbul: A Seventeenth-Century Biographer's Perspective* (New York: Routledge, 2017), 6.

18 Aslı Niyazioğlu, "Aşık Çelebi'ye Rüyaların Söyledikleri," in *Aşık Çelebi ve Şairler Tezkeresi Üzerine Yazılar*, ed. Hatice Aynur and Aslı Niyazioğlu (Istanbul: Koç University Press, 2011), 71–85.

19 Aslı Niyazioğlu, "On Altıncı Yüzyıl Sonunda Osmanlı'da Kadılık Kabusu ve Nihânî'nin Rüyası," *Journal of Turkish Studies* 31, no. 2 (2007): 133–43.

20 Aslı Niyazioğlu, "Dreams, Ottoman Biography Writing, and the Halveti Sünbüli Şeyhs of Sixteenth-Century Istanbul," in *Many Ways of Speaking About the Self: Middle-Eastern Ego-Documents in Arabic,*

Persian, and Turkish 14th–20th Century, eds. Ralph Elger and Yavuz Erköse (Wiesbaden: Harrassowitz Verlag, 2010), 177.

21 Mehmed Muhyiddin-i Gülşeni, *Menâkıb-ı İbrahim-i Gülşenî ve Şemleli-Zâde Ahmed Efendi Şive-i Tarikat-i Gülşeniye*, ed. Tahsin Yazıcı (Ankara: Türk Tarih Kurumu, 1982), 64.

22 Hagen, "Dreaming 'Osmans," 99. See also Orhan Şaik Gökyay, "Rüyalar Üzerine," in *II. Milletlerarası Türk Folklor Kongresi Bildirileri*, vol. 4 (Ankara: Kültür ve Turizm Bakanlığı, 1982), 190–95.

23 Hagen, "Dreaming 'Osmans," 108–12.

24 Evliyâ Çelebi b. Derviş Mehemmed Zıllî. *Evliyâ Çelebi Seyahatnâmesi I. Kitap Topkapı Sarayı Kütüphanesi Bağdat 304 Numaralı Yazmanın Transkripsiyonu—Dizini*, ed. Zekeriya Kurşun, Seyit Ali Kahraman, and Yücel Dağlı, vol. 1 (Istanbul: Yapı Kredi Yayınları, 1998), 12.

25 Ibid., vol. 2, 89, 120, 146, 214–15; vol. 3, 230; vol. 4, 25, 95, 113; vol. 5, 124.

26 Robert Dankoff, *An Ottoman Mentality, the World of Evliya Çelebi with an Afterword by Gottfried Hagen* (Leiden: Brill, 2004), 26.

27 Gelibolılı Yazıcızade Muhammed Efendi Merhum, *Kitab-ı Muhammediye* (Der Saadet: Hürriyet Matbaası, 1324 [1869]), 4–5.

28 Ozgen Felek, *Kitābu'l-Menāmāt: Sultan III. Murat'ın Rüya Mektupları* (Istanbul: Tarih Vakfi Yayınları, 2014).

29 Cemal Kafadar, *Rüya Mektupları/Asiye Hatun; Giriş, Çevrimyazı, Sadeleştirme* (Istanbul: Oğlak Yayıncılık ve Reklamcılık, 1994), 20.

30 Mustafa Tatcı, "Niyâzî-i Mısrî'nin Tasavvufî bir Rü'yâ Tabîr-nâmesi (inceleme-metin)," *Türk Folkloru Araştırmaları* (1989): 85–96.

31 Semra Çörekçi, "A Methodological Approach to Early Modern Self-Narratives: Representations of the Self in Ottoman Context (1720s–1820s)" (PhD diss., Istanbul Medeniyet University, 2021).

32 Ze'evi, "Dream Interpretation and Unconsciousness," 103.

33 Yūsuf Khāṣṣ Ḥājib, *Wisdom of Royal Glory (Kutadgu Bilig)*, 235–38.

34 A list of Turkish dream interpretations can be found in Adem Balaban, "Türkçe Yazma Tabirnameler," *Dil ve Edebiyat Eğitimi Dergisi* 9 (2014): 112–32. On dream interpretations in Turkish, see also Orhan Şaik Gökyay, "Tabirnâmeler," *Tarih ve Toplum* 94 (October 1991), 201–6.

35 Kafadar, *Rüya Mektupları/Asiye Hatun*.

36 Üsküdarlı Mehmed Nasuhi Halveti, *Seyr ü Sülük Mektupları*, ed. Mustafa Tatcı and Abdülmecit İslamoğlu (Istanbul: H Yayınları, 2017).

37 Dror Ze'evi has dedicated a chapter, titled "In "Dream Interpretation and Unconsciousness," to the sexual images and symbols found in the Ottoman dream interpretation tradition in his *Producing Desire*, 99–124.

Bibliography

Al-Qushayri. *Al-Qushayri's Epistle on Sufism: Al-Risala al-qushayriyyafi 'ilm al-tasawwuf*. Translated by Alexander D. Knysh. Reading: Garnet, 2007.

Aşıkpaşaoğlu Ahmed Âşıkî. *Tevārīḫ-i Āl-i Oṣmān'dan Āşıkpaşazāde Tārīḫi*. Istanbul: Matba'a-i Amire, 1332.

Balaban, Adem. "Türkçe Yazma Tabirnameler." *Dil ve Edebiyat Eğitimi Dergisi*, no. 9 (2014): 112–32.

Bang, W., and G. R. Rahmeti, eds. *Oğuz Kağan Destanı*. Istanbul: Burhaneddin Basımevi, 1936.

Başgöz, İlhan. "Dream Motif in Turkish Folk Stories and Shamanistic Initiation." *Asian Folklore Studies* 26, no. 1 (1967): 1–18.

———. "Dream Motif in Turkish Folk Stories and Shamanistic Initiation." In *Turkish Folklore and Oral Literature: Selected Essays of İlhan Başgöz*, edited by Kemal Sılay, 11–23. Bloomington: Indiana University Turkish Studies, 1998.

Çelepi, Mehmet Surur. *Türk Halk Kültüründe Rüya*. Konya: Kömen Yayınları, 2017.

Corbin, Henry. "The Visionary Dream in Islamic Spirituality." In *The Dream and Human Societies*, edited by G. E. Von Grunebaum and Roger Caillois, 381–408. Berkeley: University of California Press, 1966.

Çörekçi, Semra. "A Methodological Approach to Early Modern Self-Narratives: Representations of the Self in Ottoman Context (1720s–1820s)." PhD diss., Istanbul Medeniyet University, 2021.

Dankoff, Robert. *The Intimate Life of an Ottoman Statesman Melek Ahmed Pasha (1588–1662) as Portrayed in Evliya Çelebi's Book of Travels Translation and Commentary by Robert Dankoff with a Historical Introduction by Rhoads Murphey*. Albany: SUNY Press, 1991.

———. *An Ottoman Mentality, the World of Evliya Çelebi with and Afterword by Gottfried Hagen*. Leiden: Brill, 2004.

Evliyâ Çelebi b. Derviş Mehemmed Zıllî. *Evliyâ Çelebi Seyahatnâmesi I. Kitap Topkapı Sarayı Kütüphanesi Bağdat 304 Numaralı Yazmanın Transkripsiyonu—Dizini.* Edited by Zekeriya Kurşun, Seyit Ali Kahraman, and Yücel Dağlı. Istanbul: Yapı Kredi Yayınları, 1998.

Felek, Özgen. "(Re)creating Image and Identity Dreams and Visions as a Means of Murad III's Self-Fashioning." In *Dreams and Visions in Islamic Societies*, edited by Ozgen Felek and Alexander D. Knysh, 249–72. Albany: SUNY Press, 2011.

————. *Kitābu'l-Menāmāt: Sultan III. Murat'ın Rüya Mektupları.* Istanbul: Tarih Vakfı Yayınları, 2014.

Gökyay, Orhan Şaik. "Rüyalar Üzerine." In *II. Milletlerarası Türk Folklor Kongresi Bildirileri*, vol. 4, 183–208. Ankara: Kültür ve Turizm Bakanlığı, 1982.

————. "Tabirnâmeler." *Tarih ve Toplum*, no. 94 (October 1991): 201–6.

Green, Nile. "The Religious and Cultural Roles of Dreams and Visions in Islam." *Journal of the Royal Asiatic Society* 3, no. 13 (2003): 287–313.

Günay, Umay. *Türkiye'de Âşık Tarzı Şiir Geleneği ve Rüya Motifi.* Ankara: Akçağ Yayınları, 2005.

Hagen, Gottfried. "Dreaming 'Osmans of History and Meaning." In *Dreams and Visions in Islamic Societies*, edited by Ozgen Felek and Alexander D. Knysh, 99–122. Albany: SUNY Press, 2011.

Kafadar, Cemal. *Rüya Mektupları/Asiye Hatun; Giriş, Çevrimyazı, Sadeleştirme.* Istanbul: Oğlak Yayıncılık ve Reklamcılık, 1994.

Katz, Jonathan. "Dreams and Their Interpretation in Sufi Thought and Practice." In *Dreams and Visions in Islamic Societies*, edited by Ozgen Felek and Alexander D. Knysh, 181–97. Albany: SUNY Press, 2011.

Khan, Fareeha. "Sometimes a Dream Is Just a Dream." In *Dreams and Visions in Islamic Societies*, edited by Ozgen Felek and Alexander D. Knysh, 123–37. Albany: SUNY Press, 2011.

Kinberg, Leah. *Morality in the Guise of Dreams: A Critical Edition of Kitab Al-Manam Islamic Philosophy, Theology, and Science.* Leiden: E.J. Brill, 1994.

————. "Dreams Online: Contemporary Appearances of the Prophet in Dreams." In *Dreams and Visions in Islamic Societies*, edited by Ozgen Felek and Alexander D. Knysh, 139–57. Albany: SUNY Press, 2011.

Knysh, Alexander. "Introduction." In *Dreams and Visions in Islamic Societies*, edited by Ozgen Felek and Alexander D. Knysh, 1–15. Albany: SUNY Press, 2011.

Lamoreaux, John C. *The Early Muslim Tradition of Dream Interpretation.* Albany: SUNY Press, 2002.

Marlow, Louise, ed. *Dreaming Across Boundaries: The Interpretation of Dreams in Islamic Lands.* Washington, DC: Ilex Foundation, Center for Hellenic Studies, 2008.

Mehmed Muhyiddin-i Gülşeni. *Menâkıb-ı İbrâhim-i Gülşenî ve Şemleli-Zâde Ahmed Efendi Şîve-i Tarîkat-i Gülşeniye.* Edited by Tahsin Yazıcı. Ankara: Türk Tarih Kurumu, 1982.

Mirza, Sarah. "Dreaming the Truth in the Sira of Ibn Hisham." In *Dreams and Visions in Islamic Societies*, edited by Ozgen Felek and Alexander D. Knysh, 15–30. Albany: SUNY Press, 2011.

Niyazioğlu, Aslı. "On Altıncı Yüzyıl Sonunda Osmanlı'da Kadılık Kabusu ve Nihânî'nin Rüyası." *Journal of Turkish Studies* 31, no. 2 (2007): 133–43.

————. "Dreams, Ottoman Biography Writing, and the Halveti Sünbüli Şeyhs of Sixteenth-Century Istanbul." In *Many Ways of Speaking About the Self: Middle-Eastern Ego-documents in Arabic, Persian, and Turkish 14th–20th century*, edited by Ralph Elger and Yavuz Erköse, 171–85. Wiesbaden: Harrassowitz Verlag, 2010.

————. "Aşık Çelebi'ye Rüyaların Söyledikleri." In *Aşık Çelebi ve Şairler Tezkeresi Üzerine Yazılar*, edited by Aslı Niyazioğlu and Hatice Aynur, 71–85. Istanbul: Koç University Press, 2011.

————. *Dreams and Lives in Ottoman Istanbul: A Seventeenth-Century Biographer's Perspective.* New York: Routledge, 2017.

Özgül, Metin Kayahan. *Türk Edebiyatında Siyasi Rüyalar.* Ankara: Akçağ, 1989.

Rahman, Fazlur. "Dream, Imagination, and aʿlam al-mithāl." In *The Dream and Human Societies*, edited by G.E. Von Grunebaum and Roger Caillois, 409–19. Berkeley: University of California Press, 1966.

Sarıkaya, Erdem. *Eski Türk Edebiyatında Rüya (Başlangıçtan XV. Asra Kadar).* Ankara: Gece Kitaplığı, 2017.

Schimmel, Annemarie. *Halifenin Rüyaları & İslamda Rüya ve Rüya Tabiri.* Istanbul: Kabalcı, 2005.

Şen, Ahmet Tunç. "A Mirror for Princes, a Fiction for Readers: The Habname of Veysi and Dream Narratives in Ottoman Turkish Literature." *Journal of Turkish Literature* 8 (2011): 41–65.

Üsküdarlı Mehmed Nasuhi Halveti. *Seyr ü Sülük Mektupları.* Edited by Mustafa Tatcı and Abdülmecit İslamoğlu. Istanbul: H Yayınları, 2017.

Yüksel, Hasan Avni. *Türk İslâm Tasavvuf Geleneğinde Rüya.* Istanbul: Milli Eğitim Basımevi, 1996.

Yūsuf Khāṣṣ Ḥājib. *Wisdom of Royal Glory (Kutadgu Bilig): A Turko-Islamic Mirror for Princes, Translated, with an Introduction and Notes by Robert Dankoff.* Chicago: University of Chicago Press, 1983.

Ze'evi, Dror. "Dream Interpretation and Unconsciousness." In *Producing Desire Changing Sexual Discourse in the Ottoman Middle East, 1500–1900*, 99–124. Berkeley: University of California Press, 2006.

2

AŞIK LITERATURE IN HISTORICAL CONTEXT

Ali Aydın Karamustafa

Aşık is a term for minstrels who performed mainly in Turkish across Ottoman and Iranian lands, especially the Balkans, Anatolia, the Caucasus, and northern Iran, beginning in the sixteenth century.[1] Scholars usually consider the aşık phenomenon in a Turkish cultural framework, but it is also useful to situate it in a Eurasian context because of the diversity of linguistic and religious communities who engaged with aşık literature and performances. Eurasia is an unwieldy concept, but useful insofar as it evokes the regions from China to Europe that had close interactions with the steppe and witnessed the expansion of large bureaucratic empires in the early modern era. This chapter positions the development of aşık literature in this historical context and offers an overview of the social character of aşık performance.

The aşık was an early modern phenomenon, distinguished by the language, medium, and contents of performance. The profession did not have strict religious or linguistic dimensions, although it harbored a close relationship with Turkish. Aşık literary production was also tied to the spread of new writing traditions in sixteenth-century Ottoman and Safavid lands. Although the most constant feature in aşık poetry and song was the use of syllabic meter (Turkish, *hece veznî*), aşıks were masters of versatility who were familiar with a wide range of literary genres and navigated multiple social contexts. On an ethnographic trip to Azerbaijan in 1967, İlhan Başgöz noted how they performed poetry, prose, and music, and typically relied on a fixed repertoire of stories and songs with which audiences were familiar, although they occasionally produced original material as well.[2] These are the elements that define aşık literature and render it a sixteenth- to twentieth-century phenomenon.

Scholars have long maintained that the medieval Turkish minstrel, or *ozan*, was the predecessor to the aşık. Although the continuity between the two types is clear, the discussion has traditionally posited the former as a repository of pre-Islamic (and thus supposedly uncorrupted) Turkish culture that was remolded into the latter under the influence of the Persianate Islam in urban centers. One of the most authoritative voices in Turkish literature and a pioneer in the study of aşıks, Fuad Köprülü, wrote:

> In the sixteenth and seventeenth centuries, the aşıks whose material and spiritual culture had developed and who had grown up in large cities where Sufi lodges were widespread and which were suffused with the atmosphere of mysticism were of course unable to accept the label "ozan," which had been carried by their predecessors who

DOI: 10.4324/9780429279270-4

29

had come out of primitive villages and tribal settings; therefore, they began to use the title of *aşık* which was current among the sufi poets, who were not foreign to them in any case.[3]

For Köprülü, the tribe and the city are respective stand-ins for Turkish and Islamic culture, frameworks which he treats as incompatible. There is indeed ample evidence that there were strong cultural pressures to shed the label *ozan* by the sixteenth century, but the still current notion of an inexorable assimilation predicated on the cultural dominance of urban Islam is reductionist and ahistorical.[4] Rather than forcing aşık literature into a meta-narrative of the Islamization of the Turks, it is more useful to examine the rise of this tradition of performance in the dynamic Eurasian cultural context in the middle of the second millennium. The two most important developments in this context were the spread of Turkish and the expansion of literacy.

Writing and Speaking in Turkish

The diffusion of written and spoken Turkish is crucial to explaining the history of aşık literary production. After the sporadic written usage of the language in the medieval period in Central Asia and Anatolia, it was increasingly employed first in fourteenth-century Anatolia, and then more rapidly in the following century under the patronage of the Ottoman court in the eastern Mediterranean and the Timurid court in Central Asia. While it is unsurprising that the language of the ruling elite eventually came to be written, there is little scholarly consensus for why this change transpired in the fifteenth century. After all, the language replaced neither Persian as a literary tongue nor Arabic in the religious realm.

The political orientation of the new Turkish corpus suggests that the rise of the written Turkish may have been governed by a discursive need for new mechanisms of legitimacy. A range of new Turkish dynasties sought to convincingly insert themselves into an already established Turco-Mongol historical paradigm which had been articulated in Persian during the preceding centuries. Simply reproducing Seljuq or Mongol models would no longer suffice, but partially translating such models from Persian into Turkish and then infusing them with a new mythical slant, as did Yazıcıoğlu Ali in his *Tārīh-i Āl-i Selcūk* in the court of the Ottoman Murad II (r. 1421–1444, 1446–1451), appeared to do the trick. In Ottoman and Aq Qoyunlu Anatolia, Cemal Kafadar has also posited that the crisis engendered by the Timurid invasion of the region and continued Timurid dismissal of the legitimacy of these westerly Turkish dynasties bolstered the need among the latter for a new historical and literary idiom to strengthen their political claims.[5]

This notion is confirmed by the popularization of a historical tradition which derived political legitimacy from mythical connections to an Oghuz Turkish past, often titled the *Oğuznāme* ("Book of Oghuz"). Yazıcıoğlu Ali's work is an early example of what constituted a growing textual corpus particularly in fifteenth-century Anatolia and Iran, although it had earlier roots.[6] Thus a sort of Oghuz consciousness may have propelled the increased use of the language in written form. A variety of factors were probably at play, including an increasing number of Turkish-speaking city dwellers. The Baghdadi poet Fuzūlī's (d. 1556) composition of the story of the death of Huseyin so that "the Turkish literati [*fusahā-yi Turkī-zebān*] could find joy in listening to it and not rely on Arabs or Persians to understand its meaning" certainly suggests that among elites there was also simply a growing demand for Turkish texts.[7]

And yet Turkish came to differ from Persian in ways that elucidate its success in the aşık tradition. The history of Turkish rendered it uniquely malleable in register. Successive waves of

Turkish nomadic settlers into Azerbaijan and Anatolia during the Seljuq and Mongol periods brought a rich variety of oral traditions which became fodder for the new written language.[8] Their mobility also helped create new vectors of linguistic transmission and exchange between speakers that were tribal (pastoralists), rural (peasants), and urban (official patrons of texts and literate people). If written Persian was a standardized language produced in urban nodes of patronage and, as characterized by Nile Green, defined by a "sporadic and distant" geography as opposed to one that was "dense and localized," then Turkish texts were frequently produced within vernacular clusters which did not radiate from centers of political power.[9]

We can consider, for instance, the dervish poetry of Yunus Emre in rural Anatolia, or the tales of the Oğuz tribe in the *Book of Dede Korkut* (written ca. 1500), a popular oral rendition of the *Oğūznāme*. Unlike Persian and Arabic works in the post-Mongol period, early Turkish texts were more colloquial in register. This was even the case for Ottoman courtly texts, such as the history of Āşıkpāşāzāde (ca. late fifteenth century), the plain and unadorned language of which is a far cry from the Arabic and Persian-laced idiom that characterizes the later Ottoman court chronicles.

Knowledge of Turkish as a spoken language was also advantageous, and communities across Ottoman and Safavid lands would adopt the language during the early modern era. For instance, travelers' accounts show that many cities in Azerbaijan experienced an important degree of Turkification between the sixteenth and eighteenth centuries.[10] Spoken Turkish became widespread among non-Muslims in Anatolia, the Caucasus, and Iran in the sixteenth and seventeenth centuries—in particular among Armenians, many of whom began to use it as a first language.[11] Many Anatolian Greeks became Turkish speakers; the Ottoman traveler Evliya Çelebi (1611–1682) noted their presence in Antalya during the seventeenth century,[12] and Orthodox Greeks of the Karaman region developed a rich Greco-Turkish literature.

This linguistic trend was not only Ottoman, rather it connected Ottoman lands with those to the east. At the same time in which it was being elaborated as an imperial tongue, Turkish also offered an accessible medium for a variety of urban and rural communities. This was the foundation for the expansion of aşık literature as a trans-imperial phenomenon.

A Changing Culture of Literacy

The second crucial development at mid-millennium was the spread of a new informal practice of small books called *cönk* in Turkish (Persian, *jong*) in which aşıks were key participants. Originally a Javan and Malaysian word for a long-ruddered sailboat, *cönks* were literary collections that earned their name for their small size and narrow shape, making them easier and less costly to produce and transport. Also called by the more generic term *mecmua* (from the Arabic for anthology, *mecmū'a* in Turkish, or *majmū'eh* in Persian), these texts typically consisted of poems and versified stories, and a single *cönk* commonly included the works of multiple authors.[13]

Cönks were usually, but not exclusively, a popular tradition of book writing and compilation in that they were not commissioned for a patron, a feature noticeable from their often scrapbook-like quality. They were not always looked upon kindly by the educated elite; in the late sixteenth century, the Ottoman statesmen Mustafa 'Ālī (d. 1600) considered the arbitrary and patchwork character of *cönks* to be a manifestation of the social and moral decline of his time.[14]

One example of the structure and variety of these texts is cönk no. 74 from the Ankara National Library. It is a 98-folio book approximately 10 cm × 20 cm which opens vertically on its short axis—the latter a common feature of the *cönk*. It contains short poems in Turkish attributed to at least 30 poets, prayers in Arabic written with instructions to a Turkish reader, sermons in Arabic, sketches of objects and lines of letter-writing practice, stories of the Prophet, and various other short texts. Judging by the varieties of handwriting, at least ten people and perhaps many more contributed to the pages of this small book. Such texts, which exhibit evidence of a widespread participatory writing tradition, were typical sites for the composition and circulation of aşık poetry.

The timing of their spread parallels the expansion of print culture in Europe and underscores how the aşık tradition's connection to literacy fit broader Eurasian patterns. This spread also built on the expansion of the written word in earlier centuries, as documented by Konrad Hirschler in the case of Egypt in Syria during the period 1000–1500.[15] Historicizing the appearance of these texts and quantifying their spread could help us to better understand their historical impact; for now, the matter of cataloguing them alone is so convoluted and inconsistent as to elude such assertions. In most manuscript catalogues, conks begin to appear in the sixteenth century and increase exponentially in later centuries, but there is no established method for distinguishing them from closely related anthologies or other sorts of literary compilations.[16] Important regional manuscript libraries contain hundreds or even thousands of such texts.

In examining the contents of stories circulated by aşıks, we find that writing, and especially love letters, were a key theme. The tales of the warrior-bandit Köroğlu and the story of the amorous bard Aşık Garip, for instance, feature letter-writing as a recurrent narrative theme.[17] They are among the most widespread aşık traditions, which scholars peg to around the seventeenth century. Nineteenth-century manuscripts from the Caucasus and northern Iran show Köroğlu frequently reading epistles sent by Ottoman princesses.[18] One encounter even shows the bandit, himself an aşık, outsmarting an Ottoman religious scholar in Istanbul (*faqīh*, written *fāqī* in the text) who tries to trick him by writing a phony letter. The educated man panics after realizing his mistake: "Oh man, I'm done for—turns out this guy can read!" (*vāy vāy pidaram vāy, maʿlūm shud īn khānandih ast*).[19] Aşık Garip's story is also driven by letter-writing characters. A rendition of the story from Kars has the bard playfully lamenting in song to his lover Şah Senem, "You should have written me a letter, telling me to stay away."[20]

Performers developed a close relationship to the written word, and regularly referenced a centuries-old literary canon of Persian texts in their work, suggesting a high degree of cross-fertilization between written and oral traditions.[21] Still, scholars have not highlighted the important role of writing in aşık culture. Despite acknowledging the relevance of *cönk*s, they tend to focus on the distinct character of local traditions, oral practices such as improvisation, and institutions such as apprenticeship.[22] But the prominent role of the written word in the craft of the aşıks did not come at the expense of oral performance—sociologists have long since established that orality and written culture seem to form a simplistic binary in which they appear mutually exclusive but are in fact complementary.[23] And even if most performers remained illiterate, the writing of songs, poetry, and stories in a portable medium was becoming an increasingly common practice among them. Further research based on the study of *cönk*s and original texts, as well as contemporary observations regarding the characteristics of aşık performance, will reveal more about aşık literacy and the complementary relationship between writing, reading, and performance.

The Social Contexts of Aşık Literary Production

Although scholars have long contested the facile division of popular and elite culture, Peter Heath's tripartite classification of elite, popular, and folk literature is a useful schematic point of departure for understanding aşık literature. Heath writes that popular literature is characterized by public and accessible entertainment based on formulaic variation, while elite literature is characterized by restricted readings of unique texts for educated audiences for the purpose of edification. Both are produced by professionals and may cover wide geographies, but elite literature is only city based (by contrast, his third category of folk literature is a regional phenomenon that "exists with:n 'local' groups" and does not involve professionals).[24] Heath acknowledges the movement of texts between these categories and the regular overlapping of their audiences. Throughout its entire history, aşık literature penetrated all three categories, but it is useful to approach it chiefly as a popular tradition with a public and accessible character produced by professional performers.

Folklorists tend to divide aşıks by milieu, categorizing them as performing mainly in Sufi lodges, coffeehouses, tribes, army encampments, or urban courts. Some scholars insist on a schematic division; for instance, the Azerbaijani folklorist and musicologist Meherrem Qasımlı writes that premodern aşıks were active in three arenas: the ethnographic context, particularly folk celebrations; war and politics, where aşıks accompanied armies on their conquests; and Sufi lodges.[25] In reality, we know almost nothing about the background of most performers, many of whom may have moved freely between these environments, although the contents of their writing can offer hints about where they performed.

As a case study, the story of Köroğlu can give us a sense of the social dynamics of performers. The Köroğlu tradition is one of the most widespread in aşık literature and is found from the Balkans to Central Asia. It tells the story of a heroic youth whose family has been wronged by political leaders who takes revenge by embracing a life of lawlessness. Three nineteenth-century manuscripts from the Caucasus version of the story represent the earliest full prose and song manuscript sources we have from the tradition.[26]

The three most portrayed sites for performance in Caucasus version of the Köroğlu tradition are public squares in towns, rural army encampments, and the homes or entourages of notable men.[27] Interestingly, these manuscripts do not depict Sufi lodges or coffeehouses, which we will address separately, but we can take these three as a starting point for mapping aşık performances.

Ethnographic work and observations regarding aşıks who have performed the Köroğlu saga suggest a more complex social role than impromptu street performer. Alexander Chodźko, the Polish ethnographer and bureaucrat for the Russian Empire who first translated Köroğlu into English in 1842, described aşıks as ubiquitous:

> In northern Persia, this word [aşık] designates the professional singers, who singly, or in company of jugglers, rope-dancers, and sometimes monkeys, perambulate the towns, villages, and encampments of the nomads, attend the wedding ceremonies and festivals, amuse the people with music, puns, songs, etc.[28]

He portrayed a mobile oral tradition that spanned urban, rural, and pastoral environments, and was deeply embedded in the everyday lives and rituals of ordinary villagers and townspeople in Northern Iran and Azerbaijan.

The capacity of aşıks as hired entertainers for special occasions is commonly attested to in modern ethnographic research. A compilation of Köroğlu episodes from 2009 in Iran shows how aşıks continue to perform the tradition for large audiences at weddings and festivals in the twenty-first century.[29] In his trip to Azerbaijan, Başgöz noted how aşıks had more reliable audiences in urban centers where they could perform a set repertoire in a fixed location (typically a coffee shop), although they received the highest pay from the tribes of the region who employed musicians and singers for their wedding festivities.[30]

Marginal Performers?

Scholars have claimed that aşıks were on the fringes of Ottoman and Iranian society. About the Azerbaijani context, Qasımlı writes that performers were frequently looked down upon even by the general population.[31] Mehmet Bayrak writes that aşıks in Ottoman lands tended to be uneducated and itinerant, and many were blind.[32] Inevitably, traveling entertainers were perpetual outsiders and exclusively male.

The Köroğlu manuscripts also portray aşıks as socially marginal. When Köroğlu uses his aşık guise to gain access to the court of an Ottoman governor's daughter named Leyli Xanım, she is won over by his good looks and noble features but secretly laments, "What a shame that this young man is an aşık!"[33] On another occasion, the bandit's same disguise falls through when he is too generous with his finances and leads a dubious townsman to quip, "Pal, don't take me for a fool, a minstrel would never spend his money like you unless he had to."[34] Aşıks were also suspicious and even nefarious characters. In another instance, a pasha and his court are so surprised at Köroğlu's prodigious wine consumption that they exclaim, "This *yanşak* must be a spirit!" The lowbrow substitute for aşık, *yanşak*, indicated a person who would talk too much and was a teller of tall tales.[35]

Poets frequently tangled with one another over their status, and some deployed the concept of the common, unsophisticated performer as an insult. The court poet Sünbülzâde Vehbî (1719–1809) held Aşık Ömer (d. ca. 1730) in contempt by calling him the "seeker of rhymes in speech" (i.e., one who could not form a rhyme), and mocked aşıks Gevheri and Karacaoğlan for their simplicity ("Much praise of Gevheri circulates these days / The rare jewel of the la–la of speech," a play on Gevheri's name).[36] About a century earlier, Aşık Ömer himself had scoffed of his contemporary Karacaoğlan that "we don't consider such a blabbermouth [*ozan*] to be a poet."[37]

Although aşıks often had humble backgrounds, there was a high demand for their work among elites. The Köroğlu epic portrays Ottoman officials as appreciative of their talents, a fact which the hero frequently exploits to trick the Ottomans into positions of vulnerability.[38] The label aşık itself did not signify mean or humble extraction; at least two sixteenth-century authors with a formal education in the Ottoman schooling system (the *medrese*) and connections to the imperial elite took it on as a pen name: Aşık Çelebi (1520–1572) and Mehmed Aşık (1556–ca. 1600).

Rather than impose a social standing onto this group, it is more useful to view aşıks as actors adept at navigating a variety of social contexts. Pertev Naili Boratav wrote of their success in rural areas and in nomadic and semi-nomadic environments.[39] This is confirmed by Chodźko's testimony about the importance of the legend of Köroğlu and his songs among the tribes of Iran: "The Turkish *Iliats* [*sic*], or wandering tribes . . . carefully preserve his [Köroğlu's] poetry, and the memory of his actions. He is their model warrior—their national model bard, in the whole signification of those terms."[40] Some aşıks operated chiefly in tribal contexts, such as Dadaloğlu (d. 1868), who lived among the Afshar tribes to the east of the Taurus mountains between what is modern Syria and eastern Turkey.

Being outsiders likely permitted aşıks a greater degree of social and political freedom. Dadaloğlu wrote anti-Ottoman songs ("When the [Iranian] Shah's decree reaches Türkmen land / O! Lord have mercy on the Ottomans"), and the Köroğlu tradition in the Caucasus fiercely critiqued both Ottoman and Safavid power.[41] An outsider's position could also easily be filled by individuals of different linguistic and religious backgrounds. For instance, Armenian *ashugh*s had intimate connections with Turkish aşıks and the Turkish communities for whom they performed.[42] Examples of well-known Armenian aşıks who performed in Turkish are Aşık Civan and Aşık Vartan (act. eighteenth century, Sivas).

Perhaps the best example of aşık linguistic and cultural versatility is Sayat Nova (1712–1795), an Armenian with a father from Aleppo and a mother from Tbilisi who lived and worked in Georgia during his long career as a court performer and minstrel. During his time in the courts of T'elavi and Tbilisi, he mainly composed songs in Azerbaijani Turkish, Georgian, and Armenian, but he also had a good knowledge of Persian and his poetry displayed well-known

Persianate literary symbols such as the rose and nightingale.[43] His linguistic and musical skills in combination with his mobility (he traveled through Georgia, Armenia, and Iran) make him an ideal example of how aşıks moved between cultural and linguistic contexts to offer their services to early modern courts.

In the seventeenth century, it seems that aşıks were not yet associated with coffeehouse culture, as they would come to be in later centuries. The Caucasian Köroğlu manuscripts portray no coffeehouses in their seventeenth-century setting. What's more, Evliya Çelebi never encountered aşıks during his many visits to urban coffeehouses. Instead, he found the *ḳiṣṣahān* (storyteller), *ḥānende* (singer), *muṭrib* (entertainer, vocalist), and *sāzende* (musician) in nearly every coffeehouse he entered, and he even found *şā'ir-i şeyyāḥ* (traveling poets).[44]

Finally, the degree to which aşıks figure into the history of Sufi practice in Ottoman and Iranian realms is obscure. Musicians were a key part of the practice of some Sufi orders, just as Sufi mystical poetry was a fixture of the aşık repertoire.[45] Aşık was the term that Kizilbash communities in the Ottoman context (those today called Alevis) used for their bards as well, although the label in this context had a more obviously mystical connotation.[46] Although some aşıks came to be viewed as important mystical figures, such as Pîr Sultan Abdal (d. sixteenth century), or Hatāyī (the pen name of the Safavid Shah Ismail I, r. 1501–1524), for the most part, Sufi themes are so ubiquitous in Turkish and Persian literature that we would be hard-pressed to justify the creation of a separate category of the mystical aşık.

Over time, aşık literature and performance became more ubiquitous in the Ottoman and Caucasian contexts. It becomes increasingly easy to find examples of poets who write both in syllabic meter (*hece vezni*) and with the Persianate metrics (*aruz*) that characterized the poetry of the Ottoman court (the typically cited seventeenth-century examples of this trend are Gevheri and Aşık Ömer). By the eighteenth century, aşık styles were common in court poetry, just as aşıks with a formal scholarly education and predilection for court styles increased. The important increase in sources from this period means that there is ample material for further studying this expansion of aşık literature after 1700.

Conclusions

Aşıks became a common feature of the vast realms between Istanbul and Isfahan beginning in the sixteenth century. Although the term persistently retained the connotation of an outsider, it came to primarily denote a public performer who sang and told stories. Its many layers may explain why Turkish folklorists prefer a more academic alternative, *saz şairi*, or "poet of the saz," referring to the string instrument that most aşıks played. They performed in tribal settlements, villages, towns, and urban courts, as well as in the quintessentially early modern institutions of large army encampments, coffeehouses, and Sufi lodges.

The rise of the aşık in the sixteenth century should not be understood as simply an urban and Islamic "update" to the legacy of the Turkish *ozan*, because such an approach gives undue weight to the ahistorical universal notion of Islamization in aşık literature. The rise of the aşık was a chiefly a result of patterns noticeable across Eurasia, namely the spread of the written and spoken Turkish, as well as new forms of literary production such as the *cönk*. Aşık literature should push scholars to rethink the notion of the national literary canon and focus instead on cultural production in multiple linguistic and religious communities. This literary corpus in turn demonstrates the new generic, accessible, and shared role of the Turkish literature in the early modern era. The fact that many aşık traditions, such as those of Köroğlu and Aşık Garip, moved between Anatolia and Iran should also encourage us to connect Ottoman realms with lands further east in our historical and literary analysis.

Still, the craft of aşıks remained chiefly oral. Chodźko attests to how aşıks in nineteenth-century Iran were bewildered by his request to write the contents of the Köroğlu tales: "The task was more difficult than at first thought," he recalled, as "many Mirzas were quite surprised, nay shocked," at his insistence on having them record the stories.[47] The oral nature of performance, as well as the informal and scattered nature of *cönk*s, long considered a lesser manuscript tradition, explains why aşık literature remains such an untapped and exciting source for historical and literary scholarship.

Notes

1 For the sake of simplicity and consistency, I follow modern Turkish spelling for widely used terms. In some cases, eastern alternatives would be more accurate (e.g., Azerbaijani *aşıq* or Persian *āsheq*). The word comes from the Arabic term for lover, *'āshiq*, a concept which carries Sufi mystical connotations beyond its obvious romantic sense.

2 Ilhan Başgöz, "Turkish Hikaye-Telling Tradition in Azerbaijan, Iran," *Journal of American Folklore* 83, no. 330 (October–December): 391–92.

3 Mehmet Fuat Köprülü, *Saz Şairleri* (Ankara: Akçağ Yayınları, 2004), 43.

4 *Ozan* came to acquire the meaning of a garrulous talker as early as the fourteenth to fifteenth centuries, and this became the dominant connotation of the term in the following centuries; see Türk Dil Kurumu Yayınları 212, *Tarama Sözlüğü V* (Ankara: Ankara Üniversitesi Basımevi, 1995), 3044–45. The term also became synonymous to *yanşak*, meaning "blabbermouth"; see *Tarama Sözlüğü VI*, Türk Dil Kurumu, 4292.

5 Cemal Kafadar, *Between Two Worlds: The Construction of the Ottoman State* (Berkeley: University of California Press, 1996), 81–82, ProQuest Ebook Central.

6 Evrim Binbaş, "Oğuz Khan Narratives," in *Encyclopaedia İranica,* online s.v., accessed March 2020, www.iranicaonline.org/articles/oguz-khan-narratives.

7 Muhammad bin Suleyman Fuzūlī, *Hadikatü's-Süeda*, hazırlayan Dr. Şeyma Güngör (Ankara: Kültür ve Turizm Bakanlığı Yayınları, 1987), 16–17.

8 Mehmet Fuad Köprülü, *Türk Edebiyatı Ders Notları* (Istanbul: ALFA, 2014), 391–94.

9 Nile Green, "Introduction: The Frontiers of the Persianate World," *The Persianate World: The Frontiers of a Eurasian Lingua Franca*, ed. Nile Green (Oakland: University of California Press, 2019), 26.

10 Willem M. Floor and Hasan Javadi, "The Role of Azerbaijani Turkish in Safavid Iran," *Iranian Studies* 46, no. 4 (2013): 2–4.

11 Kevork Pamukciyan and Osman Köker, *Ermeni Kaynaklarından Tarihe Katkılar: II Cilt, Ermeni Harfli Türkçe Metinler* (İstanbul: Aras Yayıncılık, 2002), xi–xxiv, 28–31; A.J. Hacikyan, Gabriel Basmajian, Edward S. Franchuk, and Nourhan Ouzounian, *The Heritage of Armenian Literature*, vol. II (Detroit, MI: Wayne State University Press, 2000), 58–60.

12 Evliya Çelebi, *Evliya Çelebi Seyahatnâmesi*, ed. Robert Dankoff, Seyit Ali Kahraman, and Yücel Dağlı, vol. 2 (Istanbul: Yapı Kredi Yayınları, 2011), book 9, 147.

13 Orhan Şaik Gökyay, "Cönk," in *TDV İslam Ansiklopedisi*, online s.v., accessed April 2019, https://islamansiklopedisi.org.tr/conk.

14 Melis Taner, *Caught in a Whirlwind: A Cultural History of Ottoman Baghdad as Reflected in Its Illustrated Manuscripts* (Leiden: Brill, 2020), 72, online resource, www.brill.com.

15 Konrad Hirschler, *The Written Word in the Medieval Arabic Lands: A Social and Cultural History of Reading Practices* (Edinburgh: Edinburgh University Press, 2012).

16 The lack of distinction between these closely related categories is a major problem in Turkish literary studies, as is addressed in numerous essays in Hatice Aynur, Müjgân Çakır, Hanife Koncu, Selim S. Kuru, and Ali Emre Özyıldırım, eds., *Mecmûa: Osmanlı Edebiyatının Kırkambarı* (Eski Türk Edebiyatı Çalışmaları, 7) (Istanbul: Turkuaz, 2012).

17 Fikret Türkmen, *Aşık Garip Hikayesi* (Ankara: Akçağ Yayınları, 1995), 2–3; Safura Yakubova, *Azerbajdzhanskoe Narodnoe Skazanie, "Ashik Garib"* (Ankara: Akademija Nauka Azerbajdzhanskoj SSR), 6, 10; Ali Karamustafa, "The Köroğlu Epic in Trans-imperial Perspective: The Story of the Ottoman and Safavid Expansion and Crises" (PhD diss., Stanford University, 2019), 35–36, 50–54.

Aşık *Literature in Historical Context*

18 Anonymous, *Azerbaycan Folklor Külliyatı*, XV (Bakı: AMEA Folklor İnstitutu), 8, 101; Bibliothèque nationale de France, Paris, Supplément persan 994, Şādeq Beg, "Kūrūghlī Nāmih," *Recueil* (1834–1835): 39b, 84a.

19 Bibliothèque nationale de France, Supplément persan 994, 48b–49a.

20 Dursun Celvani, "Aşık Garip Hikayesi: Cevlani," in *Hikâye: Turkish Folk Romance as Performance Art: Special Publications of the Folklore Institute*, ed. İlhan Başgöz (Bloomington: Indiana University Press, 2008), 486.

21 An example of this intertextuality is found in the works of Karacaoğlan (d. seventeenth century), who wrote about the lives of saintly figures (Haci Bektaş, Mevlânâ), heroes and their exploits (Ali, Hamza), and medieval romances (Leyla and Mecnūn, Hüsrev and Şīrīn). See Köprülü, *Saz Şairleri*, 295.

22 Nurettin Albayrak, "Âşık," *TDV İslam Ansiklopedisi*, online s.v., accessed February 22, 2019, https://islamansiklopedisi.org.tr/asik; The work of other prominent folklorists such as Erman Artun also follows this pattern. Erman Artun, *Aşıklık Geleneği ve Aşık Edebiyatı*, 11. baskı (Adana: Karahan Kitabevi, 2019).

23 Walter Ong was a pioneer in this field with his work on orality and textuality in early modern Europe. Walter Ong, *Orality and Literacy: The Technologizing of the Word* (New York: Routledge, 1982).

24 Peter Heath, *The Thirsty Sword: Sirat 'Antar and the Arabic Popular Epic* (Salt Lake City: University of Utah Press, 1996), 47–50.

25 Meherrem Qasımlı, *Ozan-Aşıq Sənəti* (Baku: Uğur Neşriyyatı, 2011), 154.

26 There has been little comprehensive study of these earlier manuscripts from social or historical perspectives. See Karamustafa, "The Koroghlu Epic"; Judith Wilks, "Aspects of the Koroglu Destan: Chodzko and Beyond" (PhD diss., University of Chicago, 1995).

27 Some examples include aşık performances in town squares or markets: Anonymous, *Azerbaycan Folklor Külliyatı*, XV, 3, 94; Matenadaran, Mesrop Mashtots Institute of Ancient Manuscripts, Yerevan, MS 7318; Anonymous, "Keoroghlun Naghli," in *Untitled Codex* (1881), 114b. In army encampments: Anonymous, *Azerbaycan Folklor Külliyatı*, XVI, 322; Bibliothèque nationale de France, Supplément persan 994, 133a; Matenadaran, MS 7318, 107b. Most of the other performances, which feature regularly in the story, occur in the homes of Ottoman notables.

28 Alexander Chodźko, *Specimens of the Popular Poetry of Persia* (London: Printed for the Oriental Translation Fund of Great Britain and Ireland, and Sold by W. H. Allen, 1842), 13.

29 Ali Naseri, *Köroğlu dar Iran Zamin* (Tabriz: Yaran, 1388 [2010]). See performer biographies.

30 Başgöz, "Turkish Hikaye-Telling," 395.

31 Qasımlı, *Ozan-Aşıq*, 96–103.

32 Mehmet Bayrak, *Alevi-Bektaşi Edebiyatında Ermeni Aşıkları (Aşuglar)* (Ankara: Öz-Ge Yayınları, 2005), 108–9.

33 Anonymous, *Azerbaycan Folklor Külliyatı*, XV, 223.

34 Ibid., 351.

35 See note 4.

36 Sünbülzade Vehbi, "Sühan Kasidesi," in *Sünbül-zâde Vehbî Dîvânı*, ed. Ahmet Yenikale (London: Ukde, 2011), 274.

37 Köprülü, *Saz Şairleri*, 288.

38 For an example of this pattern, see Anonymous, *Azerbaycan Folklor Külliyatı*, XV, 223.

39 Pertev Naili Boratav, "La Littérature des 'Āšıq," in *Philologiae Turcicae Fundamenta: Iussu et Auctoritate Unionis Universae Studiosorum Rerum Orientalium*, ed. Jean Deny (Aquis Mattiacis, Steiner, 1959), 147.

40 Chodźko, *Specimens*, 3–4.

41 Köprülü, *Saz Şairleri*, 613; Karamustafa, "The Köroğlu Epic," 135–71.

42 Fikret Türkmen, *Türk Halk Edebiyatının Ermeni Kültürüne Tesiri* (Akademi, Sivas 1992), 22–33.

43 Sayat Nova, *Sayat Nova* (Bakı: Azerbaycan Devlet Neşriyyatı, 1963).

44 Evliya Çelebi, *Evliya Çelebi Seyahatnâmesi*, ed. Robert Dankoff, Seyit Ali Kahraman, and Yücel Dağlı, vol. 2 (Istanbul: Yapı Kredi Yayınları, 2006), book 8, 73.

45 Mark L. Soileau, "Âşık," in *Encyclopaedia of Islam, THREE*, online s.v., https://doi.org/10.1163/1573-3912_ei3_SIM_0099.

46 Markus Dressler, "Alevīs," in *Encyclopaedia of Islam, THREE*, online s.v., https://doi.org/10.1163/1573-3912_ei3_COM_0167.

47 Chodźko, *Specimens*, 13.

References

Albayrak, Nurettin. "Âşık." *TDV İslam Ansiklopedisi*, online resource. Accessed February 22, 2019. https://islamansiklopedisi.org.tr/asik.

Anonymous. *Azerbaycan Folklor Külliyatı, Dastanlar*, vol. XV–XVI. Bakı: AMEA Folklor İnstitutu, 2010.

Artun, Erman. *Aşıklık Geleneği ve Aşık Edebiyatı*, 11 baskı. Adana: Karahan Kitabevi, 2019.

Aynur, Hatice, Müjgân Çakır, Hanife Koncu, Selim S. Kuru, and Ali Emre Özyıldırım. *Mecmûa: Osmanlı edebiyatının kırkambarı*. Eski Türk edebiyatı çalişmaları; 7. Istanbul: Turkuaz, 2012.

Başgöz, Ilhan. "Turkish Hikaye—Telling Tradition in Azerbaijan, Iran." *Journal of American Folklore* 83, no. 330 (October–December): 391–405.

Bayrak, Mehmet. *Alevi-Bektaşi Edebiyatında Ermeni Aşıkları (Aşuglar)*. Ankara: Öz-Ge Yayınları, 2005.

Binbaş, Evrim. "Oğuz Khan Narratives." In *Encyclopaedia İranica*, online s.v. Accessed March 2020. www.iranicaonline.org/articles/oguz-khan-narratives.

Boratav, Pertev Naili. "La Littérature Des 'Âşiq." In *Philologiae Turcicae Fundamenta: Iussu et Auctoritate Unionis Universae Studiosorum Rerum Orientalium*, edited by Jean Deny, 129–47. Aquis Mattiacis, Steiner, 1959.

Cevlani, Dursun. "Aşık Garip Hikayesi: Cevlani." In *Hikâye: Turkish Folk Romance as Performance Art: Special Publications of the Folklore Institute*, edited by Ilhan Başgöz, 455–89. Bloomington: Indiana University Press, 2008.

Chodźko, Alexander. *Specimens of the Popular Poetry of Persia*. London: Printed for the Oriental Translation Fund of Great Britain and Ireland, 1842.

Dressler, Markus. "Alevīs." In *Encyclopaedia of Islam, THREE*, online resource. https://doi.org/10.1163/1573-3912_ei3_COM_0167.

Evliya Çelebi. *Evliya Çelebi Seyahatnamesi*. Edited by Robert Dankoff, Seyit Ali Kahraman, and Yücel Dağlı, vol. 2, 10 books. Istanbul: Yapı Kredi 'Yayınları, 2011.

Floor, Willem M., and Hasan Javadi. "The Role of Azerbaijani Turkish in Safavid Iran." *Iranian Studies* 46, no. 4 (2013): 569–81.

Fuzūlī, Muhammad bin Suleyman. *Hadikatü's-Süeda*. Hazırlayan Dr. Şeyma Güngör. Ankara: Kültür ve Turizm Bakanlığı Yayınları, 1987.

Gökyay, Orhan Şaik. "Cönk." In *TDV İslam Ansiklopedisi*, online resource. Accessed April 2019. https://islamansiklopedisi.org.tr/conk.

Green, Nile. "Introduction: The Frontiers of the Persianate World." In *The Persianate World: The Frontiers of a Eurasian Lingua Franca*, edited by Nile Green, 1–71. Oakland: University of California Press, 2019.

Hacikyan, A.J., Gabriel Basmajian, Edward S. Franchuk, and Nourhan Ouzounian. *The Heritage of Armenian Literature*, vol. II. Detroit, MI: Wayne State University Press, 2000.

Heath, Peter. *The Thirsty Sword: Sirat Antar and the Arabic Popular Epic*. Salt Lake City: University of Utah Press, 1996.

Hirschler, Konrad. *The Written Word in the Medieval Arabic Lands: A Social and Cultural History of Reading Practices*. Edinburgh: Edinburgh University Press, 2012.

Kafadar, Cemal. *Between Two Worlds: The Construction of the Ottoman State*. Berkeley: University of California Press, 1995.

Karamustafa, Ahmet T. *God's Unruly Friends: Dervish Groups in the Islamic Later Middle Period, 1200–1550*. Oxford: Oneworld, 2006.

Karamustafa, Ali. "The Köroğlu Epic in Trans-imperial Perspective: The Story of the Ottoman and Safavid Expansion and Crises." Doctoral diss., Stanford University Press, 2019.

Köprülü, Mehmet Fuat. *Saz Şairleri*. Ankara: Akçağ Yayınları, 2004.

———. *Türk Edebiyatı Ders Notları*. Istanbul: ALFA, 2014.

"Kūrūghlī Nāmih." *Recueil*, 1r–156v. Supplément persan 994. Şādeq Beg. Paris: Bibliothèque nationale de France, 1834–1835.

Matenadaran, Mesrop Mashtots Institute of Ancient Manuscripts, Yerevan, Armenia. Anonymous. MS 7318. "Keoroghlun Naghli." In *Untitled Codex*, 105v–19v, 1881.

Naseri, Ali. *Koroghlu dar Iran Zamin*. Tabriz: Yaran, 1388 [2010].

Ong, Walter. *Orality and Literacy: The Technologizing of the Word*. New York: Routledge, 1982.

Pamukciyan, Kevork, and Osman Köker. *Ermeni Harfli Türkçe Metinler, vol. 2 of Ermeni Kaynaklarından Ttarihe Katkılar*. İstanbul: Aras Yayıncılık, 2002.

Qasımlı, Meherrem. *Ozan-Aşıq Sənəti*. Bakı: Uğur Nəşriyyatı, 2011.

Soileau, Mark L. Âşık." In *Encyclopaedia of Islam, THREE*, online resource. https://doi.org/10.1163/1573-3912_ei3_SIM_0099.

Sünbülzade Vehbî. *Sünbül-zâde Vehbî Dîvânı*. Edited by Ahmet Yenikale. London: Ukde, 2011.

Taner, Melis. *Caught in a Whirlwind: A Cultural History of Ottoman Baghdad as Reflected in Its Illustrated Manuscripts*. Arts and Archaeology of the Islamic World, vol. 15. Online resource. Leiden: Brill, 2020. www.brill.com.

Türk Dil Kurumu Yayınları 212. *Tarama Sözlüğü*, vol. 8. Ankara: Ankara Üniversitesi Basımevi, 1995.

Türkmen, Fikret. *Türk Halk Edebiyatının Ermeni Kültürüne Tesiri*. Akademi, Sivas 1992.

———. *Aşık Garip Hikayesi*. Ankara: Akçağ Yayınları, 1995.

Yakubova, Safura Z. *Azerbaĭdzhanskoe Narodnoe Skazanie, "Ashyg Garib."* Izdatel'stvo Akademia Nauka Azerbaĭdzhanskoĭ SSR [Moscow: Publishing House of the Azerbaijan Soviet Socialist Republic Academy of Sciences], 1968.

3

SELFHOOD AND MYSTICAL LANGUAGE IN THE POETRY OF YUNUS EMRE

Zeynep Oktay

Turkish mystic poet Yunus Emre (d. 1320) was a foundational figure for the vernacularization process of Western Turkish and the dissemination of Sufi teachings and literature in Anatolia. Despite his widespread veneration by an entire spectrum of religious groups throughout Ottoman history and beyond, and despite the large body of secondary literature dedicated to him, the doctrinal content of Yunus Emre's corpus has not been fully investigated. This chapter analyzes Yunus Emre's Sufi teachings in relation to his understanding of the metaphysical status of language and how this relates to the poet's own words. A short introduction to Yunus Emre's life and works is followed by an overview of his reception during the Republican period in Turkey, tracing the politicization and the ensuing changes in his social image. This overview precedes the main body of the chapter, which includes a close reading of Yunus Emre's *Divan* (poetry collection) with regards to its conceptions of the self, focusing on the latter's relationship with language and mystical meaning. According to Yunus, the partial selves of our everyday lives and the greater selves of our absolute mystical truth each have a language of their own. While the former is based on a difference between "you" and "I," the latter is the locus of the inexpressible One, simultaneously hidden and revealed by the Sufi's poetry.

Life and Works

Recent studies on the vernacularization process of Western Turkish reveal that Anatolian Turkish as a written tradition can only be traced back to the early fourteenth century.[1] "Old Anatolian Turkish," as this language is currently named, also became spoken and written in the Balkans by the middle of the fourteenth century. Two major dynamics were at play in the development of Turkish as a literary language: The first of these was the patronage of Persophone and Arabophone authors by the Anatolian *beg*s (warlords) who rose to power after the fall of the Anatolian Seljuks and the subsequent Mongol period. These authors and their patrons led and supported a rich movement of translation and rewriting that sought to integrate this recently conquered periphery to Islamic culture and learning. The second is the role of popular Sufi figures in the same process of Islamization, wherein literature served as a medium of religious education, centered around the social space of the Sufi lodge. Yunus Emre's surviving *Divan* and *Risaletü'n-Nushiyye* are the best-known and most significant specimens of this latter process.[2]

40

DOI: 10.4324/9780429279270-5

Selfhood and Mystical Language in the Poetry of Yunus Emre

Information on Yunus' life is scarce and relies heavily on the references in his poems as well as legendary tales.[3] His dates of birth and death have been subject to various debates. A record published by Adnan Erzi, taken from a *mecmū'a* (book of miscellanea) at Beyazıt Library (n. 7912, fol. 38b), indicates that Yunus lived for 82 years and died in 720 (1320/21).[4] It is generally accepted that Yunus was born in an area near the Sakarya River and lived in the dervish lodge of his master Tapduk Emre which was located at Emrem Sultan near Nallıhan (part of today's Ankara). According to Semih Tezcan, the word *"emre"* is a Turkified version of the word *"ham-rāh"* in Persian, indicating that Yunus was a wandering dervish.[5] This is also in line with what we know of his pedigree, as indicated below. While there are graves attributed to Yunus in various places in Anatolia (most notably in Karaman) as well as in Azerbaijan, scholars generally agree on the authenticity of the grave in Sarıköy, near Sivrihisar.[6]

Although his references to being *ümmī* (illiterate) in his poems led popular legend to consider him illiterate, it is now well accepted that Yunus was fairly educated, though most likely in the context of the Sufi lodge (as opposed to an official madrasa education). Abdülbaki Gölpınarlı draws close parallels between some of Yunus' poems and those of Sa'di-i Shirazi (d. 1292) and Maulana Jalal al-din Rumi (d. 1273), concluding that Yunus knew enough Persian to do translation.[7] In his *Divan*, Yunus expresses his spiritual lineage as *"Yūnus'a Ṭapduġ u Ṣaltuġ u Barak'dandur naṣīb* [Yūnus's spiritual lot comes from Tapduk, Saltuk, and Barak]."[8] We know very little about Tapduk Emre, who is mentioned as Yunus' master in other poems as well. The hagiography of Hacı Bektaş (d. 1271?), eponym of the Bektashi order, contains an episode in which Tapduk Emre's name (which actually refers to the finding of a divine child) is explained as a response to seeing the miracles of Hacı Bektaş.[9] Sarı Saltuk (d. shortly after 1300), on the other hand, is the hero of the epic/hagiography named the *Saltuk-name*,[10] famous for his role in the Islamization of Anatolia and the Balkans. Barak Baba, his disciple, is a prominent early figure in the development of dervish piety in Anatolia, who traveled to Iran and became the close trustee of İlkhan Ghazan Khan (r. 694–703/1295–1304) and his successor Muhammad Khudabanda Uljaytu (r. 703–716/1304–1316).[11] In addition to these three masters, Yunus mentions Jalal al-Din Rumi, for whom he had great veneration, in his poems.

Yunus Emre's Turkish *Divan* is preserved in numerous manuscripts both in Turkey and abroad. According to a *mecmū'a* (miscellanea) published by Şinasi Tekin, the *Divan* was composed in 707/1307.[12] The *Divan* currently has two major scholarly editions, in addition to numerous more popular ones. The edition by Abdülbaki Gölpınarlı consists of 100 poems, whereas Mustafa Tatcı's edition includes a total of 417. This difference results from varying approaches to the difficulty in differentiating between the poems of Yunus Emre, 'Aşık Yunus, and other poets who wrote with the same pen name and imitated Yunus' style.[13]

The Gölpınarlı edition of the *Divan* consists of the transliteration of a fifteenth-century manuscript, which also includes selections from other manuscripts at the end. In contrast, the Tatcı edition contains 12 manuscripts (as well as poetry in some miscellanea books) of varying dates, and should thus be considered as representative of the "Yunus tradition," the entire tradition of poets who wrote with the pen name of Yunus. We currently have knowledge of five fifteenth-century manuscripts of Yunus' *Divan*.[14] A comparative edition of these manuscripts can yield more accurate results regarding the identification of Yunus' poetry. In this study, I cite and elaborate on poetry found in these five manuscripts while excluding parts of the Gölpınarlı and Tatcı editions that do not feature there.

Yunus Emre is also the author of the *Risaletü'n-Nushiyye*, a 600-couplet work in the form of a *mesnevi* composed in the year 707/1307. A didactic work lacking the lyrical quality and mystical content of Yunus' poems, it is considered by some scholars to be misattributed on the basis of its content, language, and vocabulary. On the other hand, a close analysis of the work, in addition to an examination of the manuscripts, suggests that differences in language and teaching between the two works stem from differences in genre and audience. While the didactic and prescriptive nature of the *Risaletü'n-Nushiyye* makes it a typical example of works written for the education of the novice in the Sufi path, the lyrical poetry found in the *Divan* appears as a spiritual conversation with spiritual directors of equally high rank, with one's deepest self, and finally, with God. Moreover, a close look reveals that the *Divan* also includes poetry with prescriptive content, although significantly low in number.

Modern Reception and Politicization

Due to the political dynamics behind the formation of the Republic of Turkey, from the early Republican period onwards Yunus Emre became a highly politicized figure. This resulted in a great discrepancy between the various identities attributed to Yunus Emre, ranging from his depiction as a secular humanist or a founder of Turkishness to a model for modern Islam. Among the scholars who have investigated the reception of Yunus Emre in modern Turkey, Beşir Ayvazoğlu's monograph *Yunus, Ne Hoş Demişsin: Cumhuriyet Sonrası Yunus Emre Yorumları* (Yunus, How Well You Have Spoken: Republican Interpretations of Yunus Emre) is the most extensive.[15] This work narrates the modern interpretations of Yunus up to the early 2000s, beginning with the modern "discovery" of Yunus Emre by early Republican scholar Fuad Köprülü and his monumental work *Türk Edebiyatında İlk Mutasavvıflar* (Early Mystics in Turkish Literature).[16] In its investigation of a wide array of sources ranging from official festivals to music to the plastic arts, Ayvazoğlu demonstrates the intricate relationship of Yunus Emre's image to governmental politics at each turn of modern Turkish history, while also underlining dissident voices within this politicization. Thus, in the early Republican period, Yunus was praised as a founder of Turkishness and the Turkish language. His poetry (to which few have access in its original form) provides historical identity and continuity to a modern Turkish public that was stripped of its history through cultural politics based on the rejection of the entire Ottoman period. With the humanist cultural politics of the 1940s, the most prominent interpretation of Yunus stressed his "universal" character as a secular humanist beyond Islam, a trend that lasted with lesser force until the 1990s, when the centralization of Islam and Islamism in Turkish politics put forth a decidedly Muslim Yunus. Yet this Muslim mystic, while seemingly more historically accurate, is one who exceedingly resembles modern and contemporary understandings of Islam and is made to serve Islamist ideology and politics up to our day.

Perhaps the most intriguing aspect of this account is the fact that, at every turning point in modern Turkish history, governments needed to fit Yunus into their ideological positions and intellectuals had to position Yunus and his worldview in relation to their own. Being indifferent to Yunus was not an option for either. At the same time, this preoccupation with Yunus did not translate into actual academic work; the body of scholarly work on Yunus (that of actual merit, which does not serve primarily to voice ideology) remained scarce compared to the influence of his social image. The above-mentioned issue with the editions of his *Divan* is perhaps the most obvious example of this. However, the doctrinal content of his work has received even less attention, with fewer than a handful of scholars taking a serious look at this subject throughout the Republican period. In this regard, the following part of this chapter is an attempt to help fill an important void. As a close investigation of Yunus Emre's religious doctrine and its relationship to his understanding of his own poetry, the chapter aims to offer a reading that goes beyond ideological positions on Yunus Emre to take a direct look at his own corpus.

Selfhood and Language

Modern theoretical discussions on mystical experience often describe it as a matter of selfhood and language. In his article titled "Mystique [Mysticism]," Michel de Certeau characterizes mystical experience as a transformation of consciousness that is identical to an annihilation of consciousness, where one is outside of oneself as a greater Self is asserted.[17] Inherent in this experience is a paradox: Mystical experience itself, as a position of radical interiority, is beyond the social; yet to be able to speak of it, one needs to move outside of the event into history, society, language.[18]

The mystical poet thus has a daunting task at hand: to say the unsayable, to create within the particular social language he has inherited a space in which reference can be made to the beyond, to the absolute. When de Certeau says "mystical language is a social language," he is formulating a definition of language that encompasses the mystic's entire ontological and epistemological field of experience:

> "Language" refers not only to the syntax and vocabulary of a certain tongue—that is to say, the combination of apertures and closures that determine the possibilities of comprehension—but also to the codes of recognition, the organization of the imaginary, the sensory hierarchizations in which smell or sight predominate, the fixed constellation of institutions or doctrinal references, and so forth.[19]

Hence language can be defined as the entire semantic system that configures our individual consciousness. Transcending this received language and transcending one's socially constructed self appear to be interlinked processes.

A central aspect of Yunus Emre's mystical experience and language is the concept of divine love.[20] Yunus posits divine love as not only the necessary fuel in the mystic's spiritual advancement but also, and more importantly, the source of creation, the truth of existence as the locus of the divine beloved's self-contemplation. This central tenet of Yunus' religious doctrine is analyzed by Ahmet Karamustafa in his article "İslam Tasavvuf Düşüncesinde Yunus Emre'nin Yeri" (The Place of Yunus Emre in the Sufi Thought of Islam), where he connects Yunus Emre to the path of love (*mazhab-i 'ishq*) in Sufism, initiated by Ahmad al-Ghazzali (d. 1126) and developed by figures such as Najm al-Din Daye (d. 1256), Fahr al-din Iraqi (d. 1289), and most famously, Jalal al-Din Rumi.[21] In this regard, Yunus Emre's vast yet unexplored influence on Sufi poetry in Turkish can also be traced in the dissemination of the doctrine of divine love, which permeated almost all aspects of Muslim religious discourse in the Ottoman realm. The chapter at hand will focus on a much less known, yet equally central aspect of Yunus' thought: the quest for the absolute Self and a language able to refer to it.

Experiencing and expressing the self is an essential problematic in Yunus' *Divan*, where a multiplicity of selves appear to speak at the same time. In this regard, tracking the pronouns "*sen*" (you) and "*ben*" (me/I) offers us a venue for penetrating Yunus' religious doctrine. For Yunus, the search for God is an inward journey, a fact frequently repeated with phrases such as "*nite kim ben beni buldum; bu oldı kim Ḥaḳḳı buldum*" (when I found my own self, that is when I found God; G141)[22] and "*sen sende bulmazısañ ḳanda bulasın anı*" (If you cannot find Her[23] in your own self where will you find Her?; G198, T416). Although less pronounced in the *Risaletü'n-Nushiyye* due to the work's prescriptive approach and focus on moral values, the discovery of the self is also identified here as the true remedy for salvation.[24]

Yunus often juxtaposes two notions of self: the base self (i.e., the *nefs*) and the true self, which is identical to God's selfhood. The pronouns "*ben*" (me) and "*sen*" (you) may refer to either of these, depending on the couplet's particular message. They also often refer to both simultaneously, thus creating a double meaning possibly intended for disciples at different levels of spiritual accomplishment. Yunus frequently plays with these two "*sen*"s:

Gel imdi ḥicābuñ aç senden ayrıl saña ḳaç
Sende bulasın miʿrāc saña gelür cümle yol

Come and open up your veil; leave yourself and run to yourself
You shall find the ascension in your own self; all roads lead to you
(G81, T168)

The pronoun "*ben*" also carries a similar multivalence. The first of these is the poet's own selfhood, identified with the name "Yunus," while the second is once again the poet's true self, who is no longer Yunus but something that encompasses Yunus and all other partial selves within creation:

Benüm degül bu keleci varlıḳ senüñ Yūnus neci
Çün dilüme ḳadīr sensin sensüz dilüm uzatmayam[25]

These are not my words; existence is yours, what is Yunus for?
Since you are the one holding the power of my tongue, I shall not speak without you
(G88, T200)

These examples clarify that the identities of the speaker and listener are in constant flux, depending on how Yunus understands and presents his own selfhood.

The transformation of the Sufi's selfhood as the central experience of his spiritual journey is explained by Ahmad Ghazzali in his metaphysical treatise on love, the *Sawanih* (ca. 1114). Accordingly, the changing emotional and experiential states of the lover of God result from the persistence of his partial self, while the lover's erasure of his own selfhood is an act of transcending the dictates of time:

> So long as the lover subsists through his own self, he is subject to separation and union, acceptance and refusal, contraction (*qabḍ*) and expansion (*basṭ*), sorrow and delight, etc. . . . Once he comes in himself to the (real) self from her, his way to the (real) self starts from her and leads to her, he will not be subject to those states. . . . In this (sublime) station he is the master of Time. When he descends to the sky of this world, he will have supremacy over Time, instead of Time having supremacy over him, and he will be free from (the dictates of) Time.[26]

Ghazzali's conceptualization of Time (*vaqt*) identifies it with creation itself, which is subject to change, origination, and decay. Ghazzali describes the capacity to transcend time as a type of spiritual power that allows the lover of God to become the locus and actor of God's will. As a follower of the spiritual path of Ghazzali, Yunus also devotes significant portions of his poetry to the motif of being beyond time. This is expressed most vividly in the poems where the poet's self travels through time and identifies itself with various aspects of creation, most often with past prophets. The final lines of one of these poems read:

Şimdi adum Yūnusdurur ol demde İsmāʿīl idi
Ol dost içün ʿArafāta ḳurbān olup çıkan benem

Now my name is Yunus; at that time it was Ismail
I am the one who climbed Mount Arafat as sacrifice
(G92, T208)

This couplet is taken from a *şaṭḥiyye*, a genre originating from the classical genre of *shaṭḥ* in Arabic, wherein the author's self is substituted for God, who is expressed to be the true speaker. There are many such poems in Yunus' *Divan*; these typically end with the repeated rhyme (*redif*) of "*benem*" (I am).[27] In one such poem where the speaker identifies himself with the names of God, the creator of the universe, the faith in the believer's heart, and the author and content of the Qur'an; this true and absolute self is once again juxtaposed with "Yunus": "*Yūnus degül bunu diyer kendülügidür söyleyen / Kāfir olur inanmayan evvel āḫir heman benem*" (The One who says this is not Yunus; it is her own Selfhood / Those who do not believe become infidels; I am the First and the Last; G94, T215).[28]

In fact, these pronouns only exist in the world of the created; their very existence points to a vision of multiplicity, hence a lack in the spiritual accomplishment of the speaker, as when Yunus says: "*Ya niçe bir ben diyem sensin diyem utanmadın*" (Until when will I keep saying "I" and "you are" without being ashamed?; G99). The pronouns themselves are thus a sign of the world of multiplicity, in contrast with the Oneness of God. Yunus frequently refers to a time and place prior to the Pre-eternal Pact (*bezm-i elest*), in which the believers attested to God's sovereignty by saying "Yes indeed" to the question of "Am I not your Lord?" (7:172). This time and place, which Yunus describes with phrases such as "*ben olıdum ol benidüm*" (I was her and she / I was me; G95, T186) and "*ġayr-ı sen ü ben idük*" (we were beyond "you" and "me"; G136, T379), was prior to creation and the differentiation between the lover and the beloved. All speech (*söz*) was abolished (*mensūḫ*); all that existed was God's Self in its absolute transcendence (*sübḥān*), the true object of veneration for the lovers of God.

At this time, Yunus himself, together with all the other lovers, was hidden in God. Yunus describes this as the place of oneness (*vaḥdet*) and sometimes refers to it simply as "*bir*" (one). In its definition as prior to pronouns and prior to the dialogue in the Pre-eternal Pact, we can identify this unity as prior to language. Creation itself is a loss of this experience of oneness. In separation, the beloved's silent self-contemplation becomes a fervent dialogue between the beloved and the lover. Yunus tells God: "*Senden yana varur yolum senden seni söyler dilüm / İlle saña irmez elüm bu ḥikmete ḳaldum ṭaʿna*" (My path leads towards you; you are spoken on my tongue that is given by you / Yet no matter what I cannot reach you; I am bewildered by this divine wisdom; G41, T29).

Love and longing lead to the erasure of Yunus' self, a process that is identified with the erasure of fear and anxiety, expressed with the words *ḳorḳu*, *ġuṣṣa*, *ḳayġu*, and *endīşe*. In a fashion similar to the passage above by Ahmad Ghazzali, Yunus also underlines that pre-eternal oneness was beyond these emotions, which are themselves signs of creation, hence separation. Once these emotions are gone and the created self is fully consumed by the beloved's love, an existential change occurs in his/her language. Yunus expresses this new language with the following words:

Yūnus saña ṭutdı yüzin unutdı cümle kendözin
Cümle saña söyler sözin söz söyleden sensin baña

Yunus turned his face towards you and completely forgot his own self
All beings speak to you in their tongues, yet when it comes to me you
   are the one who speaks

(G42)

Yunus thus moves from the vantage point of the supplicant to that of the beloved. This new language beyond pronouns erases all differentiations of identity and leaves its listeners stupefied. It is repeatedly referred to as *kudret dili* (the language of power)[29] and *kuş dili* (the language of birds; G185, T190), equated with unveiling a hidden secret, a language that nobody knows. Despite knowing that the people will fail to understand him, Yunus cannot hold himself back due to his intoxication with love:

Yūnusuñ ḥavşalası 'ışḳıla ṭolmışdurur
Derdin şaḳlıyamadı geñsüz söyler 'ışḳ dilin

Yunus's mental grasp is filled with love
He has been unable to hide his suffering; he
   speaks the tongue of love despite himself
                (G113, T275)

He juxtaposes this language of love and power with the language of created beings. According to Yunus, the tongue is the exoteric dimension of the heart. He often repeats that the tongue cannot express what the heart feels. Yet there is a path beyond this apparent impossibility: a path from the heart to the tongue, from the esoteric to the exoteric, from the hidden to the apparent. It is through a language capable of carrying the hidden secret, a tongue of the esoteric, where the truth can be expressed as it is. This language of the heart forms a stark contrast with the language of science and religious practice, which lack this multidimensional quality:

'İlm ü 'amel sözi degül Yūnus dili söyledügi
Dil ne bilür dost ḥaberin ben dostıla nice birem

What Yunus speaks is not the language of science and deed
How can the tongue have news of the beloved; how can it know
   my oneness with the friend?
                (G103, T232)

This separation between languages in their varying existential capacities underlies Yunus' frequent criticisms of exoteric representatives of Islam, namely the qadi, mufti, *müderris* (schoolteacher), *zāhid* (ascetic), and *ṣofu* (derogatory term for Sufi).[30]

The esoteric language that emerges as Yunus transforms is none other than the language of God. In addition to the above-mentioned poems in which God speaks through the first person, in several instances Yunus reveals God to be the actual speaker behind his words. In fact, in several poems Yunus reveals that all languages spoken on all tongues are the language of God and express the love of God as their sole referent.[31] He refers to this language as "*tesbīḥ dili*" (the language of the profession of God's glory; G47, T47).[32] This is the language of the One; its content is the One, its referent the One. All tongues speak this One in their own unique way:

Onsekiz biñ 'ālem ḥalḳı cümlesi bir içinde
Kimse yoḳ birden artuḳ söylenür dil içinde

Cümle bir anı birler cümle ana giderler
Cümle dil anı söyler her bir tebdīl içinde[33]

All created beings in the eighteen thousand universes are all in unison
The One is all that is spoken on all tongues; there is nothing else

All the ones profess his unity; all lead the path to the One
All languages speak the One in different forms

(G122, T326)

There thus seems to be a paradox here: If all beings already speak the language of God, how is it they are incapable of understanding this language and knowing God? How can we speak of a difference between the language of the heart and the language of science? Yunus resolves this matter through an intricate definition of the concept of "meaning."

Poetry and Meaning

The relationship between the language of created beings and the language of God is a major theme in the Persian authors who formed Yunus Emre's pedigree. In *Fihi ma fih*, Jalal al-Din Rumi underlines the above-mentioned paradox between the two languages and defines it as an issue of knowing.[34] All beings seek the same God; however, they are not aware of this fact. It is only on judgment day that all beings become aware of what they were actually seeking. Until then, Rumi says:

> *Ārī, īn shakhṣ muʿtaqidast ammā iʿtiqād rā namīdānad. Hamchunānke kūdakī muʿtaqid-i nānast ammā namīdānad ka cha chīz rā muʿtaqidast. Va hamchunīn az nāmiyāt. Dirakht zard u khushk mīshavad az tashnagī va namīdānad ke tashnagī chīst.*

> Indeed, this man has faith, but he does not know what faith is. This is like the child who has faith in bread but does not know this. Plants are like this, too. The tree turns pale, dries up from dehydration but it does not know what dehydration is.[35]

This ignorance is the result of a vision that can only grasp the exoteric, incapable of penetrating the surface of reality to access its inner meaning. Yet such ignorance appears and takes form only in speaking; it is only through our speech that the truth of our worship becomes hidden beneath the veil of the dichotomy of faith and infidelity. Prior to language, our thoughts are beyond faith and infidelity, in the realm of the absolute truth of our worship.[36]

A similar perspective is put forth by Rumi's precursor Farid al-Din ʿAttar (d. 1221) in *Manṭiq al-Tayr* (The Conference of the Birds), which begins with a section praising God, where all beings are described as intoxicated in their profession of God's glory and transcendence. In the initial layer of ʿAttar's famous allegory, the hoopoe is identified with the spiritual director who leads the disciples towards spiritual perfection by transforming them through his words. On a second level, it is ʿAttar himself who transforms the reader with the language of birds, a language beyond logic and beyond opposites. The hoopoe tells the birds: "*Mard-i maʿnā bāsh! Dar ṣūrat mapich! Chīst maʿnā? Aṣl. Ṣūrat chīst? Hich!*" (Be a Man of Meaning! Do not become entangled in the form! What is meaning? The foundation. What is form? Nothing!)[37] In fact, the word "meaning" appears at several instances in the work in opposition to the word *ṣūrat* (form, appearance), as its hidden inner dimension, the goal of spiritual achievement.

This definition of "*maʿnā*" (meaning) by ʿAttar has close parallels in the poetry of Yunus Emre, whose use of the word reveals a strong preoccupation with defining and locating meaning.[38]

The central notion in the poet's various uses of the word is that meaning is the esoteric, hidden dimension of language, and thus of creation. Meaning is also the hidden dimension of the partial self, equated with Yunus or the listener; access to meaning is thus identified with access to God's selfhood, hence with salvation.

The word "meaning" also appears as part of a tripartite notion of theophany (*tecellī*), in which God manifests herself first in the divine names and attributes (*ṣıfāt*), then through these in the forms (*ṣūret*) of creation. This central tenet of Sufi thought formulated most profoundly by Ibn 'Arabi (d. 1240) relies on a progression from the esoteric to the exoteric, in which God's Selfhood is defined as the absolute esoteric (referred to as the *bāṭınu'l-bāṭın*, the esoteric of the esoteric). Yunus identifies this absolute hidden with "meaning" and presents the attributes as a way of accessing it:

Ṣūretden gel ṣıfāta anda ma'nī bulasın
Ḥayāllerde ḳalmaġıl erden maḥrūm ḳalasın[39]

Travel from the form to the attribute; there you will find meaning
Do not remain in visions; or you will remain deprived of the Perfect Man
(G105, T263)

Similar to the differentiation between the language of the heart and the language of science, Yunus juxtaposes this "meaning" with a language of the exoteric, which fails to carry it and thus consists of nothing but a façade: "*Dört kitābuñ ma'nīsi bellidür bir elifde / Sen elif dirsün ḫoca ma'nīsi ne dimekdür*" (The meaning of the four holy books is visible in one Alef[40] / O khoja! You say Alef but tell me, do you know what it means?; G163, T114). In this regard, the language of the exoteric is in truth a language of hypocrisy, a language that veils not the hidden meaning but the hidden ignorance. Yunus stresses this perspective by juxtaposing the word *ma'nā* (meaning) with the word *da'vā* (claim), identified with the act of making a false claim to a greater access to truth:

Bize dīdār gerek dünyā gerekmez
Bize ma'nā gerek da'vā gerekmez

What we want is the beloved's face; we have no need for the world
What we want is the meaning; we have no need for the claim
(G67, T120)

These hypocrite representatives of religion are identified in Yunus' poetry with the *müftī* (religious official), *müderris* (madrasa teacher), *faḳīh* (scholar of law), and Sufi (who at this time had already become a figure of worldly power).[41] In their attachment to exoteric observance and science, these figures have lost the true purpose of worship. As a result, the meaning behind Yunus' words is hidden to them, appearing meaningless and scandalous. Yunus expresses this in one of his famous poems:

Ben bir kitāb oḳudum ḳalem anı yazmadı
Mürekkeb eyler isem yetmiye yidi deñiz

Ben oruç namāz içün süci içdüm esridüm
Tesbīḥ ü seccādeyçün diñledüm çeşte ḳopuz

Yūnus'uñ bu sözinden sen ma'nī añlarısañ
Ḳonya menāresini göresin bir çuvalduz

I read a book no pen has ever written
If I were to put it into ink, seven seas would not suffice

For fasting and daily prayer I drank wine and became drunk
For the rosary and prayer rug I listened to *çeşte* and *ḳopuz*[42]

If you understand the meaning of these words by Yunus
You shall see the minaret of Konya as a packing needle
(G70, T125)

Like 'Attar's use of the phrase *mard-i ma'nā* (the men of meaning), Yunus juxtaposes the hypocrite representatives of religion with those he calls "*ma'nā eri*" (the men of meaning; G80, T174), the true spiritual directors who reveal the hidden meaning and bring salvation upon those who hear them. These Perfect Men are those who make the spiritual journey (the archetype of which is the Prophet's Ascension) through the entirety of existence inside the vehicle of their own bodies, which Yunus refers to as "*ma'nā evi*" (the house of meaning; G170).[43] "Meaning" is also what is shared among these Perfect Men, their common language. Yunus expresses this in a couplet expressing his reverence for Jalal al-Din Rumi: "*Mevlānā ṣoḥbetinde sāzıla 'işret oldı / 'Ārif ma'nīye ṭaldı çün biledür ferişte*" (In the company of Maulana musical instruments brought joy and intoxication / The gnostic immersed himself in meaning, because the angels were present; G121, T321).

The poet Yunus Emre is one such spiritual director, whose speech (identical to "meaning") has become famous among the people (G120, T324). Yunus also identifies himself with his own master, Tapduk Emre, under whose spiritual guidance he became capable of revealing the hidden truth (G104, T235). In one of his poems, Yunus describes the replacement of his base self with his true self as a replacement of the person of Yunus with that of Tapduk Emre:

Yarın maḥşer ḳopıcaġaz ḳamu ḳul nefsüm diyiser
Ben Yūnusı hiç anmayam Ṭapduġı getürem dile[44]

Tomorrow when the apocalypse comes all servants of God will say "my self"
I will not think of Yunus for even a moment; Tapduk will be the name on my tongue
(G126, T330)

In this sense, the words of the spiritual director (i.e., his esoteric language) have a transformative power to engender and strengthen the divine love in the listener, thus helping to tear away the veil of the base self, the veil of the pronouns "you" and "me." This transformation of selfhood goes hand in hand with a moral transformation:

Sen saña ne ṣanursañ ayruġa da anı ṣan
Dört kitābuñ ma'nīsi budur eger varısa

Bildük gelenler gelmiş ḳonanlar girü göçmiş
'Işḳ şarābından içmiş kim ma'nī ṭuyarısa

Whatever you wish for yourself, wish the same for others
If there is a meaning to the four books, this must be it

We know that whoever has come to earth is to go back
Whoever hears the meaning has drunk from the wine of love
(G119, T318–319)

Elsewhere in Yunus' poetry, the phrase "*ışḳ şarābı*" (the wine of love) is replaced with "*ma'nī şarābı*" (the wine of meaning; G130, T366). In this regard, the wine of divine love can be identified with the spiritual director's words, which reinstate the true faith in the believer and lead him from a vision of multiplicity to an experience of the One (G132, T323).

Such an interpretation also allows us to resolve the apparent paradox mentioned earlier, in between created beings' ignorance of God's language and their constant expression of it. Just as the true selves of all beings are identical to God's selfhood, the languages of all beings are identical in meaning to the language of God. This is because meaning itself is not an attribute of the world of multiplicity, but holds the One as its sole referent. When the meaning is hidden, we see and hear the numerous languages of created beings, signifying a plurality of spiritual levels. These languages and the various partial selves they denote seem alien to one another, like foreign languages whose meanings are obscure to us. This results from a discrepancy between the meaning and the form of language, between the One and the many, opposites that signify an impossibility: the impossibility of the many to express the One, the failure of language to access and express the One. Yunus' poetry is filled with expressions stressing the impossibility of his task.

In this regard, the Perfect Man's language is the only language where the face/form of language and its meaning are not in opposition but harmony. This language of birds is a language that transcends duality, and in so doing, becomes ontologically identical to the language of God. As a language of divine power, it has the capacity to transform its listeners, to shatter their base selves and allow the hidden truth to appear. On the other hand, the language of the men of love only transcends duality because these men let go of their adherence to their partial selves, and thus move from a position of *da'vā* to one of *ma'nā*.

In his article "Mystical Speech and Mystical Meaning," Stephen Katz defines three main properties of mystical language: language as transformational, language as power, and language as information.[45] In Yunus Emre's poetry, these three aspects appear deeply intertwined: As the carrier of *ma'nā*, poetry instructs, acts upon, and transforms its listener. It thus acts upon the world itself and takes part in God's act of creation. In this regard, poetry has a special significance: It is only with poetry that we are able to transcend the languages of created beings, because only poetry can carry the ambiguity inherent in the existence of multiple levels of meaning. The face of poetry is a veil, like every other language that veils the oneness of the truth, but poetry does something more: It reveals while hiding at the same time. It uses the plurality of language to refer beyond it, to turn towards its impossible referent.

Conclusion: The Lyrical and the Mystical

Our discussion of Yunus Emre's notions of selfhood, language, and meaning demonstrates that Yunus was deeply preoccupied with the paradox of expressing the inexpressible, with creating a language where the impossible could be achieved. He defined this language as a tongue of the esoteric that refers to the One as its sole referent, hidden and revealed at the same time by the multiplicity of speaking selves and their polyvalent pronouns. Yet one question remains: How did this endeavor for a transcendental language play into Yunus' lyricism for which he became widely famous and influential?

To understand the role of the lyrical in Yunus Emre's poetry, we must return to our initial discussion, to the concept of love. In her discussion of the role of paradox in the poetry of Rumi, Fatemeh Keshavarz states that for Rumi, love itself is a paradox, "the contradiction inherent in the oneness of the two, the concurrent separation and unity of the lover and the beloved."[46] As a "linguistic manifestation of bewilderment," Rumi's poetry is "an extended linguistic paradox that operates at the limits of discourse."[47] According to Keshavarz, this linguistic paradox operates through its emotional component, an enchantment of the senses that demolishes the categorical boundaries of existing discourse.

Yunus Emre's poetry creates a similar emotional and suprarational experience in its audience through a juxtaposition of its two referents: the multiple, exemplified by the structure of language itself, and the One, the silent and absolute Other. Through a juxtaposition of multiple form and singular meaning, poetry brings together what cannot be brought together. It thus makes it possible to reveal while hiding, to speak while remaining silent.[48] Indeed, the tension between speaking and remaining silent is prevalent throughout Yunus' poetry. In this regard, we can say that Yunus' poetry approaches silence in its capacity to carry absolute meaning, to refer to nothing but the Absolute itself. It is this self-referential truth that carries the weight of the lyrical in his poetry. The absolute Object is in fact an absolute Subject that can only be approached through an absolute act of self-referentiality, in which the self is simultaneously erased and reestablished. This constant act of becoming, identical to love itself, is true as much for the audience as it is for the poet. As the embodiment of this dynamic love, the lyrical is a transformative force, a creative act that mirrors the creative act of God.

Acknowledgment

The research leading to these results has received funding from the European Research Council under the European Union's Seventh Framework Programme (FP/2007–2013) / ERC Grant Agreement n.208476, "The Islamisation of Anatolia, c. 1100–1500." I would like to thank Hatice Aynur for reading and commenting on my article.

Notes

1 For a concise and critical account, see A.C.S. Peacock and Sara Nur Yıldız, "Introduction: Literature, Language and History in Late Medieval Anatolia," in *Literature and Intellectual Life in Fourteenth- and Fifteenth-Century Anatolia*, ed. A.C.S. Peacock and Sara Nur Yıldız (Würzburg: Ergon Verlag, 2016), 19–35. For a recent reevaluation of the subject with access to new sources, see A.C.S. Peacock, *Islam, Literature and Society in Mongol Anatolia* (Cambridge: Cambridge University Press, 2019), 147–87.

2 On Yunus Emre's language, see Fahir İz, "Yunus Emre'nin Dili," in *Uluslararası Yunus Emre Semineri 6–7–8 Eylül-İstanbul: Bildiriler* (Istanbul: Baha Matbaası, 1971), 124–30, among others.

3 For information on Yunus' life, see Edith G. Ambros, "Yunus Emre," *The Encyclopedia of Islam*, vol. 11 (Leiden: Brill, 2002), 349–50; Abdülbaki Gölpınarlı, *Yunus Emre ve Tasavvuf* (Istanbul: Remzi Kitabevi, 1961 [Reprint İnkılap, 2008]); Mustafa Tatcı, "Yûnus Emre," in *TDV İslam Ansiklopedisi*, vol. 43 (Ankara: Türkiye Diyanet Vakfı, 2013), 600–6; Mustafa Tatcı, *Yûnus Emre Külliyâtı, vol. I: Yûnus Emre Dîvânı İnceleme* (Istanbul: H Yayınları, 2008 [First Edition Kültür Bakanlığı, 1990]).

4 Adnan Sadık Erzi, "Türkiye Kütüphanelerinden Notlar ve Vesikalar I: Yûnus Emre'nin Hayatı Hakkında Bir Vesika I," *TTK Belleten* 14, no. 53 (1950): 85–89.

5 See Semih Tezcan, "Eski Anadolu Türkçesi ve Yunus Emre Şiirlerinin Dili Üzerine," in *Yunus Emre*, ed. Ahmet Yaşar Ocak (Ankara: Kültür ve Turizm Bakanlığı, 2012), 101.

Zeynep Oktay

6 This grave was moved in 1946 in the building of the railway between Ankara and Eskişehir and was subsequently transferred to its newly built mausoleum in 1970.

7 Gölpınarlı, *Yunus Emre ve Tasavvuf*, 100–1. For a comparison between Rumi and Yunus, see Yvon Le Bastard, "Mevlânâ et Yunus Emre," in *Yunus Emre: Message Universel*, ed. Michel Bozdemir (Paris: Inalco, 1992), 93–104. Also see Ahmet Yaşar Ocak, "13–14. Yüzyıllar Anadolu'sunun İki Büyük Cezbeci ve Estetikçi Şair Sûfîsi: Celâleddîn-i Rûmî ve Yunus Emre," in *Türk Sûfîliğine Bakışlar* (Istanbul: İletişim Yayınları, 1996), 122–36.

8 Yûnus Emre, *Risâlat al-Nushiyya ve Dîvân*, ed. Abdülbaki Gölpınarlı (Istanbul: Eskişehir Turizm ve Tanıtma Derneği Yayınları, 1965), 100; Yunus Emre, *Yûnus Emre Dîvânı, vol. II: Tenkitli Metin*, ed. Mustafa Tatcı (Istanbul: H Yayınları, 2008 [First Edition Kültür Bakanlığı, 1990]), 227. These two editions will be shortened as "G" and "T" throughout the chapter and will be accompanied by the page numbers for references.

9 See Hamiye Duran, ed., *Velâyetnâme: Hacı Bektâş-ı Velî* (Ankara: Türkiye Diyanet Vakfı, 2007), 184–87. Although Yunus Emre also appears in Hacı Bektaş' hagiography, the lack of references to Hacı Bektaş in Yunus' poetry indicates that Yunus was not directly related to him.

10 See Ahmet T. Karamustafa, "Islamisation Through the Lens of the Saltuk-Name," in *Islam and Christianity in Medieval Anatolia*, ed. A.C.S. Peacock, Bruno De Nicola, and Sara Nur Yıldız (Surrey: Ashgate, 2015), 349–64.

11 See Ahmet T. Karamustafa, "Baraq Baba," in *Encyclopaedia of Islam, vol. 3*, ed. Kate Fleet, Gudrun Krämer, Denis Matringe, John Nawas, and Everett Rowson (Boston: Brill); Ahmet T. Karamustafa, *God's Unruly Friends: Dervish Groups in the Islamic Later Middle Period 1200–1550* (Salt Lake City: University of Utah Press, 1994), 62–63; Hamid Algar, "Baraq Baba," *Encyclopaedia Iranica* III, fasc. 7 (1988): 754–55.

12 See Şinasi Tekin, "İkinci Bâyezît Devrine Ait Bir Mecmûa," *Journal of Turkish Studies/Türklük Bilgisi Araştırmaları* 3 (1979): 354.

13 Faruk K. Timurtaş was the first scholar to indicate that Yunus Emre and 'Aşık Yunus were two separate poets. See Yunus Emre, *Yunus Emre Dîvânı*, ed. Faruk Timurtaş (Ankara: Başbakanlık Basımevi, 1986), 19. The poet 'Aşık Yunus lived in Bursa and died in the beginning of the fifteenth century. The fact that Yunus Emre used adjectives such as *'âşık, miskîn*, and *dervîş* (lover of God, poor, dervish) to refer to himself resulted in the mixing of the poems attributed to the two poets. This is visible in a majority of the manuscripts.

14 These five manuscripts are the following: Berlin Staatsbibliothek Ms. Or. October 2575, fol. 1a–89b; Süleymaniye Library Fatih Collection No. 3889, 210 ff.; Hacı Selim Ağa Library Kemankeş Collection No. 316, fols. 1b–3b, 19b–32b; manuscript in the private collection of Raif Yelkenci; Bursa İnebey Manuscript Library General Collection No. 882, 53 ff. For information on the manuscripts of Yunus Emre's poetry and a detailed description of the recently discovered manuscript at the Hacı Selim Ağa Library, see Zeynep Oktay-Uslu, "Yunus Emre Şiirleri ve Kemal Ümmî'nin Kırk Armağan'ının 15. Yüzyıla Ait Bilinmeyen Bir Yazması Üzerine," *Journal of Turkish Studies/Türklük Bilgisi Araştırmaları* 50 (2018): 389–98.

15 Beşir Ayvazoğlu, *Yunus, Ne Hoş Demişsin: Cumhuriyet Sonrası Yunus Emre Yorumları* (Istanbul: Kapı Yayınları, 2014). On this subject also see Ahmet Yaşar Ocak, "Türkiye'de Yunus Emre Araştırmaları Üzerinde Genel Bir Değerlendirme ve Yunus Emre Problemi," in *Türk Sûfîliğine Bakışlar* (Istanbul: İletişim Yayınları, 1996), 98–108; Ahmet Yaşar Ocak, "Türkiye'de Kültürel İdeolojik Eğilimler ve Bir 13–14. Yüzyıl Halk Sûfîsi Olarak Yunus Emre'nin Kimliği," in *Türk Sûfîliğine Bakışlar* (Istanbul: İletişim Yayınları, 1996), 109–21.

16 See Köprülüzade Mehmed Fuad, *Türk Edebiyatında İlk Mutasavvıflar* (Istanbul: Matbaa-i Âmire, 1918); translated as *Early Mystics in Turkish Literature*, ed. and trans. Gary Leiser and Robert Dankoff (London: Routledge), 2006.

17 Michel de Certeau, "Mystique," in *Encyclopaedia Universalis*, vol. XI (Paris: Encyclopaedia Universalis, 1971), 521–26; translated as "Mysticism," trans. Marsanne Brammer, *Diacritics* 22, no. 2 (1992): 17–18.

18 For a detailed discussion of the same paradox, see Lowry Nelson, "Towards a Definition of Mystical Poetry," in *Poetic Configurations: Essays in Literary History and Criticism* (University Park: Pennsylvania State University Press, 1992), 53–71.

19 De Certeau, "Mystique," trans. Brammer, 21.

20 For a comparison between Yunus Emre and various European mystics, see Andreas Tietze, "Yunus Emre ve Çağdaşları," in *Uluslararası Yunus Emre Semineri 6–7–8 Eylül-İstanbul: Bildiriler* (Istanbul: Baha Matbaası, 1971), 259–87. For an overview of Yunus Emre's mystical doctrine, see Mehmet Kaplan, "Yunus Emre's Views on Time, Life, and the Meaning of Existence," in *Yunus Emre and His Mystical Poetry*, ed. Talat Halman (Bloomington: Indiana University Turkish Studies, 1981), 41–57. For Mehmet

Kaplan's collected work on Yunus Emre, see Mehmet Kaplan, *Yunus Bir Haber Verir* (Istanbul: Dergah Yayınları, 2015).

21 Ahmet T. Karamustafa, "İslam Tasavvuf Düşüncesinde Yunus Emre'nin Yeri," in *Yunus Emre*, ed. Ahmet Yaşar Ocak (Ankara: T. C. Kültür ve Turizm Bakanlığı, 2012), 287–304.

22 For a different rendition of the line, see T393. The word "*ḥaḳḳ*" can also be translated as Truth; it denotes God as the Absolute Truth.

23 Turkish does not have gendered pronouns. My use of she/her over he/him intentionally breaks with the Western tradition of translating, which relies on pronoun use in Arabic as well as in various Western languages.

24 See Gölpınarlı, *Yunus Emre ve Tasavvuf*, 29, 35; Yunus Emre, *Yunus Emre Külliyatı, vol. III: Risaletü'n-Nushiyye Tenkitli Metin*, ed. Mustafa Tatcı (Istanbul: H Yayınları, 2008 [First Edition Kültür Bakanlığı, 1990]), 107, 122–23.

25 The word "existence" appears as "felicity" (*devlet*) in the Gölpınarlı edition. The second line differs but has the same meaning in the Tatcı edition.

26 Ahmad Ghazzali, *Sawanih: Inspirations from the World of Pure Spirits*, trans. Nasrollah Pourjavady (London: Routledge, 1986 [2013]), 39; for the Persian original see Ahmad Ghazzali, *Kitab-i Savanih*, ed. Hellmut Ritter (Istanbul: Matbaa-i Maarif, 1942), 36.

27 See Gölpınarlı, *Yunus Emre ve Tasavvuf*, 92–94, 96–97, 179–80; Tatcı, *Yûnus Emre Külliyâtı, vol. 1*, 207–8, 214–15, 217–18, 237–38. This genre is different in content and style from another genre of poetry by Yunus and his successors, also called *şaṭhiyye*. On the latter see Zeynep Oktay-Uslu, "The *şaṭhiyye* of Yūnus Emre and Ḳayġusuz Abdāl: The Creation of a Vernacular Islamic Tradition in Turkish," *Turcica* 50 (2019): 9–52; Emine Sevim, *Yunus Emre Şerhleri: Çıktım Erik Dalına* (Istanbul: Bilge Kültür Sanat, 2014); Mustafa Tatcı, *Yûnus Emre Külliyatı 5: Yûnus Emre Şerhleri* (Istanbul: H Yayınları, 2008 [First Edition Kültür Bakanlığı, 1990]).

28 The "First" and the "Last" are two of the Ninety-Nine Names of God in Islamic tradition.

29 See Gölpınarlı, *Yunus Emre ve Tasavvuf*, 47, 97, 180, 183; Tatcı, *Yûnus Emre Külliyâtı, vol. 1*, 46, 237, 248.

30 On this subject, see Oktay-Uslu, "The *şaṭhiyye* of Yūnus Emre."

31 See Gölpınarlı, *Yunus Emre ve Tasavvuf*, 92, 147; Tatcı, *Yûnus Emre Külliyâtı, vol. 1*, 207, 402. Also see note 32 below.

32 This conceptualization can be considered as a reference to the Qur'anic verse 17:44, translated as follows: "The seven heavens and the earth and everyone in them glorify Him. There is not a single thing that does not celebrate His praise, though you do not understand their praise." See M.A.S. Abdel Haleem, *The Qur'an: A New Translation* (Oxford: Oxford University Press, 2004), 177–78.

33 The word *tebdîl* appears as *menzil* (stopping place) in the Tatcı edition.

34 For the role of paradox in Persian poetry including Rumi, see Fatemeh Keshavarz, *Reading Mystical Lyric: The Case of Jalal al-Din Rumi* (Columbia: University of South Carolina Press, 1998), 31–48. For paradox and the genre of *shaṭh*, see Paul Ballanfat, "Réflexions sur la Nature du Paradoxe," *Kâr Nâmeh* 12, no. 3 (1995): 25–40.

35 Maulana Jalal al-Din, *Kitab-i fihi ma fih*, ed. Badiʿ al-zaman Furuzanfar (Tehran: Danishgah-i Tahran, 1362), 30. The translation is mine.

36 Ibid., 97–99.

37 Farid al-Din ʿAttar, *Mantiq al-tayr*, ed. Dr. Sayyid Sadiq Gavharin (Tehran: Bungah-i Tarjama va Nashr-i Kitab, 1969), 116. The translation is mine.

38 For a recent valuable study on the concept of *maʿnā* in various Arabic scholarly traditions in the eleventh century, see Alexander Key, *Language Between God and the Poets: Maʿnā in the Eleventh Century* (Oakland: University of California Press, 2018).

39 There are some minor variations in the Tatcı edition.

40 The first letter of the Arabic alphabet that symbolizes Oneness.

41 For a detailed discussion of this matter, see Oktay-Uslu, "The *şaṭhiyye* of Yūnus Emre."

42 Classical musical instruments; the poem is thus in reference to the practice of *semāʿ* (Sufi ritual of music and dance).

43 The phrase appears as "*maʿnā baḥri*" (the ocean of meaning) in the Tatcı edition; see Tatcı, *Yûnus Emre Külliyâtı, vol. 1*, 150.

44 There is some variation in the second line in the Tatcı edition.

45 Stephen Katz, "Mystical Speech and Mystical Meaning," in *Mysticism and Language*, ed. Stephen Katz (New York: Oxford University Press, 1992), 3–41.

46 Keshavarz, *Reading Mystical Lyric*, 38.

47 Ibid.

48 The fourth chapter of Keshavarz's above-mentioned work is on Rumi's poetics of silence; see ibid., 49–71.

References

Abdel Haleem, M.A.S. *The Qu'ran: A New Translation*. Oxford: Oxford University Press, 2004.

Ahmad Ghazzali. *Kitab-i Savanih*. Edited by Hellmut Ritter. Istanbul: Matbaa-i Maarif, 1942; Translated as *Sawanih: Inspirations from the World of Pure Spirits*. Translated by Nasrollah Pourjavady. London: Routledge, 1986 [2013].

Algar, Hamid. "Baraq Baba." *Encyclopaedia Iranica* III, fasc. 7 (1988): 754–55.

Ambros, Edith G. "Yunus Emre." In *The Encyclopedia of Islam*, vol. 11, 349–50. Leiden: Brill, 2002.

Ayvazoğlu, Beşir. *Yunus, Ne Hoş Demişsin: Cumhuriyet Sonrası Yunus Emre Yorumları*. Istanbul: Kapı Yayınları, 2014.

Ballanfat, Paul. "Réflexions sur la Nature du Paradoxe." *Kâr Nâmeh* 12 no. 3 (1995): 25–40.

De Certeau, Michel. "Mystique." In *Encyclopaedia Universalis*, vol. XI, 521–26. Paris: Encyclopaedia Universalis, 1971; translated by Marsanne Brammer in *Diacritics* 22, no. 2 (1992): 11–25.

Duran, Hamiye, ed. *Velâyetnâme: Hacı Bektâş-ı Velî*. Ankara: Türkiye Diyanet Vakfı, 2007.

Erzi, Adnan Sadık. "Türkiye Kütüphanelerinden Notlar ve Vesikalar I: Yûnus Emre'nin Hayatı Hakkında Bir Vesika I." *TTK Belleten* 14, no. 53 (1950): 85–89.

Farid al-Din 'Attar. *Mantiq al-tayr*. Edited by Dr. Sayyid Sadiq Gavharin. Tehran: Bungah-i Tarjama va Nashr-i Kitab, 1969.

Gölpınarlı, Abdülbaki. *Yunus Emre ve Tasavvuf*. Istanbul: Remzi Kitabevi, 1961 [Reprint İnkılap, 2008].

İz, Fahir. "Yunus Emre'nin Dili." In *Uluslararası Yunus Emre Semineri 6–7–8 Eylül-İstanbul: Bildiriler*, 124–30. Istanbul: Baha Matbaası, 1971.

Kaplan, Mehmet. *Yunus Bir Haber Verir*. Istanbul: Dergah Yayınları, 2015.

———. "Yunus Emre's Views on Time, Life, and the Meaning of Existence." In *Yunus Emre and His Mystical Poetry*, edited by Talat Halman, 41–57. Bloomington: Indiana University Turkish Studies, 1981.

Karamustafa, Ahmet T. *God's Unruly Friends: Dervish Groups in the Islamic Later Middle Period 1200–1550*. Salt Lake City: University of Utah Press, 1994.

———. "İslam Tasavvuf Düşüncesinde Yunus Emre'nin Yeri." In *Yunus Emre*, edited by Ahmet Yaşar Ocak, 287–304. Ankara: T. C. Kültür ve Turizm Bakanlığı, 2012.

———. "Islamisation Through the Lens of the Saltuk-Name." In *Islam and Christianity in Medieval Anatolia*, edited by A.C.S. Peacock, Bruno De Nicola, and Sara Nur Yıldız, 349–64. Surrey: Ashgate, 2015.

———. "Baraq Baba." In *Encyclopaedia of Islam, Three*, edited by Kate Fleet, Gudrun Krämer, Denis Matringe, John Nawas, and Everett Rowson. Boston: Brill.

Katz, Stephen T. "Mystical Speech and Mystical Meaning." In *Mysticism and Language*, edited by Stephen T. Katz, 3–41. New York: Oxford University Press, 1992.

Keshavarz, Fatemeh. *Reading Mystical Lyric: The Case of Jalal al-Din Rumi*. Columbia: University of South Carolina Press, 1998.

Key, Alexander. *Language Between God and the Poets: Ma'nā in the Eleventh Century*. Oakland: University of California Press, 2018.

Köprülü(zade), Mehmed Fuad. *Türk Edebiyatında İlk Mutasavvıflar*. Istanbul: Matbaa-i Âmire, 1918; Translated as *Early Mystics in Turkish Literature*. Edited and translated by Gary Leiser and Robert Dankoff. London: Routledge, 2006.

Le Bastard, Yvon. "Mevlânâ et Yunus Emre." In *Yunus Emre: Message Universel*, edited by Michel Bozdemir, 93–104. Paris: Inalco, 1992.

Maulana Jalal al-Din. *Kitab-i fihi ma fih*. Edited by Badi ' al-zaman Furuzanfar. Tehran: Danishgah-i Tahran, 1362 [1946].

Nelson, Lowry. "Towards a Definition of Mystical Poetry." In *Poetic Configurations: Essays in Literary History and Criticism*, 53–71. University Park: Pennsylvania State University Press, 1992.

Ocak, Ahmet Yaşar. "13–14. Yüzyıllar Anadolu'sunun İki Büyük Cezbeci ve Estetikçi Şair Sûfisi: Celâleddîn-I Rûmî ve Yunus Emre." In *Türk Sûfîliğine Bakışlar*, 122–36. Istanbul: İletişim Yayınları, 1996.

———. "Türkiye'de Kültürel İdeolojik Eğilimler ve Bir 13–14. Yüzyıl Halk Sûfisi Olarak Yunus Emre'nin Kimliği." In *Türk Sûfîliğine Bakışlar*, 109–21. Istanbul: İletişim Yayınları, 1996.

———. "Türkiye'de Yunus Emre Araştırmaları Üzerinde Genel Bir Değerlendirme ve Yunus Emre Problemi." In *Türk Sûfîliğine Bakışlar*, 98–108. Istanbul: İletişim Yayınları, 1996.

Oktay-Uslu, Zeynep. "Yunus Emre Şiirleri ve Kemal Ümmî'nin Kırk Armağan'ının 15. Yüzyıla Ait Bilinmeyen Bir Yazması Üzerine." *Journal of Turkish Studies / Türklük Bilgisi Araştırmaları* 50 (2018): 389–98.

———. "The *şaṭhiyye* of Yūnus Emre and Ḳayġusuz Abdāl: The Creation of a Vernacular Islamic Tradition in Turkish." *Turcica* 50 (2019): 9–52.

Peacock, A.C.S. *Islam, Literature and Society in Mongol Anatolia*. Cambridge: Cambridge University Press, 2019.

Peacock, A.C.S., and Sara Nur Yıldız. "Introduction: Literature, Language and History in Late Medieval Anatolia." In *Literature and Intellectual Life in Fourteenth- and Fifteenth-Century Anatolia*, edited by A.C.S. Peacock and Sara Nur Yıldız, 19–35. Würzburg: Ergon Verlag, 2016.

Sevim, Emine. *Yunus Emre Şerhleri: Çıktım Erik Dalına*. Istanbul: Bilge Kültür Sanat, 2014.

Tatcı, Mustafa. *Yûnus Emre Külliyâtı, vol. I: Yûnus Emre Dîvânı İnceleme*. Istanbul: H Yayınları, 2008 [First Edition Kültür Bakanlığı, 1990].

———. *Yûnus Emre Külliyâtı, vol. 5: Yûnus Emre Şerhleri*. Istanbul: H Yayınları, 2008 [First Edition Kültür Bakanlığı, 1990].

———. "Yûnus Emre." In *TDV İslam Ansiklopedisi*, vol. 43, 600–6. Ankara: Türkiye Diyanet Vakfı, 2013.

Tekin, Şinasi. "İkinci Bâyezît Devrine Ait Bir Mecmûa." *Journal of Turkish Studies / Türklük Bilgisi Araştırmaları* 3 (1979): 354.

Tezcan, Semih. "Eski Anadolu Türkçesi ve Yunus Emre Şiirlerinin Dili Üzerine." In *Yunus Emre*, edited by Ahmet Yaşar Ocak, 97–123. Ankara: Kültür ve Turizm Bakanlığı, 2012.

Tietze, Andreas. "Yunus Emre ve Çağdaşları." In *Uluslararası Yunus Emre Semineri 6–7–8 Eylül-İstanbul: Bildiriler*, 259–87. Istanbul: Baha Matbaası, 1971.

Yunus Emre. *Risâlat al-Nushiyya ve Dîvân*. Edited by Abdülbaki Gölpınarlı. Istanbul: Eskişehir Turizm ve Tanıtma Derneği Yayınları, 1965.

———. *Yunus Emre Dîvânı*. Edited by Faruk Timurtaş. Ankara: Başbakanlık Basımevi, 1986.

———. *Yûnus Emre Dîvânı, vol. II: Tenkitli Metin*. Edited by Mustafa Tatcı. Istanbul: H Yayınları, 2008 [First Edition Kültür Bakanlığı, 1990].

———. *Yunus Emre Külliyatı, vol. III: Risaletü'n-Nushiyye Tenkitli Metin*. Edited by Mustafa Tatcı. Istanbul: H Yayınları, 2008 [First Edition Kültür Bakanlığı, 1990].

———. *Divan*. Berlin: Staatsbibliothek Ms. Or. Oct., 2575, fol. 1a-89b; also Süleymaniye Library Fatih Collection No. 3889, 210 ff.; Hacı Selim Ağa Library Kemankeş Collection No. 316, fol. 1b-3b, 19b-32b; Bursa İnebey Manuscript Library General Collection No. 882, 53 ff.

SECTION II

Ottoman Poetics

4

WORDS THAT ARE DAGGERS

Reassessing the Historical Dimensions of the Ottoman *Kaside*

Oscar Aguirre-Mandujano

In the introductory section of a famous *kaside*[1] composed in praise of Ottoman Sultan Bayezid II (r. 1481–1512) and known by its repeated rhyme word "*hançer*," Ottoman poet Necatî (d. 1509) compares the hair and glances of the beloved to a dagger, the word and image that gives thematic unity to the poem.[2] He quickly presents both sides of the sultan, warrior and beloved, whose ire is as dangerous on the battlefield as his munificence is at court:

> *Eğer ki lûtf ide nāzuñ eger ki ḳahr ide lûtf*
> *Ki bezme rezme yaraşur bu dil-sitān ḥançer*

> Whether you show grace playfully, or your grace causes suffering,
> this heart-stealing dagger befits both feasts and battles

The bellicose representation of the beloved's body and his power over the suffering and well-being of the lover was not an uncommon trope in Ottoman poetry in the fifteenth and sixteenth centuries, and even less so when praising a sultan. Indeed, here the dagger may be both playful and wrathful. Necatî links the sultan's military prowess and beauty to the power of words. It is unclear, however, whether he means the sultan's words or his own:

> *Egerçi tīr-i ciğer-dūzuñ ağzı var dili yoḳ*
> *'Aceb budur kim olur cümleten zebān ḥançer*

> Although the heart-piercing arrow has a mouth it has no tongue,
> It's a wonder that it constantly speaks, this dagger

Scholars of Ottoman poetry during the nineteenth and twentieth centuries could not have agreed more with Necatî, if probably for a different reason, as many saw the *kaside* as a series of dishonest and uninventive verses. Necatî, however, may be talking as much about himself as about what he hoped the sultan to be, confessing that

> *Dilindedür nesi var ise ḳalbi ṣāfīdür*
> *Ne deñlü tizlenür ise geçer hemān ḥançer*

DOI: 10.4324/9780429279270-7

Whatever the dagger has in its tongue, its heart is pure
No matter how sharp it is, it immediately succeeds

For Necatî reminds us:

Dilinden āyet-i naṣrun mina'llāh olmaz dūr
Hemīşe hem-dem-i fetḥun ḳarīb olan ḫançer[3]

It constantly repeats the verse "Victory derives only from Allah"
It is always the friend of "Conquest is near," that dagger

In these few verses of Necatî's 40-couplet *kaside*, we can see the tensions that led to some of the major issues in the study of Ottoman *kaside*: the use of imagery and formal elements that echo (or indeed borrow and adapt) the Persian and Arabic panegyric tradition, at times raising the question of what is distinctively Ottoman in it; the close and direct connection to rulers and patrons and, thus, its allegedly unique relation to power, desire, and politics in contrast to other more strictly aesthetic poetic forms and literary genres; and, last but not least, the question of sincerity, both as it affects the poem's stature as art or its reliability as a historical source. In this chapter, I discuss how scholars, mostly writing in English, have approached these questions, and suggest, albeit briefly, how we can reassess the attention we ought to give to Ottoman *kaside*, whose importance never seemed to have been questioned by the Ottomans themselves, at least not until the nineteenth century.

The most influential account of Ottoman literary history is the six-volume work of E.J.W. Gibb, of which only the first volume was published while the author was still alive, in 1900. In it, Gibb dismissed Ottoman *kaside* as a "waste of time and talent."[4] While Gibb recognized certain elements within the Ottoman tradition of praise poetry as extremely beautiful, these were limited to the so-called exordium (*nasīb*) of the poem, which is the introductory section dealing not with the eulogy (*medḥiye*) itself, but with the lyric element that sets the poem's central theme, such as spring, winter, the holy month of Ramadan, or an object like Necatî's dagger. Accordingly, in Gibb's view, the beauty of the *nasīb* derives from its apparent independence from the *kaside* proper (*maḳṣūd*) and its use of more poetic elements, such as nature-inspired themes.[5] Ironically, while Ottoman *kaside* clearly left Gibb uninspired, his monumental survey confirms the central role of the *kaside*, recognizing its value in the professional path of Ottoman court poets during the fourteenth and fifteenth centuries. This involuntary affirmation of the centrality of Ottoman *kaside* results from Gibb's sources, namely, poetry collections (*dīvāns*) and biographical dictionaries (*teẕkīres*).

Similar to Gibb's dismissal of Ottoman *kaside* for its lack of originality, Turkish scholars of the first half of the twentieth century downplayed its social and artistic value. Early Republican Turkish scholarship attempted to record the literary monuments of Turkish civilization. Historians of Turkish literature such as Mehmet Fuad Köprülü (d. 1966) and Vasfi Mahir Kocatürk (d. 1961) focused their efforts on recovering the imagined historical continuity of Turkish folk literature as opposed to the Persian-inflected literature of the learned elite.[6] Ottoman *kaside* represented a core foreign element in the Turkish literary tradition representative of an isolated palace culture imagined by these literary historians. The practical elements of Ottoman *kaside*, such as requests for patronage or royal favor, combined with its Arabic origins, reinforced the nationalist discourse that conceptualized the literature of the Ottoman learned elite as a mechanical and unsuccessful attempt to impose Arabic and Persian forms upon the national genius of the Turkish people. Literary historians of this time faced the difficult task of defining a national literature at the time of the fragmentation of former Ottoman territories into new nations and kingdoms while trying to rescue what they believed was the neglected and oppressed Turkish spirit in their literature. In this paradigm, Ottoman *kaside* was a poetic form that represented artifice, pretension, and ultimately, failure. The *kaside* was deemed so, of course, only inasmuch as it was evaluated with a European derived romantic poetics that considered true art an independent form of expression produced by the artist's genius. This approach did not consider that poems may be valuable not only as an aesthetic product derived from the poet's/artist's individuality. It ignored the fact that Ottoman poetry, panegyric or otherwise, was a group activity and an act of communication that was first and foremost social, thus entangled with the political, cultural, and spiritual realities of poets, patrons, and literary audiences.

Since the 1990s, discussion of panegyric in Arabic and Persian poetry (*qaṣīdah/qaṣīdeh*) has centered around questions of power, pragmatism, sincerity, and aesthetics. Julie Scott Meisami, in her study of Persianate court poetry, highlighted that the poetry of praise (*qaṣīdah*) provided poets and intellectuals with a space to present idealized versions of rule, not only in their attempt to complement the ruler but also to guide him by illustrating the ruler's potential for better, more just rule.[7] The understanding of hyperbole as a rhetorical strategy with functions more complex than blatantly lying to the ruler in expectation of material reward complicates the study of *kaside* and brings to the fore questions about meaning, form, genre, and also of intention, sincerity, and agency.[8] Considering *kasides* as more than empty compliments forces contemporary readers to approach Ottoman *kasides* more carefully. Understanding them as sincere offerings of appreciation reveals each poem's subtly implied judgments and signs of approval and reproach, as well as the aspirations of a governing elite. This is not to say that all panegyrists were honest or that sincere compliments did not mingle with exaggeration and commonplaces. Instead, taking into account the multiple layers of truth, meaning, and tradition suggests that praise must be considered an early modern poetics intrinsically related to power, rule, and governance.[9] The Ottoman *kaside* could also be used to vituperate enemies and rivals, substituting insults for compliments and using the formal elements of the *kaside* to produce a satirical effect in the invective.[10] The early twentieth-century scholars interested in distilling what was Turkish in Ottoman literature marginalized Ottoman *kasides* in relation to other forms such as lyric poetry (*gazel*), mystical (Sufi or Tekke) poetry, and long versified narratives (*mesnevi*).[11] It also put Turkish scholars in the difficult position of defending the Ottoman/Turkish literary genius as something more than a derivation of Persian and Arabic literature—a question that, unfortunately, is still asked when Ottoman literature is theorized independently of its Arabic and Persian counterparts.[12]

The assumption that Ottoman *kaside* replicated Arabic and Persian panegyrics (*qaṣīdah/qaṣīdeh*) in form and content has limited the scope of scholarship to analysis of the work of individual poets or compilations of *kasides* grouped by period of composition.[13] One of the major questions in the field relates to the traditional constitutive parts of the *kaside*, which do not quite correspond to the Ottoman case.[14] In his article "Speaking of Power: The Ottoman Kasîde," Walter Andrews argued for a reassessment of the genre with more attention to the context of its production. He identified a practical dimension in the poem as a gift, an element of a larger palace economy, wherein *kasides* constituted a "genre of expression for addressing a group of [specific] people."[15] Recently, Yorgos Dedes and Stefan Sperl discussed Andrews' argument against the continuity of Persian and Arabic elements in Ottoman *kaside* and successfully placed the genre within the larger literary tradition of the Islamic world.[16] Andrews' invitation to rethink Ottoman *kaside* as a product of Ottoman palace culture remains relevant, regardless of its connection to other literary traditions. He correctly stressed the creative use of traditional literary forms in this context, which can reveal historically specific meanings within these poems.

More recently, Andrews and Kalpaklı further argued that Ottoman *kaside* allowed poets to prove their own value to their literary and intellectual communities. The *kaside*—or rather, the act of writing one—served as a public examination of the poet's ability to participate in the emotional investment of his social group.[17] In this reading, the poet's literary community is at the same time his social world: an elite with a particular emotional economy based on patronage and gift exchange. Andrews and Kalpaklı consider *kaside* as a poetic form about love and separation as the two poles of Ottoman emotional and social interaction.[18] They argue that the depiction of the characteristics of the patron/beloved is not as important for understanding Ottoman *kaside* as the implication of an act of negotiation between poet/lover and patron/beloved, which is ultimately based upon an Ottoman ecology of love and an ever-present expectation of reunion. Andrews and Kalpaklı's approach contrasts with other historical readings of *kaside*.[19]

Historians have long recognized that poems can also prove helpful in corroborating dates and social relations beyond their poetic value. While Andrews and Kalpaklı attempt to reconstruct a cultural history of Ottoman emotions against which *kasides* and poetic composition can be analyzed together with the social actions that they imply (such as singing/reciting, meeting with others, and communicating), others have attempted to mine Ottoman *kasides* for references to Ottoman imperial political history.[20] This scholarship provides us with a helpful index of historical events mentioned in *kaside* poetry, but by and large it does not integrate these events with the surrounding poetry and leaves out important questions: How were the events mentioned in *kasides* integrated into the larger structure of the specific poems? How were *kasides* read in relation to other literary products recording the same events, such as chronicles and dynastic histories?[21] Some scholars have successfully incorporated the use of historical sources in reading, or rather cross-reading, the poems. This approach puts particular emphasis on dissecting historical objects within the poem, and it has produced fascinating inventories of the material culture that inspired poetic imagery in the early modern Ottoman world.[22] Nonetheless, this approach has also turned poems into an archive of their own, an Ottoman ethnography removed from the intellectual environment that made it meaningful.

If too close a study of form and image has led to the musealization of Ottoman poetry, how can we return to the Ottoman *kaside* the dynamism and importance that it must have had among the early Ottomans? Ottoman *kaside* remained close in its formal elements to Persian and Arabic models but was more flexible in incorporating all the elements of panegyric. What made Ottoman *kaside* unique was the occasion in which it was produced, the meanings it conveyed, and its connection with other contemporary texts. I believe that reexamining patronage in relation to poetry, panegyric or otherwise, will help us appreciate Ottoman poems and will also clarify the social and political context in which they were produced.

The history of Ottoman *kaside*, and Ottoman poetry in general, need to be reconsidered following models recently developed for other intellectual practices in the Ottoman Empire. Two studies by Halil İnalcık renewed a century-old reaction to Ottoman literary culture that had been developed by late Ottoman and early Republican literary historians.[23] İnalcık's study of poetry was important because it discussed the economic and sociological aspects of the production of Ottoman poetry in the early modern period. Before İnalcık, literary historians had discussed patronage as part of general descriptions of literature or biographical works of specific poets.[24] Haluk İpekten studied poetic gatherings and their relation to imperial patronage in his analysis of social circles of court poets during the fifteenth and sixteenth centuries. While İpekten did not employ the category of patronage, he established the ground for future studies of both Ottoman patronage and literary criticism.[25] Following this scholarship, İnalcık attempted a sociological and historical approach to Ottoman literary patronage, first by dissecting the relationship between patrons and poets and later by drawing a general picture of the origins of Ottoman literature in the fifteenth century. Relying heavily on the only two available, yet incomplete, registers of rewards given by the court to poets and other craftsmen,[26] İnalcık based his analytical insights on the distinction between a patrimonial state in the East and the development of a powerful bourgeoisie in the West, following Weberian models of state formation, authority, and monopoly of power.[27] İnalcık's use of literary sources in *Poet and Patron* (*Şair ve Patron*) stirred objections among Turkish scholars of Ottoman literature.[28]

In his "Origins of Classical Ottoman Literature," İnalcık parts from the sociological model explored in *Poet and Patron* to develop the idea that the origin of patronage in the Ottoman literary tradition was closely tied to the culture of the *meclis* (Ar. *majlis*), the public drinking gathering of poets. The abundance of poetic gatherings correlates in İnalcık's study to the migration of Persian poets and practices to Ottoman lands. The movement of poets from Persian courts during the late Seljuk and Beylik periods in the fourteenth and fifteenth centuries, he argues, led to the adaptation of models derived from the Persian canon. İnalcık's argument is based on the association of literary work and material rewards; he establishes a teleology of increasingly centralized patronage, a system based on the proportional relation between the imperial court's development and the production of a literary tradition. With his focus on the sultan, İnalcık's model of patronage echoes historiographical accounts of artistic patronage in the Ottoman Empire from the sixteenth century onward.[29] While İnalcık was right to look for a social space wherein poetic composition was performed, enacted, and shared, his work presents a mechanical causation between what he identifies as a patrimonial state and the increase of Ottoman literary production, similar to Gibb's assessment of the Ottoman *kaside* as a purely pragmatic literary product discussed above.

İnalcık's sociological model of court patronage places the sultan as the source of wealth distribution and literary production as the direct outcome of subjects benefiting from the sultan's generosity. This model disregards class and political change as factors of intellectual and cultural production. It also ignores the fact that up to the sixteenth century, most poets in the Ottoman Empire were not only poets but had other occupations as well. As İnalcık's critics point out, his exclusive focus on *kaside* ignores other forms of literary expression beyond those that were solely intended to mediate the relation between patron and poet. Indeed, his model presumes that the composition of poetry is a social mechanism resulting from the interaction of two social blocs, one at the center and one at the periphery. Even when the intellectual elites of the empire were at the core of the imperial court, this interpretation positions the sultan in opposition to any other social actor, artificially creating a division between the ruler as the sole agent behind the political project of the empire and his subjects reacting mechanically to the imperial mastermind. I would insist that the assumption (and rarely an argument) that all political, cultural, and social projects in the empire depended on or derived from the monarch or at least from the grand vizier's office, and thus depended mostly on each powerful individual's personality, limits our understanding of how Ottoman subjects other than the sultan and his most powerful ministers participated in the configuration of the emerging empire.

The transformations of the late fifteenth century and early sixteenth century point to the emergence of new social groups among the subjects of the empire. Recent scholarship has demonstrated the creation of a new scholarly class, a group of individuals with shared political and social modes of self-identification, particularly among religious and legal scholars, many of whom wrote *kasides*. Sooyong Kim has shown the transformation of literary patronage and the creation of professional poets in the late sixteenth century through the study of Ottoman poet Zatî, his biography, and poems.[30] The emergence of the professional poet was part of other intellectual innovations that led to the formation of an Ottoman literary community throughout the fifteenth and sixteenth centuries.[31] These changes in literary patronage and the transformation of the Ottoman literary community in Istanbul coincided with the other changes in the Ottoman capital and among the Ottoman elite. At the turn of the sixteenth century, scholars became aware of their social group as a self-sustaining class based mostly on their profession and with some political power. Abdurrahman Atçıl has traced the institutional transformations in the religious hierarchy during the fifteenth and sixteenth centuries, in particular the bureaucratization of legal and religious scholarly production.[32] Guy Burak also identifies the consolidation of religious scholars into a new social class. In contrast to Atçıl's work, Burak focuses on explaining the legal, ideological, and intellectual repercussions that the centralization of scholarly work on religious law had on the empire.[33] Not only the political but also the institutional changes, shifting class dynamics, and the professionalization of the Ottoman elite constitute an important part of the history of literary transformations.

While it is important to question whether there is a direct correlation or parallel between the development of an Ottoman literary culture and the political culture at the imperial court, understanding the importance of class formation in the early modern Ottoman Empire adds considerable depth to the discussion of patronage and the Ottoman *kaside* as it provides collective and individual agency to political actors other than the sultan or the imperial court. Scholarly works that have reconstructed how the court and other elites promoted the creation of cultural and material wealth in the empire point to complex power relations among the Ottoman educated elite. Gülru Necipoğlu's analysis of artistic patronage during the age of Suleiman I demonstrates the centrality of the office of the grand vizier in promoting particular forms of arts and crafts according to specific political agendas.[34] Gönül A. Tekin's survey of Ottoman literature under Mehmet II provides an overview of the creation of a court literature by a group of elites in competing literary salons.[35] More importantly for the purposes of this chapter, Walter G. Andrews and Mehmet Kalpaklı have mapped an Ottoman emotional ecology in the poetic worldview of the early modern Ottoman world, particularly as it appears in the tropes of lyric poetry.[36]

These dynamics were reproduced beyond the imperial court and determined power and patronage at other levels of Ottoman society. In a recent article, Fatma M. Şen collects the various *kasides* that poets of renown, then still making their way upwards in Istanbul's literary community—such as Zatî (d. 1546), Mesihî (d. 1512), and Necatî (d. 1509)—wrote to Bayezid II's imperial chancellor, Tacizade Ca'fer Çelebi (d. 1512), himself a poet who had presented *kasides* to the sultan.[37] Şen's selection of poets surrounding a member of the imperial court as patron is an important contribution to the study of Ottoman *kaside*. Although Şen does not explore the social and intellectual context and ramifications of this relation between poets, *kasides*, and patronage, her decision to study all the *kasides* addressed to a single figure in the Ottoman capital illustrates the close connection between the various *kasides* and the poets who wrote them. Together with the work of Walter G. Andrews, Mehmet Kalpaklı, Attila Şentürk, Mehmet Karavelioğlu, and others, the multiple approaches to the study of *kaside* and the still incomplete picture of the Ottoman *kaside* and its dynamics within Ottoman society in the fifteenth and sixteenth centuries illustrate the main point raised here: There is a need to see the poems not as individual products, but as a series of coexisting voices and dissonances around the Ottoman imperial project and its actors. It is also important to consider *kasides* both within and across genres.

Approaching Ottoman *kaside* not as individual texts, sincere or otherwise, but rather as a series of interrelated texts, highlights the multiple layers of agency and communication present in the public acts of writing, reciting, and receiving praise. It also underlines the need to reassess *kaside* together with other changes in literary canon, patronage, elite culture, and class formation. The performative aspect with which poetry was presented, the economic rewards it entailed, the length and time it consumed, and the literary skill and political savviness a poet had to command to successfully write a *kaside* speak to the central role of *kaside* in the constant negotiation of power within the court, be that performatively, intellectually, or pragmatically: performatively, as it reinforced elements of court culture and public dynamics of power; intellectually, in the idealized images and prescriptive elements it provided and publicly broadcasted as it was recited and presented; and pragmatically, in the material and political relations it established between patrons and poets.

Acknowledgment

I am thankful to Robert Dankoff and Selim S. Kuru for their comments and suggestions.

Notes

1 The word *kaside* refers to the poetic form of praise poems. In this chapter, I have preferred to use the Turkish word to avoid the historical implications of panegyric poetry in European history and literary traditions, and to invoke the specifics of the Ottoman context and its relation to Persian and Arabic literary traditions. When talking about the poetry of praise and panegyric in a general sense I have used the English word. For the *kaside* in Arabic and Persian contexts, I have added the transliteration in parenthesis to reflect the Arabic and Persian transliteration respectively.
2 I have followed Ali Nihat Tarlan's edition and transcription of Necati's Divan. For this *kaside* see Necatî, *Divan*, ed. Ali Nihat Tarlan (Ankara: Akçağ Yayınları, 1992), 61–63.
3 Both quotations come from Qur'an 61:13.
4 E.J.W. Gibb, *A History of Ottoman Poetry*, 2nd ed. (London: Messrs Lucac, 1958), 1:87.
5 Ibid., 1:82.
6 Some of the most influential works in this sense are: Mehmet Fuat Köprülü, *Early Mystics in Turkish Literature* (London: Routledge, 2006); Mehmet Fuat Köprülü, *Edebiyat Araştırmaları* (Ankara: Türk Tarih Kurumu Basımevi, 1999); Vasfi Mahir Kocatürk, *Türk Edebiyatı Tarihi; Başlangıçtan Bugüne Kadar Türk Edebiyatının Tarihi, Tahlil ve Tenkidi* (Ankara: Edebiyat Yayınevi, 1970).
7 Julie Scott Meisami, *Medieval Persian Court Poetry* (Princeton, NJ: Princeton University Press, 1987), 40–76.
8 Franklin Lewis, "Sincerely Flattering Panegyrics: The Shrinking Ghaznavid Qasida," in *The Necklace of the Pleiades: 24 Essays on Persian Literature, Culture and Religion*, ed. Franklin Lewis and Sunil Sharma (Leiden: Leiden University Press, 2010), 228–29.
9 For a similar call to consider the panegyric as central to an early modern poetics see Rebecca Gould, "The Much-Maligned Panegyric: Towards a Political Poetics of Premodern Literary Form," *Comparative Literature Studies* 52, no. 2 (2015): 254–84.
10 Invective and satire (*hicv*) have been little explored in Ottoman literary history, and more so its entanglements with other genres, such as panegyric or long narrative poems (*mesnevi*). Recently, Michael Sheridan has explored the mechanics of invective and shown how the use of invective in the late sixteenth and seventeenth centuries had important implications in othering enemies and defining the Ottoman elite of the time. Michael Sheridan, "Defining and Defaming the Other in Early Seventeenth-Century Ottoman Invective," in *Disliking Others: Loathing, Hostility, and Distrust in Premodern Ottoman Lands*, ed. Hakan Karateke, Erdem Çıpa, and Helga Anetshofer (Boston: Academic Studies Press, 2018), 296–320.
11 Talat Halman's overview of Ottoman literature is a good example of how the sharp distinction between Turkish and foreign, as well as between popular and elite, shape the history of Ottoman literature. While folk poetry is considered the voice of the people and resistance, court poetry, and panegyric most of all, is presented as the voice of the powerful. This dichotomy fails to see the more complex interactions among the educated elite of the Ottoman world. See Talat S. Halman, "Ottoman Glories," in *A Millennium of Turkish Literature*, ed. Jayne L. Warner (Syracuse, NY: Syracuse University Press, 2011), 25–53. For a discussion of the relation and overlap of Ottoman panegyrics and Sufi poetry see Oscar Aguirre-Mandujano, "The Social and Intellectual World of a Fifteenth-Century Poem," *Journal of the Ottoman and Turkish Studies Association* 7, no. 2 (2020): 55–79.

12 For a new literary history of Medieval Anatolia that recognizes and analyzes the entanglements of various literary traditions in Anatolia, including Turkish Persian, Arabic, and Armenian, see Michael Pifer, *Kindred Voices: A Literary History of Medieval Anatolia* (New Haven, CT: Yale University Press, 2021).

13 See, for instance, Ceyhun Arslan's recent attempt to propose a new paradigm for comparative literature based on his readings of nineteenth-century Ottoman scholar Ziya Pasha. Arslan's call to reconsider the Arabic and Persian traditions not as distinct national literature but as a "reservoir" of literary canon(s) that were available to Ottoman elite men, while not directly devised for the study of panegyric, addresses one of the main problems when studying Ottoman literary history in general. See Ceyhun Arslan, "Canons as Reservoirs: The Ottoman Ocean in Ziya Pasha's *Harabat* and Reframing the History of Comparative Literature," *Comparative Literature Studies* 54, no. 4 (2017): 731–48.

14 Some of the discussions regarding Persian and Arabic *qaṣīdah* deal with the substitution of traditional themes in the exordium (*nasīb*) and the way Persian poets adapted the Arabic form to suit the courtly context of the Persianate Islamic literary world. Scholars of earlier Islamic literature have also paid attention to the uses of *qaṣīdah* in courtly contexts and its transformation in relation to historical changes of the region. See Stefan Sperl, "Islamic Kingship and Arabic Panegyric Poetry in the Early 9th Century," *Journal of Arabic Literature* 8, no. 1 (1977): 20–35; Julie Scott Meisami, "The Uses of Qaṣīda: Thematic and Structural Patterns in a Poem of Bashshār," *Journal of Arabic Literature* 16, no. 1 (1985): 40–59.

15 Walter G. Andrews, "Speaking of Power: The Ottoman Kasîde," in *Qasida Poetry in Islamic Asia and Africa*, ed. Stefan Sperl and Christopher Shackle, vol. 2 (Leiden: Brill, 1996), 281–300. The entire volume is an excellent attempt to consider the *qasida* across the Islamic world.

16 Yorgos Dedes and Stefan Sperl, "'In the Rose-Bower Every Leaf Is a Page of Delicate Meaning': An Arabic Perspective on Three Ottoman Kasides," in *Kasîdeye Medhiye: Biçime, İşleve ve Muhteveya Dair Tespitler*, ed. Hatice Aynur et al. (Istanbul: Klasik, 2013), 240–313.

17 Walter G. Andrews and Mehmet Kalpaklı, "Ottoman Love: Preface to a Theory of Emotional Ecology," in *A History of Emotions 1200–1800*, ed. Jonas Lilequist (London: Pickering & Chatto, 2012), 21–47.

18 See also Walter G. Andrews and Mehmet Kalpaklı, *The Age of Beloveds: Love and the Beloved in Early-Modern Ottoman and European Culture and Society* (Durham, NC: Duke University Press, 2005).

19 In addition to the more theoretical article of 2012, Andrews and Kalpaklı further illustrate their reading of the Ottoman panegyric as an expression of an Ottoman emotional ecology by reading closely and analyzing one of Tacizade Cafer Celebi's (d. 1512) panegyrics to Bayezid II. See Walter G. Andrews and Mehmet Kalpaklı, "Poet, Panegyric and Patron: A Bahariye Kaside by Tacizade Ca'fer Çelebi for Sultan Bayezit II," in *Turkish Language, Literature, and History. Travelers' Tales, Sultans and Scholars Since the Eighth Century*, ed. Bill Hickman and Gary Leiser (London: Routledge, 2016), 16–32.

20 For instance, Murat Karavelioğlu has recently identified historical events explicitly mentioned in Ottoman panegyrics of the fifteenth and sixteenth centuries, mostly victories and military campaigns. See Murat Karavelioğlu, "Tarihin Edebiyatı: 15. ve 16. Yüzyıl Kasîdelerinde Tarihî Arka Plan," in *Kasîdeye Medhiye: Biçime, İşleve ve Muhteveya Dair Tespitler* (Istanbul: Klasik, 2013), 380–454.

21 Recent scholarship of Persian and Arabic literatures has introduced new approaches to the study of panegyric, mainly with a focus on cultural history or biography. See Sunil Sharma, *Amir Khusraw: The Poet of Sultans and Sufis* (Oxford: Oneworld, 2005); Sunil Sharma, "Forbidden Love, Persianate Style: Re-Reading Tales of Iranian Poets and Mughal Patrons," *Iranian Studies* 42 (2009): 765–79.

22 A perfect example of this approach can be seen in Attila Şentürk, "Okçuluk tarihine yeni bir kaynak olarak Osmanlı şiiri," in *M. Ali Tanyeri'nin Anısına Makaleler*, ed. Hatice Aynur et al. (Istanbul: Ülke Kitapları, 2015), 71–142.

23 Halil İnalcık, *Şair ve Patron* (Ankara: Dogu Bati Yayınları, 2003); Halil İnalcık, "Klasik Edebiyat Menşei: İranî Gelenek, Saray Işret Meclisleri ve Musâhib Şâirler," in *Türk Edebyatı Tarihi*, ed. Talât Sait Halman et al., vol. 1 (Ankara: Külür ve Turizm Bakanlığı Yayınları, 2006), 221–31. For an English translation of the latter, see Halil İnalcık, "The Origins of Classical Ottoman Literature: Persian Tradition, Court Entertainments, and Court Poets," *Journal of Turkish Literature*, no. 5 (2008): 5–75.

24 Most major surveys of Ottoman literature reproduce ideas of patronage as portrayed in biographical dictionaries of the fifteenth century, and many of them are explicit critiques of the state of literary patronage in the age of Suleiman I, particularly after the execution of Grand Vizier İbrahim Paşa. See, for instance, Günay Kut, "Turkish Literature in Anatolia," in *History of the Ottoman State, Society & Civilisation*, ed. Ekmeleddin İhsanoğlu, vol. 2 (Istanbul: Research Centre for Islamic History, Art and Culture, 2002), 25–45; Gönül Alpay Tekin, "Fatih Devri Edebiyatı," in *İstanbul Armağanı: Fetih ve Fatih*, ed. Mustafa Armağan (Istanbul: İstanbul Büyükşehir Belediyesi Kültür İşleri Daire Başkanlığı,

1995), 161–235; Harun Tolasa, Sehî, Latîfî, *Âşık Çelebi Tezkirelerine Göre 16. Y.y.'da Edebiyat Araştırma ve Eleştirisi* (Izmir: Ege Üniversitesi Matbaası, 1983); Haluk İpekten, *Divan Edebiyatında Edebî Muhitler* (Istanbul: Milli Eğitim Bakanlığı, 1996).

25 İpekten, *Divan Edebiyatında Edebî Mühitleri*; Tolasa, Sehî, Latîfî, *Âşık Çelebi Tezkirelerine Göre 16. Y.y.'da Edebiyat Araştırma ve Eleştirisi*; Hanna Sohrweide, "Dichter und Gelehrte aus dem Osten im Osmanischen Reich (1453–1600)," *Der Islam* 46, no. 1 (1970): 263–302.

26 This document, a draft copy of a court register of gifts, was first published in İsmail E. Erünsal, "Türk Edebiyati Tarihi'nin Arşiv Kaynakları I. II. Bayezid Devrine Ait Bir In'amat Defteri," *İstanbul Üniversitesi Edebiyat Fakültesi Tarih Dergisi* 10–11 (1981): 303–42.

27 İnalcık, *Şair ve Patron*, 13. See also Halil İnalcık, "Comments on 'Sultanism': Max Weber's Typification of the Ottoman Polity," *Princeton Papers in Near Eastern Studies* 1 (1992): 49–72.

28 Scholars of Ottoman literature have considered İnalcık's approach too limited because it focuses exclusively on the Ottoman panegyric. For a summary of this debate, see Kemal Kahramanoğlu, "Divan Şiirinde Şair, Hükümdar ve Yabancılaşmış Ben," *Türk Edebiyatı* 359 (2003): 18–23. For İnalcık's response to his critics, see Halil İnalcık, "Şair ve Patron Hakkında," *Zaman*, June 12, 2003.

29 İnalcık brings together work on artistic patronage and social gatherings done particularly for the sixteenth century. This includes the work of Walter G. Andrews and Mehmet Kalpaklı on poetic gatherings. See Andrews and Kalpaklı, *The Age of Beloveds*. For a discussion on the importance of poetic responses and the community of Ottoman poets, see Walter G. Andrews, "Starting Over Again: Some Suggestions for Rethinking Ottoman Divan Poetry in the Context of Translation and Transmission," in *Translations: (Re)shaping of Literature and Culture*, ed. Saliha Paker (Istanbul: Boğaziçi University Press, 2002), 15–40.

30 Sooyong Kim, *The Last of an Age: The Making and Unmaking of a Sixteenth-Century Ottoman Poet* (London: Routledge, 2018).

31 For the formation of an Ottoman literary community and the poets of Rum in the fifteenth and sixteenth centuries, see Selim S. Kuru, "The Literature of Rum: The Making of a Literary Tradition (1450–1600)," in *Cambridge History of Turkey 2: The Ottoman Empire as a World Power, 1453–1603*, ed. Suraiya Faroqhi and Kate Fleet (Cambridge: Cambridge University Press, 2013), 548–92.

32 Abdurrahman Atçıl, *Scholars and Sultans in the Early Modern Ottoman Empire* (Cambridge: Cambridge University Press, 2017).

33 Guy Burak, *The Second Formation of Islamic Law: The Ḥanafī School in the Early Modern Ottoman Empire* (New York: Cambridge University Press, 2015).

34 Gülru Necipoğlu, "A Kanun for the State, a Canon for the Arts: The Classical Synthesis in Ottoman Art and Architecture During the Age of Süleyman," in *Soliman Le Magnifique et Son Temps, Actes Du Colloque de Paris Galeries Nationales Du Grand Palais, 7–10 Mars 1990*, ed. Gilles Veinstein (Paris: Rencontres de l'École du Louvre, 1992), 195–216.

35 Gönül A. Tekin, "Fatih Devri Edebiyatı," in *İstanbul Armağanı: Fetih ve Fatih*, ed. Mustafa Armağan (Istanbul: İstanbul Büyükşehir Belediyesi Kültür İşleri Daire Başkanlığı, 1995), 161–235.

36 Walter G. Andrews and Mehmet Kalpaklı, "Ottoman Love: Preface to a Theory of Emotional Ecology," in *A History of Emotions 1200–1800*, ed. Jonas Lilequist (London: Pickering & Chatto, 2012), 21–47.

37 Fatma Meliha Şen, "Tâcîzâde Ca'fer Çelebi'nin (ö. 921/1515) Çevresindeki Şairler ve Onun İçin Yazılmış Şiirler," in *Kitaplara Vakfedilen Bir Ömre Tuhfe. İsmail Erünsal'a Armağan*, ed. Hatice Aynur et al., vol. 2 (Istanbul: Ülke Kitapları, 2014), 1133–54.

References

Aguirre-Mandujano, Oscar. "The Social and Intellectual World of a Fifteenth-Century Poem." *Journal of the Ottoman and Turkish Studies Association* 7, no. 2 (Winter 2020): 55–79.

Andrews, Walter G. "Speaking of Power: The Ottoman Kasîde." In *Qasida Poetry in Islamic Asia and Africa*, edited by Stefan Sperl and Christopher Shackle, 281–300. Leiden: Brill, 1996.

———. "Starting Over Again: Some Suggestions for Rethinking Ottoman Divan Poetry in the Context of Translation and Transmission." In *Translations: (Re)shaping of Literature and Culture*, edited by Saliha Paker, 15–40. Istanbul: Boğaziçi University Press, 2002.

Andrews, Walter G., and Mehmet Kalpaklı. *The Age of Beloveds: Love and the Beloved in Early-Modern Ottoman and European Culture and Society*. Durham, NC: Duke University Press, 2005.

————. "Ottoman Love: Preface to a Theory of Emotional Ecology." In *A History of Emotions 1200–1800*, edited by Jonas Lilequist, 21–47. London: Pickering & Chatto, 2012.

————. "Poet, Panegyric and Patron: A Bahariye Kaside by Tacizade Ca'fer Çelebi for Sultan Bayezit II." In *Turkish Language, Literature, and History. Travelers' Tales, Sultans and Scholars Since the Eighth Century*, edited by Bill Hickman and Gary Leiser, 16–32. London: Routledge, 2016.

Arslan, Ceyhun. "Canons as Reservoirs: the Ottoman Ocean in Ziya Pasha's *Harabat* and Reframing the History of Comparative Literature." *Comparative Literature Studies* 54, no. 4 (2017): 731–48.

Atçıl, Abdurrahman. *Scholars and Sultans in the Early Modern Ottoman Empire*. Cambridge: Cambridge University Press, 2017.

Burak, Guy. *The Second Formation of Islamic Law: The Ḥanafī School in the Early Modern Ottoman Empire*. New York: Cambridge University Press, 2015.

Dedes, Yorgos, and Stefan Sperl. "'In the Rose-Bower Every Leaf Is a Page of Delicate Meaning': An Arabic Perspective on Three Ottoman Kasides." In *Kasîdeye Medhiye: Biçime, İşleve ve Muhteveya Dair Tespitler*, edited by Hatice Aynur et al., 240–313. Istanbul: Klasik, 2013.

Erünsal, İsmail E. "Türk Edebiyati Tarihi'nin Arşiv Kaynakları I. II. Bayezid Devrine Ait Bir In'amat Defteri." *İstanbul Üniversitesi Edebiyat Fakültesi Tarih Dergisi* 10–11 (1981): 303–42.

Gibb, E.J.W. *A History of Ottoman Poetry*. London: Messrs Lucac, 1958.

Gould, Rebecca. "The Much-Maligned Panegyric: Towards a Political Poetics of Premodern Literary Form." *Comparative Literature Studies* 52, no. 2 (2015): 254–84.

Halman, Talat S. *A Millennium of Turkish Literature*. Edited by Jayne L. Warner. Syracuse, NY: Syracuse University Press, 2011.

Hanna Sohrweide. "Dichter und Gelehrte aus dem Osten im Osmanischen Reich (1453–1600)." *Der Islam* 46, no. 1 (1970): 263–302.

İnalcık, Halil. "Comments on 'Sultanism': Max Weber's Typification of the Ottoman Polity." *Princeton Papers in Near Eastern Studies* 1 (1992): 49–72.

————. *Şair ve Patron*. Ankara: Dogu Bati Yayınları 2003.

————. "Şair ve Patron Hakkında." *Zaman*, June 12, 2003.

————. "Klasik Edebiyat Menşei: İranî Gelenek, Saray Işret Meclisleri ve Musâhib Şâirler." In *Türk Edebiyatı Tarihi*, edited by Talât Sait Halman et al., 221–31 Ankara: Külür ve Turizm Bakanlığı Yayınları, 2006.

————. "The Origins of Classical Ottoman Literature: Persian Tradition, Court Entertainments, and Court Poets." *Journal of Turkish Literature*, no. 5 (2008): 5–75.

İpekten, Haluk. *Divan Edebiyatında Edebî Muhitler*. Istanbul: Milli Eğitim Bakanlığı, 1996.

Kahramanoğlu, Kemal. "Divan Şiirinde Şair, Hükümdar ve Yabancılaşmış Ben." *Türk Edebiyatı* 359 (2003): 18–23.

Karavelioğlu, Murat. "Tarihin Edebiyatı: 15. ve 16. Yüzyıl Kasîdelerinde Tarihî Arka Plan." In *Kasîdeye Medhiye: Biçime, İşleve ve Muhteveya Dair Tespitler*, edited by Hatice Aynur et al., 380–454. Istanbul: Klasik, 2013.

Kim, Sooyong. *The Last of an Age: The Making and Unmaking of a Sixteenth-Century Ottoman Poet*. London: Routledge, 2018.

Kocatürk, Vasfi Mahir. *Türk Edebiyatı Tarihi; Başlangıçtan Bugüne Kadar Türk Edebiyatının Tarihi, Tahlil ve Tenkidi*. Ankara: Edebiyat Yayınevi, 1970.

Köprülü, Mehmet Fuat. *Edebiyat Araştırmaları*. Ankara: Türk Tarih Kurumu Basımevi, 1999.

————. *Early Mystics in Turkish Literature*. London: Routledge, 2006.

Kuru, Selim S. "The Literature of Rum: The Making of a Literary Tradition (1450–1600)." In *Cambridge History of Turkey 2: The Ottoman Empire as a World Power, 1453–1603*, edited by Suraiya Faroqhi and Kate Fleet, 548–92. Cambridge: Cambridge University Press, 2013.

Kut, Günay. "Turkish Literature in Anatolia." In *History of the Ottoman State, Society & Civilisation*, edited by Ekmeleddin İhsanoğlu, 25–45. Istanbul: Research Centre for Islamic History, Art and Culture, 2002.

Lewis, Franklin. "Sincerely Flattering Panegyrics: The Shrinking Ghaznavid Qasida." In *The Necklace of the Pleiades: 24 Essays on Persian Literature, Culture and Religion*, edited by Franklin Lewis and Sunil Sharma, 228–29. Leiden: Leiden University Press, 2010.

Meisami, Julie Scott. "The Uses of Qaṣīda: Thematic and Structural Patterns in a Poem of Bashshār." *Journal of Arabic Literature* 16, no. 1 (1985): 40–59.

————. *Medieval Persian Court Poetry*. Princeton, NJ: Princeton University Press, 1987.

Necatî. *Divan*. Edited by Ali Nihat Tarlan, 61–63. Ankara: Akçağ Yayınları, 1992.

Necipoğlu, Gülru. "A Kanun for the State, a Canon for the Arts: The Classical Synthesis in Ottoman Art and Architecture During the Age of Süleyman." In *Soliman Le Magnifique et Son Temps, Actes*

Du Colloque de Paris Galeries Nationales Du Grand Palais, 7–10 Mars 1990, edited by Gilles Veinstein, 195–216. Paris: Rencontres de l'École du Louvre, 1992.

Pifer, Michael. *Kindred Voices: A Literary History of Medieval Anatolia*. New Haven, CT: Yale University Press, 2021.

Şen, Fatma Meliha. "Tâcîzâde Ca'fer Çelebi'nin (ö. 921/1515) Çevresindeki Şairler ve Onun İçin Yazılmış Şiirler." In *Kitaplara Vakfedilen Bir Ömre Tuhfe. İsmail Erünsal'a Armağan*, edited by Hatice Aynur, Bilgin Aydın, and Mustafa Birol Ülker, vol. 2, 1133–54. Istanbul: Ülke Kitapları, 2014.

Şentürk, Attila. "Okçuluk tarihine yeni bir kaynak olarak Osmanlı şiiri." In *M. Ali Tanyeri'nin Anısına Makaleler*, edited by Hatice Aynur et al., 71–142. Istanbul: Ülke Kitapları, 2015.

Sharma, Sunil. *Amir Khusraw: The Poet of Sultans and Sufis*. Oxford: Oneworld, 2005.

———. "Forbidden Love, Persianate Style: Re-Reading Tales of Iranian Poets and Mughal Patrons." *Iranian Studies* 42 (2009): 765–79.

Sheridan, Michael. "Defining and Defaming the Other in Early Seventeenth-Century Ottoman Invective." In *Disliking Others: Loathing, Hostility, and Distrust in Premodern Ottoman Lands*, edited by Hakan Karateke, Erdem Çipa, and Helga Anetshofer, 296–320. Boston: Academic Studies Press, 2018.

Sperl, Stefan. "Islamic Kingship and Arabic Panegyric Poetry in the Early 9th Century." *Journal of Arabic Literature* 8, no. 1 (1977).

Tekin, Gönül Alpay. "Fatih Devri Edebiyatı." In *İstanbul Armağanı: Fetih ve Fatih*, edited by Mustafa Armağan, 161–235. Istanbul: İstanbul Büyükşehir Belediyesi Kültür İşleri Daire Başkanlığı, 1995.

Tolasa, Harun. *Sehî, Latîfî, Âşık Çelebi Tezkirelerine Göre 16. Y.y.'da Edebiyat Araştırma ve Eleştirisi*. Izmir: Ege Üniversitesi Matbaası, 1983.

5

GAZEL AS GENRE AMONG THE OTTOMAN RULING ELITE

Selim S. Kuru[*]

The inflection of *gazel* (ghazal) as a genre in Anatolia and the Balkans—or as it was termed then, Rum—represents one of the many manifestations of this resilient form of lyric poetry that took its now familiar shape in the twelfth century in Persian.[1] While the first examples of the form appeared in the Turkish language in fourteenth-century Rum, the gazel was integrated into Ottoman court culture by the late fifteenth century, when it distinguished itself from other manifestations of the form used for other groups and established itself as a genre that informed the prevalent forms of poetry and prose.[2] The gazel genre in the Ottoman court established itself as a core form with a queering impact on the learned, bureaucratic, and military elite, which will be explained later in the chapter. Tens of thousands of gazels are today preserved in manuscripts in various libraries and private collections across the world. This dispersed yet expansive archive is a testimony to the important place of the gazel in the Ottoman court, while only a fraction of this massive archive is available in reliable modern editions.[3]

Gazel is a short poem of 5 to 15 couplets that starts with a rhymed couplet and continues with the following one rhyming with the first at the end of the second hemistich. Each couplet accommodates up to 32 syllables according to established patterns in *aruz* meter, which originated in Arabic prosody.[4] Starting in the second half of the fifteenth century, unlike the 11- to 15-couplet Anatolian gazels of the earlier decades, courtly gazels comprised five or seven couplets. While, formally, the gazel may sound deceptively simplistic, the rules were rather ambiguous with respect to rhetorical figures and the content to which they gave form. In a sense, this contrast between the rigid form and the supple content turned composing gazel into a competitive game that lasted for centuries.[5] For its content, focusing on love as the invisible truth behind the visible cosmos, the courtly gazel piggybacked on forms of knowledge that could be gained through specialized theological, mythological, scientific, historical, and rhetorical practice. These converging ways of knowing through signification conjured up a cosmology that informed, as it was altered by, the experiences of the courtly elite. The narrow container of the form became a vehicle for the sprawling gazel genre, which orbited a particular understanding of love as a discursive experience.

---

[*] I presented this article as a part of the "Ottomans Online: Skilliter Centre Seminars on the Ottoman Empire and Early Turkish Republic," Accessed November 17, 2022, https://skilliter.newn.cam.ac.uk/ottomans-online-7/

70

DOI: 10.4324/9780429279270-8

The adjective "courtly" that I use here to qualify this variation of the genre refers by no means to a homogenizing space; the Ottoman court hosted a heterogeneous system of fragile hierarchies that defined particular positionalities for its members that were painstakingly redefined as the larger contexts shifted. As will be discussed later, the gazel genre as produced by the Ottoman courtly elite offered those who were individuated by their hierarchical and/or social positions a possibility of queering the existing hierarchical boundaries.[6]

In his foundational theoretical work on Ottoman literary culture, Walter G. Andrews painstakingly interrogated the links between courtly literary production and larger Ottoman society focusing on lyric in its gazel, *kaside*, and *mesnevi* forms.[7] Starting with his first major article, Andrews cultivated "critical standards and aesthetic principles for Ottoman poetry" for a theoretical though ahistorical frame in order to understand the lyric form in Ottoman Turkish.[8] Andrews' work, while underpinning the difference of "Ottoman" lyric, investigating its position in the wider "Ottoman culture," does not interrogate the hierarchies among different forms that hosted lyric. It still opens the way for more focused interrogations of historicity and singularity of this particular linguistic and literary experience and the function of different genres that peruse similar forms in the literary system of Rumi culture.[9] Building upon Andrews' work, I consider gazel as a core literary form that established a genre in communication with categorically distinct forms such as kaside and mesnevi as it altered their thematic conventions. This gazel genre fulfilled a queering function within the etiquette of the Ottoman court and a queering affect in Ottoman studies.

I argue that the courtly gazel evolved in the form of a competitive game and reformulated Islamicate cosmology for the Ottoman court, subverting the theater of the court thanks to a specialized nebulous imagery that signified a story that was impossible to tell straight—a story of (1) creation by, (2) separation from, and (3) yearning to return to the Divine; in short, the human experience in the universe, as codified by Islamicate mystical cosmologies. In the court, the gazel form functioned as the core device to express this experience in a repetitive yet fragmentary fashion and, thanks to the long continuation of the Ottoman court, to the point of exhausting the intricate system of imagery it engendered. The courtly gazel affected a parallel yet subversive cosmology in the form of a fragmented discourse on love. Each gazel was a building block in the reconstruction of the cosmos in the form of a lover's discourse, and presented a puzzle that was meant to be experienced and never resolved. Instead of providing a well-ordered image system that targeted the construction of a direct statement, courtly gazel targeted a multiplication of meaning to dazzle the reader, triggering their imagination and forcing them to be creative readers. The courtly gazel, as such, when directed to a particular learned readership, moreover, encouraged its readers to interpret and compose gazels. It also established a genre, spilling into other forms of literature running them to the work of expressing divine love.

Genre in Ottoman literary studies is generally confused with content with respect to verse narratives, the mesnevi form. There are approaches that classify verse narratives in a categorical rather than an analytical fashion.[10] Unlike modern scholars, however, contemporary critics have concentrated on gazel in a manner stressing the centrality of the "gazel genre" for "*şi'r*," lyric poetry, while citing other genres in verse as "*nazm*," versification. While the gazel form established the core of the genre, mesnevi, kaside, and others were occasionally employed for its service. *Şi'r* referred to strictly poetic performances defined by the experience of metaphorical love, *aşk-ı mecazi*, on the path of *aşk-ı hakiki*, the Divine Love. In a queer manner, while the gazel genre reflected on this experience, it was also the main vehicle for the courtly poet to experience *aşk-ı mecazi*. Cem Dilçin and Harun Tolasa identified a terminology employed by premodern literary critics to delineate different modes in gazel form, paving the way to investigate it within the different literary forms. The major vocabulary employed—*aşıkane* (amorous), *rindane* (worldly), *şuhane* (playful/wicked), *hakimane* (philosophical), and *sufiyane* (mystical)—points to the modes that are at the basis of what I call the gazel genre.[11] These modes determined different forms based on the imagery developed in the particular contexts of the court.

Two kinds of works, biographical dictionaries of poets and parallel poetry anthologies, are major sources for understanding the courtly gazel genre. The sixteenth-century biographical dictionaries of poets (*tezkire-i şuara*), major sources for literary criticism in Turkish, include observations about the composition, function, and transmission of poetry among the Ottoman courtly elite with a focus on *şi'r*. These biographical dictionaries started with *Heşt Bihişt* (ca. 1538) by Sehî Bey (d. 1548) and included elite poets linked to the Ottoman court.[12] These poets were distinguished from other poets, such as urban and sufi poets, as "the poets of Rum," *şuara-i Rum*, which were juxtaposed with the "poets of Persia" or "poets of Acem" or *şuara-i Fürs/Acem*. The word "Rum" implied somewhat vague geographical boundaries, Western Anatolia and the Balkans under Ottoman rule with Istanbul as its center after the conquest of the city in 1453.[13] This date coincides with the transformation of the gazel genre along with elite organization, pointing to the entanglement of the courtly gazel with the political stratification of the Ottoman male elite.[14] Biographical dictionaries of poets, as a matter of fact, appear to keep a record of poets that signify this courtly formation during its early stages, and they establish a chain of continuation volumes by various authors that continues until the end of the empire. These volumes, while not comparable to the size of the extensive Arabic biographical dictionaries of earlier eras, were large compendiums that focused on Muslim male poets who were linked to the court. As Didem Havlioğlu demonstrated in her trailblazing work, when few women poets were included in biographical dictionaries, the male authors of biographical dictionaries raised the topic of gender in poetry in a manner that stratified the male-centric nature of composing poems in the gazel genre.[15]

The rules dictating the composition, communication, and reception of courtly gazels were also signified by the large parallel poetry anthologies (*mecmua-i nezair*) that appeared around the same time as the biographical dictionaries. These contributed to the establishment of a strict Ottoman Turkish canon.[16] Both included only those poets who appeared in Rum, who sang their poems in Turkish, and who were related to the Ottoman court. Together, these works provided models for poets and readers, and at times fabricated continuities for topics otherwise difficult to trace in gazels. Biographical dictionaries and parallel poetry anthologies are literary tools that bear witness to the transformation of the gazel as a learned form, altering its oral nature, making it more historical and more available to establish lineages.

The poets of Rum fashioned themselves to be a discrete community of poets who developed a distinct genre about metaphorical love, the core generative form of which was the gazel. Sixteenth-century biographical dictionary composers identified Şeyhî (d. 1431) as an ancient poet who moved from the Germiyan court to the Ottoman court. Post-conquest poets Ahmed Paşa (d. 1497) and Necatî (d. 1509) were designated as the fountainheads of two distinct styles. Aşık Çelebi (1520–1572), author of one of the major biographical dictionaries of poets, compared the latter two as follows:

> Necatî is the matter of life for the art of poetry in Rum and he delivered the Poets of Rum from the Poets of Fars's merciless jibes that are like stones opening wounds. Ahmed Paşa is the unique leader in this art and when one considers the craft of poetry, the heart goes back to his poems. Yet, his difference from Necatî is like the comparison of the wonders to magic and the light of the sun to the flame of a candle.

After praising Ahmed Paşa for his universalizing wondrous poetry, Aşık Çelebi appreciates Necatî as the localizing master for the poets of the Rum: Necatî established "a heart-fetching mansion that is the envy of the heavenly gardens by breaking the ground for poetry for the first time in Rum."[17] Many such commentaries reflect the universal versus local as a major stress point behind the Turkish courtly gazel.

While corresponding with the gazel in other languages, like Ahmet Paşa, and localizing the genre, like Necatî, the Poets of Rum were involved in a competition with each other, making the composition of gazels into a game. When they appreciated a poem or when a poem presented a challenge for them, or for many other reasons, they responded by composing a similar one mimicking the meter and rhyme while seeking to surpass its predecessor.[18] Bakî, a military judge who would later publish his poetry collection central to understanding gazel in Western Turkish, wrote a parallel for a poem by Muhibbî (i.e., Sultan Süleyman I; r. 1520–1566). In a letter to the Sultan, Bakî, who was then probably an assistant judge in Aleppo (ca. 1556–1560), likened his repeated attempts to surpass the Sultan's poem to a game in which the defeated never concedes. The letter, delivered by an intermediary at the court, preserved an intimate communication between a sultan and an assistant judge that was possible thanks to their mutual interest in poetics, yet it must have been seen as important enough to be kept in the Topkapı Palace archives.[19]

One productive question about the Ottoman courtly gazel may be how the gazel genre sustained itself as the core literary product under the patronage of Ottoman rulers for more than 500 years. Gazel became a growingly competitive form of play in the Ottoman court and the form certainly benefited from the longevity of a centralized empire. The performance of gazel by Ottoman sultans, and their *kul*s or "subjects" (e.g., viziers, scholars, judges, soldiers) displayed a distinct character by the turn of the sixteenth century, the so-called classical age of the Ottoman Empire. From this period on, intricately designed courtly rituals pronounced a sacred order that enchanted the realm of "work," somewhat similar to the work realm of a lawyer or a doctor today that is mystified for outsiders with its specialized vocabulary, techniques, offices, and routines. Yet the court's aura was much more restrictive and individuating. While distinct sets of knowledge informed other poetic forms and genres, mesnevi and kaside, the gazel pushed the boundaries of poetics by teasing out the impossible-to-tell story of a cosmology that connected the Ottoman elite in another manner. This cosmology provided them with a different collective subjectivity as a surplus of the courtly realm. In the end, writing a praise poem for a patron may, on the surface, be accepted as a display of superior skills in poetry for the sake of financial gain, but it also communicated the acceptance by the poet of his inferior *kul*/subject position. However, unlike the kaside, the gazel was a song of transgression. There is more than one argument behind this statement: In a gazel, the poet appears as the rebel lover who rebels against the mundane, repetitive, bland, ambiguous, and at times violent forms of experience defined by (1) service at the court, (2) creed in religion, and (3) etiquette in social engagement. In short, gazel performs a defiance of these rules of courtliness. To understand the significance of gazel in the construction of Ottoman courtly identity, how it was embedded into courtly life, one may refer to the rejection of it as degenerate "palace literature" by early modernist/nationalist critics.

As I argued above, the function of Ottoman Turkish gazel experienced a transformation during the late fifteenth century and, further, functioned as a vehicle that complicated elite hierarchies through a queering cosmology expressed/experienced by the poet/lover in this period. Consequently, the form evolved into a major yet subversive marker of Ottoman elite status. The members of the court might have had different educational, ethnic, religious, or social backgrounds; however, they submitted to the unifying rules of governance and ritual that defined the court. For the elite, the court was the realm of work, and while the gazel writing was definitely a function of the court, it had no serious consequences for this ritualistic realm.

Considering the inexplicably enormous number of gazels that were recorded, material gain or professional goals cannot be the sole motivation behind gazel writing and sharing. There were two other genres of poetry: kaside, the praise poems written for notables; and mesnevi, verse narratives to develop learned, historical, or amorous discourses that might have transactional value in a gift economy. Unlike those, composing gazels did not have any direct bearing on the daily routines of sultans, scholars, judges, and bureaucrats. The lack of any particular motivation behind it makes gazel writing seem like a purposeless leisure activity, beyond practicing rhetorical figures and imagery, but then why record and preserve those so systematically? Why were they evaluated as the central important products of a poet?

While Walter G. Andrews brilliantly described the emotional economy of Ottoman Turkish poetry with a focus on the notion of gazel as "play" in the seventh chapter of his *Poetry's Voice, Society's Song* titled "Ecology of the Song," he chose not to address the exclusionary power of gazel as a technology of the self.[20] In that sense, Andrews was joining forces to defend Ottoman Turkish literature against reductive formulations by modernist critics who condemned the literature produced in courtly contexts as an elite occupation without any social function. Gazel, on the other hand, was ultimately a social act that secreted a group ethos (masters of love and poets of Rum); furthermore, in a queering manner, it was also an individuating act (the poet/lover). With the help of the above-mentioned literary tools, the courtly gazel became part of the exclusionary technologies of the courtly elite in the form of a puzzle only the masters of sight, *ehl-i nazar*, could fully grasp. The sounds and surface meaning allowed these songs to capture the attention of outsiders, yet the intricate culture of the gazel also created knots in the texture of an intertextual cosmography in the form of a written archive providing the sense of a parallel history of poets, making its deeper meanings and genealogies available but only for the courtly elite. This was an ongoing process that lasted, with some transformations, until the late nineteenth century.

The object of the *gazel* is the beloved's created beauty as a signification of the Divine and the poet/lover's only request is annihilation through direct attention by the beloved. This approach separates the gazel genre from "palace allegory," a term introduced by Ahmet Hamdi Tanpınar and detailed by Walter G. Andrews.[21] According to this concept, the beloved defined not only beautiful young men but also the Sultan and God, creating multiple layers of signification in one literary work. While this generalizing view may hold true for some literary works where the person of the Sultan may inflict desire in the poets, like a young man with his physical qualities, and yearning for God whom he represented as the Caliph in this world, palace allegory did not require the existence of the Ottoman court as such. Palaces, gardens, or any organized space had already been a part of the poetic imagery, which may have influenced the courtly space and imagination.

Another aspect of gazel-play that explains its longevity was that it not only allowed members of the Ottoman elite to step out of the daily drudgery of their work realm but also subverted their *kul*/subject status and disrupted their masculinity: the emasculated lover surrenders to the beauty of the beloved, who combines the beauty and the wrath (*Celal* and *Cemal*) of the Creator. The constantly crying rebel lover is in a sense emasculated, yet he is also empowered by a strong emotion of love that in his yearning for ultimate union with the beloved enables him to deny the material world and all the obligations his status required. Emasculation was not a loss, as experienced through gazel-play, but rather a form of empowerment delivering the poet through his poem and beyond the gendered hierarchy of the court and all the worldly markers of identity, such as ethnicity, class, or race.

The beloved—who is generally defined as the Other, a non-Muslim young man, from outside the court—lures the poet into the darkness of disbelief (where, according to the legends, the elixir of life is found). Once the lover is afflicted by the side glance of the disinterested

Gazel as Genre Among the Ottoman Ruling Elite

and cruel beloved that is depicted as a war machine (e.g., his eyebrows are bows, his eyelashes arrows, the curls of his hair hooks carrying pieces of lovers' crushed hearts, the beauty mark on his cheek a maelstrom of promises, his dimple a dungeon), there is no escape from the centripetal force of what was captured by the beloved's discerning eye that seals the poet/lover's heart. Like a virus, this image instigates the poet/lover to produce gazels to express an incommunicable emotion. Each depiction ends up becoming a queer act that renders the courtly elite to his poetic persona, which he would boast through claims to be the best poet/lover.[22] Through the power of his true vision, the poet/lover tore apart the illusions of the wretched created world in his gazels. Taking part in the gazel game elevated the poet/lover to a *sahib-nazar*, master of vision, which also meant being in a lonely position. However, the heated competition kept elite men fighting for this position, gaining and losing score with each gazel.

What became visible for the masters of vision through gazels was a queer cosmology. Queer because, for the members of the elite, the cosmology that was wrought in the highly referential gazel genre through centuries of Islamicate sacred texts, traditions, legends, and stories had a destabilizing effect on the perception of time and space. The story of the gazel was originally about mystical love; however, the gazel also became a generator of imagery, as mentioned above. Words gained new signification within a further specialized language through new associations assigned to the basic vocabulary of love, adoration, and submission. The imagery that signified an ever-detailed story occasionally seeped into the letters, histories, and other kinds of narratives composed by the courtly elite. This influence of the gazel on the Anatolian Turkish literary system may not be a conscious act, but through the pens of the poets of the Ottoman court the gazel-game transformed the literary language and, thanks to the relatively stable longevity of the dynasty, allowed for the detailing of the gazel genre's rules. The joys that the genre inflicted on poets and their readers expanded the boundaries of Turkish rhetorical instantiations of love by refreshing age-old Islamicate imagery through a series of adjustments. Each act of composing a gazel relied on a mastery of the genre while the rhetorical inventiveness of the poet kept the game fresh.

Ottoman sultans and their subjects (viziers, bureaucrats, judges, scholars, financial administrators, provincial governors, janissary officers, and all those people who are defined as Ottoman governing elite) took a growing part in the game, which is attested by an enormous yet dispersed archive of Ottoman gazels. Composing gazels must have taken an important part in the lives of these men. Just to give an idea about the magnitude of gazel production in the empire, one of the parallel poetry anthologies, *Mecmau'n-nezair* by Nazmî of Edirne from the early sixteenth century, compiled 5,527 gazels by 357 poets.[23] Süleyman the Magnificent, the tenth and the longest-reigning Ottoman sultan, for example, composed around 4,000 gazels.[24]

The following anecdote provides a glimpse into how the gazel genre served as a heated arena of competition and frustrations that encouraged the poet/players to persevere in the game. Aşık Çelebi asked Hayalî (d. 1557), a major poet, about his favorite poem. Hayalî expressed his frustration upon encountering a couplet by another scholar and judge, İshak Çelebi (d. 1537): "It's been years that I am drunk with the wine of envy that this couplet feeds me with, and I get devastated by the wine of frustration whenever I attempt to compose a parallel to it." The following is the couplet that troubled Hayalî so much:

Gönül âyinesi sâfidür ammâ, temâşâ bu ki bir sâhib-nazar yok[25]

İshak Celebi was already dead and Hayalî was not seeking any favors from Aşık Çelebi, so his expression of wonder appears sincere. Modern readers may not have the tools to see the intrinsic quality of this seemingly simple verse and why it caused Hayalî such intense frustration. The line may be explicated through translation as, "The mirror of the heart is pure, yet it puts on such a show that there is no master of gaze to appreciate what it reflects."

In the sixteenth century, gazel as a game was being corrupted as it became "an instrument of the fecund and decisive culture" of the Ottoman elite through large parallel poetry collections and biographical dictionaries.[26] Writing parallel poems transformed the gazel into a rhetorical performance of the lyric "I." However, rather than being an expression of individual experience, the lyric I sounded out an expression of impossible desires, which was made possible by taking part in the collective of the "masters of Love" (ehl-i ışk) as the poets of Rum. The gazel connected each sahib-nazar of Rum in a community that enabled him to step out of his individuality, as determined by the hierarchies that framed the court space.

The gazel eschewed the patriarchal lineages and courtly hierarchies that ordered the male ruling elite, who deployed pen names to mark a poetic subjecthood/persona. One of the distinguishing components of the player's pen name is that it was generally an adjectival construct that assigned a particular feature to the poet, such as with Şeyhî (sheikhly or "sheik-like") or Bakî (permanent), and so on. Poets signed their gazels with this chosen or given pen name. Called mahlas in Rum, this pen name helped them appellate a persona as a significant supplement to their courtly elite personhood.[27] The power of this supplemental identity was indicated by the fact that courtly poets never included their full names in their poetry collections. The mahlas that appeared in the final couplet of a gazel was the ultimate marker that kept the players distinguishable in the game. Paradoxically, the mahlas, as a mask, immortalized them while effacing their courtly identity. The lover, the subject of this competitive role-play in the gazel, was nominally separated from the person, the courtly notable, through the pen name. The gazel-game enchanted the capacious and contentious theater of the Ottoman court. What then was the motivation to take part in this game, which was subversive on many levels, starting with the establishment of a poet/lover persona?

Latifî (d. 1582), a mid-sixteenth-century biographer of poets, claimed that poets, in his time, were as many as flies, each claiming to be the Simurg, the mythological bird that is reborn from its ashes. Latifî is the only Ottoman literary critic who distinguished the courtly gazel from the mystical gazel. Before starting his biographical dictionary, which included biographies of over 300 poets, Latifî described 13 Anatolian mystic poets, who lived before the rise of the Ottomans and composed poetry in different languages and genres, as true lovers, pointing to a perception of different registers of composing gazels, among which the courtly variety I refer to in this chapter ended up being the best recorded, transmitted, and discussed.[28] Latifî would burn the products of his involvement in courtly gazel-play as worthless artifacts compared to the songs of the true love (aşk-ı hakiki) by previous generations. He appears to be a rare spoilsport, who still left an original record of the game.

Playing within the boundaries of this scheme, bound by the impossibility of direct expression of the alluded visionary experience, poet/lovers created a new puzzle with each gazel they composed. A gazel is not a direct expression of his experience since it has to be veiled by language. Rather, the gazel is mere implication. It provided the excuse for the poet/lover's denial of the established world, including courtly rituals. Gazel is the mirror that reflects the beauty of the dil-ber, the heart-snatcher, who threw the courtier, officer, or scholar off their orderly paths. The remembrance of Creation that the beloved inadvertently activates is delivered in fragments gazel by gazel, each providing an instance of the overall rhetorical experience of love. The side glance that thrashes the hearts of the elite male poet/lover transforms him into a lover whose wailings become the gazel. Gazel pushed aside service, creed, and etiquette—the main markers of Ottoman elite status—and in a queering manner established the courtly elite person as a poet/lover under his assumed poetic signature.

In the theater of the court, gazel-play lost its ritualistic function which Latifî underscored as a sacred performance signifying the later stages of the mystical path. Transmission and canonization, traces of which were preserved in the anthologies and biographical dictionaries composed in growing bureaucratized and institutionalized courtly contexts, drew in the reins on the enchanted and enchanting forms of gazel, transforming it into a queer yet inevitable part of the court ritual. The ecstatic song of the unseen, in a process similar to the transition from icon painting to allegorical oil paintings, from sacred allegory to disenchanted realistic depictions of religious themes, transformed into a calculated image-making contest as a courtly practice.

Losing its sacred origins in courtly circles, the gazel also subverted the strong patriarchal system centered around forms of masculinity, whereas a particular form of submissive masculinity came to be a heightened expression of the poet's *kul*/subject status, since the play involved the expression of the joy of being the slave of love, a love for an enchanted world that constantly flowed through the face and body of the beloved and which signified the queer cosmology of the Unseen. For Ottoman scholars and bureaucrats of all ages, gazel-play was mostly a form of competitive role-play, as they restricted the state of being the lover, or speaking as the lover, to the space of gazel. Going beyond its written archive to reconstruct/reimagine the processes of gazel play, the composition and sharing of gazels is very difficult today.

Poets wrote more and more gazels, almost like an addiction, transforming themselves from sultans, bureaucrats, scholars, or judges into base and lowly poet-lovers, who are constantly proud of being able to fall so low for love. Remarkably, this queering effect of gazel-play on male poets is explained in pragmatic terms by Aşık Çelebi. In the introduction to his biographical dictionary of poets, he stated that one of the aspects of poetry was alchemy, as it transformed everyone from sultans to beggars to lovers. Even though he did not specify any one form in his discourse on poetry, it was definitely the gazel genre that he had in mind. In gazel-play, the sultans, courtiers, and the learned competed with each other behind the mask of lover in order to gain the position of "best lover." The best lover accepted having the power to re-enchant the world by reflecting in his gazels the unseen power behind it; the strife in the play was designed to consciously represent that yearning for the known-but-not-to-be-experienced, unless annihilated by the sun-like, burning gaze of the beloved. This unifying power of the play further complicated the *kul*/subject status subverted by the queer discourse of gazel-play.

The gazel can be taken as an addictive hobby since, as I implied above, there are some pragmatic ends to this skill-based game. Skill, in this case, involved becoming an expert in a specialized language with the strict rules of establishing one image in one couplet, and then setting together five to seven couplets in mono-rhyme and meter. The player did not aim to resolve but rather to complicate the linguistic associations to exalt metaphors in order to implicate the invisible, inexplicable, unknowable, unreachable by constructing a paradoxical puzzle. The story remained, however; innumerable gazels were composed to tell it in the form of a beautiful implication. The learned readers of the gazel were to be surprised by the puzzle that each couplet veiled: the blinding light of the unwitnessable within was veiled by the darkness of visible letters that formed words tasked with conveying multiplying meanings, so much so that all meaning ended in a heightened metaphor. The gazel was composed to tease, provoke, and instigate other poets, stratifying a community of the masters of love as the poets of Rum, distinguishing them within the global genre of gazel as part of an elite performance.

The gazel genre needs to be located within the wider context of Anatolian Turkish poetics. Instead of discussing the sacred origins of the gazel genre, I have discussed how it was transformed into a competitive role-playing game. The gazel was not individualistic but rather a subjective, first-person narrative and there was only one role to play in this game: the Lover which pointed to an emasculated *kul*. Based on this, I argue that for the Ottoman learned elite, the joy of composing gazels was similar to running marathons with respect to training and performance; however, it differed with respect to the transgression it allowed for the player. So as Bakî stated, the gazel fashioned a game in which losing encouraged one to strive for more, and it may be argued that winning was hardly possible. There were no boundaries for establishing linguistic associations related to the core narrative of Creation by, Separation from, and Yearning for the divine. Learned elite, at play with words, were able to deny submission to their courtly world through the gazel. While high officers, sultans, viziers, judges, and scholars asked for suffering, expressed desire for annihilation, and shed bloody tears in their gazels, they were composing ambiguous, multilayered images that made the created world a more interesting place, where natural or man-made objects played a game of mirrors that signified an invisible and unknowable world. This unknowable world established a cosmology experienced by composing gazels through synchronic communication with fellow poets from various ranks and diachronically with past poets. Like a stream that flows backwards and sideways, expanding like celestial spheres, gazels sang a queer realm into existence—one in which taverns are mosques, a beloved's eyebrows are altars to pray towards, and pious believers are hypocrites.

Among many the possibilities for "rescuing" Ottoman Turkish poetry, one may describe the Ottoman Turkish gazel as a symbolic system, a semiosis, developed by a centrally located "social life" or "palace culture." However, this creates a determination by a center and an understanding of the gazel, which Andrews challenged in his work, by despotic rule. As a way of escaping the thesis of determination and appreciating the subversive aspects of Ottoman poetry, especially the gazel, one may also start from its core themes, which establish a constellation centered around an idea of oneness. From the core themes, one may reach various links in the social order that might or might not be signified by individual gazels, which may however subvert our understanding of the poets of Rum and their patrons. The concept of entanglement may provide such an approach wherein spooky nodes of literary production and production of a bureaucratic rule entangled within an indescribable relationship between the two. This approach then, while identifying gazel as a node of its own, focuses on one particular inflection when it was performed by the Ottoman ruling elite.

Notes

1 For the evolution of the term "Rum" to signify Western Anatolia and Rumelia for the Ottoman elite, see Salih Özbaran, *Bir Osmanlı Kimliği: 14–17. Yüzyıllarda Rûm/Rûmi Aidiyet ve İmgeleri* (Istanbul: Kitap Yayınevi, 2004); Cemal Kafadar, "A Rome of One's Own: Reflections on Cultural Geography and Identity in the Lands of Rum," *Muqarnas* 24 (2007): 7–25. For a more detailed discussion of Rum see Michael Sheridan, "'I Curse No One Without Cause': Identity, Power, Rivalry, and Invective in the Early 17th-Century Ottoman Court" (PhD diss., Bilkent University, 2018), 343–56.

2 For a succinct evaluation of form and genre with a focus on the gazel in the Persian language see Julie Scott Meisami, *Medieval Persian Court Poetry* (Princeton, NJ: Princeton University Press, 1987), 237–98. For a general survey of Ottoman Turkish literature see Selim S. Kuru, "The Literature of Rum: The Making of a Literary Tradition (1450–1600)," in *Cambridge History of Turkey*, ed. Suraiya N. Faroqhi, vol. 2 (Cambridge: Cambridge University Press, 2012), 548–92. For a history of premodern Turkish literature in Anatolia with information about major literary forms, see Ömer Faruk Akün, "Divan Edebiyatı," in *TDV İslam Ansiklopedisi* (Istanbul: Türkiye Diyanet Vakfı Yayınları, 1994), https://islamansiklopedisi.org.tr/divan-edebiyati. In this chapter, I do not comment on the important topic of the influence of Persian on the Ottoman Turkish gazel., For an excellent evaluation, see Murat Umut İnan, "Rethinking the Ottoman Imitation of Persian Poetry," *Iranian Studies* 50, no. 5 (2017): 671–89.

3 For an overview of and future prospects for editing Ottoman Turkish manuscripts, see Walter G. Andrews and Gülşah Taşkın, "The Fourth Wave: The Digital Future of Ottoman Manuscripts, Manuscript Transcription, Edition, and Textual Studies," in *Âb-ı Hayatı Aramak: Gönül Tekin'e Armağan*, ed. Ozan Kolbaş and Orçun Üçer (Istanbul: Yeditepe Yayınevi, 2018), 345–72.

Gazel as Genre Among the Ottoman Ruling Elite

4 For a detailed description of the form in English along with translation and analysis of a gazel, see Walter G. Andrews, *An Introduction to Ottoman Poetry* (Minneapolis: Bibliotheca Islamica, 1976), 136–45. See pp. 177–80 of the same text for *aruz* feet and patterns. See also Cem Dilçin, "Divan Şiirinde Gazel," *Türk Dili*, no. 416–18 (1986): 78–247.

5 Gazel as play was first taken up by Andrews with reference to Huizinga's work. Walter G. Andrews, *Poetry's Voice, Society's Song: Ottoman Lyric Poetry* (Seattle: University of Washington Press, 1985), esp. chap. 7. See also Johan Huizinga, *Homo Ludens; a Study of the Play-Element in Culture.* (London: Routledge & Kegan Paul, 1949). My approach incorporates Caillois' division between work and leisure in Roger Caillois, *Man, Play, and Games* (New York: Free Press of Glencoe, 1961).

6 For a historical analysis of Ottoman households, see Metin Kunt, "Royal and Other Households," in *The Ottoman World*, ed. Christine Woodhead (New York: Routledge, 2011), 119–31. On the palace system, see Rhoads Murphey, *Exploring Ottoman Sovereignty: Tradition, Image and Practice in the Ottoman Imperial Household, 1400–1800* (London: Continuum, 2008). For an evaluation of the *kul* status, see Dror Ze'evi, "Kul and Getting Cooler: The Dissolution of Elite Collective Identity and the Formation of Official Nationalism in the Ottoman Empire," *Mediterranean Historical Review* 11, no. 2 (1996): 180–86.

7 Andrews, *Poetry's Voice, Society's Song*; Walter G. Andrews and Mehmet Kalpaklı, *The Age of Beloveds: Love and the Beloved in Early-Modern Ottoman and European Culture and Society* (Durham, NC: Duke University Press, 2005). For more on the kaside, see Oscar Aguirre-Mandujano's chapter in this volume.

8 Walter G. Andrews, "A Critical-Interpretive Approach to the Ottoman Turkish Gazel," *International Journal of Middle East Studies* 4, no. 1 (1973): 110.

9 Oscar Aguirre Mandujano's approach to the historicity and function of poetic production develops on cues by Andrews in "Poetics of Empire: Literature and Political Culture at the Early Modern Ottoman Court" (PhD diss., University of Washington, 2018). For a review of manifestations of Rumi identity and how the term was employed by litterateurs, see Özbaran, *Bir Osmanlı Kimliği*, 109–20.

10 For a general evaluation and references, see Fatma S. Kutlar, "Mesnevî Nazım Şekline bir Bakış ve Türk Edebiyatında Mesnevî Araştırmalarıyla İlgili bir Araştırma," *Türkbilig* 1 (2000): 102–57.

11 Dilçin, "Divan Şiirinde Gazel," 140–44; Harun Tolasa, *Sehî, Latîfî, Âşık Çelebi Tezkirelerine Göre 16. y.y.'da Edebiyat Araştırma ve Eleştirisi* (Izmir: Ege Üniversitesi Matbaası, 1983). For a brief introductory evaluation of how these modes that incorporated the long verse-narrative form mesnevi into the gazel genre, see Selim S. Kuru, "Mesnevi Biçiminde Aşk Hali: Birinci Tekil Şahıs Anlatılar Olarak Fürkat-Nâme, Heves-Nâme Üzerinden Bir Değerlendirme," in *Nazımdan Nesire Edebî Türler*, ed. Hatice Aynur et al., Eski Türk Edebiyatı Çalışmaları 4 (Istanbul: Turkuaz, 2009), 168–33.

12 For an evaluation of sixteenth-century biographical dictionaries, see Kuru, "The Literature of Rum," 586–92.

13 Özbaran, *Bir Osmanlı Kimliği*; Kafadar, "A Rome of One's Own."

14 For the formation of Ottoman court, see Gülru Necipoğlu, *Architecture, Ceremonial, and Power: The Topkapi Palace in the Fifteenth and Sixteenth Centuries* (New York: MIT Press, 1991).

15 Didem Havlioğlu, "On the Margins and Between the Lines: Ottoman Women Poets from the Fifteenth to the Twentieth Centuries," *Turkish Historical Review* 1, no. 1 (2010): 25–54. Also see Didem Havlioğlu, *Mihrî Hatun: Performance, Gender-Bending, and Subversion in Ottoman Intellectual History* (Syracuse, NJ: Syracuse University Press, 2017). On women poets in biographical dictionaries, see pp. 33–56.

16 Selim S. Kuru, "Sex in the Text: Deli Birader's Dâfi'ü 'l-Gumûm ve Râfi'ü 'l-Humûm and the Ottoman Literary Canon," *Middle Eastern Literatures* 10, no. 2 (2007): 158–61. Kuru, "The Literature of Rum." For a recent evaluation of literary canon in the Ottoman Empire see also Ferenc Csirkés, "Turkish/Turkic Books of Poetry, Turkish and Persian Lexicography: The Politics of Language under Bayezid II," in *Treasures of Knowledge: An Inventory of the Ottoman Palace Library (1502/3–1503/4)*, ed. Gülru Necipoğlu, Cemal Kafadar, and Cornell H. Fleischer (Leiden: Brill, 2019), 673–733.

17 For a categorical evaluation of major sixteenth-century Ottoman Turkish biographical dictionaries of poets, see Tolasa, *Sehî, Latîfî, Âşık Çelebi.*

18 Walter G. Andrews, "Starting Over Again: Some Suggestions for Rethinking Ottoman Divan Poetry in the Context of Translation and Transmission," in *Translations: (Re)Shaping of Literature and Culture*, ed. Saliha Paker (Istanbul: Boğaziçi University Press, 2002), 15–40.

19 For references to scholarship on this letter, see Selim S. Kuru, "Kâfiri Mihrabda Eğrilik: Baki'nin Mektubu Muhibbî'nin Beyti," *Journal of Turkish Studies* 54 (December 2020): 235–48.

20 Andrews, *Poetry's Voice, Society's Song*, 143–74.

21 Walter G. Andrews, "Singing the Alienated 'I': Guattari, Deleuze, and Lyrical Decodings of the Subject in Ottoman Divan Poetry," *Yale Journal of Criticism* 6, no. 2 (1993): 217, ft. 7. For an original evaluation of "palace allegory," see Walter G. Andrews and Irene Markoff, "Poetry, the Arts and Group Ethos in the Ideology of the Ottoman Empire," *Edebiyat* 1, no. 1 (1987): 28–71.

22 "In fact, the persona of the Ottoman poet was quite distinct from the actual personality of the man, and this distinction is deliberately maintained." See İsmail E. Erünsal, *The Life and Works of Tâcî-zâde Ca'fer Çelebi* (Istanbul: Edebiyat Fakültesi Basımevi, 1983), xviii.

23 Mustafa Özkan, "Edirneli Nazmî," in *TDV İslam Ansiklopedisi* (Istanbul: Türkiye Diyanet Vakfı Yayınları, 1994); M. Fatih Köksal, "Nazîre: Türk Edebiyatı," in *TDV İslam Ansiklopedisi* (Istanbul: Türkiye Diyanet Vakfı Yayınları, 2006). For a survey of parallel poetry anthologies, see M. Fatih Köksal, *Sana Benzer Güzel Olmaz: Divan Şiirinde Nazire* (Ankara: Akçağ, 2006).

24 I. Süleyman, *Muhibbî Dîvânı: Bütün Şiirleri (İnceleme—Tenkitli Metin)*, ed. Kemal Yavuz and Orhan Yavuz (Istanbul: Türkiye Yazma Eserler Kurumu Başkanlığı, 2016).

25 Âşık Çelebi, *Âşık Çelebi—Meşâ'irü'ş-şu'arâ: İnceleme—Metin*, ed. Filiz Kılıç, vol. 3 (Istanbul: İstanbul Araştırmaları Enstitüsü, 2010); İshak Çelebi, *Dîvan: Tenkidli Basım*, ed. Mehmed Çavuşoğlu and M. Ali Tanyeri (Istanbul: Mimar Sinan Üniversitesi Fen-Edebiyat Fakültesi Yayınları, 1989), 203.

26 Caillois, *Man, Play, and Games*, 27.

27 On use of poetic signature, see Âşık Çelebi, *Âşık Çelebi*.

28 Selim S. Kuru, "Latifi Tezkiresinde Mutasavvıflar," in *Bursa'da Dünden Bugüne Tasavvuf Kültürü-3*, ed. Hasan Basri Öcalan (Bursa: Bursa Kültür Sanat ve Turizm Vakfı, 2004), 197–207.

References

Aguirre Mandujano, Oscar. "Poetics of Empire: Literature and Political Culture at the Early Modern Ottoman Court." PhD diss., University of Washington, 2018.

Akün, Ömer Faruk. "Divan Edebiyatı." In *TDV İslam Ansiklopedisi*. Istanbul: Türkiye Diyanet Vakfı Yayınları, 1994. https://islamansiklopedisi.org.tr/divan-edebiyati.

Andrews, Walter G. "A Critical-Interpretive Approach to the Ottoman Turkish Gazel." *International Journal of Middle East Studies* 4, no. 1 (1973): 110.

———. *An Introduction to Ottoman Poetry*. Minneapolis: Bibliotheca Islamica, 1976.

———. *Poetry's Voice, Society's Song: Ottoman Lyric Poetry*. Seattle: University of Washington Press, 1985.

———. "Singing the Alienated 'I': Guattari, Deleuze, and Lyrical Decodings of the Subject in Ottoman Divan Poetry." *Yale Journal of Criticism* 6, no. 2 (1993): 191–219.

———. "Starting Over Again: Some Suggestions for Rethinking Ottoman Divan Poetry in the Context of Translation and Transmission." In *Translations: (Re)shaping of Literature and Culture*, edited Saliha Paker, 15–40. Istanbul: Boğaziçi University Press, 2002.

Andrews, Walter G., and Mehmet Kalpaklı. *The Age of Beloveds: Love and the Beloved in Early-Modern Ottoman and European Culture and Society*. Durham, NC: Duke University Press, 2005.

Andrews, Walter G., and Irene Markoff. "Poetry, the Arts and Group Ethos in the Ideology of the Ottoman Empire." *Edebiyat* 1, no. 1 (1987): 28–71.

Andrews, Walter G., and Gülşah Taşkın. "The Fourth Wave: The Digital Future of Ottoman Manuscripts, Manuscript Transcription, Edition, and Textual Studies." In *Âb-ı Hayatı Aramak: Gönül Tekin'e Armağan*, edited by Ozan Kolbaş and Orçun Üçer, 345–72. Istanbul: Yeditepe Yayınevi, 2018.

Âşık Çelebi. *Âşık Çelebi—Meşâ'irü'ş-şu'arâ: İnceleme—Metin*. Edited by Filiz Kılıç, vol. 3. Istanbul: İstanbul Araştırmaları Enstitüsü, 2010.

Caillois, Roger. *Man, Play, and Games*. New York: Free Press of Glencoe, 1961.

Csirkés, Ferenc. "Turkish/Turkic Books of Poetry, Turkish and Persian Lexicography: The Politics of Language Under Bayezid II." In *Treasures of Knowledge: An Inventory of the Ottoman Palace Library (1502/3–1503/4)*, edited by Gülru Necipoğlu, Cemal Kafadar, and Cornell H. Fleischer, 673–733. Leiden: Brill, 2019.

Dilçin, Cem. "Divan Şiirinde Gazel." *Türk Dili* 416–18 (1986): 78–247.

Erünsal, İsmail E. *The Life and Works of Tâcî-zâde Ca'fer Çelebi*. Istanbul: Edebiyat Fakültesi Basımevi, 1983.

Havlioğlu, Didem. "On the Margins and Between the Lines: Ottoman Women Poets from the Fifteenth to the Twentieth Centuries." *Turkish Historical Review* 1, no. 1 (2010): 25–54.

―――. *Mihrî Hatun: Performance, Gender-Bending, and Subversion in Ottoman Intellectual History*. Syracuse, NY: Syracuse University Press, 2017.

Huizinga, Johan. *Homo Ludens; a Study of the Play-Element in Culture*. London: Routledge and Kegan Paul, 1949.

İnan, Murat Umut. "Rethinking the Ottoman Imitation of Persian Poetry." *Iranian Studies* 50, no. 5 (2017): 671–89.

İshak Çelebi. *Dîvan: Tenkidli Basım*. Edited by Mehmed Çavuşoğlu and M. Ali Tanyeri. Istanbul: Mimar Sinan Üniversitesi Fen-Edebiyat Fakültesi Yayınları, 1989.

Kafadar, Cemal. "A Rome of One's Own: Reflections on Cultural Geography and Identity in the Lands of Rum." *Muqarnas* 24 (2007): 7–25.

Köksal, M. Fatih. "Nazîre: Türk Edebiyatı." In *TDV İslam Ansiklopedisi*. Istanbul: Türkiye Diyanet Vakfı Yayınları, 2006.

―――. *Sana Benzer Güzel Olmaz: Divan Şiirinde Nazire*. Ankara: Akçağ, 2006.

Kunt, Metin. "Royal and Other Households." In *The Ottoman World*, edited by Christine Woodhead, 119–31. New York: Routledge, 2011.

Kuru, Selim S. "Latifi Tezkiresinde Mutasavvıflar." In *Bursa'da Dünden Bugüne Tasavvuf Kültürü-3*, edited by Hasan Basri Öcalan, 197–207. Bursa: Bursa Kültür Sanat ve Turizm Vakfı, 2004.

―――. "Sex in the Text: Deli Birader's Dâfi'ü 'l-Gumûm ve Râfi'ü 'l-Humûm and the Ottoman Literary Canon." *Middle Eastern Literatures* 10, no. 2 (2007): 158–61.

―――. "Mesnevi Biçiminde Aşk Hali: Birinci Tekil Şahıs Anlatılar Olarak Fürkat-Nâme, Heves-Nâme Üzerinden Bir Değerlendirme." In *Nazımdan Nesire Edebî Türler*, edited by Hatice Aynur et al., 168–233. Istanbul: Turkuaz, 2009.

―――. "The Literature of Rum: The Making of a Literary Tradition (1450–1600)." In *Cambridge History of Turkey*, edited by Suraiya N. Faroqhi, vol. 2, 548–92. Cambridge: Cambridge University Press, 2012.

―――. "Kâfiri Mihrabda Eğrilik: Baki'nin Mektubu Muhibbî'nin Beyti." *Journal of Turkish Studies* 54 (December 2020): 235–48.

Kutlar, Fatma S. "Mesnevî Nazım Şekline bir Bakış ve Türk Edebiyatında Mesnevî Araştırmalarıyla İlgili bir Araştırma." *Türkbilig* 1 (2000): 102–57.

Meisami, Julie Scott. *Medieval Persian Court Poetry*. Princeton, NJ: Princeton University Press, 1987.

Murphey, Rhoads. *Exploring Ottoman Sovereignty: Tradition, Image and Practice in the Ottoman Imperial Household, 1400–1800*. London: Continuum, 2008.

Necipoğlu, Gülru. *Architecture, Ceremonial, and Power: The Topkapi Palace in the Fifteenth and Sixteenth Centuries*. New York: MIT Press, 1991.

Özbaran, Salih. *Bir Osmanlı Kimliği: 14.-17. Yüzyıllarda Rûm/Rûmi Aidiyet ve İmgeleri*. Istanbul: Kitap Yayınevi, 2004.

Özkan, Mustafa. "Edirneli Nazmî." In *TDV İslam Ansiklopedisi*. Istanbul: Türkiye Diyanet Vakfı Yayınları, 1994.

Sheridan, Michael. "'I Curse No One Without Cause': Identity, Power, Rivalry, and Invective in the Early 17th-Century Ottoman Court." PhD diss., Bilkent University, 2018.

Süleyman, I. *Muhibbî Dîvânı Bütün Şiirleri (İnceleme—Tenkitli Metin)*. Edited by Kemal Yavuz and Orhan Yavuz. Istanbul: Türkiye Yazma Eserler Kurumu Başkanlığı, 2016.

Tolasa, Harun. *Sehî, Latîfî, Âşık Çelebi Tezkirelerine Göre 16. y.y.'da Edebiyat Araştırma ve Eleştirisi*. Izmir: Ege Üniversitesi Matbaası, 1983.

Ze'evi, Dror. "Kul and Getting Cooler: The Dissolution of Elite Collective Identity and the Formation of Official Nationalism in the Ottoman Empire." *Mediterranean Historical Review* 11, no. 2 (1996): 180–86.

6

TOWARDS A THEORY OF OTTOMAN ALLEGORY

Allegorical Narratives From *Ḥüsn ü Dil* to *Ḥüsn ü ʿAşq*

Berat Açıl

With only sporadic mention here and there, Ottoman allegory remains an area of study that has received inadequate attention, particularly in English.[1] Among works that have addressed this field, Peter Heath's chapter on allegory in Islamic literature(s) constitutes the most comprehensive synopsis that also touches upon Ottoman allegory.[2] Hence, the foremost purpose of this chapter is to provide an overview of Ottoman allegorical narratives, most of which are written in *mathnawi* form.[3] First, the chapter presents the general characteristics of allegorical writing and those unique to classical Ottoman literature, which will result in a (re)definition of allegory. Second, this chapter provides a synopsis of the Ottoman allegorical style of writing by presenting a list of allegorical works. The chapter argues that allegories composed in classical Ottoman literature are not allegorical interpretation[4] but examples of allegorical writing,[5] as they bear the quintessential mark of allegorical writing, which is all the more apparent in the various renditions of the romance called *Ḥüsn ü Dil* (Beauty and Heart) and in *Ḥüsn ü ʿAşq* (Beauty and Love), a mathnawi written by Şeyḫ Ġalib.

It seems that eastern and western allegories share three common characteristics in the premodern period; namely, personifying concepts to include them as characters in the narrative, which is called personification; *bellum intestinum* (inner war), which can be defined as "personified vices and virtues that engaged in battle upon a field of abstractions";[6] and quest (journey). Of all the exquisite and influential works that have been put to pen, *Le Roman de la Rose* (*the Roman of the Rose*) by Guillaume de Lorris (written in 1237) is the work most deserving of being deemed the primary example of allegorical personification. Indeed, *Le Roman de la Rose* started a succession of literary works recounting the story of the rose and the nightingale.[7] On the other hand, of all allegorical works written in European languages, *The Faerie Queene* written by Edmund Spenser in the medieval period (published in 1590) best epitomizes *bellum intestinum* for its important use of inner war. Among allegories, one of the most lucid depictions of a quest is *The Pilgrim's Progress* (published in 1678), a work that brilliantly depicts a journey of spiritual maturation.

These three characteristics of personification, *bellum intestinum*, and quest are shared by nearly all allegorical works and pervade the very fabric of classical allegories. As these features likewise apply to Islamic and Ottoman allegories, I will not repeat them in this context. Rather, I will

82

DOI: 10.4324/9780429279270-9

itemize the characteristics that are common in classical Ottoman allegories but not universally shared with allegories of non-Ottoman literary traditions.

Characteristics of Ottoman Allegories

When discussing Islamic literature(s), and especially classical Ottoman literature, it is essential to determine what the first allegorical texts were and when they were written. Is allegory native to Islamic literature, or was it inherited from another literary tradition? Since Greek philosophy was transmitted to Islamic philosophy through extensive translation projects,[8] allegorical modes of narration were also inherited from the Greeks and subsequently "integrated and developed in Islamic culture," as Heath argues.[9]

One challenge to determining the origins of allegorical texts in Ottoman literature is the loose and hence ambiguous definition of the term in earlier scholarship. Although Ottomans did not self-consciously coin a neologism for what later be called allegory, *istiare-I temsiliyye* might best cover its meaning, whereas the term preferred in modern Turkish is *alegori*, which is similar to its English original. In addition, the term *temsilî* is used for "allegorical" both in Ottoman and modern Turkish.[10] Accordingly, I will narrow the scope of the term's meaning so that it is more conducive for analyzing Ottoman allegorical narratives. With this objective in mind, I will redefine allegory to denote works containing a single, continuous story that has at least two separate layers enmeshed in the narrative itself without interruption.[11] I will use the term "allegorical" for works that are essentially allegorical and not for those that simply incorporate allegory in one or more places in the narrative. This redefinition may be deemed "literary allegory" since it is based on the study of Ottoman romances.

It is refr necessary to identify the characteristics of Ottoman allegory shared across the overwhelming majority of narratives.[12] Whereas personification, *bellum intestinum*, and the journey are three features common in eastern and western allegories alike, the following features that will be discussed are, for the most part, unique to Ottoman allegorical narratives in the sense that Ottoman narratives take advantage of them consistently and insistently. Moreover, Ottoman allegories make use of all of these features at once in the same narrative, something that differentiates Ottoman narrative style from its Western, Arab, Persian, and Urdu counterparts. These features may be labeled as the following: multilayered, harmony, obscurity or vagueness, intertext, and manifesting the allegorical way of writing at the end of the text.

Because allegory is to say one thing on the lexical level while meaning another in the mode of expression, allegorical narratives must contain at least two different and autonomous stories told in a single text. Therefore, while on the surface structure, the lexical dimension pertaining to the meaning of words themselves, one may find a single story, an allegory should contain at least one more story in the deep structure, which is the narrative dimension of the text. As a result, narrating more than one story with exactly the same words makes Ottoman allegories multilayered. Accordingly, being multilayered is one of the foremost characteristics of Ottoman allegorical narratives.

The next characteristic of Ottoman allegories is *tenasüp* (harmony). This has some common features with the first universal feature of allegory, personification. One of the leading researchers reevaluating the literature on allegory, Deborah L. Madsen, correctly stated that "[in] allegorical personifications, [the] character is indicated by [its] etymology or linguistic genealogy."[13] This understanding of allegorical personification leads us to the concept of *tenasüp* (harmony), which despite being a universal characteristic of Ottoman allegorical narratives, is also a common feature of Ottoman poetry in general. Nearly all hemistiches of Ottoman *gazels* exhibit internal harmony wherein poets use words, terms, or concepts that are related in their etymologies, meanings, connotations, and so on to compose a harmonious work of poetry. In the case of allegorical narratives where a character personifies a specific concept, the name given to the character is etymologically related to the concept personified, which makes the use of harmony possible or necessary. For example, the personified character *Mihr*, which literally means both "sun" and "love," should behave accordingly. Friends of *Mihr* should be either other celestial bodies or love-related personifications like affection, fidelity, and so on. These connections build up harmony in the poetry.

Allegorical potential is inversely related to real-world specification. The more a narrative is disassociated from real individuals affiliated with a certain time or place, the more allegorical the text becomes. Obscurity or vagueness are also techniques designed to create this effect. Ottoman narratives perfectly embody this feature. As C. S. Lewis specifies in the case of medieval allegorical literature from Europe, "Allegory, in some sense, belongs not to medieval man but to man, or even to mind, in general. It is of the very nature of thought and language to represent what is immaterial in picturable terms."[14] The "medieval man" Lewis mentions, could also be interpreted as a humankind in general instead of just Europeans, which makes allegory universal. Indeed, Ottoman allegorical narratives obfuscate the geographical and temporal location of their characters, thereby rendering both time and place tropological.

Another characteristic of Ottoman allegorical narratives is that they are intertexts, in the same way that Lewis uses the term: "Perhaps allegories would be more accurately termed *intertexts* than texts: from the allegorical quest structure to the narrative paradigms that constitute the structure, allegories produce their generic mark as the interpretation of prior texts."[15] This usage here is not to be confused with how poststructuralists and others identified this same term; here, intertext describes texts that know and refer to each other. In fact, retelling/rewording a narrative, or writing a parallel to it and thereby reinterpreting a prior text, is a common feature of various Islamic literatures, including Arabic, Persian, Chagatai, Urdu, and Ottoman. This makes them all intertexts. The uniqueness of the Ottoman case is that Ottoman allegorical narratives use this style of writing more consistently than any other literary tradition.

The final common feature of Ottoman allegorical narratives is that they manifest, in most cases, their allegories at the end of the narrative, a characteristic rarely found in Western allegorical narratives.[16] This feature facilitates to classify them as allegorical writing in which the author of the narrative is aware that he is specifically designing his narrative/text as an allegory—not as interpretations that commentators interpret as allegory but which are not necessarily written allegorically. In addition, those narratives that might be called "allegorical writing" generally admit or express explicitly that they are allegories at the end of the text.

To conclude, these features of Ottoman allegories clearly demonstrate that Ottoman allegory is decidedly different from other literary traditions, and particularly from medieval western literature. The Ottoman allegorical narratives that will be analyzed in this chapter are allegories that fit almost all of the characteristics discussed above.

Ottoman Allegorical Narratives

Allegorical narratives in Islamic literature have a long history reaching all the way back to Ibn Sīnā (d. 1037),[17] whose allegorical narrative *Ḥayy bin Yaqẓān* is held to be the first Islamic allegorical narrative.[18] *Ḥayy bin Yaqẓān* is allegorical in its mode of narration in that it personifies several concepts like the intellect and imagination. The other narrative by Ibn Sīnā argued to be allegorical is *Salāmān and Absāl*. Analyzing the text, however, we observe that it does not seem to be allegorical, as it does not bear even the most basic characteristics of the genre (i.e., personification and *bellum intestinum*).[19] After Ibn Sīnā, it appears that Muslim authors began to emulate his style of narration, with Suhrawardī (d. 1191) and Ibn al-Nefīs (d. 1288) writing allegorical narratives in Arabic and Suhrawardī, Ahlī-I Shirāzī (d. 1538), and Fattāhī (d. 1448) in Persian.[20] In Heath's synopsis of allegory in Islamic literature(s), he devotes only a few paragraphs to Ottoman allegories, mentioning a select number of narratives of which many cannot be considered allegorical in the sense I am using here.[21] Among those narratives that Heath counts as allegorical and that also satisfy my criteria, there are *Beauty and Heart*[22] by Lamiʿī (d. 1531/32) and Āhī (d. 1517),[23] *the Rose and the Nightingale* by Fażlī (d. 1563/64), and *Beauty and Love* by Şeyḫ Ġalib (d. 1799).[24]

In the following paragraphs, I will categorize Ottoman allegorical narratives in three groups, which all bear the characteristics I have mentioned. The first group includes the story *Şemʿ u Pervāne* (The Candle and the Moth) written by Ahlī in Persian in 1489. A work of the same title written after 1603 by Feyżī Çelebi (d. seventeenth century) is a unique allegorical story in classical Ottoman literature written in syllabic meter whereas all other narratives are written in *aruz* meter.[25] In her analysis of Feyżī Çelebi's text, Tekin elucidates the meaning of each one of the personified mystical concepts that make this work allegorical.[26] The narrative demonstrates yet another shared characteristic of Ottoman allegories: namely, they depict an exposition of mutual love between two personified concepts. Moth comes to Şebistān (The Land of Evening) from another country only to encounter Candle and fall in love with her. There are also several other characters, like Şeb-i Ṭāriq (Dark Night) and those who would seek to prevent Moth from union with Candle, like Fānūs (Lantern). This is a melancholy story because, just as in the natural world, Moth is forever deprived of union with Candle, which is an allegory for melting away in the absolute Being. Indeed, *The Candle and the Moth* is the embodiment of a spiritual journey narrated using mystical concepts.

The second type of allegorical narrative relates to seasons and uses depictions of roses, nightingales, and the vernal equinox. There are many narratives under the name *Gül ü Nevrūz* (The Rose and the Vernal Equinox), among them Muḥibbī's (d. sixteenth century), written around 1536–1537. In this spiritual journey, the main content pertains to the mystical maturation of men. The rose and the vernal equinox are personified and the themes of the journey, *bellum intestinum*, quest, and harmony all contribute to the narrative's allegorical nature. Another allegory of the same name was written in 1670 by Pārsā Ṣābir (d. 1679/80). Ṣābir began translating the text by fourteenth-century Persian poet Jalāl Ṭabīb (d. 1333) into Turkish; however, the translation remains unfinished. The story resembles that of the previous version in that it depicts the mutual love between the Vernal Equinox, the prince of Şarq (the East), and Rose, the princess of China.[27] Nightingale, who also hails from China, is a character who comes between the two lovers. The Vernal Equinox falls in love with Rose after seeing her in a dream whereas Rose falls in love with the Vernal Equinox based upon Nightingale's portrayal of him. Though unfinished, this story also incorporates personification, *bellum intestinum*, quest, harmony, and both geographical and temporal ambiguity. It is therefore safe to say that Ṣābir's *Gül ü Nevrūz* is an allegory.

In a similar manner, *Gül ü Bülbül* (Rose and Nightingale) narratives employ a story of mutual love through allegories of season. The *Rose and Nightingale* narratives by Fażlī (d. 1564) in 1533 and by Beqāyī (d. 1595) in 1565 resemble each other.[28] Another rendition of *Rose and Nightingale*, composed by Ġāzī Giray (d. 1607), appears to have been lost, only existing through the summary of İsmail Hikmet Ertaylan.[29] These allegorical narratives use seasons to depict a spiritual journey. All the characters in Fażlī's narrative are personifications—Rose, Nightingale, Diken (Thorn), and Shāh-ı Bahār (Prince Spring)—whereas the characters in Beqāyī's rendition include Nightingale, Bād (Wind), Shāh-ı Bahār (Prince Spring), Rose, Ṭūtī (Parrot), and

Qumri (Dove), among others.[30] Ömer Fu'ādī's (1560/1636) *Bülbüliyye* (the Book of Nightingale), written in 1623/24, resembles other fables related to the story of the Nightingale who strives to demonstrate his love for the Rose through song. Disturbed by these incessant songs, the other birds in the forest level a complaint against the Nightingale to Prophet Solomon. This narrative is an allegory of the seven manners (*eṭvār-ı seb'a*), which is a way of demonstrating mystical maturation in taṣawwuf (mysticism). Ömer Fu'ādī himself explicates the allegorical nature of the narrative at the end of his work.[31] Another rendition of *Bülbüliyye* is a translation or retelling of Fu'ādī's version written in verse by Manisalı Birrī (d. 1715) in 1706. Birrī then rewrote the same story in prose and affirmed the allegorical nature of his rendition.[32] Sıdqī Paşa (d. after 1660/61) authored an original allegory titled *Berf ü Bahār* (Snow and Spring), which depicts the struggle of King Snow and King Spring to conquer the city Gülşen-ābād (Rosery). This is an allegory in which seasons are intersected with a journey that involving *bellum intestinum*. In that sense, the work resembles both *Gül ü Bülbül (Rose and Nightingale)* and *Sıhhat u Maraz (Health and Disease)* in their style of narration and structure because are all structured around *bellum intestinum*.

In additional to allegories related to seasons, the third group of original narratives exists that includes narratives like *Mihr ü Māh* (the Sun and the Moon), *Ḥayāl u Yār* (Imagination and Beloved), *Ḥasb-i Ḥāl* (The Conversation), and *Ġamze vü Dil* (Glance and Heart). One of the most well-structured allegories of the sixteenth century, *The Sun and the Moon*, written by famous statesman and poet Muṣṭafā 'Ālī (1541–1600), is a three-layered narrative structured, on the first level, as a love story between two personified concepts, Sun and Moon. On the second level, it is about celestial bodies, and on the third level, it is simultaneously an inner journey to spiritual maturation.[33] This narrative contains all the characteristics specific to Ottoman allegories, and the author clearly states that the text is an allegory at the end of the story. Written by Nev'ī (1533/34–1599) in 1555 and 1556, *Ḥasb-i Ḥāl* appears at first glance not to be a romance between two personified concepts; however, upon further scrutiny, it personifies characters like 'Āşıq (Lover), Ma'şūq (Beloved), Ṣabr (Patience), Mekr (Ruse), Irşād (Guidance), and Meyl (Inclination). An inner spiritual journey with mystical dimensions, *Ḥasb-i Ḥāl* relates the allegorical story of the lover and the beloved seeking to be united. The distinguishing feature of this narrative is that the very names of the main characters mean "lover" and "beloved," thereby making the allegorical quality even more concrete. Written in 1573 by Vücūdī (d. 1612), *Ḥayāl u Yār* resembles *Ḥasb-i Ḥāl* in basing the main characters on pure concepts. Imagination (Ḥayāl), the protagonist of the story, has fallen in love with Beloved (Yār) without ever seeing him/her.[34] Imagination travels to the city Gönül (Heart) to find Beloved. Reaching a dervish lodge known as 'Uzlet (Solitude), the sheikh 'Aql (Reason) residing there recommends patience (Ṣabr). After a long journey through Muḥabbet (Affection) valley and Melāḥat (Charm) vineyard and after confronting antagonists like Raqīb (Rival lovers), Imagination is united with his/her beloved and understands that the entire journey was but a metaphysical vision. Written by Sīmkeş-zāde Feyżī (d. 1690) in 1654, *Ġamze vü Dil* is a mystical allegorical narrative that uses a spiritual journey whose main character is Heart (Dil), a traveling dervish. Heart reaches the city Vücūd (Body) ruled by Naẓar (Sight). Heart then approaches 'Aşq (Love), the foster brother of Sight, who then brings Heart to Dīde (Eye) to go hunting, during which time they come across Ġamze (Glance), the son of Sight, with whom Heart falls in love. Love then delivers Glance a declaration of love from Heart, upon which Imagination becomes the mediator between Heart and Sight. Although Sight initially rejects Heart's declaration of love, after many years of pain and with the aid of characters like Dāniş (Knowledge), Fikr (Idea), Fehm (Understanding), Vehm (Illusion), 'Aql (Reason), and Love, the two lovers are finally united. This mystical narrative relates the seven manners (*eṭvār-ı sebʿa*) through personification, *bellum intestinum*, and a quest. Together with its multilayered story, it is truly an allegory.

From *Ḥüsn ü Dil* to *Ḥüsn ü ʿAşq*

I will now discuss the textual adventure of *Ḥüsn ü Dil* (Beauty and Heart) by Fattāḥī of Nīshābūr, as it is a work that triggered one of the most extensive chains of influence cutting across centuries, languages, and cultures. It may also be classified under the third group of allegories. The famous allegorical narrative by Fattāḥī was initially titled *Dastūr-i ʿUshshāq* (The Counselor of Lovers)[35] in verse and then summarized by the author himself in prose under the name *Ḥüsn ü Dil* in 1434.[36]

The story *Ḥüsn ü Dil*, summarized here, is a sophisticated one. The hero of the story is Prince Dil (Heart), the son of Aql (Reason) who rules the city Ten (Body). Heart learned about Āb-i Ḥayāt (the Elixir of Life) in a *majlis* (gathering) and wanted to obtain it for himself but does not know where it may be found. His spy, Naẓar (Sight), offers to find it for him, thereby setting the stage for a journey. Sight, passing through the city ʿĀfiyet (Well-being) whose king is Nāmūs (Law or Reputation), crosses the Zuhd (Asceticism) mountains governed by Rāhib Zerq (The Monk Hypocrisy). Finally, he reaches King Himmet (Favor) in the city of Hidāyet (Guidance), who informs him that the elixir of life is real, and that one can find it at the Mountain Qaf in the Far East, which is under the dominance of King ʿAşḳ (Love), the father of Ḥusn (Beauty). Beauty lives in the city Dīdār (Aspect), where the elixir of life exists in the fountain Āb-i Āşīnāyī (The River of Familiarity). Upon learning this and venturing to Dīdār, Sight tells Beauty about Heart, causing her to fall in love with him. Characters on Beauty's side include Zülf (Lovelock), Ġamze, Imagination, Affection, Nāz (Coquetry), Vefā (Fidelity), Rival, and Ġayr (Outsider), whereas those on Heart's side include Vehm (Fancy), Tevbe (Repentance), and Ṣabr (Patience).

All these characters are some sort of abstraction or personification, so as to make it easier to narrate allegorically. The personifications are both vices and virtues that make *bellum intestinum* possible. This story also masterfully interweaves personification, journey, and quest throughout its narrative. As Reason's ultimate objective is to conquer the body, through the intermediation of Favor it becomes the vizier of Love who is, in fact, Reason's brother, and Beauty and Heart are married so that Heart may find the elixir of life. During the final episode, Ḫıżr (an immortal person believed to be a prophet) appears and reveals the secrets of the story, thereby demonstrating it to be an allegory.

The narrative was translated, or, more accurately, rewritten in Ottoman Turkish by Lamiʿī (d. 1532) in 1512, Āhī (d. 1517) in 1517, Muḥyī-i Gülşenī (d. 1604) in 1578, Yenipazarlı Vālī (d. 1598/99) in 1593 and 1594, and Keşfī (d. 1538/39), most probably at the very beginning of the sixteenth century.[37] As the summary of the story shows, *Ḥüsn ü Dil* incorporates all of the features of Ottoman allegories in addition to the three universal characteristics shared by all allegories (i.e., personification, *bellum intestinum*, and quest).

Simply looking at the names of the characters who are Beauty's close friends, namely Affection, Coquetry, and Fidelity, one realizes that there is *tenasüp* (harmony) at work both in terms of their etymology and deeds. *Ḥüsn ü Dil* is a multilayered narrative and thus, as Greenshields asserts, "contains a double allegory, . . . based on spiritual qualities, of the search of the human heart for beauty, physical and spiritual."[38] Both the time and location in the story are left vague so as to preclude the reader from appropriating it to any specific geographical location. Most renditions of *Ḥüsn ü Dil* reworked by Ottoman authors make references to previous narratives with the same name, thereby making them intertexts. Last, their allegorical nature is further reinforced when, at the end of the story, Ḫiżir approaches Heart to elucidate the secrets of the narrative both for himself and the reader. To sum up, the *Ḥüsn ü Dil* narratives written in Ottoman Turkish constitute a single allegorical narrative that, through their incorporation of all the above-delineated characteristics, represent exemplary allegories. Though they are all rewrites and retellings based on translations of Fattāḥī's *Ḥüsn ü Dil*, it is unclear whether the allegorical narrative by Lāmiʿī (1472–1532) or Keşfī's (d. 1538/39) version of the same name was written first. Although we know that Lāmiʿī wrote his rendition in 1512,[39] it is not known when Keşfī completed his.[40] While Keşfī's *Ḥüsn ü Dil* more clearly resembles a genuine translation of Fattāḥī's, Lāmiʿī made certain revisions to render it more Ottoman. For example, Lāmiʿī added Faḫr (Pride) who lives in Şöhret (Reputation), an important character who Sight encounters on his way to Beauty. All subsequent *Ḥüsn ü Dil* romances adopted this character and encounter. Since Āḥī, another writer of *Ḥüsn ü Dil*, died in 1517, his allegory remains unfinished; however, many Ottoman literature specialists agree that it is the most exemplary rendition of *Ḥüsn ü Dil* in terms of style and narration.[41] The next *Ḥüsn ü Dil* was written by Muḥyī Gülşenī in 1578, which was the last Ottoman rendition of Fattāḥī's work in prose. In his rendition, Gülşenī increased the number of personified characters to approximately 70.

Tracking the additional characters either adopted or omitted over time can help us compare of the influence of the different renditions on the others. For instance, another character added by Lāmiʿī was Nefs (Self/Desire), the wife of Reason, who was then adopted by subsequent authors. That said, not all of the characters added by Lāmiʿī were perpetuated in the works of other authors. For example, Ġayret-i Nāmdār (Renowned Effort), one of the warriors in Love's army, was not used by other writers. Similarly, Āḥī added several new characters to the narrative, such as the cupbearer Būse-i Dehān (Kiss of the mouth) and Mütefekkire (Contemplation), the grand vizier of Reason. The final Ottoman rendition of *Ḥüsn ü Dil* was written by Wālī in 1593–1594. He also added several characters, such as ʿAyn (Eye), the head soldier of Glance, and Ḍamīr (Heart), the head soldier of Heart. Among them, Muḥyī added more characters than any of the other authors. These serve the harmony of the narrative, specifically when Self/Desire and Love fight each other.[42]

Some scholars rightfully argue that *Ḥüsn ü Dil* is a model for subsequent Ottoman allegories, beginning with *Sıhhat u Maraz* (Health and Disease) by Fużūlī (1483/1556) in the sixteenth century up to *Cān u Cānān* (The Lover and the Beloved) by Refīʿ-i Āmidī (1756–1816) in the nineteenth. Among them, İskender Pala asserts that *Ḥüsn ü Dil* influenced *Gül ü Bülbül* by Fażlī, *Sıhhat u Maraz* by Fużūlī, and *Ḥüsn ü ʿAşq* by Şeyḫ Ġalib.[43]

Fużūlī's *Sıhhat u Maraz*, as stated earlier, is one of the finest allegories in Ottoman Turkish,[44] and some have argued it adapts the allegorical writing and structure used in *Ḥüsn ü Dil* to the area of medicine.[45] This narrative allegorizes the Body (Beden) as the city under siege. Health and Disease attempt to invade the city with the aid of Affection, Love, Reason, Spirit (Rūḥ), and several others. The narrative incorporates Ibn Sīnā's concepts related to the soul (*nefs*) and psychology in general. Thus, this narrative contains the main characteristics shared by all allegories mentioned here: personification, *bellum intestinum*, quest, and harmony.

Most scholars agree that the best allegorical narrative in classical Ottoman literature, if not all classical Islamic literatures, is *Ḥüsn ü ʿAşq* written by Şeyḫ Ġalib (1757–1799) in 1782–1783. This narrative is a story of mutual love between the personified characters Beauty and Love,[46] and all other characters are also personifications of various concepts.[47] *Ḥüsn ü ʿAşq* is a spiritual journey on the path to mystical maturation. Beauty and Love are born to a society called Benī Muḥabbet (Sons of Affection) on the same day, go to the same school called Edeb (Decency), and have the same teacher Mollā-yi Cünūn (Mullah of Madness). First, Beauty falls in love with Love, contrary to most Ottoman romances. They see each other in a garden called Maʿnā (Meaning) through the mediation of Suḫan (Word/Poetry). Love asks for Beauty's hand; however, society wants him to retrieve (the knowledge of) alchemy from the Land of the Heart, which turns out to be the knowledge or the secret of the journey for the maturation. After a long journey filled with numerous adventures that include a fight against a Witch, a well, and ruins, Love achieves (the knowledge of) alchemy. In the end, we learn that Beauty and Love are one and the same: Love never traveled physically, only spiritually.

Because *Ḥüsn ü ʿAşq* has all the allegorical characteristics listed earlier, I agree with scholars who argue that it is the most proficiently established allegorical romance in classical Ottoman Turkish in terms of its narrative strategies. Indeed, with its multilayered narrative and numerous interpretations, it is the most well-crafted allegory. In line with Islamic mysticism, it is first and foremost an allegory showcasing the relationship between God and humankind, with Beauty being the beauty of God and Love being the human in love with God. Second, it narrates the spiritual maturation process undergone by Mawlawī dervishes. Third, it allegorizes the relationship between Shams and Rūmī using, respectively, beauty and love to symbolize them. Fourth, it is the allegory of the whirling (*semā*) of Mawlawī dervishes. Fifth, it allegorizes all classical Ottoman romances in general and Mawlawī romances in particular. Finally, it is a story of mutual love between the characters Beauty and Love.

The last allegorical narrative, which includes all the aforementioned characteristics, is a parallel of *Ḥüsn ü ʿAşq* titled *Cān u Cānān* written by Refīʿ-i Āmidī (1756–1816) in 1790 and 1791. The story is structured similarly to *Ḥüsn ü ʿAşq*, with the only important difference being that Āmidī has society ask Love to retrieve the water of life from Lā-mekān (No-land) instead of (the knowledge of) alchemy from the Land of the Heart. All the characters are personifications, and the narrative harmoniously interweaves an internal conflict and spiritual journey. Contrary to Āmidī's claim to have written a better allegory than *Ḥüsn ü ʿAşq*, as academics assert,[48] it is not better than Şeyḫ Ġālib's work since it is just a retelling of the same story without containing the multilayers *Ḥüsn ü ʿAşq* employs. Nevertheless, it is still one of the most well-structured allegories in classical Ottoman literature.

Conclusion

Ottoman allegories have received very little critical study in modern academic literature and this is no less the case in English. Consequently, it is difficult to write exhaustively about Islamic/Ottoman allegorical mathnawis in particular or narratives in general. The first difficulty arises in defining the term itself: The concept has been defined and used so loosely that it generally signifies any part of a literary, philosophical, or mystical text whether it be a single word, sentence, paragraph, or whole story. Hence, I redefined and narrowed the definition of the term for clarity. In this chapter, I used allegory to describe saying one thing while meaning another—and not simply in a few parts of the narrative but enmeshed in the very fabric of the whole story itself.

As my theoretical abstraction of Ottoman allegory manifests several fundamental characteristics that distinguish it from its European counterpart, it is necessary to identify the characteristics specific to Ottoman allegories. Ottoman allegorical mathnawis, romances, or narratives are generally stories between two personified concepts and incorporate a journey or quest in which the protagonist travels spiritually, as almost all of them are mystical narratives. Because the very nature of mystical maturation quests involves a traveler who is party to the struggle of vices and virtues that try to control the body, this is an example of *bellum intestinum*. Allegories, by definition, should apply to all humankind. The universalistic appeal is created by avoiding spatial and temporal specificities; hence, the time and place of the narrative are left vague. Ottoman allegories and poetry hold fast to the rule that successive personified concepts or words used in the same hemistich or episode should be in harmony. Thus, Beauty, Fidelity, Smile, Affection, and Love live in the same country. Ottoman allegories are multilayered narratives in which at least two stories are narrated in the same textual body and authors generally reveal the allegorical nature of their narrative at the end of the story. The final common feature of Ottoman allegories is that they are intertexts, in that they reference previous narrative(s) by name.

Ottoman allegorical practices contain both similarities and differences when compared with other similar traditions. Concerning similarities, Ottoman allegories employ the common techniques of personification, the *bellum intestinum*, and journey as their European or other Islamic counterparts do in their narratives. Nevertheless, what distinguishes Ottoman allegories from other allegorical narratives is that they employ all of those features/techniques at once whereas other allegorical traditions, for the most part, prefer one technique over the others. Concerning differences, Ottoman allegories were marked by such uniquely Ottoman techniques as manifesting their allegories (allegorical writing), being intertexts, obfuscating their geographical and temporal location, being multilayered, narrating a single story in the work, and harmony. Consequently, Ottoman allegories have some similarities with and differences from both eastern and western allegories, which make the theory of Ottoman allegory possible.

Acknowledgment

I want to thank Ercüment Asil, who read the draft of this chapter and offered valuable commentary.

Notes

1 For an introduction to allegory in English, see C. S. Lewis, *The Allegory of Love: A Study in Medieval Tradition* (Oxford: Oxford University Press, 1958); Jon Whitman, *Allegory* (Cambridge, MA: Harvard University Press, 1987).
2 Peter Heath, "Allegory in Islamic Literatures," in *The Cambridge Companion to Allegory*, ed. Rita Copeland and Peter T. Struck (Cambridge: Cambridge University Press, 2010), 83–100.
3 On Ottoman allegory, see Berat Açıl, *Klasik Türk Edebiyatında Alegori*, 2nd ed. (Istanbul: Küre Yayınları, 2018). For a discussion on whether allegory is a genre or style in Turkish literature, see Berat Açıl, "Bir Tür mü Tarz mı? Klasik Türk Edebiyatında Alegori," *Divan: Disiplinlerarası Çalışmalar Dergisi*, no. 37 (December 2014): 145–67.
4 Allegorical interpretation means narratives that are not necessarily intended to be allegorical by their authors but interpreted as allegorical by commentators.
5 Allegorical writing means narratives that are intended to be allegorical by their authors.
6 Deborah L. Madsen, *Rereading Allegory* (New York: St. Martin's Press, 1994), 65.
7 See D'Istria Dora, "Osmanlılar'da Şiir: İstiareli Destanlar," in *Osmanlı Divan Şiiri Üzerine Metinler*, ed. Mehmet Kalpaklı (Istanbul: YKY, 1999), 48–50.
8 Dimitri Gutas, *Greek Thought Arabic Culture: The Graeco-Arabic Translation Movement in Baghdad and Early 'Abbasid Society (2nd–4th/8th–10th Centuries)* (London: Routledge Press, 1999).
9 Heath, "Allegory," 86.
10 For a detailed discussion of conceptual framework of allegory and its counterparts in Ottoman and modern Turkish, see Açıl, *Klasik Türk Edebiyatında Alegori*, 95–109.
11 Berat Açıl, "Bir Tür mü Tarz mı?" 146–47.
12 The characteristics that will be itemized were identified after having examined nearly every Ottoman romance. See Berat Açıl, "Muhyi's Hüsn ü Dil: An Allegorical Work" (PhD diss., Boğaziçi Üniversitesi, 2010).
13 Madsen, *Rereading Allegory*, 83.
14 Lewis, *Allegory*, 44.

15 Ibid., 91.

16 *The Faerie Queene*, in which the author Edmund Spenser states that his work is an allegory in a letter to Sir Walter Raleigh, is the only example to my knowledge. See Edmund Spenser, *The Faerie Queene*, ed. P. C. Bayley (Oxford: Oxford University Press, 1970), 39.

17 Heath treats the Brethren of Purity as the first writers of allegory in the Islamic tradition. According to the (re)definition of the term, the Brethren of Purity has no allegorical narrative but fragmental allegorical pieces.

18 Ibn Sina and Ibn Tufeyl, *Hayy Bin Yakzan*, ed. N. Ahmet Özalp, trans. M. Şerefettin Yaltkaya and Babanzade Reşid (Istanbul: YKY, 1996), 7; Mehmet Harmancı, *İslam Felsefesinde Metaforik Üslup* (Ankara: Hece, 2012), 90.

19 Ebû Ali b. Sînâ, *El-İşârât ve't-Tenbîhât Maa Şerhi Nasîrüddin et-Tûsî*, ed. Süleyman Dünya, vol. 3 (Beirut: Müessesetü'n-Numan, 1992), 48–57.

20 For a list of allegorical narratives bearing all the allegoric features in every linguistic current of Islamic Literature, see Açıl, *Klasik Türk Edebiyatında Alegori*, 88–89.

21 The sole source pertaining to Ottoman allegories that Heath mentions is Gibb's history of Ottoman poetry. The narratives that he treats as allegorical are *Joseph and Zulaikhā* and *Lailā and Majnūn* by Ḥamdī (d. 1509); *The Candle and the Moth, The Ball and the Polo Stick*, and *Salāmān and Absāl* by Lamiʿī (d. 153/32); *The King and the Beggar* by Yehyā Beg (d. 1575/76); and *Leilā and Mejnūn* by Fużūlī (1483/1556).

22 Heath has written the name of the narrative as *Beauty and Love* by mistake. See Heath, "Allegory," 98.

23 Contrary to Heath's assertion, Lamiʿī had written his version before Āhī. See Heath, "Allegory," 98.

24 Several scholars provide more concise lists of alleged allegorical narratives. See, e.g., Osman Horata, *Mesneviler*, vol. 2, 4 (Ankara: Kültür ve Turizm Bakanlığı, 2007); Ali Fuat Bilkan, "Mesneviler," in *Türk Edebiyatı Tarihi*, ed. Talat Sait Halman, vol. 2 (Ankara: Kültür ve Turizm Bakanlığı, 2007), 296; Muhsin Macit, "Temsilî (Alegorik) Mesneviler," in *Türk Edebiyatı Tarihi*, ed. Talat Sait Halman, vol. 2 (Ankara: Kültür ve Turizm Bakanlığı, 2007), 57–59.

25 For a comprehensive analysis of the text, see Feyzî Çelebi, *Şemʿ u Pervâne*, ed. Gönül Alpay Tekin (Cambridge, MA: Harvard University Department of Near Eastern Languages and Civilizations, 1991).

26 Ibid., 1–35.

27 China is used as an imaginative geography in classical Ottoman literature rather than a concrete place as Ahmet Hamdi Tanpınar asserts. See Ahmet Hamdi Tanpınar, *19. Asır Türk Edebiyatı Tarihi* (Istanbul: Çağlayan Kitabevi, 1997), 4–5.

28 Likewise, *Le Roman de la Rose* shares many parallels with these two renditions, as earlier stated by Dora d'Istria, specifically, in terms of personification. See D'Istria, "Osmanlılar'da Şiir," 48–50.

29 See İsmail Hikmet Ertaylan, *Gâzi Geray Han: Hayatı ve Eserleri* (Istanbul: Ahmed Said Basımevi, 1958), 50.

30 Açıl, *Klasik*, 70–71.

31 Ibid., 84–85.

32 Ibid., 88.

33 Zeynep Sabuncu, "Âli'nin Mihr ü Mâh Ile Feyzî'nin Şemʿ ü Pervâne'si Arasındaki Benzerlikler: İntihal Mi, Gelenek Mi?," *Türk Kültürü İncelemeleri Dergisi* 13 (2005): 140.

34 Pronouns in Turkish do not express gender, which works to obscure the gender of the characters.

35 Muḥammad Yaḥyā ibn Sībak, *Dastūr-i ʿUshshāq: The Book of Lovers*, ed. Robert S. Greenshields (London: Luzac, 1926).

36 Muḥyi-i Gulshanī, *Ḥusn u Dil*, trans. Ġulām Riżā Ferzānepūr (Tehran: Shirkat-i Sehāmī, 1932), 3.

37 I will restrict this chapter to Ottoman renditions. For a more detailed analysis and information related to other languages, see Açıl, "Muhyi's Hüsn ü Dil," 30–47.

38 Muḥammad Yaḥyā ibn Sībak, *Dastūr-i ʿUshshāq*, Preface, para. 6.

39 Yenipazarlı Vâlî, *Hüsn ü Dil*, ed. M. Fatih Köksal (Istanbul: Kitabevi, 2003), 13.

40 It is probable that he had written his work before Lamiʿī. See Sadık Yazar, "XVI. Yüzyıl Şairlerinden Gedizli Keşfî ve Hüsn ü Dil Tercümesi," *Journal of Turkish Studies/Türklük Bilgisi Araştırmaları* 33, no. 2 (2009): 245–86.

41 Âlî, *Künhü'l-Ahbârın Tezkire Kısmı*, ed. Mustafa İsen (Ankara: Atatürk Kültür Merkezi, 1994), 174.

42 For a detailed comparison of these five renditions of *Ḥüsn ü Dil*, see Açıl, "Muhyi's Hüsn ü Dil." Nevertheless, this is not an exhaustive history of *Ḥüsn ü Dil* because it has also been translated into, retold, and reworded in other languages. Specifically, it has been retold or parallelized in Persian by Dâvûd Elçi and Hace Mahmud Bîdîl and in Urdu by Vajhi, Dhawqi, Mujrimi, and Qādiri at different times. It was later translated into German in 1889 by Rudolf Dvorak and into English by both A. Brown in

1801 and William Price in 1828. See Tahsin Yazıcı, "Fettâhî," in *TDV İslâm Ansiklopedisi* (Istanbul: TDV Yayınları, 1995), 582.

43 Pala İskender, "Hüsn ü Dil," in *Akademik Divan Şiiri Araştırmaları* (Istanbul: Kapı Yayınları, 2005), 96.

44 I argue that the first allegory in the Ottoman literature is *Ḥüsn ü Dil* and that the last one (if not the best) is *Ḥüsn ü ʿAşq* and its parallel *Cān u Cānān. Sıhhat u Maraz* is an intermediate allegory between *Beauty and Love* and *The Lover and the Beloved*.

45 Yazıcı, "Fettâhî," 485.

46 For the translation of the text see Şeyh Galip, *Beauty and Love*, trans. Victoria R. Holbrook (New York: Modern Language Association of America, 2005).

47 For an exemplary analysis of the narrative in book form, see Victoria Rowe Holbrook, *The Unreadable Shores of Love: Turkish Modernity and Mystic Romance* (Austin: University of Texas Press, 1994).

48 See Refî-i Âmidî, *Cân u Cânân*, ed. Nihat Öztoprak (Istanbul: Türkgev, 2000), 93–101.

References

Açıl, Berat. "Muhyi's Hüsn ü Dil: An Allegorical Work." PhD diss., Boğaziçi University, 2010.

———. "Bir Tür mü Tarz mı? Klasik Türk Edebiyatında Alegori." *Divan: Disiplinlerarası Çalışmalar Dergisi*, no. 37 (December 2014): 145–67.

———. *Klasik Türk Edebiyatında Alegori*, 2nd ed. Istanbul: Küre Yayınları, 2018.

Âlî. *Künhü'l-Ahbârın Tezkire Kısmı*. Edited by Mustafa İsen. Ankara: Atatürk Kültür Merkezi, 1994.

Bilkan, Ali Fuat. "Mesneviler." In *Türk Edebiyatı Tarihi*, edited by Talat Sait Halman, vol. 2, 293–308. Ankara: Kültür ve Turizm Bakanlığı, 2007.

D'Istria, Dora. "Osmanlılar'da Şiir: İstiareli Destanlar." In *Osmanlı Divan Şiiri Üzerine Metinler*, edited by Mehmet Kalpaklı, 48–50. Istanbul: Yapı Kredi Yayınları, 1999.

Ebû Ali b. Sînâ. *El-İşârât ve't-Tenbîhât Maa Şerhi Nasîrüddin et-Tûsî*. Edited by Süleyman Dünya, vol. 3, 48–57. Beirut: Müessesetü'n-Numan, 1992.

Ertaylan, İsmail Hikmet. *Gâzi Geray Han: Hayatı ve Eserleri*. Istanbul: Ahmed Said Basımevi, 1958.

Feyẓī Çelebi. *Şem ʿu Pervâne*. Edited by Gönül Alpay Tekin. Cambridge, MA: Harvard University Department of Near Eastern Languages and Civilizations, 1991.

Gutas, Dimitri. *Greek Thought Arabic Culture: The Graeco-Arabic Translation Movement in Baghdad and Early ʿAbbasid Society (2nd–4th/8th–10th Centuries)*. London: Routledge Press, 1999.

Harmancı, Mehmet. *İslam Felsefesinde Metaforik Üslup*. Ankara: Hece, 2012.

Holbrook, Victoria Rowe. *The Unreadable Shores of Love: Turkish Modernity and Mystic Romance*. Austin: University of Texas Press, 1994.

Horata, Osman. "Mesneviler." In *Türk Edebiyatı Tarihi*, edited by Talat Sait Halman, vol. 2, 545–62. Ankara: Kültür ve Turizm Bakanlığı, 2007.

Ibn Sina, and Ibn Tufeyl. *Hayy Bin Yakzan*. Translated by M. Şerefettin Yaltkaya and Babanzade Reşid and edited by N. Ahmet Özalp. Istanbul: YKY, 1996.

Macit, Muhsin. "Temsilî (Alegorik) Mesneviler." In *Türk Edebiyatı Tarihi*, edited by Talat Sait Halman, vol. 2, 57–59. Ankara: Kültür ve Turizm Bakanlığı, 2007.

Madsen, Deborah L. *Rereading Allegory*. New York: St. Martin's Press, 1994.

Muḥammad Yaḥyā ibn Sībak. *Dastūr-i ʿUshshāq: The Book of Lovers*. Edited by Robert S. Greenshields. London: Luzac, 1926.

Muḥyi-i Gulshanī. *Ḥusn u Dil*. Translated by Ġulām Riżā Ferzānepūr. Tehran: Shirkat-i Sehāmī, 1932.

Pala, İskender. "Hüsn ü Dil." *Akademik Divan Şiiri Araştırmaları* (2005): 93–99.

Refî-i Âmidî. *Cân u Cânân*. Edited by Nihat Öztoprak. Istanbul: Türkgev, 2000.

Sabuncu, Zeynep. "Âlî'nin Mihr ü Mâh İle Feyzî'nin Şem' ü Pervâne'si Arasındaki Benzerlikler: İntihal Mi, Gelenek Mi?" *Türk Kültürü İncelemeleri Dergisi* 13 (2005): 129–66.

Şeyh Galip. *Beauty and Love*. Translated by Victoria R. Holbrook. New York: Modern Language Association of America, 2005.

Spenser, Edmund. *The Faerie Queene*. Edited by P. C. Bayley. Oxford: Oxford University Press, 1970.

Tanpınar, Ahmet Hamdi. *19 Asır Türk Edebiyatı Tarihi*. Istanbul: Çağlayan Kitabevi, 1997.

Yazar, Sadık. "XVI. Yüzyıl Şairlerinden Gedizli Keşfî ve Hüsn ü Dil Tercümesi." *Journal of Turkish Studies/Türklük Bilgisi Araştırmaları* 33, no. 2 (2009): 245–86.

Yazıcı, Tahsin. "Fettâhî." *TDV İslâm Ansiklopedisi* 12 (1995): 485–86.

Yenipazarlı Vâlî. *Hüsn ü Dil*. Edited by M. Fatih Köksal. Istanbul: Kitabevi, 2003.

7

HUMAN VOICE ECHOING IN THE SILENCE OF GOD

Tevfik Fikret and Modern Ottoman Poetry

Deniz Aktan Küçük

The Ottoman literature of the second half of the nineteenth century has almost always been evaluated within the framework of a certain modernization discourse, which features a close connection with the post-Tanzimat Westernization process. This process is considered a rupture in the history of Ottoman literature, one determining the "beginning" of the modern and the "end" of the classical period. Within this discourse, the modernization of Ottoman literature is illustrated and revealed directly by Western influence and the "new" Ottoman literature is described as having emerged in the footsteps of the Western model as a one-sided and unattainable imitation. Accordingly, late nineteenth-century texts are coerced into revealing what is expected or predetermined in the context of being non-Western, peripheral, belated, or forcibly Westernized. In other words, the "new" Ottoman literature is situated within a history where the effects of traumatic Westernization held sway and the very experience of modernity is thus pushed aside. As Daryush Shayegan puts it, in the "Eastern" world, modernity has never been considered as a new paradigm, as it is within its own philosophical content, but always something responded to in terms of the traumatic changes it has wrought in traditions and ways of living and thinking.[1]

In this chapter, I will suggest a potential reading of the poems of Tevfik Fikret (1867–1915), one of the most prominent poets of Ottoman literature's fin de siècle, in order to see how Ottoman poetry relates to modernity in its own way. By taking modernity as an adventure of displacement and reconstruction in general, my contribution analyzes Fikret's oeuvre from the perspective of the gradual retreat of God and the human subject's assignment as the substitute. In other words, this chapter covers the poems of Fikret and the literary atmosphere surrounding them by shedding light on the radical changes in the conceptualization of the subject, the world, and its regulating principles and values in the context of the experience of groundlessness when God ceased to be the ground for determining poetry.

From the first poems that he wrote and published around the mid-1880s to his final works, Tevfik Fikret was on the quest for an authentic poetry that centered the human subject in its worldly/material existence, unique experiences and deepest thoughts, feelings, and imagination. However, not being able to justify this very centralization of the human, the poems first called on help from both the Ottoman and Western poetic traditions and tried to find ways to compromise with the theological paradigm. Then, with the gradual elimination of God from poetry, as in the period of the influential journal *Servet-i Fünun* (1896–1901), poets plunged into

DOI: 10.4324/9780429279270-10

93

a deep abyss of melancholy. The melancholy of being in a world abandoned by God and not being able to fill the gap left behind was eventually mastered by Fikret in the poems published between his departure from *Servet-i Fünun* in 1901 and his death in 1915. It was the acceptance of "science" or, more precisely the "theory of evolution," that made it possible to validate the human subject's sovereignty.

Swinging Between Traditions: The Early Poems of Tevfik Fikret

Tevfik Fikret wrote his first poems in the mid-1880s when he was a pupil at Mekteb-i Sultani and they were published in the newspaper *Tercüman-ı Hakikat* and its anthologies. As the products of a fledgling poet looking for recognition, these poems fit perfectly in the general outlook of late Ottoman poetry. They display an explicit engagement with Ottoman *divan* poetry by exemplifying its specific genres and using its strictly determined poetic vocabulary. However, this was, in a way, a pseudo-engagement. While the impression given is one of respect for classical literary conventions following its semantic realm, these conventions are in fact bent or even broken with an intention of updating them. In spite of these first impressions, Fikret's early poems are shaped by many, even contradictory poetic traditions intertwining, intermingling, and finally uniting in the production of a human subject–centered, worldly poetry.

The plurality or coexistence of different literary traditions can be detected in Tevfik Fikret's "Tevhid" (Tawhid) published in 1885 in *Tercüman-ı Hakikat*. First of all, *tawhid qasidas* in general correspond to a specific genre in the Ottoman classical poetry, aiming to present the unity or oneness of God.[2] Writing and publishing a tawhid, Fikret reproduces the generic conventions in a manner that "Tevhid" appears to fit into this particular genre while making it implicitly divergent. In other words, rather than professing belief in the unity of God, the poem gives prominence to the human subject by devoting itself to the way one knows, feels about, or connects with God. It is this shift that brings about the upending of tradition. The poem first appears to depend on the mystical tradition of Sufism (*tasawwuf*) and then, midway, presents a transition to the rationality of Islamic scholastic theology (*kalam*). The opening couplets of the poem reflect the Sufi mystical account of love, in which God is represented as the beloved and the speaker of the poem as the lover. While the love of God is the ultimate end of the spiritual journey, the correct path to follow is proposed as the one of the heart.[3] Following these couplets, the poem goes on to engage with the subject's efforts to "know" or "prove" God. It deliberately focuses on how he perceives his environment, the material world itself, using his own capabilities, how he reflects on it, and how the thoughts he derives from the world help him reach God. The empirical observation and reasoning that the mystical tradition had pushed to the periphery due to their defectiveness and deficiency gradually proceed to the center of the poem by displacing the heart.[4]

The concrete, material world itself and the authentic experiences and feelings of the subject therein are also emphasized in the love poem "Mes'ûdiyet-i Aşk." This differs from the other love poems of the young Fikret,[5] which echo the absolute definition of love in classical Ottoman poetry with its precisely drawn boundaries and strictly set rules.[6] The dual dimension of classical poetry, which makes mystical and profane interpretations possible all at once and allows for reading "the beloved" also as the sultan, the prophet, or God, is not applicable to "Mes'ûdiyet-i Aşk." While in these other poems love is always unrequited, painful, burning, and destructive, the trademark of "Mes'ûdiyet-i Aşk" is the "joy of love," as its title attests. Moreover, instead of seeking to praise the beloved, the poem accentuates the lover, the speaker of the poem. The opening couplets are centered around the speaker's feelings and how they change the way he sees the world around him. As can be observed in Fikret's other poems written contemporaneously, like "Şeyh Vasfî'nin Bir Gazelini Tahmis,"[7] although the strictly determined poetic vocabulary of the classical tradition is preserved, there are significant alterations in the way the *mazmun*s, the poetic themes, are used. For example, the nightingale that always refers to the lover who isolates himself from the world and hopelessly longs for the beloved while constantly singing his woes,[8] loses all these characteristics in this particular poem. The nightingale becomes instead cheerful and lively, deeply attached to the world and focusing solely on his own experience of love without even mentioning "the rose," the beloved. On the other hand, the coexistence of different literary tendencies or styles shaped by different traditions is also apparent in "Mes'ûdiyet-i Aşk," in that the divine love of mystical tradition suddenly interferes with the human-centered, worldly tone of the poem. This new, mystical context, which does not fit with or even contradicts the general spirit of the poem, abruptly takes back all the value given to what is worldly, temporary, and subjective, reducing all the profane content to a stage towards reaching the "real," divine love.[9]

The ebbs and flows between different literary traditions display both the confusions and quests of the early works of Fikret. An inclination towards a human-centered, worldly poetry and an ambivalent conversation with the God-centered paradigm shape these poems by creating conflicts and contradictions. Although it is possible to see these early poems at first glance as a continuation of Islamic Ottoman poetry, they actually reflect the need to employ valid literary conventions to find a legitimate way to create an authentic poetry based on the human subject with its worldly/material existence. The same need continues to operate in the poems written and published between 1890 and 1895 in the journals *Mirsâd* and *Malumât*. However, this time, in addition to seeking assistance from classical God-centered poetry, Fikret leans towards Romanticism under the guidance of Recaizâde Mahmut Ekrem, to whom he refers as the theorist who transformed his poetry.

Centering the Human Subject in God's World

In the first article Fikret wrote as editor-in-chief of the *Servet-i Fünun*, he criticizes his early works for being "not authentic enough" and himself for incorrectly assuming a poem to be just a collection of meticulous, rhyming, imaginary, and elegant words. He announces Recaizâde Mahmud Ekrem as the literary theorist that changed his attitude towards poetry. According to Fikret, Recaizâde Ekrem's theory of poetry helped ending the turmoil in poetry and updating Ottoman rhetoric, which no longer functioned to determine the conditions of artistic creation and reception.[10]

For Recaizâde Ekrem, poetry primarily aims to express the thoughts, feelings, and imagination of the poet himself. While a new type of poet who observes, thinks, imagines, and has intense feelings is introduced, he is expected to adhere to both external and internal reality. Recaizâde Ekrem defines external reality within and with respect to the material world, which he designates in his theory as "nature." Similarly, like reality, beauty is defined in terms of the sensible world and "absolute beauty" (*hüsn-i mutlak*) matches up with "the beauty of nature" (*hüsn-i tabiat*). Moreover, the new poet, who creates in accordance with nature, should as well turn his gaze towards the depth of his inner reality such that introspection, like observation, emerges as a privileged principle of the new, autonomous poetry.[11]

Recaizâde Ekrem's emphasis on nature is also decisive in the way his theory connects to the God-centered paradigm. He defines nature itself as "poetry," and God is added automatically to the picture as the poet of nature. By repeating the Islamic Ottoman poetic tradition's idea that everything is an art or a poem of God, Recaizâde Ekrem's theory may seem like it compromises its profane aspects. However, instead of foregrounding a transcendental or otherworldly beauty—or treating nature as a trap that makes believers latch onto its imperfect, temporal, defective, deficient beauties and interrupt their spiritual journeys—Recaizâde Ekrem defends the definition of beauty within the sensory world by stressing its character as a reflection of God's beauty. In other words, because God expresses Himself in nature, nature can be taken as participating in divine beauty. This is what Fikret highlights to justify the value given to the sensual, material world itself.

The mystification of nature, on the other hand, does not only pertain to the Islamic Ottoman poetic tradition. It also shows the influence of European Romanticism, especially the Romantic enchantment of nature, on Recaizâde Ekrem.[12] With the help of the overlap between the conceptualization of nature in the God-centered paradigm[13] and Romantic poetry, Recaizâde Ekrem contrives a way of constructing a theory of a subject-centered, worldly Ottoman poetry that is also consonant with the God-centered paradigm.[14]

As a passionate follower of Recaizâde Ekrem, Fikret mimics his works by repeating the main principles of his theory in prose and trying to put them in application in his verse. As we see in his essay "Hepimiz Tabi'atın Birer Acemi Şâkirdiyiz" (We Are All Novice Disciples of Nature) published in the journal *Ma'lûmat* in 1894, every crucial point Fikret touches on, even the title itself, comes from Ekrem's works. The essay focuses on the beauty that exists genuinely in nature and defends observation and introspection as the sources of poetry dependent on this beauty. The first-person narrator of the essay is portrayed as a poet seeking refuge in both natural beauty and poems that manage to imitate it. The observation of natural scenes and the examination of the thoughts, feelings, and imagination they awaken serve as the criteria of literary criticism as well. Fikret especially admires Lamartine among a group of poets including Baudelaire, Musset, Hugo, Baunivalle, Prudhomme, and Coppeé. He dubs Lamartine "a mighty poet" (*edib-i muktedir*) and explains that this might lie in his ability to represent the beauty of nature, which is the reflection of divine beauty itself, without decentering the thoughts, feelings, and imagination of the poet.[15]

The poet himself has a central place in the poem "Şâire Dair" (On the Poet) too. Fikret addresses not only the observation of the beauty of nature at different moments of the day but also their effects on the beholder, "the poet." The examination and expression of the inner world of the "human-poet" are dominant in the poem, whereas God is implicitly referred to as "the real poet" and sunrise, sunset, and midnight are called His "poems." Only at the end of "Şâire Dair" is the connection between these two poets stressed, namely the human-poet and God. The human-poet as an apprentice of the real one, and as an imitator of nature, falls in love with the divine beauty manifest in all creation—so much so that with the intensity of his feelings and his fascination with the beautiful, the human-poet himself is defined as a poem of the "master," God, as well.[16]

Under the guidance of Recaizâde Mahmut Ekrem, the presence of God or religious elements in general in Fikret's poetry become, to some extent, epiphenomenal, that is, "functional to other distinct goals or purposes."[17] In spite of its divine content, which seems like a patch placed over the poem, "Şâire Dair" contemplates the human poet whose thoughts, feelings, and imagination are brought to light along with this epiphenomenality or functionality that signals the oncoming erasure of God's presence from poetry.

The Retreat of God and the Melancholic Experience of Groundlessness

In 1896, Tevfik Fikret was appointed as editor-in-chief of *Servet-i Fünun* at Recaizâde Mahmut Ekrem's request. During his editorship (1896–1901), *Servet-i Fünun* became a hub for literary innovators. It left its mark on Ottoman-Turkish cultural and literary history not only as a journal but also most notably as a literary movement generating a "New Literature" (*Edebiyat-ı Cedîde*).[18]

During the *Servet-i Fünun* period, the emphasis on God lost its strength in Fikret's poetry. Appreciating Recaizâde Ekrem's theory of a subject-centered, worldly poetry at first and then going beyond the limits of subjectivity Ekrem had in mind, Tevfik Fikret, along with other members of the *Servet-i Fünun* movement, challenged Ekrem's theory by eliminating God from poetry. This is reflected in poems as the awareness of the absence of the ground providing a certain way of thinking, a means for producing knowledge, a model for judgment, and a conceptual framework of fundamental questions and their answers.

The elimination of God from poetry corresponds to the loss of "the absolute" for the *Servet-i Fünun* circle and what it brings into being is pure relativity. As Fikret discussed in his "Hafta-i Edebî" (Literature Weekly), the subject, unable to articulate a truth valid for or applicable to everyone, everywhere, and at every moment, is aware that what he can utter will only be a claim of subjective truth among several others.[19] While the retreat of God primarily brings the problem of subjective claims of truth and the legitimacy of relativity, it also problematizes the issue of beauty. "The absolute beauty of nature" is severely criticized and replaced with the subjective judgment of taste in this period.[20] When beauty is no longer something to be found in the object but depends on the subject, there arises another question: What is it, then, that determines the subject himself with his judgments in general, including taste? The search for an answer led the *Servet-i Fünun* members to positivist criticism, especially that of Hippolyte Taine. Taine's theory meant more than a method for analyzing or criticizing literary texts by considering "race, environment, and time." It also provided a way of making sense of subjectivity and relativity.[21] Moreover, the underlying idea of redefining poetry at the turn of the century can be found in the emphasis on time. In other words, the "spirit of time" is taken as requiring a new poetry based on the exploration and expression of the inner world of the subject and a new, subjective language appropriate for it.[22] The path of the *Servet-i Fünûn* circle intersected with Symbolism and Decadence at this point in a way that these two movements showed how every element of poetry can be dissipated for the sake of self-expression.[23]

The "self" expressed in the poems is a very melancholic one. Both Fikret and other *Servet-i Fünun* poets emphasize melancholy and appropriate it as a distinctive feature of their era and its poetry. As seen in his essay "Musâhabe-i Edebiyye: Bir Mülâhaza" (Literary Conversation: A Contemplation), Fikret defines melancholy as an illness spread across contemporary literature, affecting or even shaping it as a whole. With an implicit reference to "Mal du Siécle," he evaluates melancholy not as a personal problem but as a mood experienced collectively.[24] Starting from this collectivity assigned to melancholy, a close reading of poems gives several hints that the fin-de-siècle Ottoman melancholy in all its connotations can be read from the perspective of "the pain of groundlessness." When God retreats, He still exists or reminds humans of himself in poems via the gap left behind. What manifests itself through melancholy is the vigorously contested "inability" of the human subject to fill this particular gap by justifying his sovereignty or his own assignment as the new ground of meaning. As we see in Fikret's poetry and particularly in poems like "İnanmak İhtiyacı" (The Need to Believe), "Yine Halûk" (Haluk Again), "Perde-i Tesellî" (The Curtain of Consolation) and "Buda" (Buddha),[25] the melancholic tone of the poems unites in the experience of groundlessness, which is revealed by images like emptiness, nothingness, void, abyss, drifting, stumbling, mourning, exitlessness, meaningless, aimlessness, solitude, and especially finitude. All these images expressing the melancholy of groundlessness also reveal an intense need that is finally met with science in the poems Fikret wrote in the twentieth century.

From Heaven to Earth: The Last Poems of Tevfik Fikret

From the time of his separation from the *Servet-i Fünun* circle in 1901 and until his death in 1915, Fikret's poems are marked with a transformation that enables the groundless subject to fill the gap God left behind. Science is the enabler of this transformation: In science, Fikret discovers the legitimacy of articulating the absolute. As science was conceptualized by twentieth-century Ottoman intellectuals with reference to Darwin's evolutionary thought, so are Fikret's poems based on the framework drawn up especially by Charles Darwin in conjunction with Ludwig Büchner and Ernst Haeckel.[26]

Human nature, which evolutionists depicted as a constant struggle that gives only the strongest a chance to survive and harboring no value other than their own survival, is reflected in Fikret's poems as the demystification of the human being. The value attached to the humans in the God-centered paradigm is lost when Darwinism is taken up, just as the boundaries between humans and animals are erased. When life is explained by science (especially by biology, which was translated as "*hayâtiyyât*") as an event of nature ("*hâdise-i tabî'iyye*") whose basis is the protoplasm, humans are no longer the noblest of the created ("*eşref-i mahlûkat*") or the apple of the eye of beings ("*merdüm-i dîde-i ekvân*"). As Büchner stated, humans, as a collection of atoms no different from those, which make up the universe, are subject to the same laws, especially the struggle for existence, as the others. While this perspective, which demystifies human beings by relating all their acts to survival, is repeated in Fikret's poem "Cevâb" (The Answer),[27] it is used specifically for interpreting the past (i.e., human history), as in the poems "Târîh-I Kâdim" (Ancient History) and "Hilâl-i Ahmer" (Red Crescent).[28]

The evolutionary approach's emphasis on progress also makes it possible to envision the future as a human-made paradise with a human-centered morality. It is a future in which there is no place for struggle or wars and in which selfishness is replaced by solidarity. This vision is the source of the hope observed in Fikret's last poems. In poems such as "Sabah Olursa" (If the Morning Comes) and "Halûk'un Amentüsü" (Haluk's Credo),[29] progress is considered a road to a future marked by freedom and enlightened by science, in which human beings take the place of God. The experience of groundlessness of the *Servet-i Fünun* period turns into a criticism of religion in these late poems. There, the retreat of God is defined in accordance with the new paradigm and is conceptualized as a "displacement" by the human mind. Science reshaped the perception of God as well as the perception of the world as it regards what cannot be explained rationally to be superstitious. As in "Târîh-i Kadîm'e Zeyl" (Addendum to Ancient History), God turns into something that is sought but cannot be found empirically. While the existence of God is pronounced to be fake, this deception is attributed to the fears or ambitions of human beings who have not sufficiently evolved.

Human beings' adventure from darkness to light, from captivity to sovereignty is also at the focus of Fikret's poems, as we see in "Gökten Yere" (From Heaven to Earth), written in this period. Echoing Büchner, who had said "there is no 'absolute silence' in nature,"[30] the poem relates the gradual progress of human beings by illustrating the history of humanity in a continuous, linear movement. As humans achieve progress by means of questioning and searching, Fikret reckons that they will come to see the truth clearly and replace divinity with humanity and emerge as the new God.[31]

Conclusion

When we take for granted the idea of modernization in which the state of being modern is labeled as being "Western," and being "Western" as an ideal or project shaped by a compensating ideology to eliminate "historical belatedness," we silence the possibility of texts expressing

Human Voice Echoing in the Silence of God

their own, authentic experience of modernity. That is why, instead of starting with the idea of modernization, directly focusing on the texts from the perspective of modernity itself can pave the way for an alternative understanding of fin-de-siècle Ottoman literary history. In this respect, Tevfik Fikret's works bear the traces of the turmoil Ottoman poetry experienced at the turn of the century. Heralding God's retreat with the prominence given to the human subject and his existence in the world, which is gradually stripped of its spiritual connotations, becomes the trademark of the new Ottoman poetry. Along the same lines, Fikret's poetry is generated from the experience of groundlessness in which God ceased to be the ground for determining poetry. In other words, his poetry feeds on the modern tension between the retreat of God and the assignment of the human subject as the substitute or as the new God.

Author's Note

This chapter is based on my dissertation, "Tanrısal Sessizlikte Yankılanan İnsan Sesi: Tevfik Fikret Şiirinde Dünyevileşme ve Ölüm," completed in 2014 under the supervision of Zeynep Uysal at Boğaziçi University.

Notes

1 Daryush Shayegan, *Cultural Schizophrenia: Islamic Societies Confronting the West*, trans. John Howe (Syracuse, NY: Syracuse University Press, 1997), 3.
2 Cem Dilçin, *Örneklerle Türk Şiir Bilgisi* (Ankara: Türk Dil Kurumu Yayınları, 1997), 251.
3 For a comprehensive discussion on Tevhid and Sufism, see Mustafa İsen and Muhsin Macit, eds., *Türk Edebiyatında Tevhidler* (Ankara: Türkiye Diyanet Vakfı, 1992); Ali Nihad Tarlan, *Divan Edebiyatında Tevhidler: Fasikül III* (Istanbul: İstanbul Üniversitesi Yayınları, 1936). For the aforementioned couplets, see Tevfik Fikret, *Bütün Şiirleri*, ed. İsmail Parlatır and Nurullah Çetin (Ankara: Türk Dil Kurumu Yayınları, 2004), 27.
4 For a comprehensive discussion on Tevhid and Kalam, see Halûk Gökalp, "İslam Felsefesinin ve Kelâmının Divan Şiirine Yansımaları: Tevhid Kasidelerinde İsbât-ı Vâcib," *Osmanlı Araştırmaları* 27 (2006): 47–82. For aforementioned couplets see Tevfik Fikret, *Bütün Şiirleri*, 27–28.
5 For examples, see Tevfik Fikret, *Bütün Şiirleri*, 5, 10–11, 13.
6 Mehmet Kalpaklı, "Divân Şiirinde Aşk," in *Osmanlı Divân Şiiri Üzerine Metinler*, ed. Mehmet Kalpaklı (Istanbul: Yapı Kredi Yayınları, 1999), 454.
7 Tevfik Fikret, *Bütün Şiirleri*, 36–37.
8 İskender Pala, *Ansiklopedik Divan Şiiri Sözlüğü* (Istanbul: Leyla ve Mecnun Yayıncılık, 2003), 87.
9 For these couplets, see Tevfik Fikret, *Bütün Şiirleri*, 21–23.
10 Tevfik Fikret, "Musâhabe-i Edebiyye," in *Dil ve Edebiyat Yazıları*, ed. İsmail Parlatır (Ankara: Türk Dil Kurumu Yayınları, 1987), 3–4.
11 See Recaizâde Mahmud Ekrem, *Ta'lîm-i Edebiyat*, ed. Murat Kacıroğlu (Sivas: Asitan Yayıncılık, 2011); Recaizâde Mahmud Ekrem, "Zemzeme (Üçüncü Kısım) Mukaddime," in *Bütün Eserleri II*, ed. İsmail Parlatır, Nurullah Çetin, and Hakan Sazyek (Istanbul: Milli Eğitim Bakanlığı Yayınları, 1997); Recaizâde Mahmud Ekrem, *Elhân –Takdîr-i Elhân: Her Güzel Şey Şiirdir*, ed. Tülin Arseven (Erzurum: Salkımsöğüt Yayınevi, 2008).
12 For a comprehensive discussion on Romantic enchantment of nature, see James C. McKusick, "Nature," in *A Companion to European Romanticism*, ed. Michael Ferber (Malden, MA: Blackwell, 2005), 413–33; Kate Rigby, *Topographies of the Sacred: The Poetics of Place in European Romanticism* (Charlottesville: University of Virginia Press, 2004); Virgil Nemoianu, "Sacrality and the Aesthetic in the Early Nineteenth Century," in *A Companion to European Romanticism*, ed. Michael Ferber (Malden, MA: Blackwell, 2005), 393–413; Isaiah Berlin, *The Roots of Romanticism*, ed. Henry Hardy (Princeton, NJ: Princeton University Press, 1999); Peter Murphy and David Roberts, *Dialectic of Romanticism* (London: Continuum, 2006).
13 For a comprehensive discussion on nature in Ottoman poetry, see Ali Yıldırım, "İslam'ın Tabiat Anlayışı ve Divan Şiirine Yansımaları," *İlmî Araştırmalar* 17 (Fall 2004): 155–73; Shirine Hamadeh,

The City's Pleasures: Istanbul in the Eighteenth Century (Seattle: University of Washington Press, 2008); Veysel Öztürk, "The Romantic Roots of Turkish Poetry: Romantic Subjectivity in Abdülhak Hâmid Tarhan's Poetry" (PhD diss., Boğaziçi University, 2010); Walter G. Andrews, *Poetry's Voice, Society's Song: Ottoman Lyric Poetry* (Seattle: University of Washington Press, 1995).

14 See Recaizâde Mahmud Ekrem, *Elhân –Takdîr-i Elhân: Her Güzel Şey Şiirdir*, ed. Tülin Arseven (Erzurum: Salkımsöğüt Yayınevi, 2008).

15 Tevfik Fikret, "Hepimiz Tabi'atın Birer Acemi Şâkirdiyiz," in *Dil ve Edebiyat Yazıları*, ed. İsmail Parlatır (Ankara: Türk Dil Kurumu Yayınları, 1987), 228–29.

16 Tevfik Fikret, *Bütün Şiirleri*, 90–91.

17 For a comprehensive discussion on the independent motivation to religious belief and action in conditions of modernity, see Charles Taylor, *A Secular Age* (Cambridge, MA: Belknap Press of Harvard University Press, 2007), 433–34.

18 For a comprehensive examination, see "Osmanlı Kültür Tarihinde Servet-i Fünun Dergisi TÜBİTAK Araştırma Projesi Veritabanı," www.servetifunundergisi.com/.

19 Tevfik Fikret, "Hafta-i Edebî I," in *Dil ve Edebiyat Yazıları*, ed. İsmail Parlatır (Ankara: Türk Dil Kurumu Yayınları, 1987), 142–47.

20 For a comprehensive discussion on the denial of the absolute beauty of nature and Servet-i Fünun movement's defense of subjective taste, see Bilge Ercilasun, *Servet-i Fünûn'da Edebî Tenkit* (Ankara: Kültür Bakanlığı Yayınları, 1981); Hasan Akay, *Servet-i Fünûn Şiir Estetiği: Cenab Şahabeddin'in Gözüyle* (Istanbul: Kitabevi Yayınları, 1998); Emine Tuğcu, *Osmanlı'nın Son Döneminde Şiir Eleştirisi* (Istanbul: İletişim Yayınları, 2013). For a comprehensive examination of the relation between subjective taste and modernity, see Luc Ferry, *Homo Aestheticus: The Invention of Taste in the Democratic Age*, trans. Robert de Loaiza (Chicago: University of Chicago Press, 1993); Rüdiger Safranski, *Romanticism: A German Affair*, trans. Robert E. Goodwin (Evanston, IL: Northwestern University Press, 2014); Matei Calinescu, *Five Faces of Modernity: Modernism, Avant-Garde, Decadence, Kitsch, Postmodernism* (Durham, NC: Duke University Press, 1987).

21 For a comprehensive discussion on *Servet-i Fünun*'s attitude towards positivist criticism, see Çiğdem Kurt, "Edebiyatı Yeniden Şekillendirmek: Ahmed Şuayb'ın Edebiyat Eleştirisi" (MA thesis, Boğaziçi University, 2008). For Tevfik Fikret in particular, see Tevfik Fikret, "Musâhabe-i Edebiyye 5," "Romanların Te'sîri," and "Hafta-i Edebî 5," in *Dil ve Edebiyat Yazıları*, ed. İsmail Parlatır (Ankara: Türk Dil Kurumu Yayınları, 1987), 24–29, 131–32, 158–62.

22 See Tevfik Fikret, "Nazîre-perdâzlık," in *Dil ve Edebiyat Yazıları*, ed. İsmail Parlatır (Ankara: Türk Dil Kurumu Yayınları, 1987), 12–15. As a manifesto of *Servet-i Fünun* poetry, see Halid Ziya Uşaklıgil, *Mai ve Siyah* (Istanbul: Özgür Yayınları, 2004).

23 For a comprehensive discussion, see Fazıl Gökçek, *Bir Tartışmanın Hikâyesi: Dekadanlar* (Istanbul: Dergâh Yayınları, 2007).

24 Tevfik Fikret, "Musâhabe-i Edebiyye: Bir Mülâhaza," in *Dil ve Edebiyat Yazıları*, ed. İsmail Parlatır (Ankara: Türk Dil Kurumu Yayınları, 1987), 123–28.

25 See Tevfik Fikret, *Bütün Şiirleri*, 421, 416, 396, 434.

26 See Louis Büchner, *Mâdde ve Kuvvet*, trans. Baha Tevfik and Ahmed Nebil, ed. Kemal Kahramanoğlu and Ali Utku (Konya: Çizgi Kitabevi, 2012); Ernst Haeckel, *Vahdet-i Mevcûd: Bir Tabî'at 'Âliminin Dîni*, trans. Baha Tevfik and Ahmed Nebil, ed. Remzi Demir, Bilal Yurtoğlu and Ali Utku (Konya: Çizgi Kitabevi, 2014).
Tevfik Fikret, *Bütün Şiirleri*, 570.

27 Ibid., 465–66.

28 Ibid., 639–45, 569–71.

29 Ibid., 461–62, 541–42.

30 Büchner, *Mâdde ve Kuvvet*, 89.

31 Tevfik Fikret, *Bütün Şiirleri*, 572–74.

References

Akay, Hasan. *Servet-i Fünûn Şiir Estetiği: Cenab Şahabeddin'in Gözüyle*. Istanbul: Kitabevi Yayınları, 1998.

Andrews, Walter G. *Poetry's Voice, Society's Song: Ottoman Lyric Poetry*. Seattle: University of Washington Press, 1995.

Berlin, Isaiah. *The Roots of Romanticism*. Edited by Henry Hardy. Princeton, NJ: Princeton University Press, 1999.

Büchner, Louis. *Mâdde ve Kuvvet*. Translated by Baha Tevfik ve Ahmed Nebil and edited by Kemal Kahramanoğlu and Ali Utku. Konya: Çizgi Kitabevi, 2012.

Calinescu, Matei. *Five Faces of Modernity: Modernism, Avant-garde, Decadence, Kitsch, Postmodernism*. Durham, NC: Duke University Press, 1987.

Dilçin, Cem. *Örneklerle Türk Şiir Bilgisi*. Ankara: Türk Dil Kurumu Yayınları, 1997.

Ercilasun, Bilge. *Servet-i Fünûn'da Edebî Tenkit*. Ankara: Kültür Bakanlığı Yayınları, 1981.

Ferry, Luc. *Homo Aestheticus: The Invention of Taste in the Democratic Age*. Translated by Robert de Loaiza. Chicago: University of Chicago Press, 1993.

Gökalp, Halûk. "İslam Felsefesinin ve Kelâmının Divan Şiirine Yansımaları: Tevhid Kasidelerinde İsbât-ı Vâcib." *Osmanlı Araştırmaları* 27 (2006): 47–82.

Gökçek, Fazıl. *Bir Tartışmanın Hikâyesi: Dekadanlar*. Istanbul: Dergâh Yayınları, 2007.

Haeckel, Ernst. *Vahdet-i Mevcûd: Bir Tabî'at 'Âliminin Dîni*. Translated by Baha Tevfik and Ahmed Nebil and edited by Remzi Demir, Bilal Yurtoğlu, and Ali Utku. Konya: Çizgi Kitabevi, 2014.

Hamadeh, Shirine. *The City's Pleasures: Istanbul in the Eighteenth Century*. Seattle: University of Washington Press, 2008.

İsen, Mustafa, and Muhsin Macit, eds. *Türk Edebiyatında Tevhidler*. Ankara: Türkiye Diyanet Vakfı, 1992.

Kalpaklı, Mehmet. "Divân Şiirinde Aşk." In *Osmanlı Divân Şiiri Üzerine Metinler*, edited by Mehmet Kalpaklı, 454–55. Istanbul: Yapı Kredi Yayınları, 1999.

Kurt, Çiğdem. "Edebiyatı Yeniden Şekillendirmek: Ahmed Şuayb'ın Edebiyat Eleştirisi." MA thesis, Boğaziçi University, 2008.

McKusick, James C. "Nature." In *A Companion to European Romanticism*, edited by Michael Ferber, 413–33. Malden, MA: Blackwell, 2005.

Murphy, Peter, and David Roberts. *Dialectic of Romanticism*. London: Continuum, 2006.

Nemcianu, Virgil. "Sacrality and the Aesthetic in the Early Nineteenth Century." In *A Companion to European Romanticism*, edited by Michael Ferber, 393–413. Malden, MA: Blackwell, 2005.

"Osmanlı Kültür Tarihinde Servet-i Fünun Dergisi TÜBİTAK Araştırma Projesi Veritabanı." www.servetifunundergisi.com/.

Pala, İskender. *Ansiklopedik Divan Şiiri Sözlüğü*. Istanbul: Leyla ve Mecnun Yayıncılık, 2003.

Recaizâde Mahmud Ekrem. "Zemzeme (Üçüncü Kısım) Mukaddime." In *Bütün Eserleri II*, edited by İsmail Parlatır, Nurullah Çetin, and Hakan Sazyek. Istanbul: Milli Eğitim Bakanlığı Yayınları, 1997.

———. *Elhân –Takdîr-i Elhân: Her Güzel Şey Şiirdir*. Edited by Tülin Arseven. Erzurum: Salkımsöğüt Yayınevi, 2008.

———. *Ta'lîm-i Edebiyat*. Edited by Murat Kacıroğlu. Sivas: Asitan Yayıncılık, 2011.

Rigby, Kate. *Topographies of the Sacred: The Poetics of Place in European Romanticism*. Charlottesville: University of Virginia Press, 2004.

Safranski, Rüdiger. *Romanticism: A German Affair*. Translated by Robert E. Goodwin. Evanston, IL: Northwestern University Press, 2014.

Shayegan Daryush. *Cultural Schizophrenia: Islamic Societies Confronting the West*. Translated by John Howe. Syracuse, NY: Syracuse University Press, 1997.

Tarlan, Ali Nihad. *Divan Edebiyatında Tevhidler: Fasikül III*. Istanbul: İstanbul Üniversitesi Yayınları, 1936.

Tevfik Fikret. *Dil ve Edebiyat Yazıları*. Edited by İsmail Parlatır. Ankara: Türk Dil Kurumu Yayınları, 1987.

———. *Bütün Şiirleri*. Edited by İsmail Parlatır and Nurullah Çetin. Ankara: Türk Dil Kurumu Yayınları, 2004.

Tuğcu, Emine. *Osmanlı'nın Son Döneminde Şiir Eleştirisi*. Istanbul: İletişim Yayınları, 2013.

Uşaklıgil, Halid Ziya. *Mai ve Siyah*. Istanbul: Özgür Yayınları, 2004.

Veysel Öztürk. "The Romantic Roots of Turkish Poetry: Romantic Subjectivity in Abdülhak Hâmid Tarhan's Poetry." PhD diss., Boğaziçi University, 2010.

Yıldırım, Ali. "İslam'ın Tabiat Anlayışı ve Divan Şiirine Yansımaları." *İlmî Araştırmalar* 17 (Fall 2004): 155–73.

SECTION III

Cultures of Reading

8

READING AND WRITING PRACTICES IN THE OTTOMAN EMPIRE

İrvin Cemil Schick

According to a saying attributed to the Prophet Muḥammad (d. Medina, 632), known as a *ḥadīth*:

> The first thing that God created was the pen. And He said to it: "Write!" It said: "Lord, what should I write?" He said: "Write down the destiny of all things until the final hour."
>
> *(Sunan Abī Dāwūd, Sunnah 42:105)*

Moreover, the first few verses of *Sūrah al-'Alaq*, the 96th chapter of the Qur'ān, considered the beginning of the Divine Revelation, are as follows:

> Read! in the name of thy Lord who has created—created man from a clot. Read! And thy Lord is the most bounteous, Who teaches by the pen, taught man that which he knew not.
>
> *(al-'Alaq 96: 1–5)*

These two remarkable statements tell us a great deal about the centrality of reading and writing in the Islamic cosmology. If God first created the pen and ordered it to write everything that will ever be, then all of creation is fundamentally a written text. The Qur'ān is a "user's manual" that helps believers read and comprehend that text by explicating the signs that God has placed all around them and, conversely, the material world helps believers read and interpret the message of the Qur'ān. Together, the universe and the Scripture constitute an "intertext" that guides believers in worshipping God with a fuller understanding of His power and grace.[1]

The Qur'ān is believed to be the verbatim record of the word of God as revealed to the Prophet, a unique and miraculous text the likes of which could not have been written by mere mortals. It subdivides non-Muslims into those who have received a revelation, known as "People of the Book" (Jews and Christians), and those who have not, the unbelievers.

Although the Qur'ān was revealed to the Prophet gradually, in fact it is generally believed to have preexisted the Revelation, indeed to be "uncreated." Verses like "Nay but it is a glorious Qur'ān in a Preserved Tablet" (*al-Burūj* 85:21–22) and "With Him is the Mother of the Book" (*al-Ra'd* 13:39) are taken to indicate that the text of the Qur'ān is conserved, perhaps in

DOI: 10.4324/9780429279270-12

archetypical form, by the side of God. Moreover, everything that has happened, is happening, and will happen is recorded on the Preserved Tablet, and this is why Muslims often refer to fate in terms of writing—in colloquial Turkish, for example, "what is written" (*yazgı*) and "the writing on the forehead" (*alın yazısı*).

In short, reading and writing are inextricably linked with the Islamic faith, and this fact constitutes the foundation of the Ottoman practices of reading and writing. A revealing anecdote is told about the scholar and Qur'ān commentator Elmalılı Muhammed Hamdi Yazır (d. Istanbul, 1942). When a young boy, so the story goes, he placed a discarded container on the floor to help his elderly teacher step over a high threshold. The latter exclaimed that it would be a grave sin for him to do so, because there were inscriptions on the container. The boy said, "But this is not Islamic writing," meaning that the inscription was in Latin script. His teacher responded: "Muslims and infidels both have writing, but there is no such thing as Muslim writing and infidel writing. Can what is done with one not be done with the other? All writing deserves respect, provided that it is used not for evil but for good."[2]

The Caliph 'Alī ibn Abī Ṭālib (d. Kufa, 661) is reported to have said, "Knowledge is fugitive; tie it down with writing," while his contemporary and rival Mu'āwīyah ibn Abī Sufyān (d. Damascus, 680) similarly said, "He who relies on memory is deceived, and he who relies on the record is contented."[3] These are forceful statements in support of textual practices in early Islam and it is clear that many Muslims took them to heart: bibliographical dictionaries such as *Kitāb al-Fihrist* by al-Nadīm (d. Baghdād, 990) and *Kashf al-ẓunūn 'an asāmī al-kutub wa al-funūn* by Kâtip Çelebi (a.k.a. Hacı Halîfe, d. Istanbul, 1657) list many thousands of titles, underscoring both the importance of scholarship in the Muslim world and the proliferation of written records of that scholarship.[4]

In addition, keeping written records of financial transactions was mandated by the Qur'ān, which declares, in part:

> O you who believe! When you contract a debt for a fixed term, record it in writing. Let a scribe record it in writing between you in [terms of] equity. No scribe should refuse to write as God has taught him, so let him write, and let him who incurs the debt dictate, and let him observe his duty to God his Lord, and diminish nothing of it. But if he who owes the debt is of low understanding, or weak, or unable himself to dictate, then let the guardian of his interests dictate in [terms of] equity. . . . Do not be averse to writing down [the contract] whether it be small or great, with [record of] its term. That is more equitable in the sight of God and more sure for testimony, and the best way of avoiding doubt between you.
>
> *(al-Baqara 2:282)*

Similarly, the Prophet had 'Alī prepare a written document to record the terms of the Treaty of Ḥudaybiyya (*Ṣaḥīḥ Bukhārī, al-Jizya wa al-mawāda'a* 58:26). Such rulings can only have encouraged the maintenance of written records,[5] and that may explain, at least in part, the enormous wealth of Ottoman archival sources available to the historian today.

Received opinion has it that the process of modernization involves, among other things, a definitive transition from oral to written culture. There are good reasons to question this premise, not least because of the persistence of orality in developed societies even today, and indeed Ottoman history provides many examples of the continuing imbrication of orality and literacy. In addition to the important place of orality in certain types of specialized training, such as calligraphy[6] and music,[7] and in certain sectors of officialdom, such as public administration[8] and jurisprudence,[9] literature too continued to straddle the line between oral and written.

Reading and Writing Practices in the Ottoman Empire

In this respect, it is important to bear in mind that reading has not always been the solitary occupation it often is today. Classical poetry, for example, was typically recited and discussed in literary salons known as *meclis* (from the Arabic verb *jalasa*, to sit).[10] In other words, there was not always a clear-cut distinction between reading and performance.[11] An important consequence of this persisting orality was that reading inevitably remained an exclusive occupation: women, for example, were generally not allowed in the *meclis* and were therefore largely locked out of such literary pursuits.[12] Likewise, public readings of popular literary works were fairly common, as attested not only by marginal notes scribbled into the manuscripts[13] but also by some European travelers' accounts. For example, Ottaviano Bon, a Venetian envoy who spent some two and a half years in Istanbul during the first decade of the seventeenth century, wrote:

> And among the *Turks*, he that can but read, and write, is held a very learned man, and esteemed far above others, by the common ignorant people; insomuch that when a craft fellow hath got a book, which he knows will please their humours . . . he forthwith gets him with his book to some *Cahve* house [i.e. coffee house], or other, where there is always great resort, and there, being set down in the middle of them, he falls to reading, the people evermore giving credit to whatsoever he says; and so having spent an hour, or two, he takes their benevolences, which is usually more than the price of his book comes to; such is their simplicity, and such is their delight in hearing a man read fables.[14]

In other words, reading was often a collective activity that included audience participation in the form of public comments as well as expressions of approval or displeasure. As coffeehouses—even more than literary salons—were fundamentally homosocial spaces, these public readings too played a role in enforcing the gendered nature of literary activities in the Ottoman Empire.

Another way in which the masses, whether literate or not, interacted daily with written texts was by navigating among the countless architectural inscriptions that dotted the Ottoman urban landscape.[15] Although such inscriptions have been studied for their documentary content as well as their artistic merit, the way in which they were articulated with reading and writing practices has not been given the attention it deserves. It has been suggested, for example, that the difficulty in deciphering complex calligraphic compositions, their sometimes inaccessible positioning, and the occasional presence of textual or orthographical errors together suggest that architectural inscriptions were primarily decorative and not intended to be read.[16] This, however, overlooks the fact that reading and writing are culturally specific activities and that the way an Ottoman might have approached an inscription is not necessarily identical to the way we might today.

In particular, it must be borne in mind that people were far less mobile in the past, so that a given person would have been exposed to the same architectural inscriptions day in, day out, for months or years, and would thus have had ample opportunity to parse even a complex composition or at least ask others for help in doing so; and that many architectural inscriptions contain texts—such as certain popular Qur'ānic verses—that would have been familiar to most Ottomans and could therefore be reconstructed once no more than a couple of words had been deciphered. The same may be said for the myriad everyday objects that bore inscriptions, from scarves to swords, from copper bowls to mirrors. The texts with which such objects were inscribed were, once again, often fairly well known, so that a reader would have had no difficulty recognizing them, even if not by actually making out each and every individual letter of which they were composed.

So one may justifiably ask, if many of the texts inscribed onto objects and buildings were likely to be known by both the writers and the potential readers, what was the purpose of writing and reading them in the first place? The answer lies once again in the various culturally specific meanings ascribed to the acts of reading and writing in Ottoman society. In some cases, books served as vectors for the transmission of knowledge, whether they were read from cover to cover or simply used for reference.[17] In other cases, however, their function could be ritual or devotional, and for such objects "reading" meant something quite different. For example, reading (and rereading) the Qur'ān, popular books like al-Jazūlī's (d. Āsafī, 1465) *Dalā'il al-Khayrāt* or Yazıcıoğlu Meḥemmed's (d. Gelibolu, 1451) *Muḥammediyye*, or one's favorite book of daily prayers (*evrād/awrād*) was an act of affirmation, worship, and meditation as much as communication or education. Likewise, Qur'ānic verses, *ḥadīth*s, or bon mots (*kelâm-ı kibar*) inscribed on everyday objects were not purely informative. They could also be moralistic, say, or devotional; not least, they were a confirmation of Islam's religious and cultural sovereignty over the material world.

Most inscriptions by far have always consisted of ordinary writing; only some have been bona fide works of calligraphy, that is, beautiful writing. It is important to distinguish one from the other not only on aesthetic grounds but also functionally. Born of the imperative to preserve the word of God in the most beautiful form, calligraphy is arguably the most recognizably "Islamic" of the arts practiced in the Muslim world. Its abstract nature, moreover, appears to have been found especially appealing by Ottomans, who excelled at writing several scripts and even invented a number of their own. But calligraphy is more than just artistic writing: the form of calligraphy often conveys meanings above and beyond that contained in the text itself.[18] For example, different scripts were sometimes used for different purposes, as were different formats, and readers' responses to the texts before them would inevitably be influenced by such seemingly purely formal factors.

The most widely used script during the Ottoman period was *nesih* (*naskh*), the "book script" par excellence. Unlike some other scripts, *nesih* can be fully vocalized (i.e., diacritics indicating short vowels can be added to the consonants), making the texts easier to read as well as less ambiguous. It was used primarily for texts in Arabic and Ottoman, and for religious and scholarly works, as well as popular prose. By contrast, *ta'lîk* (*nasta'līq*) is very seldom vocalized. In the Ottoman context, it was used primarily for texts in Persian as well as for literary prose and poetry in Ottoman. It is an extremely graceful script but achieves its beauty at the cost of some legibility. These two scripts were responsible for the virtual totality of book production in the Ottoman Empire, at least until the nineteenth century when *rık'a* (*riq'a*) script gained popularity. Designed for speed rather than aesthetics, *rık'a* was initially used in official correspondence but gradually became the standard everyday script of educated Ottomans. Like *rık'a*, *dîvânî* (*dīwānī*) script too was used in Ottoman official correspondence; it was never used by ordinary people, however. Finally, *sülüs* (*thulth*) was principally a calligraphic script. Its large version, *celî* (*jalî*) *sülüs*, as well as the similarly large *celî ta'lîk* script, were most commonly used on Ottoman architectural inscriptions. One often encounters references to Arabic script written on objects as "calligraphy"; it is important, however, not to lose sight of the fact that calligraphy is a very specific kind of inscription, one in which certain rules are followed with the aim of producing something that is more than just the record of a particular text: it is a beautiful rendition of the text.[19]

Like different scripts, different formats can also sometimes suggest the nature of the texts' contents.[20] For example, vertical oblong albums with horizontally oriented spines at the top, known in Turkish as *cönk*, were typically used to collect folk poetry. Albums with a vertically oriented spine on the right, known as *mecmû'a* (from the Arabic for "collected") were likewise used to compile all sorts of materials, from anecdotes to poetry, from treatises to prayers.[21] Both formats are highly idiosyncratic in that they contain material that individuals found interesting and worth recording. They also bridged the gap between written and oral: on the one hand, they recorded oral communications such as folk poetry, much of which was orally transmitted; on the other, they served a performative function by providing material to be read in social gatherings.

The word *mushaf* (from the Arabic for "composed of pages") signified a codex, and the construct *mushaf-ı şerîf* (noble codex) meant specifically a manuscript of the Qur'ān. However, the "*şerîf*" part was often dropped, so that *mushaf* is frequently used (albeit inaptly) as shorthand for the Qur'ān. By contrast, *kitâb* (from the Arabic verb "to write") simply means "book" and often figures in the title of books, as, for instance, in *Kitâb ta'bîri'r-ru'yā* (Book of Dream Interpretation). Another term that sometimes figures in titles is *risâle*, an Arabic word that means "treatise" or "booklet," as, for instance, in *Risâle fi'n-nisā* (Treatise on Women). One also rarely encounters scrolls, particularly in the case of sufi and other genealogies (*silsilenâme*).

In the case of works of calligraphy, the most frequently encountered formats—besides books—are small single pieces known as *kıt'a* (*qiṭ'a*) and larger panels known as *levha* (*lawḥa*). Often such items served talismanic/apotropaic purposes. Sometimes several *kıt'as* were collected together in book or concertina (accordion-like) form; such albums are known as *murakka'a* (from the Arabic for "patched"). In addition, disparate pages of calligraphy and sometimes also miniatures were pasted into notebooks to form albums (*mecmû'a*); such manuscripts may have been assembled for educational purposes or simply to preserve collections of specimens.[22]

Until the late nineteenth century, books were expensive and few could afford them.[23] Add to that the generally low rate of literacy,[24] and it becomes clear that large private libraries were rare. Precious collections assembled by sultans[25] and by dedicated scholars and bibliophiles such as Veliyüddîn Cârullâh Efendi (d. Istanbul, 1738)[26] and Ali Emîrî Efendi (d. Istanbul, 1924)[27] are extant, and studies often based on probate registers (*tereke kaydı*) have shed light on the personal libraries of ordinary people.[28] In addition to such private libraries, many pious foundations (*vakıf/waqf*) established and maintained libraries.[29] Some of these libraries were located in mosques and dervish lodges, while others were independent. Studies have shown that lending and renting made books available to a wider public than could have afforded to own them. Nevertheless, a relatively brisk book market did exist in Istanbul and other major Ottoman cities.[30]

Although printing presses were established by non-Muslim Ottomans as early as the 1490s, they did not print books in Ottoman or Turkish; moreover, it was long forbidden to import books printed in the languages of the Muslim world. When the first printing press officially sanctioned to print books in Ottoman was established in 1728 by the Hungarian-born İbrahim Müteferrika (d. Istanbul, 1745), its products were so expensive that manuscript books continued to be produced in large numbers.[31] Thus, printing did not bring about significant changes until the early part of the twentieth century, when increased literacy, free enterprise ("print capitalism"), and the climate of freedom ushered in by the proclamation of Constitutional Monarchy in 1908 combined to create a whole new set of reading and writing practices.

Notes

1 For a more detailed discussion, see İrvin Cemil Schick, "Text," in *Key Themes for the Study of Islam*, ed. Jamal J. Elias (Oxford: Oneworld, 2010), 321–35, 420–22.
2 Mahmud Bedreddin Yazır, *Medeniyet Âleminde Yazı ve İslâm Medeniyetinde Kalem Güzeli*, ed. Uğur Derman, vol. 1 (Ankara: Diyanet İşleri Başkanlığı Yayınları, 1972–1989), 74–75.
3 Cited in Nefes Zade İbrahim, *Gülzarı Savab*, ed. Kilisli Muallim Rifat [Bilge] (Istanbul: Güzel Sanatlar Akademisi Neşriyatı, 1939), 32, 38.
4 See Franz Rosenthal, "'Of Making Many Books There Is No End': The Classical Muslim View," in *The Book in the Islamic World: The Written Word and Communication in the Middle East*, ed. George N. Atiyeh

(Albany: SUNY Press, 1995), 33–55. This is not to say, of course, that everything was committed to writing, immediately and all at once, upon the advent of Islam. On the gradual transitions from oral to written and from aural to read, see Gregor Schoeler, *The Genesis of Literature in Islam: From the Aural to the Read*, rev. and trans. Shawkat Toorawa (Edinburgh: Edinburgh University Press, 2009). On the persistence of orality, particularly in the context of Shi'ī Islam, see Seyyed Hossein Nasr, "Oral Transmission and the Book in Islamic Education: The Spoken and the Written Word," in *The Book in the Islamic World: The Written Word and Communication in the Middle East*, ed. George N. Atiyeh (Albany: SUNY Press, 1995), 57–70; on Mamluk Egypt, see Jonathan Porter Berkey, *The Transmission of Knowledge in Medieval Cairo: A Social History of Islamic Education* (Princeton, NJ: Princeton University Press, 1992), 24–31, 59–60.

5 See, e.g., Jeanette A. Wakin, "Introduction," in *The Function of Documents in Islamic Law: the Chapters on Sales from Taḥāwī's* Kitāb al-shurūṭ al-kabir, ed. Jeanette A. Wakin (Albany: SUNY Press, 1972), 1–10. For an interesting study of writing and authority in the modern era, see Brinkley Messick, *The Calligraphic State: Textual Domination and History in a Muslim Society* (Berkeley: University of California Press, 1993); note, however, that "calligraphic" in the title is an unfortunate misnomer, as the subject of the book is the written text, not the art of beautiful writing.

6 İrvin Cemil Schick, "Bedensel Hafıza, Zihinsel Hafıza, Yazılı Kaynak: Hat Sanatının Günümüze İntikalinin Bazı Boyutları," in *Nasıl Hatırlıyoruz? Türkiye'de Bellek Çalışmaları*, ed. Leyla Neyzi (Istanbul: Türkiye İş Bankası Kültür Yayınları, 2011), 12–39.

7 Cem Behar, *Zaman, Mekân, Müzik: Klâsik Türk Musıkisinde Eğitim (Meşk), İcra ve Aktarım* (Istanbul: AFA Yayıncılık, 1993).

8 Nicolas Vatin, "Remarques sur l'oral et l'écrit dans l'administration ottomane au XVIᵉ siècle," *Oral et écrit dans le monde turco-ottoman, Revue du Monde Musulman et de la Méditerranée* 75–76 (1995): 143–54.

9 Işık Tamdoğan-Abel, "L'écrit comme échec de l'oral? L'oralité des engagements et des règlements à travers les registres de cadis d'Adana au XVIIIᵉ siècle," *Oral et écrit dans le monde turco-ottoman, Revue du Monde Musulman et de la Méditerranée* 75–76 (1995): 155–65.

10 See, e.g., Belkıs Gürsoy, "XV. Yüzyıldan İtibaren İstanbul'daki Edebî Muhitlere Genel Bir Bakış," *Bilig: Türk Dünyası Sosyal Bilimler Dergisi* 2 (1996): 188–202. For a useful account of pre-Ottoman Islamic salons, see Samer M. Ali, *Arabic Literary Salons in the Islamic Middle Ages: Poetry, Public Performance, and the Presentation of the Past* (Notre Dame, IN: University of Notre Dame Press, 2010).

11 For an interesting account in a pre-Ottoman context, see Konrad Hirschler, *The Written Word in the Medieval Arabic Lands: A Social and Cultural History of Reading Practices* (Edinburgh: Edinburgh University Press, 2012).

12 Didem Havlioğlu, *Mihrî Hatun: Performance, Gender-Bending, and Subversion in Ottoman Intellectual History* (Syracuse, NY: Syracuse University Press, 2017), 101–14.

13 See, e.g., Tülün Değirmenci, "Bir Kitabı Kaç Kişi Okur? Osmanlı'da Okurlar ve Okuma Biçimleri Üzerine Bazı Gözlemler," *Tarih ve Toplum: Yeni Yaklaşımlar* 13 (2011): 7–43; Elif Sezer, *The Oral and the Written in Ottoman Literature: The Reader Notes on the Story of Fîrûzşâh* (Istanbul: Libra Kitapçılık, 2015), 67–84. For pre-Ottoman examples, see Pierre A. MacKay, "Certificates of Transmission on a Manuscript of the *Maqāmāt* of Ḥarīrī (MS. Cairo, *Adab* 105)," *Transactions of the American Philosophical Society* n.s. 61, no. 4 (1971); Jan Just Witkam, "The Human Element Between Text and Reader: The *ijāza* in Arabic Manuscripts," in *The Codicology of Islamic Manuscripts: Proceedings of the Second Conference of Al-Furqān Islamic Heritage Foundation, 4–5 December 1993*, ed. Yasin Dutton (London: Al-Furqān Islamic Heritage Foundation, 1995), 123–36; Stefan Leder, "Understanding a Text Through Its Transmission: Documented *Samā'*, Copies, Reception," in *Manuscript Notes as Documentary Sources*, ed. Andreas Görke and Konrad Hirschler (Beirut: Ergon Verlag Würzburg, 2011), 59–72.

14 Ottaviano Bon, *The Sultan's Seraglio: An Intimate Portrait of Life at the Ottoman Court*, trans. John Withers, intro. and annot. Godfrey Goodwin (London: Saqi Books, 1996), 143–44. For a survey of Ottoman book culture as described by European travelers, see Engin Cihad Tekin, *Osmanlı'da Kitap Kültürü ve Batı Dünyası: Avrupalı Seyyahların Bakış Açısından Osmanlı'da Kitap ve KütüphaneKültürü (1453–1699)* (Istanbul: Hiperlink Yayınları, 2018).

15 See, e.g., the contributions to Mohammad Gharipour and İrvin Cemil Schick, eds., *Calligraphy and Architecture in the Muslim World* (Edinburgh: Edinburgh University Press, 2013).

16 See, e.g., Richard Ettinghausen, "Arabic Epigraphy: Communication or Symbolic Affirmation," in *Near Eastern Numismatics, Iconography, Epigraphy and History: Studies in Honor of George C. Miles*, ed. Dickran K. Kouymjian (Beirut: American University of Beirut, 1974), 299–300, 304. For a critique, see İrvin Cemil Schick and Mohammad Gharipour, "Introduction," in *Calligraphy and Architecture in the Muslim World* (Edinburgh: Edinburgh University Press, 2013), 1–2.

Reading and Writing Practices in the Ottoman Empire

17 Christoph K. Neumann, "Üç Tarz-ı Mütalaa: Yeniçağ Osmanlı Dünyası'nda Kitap Yazmak ve Okumak," *Tarih ve Toplum: Yeni Yaklaşımlar* 1 (2005): 51–76.

18 See İrvin Cemil Schick, "The Iconicity of Islamic Calligraphy in Turkey," *RES: Anthropology and Aesthetics* 53–54 (2008): 211–24; İrvin Cemil Schick, "The Content of Form: Islamic Calligraphy Between Text and Representation," in *Sign and Design*, ed. Brigitte Bedos-Rezak and Jeffrey Hamburger (Washington, DC: Dumbarton Oaks Research Library and Collection, 2016), 169–90.

19 For useful surveys in English, see Sheila S. Blair, *Islamic Inscriptions* (New York: New York University Press, 1998); Sheila S. Blair, *Islamic Calligraphy* (Edinburgh: Edinburgh University Press, 2008).

20 Recent years have witnessed the publication of several important works on Islamic codicology (i.e., on Islamic books as objects). Although most focus on Arabic manuscripts, much of what they describe applies equally well to Ottoman works. Johannes Pedersen's *The Arabic Book*, trans. Geoffrey French, ed. Robert Hillenbrand (Princeton, NJ: Princeton University Press, 1984) was first published in Danish in 1946 and is a pioneering, if somewhat dated, source. More recent works include François Déroche and Francis Richard, eds., *Scribes et manuscrits du Moyen-Orient* (Paris: Bibliothèque nationale de France, 1997); François Déroche et al., *Manuel de codicologie des manuscrits en écriture arabe* (Paris: Bibliothèque nationale de France, 2000); Adam Gacek, *The Arabic Manuscript Tradition: A Glossary of Technical Terms and Bibliography* (Leiden: Brill, 2001); Adam Gacek, *The Arabic Manuscript Tradition: A Glossary of Technical Terms and Bibliography—Supplement* (Leiden: Brill, 2012); Adam Gacek, *Arabic Manuscripts: A Vademecum for Readers* (Leiden: Brill, 2012). There are also a number of dictionaries of bookmaking terminology in Turkish, Persian, and Arabic, notably Mine Esiner Özen, *Yazma Kitap Sanatları Sözlüğü* (Istanbul: İstanbul Üniversitesi Fen Fakültesi, 1985); İrvin Cemil Schick, "Taczâde Risâlesine Göre Sülüs Hattına Dair Bazı Istılâhat," in *M. Uğur Derman 65 Yaş Armağanı*, ed. İrvin Cemil Schick (Istanbul: Sabancı Üniversitesi Yayınları, 2000), 457–82; Hasan Özönder, *Ansiklopedik Hat ve Tezhip Sanatları Deyim ve Terimleri Sözlüğü* (Konya: Yeni Zamanlar Dağıtım, 2003); Abdülkadir Yılmaz, *Türk Kitap Sanatları Tabir ve Istılahları* (Istanbul: Damla Yayınevi, 2004); 'Afīf al-Bahnasī, *Mu'jam muṣṭalaḥāt al-khaṭṭ al-'Arabī wa al-khaṭṭāṭīn* (Beirut: Maktaba Lubnān, 1995); Māyil Haravī, *Lughāt va-iṣṭilāḥāt-i faan-i kitābsāzī: hamrāh bā iṣṭilāḥāt-i jildsāzī, taẕhīb, naqqāshī* (Tehran: Bunyād-i Farhang-i Irān, 1353 [1974]); Ḥamīd Riżā Qilichkhānī, *Farhang-i vāzhagān va iṣṭilāḥāt-i khvushnivīsī va hunarhā-yi vābastah* (Tehran: Intishārāt-i Rawzanah, 1390 [2011]).

21 See, e.g., the contributions to Hatice Aynur, Müjgân Çakır, Hanife Koncu, Selim S. Kuru, and Ali Emre Özyıldırım, eds., *Mecmûa: Osmanlı Edebiyatının Kırkambarı* (Istanbul: Turkuaz, 2012).

22 See, e.g., Wheeler M. Thackston, *Album Prefaces and Other Documents on the History of Calligraphers and Painters* (Leiden: Brill, 2001); David J. Roxburgh, *Prefacing the Image: The Writing of Art History in Sixteenth-Century Iran* (Leiden: Brill, 2001).

23 For a useful brief summary of Ottoman book culture, see Frédéric Hitzel, "Manuscrits, livres et culture livresque à Istanbul," *Livres et lecture dans le monde ottoman, Revue du Monde Musulman et de la Méditerranée* 87–88 (1999): 19–38.

24 See, e.g., Benjamin C. Fortna, *Learning to Read in the Late Ottoman Empire and the Early Turkish Republic* (Basingstoke: Palgrave Macmillan, 2012); Orhan Koloğlu, *Osmanlıcadan Türkçeye Okuryazarlığımız* (Istanbul: Tarihçi Kitabevi, 2015).

25 See, e.g., İsmail Baykal, "Fatih Sultan Mehmed'in Hususi Kütüphanesi ve Kitabları," *Vakıflar Dergisi* 4 (1958): 77–79; Emine Fetvacı, *Picturing History at the Ottoman Court* (Bloomington: Indiana University Press, 2013): 25–57; Gülru Necipoğlu, Cemal Kafadar, and Cornell H. Fleischer, eds., *Treasures of Knowledge: An Inventory of the Ottoman Palace Library (1502/3–1503/4)* (Leiden: Brill, 2019).

26 Berat Açıl, ed., *Osmanlı Kitap Kültürü: Cârullah Efendi Kütüphanesi ve Derkenar Notları* (Istanbul: İLEM Kitaplığı and Ankara: Nobel Akademik Yayıncılık, 2015).

27 Ekrem Işın, ed., *Ali Emîrî Efendi ve Dünyası: Fermanlar, Beratlar, Hatlar, Kitaplar* (Istanbul: Pera Müzesi Yayınları, 2007).

28 See, e.g., Ali İhsan Karataş, "Tereke Kayıtlarına Göre XVI. Yüzyılda Bursa'da İnsan-Kitap İlişkisi," *Uludağ Üniversitesi İlâhiyat Fakültesi Dergisi* 8, no. 8 (1999): 317–28; Ali İhsan Karataş, "Şer'iyye Sicilleri Bağlamında Klasik Dönem Bursa Halkının Kitap Dünyası," *38. ICANAS/Uluslararası Asya ve Kuzey Afrika Çalışmaları Kongresi Ankara* (2007): 119–36; Meropi Anastassiadou, "Livres et 'bibliothèques' dans les inventaires après décès de Salonique au XIXᵉ siècle," *Livres et lecture dans le monde ottoman, Revue du Monde Musulman et de la Méditerranée* 87–88 (1999): 111–41; Abdullah Saydam, "Trabzon'da Halkın Kitap Sahibi Olma Düzeyi (1795–1846)," *Milli Eğitim* 176 (2006): 187–201; Henning Sievert, "Verlorene Schätze—Bücher von Bürokraten in den *Muḥallefāt*-Registern," in *Buchkultur im Nahen Osten des 17. und 18. Jahrhunderts*, ed. Tobias Heinzelmann and Henning Sievert (Berlin: Peter Lang,

2010), 199–263; Faruk Doğan, "Bir Eğitim Tarihi Kaynağı Olarak Giresun Şer'iye Sicilleri: Tereke Kayıtlarına Yansıyan Kitaplar," *Turkish Studies* 10, no. 9 (2015): 153–68; Asim Zubčević, "Book Ownership in Ottoman Sarajevo, 1707–1828" (PhD diss., Leiden University, 2015); Ekrem Tak and Bilgin Aydın, "XVII. Yüzyılda İstanbul Medreselerinde Okutulan Kitaplar (Tereke Kayıtları Üzerine bir Değerlendirme)," *Dil ve Edebiyat Araştırmaları* 19 (2019): 183–236. On Ottoman Syria, see Colette Establet and Jean-Paul Pascual, "Les livres des gens à Damas vers 1700," *Livres et lecture dans le monde ottoman, Revue du Monde Musulman et de la Méditerranée* 87–88 (1999): 143–69; Colette Establet, "Les inventaires après-décès, sources d'histoire culturelle (Damas)," in *Etudes sur les villes du Proche-Orient, XVIe-XIXe siècle: Hommage à André Raymond*, ed. Brigitte Marino (Damascus: Institut français d'études arabes de Damas, 2001), 81–90. For a wide-ranging survey of Ottoman Egypt, see Nelly Hanna, *In Praise of Books: A Cultural History of Cairo's Middle Class, Sixteenth to the Eighteenth Century* (Syracuse, NY: Syracuse University Press, 2003), 79–103. For an interesting pre-Ottoman list of books studied by an educated Persian Muslim, see A.J. Arberry, *A Twelfth-Century Reading List: A Chapter in Arab Bibliography* (London: Emery Walker, 1951).

29 See, e.g., İsmail E. Erünsal, *Osmanlılarda Kütüphaneler ve Kütüphanecilik: Tarihi Gelişimi ve Organizasyonu* (Istanbul: Timaş Yayınları, 2018); Faruk Bilici, "Les bibliothèques vakıf-s à Istanbul au XVIe siècle, prémice de grandes bibliothèques publiques," *Livres et lecture dans le monde ottoman, Revue du Monde Musulman et de la Méditerranée* 87–88 (1999): 39–59. On Ottoman libraries more generally, see Meral Alpay and Safiye Özkan, *İstanbul Kütüphaneleri* (Istanbul: Ünal Matbaası, 1982); Özer Soysal, *Türk Kütüphaneciliği* (Ankara: Kültür Bakanlığı Kütüphaneler Genel Müdürlüğü, 1998–1999); Özlem Bayram et al., eds., *Osmanlı Devleti'nde Bilim, Kültür ve Kütüphaneler* (Ankara: Türk Kütüphaneciler Derneği, 1999); Mert Ağaoğlu and Ayhan Altundağ, *Osmanlı Devri Müstakil İstanbul Kütüphaneleri* (Istanbul: Cinius Yayınları, 2018). On pre-Ottoman Islamic libraries, see, e.g., Youssef Eche, *Les bibliothèques arabes publiques et semi-publiques en Mésopotamie, en Syrie et en Egypte au Moyen Age* (Damascus: Institut français de Damas, 1967); Houari Touati, *L'armoire à sagesse: Bibliothèques et collections en Islam* (Paris: Aubier, 2003); Konrad Hirschler, *Medieval Damascus: Plurality and Diversity in an Arabic Library* (Edinburgh: Edinburgh University Press, 2016); İsmail E. Erünsal, *Orta Çağ İslâm Dünyasında Kitap ve Kütüphâne* (Istanbul: Timaş Yayınları, 2018).

30 Ömer Faruk Yılmaz, *Tarih Boyunca Sahhaflık ve İstanbul Sahhaflar Çarşısı* (Istanbul: Sahhaflar Derneği, 2005); İsmail E. Erünsal, *Osmanlılarda Sahaflık ve Sahaflar* (Istanbul: Timaş Yayınları, 2013).

31 On early printing in the Ottoman Empire, see, e.g., Franz Babinger, *Stambuler Buchwesen im 18. Jahrhundert* (Leipzig: Deutscher Verein für Buchwesen und Schrifttum, 1919); Selim Nüzhet Gerçek, *Türk Matbaacılığı: İki Yüzüncü Sene-i Devriyesi Münasebetiyle* (Istanbul: Matbaa-ı Ebüzziya, 1928); Aladár V. Simonffy, *Ibrahim Müteferrika: Bahnbrecher des Buchdrucks in der Türkei* (Budapest: Dr. Vajna & Bokor, 1944); Osman Ersoy, *Türkiye'ye Matbaanın Girişi ve İlk Basılan Eserler* (Ankara: Ankara Üniversitesi Dil ve Tarih-Coğrafya Fakültesi Yayınları, 1959); William J. Watson, "İbrahim Müteferrika and Turkish Incunabula," *Journal of the American Oriental Society* 88, no. 3 (1968): 435–41; A[khmet] Kh[alilovich] Rafikov, *Ocherki istorii knigopechataniya v Turtsii* (Leningrad: Izdatel'stvo "Nauka," 1973); Wahid Gdoura, *Le début de l'imprimerie arabe à Istanbul et en Syrie: Evolution de l'environment culturel (1706–1787)* (Tunis: Publications de l'Institut Supérieur de Documentation, 1985); Orlin Sabev, *İbrahim Müteferrika, ya da İlk Osmanlı Matbaa Serüveni (1726–1746): Yeniden Değerlendirme* (Istanbul: Yeditepe Yayınları, 2006); Fikret Sarıcaoğlu and Coşkun Yılmaz, *Müteferrika: Basmacı İbrahim Efendi and the Müteferrika Press* (Istanbul: Esen Ofset, 2008).

References

Açıl, Berat, ed. *Osmanlı Kitap Kültürü: Cârullah Efendi Kütüphanesi ve Derkenar Notları* Istanbul: İLEM Kitaplığı and Ankara: Nobel Akademik Yayıncılık, 2015.

Ağaoğlu, Mert, and Ayhan Altundağ. *Osmanlı Devri Müstakil İstanbul Kütüphaneleri*. Istanbul: Cinius Yayınları, 2018.

al-Bahnasī, 'Afīf. *Mu'jam muṣṭalaḥāt al-khaṭṭ al-'Arabī wa al-khaṭṭāṭīn*. Beirut: Maktaba Lubnān, 1995.

Ali, Samer M. *Arabic Literary Salons in the Islamic Middle Ages: Poetry, Public Performance, and the Presentation of the Past*. Notre Dame, IN: University of Notre Dame Press, 2010.

Alpay, Meral, and Safiye Özkan. *İstanbul Kütüphaneleri*. Istanbul: Ünal Matbaası, 1982.

Anastassiadou, Meropi. "Livres et 'bibliothèques' dans les inventaires après décès de Salonique au XIXe siècle." *Revue du Monde Musulman et de la Méditerranée* 87–88 (1999): 111–41.

Arberry, A.J. *A Twelfth-Century Reading List: A Chapter in Arab Bibliography*. London: Emery Walker, 1951.

Aynur, Hatice, and Müjgân Çakır. *Mecmûa: Osmanlı Edebiyatının Kırkambarı*. Istanbul: Turkuaz, 2012.

Babinger, Franz. *Stambuler Buchwesen im 18. Jahrhundert*. Leipzig: Deutscher Verein für Buchwesen und Schrifttum, 1919.

Baykal, İsmail. "Fatih Sultan Mehmed'in Hususi Kütüphanesi ve Kitabları." *Vakıflar Dergisi* 4 (1958): 77–79.

Bayram, Özlem et al., eds. *Osmanlı Devleti'nde Bilim, Kültür ve Kütüphaneler*. Ankara: Türk Kütüphaneciler Derneği, 1999.

Behar, Cem. *Zaman, Mekân, Müzik: Klâsik Türk Musıkisinde Eğitim (Meşk), İcra ve Aktarım*. Istanbul: AFA Yayıncılık, 1993.

Berkey, Jonathan Porter. *The Transmission of Knowledge in Medieval Cairo: A Social History of Islamic Education*. Princeton, NJ: Princeton University Press, 1992.

Berthier, Annie, and François Déroche. *Manuel de codicologie des manuscrits en écriture arabe*. Paris: Bibliothèque nationale de France, 2000.

Bilici, Faruk. "Les bibliothèques vakıf-s à Istanbul au XVIᵉ siècle, prémice de grandes bibliothèques publiques." *Revue du Monde Musulman et de la Méditerranée* 87–88 (1999): 39–59.

Blair, Sheila S. *Islamic Inscriptions*. New York: New York University Press, 1998.

———. *Islamic Calligraphy*. Edinburgh: Edinburgh University Press, 2008.

Bon, Ottaviano. *The Sultan's Seraglio: An Intimate Portrait of Life at the Ottoman Court*. Translated by John Withers, introduction and annotations by Godfrey Goodwin. London: Saqi Books, 1996.

Değirmenci, Tülün. "Bir Kitabı Kaç Kişi Okur? Osmanlı'da Okurlar ve Okuma Biçimleri Üzerine Bazı Gözlemler." *Tarih ve Toplum: Yeni Yaklaşımlar* 13 (2011): 7–43.

Déroche, François, and Francis Richard, eds. *Scribes et manuscrits du Moyen-Orient*. Paris: Bibliothèque nationale de France, 1997.

Doğan, Faruk. "Bir Eğitim Tarihi Kaynağı Olarak Giresun Şer'iye Sicilleri: Tereke Kayıtlarına Yansıyan Kitaplar." *Turkish Studies* 10, no. 9 (2015): 153–68.

Eche, Youssef. *Les bibliothèques arabes publiques et semi-publiques en Mésopotamie, en Syrie et en Egypte au Moyen Age*. Damascus: Institut français de Damas, 1967 [1985].

Ersoy, Osman. *Türkiye'ye Matbaanın Girişi ve İlk Basılan Eserler*. Ankara: Ankara Üniversitesi Dil ve Tarih-Coğrafya Fakültesi Yayınları, 1959.

Erünsal, İsmail E. *Osmanlılarda Sahaflık ve Sahaflar*. Istanbul: Timaş Yayınları, 2013.

———. *Orta Çağ İslâm Dünyasında Kitap ve Kütüphâne*. Istanbul: Timaş Yayınları, 2018.

———. *Osmanlılarda Kütüphaneler ve Kütüphanecilik: Tarihi Gelişimi ve Organizasyonu*. Istanbul: Timaş Yayınları, 2018.

Esiner Özen, Mine. *Yazma Kitap Sanatları Sözlüğü*. Istanbul: İstanbul Üniversitesi Fen Fakültesi, 1985.

Establet, Colette. "Les inventaires après-décès, sources d'histoire culturelle (Damas)." In *Etudes sur les villes du Proche-Orient, XVIᵉ-XIXᵉ siècle: Hommage à André Raymond*, edited by Brigitte Marino, 81–90. Damascus: Institut français d'études arabes de Damas, 2001.

Establet, Colette, and Jean-Paul Pascual. "Les livres des gens à Damas vers 1700." *Revue du Monde Musulman et de la Méditerranée* 87–88 (1999): 143–69.

Ettinghausen, Richard. "Arabic Epigraphy: Communication or Symbolic Affirmation." In *Near Eastern Numismatics, Iconography, Epigraphy and History: Studies in Honor of George C. Miles*, edited by Dickran K. Kouymjian, 299–304. Beirut: American University of Beirut, 1974.

Fetvacı, Emine. *Picturing History at the Ottoman Court*. Bloomington: Indiana University Press, 2013.

Fortna, Benjamin C. *Learning to Read in the Late Ottoman Empire and the Early Turkish Republic*. Basingstoke: Palgrave Macmillan, 2012.

Gacek, Adam. *The Arabic Manuscript Tradition: A Glossary of Technical Terms and Bibliography*. Leiden: Brill, 2001.

———. *The Arabic Manuscript Tradition: A Glossary of Technical Terms and Bibliography—Supplement*. Leiden: Brill, 2012.

———. *Arabic Manuscripts: A Vademecum for Readers*. Leiden: Brill, 2012.

Gdoura, Wahid. *Le début de l'imprimerie arabe à Istanbul et en Syrie: Evolution de l'environnement culturel (1706–1787)*. Tunis: Publications de l'Institut Supérieur de Documentation, 1985.

Gerçek, Selim Nüzhet. *Türk Matbaacılığı: İki Yüzüncü Sene-i Devriyesi Münasebetiyle*. Istanbul: Matbaa-ı Ebüzziya, 1928.

Gharipour, Mohammad, and İrvin Cemil Schick, eds. *Calligraphy and Architecture in the Muslim World*. Edinburgh: Edinburgh University Press, 2013.

Gürsoy, Belkıs. "XV. Yüzyıldan İtibaren İstanbul'daki Edebî Muhitlere Genel Bir Bakış." *Bilig: Türk Dünyası Sosyal Bilimler Dergisi* 2 (1996): 188–202.

Hanna, Nelly. *In Praise of Books: A Cultural History of Cairo's Middle Class, Sixteenth to the Eighteenth Century.* Syracuse, NY: Syracuse University Press, 2003.

Haravī, Māyil. *Lughāt va-iṣṭilāḥāt-i fann-i kitābsāzī: hamrāh bā iṣṭilāḥāt-i jildsāzī, taẕhīb, naqqāshī.* Tehran: Bunyād-i Farhang-i Irān, 1353 [1974].

Havlioğlu, Didem. *Mihrî Hatun: Performance, Gender-Bending, and Subversion in Ottoman Intellectual History.* Syracuse, NY: Syracuse University Press, 2017.

Hirschler, Konrad. *The Written Word in the Medieval Arabic Lands: A Social and Cultural History of Reading Practices.* Edinburgh: Edinburgh University Press, 2012.

———. *Medieval Damascus: Plurality and Diversity in an Arabic Library.* Edinburgh: Edinburgh University Press, 2016.

Hitzel, Frédéric. "Manuscrits, livres et culture livresque à Istanbul." *Revue du Monde Musulman et de la Méditerranée* 87–88 (1999): 19–38.

Işın, Ekrem, ed. *Ali Emîrî Efendi ve Dünyası: Fermanlar, Beratlar, Hatlar, Kitaplar.* Istanbul: Pera Müzesi Yayınları, 2007.

Karataş, Ali İhsan. "Tereke Kayıtlarına Göre XVI. Yüzyılda Bursa'da İnsan-Kitap İlişkisi." *Uludağ Üniversitesi İlâhiyat Fakültesi Dergisi* 8, no. 8 (1999): 317–28.

———. "Şer'iyye Sicilleri Bağlamında Klasik Dönem Bursa Halkının Kitap Dünyası." *38. ICANAS/ Uluslararası Asya ve Kuzey Afrika Çalışmaları Kongresi, Ankara* (2007): 119–36.

Koloğlu, Orhan. *Osmanlıcadan Türkçeye Okuryazarlığımız.* Istanbul: Tarihçi Kitabevi, 2015.

Leder, Stefan. "Understanding a Text through its Transmission: Documented *Samāʿ*, Copies, Reception." In *Manuscript Notes as Documentary Sources*, edited by Andreas Görke and Konrad Hirschler, 59–72. Beirut: Ergon Verlag Würzburg, 2011.

MacKay, Pierre A. "Certificates of Transmission on a Manuscript of the *Maqāmāt* of Ḥarīrī (MS. Cairo, Adab 105)." *Transactions of the American Philosophical Society* n.s. 61, no. 4 (1971).

Messick, Brinkley. *The Calligraphic State: Textual Domination and History in a Muslim Society.* Berkeley: University of California Press, 1993.

Nasr, Seyyed Hossein. "Oral Transmission and the Book in Islamic Education: The Spoken and the Written Word." In *The Book in the Islamic World: The Written Word and Communication in the Middle East*, edited by George N. Atiyeh, 57–70. Albany: SUNY Press, 1995.

Necipoğlu, Gülru, and Cemal Kafadar, eds. *Treasures of Knowledge: An Inventory of the Ottoman Palace Library (1502/3–1503/4).* Leiden: Brill, 2019.

Nefes Zade İbrahim. *Gülzarı Savab.* Edited by Kilisli Muallim Rifat [Bilge]. Istanbul: Güzel Sanatlar Akademisi Neşriyatı, 1939.

Neumann, Christoph K. "Üç Tarz-ı Mütalaa: Yeniçağ Osmanlı Dünyası'nda Kitap Yazmak ve Okumak." *Tarih ve Toplum: Yeni Yaklaşımlar* 1 (2005): 51–76.

Özönder, Hasan. *Ansiklopedik Hat ve Tezhip Sanatları Deyim ve Terimleri Sözlüğü.* Konya: Yeni Zamanlar Dağıtım, 2003.

Pedersen, Johannes. *The Arabic Book.* Translated by Geoffrey French and edited by Robert Hillenbrand. Princeton, NJ: Princeton University Press, 1984.

Qilichkhānī, Ḥamīd Riẓā. *Farhang-i vāzhagān va iṣṭilāḥāt-i khvushnivīsī va hunarhā-yi vābastah.* Tehran: Intishārāt-i Rawzanah, 1390 [2011].

Rafikov, A[khmet] Kh[alilovich]. *Ocherki istorii knigopechataniya v Turtsii.* Leningrad: Izdatel'stvo "Nauka," 1973.

Rosenthal, Franz. "'Of Making Many Books There Is No End': The Classical Muslim View." In *The Book in the Islamic World: The Written Word and Communication in the Middle East*, edited by George N. Atiyeh, 33–55. Albany: SUNY Press, 1995.

Roxburgh, David J. *Prefacing the Image: The Writing of Art History in Sixteenth-Century Iran.* Leiden: Brill, 2001.

Sabev, Orlin. *İbrahim Müteferrika, ya da İlk Osmanlı Matbaa Serüveni (1726–1746): Yeniden Değerlendirme.* Istanbul: Yeditepe Yayınları, 2006.

Sarıcaoğlu, Fikret, and Coşkun Yılmaz. *Müteferrika: Basmacı İbrahim Efendi and the Müteferrika Press.* Istanbul: Esen Ofset, 2008.

Saydam, Abdullah. "Trabzon'da Halkın Kitap Sahibi Olma Düzeyi (1795–1846)." *Milli Eğitim* 176 (2006): 187–201.

Schick, İrvin Cemil. "Taczâde Risâlesine Göre Sülüs Hattına Dair Bazı Istılâhat." In *M. Uğur Derman 65 Yaş Armağanı*, edited by İrvin Cemil Schick, 457–82. Istanbul: Sabancı Üniversitesi Yayınları, 2000.

————. "The Iconicity of Islamic Calligraphy in Turkey." *RES: Anthropology and Aesthetics* 53–54 (2008): 211–24.

————. "Text." In *Key Themes for the Study of Islam*, edited by Jamal J. Elias, 321–422. Oxford: Oneworld, 2010.

————. "Bedensel Hafıza, Zihinsel Hafıza, Yazılı Kaynak: Hat Sanatının Günümüze İntikalinin Bazı Boyutları." In *Nasıl Hatırlıyoruz? Türkiye'de Bellek Çalışmaları*, edited by Leyla Neyzi, 12–39. Istanbul: Türkiye İş Bankası Kültür Yayınları, 2011.

————. "The Content of Form: Islamic Calligraphy Between Text and Representation." In *Sign and Design*, edited by Brigitte Bedos-Rezak and Jeffrey Hamburger, 169–90. Washington, DC: Dumbarton Oaks Research Library and Collection, 2016.

Schoeler, Gregor. *The Genesis of Literature in Islam: from the Aural to the Read*. Revised and translated by Shawkat Toorawa. Edinburgh: Edinburgh University Press, 2009.

Sezer, Elif. *The Oral and the Written in Ottoman Literature: The Reader Notes on the Story of Fîrûzşâh*. Istanbul: Libra Kitapçılık, 2015.

Sievert, Henning. "Verlorene Schätze—Bücher von Bürokraten in den *Muḫallefāt*-Registern." In *Buchkultur im Nahen Osten des 17. und 18. Jahrhunderts*, edited by Tobias Heinzelmann and Henning Sievert, 199–263. Berlin: Peter Lang, 2010.

Simonffy, Aladár V. *Ibrahim Müteferrika: Bahnbrecher des Buchdrucks in der Türkei*. Budapest: Dr. Vajna & Bokor, 1944.

Soysal, Özer. *Türk Kütüphaneciliği*. Ankara: Kültür Bakanlığı Kütüphaneler Genel Müdürlüğü, 1998–1999.

Tak, Ekrem, and Bilgin Aydın. "XVII. Yüzyılda İstanbul Medreselerinde Okutulan Kitaplar (Tereke Kayıtları Üzerine bir Değerlendirme)." *Dil ve Edebiyat Araştırmaları* 19 (2019): 183–236.

Tamdoğan-Abel, Işık. "L'écrit comme échec de l'oral? L'oralité des engagements et des règlements à travers les registres de cadis d'Adana au XVIIIᵉ siècle." *Revue du Monde Musulman et de la Méditerranée* 75–76 (1995): 155–65.

Tekin, Engin Cihad. *Osmanlı'da Kitap Kültürü ve Batı Dünyası: Avrupalı Seyyahların Bakış Açısından Osmanlı'da Kitap ve Kütüphane Kültürü (1453–1699)*. Istanbul: Hiperlink Yayınları, 2018.

Thackston, Wheeler M. *Album Prefaces and Other Documents on the History of Calligraphers and Painters*. Leiden: Brill, 2001.

Touati, Houari. *L'armoire à sagesse: Bibliothèques et collections en Islam*. Paris: Aubier, 2003.

Vatin, Nicolas. "Remarques sur l'oral et l'écrit dans l'administration ottomane au XVIᵉ siècle." *Revue du Monde Musulman et de la Méditerranée* 75–76 (1995): 143–54.

Wakin, Jeanette A. "Introduction." In *The Function of Documents in Islamic Law: The Chapters on Sales from Ṭaḥāwī's Kitāb al-shurūṭ al-kabir*, edited by Jeanette A. Wakin, 1–10. Albany: SUNY Press, 1972.

Watson, William J. "İbrahim Müteferrika and Turkish Incunabula." *Journal of the American Oriental Society* 88, no. 3 (1968): 435–41.

Witkam, Jan Just. "The Human Element between Text and Reader: The *ijāza* in Arabic Manuscripts." In *The Codicology of Islamic Manuscripts: Proceedings of the Second Conference of Al-Furqān Islamic Heritage Foundation, 4–5 December 1993*, edited by Yasin Dutton, 123–36. London: Al-Furqān Islamic Heritage Foundation, 1995.

Yazır, Mahmud Bedreddin. *Medeniyet Âleminde Yazı ve İslâm Medeniyetinde Kalem Güzeli*, edited by Uğur Derman, vol. 1, 74–75. Ankara: Diyanet İşleri Başkanlığı Yayınları, 1972–1989.

Yılmaz, Abdülkadir. *Türk Kitap Sanatları Tabir ve Istılahları*. Istanbul: Damla Yayınevi, 2004.

Yılmaz, Ömer Faruk. *Tarih Boyunca Sahhaflık ve İstanbul Sahhaflar Çarşısı*. Istanbul: Sahhaflar Derneği, 2005.

Zubčević, Asim. "Book Ownership in Ottoman Sarajevo, 1707–1828." PhD diss., Leiden University, 2015.

9

REWRITING AS AN OTTOMAN TRANSLATION PRACTICE

Two *Bīḫ-i Çīnī* Translations by Sixteenth-Century Poets

Gülşah Taşkın

Introduction

The Ottoman translation tradition lasted from the late thirteenth century to the first half of the nineteenth. During this time, the methods of translation and its practices changed and diversified as a result of changes in the Ottoman social structure and literary tradition. In recent years, in-depth academic studies on the Ottoman tradition show that translation in this tradition includes a wide variety of complex practices. The modern understanding of translation, which defines translation simply as a transfer from one language to another—often without taking into account the social or cultural context—fails to explain the complex structures of the various transfer practices of the Ottoman tradition. To fully understand these complex structures, it is necessary to undertake a close reading of Ottoman texts, which will reveal the specific conditions under which they were produced, and then to discuss the principal factors peculiar to the Ottoman tradition that shaped translators' translation strategies.

This chapter aims to reveal features that characterize Ottoman translation practices as reflected in translated texts. To accomplish this, I focus on a treatise on herbal medicinal preparation titled *Bīḫ-i Çīnī (Smilax saparna)*, which was translated by two sixteenth-century poets, Surūrī Muṣliḥ al-Dīn Muṣṭafā (d. 1561) and Maḫfī-i Gīlānī (d. after 1563), each of whom employed a different approach to translation. I highlight clues that speak to the general nature of Ottoman translation practices and to the form of dialogue and conflict the two translations shared. A comprehensive treatment of Ottoman translation practices is beyond the scope of this chapter, so I have limited my discussions to the sixteenth century, the classical period of the Ottoman literary tradition. In the first part of the chapter, I establish a historical framework and present the characteristics of the Ottoman translation tradition of the fifteenth and sixteenth centuries. In the second part, I present the theoretical framework of the article and explain the basic concepts of rewriting, poetics, and patronage, which are integral to Ottoman translation tradition. In the last section, I examine the two translations of *Bīḫ-i Çīnī* through the lens of these concepts and discuss how they reflect Ottoman translation practices. My hope is that this study will inspire more comprehensive studies on the Ottoman translation tradition.

116

DOI: 10.4324/9780429279270-13

Ottoman Translation in the Fifteenth and Sixteenth Centuries

Literary translation activities in the Ottoman period spanned from the late thirteenth to the first half of the nineteenth century. Translations and interpretations of many works in Arabic and Persian were undertaken from the late thirteenth century to the end of the fifteenth, which is considered the early period of the tradition.[1] As Saliha Paker noted, in the vast majority of these early translations, the primary purpose was to inform or educate the reader. For this reason, most often these were translations of religious, mystical, and scientific texts rather than literary ones.[2] The Turkish language of this period was dominated by Arabic and Persian vocabulary: Arabic was used primarily for scientific works and Persian for literary texts; however, there was also a steady development of Turkish as a language for literary works.[3] Although translation activity increased dramatically in the fifteenth century, sultans and statesmen had encouraged and supported translations of literary texts as early as the fourteenth century, during which time translations from Arabic and Persian played a significant role in the development of Ottoman Turkish and its literature.[4] Between 1450 and 1600, the classical age of Ottoman literature, a significant transformation occurred in the literary field that paralleled political and social changes. The existing patronage system was established and expanded in this period, Ottoman Turkish underwent a marked improvement,[5] and with new borrowings from Arabic and Persian, Ottoman Turkish became a language of both science and literature.[6]

In the sixteenth century, such changes were reflected in translation activities, as translated works increased in both number and the variety of genres. This was particularly the case with translations of literary texts, especially Persian classics, which were translated and annotated increasingly during this period and many times in the following centuries.[7] Notably, during the reign of Suleyman the Magnificent (1520–1566), language and literary activities, including translations, took on a classical tone. According to Saliha Paker, as a synthesis of the Arabic, Persian, and Turkish cultures and languages, an "Ottoman interculture" had become an independent system by the end of the sixteenth century, and poets who had mastered these three languages and were therefore intimately acquainted with the respective cultures produced literary translations.[8] To grasp the translation processes of these poets, it is necessary to touch on rewriting, poetics, and patronage, which form the basis of the close reading of the two texts analyzed here.

Rewriting, Poetics, and Patronage in the Ottoman Translation Tradition

In his theory of rewriting, André Lefevere evaluates translation practices in a social and cultural context. He maintains that language is the principal element that reflects a culture and thought system, with different languages reflecting different cultures. In all translations, changes are inevitably made to the source text in order to adapt to the culture, language, and social codes that the target readership understands or recognizes.[9] Regardless of their purpose, changes made to the source text in the translation process turn each translation into a rewriting of the source text.[10] In defining society as the environment of a literary system, Lefevere emphasizes that society and the literary system are mutually affective, so translation and rewriting practices are shaped by internal control factors of the literary system and external control factors of the society in which they are produced.[11] Internal elements (e.g., language, universe of discourse, and poetics) are part of the literary system, while external elements (e.g., patronage) operate outside it; each type has a decisive influence on translation strategies and the production of any literary text.[12] Rewriting is thus seen as directly related to the general character of the Ottoman translation tradition.

Saliha Paker's views on the Ottoman translation tradition and its relationship to rewriting overlap with Lefevere's theory. Due to the nature of translation, Paker emphasizes, it is impossible to transmit a source text "exactly." Structural differences between languages, the translator's level of knowledge of the topic, and his relationship with the source text all contribute to an inevitable change to each transfer in translation, resulting in a translation that differs somewhat from the source text.[13] This type of difference is one of the key points that define the character of the Ottoman translation tradition. According to Paker, translation in the Ottoman tradition includes a wide variety of practices, ranging from "exact" transfer to changing and reproducing the source text with additions and reductions. Unlike the modern understanding of translation, which accepts a one-to-one interdependence as the main criterion, the principal character of the Ottoman translation tradition is one in which the translation essentially overlaps with the source text but differs from it in certain respects: it is this difference which constitutes the rewriting aspect of Ottoman translation.[14] In the Ottoman translation tradition, those who transmitted texts from one language to another were generally poets, whom Paker refers to as "poet-translators."[15] Lefevere's rewriting theory is therefore particularly relevant in a context where poetics and patronage are the principal determining factors in the production process of Ottoman translations. The central question is how that influence manifests itself in the translations.

Poetics, in the broadest sense, is a collection of views on poetry, poets, and art. Ottoman translation practices are closely related to the poetics of Ottoman poetry. Saliha Paker, drawing on the works of Walter G. Andrews and Kemal Kahramanoğlu, focuses on the influence of Ottoman poetics on the translation tradition.[16] Paker attributes the poetics of Ottoman poetry to the idea of the "inimitable, divine original Qur'an," which is the common denominator of cultures in the domain of Islam. According to this idea, only one thing is original, the Qur'an, and everything that man produces is only repetition; in short, originality cannot be divined in any human product. This understanding created a dilemma for the Ottoman poets in search of originality: Tradition is based on the principle of repetition, but verbatim repetition is not acceptable and a good poet is expected to say something new—that is, to be creative.[17] As Paker emphasized, in the Ottoman translation tradition, one-to-one translation is often criticized, although it is accepted that, broadly speaking, translations are similar to the source text or contain duplication.[18] A good poet was expected to remain faithful to the original work to a degree, but he was also expected to expand on it—that is, to add cultural commentary in order to produce a translated text that displayed his skills.[19]

In the Ottoman Empire, a patronage system also influenced translation practices. Patronage had a strong influence on the production and dissemination of all forms of art, particularly literary texts. From the early days of the Empire, poets were supported by the sultans, most of whom were themselves poets, and by bureaucrats at all levels of the state.[20] Ottoman poets presented poems, especially eulogies (*qasidas*), to the sultans and the bureaucratic elite, often with the aim of receiving a state appointment or sinecure, obtaining a stipend, or securing patronage. However, patronage was not only a means of earning a stipend for the poets. It also helped establish a close relationship with the upper ranks of the state administration, a relationship that afforded a patronized poet the protection of a strong ruler, not to mention the prestige it bestowed on him in the poetry community.[21] To prove his worth, however, a poet had to differentiate himself from his competitors in a way that won him more respect.[22] As for the patron, in expressing his respect for both the art and the artist, he enhanced his own position and reputation, thus garnering prestige for both parties.[23] The patronage system thus played a significant role in the development of the Ottoman translation tradition, especially from the fifteenth century onwards

Rewriting as an Ottoman Translation Practice

when Ottoman sultans and statesmen supported translation activities and many works from Arabic and Persian were translated either with the encouragement of a patron or voluntarily by the poet.[24] The demands and expectations of the patron played an important role in the strategies a translator employed. Besides, the strategies individual translators adopted reflected their understanding of what a translation should be and in cases where these conceptualizations differed, a translation could become a tool for competing with another translator as well as a tool for gaining prestige. These factors, in conjunction with the patronage system and poetics, determined the character of rewriting practices that formed the basis of the Ottoman translation tradition.

This relationship between poetics, patronage, and rewriting in the Ottoman translation tradition is reflected in two translations of *Bīḫ-i Çīnī*, each of which illustrates a different translation strategy. *Bīḫ-i Çīnī* is a medical treatise on herbal medicine originally written in Hindī by a physician named Nūr Allāh (d. ?), who was known as ʿAlā al-Dīn.[25] In the treatise, the characteristics of the *bīḫ-i çīnī* plant, known today as *Smilax saparna*,[26] were described, along with its use in medicinal preparations. While little is known about the original author and the tract itself, we do know that the Turkish translations were based on a Persian translation that we do not currently possess. It was translated into Turkish twice during the reign of Suleyman the Magnificent. The first of these translations belongs to Surūrī Muṣliḥ al-Dīn Muṣṭafā, who was known for works such as *Sharḥ-i Mathnawī* (*Commentary on* [Jalāl al-Dīn Rūmī's] *Mathnawī*) and *Baḥr al-Maʿārif* (*Sea of Knowledge*). A noted scholar and poet, Surūrī was the teacher of Suleyman the Magnificent's son Prince Mustafa (d. 1553).[27] The exact date of his translation is unknown. The second and last known *Bīḫ-i Çīnī* translation was made by Maḫfī-i Gīlānī in 1556.[28] Maḫfī was a poet and a companion of the sultan of Gīlān, Muzaffer Khan (r. 1517–1537). Maḫfī took refuge with the Ottomans after Suleyman's two Iraqi (*Irakeyn*) campaigns.[29] He had been a highly respected poet in Gīlān but was not widely known in the Ottoman Empire.

What is particularly interesting about *Bīḫ-i Çīnī* is that it was translated into Turkish twice, which was highly unusual for a noncanonical text. The Maḫfī version is radically different from Surūrī's translation, and Maḫfī deems Surūrī's translation inadequate, citing a variety of reasons and suggesting that one of the motivations for his own translation was to challenge Surūrī. I would argue that a comparative analysis of these two translations, taking into account the criticisms that Maḫfī directed towards Surūrī's translation strategy and especially the poet's identity, will be useful in understanding (1) how rewriting, poetics, and patronage shaped translation practices and (2) how translation became a tool for competition.

Surūrī Versus Maḫfī-i Gīlānī: Two *Bīḫ-i Çīnī* Translations as Rewritings[30]

In the Ottoman translation tradition, factors such as the translator's motivation and personality, the target audience of the translator, and the individual to whom he intended to present the work all had a significant influence on translation practices.[31] In Ottoman translated texts, such information is usually found in the work's introduction (*sebeb-i teʾlīf*) and the conclusion (*ḫātime*).[32] The introduction and conclusion of the Surūrī and Maḫfī translations contain substantial clues as to how these factors shaped the translation strategies and the rewriting practices of the Ottoman translation tradition.

Why Did Surūrī Translate?

Surūrī begins his translation of *Bīḫ-i Çīnī* with the words "the humble Surūrī, who writes this work, informs and tells [the story of his reason for translating it] as follows."[33] After introducing himself only by name, he explains briefly how he came upon the work and why he chose to translate it. He states that a respected person of the period had sent him a Persian treatise and asked him to translate it into Turkish using clear and understandable expressions (*rūşen-beyān*), explanations, and exposition (*ṭarīḳ-i beyān ü şerḥ*) for the benefit of the general public.[34] As can be understood from a poem by Surūrī and a note in the margins at the beginning of the text, the respected person was ʿAbd al-Bāḳī Chelebi, a member of the privileged Fanārī-zāda family of the period with whom Surūrī had a close relationship.[35] However, following the explanation, Surūrī provides no information about the title or the content of the treatise. He finishes the introduction section with a few poems and prayers for ʿAbd al-Bāḳī Chelebi and begins the translation of the work with these words: "The author of the treatise mentioned above, whose name was Nūr Allāh, says the following."[36] Unlike the concluding section of the work, which provides several sentences giving health-related advice, this brief introduction sheds light on the translator's personality, the role of patronage, his target audience, and his approach to translation and rewriting practices.

One of the main motivations of Ottoman poets when translating was to demonstrate their poetic talent and produce a text that would surpass the source text in aesthetic terms. Poets would often set out these goals in the introduction and conclusion by comparing their own translations with the source text and by highlighting aspects of their own work. However, Surūrī, both a scholar and poet, referred neither to himself nor to the qualities of his translation, nor did he make any such claims of superiority. Surūrī was particularly famous for his commentaries and translations and was respected by the elite of the period, including Suleyman the Magnificent.[37] Having already secured a place in the patronage system, Surūrī's aim in translating *Bīḫ-i Čīnī* was to put the text, not his skills, in the foreground. This goal proved to be a factor that would shape his translation strategy and the rewriting nature of his *Bīḫ-i Čīnī* translation.

In addition, as determined by his patron, ʿAbd al-Bāḳī Chelebi, Surūrī's target audience was not a group that possessed sophisticated literary tastes, nor did they have the language skills to read the text in its Persian version. The purpose of his translation was therefore to provide a tangible benefit to the Turkish-reading public. With this in mind, the patron had stipulated that the translation must be clear and easy to understand (*rūşen-beyān*) and that an explanation must be provided in sections where Surūrī deemed it necessary (*ṭarīḳ-i beyān ü şerḥ*). To understand the production of a translation, one must pay attention to how and with what words it is defined.[38] The application of these techniques (*rūşen-beyān* and *ṭarīḳ-i beyān ü şerḥ*) in the Surūrī translation is an indication of how the patron shaped his translation.

Surūrī indeed uses simple language, with a predominance of Turkish words and phrases instead of Arabic and Persian ones. He explains the spelling and the meaning of some of the words and gives the Turkish names of common diseases in the marginal notes. He describes the plants and herbs used in producing the *bīḫ-i čīnī* medicinal preparation, where they grow, and the relative amounts of each for the herbal mixture. He also gives detailed information on the technical terms and Turkish units of measurements. This information does not appear in the Persian source text; Surūrī added it solely for the benefit of the Turkish readership specified by his patron. He also amended the source text, effectively producing a new text that resembles the source text but differs from it in many ways. As noted earlier in this chapter, any intervention in relation to the source text, regardless of the reason, means that it is rewritten. Surūrī's translation is, therefore, an example of a rewriting of *Bīḫ-i Čīnī*, where a benefit-oriented translation strategy is used in order to accommodate the expectations of the patron, the needs of the target audience, and motivations of the poet himself. Nevertheless, Surūrī's translation strategy was criticized by Maḥfī-i Gīlānī, who, challenging Surūrī, applied a different strategy that provides a different example of a rewriting of *Bīḫ-i Čīnī*.

Rewriting as an Ottoman Translation Practice

Why Did Maḥfī-i Gīlānī Translate?

Maḥfī's introduction is more detailed and thus longer than Surūrī's introductory remarks. Decorated with poems, it includes a self-introduction and an explanation of his reasons for translating *Bīh-i Çīnī* into Turkish. Maḥfī also praises Muzaffer Khan and Suleyman the Magnificent while criticizing Surūrī. In the concluding section, which includes the date of the translated text, the poet praises his translation and asks the reader for a prayer, a sharp contrast with Surūrī. And unlike Surūrī's translation, which is virtually anonymous, given that the poet's name is not mentioned throughout the translation, Maḥfī makes his presence known from the beginning to the end of the text and elevates himself throughout the translation. All of these elements indicate that different motivations underpin Maḥfī's translation. So what were Maḥfī's motivations and how did they affect his translation strategy?

Maḥfī's expresses that his reason for translating the work was that the majority of the people in the Ottoman lands prefer Turkish. He therefore strives to write in a language that will benefit Turkish readers and indicates that he will accept the prayers of the wise and thus be remembered.[39] These were among the principal motivations of virtually all Ottoman poets. However, some features that are repeatedly emphasized in Maḥfī's introduction and conclusion indicate that Maḥfī had other expectations from this translation. Maḥfī consistently emphasizes that (1) he was a poet, but not an ordinary one (he was a poet of Muzaffer Khan); (2) he translated *Bīh-i Çīnī* from the original Hindī into Persian at the behest of Muzaffer Khan; (3) he is now the prayer and servant of Suleyman the Magnificent in Istanbul (*Der-milk-i Ḳosṭanṭiniyye*); and (4) by translating *Bīh-i Çīnī* from Persian to Turkish, he reconciled the three languages (*bir iki üç dil muṭābıḳ eyledüm*).[40]

In the introduction to his *Bīh-i Çīnī* translation, he continually refers to the two sultans by name (Suleyman the Magnificent and Muzaffer Khan). At this juncture, an important point about Maḥfī should be noted: Because Maḥfī was not a widely recognized poet in the Ottoman lands, as understood from information provided in his other works and biographical sources, he was continuously in search of an influential patron. It was not only in the *Bīh-i Çīnī* translation that he tries to obtain the patronage of Suleyman the Magnificent. He aspired to ingratiate himself to the Ottoman sultan in the hope of obtaining the Suleyman's patronage in his other works.[41] It should not be forgotten that one of the factors that conferred prestige on poets in this period was a command of Arabic, Persian, and Turkish, which were esteemed languages (*elsine-i muʿtebere*).[42] He also continually emphasizes his language skills so as to drive home the point that he is a master poet who is fluent in three languages and that the languages are submissive to him, suggesting that Maḥfī completed this translation to prove that he was a talented poet. So Maḥfī's target audience is different from that of Surūrī in that the former aimed to reach an audience that had different expectations from a translation, knew esteemed languages, and possessed a taste for literature and knowledge. For this reason, Maḥfī's elevates himself through poetry, language, and patronage in his introduction, the combination of which determined the translation strategy and the general character of his translation.

Maḥfī uses artistic language in his translation of *Bīh-i Çīnī*, suffused with Arabic and Persian words, phrases, and literary depictions. He adorns the entire translation with his own Persian and Turkish poems and poetic episodes, giving the impression that it is a literary text rather than a medical treatise. In expanding the source text through poetic additions to display his creativity, Maḥfī produces a new text that resembles the source text but differs from it in many ways, as does Surūrī's translation. With his poems and poetic episodes, Maḥfī's translation is an example of a rewriting where an art-oriented strategy meets the expectations of the target audience or a patron and reflects the motivation of the poet. At this point, the most critical question is the following: If Maḥfī wanted to prove himself as a poet, he could have accomplished this by translating an "esteemed" literary work instead of a medical treatise. So why would he translate *Bīḥ-i Çīnī*, a work that was outside the corpus of the Ottoman tradition's supposedly esteemed literary or canonical texts and that had recently been translated by Surūrī, a master scholar, translator, commentator, and poet? This answer to this question leads us to the concept of retranslation.

Retranslation

Retranslation is often defined as the process of translating a previously translated text into the same language.[43] Works are sometimes retranslated because the translator is unaware of a previous translation, or because the text needs updating to reflect significant changes in language or social and cultural structure.[44] Canonical texts and classics in particular are retranslated in every culture. In the Ottoman translation tradition, it was common to retranslate religious, literary, and scientific works, especially the Qur'an and Persian classics, even in the same period. So within the span of a short period when there were no major changes in either language or the social and cultural milieu, what does it mean for a translator to translate a text that has not been traditionally regarded as a canonical work, and where the translator is aware of a previous translation?

Anthony Pym considers a retranslation produced under such circumstances an indicator of tension or conflict between translators' translation strategies.[45] Lawrence Venuti, basing his views on the concept of conflict, characterizes this type of retranslation as a challenge to the previous version(s). Through retranslation, a translator tries to prove his superiority and to make a noticeable difference through those points where his own translation departs from the previous version(s) he determines to be inadequate for any reason.[46] At this point, the concept of intertextuality, which is defined as making either explicit or implicit reference(s) to another text(s), comes into play. If the purpose of retranslation is to challenge the previous version(s), intertextuality is more intensely present in a retranslated text than in other translations. Through intertextuality, the translator highlights the differences in his own translation and proves his superiority by establishing a dialogue with the previous version(s).[47]

Intertextuality is not an alien or remote concept in the Ottoman translation tradition. Particularly in the introductions and conclusions of translated Ottoman texts, it is common for poets to compare their own translations to the source text or previous translations by making explicit or implicit references to them, sometimes for the purpose of eliciting praise or leveling criticism.

Maḥfī's translation strategy and the reasons for his retranslating *Bīḥ-i Çīnī* are also shaped by conflict, challenge, and intertextuality. Maḥfī, from the beginning of his introduction, elevates himself as a trilingual poet. Entering into direct dialogue with Surūrī's translation, Maḥfī escalates the tension between the two translation strategies, this time through poetics. This also serves to please his intended patron, Suleyman the Magnificent, who is also a prominent sultan poet.

Maḥfī launches into his criticism of Surūrī at the end of the introduction, first pointing out that the latter had translated the same treatise.[48] The reader is therefore left with no doubt that Maḥfī is aware of the previous translation. He maintains that Surūrī's translation is problematic in several respects: Surūrī was unable to translate Persian *mazmuna*s into Turkish, nor was he able to elucidate implicit meanings.[49] He also criticizes Surūrī's poetry in a poem. While conceding that these are complicated tasks, he implies that Surūrī is not acquainted with poetic editing and translating techniques. He ends his poem and the introduction with a question directed to

Rewriting as an Ottoman Translation Practice

Surūrī: "Oh Surūrī, you are a master poet! So, what style is this?"[50] In this way, Maḥfī focuses on the absence of three basic elements (essential in Ottoman poetics, especially in the sixteenth century) in the Surūrī translation: expressions/words (*lafẓ*), meaning (*ma'nā*), and style (*edā*).[51] According to Maḥfī, despite the fact that Surūrī was a poet, he did not use these elements expected in the tradition. Maḥfī's main purpose in revealing the shortcomings of the Surūrī's translation with intertextual references in the introduction was to prepare the reader for the idea that his own version met these expectations. Maḥfī then begins to translate *Bīḫ-i Çīnī*, expanding on the source text to magnify his talent, style, and literary identity through creative additions in line with the expectations of a good poet of the Ottoman translation tradition. Thus, Maḥfī creates another rewriting of the source text that uses a different strategy. In his introduction and the body of the text, he clearly stated his primary objective and, in so doing, elucidated how this would be accomplished. Finally, in the conclusion, he challenges Surūrī with the following words: "If Surūrī sees [this translation], he would bow down [before me] like the letter *mim* [in Arabic (م)]," thus concluding his own self-aggrandizement.[52]

All of the above shows that Maḥfī's motivations were not exclusively for the betterment of the public or to receive prayers. As an unrecognized poet in search of a patron, he tries to gain entrance to the system by elevating himself and by declaring deficiencies in the text of a poet such as Surūrī, who was already part of the system. In other words, Maḥfī uses translation as a competitive tool and a source of prestige.

Conclusion

I have tried to extrapolate the general characteristics of Ottoman translation practices as reflected in translated texts. The two different translations of the *Bīḫ-i Çīnī* treatise reveal the impossibility of talking about a uniform understanding of translation in the Ottoman Empire. Unlike the modern understanding of translation, translation in the Ottoman period is not just a language-to-language translation of the work. Saliha Paker pointed out that the Ottoman translation tradition has a complex structure that covers a wide range of rewriting practices.[53] Both translations examined reveal how patronage and poetics, which shaped Ottoman translation practices and strategies, had an effect on the overall character of rewritings, on the simultaneous existence of different strategies, and sometimes on the presence of tension and/or conflict. These examples, which show how competition can underlie a translation, prove that translation also functioned as a factor in the accretion of privilege and prestige in the Ottoman tradition.

Finally, the analysis of these two translations is remarkable in terms of its demonstration that tradition is not fixed and that works external to the accepted canon can contain data that shed light on the characteristic features of the Ottoman translation tradition. Much research and many studies have been undertaken on canonical works, but the most striking and interesting ones that are in need of analysis are those that are less obvious, or even hidden. It is necessary to understand what such works, which have hitherto remained on the sidelines, have to say in order for us to achieve a comprehensive understanding of the Ottoman translation tradition and to deliver a fuller analysis of the complex structure of the various transfer practices of this tradition.

Notes

1 Sadık Yazar, "Anadolu Sahası Klâsik Türk Edebiyatında Tercüme ve Şerh Geleneği" (PhD diss., Istanbul Üniversitesi, 2011), 41–42.
2 Saliha Paker, "Turkish Tradition," in *Routledge Encyclopedia of Translation Studies*, ed. Mona Baker and Gabriela Saldanha (London: Routledge, 2008), 552.

3 Selim S. Kuru, "The Literature of Rum: The Making of a Literary Tradition (1450–1600)," in *The Cambridge History of Turkey 2: The Ottoman Empire as a World Power, 1453–1603*, ed. Suraiya N. Faroqhi and Kate Fleet (Cambridge: Cambridge University Press, 2012), 558.

4 Ibid. Tijana Krstic, "Of Translation and Empire: Sixteenth-Century Ottoman Imperial Interpreters as Renaissance Go-Betweens," in *The Ottoman World*, ed. Christine Woodhead (London: Routledge, 2011), 131; Paker, "Turkish Tradition," 552; Yazar, "Anadolu," 135–36.

5 Kuru, "Literature of Rum," 550–92.

6 Mehmed Fuad Köprülü, "Anadolu'da Türk Dili ve Edebiyatının Tekâmülüne Umumî Bir Bakış, in *Türk Edebiyatı Tarihi*, ed. Mehmed Fuad Köprülü (Istanbul: Ötüken Neşriyat, 1980), 382.

7 Yazar, "Anadolu," 42–44.

8 Saliha Paker, "Translation as Terceme and Nazire: Culture-Bound Concepts and Their Implications for a Conceptual Framework for Research on Ottoman Translation History," in *Crosscultural Transgressions*, ed. Theo Hermans (Manchester: St. Jerome, 2002), 139.

9 André Lefevere, "Mother Courage's Cucumbers: Text, System and Refraction in a Theory of Literature," in *The Translation Studies Reader*, ed. Lawrence Venuti and Mona Baker (London: Routledge, 2004), 236–37.

10 André Lefevere, *Translation, Rewriting, and the Manipulation of Literary Fame* (London: Routledge, 1992), vii.

11 André Lefevere, "Why Waste Our Time on Rewrites?: The Trouble with Interpretation and the Role of Rewriting in an Alternative Paradigm," in *The Manipulation of Literature: Studies in Literary Translation*, ed. Theo Hermans (London: Routledge, 2014), 226.

12 Ibid., 232–33.

13 Saliha Paker, "Terceme, Te'lîf ve Özgünlük Meselesi," in *Metnin Hâlleri: Osmanlı'da Telif, Tercüme ve Şerh*, ed. Hatice Aynur et al. (Istanbul: Klasik, 2014), 40.

14 Ibid., 40–43.

15 Paker, "Translation as Terceme and Nazire," 120.

16 For these studies, see Walter G. Andrews, "Starting Over Again: Some Suggestions for Rethinking Ottoman Divan Poetry in the Context of Translation and Transmission," in *Translations: (Re)shaping of Literature and Culture*, ed. Saliha Paker (Istanbul: Boğaziçi University Press, 2002), 15–40; Kemal Kahramanoğlu, *Divan Şiiri: Değişen Dünyada Kaybolmuş Paradigma* (Konya: Çizgi Kitabevi, 2006).

17 Paker, "Terceme," 47–51; Saliha Paker, "On the Poetic Practices of 'a Singularly Uninventive People' and the Anxiety of Imitation: A Critical Re-appraisal in Terms of Translation, Creative Mediation and 'Originality,'" in *Tradition, Tension and Translation in Turkey*, edited by Şehnaz Tahir Gürçağlar et al. (Amsterdam: John Benjamins, 2015), 33–38.

18 Paker, "Terceme," 42–43.

19 Saliha Paker, "Translation, the Pursuit of Inventiveness and Ottoman Poetics: A Systemic Approach," in *Culture Contacts and the Making of Cultures: Papers in Homage to Itamar Even-Zohar*, ed. Rakafet Sela-Sheffy and Gideon Toury (Tel Aviv: Tel Aviv University, Unit of Culture Research, 2011), 467.

20 Halil İnalcık, *Şâir ve Patron: Patrimonyal Devlet ve Sanat Üzerinde Sosyolojik Bir İnceleme* (Ankara: Doğu-Batı Yayınları, 2003), 18–35.

21 Tûbâ Işınsu Durmuş, *Tutsan Elini Ben Fakirin: Osmanlı Edebiyatında Hamilik Geleneği* (Istanbul: Doğan Kitap, 2009), 91.

22 İnalcık, *Şâir ve Patron*, 16–17.

23 Ibid., 16; Durmuş, *Tutsan Elini Ben Fakirin*, 79–85.

24 Yazar, "Anadolu," 204–11.

25 Gülşah Taşkın, "Kanunî Döneminde 'Mahfî' Bir Şair: Mahfî-i Gilanî ve Bih-i Çinî Tercümesi," *Turkish Studies: International Periodical for The Languages, Literature and History of Turkish or Turkic* 7, no. 3 (Summer 2012): 2428–29.

26 *Smilax saparna* is a plant used today as a form of alternative medicine in the treatment of various diseases. Taşkın, "Kanunî," 2428.

27 İsmail Güleç, "Gelibolulu Musluhiddin Sürûrî, Hayatı, Kişiliği, Eserleri ve Bahrü'l-Ma'ârif İsimli Eseri," *Osmanlı Araştırmaları (The Journal of Ottoman Studies)* 21 (2001): 211–36. For the full text of the Sürûrî's translation, see Uğur Uzunkaya, "A Medical Manuscript on Sarsaparilla Translated by Surūrī: Terceme-i Risāle-i Bīḫ-i Çīnī," *Türkiyat Mecmuası* 27, no. 1 (2017): 343–65.

28 For the full text of the Maḫfî's translation, see Taşkın, "Kanunî," 2424–33.

29 Muzaffer Shāh (Emīr Dūbāc Khan) ruled in Gīlān, the administrative center of Reşt city in the north of Iran between 1517 and 1537. In 1534, he pledged obedience to Suleiman the Magnificent. Taşkın, "Kanunî," 2426.

Rewriting as an Ottoman Translation Practice

30 Unless otherwise indicated, translations from Surūrī's and Maḫfī's texts are my own. The original of this quote is as follows: "ṣāḥibü't-taḥrīr ve't-takrīr Surūrī fakīr ve ḥakīr şöyle beyān ve takrīr ve 'ayān ider ki."

31 Zehra Toska, "Evaluative Approaches to Translated Ottoman Turkish Literature in Future Research," in *Translations: (Re)shaping of Literature and Culture*, ed. Saliha Paker (Istanbul: Boğaziçi University Press, 2002), 61.

32 Cemal Demircioğlu's "Action-Oriented Discourse Analysis" methodology shows how the introduction and conclusion sections can be used in the analysis of Ottoman translated texts. Cemal Demircioğlu, *Çeviribilimde Tarih ve Tarihyazımı: Doğu-Batı Ekseninde Bir Karşılaştırma* (Istanbul: Boğaziçi Üniversitesi Yayınları, 2016), 156–93.

33 Uzunkaya, "Medical," 351.

34 Ibid.

35 Güleç, "Gelibolulu," 2.

36 Uzunkaya, "Medical," 351. The original of this quote is as follows: *"pes risāle-i mezkūrenüñ muṣannifi ve evrāḳ-ı meṣṭūrenüñ mü'ellifi Nūru'llāh ki 'alā ile meşhūr imiş dimiş."*

37 Güleç, "Gelibolulu," 211–15.

38 Paker, "Terceme," 44.

39 Taşkın, "Kanunî," 2435.

40 Ibid., 2434–35.

41 For findings, see Taşkın, "Kanunî," 2423–33; Gülşah Taşkın, "On Altıncı Yüzyıla Ait Otobiyografik Bir Eser: Arz-ı Hâl ü Sergüzeşt-i Gilanî," *Turkish Studies: International Periodical for the Languages, Literature and History of Turkish or Turkic* 8, no. 4 (Spring 2013): 1339–50; Gülşah Taşkın, "Altın Çağ'dan Yükselen Farklı Bir Ses: Mahfî-i Gilanî'nin Gözüyle Sultan Süleyman," *Journal of Turkish Studies* 43 (2015): 117–30.

42 Toska, "Evaluative," 71.

43 Şehnaz Tahir Gürçağlar, "Retranslation," in *Routledge Encyclopedia of Translation Studies*, ed. Mona Baker and Gabriela Saldanha (London: Routledge, 2008), 233.

44 Ibid., 234–35.

45 Anthony Pym, *Method in Translation History* (Manchester: St. Jerome, 1998), 82–83.

46 Lawrence Venuti, "Retranslations: The Creation of Value," *Translation and Culture: Bucknell Review: A Scholarly Journal of Letters, Arts and Sciences* 47, no. 1 (2004): 25–32.

47 Ibid., 31–34.

48 Taşkın, "Kanunî," 2435.

49 Ibid.

50 Ibid. The original of this quote is as follows: "sen ehl-i naẓmsın bu ne edādur."

51 Harun Tolasa, *Sehî, Lâtîfî, Âşık Çelebi Tezkirelerine Göre 16. Yüzyılda Edebiyat Araştırma ve Eleştirisi* (Ankara: Akçağ, 2002), 360–70.

52 Taşkın, "Kanunî," 2441. The original of this quote is as follows: "Ger göreydi bir naẓar Mollā Surūr/ Önine salar idi başın çü mīm."

53 Paker, "Terceme," 40–43.

References

Andrews, Walter G. "Starting Over Again: Some Suggestions for Rethinking Ottoman Divan Poetry in the Context of Translation and Transmission." In *Translations: (Re)shaping of Literature and Culture*, edited by Saliha Paker, 15–40. Istanbul: Boğaziçi University Press, 2002.

Demircioğlu, Cemal. *Çeviribilimde Tarih ve Tarihyazımı: Doğu-Batı Ekseninde Bir Karşılaştırma*. Istanbul: Boğaziçi Üniversitesi Yayınları, 2016.

Durmuş, Tûbâ Işınsu. *Tutsan Elini Ben Fakirin: Osmanlı Edebiyatında Hamilik Geleneği*. Istanbul: Doğan Kitap, 2009.

Güleç, İsmail. "Gelibolulu Musluhiddin Sürûrî, Hayatı, Kişiliği, Eserleri ve *Bahrü'l-Ma'ârif* İsimli Eseri." *Osmanlı Araştırmaları (The Journal of Ottoman Studies)* 21 (2001): 211–36.

Gürçağlar, Şehnaz Tahir. "Retranslation." In *Routledge Encyclopedia of Translation Studies*, edited by Mona Baker and Gabriela Saldanha, 233–36. London: Routledge, 2008.

İnalcık, Halil. *Şair ve Patron: Patrimonyal Devlet ve Sanat Üzerinde Sosyolojik Bir İnceleme*. Ankara: Doğu-Batı Yayınları, 2003.

Kahramanoğlu, Kemal. *Divan Şiiri: Değişen Dünyada Kaybolmuş Paradigma*. Konya: Çizgi Kitabevi, 2006.

Köprülü, Mehmed Fuad. "Anadolu'da Türk Dili ve Edebiyatının Tekâmülüne Umumî Bir Bakış." In *Türk Edebiyatı Tarihi*, edited by Mehmed Fuad Köprülü, 327–400. Istanbul: Ötüken Neşriyat, 1980.

Krstic, Tijana. "Of Translation and Empire: Sixteenth-Century Ottoman Imperial Interpreters as Renaissance Go-Betweens." In *The Ottoman World*, edited by Christine Woodhead, 130–42. London: Routledge, 2011.

Kuru, Selim S. "The Literature of Rum: The Making of a Literary Tradition (1450–1600)." In *The Cambridge History of Turkey 2: The Ottoman Empire as a World Power, 1453–1603*, edited by Suraiya N. Faroqhi and Kate Fleet, 548–92. Cambridge: Cambridge University Press, 2012.

Lefevere, André. *Translation, Rewriting, and the Manipulation of Literary Fame*. London: Routledge, 1992.

———. "Mother Courage's Cucumbers: Text, System and Refraction in a Theory of Literature." In *The Translation Studies Reader*, edited by Lawrence Venuti and Mona Baker, 233–49. London: Routledge, 2004.

———. "Why Waste Our Time on Rewrites?: The Trouble with Interpretation and the Role of Rewriting in an Alternative Paradigm." In *The Manipulation of Literature (Routledge Revivals): Studies in Literary Translation*, edited by Theo Hermans, 215–43. London: Routledge, 2014.

Paker, Saliha. "Translation as Terceme and Nazire: Culture-Bound Concepts and Their Implications for a Conceptual Framework for Research on Ottoman Translation History." In *Crosscultural Transgressions: Research Models in Translation Studies II, Historical and Ideological Issues*, edited by Theo Hermans, 120–43. Manchester and Northampton: St. Jerome, 2002.

———. "Turkish Tradition." In *Routledge Encyclopedia of Translation Studies*, edited by Mona Baker and Gabriela Saldanha, 550–59. London: Routledge, 2008.

———. "Translation, the Pursuit of Inventiveness and Ottoman Poetics: A Systemic Approach." In *Culture Contacts and the Making of Cultures: Papers in Homage to Itamar Even-Zohar*, edited by Rakafet Sela-Sheffy and Gideon Toury, 459–74. Tel Aviv: Tel Aviv University, Unit of Culture Research, 2011.

———. "Terceme, Te'lîf ve Özgünlük Meselesi." In *Metnin Hâlleri: Osmanlı'da Telif, Tercüme ve Şerh*, edited by Hatice Aynur, Müjgân Çakır, Hanife Koncu, Selim S. Kuru, and Ali Emre Özyıldırım, 36–71. Istanbul: Klasik, 2014.

———. "On the Poetic Practices of 'a Singularly Uninventive People' and the Anxiety of Imitation: A Critical Re-appraisal in Terms of Translation, Creative Mediation and 'Originality.'" In *Tradition, Tension and Translation in Turkey*, edited by Şehnaz Tahir Gürçağlar, Saliha Paker, and John Milton, 27–52. Amsterdam: John Benjamins, 2015.

Pym, Anthony. *Method in Translation History*. Manchester: St. Jerome, 1998.

Saraçoğlu, Tuba Nur. "Fenârî Ailesi (Fenârîzâdeler) ve Aile Vakıflarına Bağlı Yapılar." In *Uluslararası Molla Fenârî Sempozyumu Bildiriler (4–6 Aralık 2009 Bursa)*, 65–86. Bursa: Büyükşehir Belediyesi Yayınları, 2010.

Taşkın, Gülşah. "Kanunî Döneminde "Mahfî" Bir Şair: Mahfî-i Gilanî ve *Bih-i Çinî* Tercümesi." *Turkish Studies: International Periodical for The Languages, Literature and History of Turkish or Turkic (Prof. Dr. Sabahattin Küçük Armağanı)* 7, no. 3 (Summer 2012): 2423–43.

———. "On Altıncı Yüzyıla Ait Otobiyografik Bir Eser: *Arz-ı Hâl ü Sergüzeşt-i Gilanî.*" *Turkish Studies: International Periodical for The Languages, Literature and History of Turkish or Turkic* 8, no. 4 (Spring 2013): 1339–50.

———. "Altın Çağ'dan Yükselen Farklı Bir Ses: Mahfî-i Gilanî'nin Gözüyle Sultan Süleyman." *Journal of Turkish Studies (Prof. Dr. Yusuf Oğuzoğlu Armağanı)* 43 (2015): 117–30.

Tolasa, Harun. *Sehî, Lâtîfî, Âşık Çelebi Tezkirelerine Göre 16. Yüzyılda Edebiyat Araştırma ve Eleştirisi*. Ankara: Akçağ, 2002.

Toska, Zehra. "Evaluative Approaches to Translated Ottoman Turkish Literature in Future Research." In *Translations: (Re)shaping of Literature and Culture*, edited by Saliha Paker, 58–76. Istanbul: Boğaziçi University Press, 2002.

Uzunkaya, Uğur. "A Medical Manuscript on Sarsaparilla Translated by Surūrī: *Terceme-i Risāle-i Bīḫ-i Çīnī.*" *Türkiyat Mecmuası* 27, no. 1 (2017): 343–65.

Venuti, Lawrence. "Retranslations: The Creation of Value." *Translation and Culture: Bucknell Review: A Scholarly Journal of Letters, Arts and Sciences* 47, no. 1 (2004): 25–38.

Yazar, Sadık. "Anadolu Sahası Klâsik Türk Edebiyatında Tercüme ve Şerh Geleneği." PhD diss., Istanbul Üniversitesi, 2011.

10

NARRATIVE AS THE LITERARY PUBLIC

Reader and Author Figures in Modern Ottoman Turkish Literature (1866–1896)

Fatih Altuğ

In modern Ottoman Turkish literature, there is minimal information about how many books were printed, how much they were read, and to which communities, cities, and genders the readers belonged. While it is difficult to make statistical and sociological analyses based on this information, it is possible to observe and analyze the essential relationship dynamics that emerge in the literary public by closely examining the fictional texts. One can trace how Ottoman authors envisaged authorship, readership, and the multilayered relationship between reader and writer in works of fiction and their forewords.

Authorship and readership performances represented in literary texts contain clues about how the texts envisaged the modern Ottoman subject. The representations of the literary public that one finds in fictional texts also have implications for Ottoman authors' understanding of the public sphere. This chapter focuses on the texts of Namık Kemal (1840–1888), Ahmet Mithat (1844–1912), Ebuzziya Tevfik (1849–1913), Nabizade Nazım (1862–1893), and Fatma Fahrünnisa (1876–1969). I will discuss how these texts represent authorship and readership and demonstrate relations between the structure of narrative and the dynamics of the literary public.

Leaving a Mark on the World and on Readers

The widespread influence of the novel and drama, the dominant genres of modern Turkish literature in the Ottoman period, over the literary public began primarily in the 1870s. The historiography of modern Turkish literature can be imagined as a line passing through Şinasi, Namık Kemal, Recaizâde Ekrem, and Abdülhak Hamid as the central axis of literary modernization. Namık Kemal is the focal point of this axis and is seen as the "founding father" by many critics. He was also a political activist who fought for the proclamation of constitutionalism in the Ottoman Empire. He was influential in the spread of modern literary genres with his novels and theater plays written in the 1870s. The novel *İntibah* [The Awakening, 1875] and plays such as *Vatan Yahut Silistre* [Homeland or Silistra, 1873] and *Gülnihal* [1875] have been considered models that contain the standards of the genres. He published an article in 1866 titled "Lisan-i Osmaninin Edebiyatı Hakkında Bazı Mülahazatı Şamildir" [Concerning Some Views on the Literature of the Ottoman Language], which is regarded as the manifesto of modern Turkish literature. Here, Namık Kemal enumerates the characteristics of the ideal literary work from

DOI: 10.4324/9780429279270-14

127

the political, bureaucratic, national, and psychological perspectives. After pointing out the deficiencies of classical Ottoman literature from these perspectives, he introduces the reader to his project of establishing new literature. At the core of this project lies the question, "Why does a human write?" Namık Kemal builds his argumentation on the ontological meaning of writing. Here the keyword is *eser*, which means both "[literary] work" and "mark" in Turkish. Namık Kemal connects writing and leaving a mark in the world by referring to the double meaning of the word *eser*. The article begins with a quotation from Namık Kemal's poem: "Parts of the human body are heading towards extinction speedily / Leaving marks [works] brings permanence."[1] If extinction is the body's destiny, humans can only become immortal by bequeathing their work to the world. In fact, the basis of human dignity lies in leaving a souvenir in the world for the good of humanity even while living a life that fades. According to this perspective of authorship, producing a work makes up for death.

Namık Kemal regards a word stored in people's memories and passed on from one generation to another, under conditions where even the most solid architectural work can disappear in time, as the most permanent thing in the world. He forges an essential link between humankind and the word and describes the word with bodily metaphors. The word is the means of exchanging ideas, and this exchange establishes civilized relationships between people. The word, regarded as a compensation for death, is like a young body that will not get older over the years. The figure of the word is considered together with the figure of the body. The word must have two characteristics: "a neat disposition" (*tenasüb-i endam*) and "a healthy and authentic meaning" (*sıhhat-i meal*).[2] Respectively, they correspond to the evenness of the human body and a mature inner world. The harmonious unity of these two elements depends on the fact that a word affects its interlocutors and wins the hearts of its listeners/readers. This effect is permanent.

Namık Kemal considers the form, originality, and property rights of a literary work interwoven: If a work lacks beautiful expression, this means one can quickly plagiarize it. A work without unique expression is like a jewel without a case: It can easily be stolen. Hence, the beauty of form ensures the originality of the work; it makes it an author's property. The work's influence begins to spread to other areas only after the author and the work establish a tight bond. Accordingly, a word is more powerful than a sword when it comes to changing people's minds. In the public sphere, the power of expression is more crucial than military power. Literature makes its interlocutors more decent and changes their state of conscience, expanding their ideas and effectively ensuring national unity.

Writing a literary work is also a technology of power for Namık Kemal. The author leaves a mark on the world through their work, which shapes people and subjects them to truth. To understand how Namık Kemal's vision of being a writer understands the reader, let us review the foreword of his novel *İntibah*, published in 1875. Namık Kemal, who states the main aim of fiction is to make people more moral, asks why it is necessary to read novels rather than classical literature or morality books. Against a critic who claimed in a news article that Hariri's *Maqamat* or Kınalızade's *Ahlak-ı Alai*[3] was more moralizing than a novel, Namık Kemal, describing *Maqamat* as a corruptor of morality, puts the difference between a novel and a book of morality at the center of the debate. Even though he likes *Ahlak-ı Alai* in terms of moral content, he thinks that moral improvement through reading this book is like being reformed through imprisonment. However, improving one's moral state by reading novels is like being educated in a school that has a lovely and tidy garden. Morality is learned and internalized through spaciousness and fun, not through the violence of being enclosed. Namık Kemal emphasizes the importance of presenting morality or other truths to the reader by making a story out of them rather than giving them as they are.

Narrative as the Literary Public

In the parable in *İntibah*'s foreword, Namık Kemal contrasts truth and fiction with the metaphor of the female body. Truth (*Hakikat*), envisaged as a naked girl, can only become acceptable when Fiction (*Hikâye*) covers her up, and Fiction without makeup is thought of as an abject body. Having a grotesque appearance, Fiction gains acceptance from the reader first by covering her body with makeup and turning herself into a cloth covering Truth.[4] This parable also points to the method Namık Kemal followed while writing *İntibah*. Choosing to disguise wise words with love, Kemal describes the authorial act performed in the novel as veiling the "virgin dream" with an imaginary story. For him, analyzing human conscience is one of the functions of writing a novel. It is impossible to discover the secrets in a human body until we look deeply into the unknown places of the heart. Because people test the ideas they come across in novels in the experiences and affects of the heart hidden in their minds, it is necessary to know readers' psychological qualities and practices of reception to impress them. For Namık Kemal, the novel is a technique of power used to subject the reader to certain ideals. With stylistic and thematic techniques that make the reader open themselves up to other feelings, ideas, and entities, they can absorb the truth and emotion in Namık Kemal's ideal. As a type of relationship where a person experiences opening her/his heart to another person, love is at the center of the novel as a genre. In his project, producing the modern Ottoman subject and writing and reading a novel based on love are intertwined.[5]

The Imaginary Society of Authors and Readers

Late Ottoman and early Republican intellectuals ascribed a founding role to Namık Kemal, while post-1990 literary scholars centered Ahmet Mithat while analyzing modern Ottoman Turkish literature. Ahmet Mithat was the most prolific literature writer in the second half of the nineteenth century. We observe a unique assemblage of experimentalism and conservatism in his novels, stories, and articles. In all his texts, the tension between democracy and authoritarianism can be perceived. He establishes the relationship between authorship and readership by setting up a dialogue with subjectivity and sociality. Just like Namık Kemal, Ahmet Mithat also begins with the ontological dimension: The reader's encounter with a text means that she/he meets an author with a lower or higher mental capacity. Reading is meaningful only when the author has a higher moral or intellectual level. However, the reader is disturbed when they are called from a higher level because if they heed this call, they will have to give up their current state and make an effort to achieve a higher one. Like Namık Kemal, Ahmet Mithat links reading to the relationship between life and death. People want a longer life to maximize the events that they take pleasure in observing. This pleasure decreases with the death of one's friends. However, if one stops considering living as just going forward and starts turning to the past, and if one attributes past experiences to oneself, the pleasure and value of life will increase. In this regard, reading books is a practice that compensates for the absence of dead friends, helps one bring past experiences to the present, and enhances the vividness of life.[6]

One can see the competition between the desire for reading and sexual desire in Ahmet Mithat's texts in the example of Akile in his novel *Felsefe-i Zenan* [Women's Philosophy, 1870]. While Zekiye and Akile have the ideal of living autonomously without being dependent on men, Zekiye decides to marry. In the face of this decision, Akile defends an autonomous life in this way: While for a woman marrying means subjecting oneself to a man's desires and lust, being alone means being free of this trouble. A lonely woman can dream in her bed and even incorporate the dreams of others into her reveries by reading a book. Akile defines this act of reading as "having fun collectively by signing a contract to build a society in the imagination [*hayılhane*]."[7] Claiming that the world is a dream, she thinks that the imaginary society she has established through books is more earthly than sexual intercourse. While body and sexuality make women passive and subject them to a man's lust, what is gained through reading is authentic social experience.

In *Teehhül* [Marriage, 1870], Mazlum Bey, a man who involuntarily gets married off to Sabire Hanım, uses the excuse of reading a book to abstain from the wedding night.[8] In Ahmet Mithat's works, reading novels can lead to one learning about or falling into the hazards of sexuality. Reading novels can also stimulate sexual drive and encourage the reader sexually. For Ahmet Mithat, the issue is not the denial of sexuality or the prohibition of reading; rather, it is that the control achieved through novels draws sexuality into a legitimate realm.

In *Bahtiyarlık* [Happiness, 1885], Ahmet Mithat compares the attitudes of French and British people towards girls' reading novels. French people do not let their daughters read a novel since they believe novels are tempting. They also raise their daughters oppressively until they get married. Consequently, young girls have a weak loyalty to their marriage and are inclined to other "flirtations" as they have not experienced the facts of life and possible sexual deviations in their imaginations before. On the other hand, British families leave their daughters relatively free to read novels. Thus, the young girls who have experienced and contemplated the possible dangers of adulthood and marriage in their imaginations make more chaste choices when they face these dangers in reality.[9]

Ahmet Mithat argues that emphasizing the interaction between reading and imagination helps achieve education in chastity provided by reading novels helps maintain the power of social norms and control deviations from these standards. He considers the community between the author and the reader actualized in the imagination. He uses the word "*hayalhane*," the place where Karagöz plays are performed, to describe this imaginary community. While reading the events and manners in a novel, the reader simultaneously experiences them and performs them in their imagination (*hayalhane*). Through this experience, one internalizes positive or negative moral values and facts.

The traffic between the reader and the text is bidirectional. On the one hand, texts stimulate the reader's mind and imagination and affect them. On the other hand, the reader gets involved in the world of the text; they become one of the fictional characters and join the movement in this world. The narrative dynamics in Ahmet Mithat's texts incorporate readers, genres, processes of reading and writing, and social relationships. Most of his fiction is formed by incorporating oral or written language (rumors, news, literary texts) into the story's discourse. He states his source and the fundamental transformation he applied to this source, especially in his introductory sentences or forewords. For example, Ahmet Mithat's fictional discourse is full of metaphors from the construction of buildings. A text is "built" using other oral or written discourses as a "foundation." He first takes another text as a foundation to build a fictional structure, then extends and adorns (*bast* and *temhid*) that foundation, adds volume to it, and in this way the text transforms (*ifrağ*) into a novel. The literary structure is like a built space and the writer uses techniques from construction as part of his writerly approach.

Ahmet Mithat's literary production has social aspects as well as architectural dimensions. Reading his texts becomes a three-dimensional, social experience; it is an experience of a society in which authors, readers, assemblies, people, texts, and genres are intertwined, related to one other, and tied together in the process of transforming and being transformed.[10] His metafictional work *Müşahedat*[11] [Observations, 1891] represents the novel's formation, writing, and reading processes. At the beginning of the text, the authorial figure introduces the cast of characters that exemplify the cosmopolitan aspects of Ottoman Istanbul. Ahmet Mithat, listening to the conversation of three Armenian women, is curious about the heartbreaking love story they tell and wants to write a news article about it. However, as he meets the women and gathers data for his article, he realizes that the incident is much more intricate and thinks writing a novel would be more suitable. He meets the other people involved in the incident, listens to the story from their perspectives, and prepares the novel's first draft. After gathering everyone involved in the story gathered, he reads the novel to them and receives feedback. *Müşahedat* also includes the reading process itself. The protagonists become the first readers/listeners of the novel and the text's first critics. *Müşahedat* presents the intersectional and tense relationships of late nineteenth-century Istanbul and constructs itself into a community where writers, readers, and characters come together and one can follow the relationships and flows between them.

His novel *Karı Koca Masalı* [A Husband and Wife's Tale, 1875], which begins as if narrating a relationship between a husband and wife, is based on dialogue with the reader and constant digressions from the topic. While metafiction and fiction entangle in *Müşahedat*, metafiction suspends the fictional plot in *Karı Koca Masalı*.[12] As soon as the novel begins, the author attempts to talk to the reader and guess their expectations about the text. The author first discusses the question "How should a novel begin?" with the reader by evaluating the old and the new traditions of writing forewords. This discussion about the nature of the foreword is the foreword itself.

The dialogue between the author figure and the reader figure forms the basis of the novel rather than the marriage story that somehow cannot be told. There is an exchange of opinions about reading and writing conventions throughout the text. The author calls on the reader, the reader interrupts the author, and both sides are stuck together. This conversation addresses many issues regarding the author-reader relationship: It presents the differences and the similarities between old reading and writing practices and new ones. The author figure proves his authenticity by demonstrating the old and new mistakes.

As a text that does not rely on a specific plot but is rather about narration itself, *Karı Koca Masalı* recommends slow reading. The principles of narrative economy here are different from the general kind: Ahmet Mithat criticizes the form of narrative economy that relies on the best representation of events and situations using the fewest words. He supports an economy in which an abundance of words is in circulation. The fact that the relationship between the author and the reader is called an "agreement" is also a sign of the economic imagination of *Karı Koca Masalı*. This text, recommended to be consumed slowly, is also a performance. Ahmet Mithat produces a text in which the narrative voice performs various modes of reading and writing.

The Text as a Critique of Literary Public

In addition to Ahmet Mithat, the fictional texts of writers such as Ebüzziya Tevfik and Nabizade Nazım also represent the dynamics of the Ottoman literary public. In the 1880s, multi-perspective and multi-sited texts emerged, showing how a book circulated among readers, writers, critics, publishers, and bookstores. Ebüzziya Tevfik, who shared common political ideals with Namık Kemal, is known for his pioneering entrepreneurship in journalism and printing sectors rather than his literary texts. In his little-known story "Bir Kitabın Sergüzeşti" [The Adventure of a Book, 1885], Ebüzziya Tevfik describes a young poet's effort to publish his poetry book with a narrative form in which both the poet and the book are narrators. The narrative, which takes place in the poet's mind, the printing house, bookstore, newspaper office, and the grocery store, presents the conditions of the 1880s literary public by also mentioning the names of real publishers such as Arakel. The text begins by describing the psychological and social aspects of a book's formation in the poet's mind and ends with the book being sold as a paper bag in a grocery store and with the poet quitting poetry to begin selling rice.[13]

The story also shows the genre dynamics of the 1880s. It was challenging to publish a poetry book at a time when the novel was in demand. The poet, believing that he is a genius and that his book will be a bestseller, does not attract publishers, booksellers, or critics, and decides to distribute and promote his book himself. In the second half of the text, the book itself becomes the narrator. The book details the decline of its own economic and symbolic value. We read which books customers are interested in through the eyes of the book waiting to be sold on the bookstore shelf. Ebüzziya Tevfik criticizes the poet alongside the other actors of the literary public, such as critics, publishers, and readers. A romantic and idealized understanding of poetry is a topic he mocks as much as the capitalist publishing market. He strengthens his panoramic representation of the literary public of the 1880s by citing the names of real books and publishers.

Another source for observing and analyzing the dynamics of the Ottoman literary public is Nabizade Nazım, a writer who was a follower of naturalism and died very young. In his novels and novellas, he describes and analyzes sexual desires, affects, and moods from the perspective of physiological psychology. In his novella "Seyyie-i Tesamüh" [The Evils of Indulgence, 1891], the issue of a novel's writing and publishing processes are interwoven with its reception by critics and readers. Nabizade Nazım, fictionalizing his criticism of the 1880s literary public, shifts the historical plane of events to the 1860s. Although the first novels in Ottoman Turkish were published after 1870, the events in "Seyyie-i Tesamüh" occur in 1862 in a vibrant novel culture. There is an announcement in the newspaper *Tercüman-ı Ahval*[14] that the novel of a brilliant 17-year-old author, Necip Bey, will be serialized. The famous writer of the newspaper, Safvet Bey, also writes an article praising the novel for its greatness, broadness of thinking, brilliant thought, fluency, and delicacy of feeling. Afterward, the focus shifts to Vahit Bey, who reads those reviews and is quite skeptical about a 17-year-old author being this brilliant. Vahit Bey and his intellectual friends discuss rumors of the author's identity and the doubt regarding whether someone that age can be a genius. Readers get curious and impatient as the newspaper announces that the novel's serialization will begin soon. In the meantime, *Tercüman-ı Ahval* publishes Asım Bey's poem praising the young author and his novel.

In the third section, the text focuses on the young author. One can follow his writing process, primary sources, and desire for reputation. This section also describes the dynamics of picking a genre or a theme and writing a novel instead of poetry or drama. However, even though he has an intense desire to write, his authorial practice is inhibited even before it begins. The next day, while reading *Le Moulin Rouge* by Xavier de Montépin, his body becomes inflamed with envy. Elated, he starts writing. This time his pen obeys him like a sheep in a flock. As his imagination overflows his mind, his pen stains the white paper. Necip Bey feels that fame is smiling upon him as he writes. He dreams that he becomes famous in the literary world, his works are translated into French and German, he puts his stamp on history, and marries the girl he loves. However, this trance state of writing is interrupted when the maid enters. His pen starts to disobey him. With these creative instabilities, Necip Bey reaches the fifth part of his novel.

Thereafter, the focus shifts to Safvet Bey, the writer of the newspaper and editor of the novel. As a prestigious author, Safvet Bey is famous for writing commendatory prefaces (*takriz*) for new writers. Since a work can barely be published without a praise letter, and literary value is associated with these letters, writers like Safvet Bey have a powerful position in the literary field. Simply because Safvet Bey wants his daughter to get engaged to the author, the son of an influential family, he serializes the novel with excessive praises and revisions. Since Nabizade Nazım included Necip Bey's novel, the actual reader simultaneously reads the novel with the fictional readers. The novel makes waves in the literary world represented in *Seyyie-i Tesamüh*. While some think that the novel is ridiculous and inappropriate, many like it. Many people think that they should like the novel because Safvet Bey did.

By constantly shifting the focus of the narration, Nabizade Nazım presents a multi-perspective portrait of the literary public. And in fictionalizing the intricate relationships consisting of the

Narrative as the Literary Public

author, reader, critic, editor, and journalist, he revealed the literary public's interests, tensions, and desires.

Gendering the Literary Public[15]

In the 1890s, women authors became more visible in modern Turkish literature. In 1877, Zafer Hanım published *Aşk-ı Vatan* [Love for Homeland], the first novel written by a woman. The second novel written by a woman was titled *Rehyab-ı Zafer* [Victorious] and was published 13 years after *Aşk-ı Vatan*. We still do not know the author's identity as it was signed only by "A Woman."[16] In 1891, the novel *Hayal ve Hakikat* [Dream and Reality] written jointly by Fatma Aliye and Ahmet Mithat, was serialized in the newspaper *Tercüman-ı Hakikat*. Fatma Aliye was named only as "A Woman." In 1892, Fatma Aliye published her novel *Muhadarat* [Face-to-Face Conversations], but this time published it alone and under her name. In the same year, Selma Rıza began to write the novel *Uhuvvet* [Fraternity]. While women wrote no novels between 1877 and 1890, there was an increase in literary activity as of the 1890s.

In the second phase of this activity, there were introductions of female authors to the literary public by male authors. In 1893, Ahmet Mithat published a book titled *Bir Muharrire-i Osmaniyenin Neşeti* [Emergence of an Ottoman Woman Writer] about Fatma Aliye. This (auto) biographical text consisted of the letters between Fatma Aliye and the narration of Ahmet Mithat and portrayed the evolution of a young female author via the male writer. In the same year, Avanzade Mehmed Süleyman's book *Muharrir Kadınlar* [Writer-Women] was published. This book consisted of articles that collected the life stories and literary accomplishments of European female authors of the nineteenth century. In the anthology *Muharrerat-ı Nisvan* prepared by Mustafa Reşid in 1895, the male writer became the compiler and most of the work was composed of writings by women named Sabriye, Bedia, Fatma Aliye, H. Remziye, Ulviye, and Seniye. *Nevsal-i Nisvan*, a women's yearbook prepared by Avanzade Mehmed Süleyman in 1897, included the works written or translated by Nigâr Hanım, Hamiyet Zehra, Makbule Leman, Fatma Fahrünnisa, Emine Semiye, and Muallime Nazime. Female authors reached the literary public through men before 1895, and male authors represented the generation of female authors through anthologies and yearbooks. The increase in these types of works also meant an increase in female readers.

After 1895, there was a significant acceleration in the number of female authors and fictional works. Authors such as İsmet Hanım, P. Fahriye, Rana bint-i Safvet, M. Nigar, Münire, Lamia, and Dilpezir began their literary careers. Fatma Aliye and her sister Emiye Semiye had their most productive years between 1895 and 1900 and published several stories and novels one after another. Ahmet Rasim, a substantial male figure in popular literature, pretended to be a female writer under the pseudonym A. Rasime. *Hanımlara Mahsus Gazete* [Newspaper for Ladies], a newspaper published continuously from 1895 to 1908, was the primary production medium for the new generation of female authors. In this context in which women defined themselves and their readers as women and emphasized their femininity while writing and publishing their works mostly in female-specific channels, the Ottoman literary field became gendered.

The foreword of Fatma Fahrünnisa's novel *Dilharap* [Heart in Ruins],[17] serialized in *Hanımlara Mahsus Gazete* in 1896, is representative of the women's writing and readership environment at this time. What made Fatma Fahrünnisa decide to write a novel after she had stood up against both the novel and drama as genres? A year before *Dilharap*, her text "Romanlar ve Tiyatrolar" emphasized the negative potential of these two genres to influence its interlocutors. Yet *Dilharap*'s foreword presents the context of this transformation: A group of women writers and readers gathered at Fatma Fahrünnisa's house and had a collective discussion that began with a guest's desire to peruse Fatma Fahrünnisa's library books. However, the anti-novelist writer had gotten rid of all the novels in her library except for those by Jules Verne. Being much more sympathetic to the novel genre than the author, the two readers began talking about types of fiction. They both tended towards sentimental, naturalist novels that analyze characters' inner world in-depth, rather than the crime novels they used to read but then decided ruined their nerves and threw them off balance.

Fatma Fahrünnisa preserves her anti-novel attitude even against the novels that these two women regard as texts full of wisdom that allow people to get to know themselves and others. According to Fatma Fahrünnisa, novels do not refine, rehabilitate, or purge one's morals, situation, and personality. Their benefits are insignificant compared to the harm they cause. While her friend believes that examples of virtue presented in novels stimulate and awaken the mind and the heart, for Fatma Fahrünnisa, a novel may have a positive effect, involve excellent morals, and stimulate that kind of morality in the reader, its influence is temporary. It cannot be internalized and sooner or later disappears.

In this foreword, she depicts a rational public that believes in consensus through a reciprocal exchange of ideas in a free environment. The communication between different voices of the foreword replaces the judgmental voice of the article itself. This is a setting where nobody is compelled to agree. It idealizes a type of relationship where ideas change and develop through reciprocal discussion.

The change of opinion that made Fatma Fahrünnisa write *Dilharap* occurred when argumentation and personal experience come together. In the foreword, one woman in particular stands out among the female readers and authors in Fatma Fahrünnisa's living room. Describing her, one of the women says that what she lived through would make a great novel. When the author says that she could change her mind easily if she is convinced of this, the troubled woman approaches the author and they begin speaking in private. The woman wants her experiences to become a novel. She desires her misfortune to be presented to other women via the writer, thus becoming a guiding reference for women. According to Fatma Fahrünnisa, these stories are not compelling even when a more excellent author writes them because novels do not have that kind of impact. Novels try to influence readers by making women's affects and the tragedies they have suffered public, but this effort is clearly pointless as there has been no change in the situation of women. Fatma Fahrünnisa adds another dimension to her claim when she receives a reproachful objection from the woman: Even if she believed in such a novel, she would not have the necessary literary capital to write it correctly. Furthermore, she is clueless about what exactly happened to her friend.

When the private conversation between them is shared with the other women at the house, the author explains why she will not write this novel to her friends: One cannot write a feeling she has not personally experienced. To write the tragedy of another, the author must experience the exact feeling herself. However, with the insistence of the other woman and unfortunate one who will become the heroine of the novel, the author is persuaded that feelings can be translated and that they can be conveyed through writing and reading novels. The novel aims to intensify the companionship between women and begins through this collective discussion of women who address each other as "sister" and "dear." Thus, the story of the novel's formation is included in its preface. It was a discussion on the novel among female readers and authors that initiated the process through which the female heroine persuades the anti-novelist author to write the novel. The foreword presents a public based on criticism and discussion, in which the author, readers, and the novel's protagonist gather together and bond in sisterhood.

Narrative as the Literary Public

Conclusion

By focusing on the texts of Namık Kemal, Ahmet Mithat, Ebüzziya Tevfik, Nabizade Nazım, and Fatma Fahrünnisa, I tried to show how they represented the dynamics of the Ottoman literary public. In a context in which sociological and statistical data on Ottoman readers and writers are minimal, literary texts offer us ample opportunities to analyze the motivations of authors, the demands of readers, the tension and alliances of the publishing world, the anxieties and concerns about reading and writing, and the gender of the literary public. Moreover, the authors in question did not merely represent these relationships but intricately linked narrative form itself to this creation of a new society and literary relations.

The opinions and themes depicted by Namık Kemal in his "Lisan-ı Osmani" article, one of the founding texts of modern Ottoman literature, were also discussed and thematized by other writers of the period. For these authors, literary production was an activity entangled with the production of the modern Ottoman subject in its psychological, social, and existential aspects. Adopting new genres, producing new styles and discourses, and establishing new literary connections were intertwined with envisaging a new kind of society and subjecthood. Literary texts dealt with the contract between the reader and the writer and the social contract more broadly. Literature was also a cultural practice establishing new ties and conventions. The fictional or nonfictional texts of the authors describing the dynamics of the literary public also contained allusions to the power relations, critical conditions, and discussion atmosphere of the Ottoman public sphere. Ottoman writers also used experimental techniques such as metafiction and digression while fictionalizing the literary actor-network of writers, texts, readers, publishers, critics, and editors. There are parallels between aspects of the narrative form and the qualities of the literary public. At the same time, the sexual contract was conceived together with social and literary relations. Moreover, in the 1890s, the Ottoman literary public became gendered. The field of women's writing became relatively autonomous as a gendered field with its own characteristics, and literary texts represent acts of solidarity, criticism, and discussion among women.

Notes

1 *"Ecza-yı beşer câlib-i tacil-i fenadır / İbka-yı nam mucib-i tahsil-i bekâdır."* Namık Kemal, "Lisan-ı Osmaninin Edebiyatı Hakkında Bazı Mülahazatı Şamildir," in *Namık Kemal'in Türk Dili ve Edebiyatı Üzerine Görüşleri ve Yazıları*, ed. Kâzım Yetiş (Istanbul: Alfa, 1996), 57.
2 Ibid.
3 *Maqamat* is the title of the collection of Arabic stories written by al-Hariri (1054–1122). *Ahlak-ı Alai* is a 1564 book of morals written by Kınalızade Ali Efendi (d. 1572) in Turkish.
4 Namık Kemal, "Son Pişmanlık—İntibah Mukaddimesi," in *Namık Kemal'in Türk Dili ve Edebiyatı Üzerine Görüşleri ve Yazıları*, ed. Kâzım Yetiş (Istanbul: Alfa, 1996), 108.
5 For a detailed discussion of Namık Kemal's literary criticism, see Fatih Altuğ, "Namık Kemal'in Edebiyat Eleştirisinde Modernlik ve Öznellik" (PhD diss., Boğaziçi University, 2007).
6 Ahmet Mithat, "Kitap Mütalaası," in *Edebiyat Yazıları 1*, ed. Harika Durgun and Fazıl Gökçek (Istanbul: Dergâh, 2016), 24.
7 *"Hayalhanede bir cemiyet akdiyle cemiyetlice eğlenmek."* Ahmet Mithat, "Felsefe-i Zenan," in *Letaif-i Rivayat*, ed. Fazıl Gökçek and Sabahattin Çağın (Istanbul: Çağrı, 2001), 75.
8 Ahmet Mithat, "Teehhül," in *Letaif-i Rivayat*, ed. Fazıl Gökçek and Sabahattin Çağın (Istanbul: Çağrı, 2001), 46.
9 Ahmet Mithat, "Bahtiyarlık," in *Letaif-i Rivayat*, ed. Fazıl Gökçek and Sabahattin Çağın (Istanbul: Çağrı, 2001), 316–17.
10 Fatih Altuğ, "Letaif-i Rivayat'ın Hayali Cemiyeti," *Istanbul Üniversitesi Türk Dili ve Edebiyatı Dergisi* XLVII (2012): 46, 55.
11 Ahmet Mithat, *Müşahedat*, ed. Necat Birinci (Ankara: Türk Dil Kurumu, 2000 [1891]).

12 Halim Kara, "Anlatıda Bir 'Cevelan': *Karı Koca Masalı*'nda İstitrâtî-Anlatı ve İşlevi," *Istanbul Üniversitesi Türk Dili ve Edebiyatı Dergisi* XLVII (2012): 105–26.
13 Fatih Aşan and Arif Can Topçuoğlu, "Kendine Ait Bir Odadan Başkalarına Ait Bir Pazara: Bir Osmanlı Şairinin Sergüzeşti," *Metafor* 1 (2020): 1–22.
14 *Tercüman-ı Ahval*, published between 1860 and 1866, was the first private Arabic-script Turkish newspaper. Şinasi's famous theater play "Şair Evlenmesi" (1860) [Poet's Marriage] was also published in this newspaper founded by Âgâh Efendi and Şinasi.
15 This chapter was written as an output of the "Women Writers' Literary Environment in Late Ottoman Istanbul (1869–1923)" project (217K101) supported by TÜBİTAK.
16 Zehra Toska, "Bilinmeyen İlk Kadın Romanlarından Biri: Rehyâb-ı Zafer," *Kültür* 16 (2009): 126–29.
17 Fatma Fahrünnisa, *Dilharap*, ed. Fatih Altuğ and Kevser Bayraktar (Istanbul: KUY, 2017).

References

Ahmet Mithat. *Müşahedat*. Edited by Necat Birinci. Ankara: Türk Dil Kurumu, 2000 [1891].
———. "Bahtiyarlık." In *Letaif-i Rivayat*, edited by Fazıl Gökçek and Sabahattin Çağın, 282–337. Istanbul: Çağrı, 2001.
———. "Felsefe-i Zenan." In *Letaif-i Rivayat*, edited by Fazıl Gökçek and Sabahattin Çağın, 56–86. Istanbul: Çağrı, 2001.
———. "Teehhül." In *Letaif-i Rivayat*, edited by Fazıl Gökçek and Sabahattin Çağın, 42–55. Istanbul: Çağrı, 2001.
———. "Kitap Mütalaası." In *Edebiyat Yazıları 1*, edited by Harika Durgun and Fazıl Gökçek, 24–27. Istanbul: Dergâh, 2016.
Altuğ, Fatih. "Namık Kemal'in Edebiyat Eleştirisinde Modernlik ve Öznellik." PhD diss., Boğaizçi University, 2007.
———. "Letaif-i Rivayat'ın Hayali Cemiyeti." *Istanbul Üniversitesi Türk Dili ve Edebiyatı Dergisi* XLVII (2012): 35–64.
Aşan, Fatih, and Arif Can Topçuoğlu. "Kendine Ait Bir Odadan Başkalarına Ait Bir Pazara: Bir Osmanlı Şairinin Sergüzeşti." *Metafor* 1 (2020): 1–22.
Fatma Fahrünnisa. *Dilharap*. Edited by Fatih Altuğ and Kevser Bayraktar. Istanbul: KUY, 2017.
Kara, Halim. "Anlatıda Bir 'Cevelan': *Karı Koca Masalı*'nda İstitrâtî-Anlatı ve İşlevi." *Istanbul Üniversitesi Türk Dili ve Edebiyatı Dergisi* XLVII (2012): 105–26.
Namık Kemal. "Lisan-ı Osmaninin Edebiyatı Hakkında Bazı Mülahazatı Şamildir." In *Namık Kemal'in Türk Dili ve Edebiyatı Üzerine Görüşleri ve Yazıları*, edited by Kâzım Yetiş, 57–66. Istanbul: Alfa, 1996.
———. "Son Pişmanlık—İntibah Mukaddimesi." In *Namık Kemal'in Türk Dili ve Edebiyatı Üzerine Görüşleri ve Yazıları*, edited by Kâzım Yetiş, 105–10. Istanbul: Alfa, 1996.
Toska, Zehra. "Bilinmeyen İlk Kadın Romanlarından Biri: Rehyâb-ı Zafer." *Kültür* 16 (2009): 126–29.

SECTION IV

Women and Gender

11

METHODOLOGICAL CHALLENGES IN LATE OTTOMAN AND TURKISH LITERARY SCHOLARSHIP

Gender, Aesthetics, and Sociopolitical Contexts

Hülya Adak

Ottoman and Turkish literature abound with exciting discoveries. In this chapter, I explore the challenges awaiting scholars of Ottoman and Turkish literary studies in the quest to address questions related to gender, intersectionality, and sociopolitical contexts. The difficulties in the field become more pronounced as we compare the scholarship in Ottoman and Turkish literature with other (particularly European and American) scholarly canons. For various reasons, but mostly because literary scholarship and literary histories of Ottoman and Turkish literature are limited, particularly in their explorations of gender and intersectionality, the field lacks many sources critical to teaching or understanding different possibilities for canonization and periodization. A few hitherto unexplored questions, for instance, might lead to the discovery of innovative aesthetic movements among women writers and sexual minorities throughout the century.

Several insightful studies exist on gender and Ottoman and Turkish literatures, starting with the groundbreaking work by Walter G. Andrews and Mehmet Kalpaklı, *The Age of Beloveds: Love and the Beloved in Early-Modern and European Culture and Society*. İrvin Cemil Schick has also expanded our understanding of the past few centuries with analyses extended to the Balkans and Europe, in works such as *Batının Cinsel Kıyısı: Başkaldırıcı Söylemde Cinsellik ve Mekansallık* and *Women in the Ottoman Balkans: Gender, Culture and History* (edited together with Amila Buturovic). Sooyong Kim's *The Last of an Age: The Making and Unmaking of a Sixteenth-Century Ottoman Poet* is an exploration of the works of the popular poet Zâtî (1471–1576), and Didem Havlioğlu's monograph on Mihrî Hatun delineates the challenges of a woman poet in male-dominant Ottoman court culture in succinct detail.[1] All of these works shed light on a gendered critique of fifteenth- and sixteenth-century Ottoman literary history, touching upon unique histories of patronage, education, aesthetics, and social institutions (e.g., the *meclis*). Another insightful study by Marc Baer focuses on the twentieth century, exploring the marginal identities of a "novelist, poet, political activist and writer" Hugo Marcus (1880–1966).[2] Such biographical explorations and gendered histories have facilitated an understanding of earlier periods as well as the modern, but the scant list only proves how much work remains ahead.

A significant publication in the early 2000s on feminist thought, gender, and literature (Sibel Irzık and Jale Parla's *Kadınlar Dile Düşünce*), focused on *écriture féminine* and phallogocentrism in

DOI: 10.4324/9780429279270-16

139

Turkish literature. Further, a comprehensive study of masculinities in post-1970 Turkish literature, titled *Broken Masculinities: Solitude, Alienation, and Frustration in Turkish Literature after 1970*, was published recently by Çimen Günay-Erkol. Roughly 15 years after *Kadınlar Dile Düşünce*, Sema Kaygusuz and Deniz Gündoğan İbrişim's edited volume *Gaflet* incorporated chapters based on sexism and an intersectional analysis of various periods of Turkish literature. To this brief list, Nurdan Gürbilek's various critical essays may be added, including *Kötü Çocuk Türk* (2001), *Kör Ayna, Kayıp Şark* (2004), and *Mağdurun Dili* (2008) with analyses of intersectionality, and theoretical discussions of masculinity and feminist thought, as they operate in trauma and memory studies.

With this scant list in mind, we might conclude that questions relating to literature by women and LGBTQI+ writers, theoretical discussions of gender and sexuality, and intersectionality are quite limited in Ottoman and Turkish literature. For students of Turkish literature, then, without interpretive frameworks, discussions on archetypes, anxieties of influence, sexual politics, or the history of suffrage as seen in fiction, women's literature remains a rather discontinuous and sporadic laundry list. The extensive list includes certainly a wide range of authors, from Zafer Hanım in the late nineteenth century to Şair Nigar, Fatma Aliye, Sırpuhi Düssap to other generations, such as Zabel Yesayan and Halide Edib, and more contemporary writers like Sevgi Soysal, Leyla Erbil, Aslı Erdoğan, Adalet Ağaoğlu, Latife Tekin among others. Many questions remain. For instance, what are the salient characteristics in women's literature of the 1970s? Can there be new periodizations outside of the modernism/postmodernism frameworks for the twentieth century? Where are the madwomen in the attic and sex changes (Gilbert and Gubar), the hysteries (Elaine Showalter), autobiographics (Leigh Gilmore), and queer spaces and time (Jack Halberstam) in Ottoman-Turkish literature? These are suggestions and, obviously, closer scrutiny of Ottoman and Turkish literature will provide new conceptual categories beyond the ones articulated in Euro-American scholarship.

Author's choice Biographical Thinking

The absence of biographies, life histories, and oral history work on authors precludes the historical and social situatedness that is necessary to understanding their political perceptions, social standing, personal idiosyncrasies, and philosophical standpoint. Without biographical research—or with the nonpersonal narratives one reads in encyclopedias, school textbooks, and Wikipedia articles—the writer is reduced to a passport photograph born in a particular place and schooled at a variety of institutions. Several authors may have also been engaged in various professional commitments and their names exist with an addendum of a list of book titles. This skim narrative is supplemented with a list of works that the author published. Such works were not explored at all in the short biographical narrative. The writer remains a composite consisting of two lists: the first is a list of dates (birth/death, schooling, professional appointments), and the second is a laundry list of titles of works grouped in conjunction with a *famous* or sometimes even *obscure* name.

Missing, hence, is cultural, political, and historical situatedness; the analysis of particular works in conjunction with the life history of the author; the influences of other writers, texts, and genres; and the history of the texts and their publication history. The Wikipedia entry of Emine Semiye Önasya is a solid example of this point: "She also wrote a math textbook entitled *Hulasa-i Ilm-i Hesap* in 1893. . . . Her most-known novels are *Sefalet* (1908) (Poverty) and *Gayya Kuyusu* (The Pit of Hell)."[3] Without giving us clues about the content, the style, and/or the historical or aesthetic context within which scholars can make sense of Emine Semiye's works, we are provided a wide array of texts, including "a math textbook." While it is easy to criticize Wikipedia for being incomplete and for being an encyclopedia in progress, it is unfortunate that some literary histories or critical editions of Ottoman and Turkish literature do not go deeper into probing biographical details.

Undoubtedly, exceptional biographies do exist. An insightful biographical example was published by Orhan Okay, a former student of Ahmet H. Tanpınar, as *Bir Hülya Adamının Romanı, Ahmet Hamdi Tanpınar* (The Novel of a Dreamer, Ahmet Hamdi Tanpınar). The book characterizes Tanpınar as a scholar and creative writer, weaving together his sources of inspiration in art, sculpture, literary works, and poems with his fiction and prose. Another spellbinding example is Yıldız Ecevit's *Ben Buradayım. . .: Oğuz Atay'ın Biyografik ve Kurmaca Dünyası* (I am Here. . .: Oğuz Atay's Universe Between Biography and Fiction). Interweaving Atay's diary entries, life history, friendships, relationships, and sources of inspiration with his fiction, the outcome is a tour de force. Another ambitious undertaking is *Romantic Communist: The Life and Work of Nâzım Hikmet* by Saime Göksu and Edward Timms. The biography illustrates not only Nâzım's years in Turkey, his prison years, but also in the Soviet Republic. The work also explores the writer's political inclinations and poetry (and dramatic literature) in the context of the Turkish left, with comparisons to Russian literature and aesthetic movements in the Soviet context.

Prior to İpek Çalışlar's biography of Halide Edib, readers had not even heard of Halide's engagement with the Swaraj movement in India. Hence, her friendship and close collaboration with Mahatma Gandhi in the 1930s were largely unknown in Turkey and in Euro-American scholarly circles. After the biography was published, Edib's activism during the nonviolent struggle for decolonization in India was made familiar to readers and triggered the publication of *Hindistan'a Dair* (On India) in 2014, an abridged version of *Inside India* (the English original of her political commentary on India in the 1930s). İpek Çalışlar's *Biyografisine Sığmayan Kadın* (The Woman Who Doesn't Fit into Her Biography) also contextualized and responded to many significant questions relevant to the scholarship on Halide Edib: How did she spend her exile years? Where was she? What were her conditions like? What was her role in the opposition party Terakkiperver Cumhuriyet Fırkası? What was her role in and how did she write about the women's movement in early Republican Turkey?

With the exception of a few examples, such as Çalışlar's biography of *Latife Hanım* and her Halide Edib biography, feminist biographies or biographies of women, LGBTI+ writers, and/ or minorities are rare. In the last decade, the work of feminist scholars such as Meral Akkent and the Istanbul Women's Museum[4] have contributed significantly to our understanding of women's lives both within the Ottoman and Turkish context and beyond. However, biographies that narrate a life over hundreds of pages also go into detail with the challenges that women literati may have encountered because of their gender, the historical conditions against which they may have struggled, and the repercussions of biographical entanglements in particular literary works (e.g., illness, imprisonment, or political persecution) and their reverberations in fiction. One may analyze the works of a multiplicity of writers, including Sevgi Soysal, Leyla Erbil, Oya Baydar, and Aslı Erdoğan among others to be able to expound on such challenging circumstances. These issues requiring the depth and profundity of a comprehensive book-length biographical narrative remain unexplored. More biographies of women and feminist biographies of sexual and other minorities await publication.

In the Absence of Critical Editions, Paratexts, Annotated Texts, and Guides

Over the past decade, Ottoman literature, particularly late nineteenth- and early twentieth-century novels, has received much public and scholarly acclaim. As part of this growing fascination, many scholars have transliterated works (from the Arabo-Persian alphabet into the Latin script and sometimes into modern Turkish) and brought obscure writers to the interest of students, scholars, and readers alike. This is a major undertaking and should be commended. However, the speedy publication processes of such transliterations or reprints have been highly problematic and have made it difficult for instructors and teachers to carry these new editions into the classroom and for all readers who have no means or interest in conducting additional research to make sense of these works.

The jubilant process of transliterating and publishing one unknown text after another picked up from dusty shelves of libraries and archives of Ottoman literature has turned into a rather hasty effort which mostly provides very little, if any, editorial commentary, publication history, or historical background on the particular text. Missing also are etymologies of certain words and phrases, and the cultural and political context of the transliterated work in question. Without forewords, afterwords, scholarly articles, or paratexts to discuss the transliterated text in the context of one or a variety of aesthetic movements, the work makes its appearance as a godsend, a miracle of sorts. Such magical publications generously serve the scholar who has ample time to devote to conducting the research necessary to interpret the text but do not necessarily serve the teacher/instructor because it becomes highly difficult, if near impossible, to teach and situate the text into a particular context and carry it directly into the classroom. A few of these texts appear as if in an entire conceptual vacuum, sometimes dispensing with essential information, such as the time and place of publication of the work in its original edition and its significance within the context of other works by the same author.

A frequently omitted piece of vital information is that the original publication might have been published in serialized form and that differences in the book form might exist when compared to the serialized version of the work. At times, this difference is so stark that the texts might need to be categorized as two altogether different texts. Further, with the help of paratextual articles, scholars could explore the unique characteristics of the novel published in serial form, responding to issues such as the reception history and how the dialogue between readers and weekly episodes (e.g., chapters, acts) permeated the text in different temporal moments of writing and publishing. Last, the changes or editorial modifications made in the publication of a serialized novel in book form could also be discussed in paratexts.

The series of transliterated works published by the publishing houses Turkuaz and Türkiye İş Bankası fortunately incorporate introductory articles by talented scholars of Ottoman literature, such as Fatih Altuğ, Ruken Alp, and others. However, the forewords are no longer than three or four pages. The skinny introductions or brief afterwords might not be so problematic in some cases because many other scholarly works on the particular authors exist or other editions of the works have already been published. In these cases, a reader can easily find material to supplement the transliteration at hand and a teacher can bring a few editions or works to class to prepare an interesting lecture without recourse to extensive research in archives, libraries, and so on. Hence, amid an abundance of editions of Samipaşazade Sezai's *Sergüzeşt* (Adventure, 1887) and many scholarly works on Halide Edib, I find the brevity of paratexts in Samipaşazade Sezai's *Sergüzeşt* (the original version and the adaptation into modern Turkish by the publishing house Can Yayınları) and Halide Edib Adıvar's *Heyula* (also from Can Yayınları) less problematic. However, given the lack of scholarly publications on several of the prominent women writers in Ottoman history (e.g., Fatma Aliye), the brevity of such introductions makes the works difficult to comprehend or contextualize. Hence, with no other extensive supplementary scholarly materials available, the brevity of paratexts in Fatma Aliye's *Refet* by Türkiye İş Bankası (2018), *Udi* (The Ud Player) and *Levayih-i Hayat* (Scenes of Life) by Turkuaz Publishing House, and

Methodological Challenges in Late Ottoman and Turkish Literary Scholarship

Hadiye Hümeyra's *Yıkık Gönüller* (Broken Hearts), also by Turkuaz (2019), become highly problematic as they are puzzling to readers, leaving them with a myriad of unanswered questions and the need for clarifications.

In Ottoman-Turkish literary scholarship, the establishment of the Library of Women's Works and the Information Center Foundation in 1990 was a milestone in archiving, publishing, and researching women's literary works.[5] This archive has led to the publication of an outstanding series of works, including the Purple Books (Mor Kitaplık), which include most of the works of Nezihe Muhiddin. While Muhiddin's political activism has received much acclaim after the influential monograph on her work by Yaprak Zihnioğlu, particularly her role as the first suffragette of Turkey and the founder of the Women's People Party—the first political party in Turkey—her literary works have not been explored. A few scholars have referred to her literary work as a canon written after her political activism could not find an outlet, a period of depression and immobility, and so on. A four-volume series has been published that encompasses the novels, essays, and letters of Nezihe Muhiddin.[6] The four volumes have only received a few pages of an introduction, which again does not address key issues, such as how Nezihe Muhiddin's fiction is related to her political activism, the reception of her fiction or the context of her fiction within various aesthetic movements in early Turkish Republican literature.

The aforementioned propensity of not publishing critical editions or fiction with paratexts applies equally to reprints. One of the striking examples is the publication of the works of political activist, journalist, and novelist Suat Derviş (1905–1972) by Doğan Publishing House with no editorial commentary besides the fact that *Ankara Mahpusu* was the first Turkish novel published in French. The brief paragraphs that make up the entirety of the novel's paratexts include citations from a few French sources that referred to the text when the original version in French was published (citations from *Les Lettres Françaises* and *Le Monde*). This version, much like *Hiçbiri*, another novel published by Doğan Publishing House, incorporates absolutely no publishing history of the text, no editorial comments, and so on.

Moreover, in the contexts of Ottoman and Turkish literature, many guides to novels and annotated texts of fiction await publication. The works of one of the major modernists of Turkish fiction, Ahmet Hamdi Tanpınar, could be better interpreted with guides and annotated texts. For instance, a guide to classical Ottoman music following the discussion of and references to Ottoman classical music in Tanpınar's *Huzur* would be a significant resource to expand on our interpretation of the novel itself. Many literature professors find the novel challenging, precisely because of the subtle references to classical Ottoman scores and the rupture with the music of the Ottoman past in the early Republican years. Because of this rupture, Turkish readers, with the exception of music scholars, find the simplest reference to Ottoman music unintelligible. Hence, readers cannot engage with the music and cannot relate to the nuances between the scenes and references to musical scores/motifs in the novel. On the other hand, if we analyze European literature, a plethora of such guides exist, mostly for the fiction of European modernists. James Joyce's *Ulysses*—an exemplary work that has received much attention with its multiplicity of meanings, styles, and registers—abounds with such complementary guides, including William York Tindall's *A Reader's Guide to James Joyce*, Harry Blamires' *The New Bloomsday Book: A Guide through Ulysses*, and Don Gifford and Robert J. Seidman's *Ulysses Annctated: Notes for James Joyce's Ulysses*. Returning to Turkish literature, similar to the works of Tanpınar, exploring the modernists and postmodernists of Turkish fiction—including Oğuz Atay, Leyla Erbil, Sevim Burak, Aslı Erdoğan, and Latife Tekin—with the aid of annotated texts and guides might make the texts more accessible to readers while leading scholars to formulate new interpretive registers.

Missing Anthologies/Interpretive Communities

As I think of world literature or English literature throughout the centuries, I think of the Norton or Macmillan anthologies. Such works, encyclopedic in scope, not only give the reader a sense of historical change and continuity, plurality, information about a multiplicity of genres, editorial notes, and reflection on the original literary texts, but also encompass amazing possibilities for K-12 and college courses. With their gargantuan panoramas of various genres, these anthologies incorporate narrative structures, social and political contexts, authors, and particular trajectories of literary histories. In the context of a more specific anthology, say, *The Norton Shakespeare*, the discussion partly concerns the different methodologies and perspectives that "the contemporary moment of scholarship" gives to an analysis of dramatic literature coming from a myriad of periods. The question then is not exclusively the structuralist one (e.g., "How do we analyze *Othello*?"). Rather, the question evolves into why critics, readers, and scholars are interested in *Othello*. What are the means by which we approach *Othello*? In the late 1990s and early 2000s, *Othello* was pivotal in scholarship and teaching in the United States because it addressed questions related to race, gender, and intersectionality. Further, does the concern with *Othello* today, particularly because of a concern with race and gender, impose rather "contemporary" issues on dramatic literature that shifts its interpretation in profoundly different ways?[7] In other words, influenced by the legacy of Kimberlé Crenshaw and others focusing on theorizing intersectionality, were these concerns or contemporary methods of approaching *Othello* not available or less pronounced during the years of the work's conception?

As these anthologies contextualize the texts in their historical settings, as well as providing an overview of centuries of interpretive strategies and communities, having a limited number of anthologies means that texts are left outside of canons, genealogies, interpretive mechanisms, and histories of interpretations. This is not to say that Ottoman and Turkish literatures lack anthologies altogether. I should pay tribute to early efforts, including Ebüzziya Tevfik's *Nümune-i Edebiyyat-ı Osmaniyye* (Osmanlı Edebiyatı Düzyazı Antolojisi, in modern Turkish, or the Anthology of Ottoman Prose), Mehmet Fuat Köprülü's *Divan Edebiyatı Antolojisi* (Anthology of Divan Literature), Talat Sait Halman's *Anthology of Modern Turkish Drama I-II*, and Mehmet Kaplan's *Yeni Türk Edebiyatı Antolojisi* (New Turkish Literature Anthology). Other prominent examples include *Ottoman Lyric Poetry: An Anthology* (eds. Walter Andrews, Mehmet Kalpaklı, and Najaat Black) and Suat Karantay's *Contemporary Turkish Short Fiction*.

While a history of the past hundred years presenting the history of the Ottoman Empire and the Turkish Republic through anthologies of life writing and autobiographical sources has been published in German (*Hundert Jahre Türkei: Zeitzeugen erzählen*), similar volumes should also be published in Turkish. Further, as more and more literature departments in Turkey move towards gender and sexuality courses, highlighting women's and LGBTQI+ literatures, scholarly attention must be given to anthologies of such works. Every time a student decides to write a thesis on these topics, it becomes extremely difficult to draw out a canon or a select number of works that could provide useful contexts for the particular works the student intends to explore. An anthology of queer works from Turkey, or anthology of women writers' works from the late nineteenth century to the present, might help students situate the texts in question within the frameworks of other texts, periodizations, a multiplicity of styles, and historical frameworks to study the particular works and authors in question.

In the Absence of Intergeneric Analyses

In Ottoman and Turkish literature, intergeneric analyses are rather rare. Generally speaking, most of the prominent works of literary theory in contemporary Turkish literature focus exclusively on the novelistic genre. Most literary scholars, including Berna Moran's *Türk Romanına Eleştirel Bir Bakış I-II-III* (Critical Approaches to the Turkish Novel), Jale Parla in *Don Kişot'tan Bugüne Roman* (The Novel from *Don Quixote* to the Present) and *Türk Romanında Yazar ve Başkalaşım* (Author and Metamorphosis in the Turkish Novel), and Azade Seyhan in *Tales of Crossed Destinies: The Modern Turkish Novel in a Comparative Context* have chosen the novelistic genre as their basis of analysis. Divan poetry has been the source of a few very significant scholarly works, including Andrews and Kalpaklı's *The Age of Beloveds*, as previously mentioned. The few intergeneric analyses, incorporating thematic foci that cut across genres, include Ahmet Hamdi Tanpınar's *19uncu Asır Türk Edebiyatı Tarihi* (Nineteenth-Century Turkish Literary History); my special issue with Rüstem Ertuğ Altınay "Performing Turkishness: Theater and Politics in Turkey and Its Diasporas" (with attempts to explore Ottoman and Turkish dramatic repertoires in conjunction with novels, and poetry in a multiplicity of linguistic and scriptural repertoires); Erol Köroğlu's *Ottoman Propaganda and Turkish Identity: Literature in Turkey During World War I*; and Murat Belge's *Genesis: Büyük Ulusal Anlatı ve Türklerin Kökeni* (Genesis: The Grand National Narrative and the Origins of the Turks), which is an exploration of the myths of genesis.

While many significant questions and genealogies can be broached in works revolving around a single genre, many questions pertinent to cultural studies await scholars, such as memory and trauma studies, gender and sexuality, and how such questions require transcending generic categorizations and boundaries. In order to analyze the afterlives of the Armenian genocide in the Turkish literary, dramatic, and filmic scene throughout the century, a thorough analysis of memoirs and fiction by Aras Publishing House such as Zabel Yesayan's works might be analyzed parallel to dramatic works such as Duygu Dalyanoğlu and Ayşe Yıldırım's *Zabel*, the performance titled *Sen Balık Değilsin ki* by Çıplak Ayaklar Kumpanyası, and Zeynep Dadak's documentary *Ah Gözel Istanbul*. This would set the tone for a post-2000 analysis of genocidal afterlives in different aesthetic genres. Further, an exploration of sexual politics in contemporary women's works might proffer provoking examples and results if Latife Tekin's *Sevgili Arsız Ölüm* and Seray Şahiner's *Kul and Antabus* were explored with their adaptations to the stage.[8]

Plurality in Empires and Nation-States: Beyond the Nation as Categorical Paradigm

Throughout the twentieth century and beyond, literatures of the Ottoman Empire have been explored under isolated/insular "national literary traditions" constructed around dismissing the linguistic heterogeneity and literary plurality of the empire. These national literary traditions or canons have operated mostly under philological genealogies, taking monolinguistic literary products and their diachronic evolution to be the basis of their study. Such genealogies were evident in Turkish, Armenian, Greek, Arab, and Kurdish literatures that addressed not only twentieth-century works but explored such national canons under the Ottoman Empire. Only recently has scholarship paid attention to hybrid scriptural or linguistic performances, such as Armeno-Turkish literatures, the interaction between various national literary traditions, and a synchronous analysis of a multitude of literary and linguistic performances.[9] Such synchronous analyses transgress the category of one single national literature and enable us to ask questions about the Zeitgeist and predominant literary/aesthetic movements (e.g., avant-garde) across various literatures.

Lerna Ekmekçioğlu and Melisa Bilal's *Bir Adalet Feryadı: Osmanlı'dan Türkiye'ye Beş Ermeni Feminist Yazar (1862–1933)* (A Cry for Justice: Five Armenian Feminist Writers from the Ottoman Empire to Turkey [1862–1933]) has broken new ground in analyzing Ottoman-Armenian and Armenian women writers in Turkey, as well as an Armenian feminist tradition. Much work lies ahead to produce publications on Ottoman and post-Ottoman feminism that synchronically incorporate works by Ottoman-Turkish, Armenian, Arab, Kurdish, Greek, and Jewish feminists among others. For instance, Sırpuhi Düssap's fiction and thought might be juxtaposed with Fatma Aliye's novels. Similarly, the work of the contemporaries Nezihe Muhiddin, Zabel Yesayan, and Hayganuş Mark might lead us to ask questions about post-Ottoman feminism in ways that cut across various national and linguistic communities.

Theater histories might be written encompassing the many communities of the last few decades of the Ottoman Empire and even beyond. Vahram Papazyan's (1888–1968) story belongs with the life history of Muhsin Ertuğrul, and Afife Jale's life cannot be narrated without understanding the banishment from Turkish stages of the actress Elize Binemeciyan (1890–1981), who spent most of her life in the early Republican period in exile.

Queering Ottoman and Post-Ottoman Literary Landscapes

Only through proliferating sources on Ottoman and Turkish literatures and probing deeper into our analyses with innovative research questions can we begin to address a few of the challenges awaiting scholars and teachers of the field. In Halberstam's footsteps, we might begin to perform queer readings of time and space in modern Turkish literature. Gendered histories of illness and disability written in twentieth-century fiction, for example, might lead to the discovery of new movements and styles. With these and further questions, I hope that our research will evolve into new geographies, mapping queer biographies, trans lives, and gender+ imaginaries, thus outlining hitherto unacknowledged canons, unique aesthetic movements, and exciting political contexts that transcend the "national imaginary" in Ottoman and post-Ottoman literary landscapes.

Notes

1 Didem Havlioğlu, *Mihrî Hatun: Performance, Gender-Bending, and Subversion in Ottoman Intellectual History* (Syracuse, NY: Syracuse University Press, 2017), 2.
2 Marc David Baer, *German, Jew, Muslim, Gay: The Life and Times of Hugo Marcus* (New York: Columbia University Press, 2020).
3 Wikipedia, "Emine Semiye," accessed October 30, 2022, https://en.wikipedia.org/wiki/Emine_Semiye_%C3%96nasya.
4 "Welcome to the Website of the Women's Museum Istanbul," *İstanbul Kadın Müzesi*, accessed March 3, 2022, www.istanbulkadinmuzesi.org/en.
5 "About Us," *Library of Women's Works and the Information Center Foundation*, accessed March 3, 2022, http://kadineserleri.org/aabout-us/.
6 A four-volume series has been published that encompasses the novels, essays, and letters of Nezihe Muhiddin.
7 Walter Cohen, "Othello," in *The Norton Shakespeare*, ed. Stephen Greenblatt and Walter Cohen (New York: Norton, 2008), 1169.
8 The play "Sevgili Arsız Ölüm—Dirmit" is an adaptation of Latife Tekin's novel by Hakan Emre Ünal and Nezaket Erden. Seray Şahiner has adapted her own novels *Kul* and *Antabus* as plays.
9 See, e.g., Mehmet Fatih Uslu, *Çatışma ve Müzakere: Osmanlı'da Türkçe ve Ermenice Dramatik Edebiyat* (Istanbul: İletişim Yayınları, 2015); Murat Cankara, "Reading Akabi, (Re-)Writing History: On the Questions of Currency and Interpretation of Armeno-Turkish Fiction," in *Cultural Encounters in the Turkish Speaking Communities of the Late Ottoman Empire*, ed. Evangelia Balta (Istanbul: Isis Press, 2014), 53–75; Murat Cankara, "Rethinking Ottoman Cross-Cultural Encounters: Turks and the Armenian Alphabet," *Middle Eastern Studies* 51, no. 1 (2015): 1–16; Hülya Adak, "Literary Heritages of the Ottoman Empire," *in Online International Encyclopedia of the First World War (1914–1918)*, 2018, https://encyclopedia.1914-1918-online.net/article/literature_ottoman_empire.

References

Adak, Hülya. "Literary Heritages of the Ottoman Empire." In *Online International Encyclopedia of the First World War (1914–1918)*, 2018. https://encyclopedia.1914-1918-online.net/article/literature_ottoman_empire.

Adak, Hülya, and Rüstem Ertuğ Altınay, eds. "Performing Turkishness: Theater and Politics in Turkey and Its Diasporas." *Comparative Drama* 52, no. 3–4 (2018).

Adak, Hülya, and Erika Glassen. *Hundert Jahre Türkei: Zeitzeugen erzaehlen.* Zurich: Unionsverlag, 2010.

Adıvar, Halide Edib. *Heyula.* Istanbul: Can Yayınları, 2019.

Aliye, Fatma. *Refet: Kadınların Hafızası.* Istanbul: Turkuaz, 2019.

———. *Udi.* Istanbul: Turkuaz, 2019.

———. *Levayih-I Hayat: Hayattan Sahneler.* Istanbul: Türkiye İş Bankası, 2020.

Andrews, Walter G., Najaat Black, and Mehmet Kalpaklı, eds. *Ottoman Lyric Poetry: An Anthology.* Seattle: University of Washington, 2006.

Andrews, Walter G., and Mehmet Kalpaklı. *The Age of Beloveds: Love and the Beloved in Early Modern and European Culture and Society.* Durham, NC: Duke University Press, 2004.

Baer, Marc David. *German, Jew, Muslim, Gay: The Life and Times of Hugo Marcus.* New York: Columbia University Press, 2020.

Belge, Murat. *Genesis: Büyük Ulusal Anlatı ve Türklerin Kökeni.* Istanbul: İletişim, 2009.

Blamires, Harry. *The New Bloomsday Book: A Guide through Ulysses.* Abingdon-on-Thames: Routledge, 1997.

Buturovic, Amila, and İrvin Cemil Schick. *Women in the Ottoman Balkans: Gender, Culture and History.* London: I. B. Tauris, 2007.

Çakırlar, Cüneyt, and Serkan Delice, eds. *Cinsellik Muamması: Türkiye'de Queer Kültür ve Muhalefet.* Istanbul: Metis, 2012.

Çalışlar, İpek. *Latife Hanım.* Istanbul: Yapı Kredi Yayınları, 2019.

———. *Biyografisine Sığmayan Kadın: Halide Edib.* Istanbul: Yapı Kredi Yayınları, 2021.

Cankara, Murat. "Reading *Akabi*, (Re-)Writing History: On the Questions of Currency and Interpretation of Armeno-Turkish Fiction." In *Cultural Encounters in the Turkish Speaking Communities of the Late Ottoman Empire*, edited by Evangelia Balta, 53–75. Istanbul: Isis Press, 2014.

———. "Rethinking Ottoman Cross-Cultural Encounters: Turks and the Armenian Alphabet." *Middle Eastern Studies* 51, no. 1 (2015): 1–16.

Cohen, Walter. "Othello." In *The Norton Shakespeare*, edited by Stephen Greenblatt and Walter Cohen, 1169–78. New York: Norton, 2008.

Dadak, Zeynep, director. *Ah Gözel İstanbul.* Elemag Pictures and Fenafilm, 2020.

Dalyanoğlu, Duygu, and Aysel Yıldırım. *Zabel.* Istanbul: BGST Yayınları, 2018.

Derviş, Suat. *Ankara Mahpusu.* Istanbul: İthaki, 2018.

———. *Hiçbiri.* Istanbul: İthaki, 2018.

Ecevit, Yıldız. *Ben Buradayım. . .: Oğuz Atay'ın Biyografik ve Kurmaca Dünyası.* Istanbul: İletişim, 2005.

Ekmekçioğlu, Lerna, and Melissa Bilal, eds. *Bir Adalet Feryadı: Osmanlı'dan Türkiye'ye Beş Ermeni Feminist Yazar (1862–1933).* Istanbul: Aras, 2017.

Gifford, Don, and Robert Seidman. *Ulysses Annotated: Notes for James Joyce's Ulysses.* Berkeley: University of California Press, 2008.

Göksu, Saime, and Edward Timms. *Romantic Communist: The Life and Work of Nâzım Hikmet.* London: Palgrave Macmillan, 1999.

Günay-Erkol, Çimen. *Broken Masculinities: Solitude, Alienation, and Frustration in Turkish Literature After 1970.* Budapest: Central European University Press, 2016.

Gürbilek, Nurdan. *Kötü Çocuk Türk.* Istanbul: Metis, 2001.

———. *Kör Ayna, Kayıp Şark.* Istanbul: Metis, 2004.

———. *Mağdurun Dili.* Istanbul: Metis, 2015.

Halman, Talat S. *Anthology of Modern Turkish Drama I-II.* Syracuse, NY: Syracuse University Press, 2008.

Halman, Talat S., and Jane L. Warner, eds. *İbrahim the Mad and Other Plays: Anthology of Modern Turkish Drama.* Syracuse, NY: Syracuse University Press, 2008.

———. *I, Anatolia and Other Plays: Anthology of Modern Turkish Drama.* Syracuse, NY: Syracuse University Press, 2009.

Havlioğlu, Didem. *Mihrî Hatun: Performance, Gender-Bending, and Subversion in Ottoman Intellectual History.* Syracuse, NY: Syracuse University Press, 2017.

Hümeyra, Hadiye. *Yıkık Gönüller*. Istanbul: Turkuvaz, 2019.

Kaplan, Mehmet, ed. *Yeni Türk Edebiyatı Antolojisi*. Istanbul: Edebiyat Fakültesi Matbaası, 1982.

Karantay, Suat. *Contemporary Turkish Short-Fiction*. Istanbul: Çitlembik Yayınları, 2010.

Kaygusuz, Sema, and Deniz Gündoğan İbrişim, eds. *Gaflet: Modern Türkçe Edebiyatın Cinsiyetçi Sinir Uçları*. Istanbul: Metis, 2019.

Kim, Sooyong. *The Last of an Age: The Making and Unmaking of a Sixteenth-Century Ottoman Poet*. Abingdon-on-Thames: Routledge, 2018.

Köprülü, Mehmet Fuat, ed. *Divan Edebiyatı Antolojisi*. Ankara: Akçağ Yayınevi, 2006.

Köroğlu, Erol. *Ottoman Propaganda and Turkish Identity: Literature in Turkey During World War I*. London: IB Tauris, 2007.

Moran, Berna. *Türk Romanına Eleştirel Bir Bakış*, vol. 1–3. Istanbul: İletişim Yayınları, 2004.

Muhiddin, Nezihe. *Bütün Eserleri*, vol. 4. Istanbul: Kitap Yayınevi, 2006.

Okay, Orhan. *Bir Hülya Adamının Romanı Ahmet Hamdi Tanpınar*. Istanbul: Dergah, 2010.

Parla, Jale. *Don Kişot'tan Bugüne Roman*. Istanbul: İletişim Yayınları, 2003.

———. *Türk Romanında Yazar ve Başkalaşım*. Istanbul: İletişim Yayınları, 2011.

Şahiner, Seray. *Kul*. Istanbul: Can Yayınları, 2017.

———. *Antabus*: Everest Yayınları, 2019.

Schick, İrvin Cemil. *Batının Cinsel Kıyısı: Başkalıkçı Söylemde Cinsellik ve Mekansallık*. Istanbul: Tarih Vakfı, 2002.

Seyhan, Azade. *Tales of Crossed Destinies: The Modern Turkish Novel in a Comparative Context*. New York: Modern Language Association of America, 2008.

Sezai, Samipaşazade. *Sergüzeşt*. Istanbul: Türkiye İş Bankası Yayınları, 2019.

Tanpınar, Ahmet Hamdi. *Huzur*. Istanbul: Dergah, 1999.

———. *Ondokuzuncu Asır Türk Edebiyatı Tarihi*. Istanbul: Dergah, 2012.

Tekin, Latife. *Sevgili Arsız Ölüm*. Istanbul: Can Yayınları, 2019.

Tevfik, Ebuzziyya. *Nümune-i Edebiyyat-ı Osmaniyye (Osmanlı Edebiyatı Düzyazı Antolojisi)*. Istanbul: Konstantiniye Matbaa Ebuzziya, 1911.

Tindall, William York. *A Reader's Guide to James Joyce*. Syracuse, NY: Syracuse University Press, 1995.

Uslu, Mehmet Fatih. *Çatışma ve Müzakere: Osmanlı'da Türkçe ve Ermenice Dramatik Edebiyat*. Istanbul: İletişim Yayınları, 2015.

Wikipedia. "Emine Semiye." Accessed February 19, 2022. https://en.wikipedia.org/wiki/Evolutionary_history_of_life.

Ze'evi, Dror. *Producing Desire: Changing Sexual Discourse in the Ottoman Middle East, 1500–1900*. Berkeley: University of California Press, 2006.

Zihnioğlu, Yaprak. *Kadınsız İnkilap*. Istanbul: Metis, 2015.

12

GENDER IN ISLAMICATE OTTOMAN POETRY

Didem Havlioğlu

In one of her many poems addressed to her male colleagues, Mihrî Hatun (ca. 1460–1515) challenges her friend and mentor Müʿeyyedzâde Abdurrahman Çelebi (1456–1516), who composed poetry with Hâtemî as his *mahlas* or pen name. In the following couplet, she makes a radical suggestion of love between a man and a woman as she presents herself as a lover for him, an alternative to the idolic image of the gender-neutral beloved:

> *O Hâtemî, you falsely passed as a lover to Mihrî*
> *But by God, she loves you better than any boy*[1]

Mihrî most probably composed these lines in response to a poem (though there is no record of it) sent to her by Hâtemî. Her biographer, Âşık Çelebi, in particular gives a detailed account of Mihrî Hatun and her relationship with Müʿeyyedzâde. According to Âşık, she studied "love" with Müʿeyyedzâde and they had a mutual affection for each other.[2] The education of love that Âşık refers to here is the craft of poetry that can be learned from master poets and performed in the *meclis*, or poetic circle. In other words, Mihrî had learned the art of poetry from Müʿeyyedzâde, who was an influential poet and patron at the time. In her poem, she claims a space as a woman in the male-dominated world of poetry by offering herself as an alternative to the traditional beloved who is supposed to have no gender marks on the surface level. Although male poets had always composed poetry for adult men in the frame of mystical love, a woman's courtship addressed to a man is transgressive as it suggests an earthly relationship.[3] Therefore it seems surprising to our understanding of Ottoman poetry and its gender system to have a woman poet like Mihrî who challenges the accepted norms of gender. If she was one of the marginal and forgotten poets, we could still adhere to our assumptions that she was just an anomaly. However, to our surprise, she was not only accepted but also celebrated by her contemporaries, colleagues, and, last but not least, by the sovereign. Her poetry collection survives in four manuscripts copies and, according to the Topkapı palace registries, she was paid handsomely on many occasions and equal to her male colleagues.[4]

How do we explain Mihrî and her poetry in early modern Ottoman literary history with the frameworks that have never considered women as part of the picture? As women poets were a minority throughout history, and the poetic tradition and its social practice were overwhelmingly male dominated, it was once suggested that women could only imitate their male

DOI: 10.4324/9780429279270-17

colleagues.[5] However, while originality is a modern phenomenon, imitation was part of the performance of Ottoman poetry and all poets were expected to imitate each other, as apparent in the *nazire*, or parallel poetry tradition.[6] Unlike the hasty assumptions of modern scholarship in terms of dismissing the difference between men and women writers, in historical documents women were perceived as a different class and their gender was always highlighted.[7] Therefore, it is anachronistic not to take their gender into account in any form when performing analysis of their works.[8]

Although few in number, Mihrî and other women poets' existence and acceptance in poetic circles suggest a complexity in gender construction as opposed to the clear-cut male homo-sociality that until recently was still accepted as the norm.[9] As Mihrî and her female successors show, a woman poet challenges the ideas of the male-centered gender structure in the Islamicate discourse of love in Ottoman poetry. Although their minority positions were not enough to transform the male-dominated poetics of their times, they not only temporarily destabilized the male homogeneity in poetry but also crystallized the gender structure. Therefore, women poets' works offer the missing piece for us to understand the complexities of the gender matrix of Ottoman intellectual circles.

Including women in the discussion of gender not only provides a fuller picture but also has the potential to highlight missing facts about the poetic tradition. Women poets' works saturate the aesthetic and social structure of poetry in ways that may be otherwise be blurred in all-male circles. First, like any other poet, women poets have to show mastery in an aesthetic tradition that was established by and for male poets. Their ability to do so showcases something that was not discussed before: that the tradition can work for women as well. For instance, their performative uses of masculinity and femininity highlight that the contrasting values of these gender roles are not absolute truths but only social constructions. Second, as for the social dimension of poetry, a woman had to be part of a *meclis*, a fundamental part of the poetic world. *Meclis* practice points to the various dynamics of power and its relation to gender. Like any other poet, a woman had to perform before an audience. Women poets' existence in history, which was ultimately recorded by men, implies that gender segregation was not all-encompassing and that some *meclis*es did include women. Therefore, a close analysis of the works of women poets' in comparison with their contemporary male poets, and to other women poets in different periods, provides an excellent vantage point to understand the complexities of the structure of gender in poetry and how it is not only performative but also historical.

The Islamicate Discourse of Love

To understand the position of a woman poet expressing herself in Islamicate Ottoman poetry, it is imperative to situate her voice within the aesthetics of love. The Neoplatonic ideals of love in Islamic mysticism and their reflection in Persian, Ottoman, and Urdu poetry are very well studied, and the long history of their interaction is beyond the scope of this chapter.[10] It is sufficient to summarize that the idea of the One as the origin of everything is the backbone of Islamicate poetry. Based on al-Gazali's (d. 1111) *Mişkat-ül-Envar*, Walter Andrews explains the fundamental features of Islamic mysticism in poetry and summarizes it as an understanding of two worlds: the exoteric and esoteric. This world as we know it, *alem-ül-his*, is the one that is accessible through the senses in the presence of light. The other world, *alem-üt-temsil*, is the world of analogy or the celestial world. We can perceive it through insight and with the help of religious books. Everything in this world is a reflection of their reality in that world. What we see as duality, polarity, or contrast are illusions because, in that world, there is only unity as everything is part of the One (Andrews 1985, 62–69).

Therefore the poet's purpose is to unveil the truth, as this world is an illusion with all its temptations making human beings forget their ultimate purpose: to return to that world, to their beloved God. The poet is the Sufi dervish who is separated from the beloved God by coming to this world and thus yearns for unity in the other world. The best example of this concept may be the *Şeb-I Aruz* (the wedding night), the night that great Sufi master Mevlana Celaleddin Rumi's passing is celebrated instead of mourned as he was finally united with his beloved God.

As everything comes from the One and will return to the One, there is no distinction between living creatures, including binary opposites such as genders. Therefore, gender is only part of this world and it only reflects two qualities of the One. It follows that, at least theoretically, there should be no difference in value between a man and a woman. However, in practice, we see clearly defined values attached to gender. For instance, although the beloved is the representation of God and therefore should have no gender marking, he is represented by a prepubescent boy as the idealized beauty in the world of poetry. The mystical interpretations of the boy-beloved suggest that he is the reflection of the unattainable beauty of the divine. Even though the intention is to represent genderlessness, he is ultimately a male body. Likewise, Andrews and Kalpaklı have demonstrated that poetry had a physical ideal through the gender of the beloved who was accepted to be an androgynous boy.[11] The gender-neutral third-person pronoun in Turkish, as in Persian, allows this ambiguity around the beloved's gender.[12] However, the poets do not shy away from leaving clues to suggest that the beloved has a male body, such as the trope of the green line on his face as a result of the budding beard on a young man's face which disqualifies him as a beloved, thus causing agony for the poet.

Apart from the mystical take on the beloved, the linguistic and discursive ambiguity of his gender allowed poets to weave multiple meanings into their lines, including actual people as beloveds, such as the sultan or a notable patron. What is not acceptable though, is to define the beloved as a woman, young or old, rich or poor. There are only a few poems written for female beloveds.[13] However, references to mythical characters such as Leyla or Şirin are more common in poetry mostly based on the meaning of their names. It is only in women's poetry that these characters are treated as ideal lovers.[14] The most common representation of women's gender is through the treacherousness of this world, time, and destiny, which are personified as an old wretched woman. The poet is almost always a man pursuing a male youth who is ultimately silent. He pursues the ambiguous beloved and proves his devotion through a series of stylized acts to resist this world which is defined by womanliness. His virility and courage not only prove that he can resist the temptations of this world but are also evidence of his masculinity and, therefore, his poetic license.

The Troubling Love: Masculinity and Femininity

In terms of femininity and masculinity, however, we see flexibility in terms of poets taking up either gender role. In the world of poetry, although both the poet and the beloved are expected to be male, they can take turns being feminine and/or masculine. The poet possesses the language and ability to express himself to pursue love, therefore he is masculine, whereas the beloved has no voice and is ultimately the object of desire, therefore he is feminine. However, each poem will have a twist where the poet submits to love and diminishes himself as a poor soul as opposed to an almighty beloved. Selim S. Kuru discusses in his chapter on the courtly *gazel* genre in this volume this twist as an emasculation of the poet.[15] Similarly, Oscar Aguirre-Mandujano discusses the role change of the lover and the beloved specifically in the panegyric genre.[16] As I will discuss women's claim of masculinity in this chapter, we come to conclude that the possibility of a role change suggests the performativity of gender in poetry.

While the male bodies of the poet and the beloved are permanent, their behavior and stylized acts can be both feminine and masculine as they take turns to actualize love. It is worth highlighting the difference between the female body and femininity here. While femaleness is something to be resisted, being feminine can be part of the male gender. In the following examples, male poets claim manliness by resisting the "femaleness" of this world:

> Necatî, aren't you a man? Don't give in to this world
> While it [the world] is a woman, in such form, it never submits to a man.[17]

Necâtî (ca. 1444–1509) is one of the most celebrated poets of the late fifteenth century, and Mihrî wrote many parallels to his poems. He has several lines claiming manliness in his poems, as in the following:

> Hands off, if you have divorced the women of this world
> O Necâtî, a person should be a man of his word.[18]

In her parallels, Mihrî does not directly refer to Necâtî's claims of manliness. Instead, she focuses on her poetic skills in comparison to Necâtî's, underscoring her place as the true lover in the poetic world, as the following lines demonstrate:

> We are among those who came to sacrifice our lives for the beloved's sake
> We have become seekers after pain, among those who came for a cure.[19]

Although Necâtî's claim of manliness and positioning of himself is juxtaposed to a woman's subjectivity, his lines are not personal but a reflection of the poetic discourse. The following examples from different periods show that poethood is associated with manliness. From Bakî (1526–1566):

> Whoever inclines to the woman of the world, oh Bakî
> Don't think he would be considered a man among the courageous[20]

From Nâbî (1642–1687):

> Whoever doesn't fall into the traps of the woman of this world
> Comes to this battlefield of destiny as a man, and leaves as a man[21]

> The battlefield of love is quiet and empty
> The effeminate took over the place, men are forgotten[22]

From Nedîm (1681–1730):

> If you are a man, don't collect people's shame
> Make yourself a collection of good conduct for those who are looking[23]

From Şeyh Gâlib (1757–1799):

> While his precious life is impossible to spare
> Oh Galib, does the content man submit his love to the woman of this world?[24]

In this male-centered poetic world, whether an Ottoman poet is a man or a woman, their resistance to female worldliness is understandable due to its negative associations. Yet, interestingly, the women poets did not defy their gender by hiding behind a male pseudonym; instead, they challenged the negative meanings attached to it and tried to redefine them by setting positive examples.

Zeynep Hatun (d. 1450) is the earliest woman poet to appear in Ottoman biographical dictionaries. Although her poetry collection has not survived, a poem attributed to her contains the following couplet about the association of beauties of this world with femininity:

> Zeyneb, like a woman, stop yearning for the frills of this world
> Come manly, be plain-speaking and abandon all decoration.[25]

As many Ottoman poems, this couplet can be read in two ways: first, she asks herself to be a woman and stop caring for the temptations of this world. At the same time, the line may mean that she asks herself to stop caring for the temptations of this world like a woman would do. While this world is personified as a woman, the tendency to crave it is not necessarily defined as female behavior. Therefore, I translated these lines following the first meaning.

After Zeynep, we see other female poets, in particular Mihrî Hatun, following in her footsteps to construct a subversive voice in poetry. From the following examples, it is clear that when Ottoman women took on the role of the speaker, they caused a transgressive intervention in the discourse of love as they claimed manliness and reclaimed the positive connotations for the female gender. In the following couplet Mihrî Hatun challenges another poet to prove his maleness, implying that she is more of a man than he is:

> They say your rival boasts and says, "I'll kill her one day"
> If he's a man, let him come and I'll show manliness to that unmanly coward.[26]

While Mihrî is clear about her claim to manliness, her successors chose a subtler voice to prove that the feminine is not less than masculine. In the following lines, Ayşe Hubbî Hatun (d. 1589/90) recalls the feminine and masculine meanings of the sun and the moon in Arabic:

> Being feminine is no shame to the name of the sun
> Being masculine is no glory to the crescent moon.[27]

A Turning Point: The Nineteenth Century

Between the sixteenth and nineteenth centuries, there are only a couple of women poets mentioned in biographical dictionaries.[28] In the nineteenth century, there was a flourishing of women poets and among them, Moralızâde Leylâ Hanım (d. 1847) was a prominent figure who embraced her predecessors and acknowledged their names in her poetry. In so doing, she caused a shift in the poetic discourse to include ordinary women's names in poetry. Her gender awareness of the poetic world coincided with the developments in the history of women's writing. In this period, many women wrote in women's magazines, and they began publishing in various genres. This was the transition period from classical genres such as Ottoman poetry to short stories and novels. Modern ideas such as women's equality with men were the hot topics appearing in magazines. Meanwhile, only a few women poets chose to keep producing classical poetry. Leylâ Hanım was one of them. In the following lines, she echoes Mihrî's unapologetic woman's voice and challenges male-centric traditions:

> If your benevolence gives strength to the mourning heart
> Men of letters would envy my formidable poetry.[29]

The men of letters Leylâ Hanım refers to are her colleagues, both contemporaries and historical figures. Mihrî also entered into dialogue with her colleagues, though she did not have a sense of history. In the nineteenth century, we encounter a sense of history and understanding of gender that we can trace in women's poetry. Moreover, being a woman has a specific meaning for Leylâ Hanım and her female colleagues, as they intentionally embrace and celebrate their gender.

Subversive Masculinities and Femininities

Throughout Ottoman literary history, women challenged the meanings of masculinity and femininity. However, they did not redefine the beloved's gender. In other words, they did not propose an all-female world as an alternative to male homosociality. Rather, as women, they assumed the role of the lover/poet who was expected to be a man. Then, just like a male poet, they took on both masculine and feminine roles. The women were able to do this because gender in poetry is performative. They do not need to hide their gender, but as they take the role of the poet/lover, they redefine not only the gender of the poet but also the meanings of femininity. Furthermore, as they compose poetry for the male beloved, even though it may disrupt the male-dominated love structure among men, they introduce an alternative spiritual love, the one between a man and a woman, which was assumed to belong only to the earthly world rather than the aesthetic.

Moralızâde Leylâ Hanım is one of a few final Ottoman poets. By the end of the nineteenth century, women choose to write primarily in prose, just like their male colleagues. This was a reflection of changing times rather than a choice primarily among women. For instance, Fatma Aliye Hanım, the pioneering Ottoman Turkish novelist, refrained from writing poetry as her mentor Ahmet Mithat warned her against it.[30] Yet Fatma Aliye related the divorce story of Moralızâde Leylâ Hanım for Ibnülemin, implying the grievance of an intellectual woman who was married off to an ignorant man.[31]

While Ottoman poetry was losing its allure and prose was emerging as the preferred genre, the last representatives of Ottoman women's poetry adapted the new women's culture and reflected it in their poetry. They represent women's solidarity in their works by, for example, reflecting the consciousness of sisterhood by acknowledging women poets in their poems. In the following poem, Moralızâde Leylâ Hanım pays homage to the poet Fıtnat (1720–1780):

> How should I not be pleased by the blessings of that court?
> All the divine gifts in Fıtnat were granted me by Mevlânâ[32]

Other women poets followed Moralızâde Leylâ Hanım's lead, although male biographers attacked her for being a lesbian.[33] Even though women had always socialized in segregated circles and claimed masculinity by comparing themselves to Mecnun, Ferhâd, or Yusuf, the suggestion of a same-sex desire in poetry among women appears only in Moralızâde Leylâ Hanım's case. The change in discourse on sexuality and a tendency towards a firmer gender binary suggests a paradigmatic shift. During this transitional period from classical Islamicate aesthetics to Ottoman modernity, literary works reflected a modernist romance between men and women.

Gender in Islamicate Ottoman Poetry

The shift in the late nineteenth century was not only in genres and attitudes towards the past; it was clear in the way literature was produced and consumed. Before the printing press became prevalent in the late nineteenth century, literary works were produced and consumed in the *meclis*es. They were most probably performed in front of an audience and later recorded on paper. The *meclis* could physically be a public or semi-public place such as a garden, a coffee house, someone's living room, or a palace court for that matter. The perception, conception, and experience of it, however, were essentially related to power relations. For instance, the particular choices of the host/patron in his/her constitution of the *meclis* were fundamentally related to his/her gender and socioeconomic background.[34] To be included in a certain *meclis*, on the other hand, was dependent not only on the poet/artists' talents but more so on his/her networking skills.

The ultimate *meclis* that all poets compete with each other to be part of is the one held by the sultan in his palace. Aside from professional recognition, the protection of the palace, either through a stable job and salary or occasional monetary awards, was the ultimate success of a poet. Presenting panegyrics (*kaside*) to sultans on specific occasions such as religious festivals (*bayrams*) was an established practice of the Ottoman court and can be traced in palace registries.[35] An excellent example of such glamourous success was Bakî's *Sultan-ı Şu'ara* (Sultan of Poets) as opposed to the work of his contemporary Fuzulî, for instance, who was just as well educated and productive. The fundamental difference between these two great poets of the sixteenth century was their relative proximity to power. While Bakî lived most of his life in Istanbul under the protection of influential men, mainly Sultan Süleyman, the Baghdad resident Fuzulî spent most of his older age searching out his livelihood. In his petition to Sultan Süleyman, Fuzulî criticizes the patronage system and reminds him that his job as the sovereign is to distribute God's blessings equally. The letter is a reflection of the disappointment of a great poet in the "unjust" and "dishonorable" systems of the poetic world.[36]

A woman poet had to overcome spatial boundaries prescribed to her gender either virtually, through the act of writing poetry, or physically, through presenting it in a *meclis*. To be a legitimate poet, she had to be included in this overwhelmingly male world. Although this might have been the reason for the small number of women poets we know of today, the survivors show that their strategic use of the tradition allowed them to enter and exist in that world. Based on the life stories of women poets, they were either related to influential men through their family or professional relationships. Apart from the aforementioned poem by Mihrî Hatun as evidence of such a relationship with an influential man, there are several similar cases recorded in history. For instance, 'Ayşe Hubbî Hâtun achieved unprecedented success in the history of women's literary practice by serving as a *musahibe*, female boon companion, to Selim II.[37] The limited information we have about Tutî Hatun in the sixteenth century suggests that she was a resident of the harem in the palace.[38] From the later periods, Nigâr Hanım (1862–1918), Adile Sultan (1826–1899), and Leylâ Saz Hanım (1850–1936) relate harem stories in their memoirs.[39]

Another way a woman poet could achieve success was to establish relationships with influential women. Unfortunately, we do not know much about female *meclis*es in the early modern period other than the scant implications in poetry about their existence. For instance, in the sixteenth century, the poet Cinânî wrote many poems praising Hubbî Hatun and the Vâlide Safiye Sultan. In later periods, both in Ottoman and Persian literature, we see further examples of poems written for female patrons and women commemorating other women.[40]

Towards the end of the nineteenth century, the Tuesday meetings of Nigâr Hanım represent the transformation of the *meclis* culture and an Ottoman take on the modern literary salon. As one of the principal patrons of the time, Nigâr influenced many male and female poets, musicians, and intellectuals. Nigâr's meetings were for all genders as well as a separate room for those women who preferred a separate place. This may have allowed women from all walks of life to be included in the meetings. Moreover, children were also welcome, as Ercüment Ekrem Talu recalls his childhood memories of the Tuesday meetings, which he used to go with his father Recaizâde Mahmut Ekrem (1847–1914) and felt the sweet taste of poetry and music as he enjoyed the candy offered to him.[41] Although we do not have documentary evidence for women's *meclis*es from earlier periods, Nigâr's salon may give an idea about how they were constructed.

Conclusion

Women poets and writers had been treated by modern scholarship as exceptions or imitations of the "real" male literature. The reasoning is that they were very few in number—or else their poems were rarely recorded. However, as I have briefly tried to show here, the marginal voice of a woman crystallizes the male-centric discourse and its gender structure, making her quite different than a male poet. Her survival strategies in a discourse that sidelines her gender are ultimately transgressive and inspirational for her successors. The similarity in women's stories throughout literary history suggests that their exceptionality is comparable. Otherwise, as we have seen through several examples, there is nothing exceptional about a woman engaging in intellectual activities.

Women poets' existence in Ottoman poetry challenges the ideas of gender segregation in socializing and suggests that not all *meclis*es were exclusively male. Privileged men and women enjoyed some leeway in their private lives, and it follows that it is no coincidence that all the women poets we know came from privileged backgrounds. Furthermore, if women were only socializing among themselves, they would not have been known to male circles, and if they were not known among male circles, they would not appear in historical documents.

This chapter attempted to provide an introductory discussion of major issues and concepts of gender in the history of Ottoman courtly literature as they were reflected in the practice of literature both on the aesthetic and social levels. The main argument is that the concepts of gender continuously change with time and space. The values of ambiguity of the early modern period worked well for constructing gender fluidity in poetry. While women poets' entry into the literary world allowed for a crystallization of the meanings of masculinity and femininity, they also revealed the performative nature of these constructs. Compared to their male colleagues, women poets showed the multiple possibilities of love and gender roles in their works. The spatial dimensions of poetry, on the other hand, as it was partially related to a physical space, suggests the connection between poetry and real life. In this light, later periods, in particular the nineteenth century and its radical change in the construction of gender in literature, suggest both transformation and continuity. On the aesthetic level, the enforcement of the gender binary, and strictly prescribed femininity and masculinity to respective bodies are the immediate outcomes of the modernization period. As the printing press replaced *meclis* culture, the boundaries of the world of letters were reconstructed with new ideals and values of gender.

Notes

1 For the transcription of the full Gazel 133 in Mihrî's Divan, see the Ottoman Text Archive Project website, http://courses.washington.edu/otap/archive/data/arch_txt/texts/Mihrî_work/lnk_m121_140.html. For its translation, see Didem Havlioğlu, *Mihrî Hatun: Performance, Gender-Bending, and Subversion in Ottoman Intellectual History* (Syracuse, NY: Syracuse University Press, 2017), 178.
2 Havlioğlu, *Mihrî Hatun*, 178–81.

3 Selim S. Kuru suggests that male poets occasionally mentioned the names of their male beloveds. See Selim S. Kuru, "Naming the Beloved in Ottoman Turkish Gazel: The Case of İshak Çelebi (d. 1537/8)," in *Ghazal as World Literature II: From a Literary Genre to a Great Tradition: The Ottoman Gazel in Context*, ed. Angelika Neuwirth et al. (Beirut: Beiruter Texte und Studien), 163.

4 *Mihrî* received monetary rewards five times from the palace. For details, see Havlioğlu, *Mihrî Hatun*, 87.

5 Kemal Silay suggested that in a male-dominated poetics of the Ottoman literary history, the only thing women poets could do was mimic their male colleagues; see Kemal Silay, "Singing His Words: Ottoman Women Poets and the Power of Patriarchy," in *Women in the Ottoman Empire: Middle Eastern Women in the Early Modern Era*, ed. Madeline C. Zilfi (Leiden: Brill, 1988), 197–213. For my critique of his claims, see Havlioğlu, *Mihrî Hatun*, 10–11.

6 Victoria Holbrook discusses the idea of the new in her influential work on Şeyh Gâlib's *Hüsn ü Aşk* and suggests that Galib's claim of the new Ottoman mesnevi is a unique position. Virginia Holbrook, *The Unreadable Shores of Love: Turkish Modernity and Mystic Romance* (Austin: University of Texas Press, 1994).

7 In early modern biographical dictionaries, either by classification or discursive treatment, women poets are treated as a separate category. For a detailed discussion, see Didem Havlioğlu, "On the Margins and Between the Lines: Ottoman Women Poets from the Fifteenth to the Twentieth Centuries," *Turkish Historical Review* 1 (2010): 25–54.

8 Among the scholarly works that paved the way for a critical analysis of women poets, see Nazan Bekiroğlu, "Osmanlıda Kadın Şairler," in *Osmanlı: Kültür ve Sanat*, ed. Güler Eren (Ankara: Yeni Türkiye Yayınları, 1993), 802–12; Mübeccel Kızıltan, "Dîvân Edebiyatı Özelliklerine Uyarak Şiir Yazan Kadın Şairler," *Sombahar* 21–22 (January–April 1994): 104–69; Zehra Toska, "Divan Şiirinde Kadın Şairlerin Sesi," in *Türk Edebiyatı Tarihi*, ed. Talat Halman et al. (Ankara: KTB, 2006), 663–74.

9 The male-centered homosocial poetic circles are discussed in detail in Walter Andrews and Mehmet Kalpaklı, *The Age of Beloveds: Love and the Beloved in Early-Modern Ottoman and European Culture and Society* (Durham, NC: Duke University Press, 2005).

10 For a further discussion on the mystical concept of love, see Jamal Elias, *Aisha's Cushion: Religious Art, Perception, and Practice in Islam* (Boston: Harvard University Press, 2012); Doris Behrens-Abouseyf, *Beauty in Arabic Culture* (Princeton, NJ: Princeton University Press, 1999); Annemarie Schimmel, *Mystical Dimensions of Islam* (Chapel Hill: University of North Carolina Press, 1975). For a discussion of Neoplatonism and Ottoman poetry, see Walter Andrews, "Ottoman Poetry: Where the Neoplatonic Dissolves into an Emotional Script for Life," in *Faces of the Infinite: Neoplatonism and Poetry at the Confluence of Africa, Asia and Europe*, ed. Stefan Sperl and Yorgos Dedes (London: The British Academy, 2021), 165–83; Didem Havlioğlu, "Mihrî Hatun and Neoplatonic Discourse: Legitimation of Women's Writing in Early Modern Ottoman Poetry," in *Faces of the Infinite: Neoplatonism and Poetry at the Confluence of Africa, Asia and Europe*, ed. Stefan Sperl and Yorgos Dedes (London: The British Academy, 2021), 188–202.

11 See Andrews and Kalpaklı, *Age of Beloveds*, 37 for a detailed discussion of the gender of the beloved in the Ottoman tradition.

12 Irvin Cemil Schick discusses three genders in Ottoman history based on linguistic and literary research: "Three Genders, Two Sexualities: The Evidence of Ottoman Erotic Terminology," in *Sex and Desire in Muslim Cultures: Beyond Norms and Transgression from the Abbasids to the Present Day*, ed. A. Kreil, L. Sorbera, and S. Tolino (London: Bloomsbury, 2020), 87–110.

13 For a discussion of the female beloved in poetry and poets who prefer women, see Andrews and Kalpaklı, *Age of Beloveds*, 44–45.

14 This is one of the ways women's works set significantly apart from the male poets' works. For Mihrî's use of Züleyha, see Havlioğlu, *Mihrî Hatun*, 129–37.

15 See Selim S. Kuru's chapter in this volume.

16 See Oscar Aguirre-Mandujano's chapter in this volume.

17 *Er degül misin Necatî olma dünyāya mufî'/ 'Avret iken ol şu şūretle mufî' olmaz ere.* The translation appears in Havlioğlu, *Mihrî Hatun*, 122.

18 *El çek boşaduñ ise zenini zemānenüñ/ Olmaḳ gerek Necatî kişi sözinüñ eri*, translation appears in Havlioğlu, *Mihrî Hatun*, 123.

19 For a comparative discussion of the poems by Necâtî and Mihrî, see Havlioğlu, *Mihrî Hatun*, 115–38.

20 *Her kim ki meyl ider zen-i dünyâya Bâkıyâ Merdâneler içinde anı sanma er geçer (Bakî Divanı, Gazel 62).*

21 *Kim ki mekr-i zen-i dünyâya zebûn olmaz ise Rezm-gâh-ı feleğe merd gelir merd gider (Nâbî Divanı, Gazel 187).*

22 *Kalmış ser-i meydân-ı mahabbet tek ü tenhâ Zen-tablar almış yeri merdân unutulmuş (Nâbî Divanı, Gazel 345).*

23 *Defter-keş-i meâ'yib-i nâs olma merd isen Kıl zâtını nazarlara mecmû'a-yı edeb (Nedîm Divanı, Gazel 7).*

24 *Hemân nakd-i hayâti bî-dirğ iken anın mihrî Zen-i dünyâya Gâlib râm olur mu merd-i istiğnâ (Seyh Gâlib Divanı, Gazel 10).*

25 *Zeyneb ko meyli ziynet-i dünyâya zen gibi / Merdâne var sâde-dil ol terk-i zîver ėt* (Âşık Çelebi, *Âşık Çelebi—Meşâ'irü'ş-şu'arâ: İnceleme—Metin*, ed. Filiz Kılıç, vol. 3 (Istanbul: İstanbul Araştırmaları Enstitüsü, 2010), 591).

26 For the transcription of the poem, see OTAP, http://courses.washington.edu/otap/archive/data/arch_txt/texts/Mihrî_work/lnk_m81_100.html; for the translation, see Havlioğlu, *Mihrî Hatun*, 187.

27 Andrews and Kalpaklı, *Age of Beloveds*, 209.

28 For an inclusive list of poets and a critical discussion, see Havlioğlu, "On the Margins," 25–54.

29 Mehmet Arslan, ed., *Leyla Hanım Divanı* (Istanbul: Kitabevi, 2003), 104.

30 Nüket Esen discusses the relationship between Fatma Aliye and Ahmet Mithat in detail; see Nüket Esen, *Hikaye Anlatan Adam: Ahmet Mithat* (Istanbul: İletişim, 2014).

31 For an overall discussion of the Ottoman women poets from the fifteenth to twentieth centuries, see Havlioğlu, "On the Margins."

32 Arslan, *Leyla Hanım Divanı* (gazel 2); translation mine.

33 Among her biographers, Mehmed Zihni is insistent on her sexual orientation as a lesbian; see Mehmed Zihni, *Meşahirü'n-Nisa* (Istanbul: Matbaa-I Amire, 1878), 195.

34 For the significance of the *meclis* culture for the Ottomans, see Halil İnalcık, *Şâir ve Patron: Patrimonyal Devlet ve Sanat Üzerinde Sosyolojik Bir İnceleme* (Ankara: Doğu-Batı Yayınları, 2003).

35 For instance, Bayezid II, who was a poet himself, was a generous patron of the arts, and his palace registry is evidence of his dedication to supporting literature and the arts during his reign. See, Hilal Kazan, *16. Asırda Sarayın Sanatı Himayesi* (Istanbul: İsar Vakfı Yayınları, 2010).

36 For a detailed discussion of the case of Fuzulî, see Halil İnalcık, *Has-bağçede 'ayş u tarab: Nedimler, Şairler, Mutripler* (Istanbul: Türkiye İş Bankası Yayınları, 2011), 283–92.

37 For a discussion of the Ottoman women patrons in the literature of the sixteenth and seventeenth centuries, see Hatice Aynur and Didem Havlioğlu, "Medhiyenin Cinsiyeti: Kadınlara Yazılmış Kasideler," in *Eski Türk Edebiyatı Çalışmaları/Kasideye Medhiyye: Biçime, İşleve ve Muhtevaya Ait Tespitler*, ed. Hatice Aynur et al. (Istanbul: Klâsik, 2013), 76–123; for a discussion of women patrons of poetry in nineteenth-century Iran, see Dominic Brookshaw, "Odes of a Poet-Princess: The Ghazals of Jahān-Malik Khātūn," *Iran* 43 (2005): 173–95.

38 Havlioğlu, "On the Margins," 2010.

39 Bekiroğlu, "Osmanlıda Kadın Şairler"; Hikmet Özdemir, ed., *Adile Sultan Divanı* (Ankara: Kültür Bakanlığı Yayınları, 1996); Leyla Saz Hanım, *Haremin İç Yüzü* (Istanbul: Milliyet Yayınları, 1974).

40 There are similar incidents in Persian poetry. Dominic Brookshaw suggests that the prominent women poet Jahan-Malik Khatun was not only an accepted and celebrated poet in the literary circles of sixteenth-century Shiraz, but also "zurafa and nudama always gathered in her majlis." See Brookshaw, "Odes of a Poet-Princess," 174.

41 For a detailed discussion of salons (*meclis*) in modern Turkish literature, see Turgat Anar, *Mekandan Taşan Edebiyat: Yeni Türk Edebiyatında Edebiyat Mahfilleri* (Istanbul: Kapı, 2012), 121.

References

Anar, Turgay. *Mekandan Taşan Edebiyat: Yeni Türk Edebiyatında Edebiyat Mahfilleri*. Istanbul: Kapı. 2012.

Andrews, Walter G. *Poetry's Voice, Society's Song: Ottoman Lyric Poetry*. Seattle: University of Washington Press, 1985.

———. "Ottoman Poetry: Where the Neoplatonic Dissolves into an Emotional Script for Life." In *Faces of the Infinite: Neoplatonism and Poetry at the Confluence of Africa, Asia and Europe*, edited by Stefan Sperl and Yorgos Dedes, 165–83. London: The British Academy, 2021.

Andrews, Walter G., and Mehmet Kalpaklı. *The Age of Beloveds: Love and the Beloved in Early-Modern Ottoman and European Culture and Society*. Durham, NC: Duke University Press, 2005.

Arslan, Mehmet, ed. *Leyla Hanım Divanı*. Istanbul: Kitabevi, 2003.

Âşık Çelebi. *Meşâ'irü'ş-Şuarâ*. Edited by Filiz Kılıç. Istanbul: İstanbul Araltırmaları Enstitüsü, 2010.

Behrens-Abouseyf, Doris. *Beauty in Arabic Culture*. Princeton, NJ: Princeton University Press, 1999.

Bekiroğlu, Nazan. "Osmanlıda Kadın Şairler." In *Osmanlı: Kültür ve Sanat*, edited by Güler Eren. Ankara: Yeni Türkiye Yayınları, 1993.

————. *Şair Nigar Hanım*. Istanbul: Kitap Yurdu, 2014.

Bilkan, A. F. *Nâbî Divanı*. Ankara: Akçağ Yayınları, 2011.

Brookshaw, Dominic. "Odes of a Poet-Princess: The Ghazals of Jahān-Malik Khātūn." *Iran* 43 (2005): 173–95.

Elias, Jamal. *Aisha's Cushion: Religious Art, Perception, and Practice in Islam*. Boston: Harvard University Press, 2012.

Esen, Nüket. *Hikaye Anlatan Adam: Ahmet Mithat*. Istanbul: İletişim, 2014.

Havlioğlu, Didem. "On the Margins and Between the Lines: Ottoman Women Poets from 15th to 20th Century." *Turkish Historical Review* 1 (2010): 25–54.

————. *Mihrî Hatun: Performance, Gender-Bending, and Subversion in Ottoman Intellectual History*. New York: Syracuse University Press, 2017.

————. "Mihrî Hatun and Neoplatonic Discourse: Legitimation of Women's Writing in Early Modern Ottoman Poetry." In *Faces of the Infinite: Neoplatonism and Poetry at the Confluence of Africa, Asia and Europe*, edited by Stefan Perl et al., 188–202. London: The British Academy, 2021.

Havlioğlu, Didem, and Hatice Aynur. "Medhiyenin Cinsiyeti: Kadınlara Yazılmış Kasideler [Gender of the Ode: Qasidas Written for Women]." In *Eski Türk Edebiyatı Çalışmaları/Kasideye Medhiyye: Biçime, İşleve ve Muhtevaya Ait Tespitler*, edited by Hatice Aynur et al., 76–123. Istanbul: Klâsik, 2013.

Holbrook, Virginia. *The Unreadable Shores of Love: Turkish Modernity and Mystic Romance*. Austin: University of Texas Press, 1994.

İnalcık, Halil. *Şair ve Patron*. Ankara: Dogu Bati Yayınları, 2003.

————. *Has-bağçede 'ayş u tarab: Nedimler, Şairler, Mutripler*. Istanbul: Türkiye İş Bankası Yayınları, 2011.

Kazan, Hilal. *16. Asırda Sarayın Sanatı Himayesi*. Istanbul: İsar Vakfı Yayınları, 2010.

Kızıltan, Mübeccel. "Dîvân Edebiyatı Özelliklerine Uyarak Şiir Yazan Kadın Şairler." *Sombahar* 21–22 (January–April 1994): 104–69.

Küçük, Sabahattin, ed. *Bakî Divanı*. Ankara: Türk Dil Kurumu Yayınları, 1994.

Kuru, Selim. "Naming the Beloved in Ottoman Turkish Gazel: The Case of İshak Çelebi (d. 1537/8)." In *Ghazal as World Literature II. From a Literary Genre to a Great Tradition. The Ottoman Gazel in Context*, edited by Angelika Neuwirth, Michael Hess, Judith Pfeiffer, and Boerte Sagaster, 163–73. Beirut and Würzburg: Beiruter Texte und Studien, 2006.

Leyla Saz Hanım. *Haremin İç Yüzü*. Istanbul: Milliyet Yayınları, 1974.

Mehmed Zihni. *Meşahirü'n-Nisa*. Istanbul: Matbaa-i Amire, 1878.

Özdemir, Hikmet, ed. *Adile Sultan Divanı*. Ankara: Kültür Bakanlığı Yayınları, 1996.

Schick, Irvin C. "Three Genders, Two Sexualities: The Evidence of Ottoman Erotic Terminology." In *Sex and Desire in Muslim Cultures: Beyond Norms and Transgression from the Abbasids to the Present Day*, edited by A. Kreil, L. Sorbera, and S. Tolino, 87–110. London: Bloomsbury, 2020.

Schimmel, Annemarie. *Mystical Dimensions of Islam*. Chapel Hill: University of North Carolina Press, 1975.

Silay, Kemal. "Singing His Words: Ottoman Women Poets and the Power of Patriarchy." In *Women in the Ottoman Empire: Middle Eastern Women in the Early Modern Era*, edited by Madeline C. Zilfi, 197–213. Leiden: Brill, 1988.

Sperl, Stefan, and Yorgos Dedes. "'In the Rose-Bower Every Leaf Is a Page of Delicate Meaning': An Arabic Perspective on Three Ottoman Kasides." In *Kasîdeye Medhiye: Biçime, İşleve ve Muhteveya Dair Tespitler*, edited by Hatice Aynur, Müjgân Çakır, Hanife Koncu, Selim S. Kuru, and Ali Emre Özyıldırım, 240–313. Istanbul: Klasik, 2013.

Tarlan, Ali Nihad, ed. *Necati Bey Divanı*. Washington University, 1963. http://courses.washington.edu/otap/archive/data/arch_txt/texts/a_necati1.html.

Toska, Zehra. "Divan Şiirinde Kadın Şairlerin Sesi." In *Türk Edebiyatı Tarihi*, 663–74. Ankara: KTB, 2006.

13

GENDERED NARRATIVES OF OTTOMAN PROSE FICTION

The "Wiles of Women" Stories

N. İpek Hüner Cora

This chapter discusses gendered narratives in Ottoman prose fiction in the early modern context. Its aims are twofold. First, it draws attention to the sources and studies on prose fiction, which is commonly regarded as a genre of secondary importance both in contemporary Ottoman literary sources and by modern scholarship. Second, it describes stereotypical gendered representations in prose fiction, with a special focus on trickster stories and the "wiles of women" genre. The chapter also emphasizes how different genres in Ottoman literature contain diverse representations of gendered stereotypes. I will focus on a limited sample of trickster stories to draw some preliminary conclusions regarding stereotypical gendered representations. From a wider perspective, this chapter proposes that we should consider genre while discussing gendered representations in the Ottoman literary world—as well as the intersectional character of the gender, affected by age and class.[1]

Several studies on the intersection of literary studies and gender focus on Ottoman poetry, especially *ghazal* and *qasida*. For instance, in the *Age of the Beloved*, Walter Andrews and Mehmet Kalpaklı focus mostly on poetry to discuss beloveds and their reception in the early modern period. The beloveds represented in poetry are primarily idealized young males who partake in age-structured, same-sex relationships.[2] The representations of same-sex desire within the cultural context are further discussed by Khaled Al-Rouayheb in *Before Homosexuality* with a focus on poetry in the Arabic-speaking lands of the Ottoman Empire.[3] The scholarship on Ottoman poetry not only prioritizes men's desires towards idealized young males due to the characteristics of commonly studied genres but also focuses consequently on male authors, poets, and readers as the most visible actors of the literary scene. The available sources for Ottoman literary history—mainly the biographies of poets—also prioritize poetry over other genres given their aims and context, listing elite male poets and leaving women out of the picture. Few women poets find their place among these lists.[4] The limited number of women in these compilations is not surprising, as the official paths to education and consequently to the literary elite were accessible only to a limited number of privileged women. Didem Havlioğlu's study of the poetess Mihrî Hatun exemplifies such a case, depicting how a woman poet negotiates her position in such a male environment and how her gender identity is reflected in her literary encounters and production.[5]

The primary position of poetry is not unique to Ottoman sources, but its legacy continues in contemporary academic studies by treating works of prose fiction as secondary. While the

160

DOI: 10.4324/9780429279270-18

elevated position of poetry might have been a reality of the Ottoman world, there is sufficient evidence that prose fiction was popular among both the elite and common folk. The sheer number of manuscripts containing prose stories speaks to this. Furthermore, these manuscripts are of various registers and scribal quality, which indicates that they were consumed by people of different social strata at various locations—be it the imperial palace or an occasional gathering at someone's home.[6] Within this mobility and fluidity, the stories themselves further defy neat categorizations of folk and high literature, as the same story might find its place in a book prepared for the sultan and a low-quality manuscript circulating in the city. Consequently, I use the term "prose fiction" as an umbrella term for stories written in prose in order to be inclusive of stories defined by varying themes, registers, lengths, and linguistic characteristics. Here, I should also note that prose was not the only form of storytelling; different forms of poetry (such as *mesnevi*) were also popular for narrative purposes.[7]

Studies that touch on gendered representations in prose works are scattered and cover different facets of the available corpus. Selim S. Kuru's study on an elaborate prose-work, *Dāfi'ü'l-gumūm ve rāfi'ül-humūm* [The Book that Repels Sorrow and Removes Grief], focuses on sexually explicit stories in prose for edification, primarily focusing on same-sex activities and practices.[8] Kuru's study is significant for gender studies as it questions the supposed "marginality" of explicit sources. From the perspective of form and genre, it also shows the artificiality of a rigid division between prose and poetry, given the shared vocabulary and imagery shaping these sources. Not only stories but other genres in prose give literary historians clues about gendered representations. For instance, in *Producing Desire*, Dror Ze'evi uses sources in different genres to discuss the history of the body and sexuality from the seventeenth to twentieth centuries, and he includes medical manuals, sharia, *qanun*, poetry, prose, dream manuals, shadow theater, and travel accounts in his analysis. This overview of gendered representations should be read with an awareness of the variety of sources and their specific modes of representation.[9] A lengthy survey by Schick offers a literary overview on erotica by tracing the representation of gender and sexuality in Ottoman and Turkish erotic literature with a focus on *bāhnāme*s, classical and folk poetry, theater works, and popular literature.[10]

The studies analyzing gendered representations in prose fiction in the early modern context are limited in number. For example, David Selim Sayers' dissertation, "The Wiles of Women in Ottoman and Azeri Texts," introduces men's and women's representation in women's wiles stories. With a focus on fairy tales, Evrim Ölçer Özünel makes a gendered and spatial reading in *Masal Mekanında Kadın Olmak* (Being a Woman in the Space of Fairy Tales). In a short article, Helga Anetshofer discusses the Nasreddin Hoca stories from a gendered perspective in which she observes a change in representation and visibility of women throughout the centuries.[11] Further publications, while not delivering a gendered analysis, provide an invaluable source for making prose stories accessible.[12]

Wiles of women stories can be considered as a thematic subgenre of prose stories or trickster stories.[13] They are a part of the shared literary culture of the Islamicate world, as studies on Arabic and Persian stories reveal. In these stories, female protagonists trick men in ways that will alarm, astonish, and entertain the readers. While the stories end in moral lessons that warn men against women and their wiles, in most stories women get away with their tricks. There is also no direct chastisement against the woman character or her specific actions, but a warning against the evil nature of all women and that they should be avoided.[14] The wiles of women stories can be considered part of a larger storytelling tradition of trickster tales, where a (male) trickster gets away with his trick, usually with significant financial gain.[15]

The difference in the treatment of trickster stories versus wiles of women stories in the scholarship reflects gendered presumptions even before we delve into close readings. Stories

161

of male tricksters are treated under rather fashionable titles such as "underworld," and they are often treated as stories that give us ideas about the dark side of daily life.[16] The stories are of more practical use: the readers are not warned against the "evil" nature of men, nor they are cautioned against consulting men. Rather they are told to be quick-witted, never give their goods without getting the payment first, and so on. The stories focusing on women tricksters, in contrast, are categorized under "wiles of women" and as a corpus. They reveal an image of women—or rather of womanhood—that is devilish, wily, and to be shunned. The advice of these stories is not only to avoid women; they also comment on the nature of women. A close reading of these stories, however, complicates our understanding of the representations of masculinity and femininity in fiction by both challenging and reproducing different stereotypes.

Wiles of women stories challenge the stereotype of the absent, silent, and/or passive woman. To pursue their vile schemes, the women in the stories show their uncanny wits, even though they may appear silent and passive at first glance. The wily women are also not women of a different world, as these stories show that any woman may use tricks depending on the circumstances. For instance, a loyal but cuckolded wife may confront her husband by borrowing his lover's clothes and pretending to be her. In that story, the husband mistakenly follows his wife—assuming she is his lover—and ends up being beaten by her.[17] In many other instances, women choose schemes not simply to trick men but also to challenge and ridicule them. For example, in one of the stories, the trickster wife gives clothes to her lover and sends him to her husband's shop to sell them, making sure that her husband gets wind of the affair.[18] To emphasize women's ability to ridicule, the stories also mock men who undermine their wits and wiles. For instance, to teach her husband a lesson, one wife buries fish in her husband's field and creates a scheme that causes him to be declared insane and suffer public consequences.[19] In another story, a young lover mocks the genre of wiles of women stories and declares them unworthy of being recorded in writing. So she teaches him a lesson that causes him to be frightened for his life.[20]

These stories also subvert the image of the women imprisoned in their homes. Women in the stories are bound by the norms of the marital bond and society, but they can transgress the boundaries easily through ruses. The transgression of physical or temporal boundaries lies at the center of many tricks. One of the most common plots starts with the wife who is locked up by her jealous husband. In those instances, the wife's transgression is not only an act of following her desires but also of revenge and daring. For example, a porter who is even "jealous of the ant at home and the spider on the wall" falls victim to a trick and ends up carrying his wife's lover on his back locked in a chest.[21] Not knowing what he has done, he even locks the door on them; thus the imposed boundaries end up serving the lovers by ensuring their privacy. In another story, a wife instructs her lover to move into a house in the street behind hers and dig a tunnel so that the couple will be able to meet while the door remains locked. In this story, the initial motivation behind the trick is not the wife's desires for the lover but her resentment at being locked up at home.[22] The women also infringe on social boundaries regulating time. For instance, they enjoy their lovers' company during the daytime when their husbands are absent.[23] Or if they are encountered on a street at night, they simply pretend to be lost and helpless.[24]

Remarkably, the stories remind us that the temporal regulations with regards to the use of space were not unique to women. Men also need to find excuses to legitimize their presence in spaces and at times not designated for them. For instance, a merchant must make excuses to return home during the day. In one story, the wife even declares "women rule inside the home and its outside is at men's disposal" when her husband comes home during the day unannounced.[25] Both men and women need to justify their presence on the streets at night. In one story, a man who goes out at night seeking illicit encounters is apprehended by the chief of the police. To legitimize his presence out at night, he pretends to be looking for the chief of the

Gendered Narratives of Ottoman Prose Fiction

police to report immoral actions at a house in his neighborhood. With this pretense, he manages to escape to home and blames the police superintendent for trespassing, thus using the normative measures of society to save himself.[26] In another story, when a woman's husband does not allow her in late at night, she feigns suicide, pretending she cannot endure being ashamed by the neighbors. Like the man in the aforementioned story, she successfully uses neighborhood watch and social norms to trick her husband.[27] These stories and others show not only the imposed societal gender norms but also how these characters use (and abuse) these norms for their own purposes. Thus, the women in the stories—as well as the narration—serve simultaneously to subvert the existing social values and to perpetuate them. As a consequence, in this fictional world, women use locked doors and their virtual imprisonment at home to secure privacy with their lovers, or else veiling becomes a way to assume another's identity or even to smuggle a lover in under the husband's nose.[28]

The wiles of women stories create devious and guileful stereotypes of women whose sexual (and also sometimes financial) desires cannot be satisfied. However, their representation of men is similarly unflattering. In many instances, the men do not even realize they are the target or victim of the trick, so the woman gets away with it. Remarkably, the stories do not explicitly criticize women or deliver a moral judgment against them; instead, they poke fun at the man's lack of wit.[29] The tricked men are stereotypical, mostly lacking description. The representation of lovers similarly lacks any depth; in some stories, their physical attractiveness and youth are mentioned, but that is all.[30] Men are rather defined by their professions as an indication of wealth and social status.

Focusing on representations of gender relations also reveals the importance of intersectionality. Above all, age is a key factor but only with regard to women. The tricksters are usually married younger women. Their mobility is limited by their marital status. The older trickster women—who are presumably widows—have a different social status and increased mobility. While they may seem less respectable, they roam streets freely and have access to strangers, including men. Older women also design tricks or help younger women to create them.[31] Unmarried free females of younger age rarely feature as tricksters or even as main characters in the stories.[32] Slave women and concubines also appear in stories, but mostly in the background, opening doors or waiting on women while they entertain their lovers.[33] They serve their female masters in different errands or are objects of desires for male characters, but they are not protagonists with agency.[34] Considering all the above examples, in the stories, the gendered stereotypes are shaped by the same criteria that organize the social encounters—in other words, age, social status, and wealth determine the visibility and mobility of women.[35]

Wealth or class is another remarkable aspect in the representation of both men and women in trickster stories. For instance, women who entertain lovers at home are typically merchants' wives who have the means to spend the day idly at home hosting feasts.[36] Appearing wealthy is also a significant factor in the public visibility of both women and men. For instance, a female trickster may dress up to appear rich and proper.[37] Thus, in one story, a woman pretends to be of higher social (and thus moral) status by putting on all her jewels so that she can convince the police superintendent that she is a chaste woman behaving within the codes of moral conduct.[38] In another story, one of the male protagonists uses his own "lesser" appearance to his advantage. In this story, the woman is entertaining her lover in the absence of her husband when her other lover comes to visit her. The first lover, who is of a lesser social status, goes into hiding upon his arrival. The second lover, however, has to hide, too, when the husband comes home unexpectedly. As the story goes, the first lover is discovered by the husband. He pretends to be a slave to the woman's (second) lover who is of higher social standing and thus of more distinguished appearance and saves the day.[39] Thus, a man's financial and social capital dictates his appearance as well as his visibility in public places. For instance, a rich man is not expected to be present in the marketplace conducting his own business. As a common plot device, tricksters prepare clueless slaves to appear like a rich country man who does not know the ways of the big city, a common social type, to fool merchants. To pull off this trick, a well-built slave is purchased and dressed up in a wealthy man's clothes. The tricksters then pretend to serve this illustrious master. They ensure that others assume he is a man of the utmost significance so that the shop owners are simply happy to serve him and deliver his goods without being paid in advance. In the end, the tricksters disappear with the goods and the merchants are left with a well-dressed slave whose price is insufficient to cover their loss.[40] These examples show that the fictional world of stories is not devoid of the social and class barriers that dictate the conduct of everyday life.

In terms of everyday life, one remarkable aspect of the sexual encounters in the wiles of women and trickster stories is that couples fulfill their desires through sexual intercourse— despite the lack of explicit details. The stories might have been titillating for their audiences, as one of the common tropes is that female desire that cannot possibly be satisfied. As an extreme example, one story in *Bedāyi'ü'l-āsār* tells of a woman who domesticates a bear so that her sexual urges can be sexually satisfied, something no human can do.[41] Of course, what readers would find to be arousing, titillating, or irritating would strongly depend on the historical context as well as the setting in which the stories are told.[42]

Yet it can be said that these sexual fantasies in the wiles of women stories present a rather heteronormative world consisting of women, their husbands, and male lovers.[43] This, of course, is not to say that the Ottoman world was strictly heteronormative or that these stories reflect the sexual preferences as they were really lived. Still, this observation underlines the significance of the genre in the representation of desires and sexual encounters. While forms of love poetry such as the *ghazal* present a world of same-sex desires, the prose stories in wiles of women predominantly present heterosexual relationships.

The predominance of heterosexual relationships alongside the vilification of women seems to favor the male gaze and fantasies. As men are seen as the primary producers and consumers of literary production, it can be safely assumed that these stories were written by and for men. Also, as mentioned above, the vilification of women and the constant warning against interacting with them points to a male approach, as these stories provide men with advice as well as entertainment. In some stories, there is an implied reference towards the wisdom of preferring men to women as sexual partners, but this does not seem to be as common enough to be described as a general trend.[44]

If one approaches the wiles of women stories as male fantasies, then they can be interpreted as the misogynistic musings of men who use the stories both to fantasize about and express their anxieties towards women. The male anxieties of being outwitted and cuckolded are embodied in the imbecile and ignorant male protagonist who is likely meant to be pitied or laughed at. The stories continuously remind men that the wiles of women are to be taken seriously; otherwise, they may lead to significant inconvenience.[45]

While men are the usual suspects behind the creation and proliferation of these stories, there is no reason to think that women were unaware of these stories and did not contribute to their proliferation or circulation. Their contribution might be primarily oral; however, unfortunately, our access to the oral narratives of the early modern period is solely mediated through written sources and thus significantly limited. The question of how women might have responded to these stories gives us further possibilities for speculation. Were they alarmed by women's wits ignited by unchaste motivations? Did they enjoy these stories and fantasize about illicit encounters? Did the stories create a space where they could transgress the boundaries of social norms? Were they inspiring? While these questions are worth asking, it is impossible to give a definite

Gendered Narratives of Ottoman Prose Fiction

answer. However, most of these possibilities must have made men anxious, as Merguerian and Najmabadi's study on the story of Joseph and Zulaikha shows: the author of one of the canonical thirteenth-century advice books remarks that women should not read the story, lest they be led astray.[46]

As these stories are imbued with values and rules that regulated daily life and social relations, they may easily give the impression of being "realistic," especially if readers believe the authors' claims that these events actually have occurred—however impossible the individual trick may seem.[47] My concern here is not to show that the stories were realistic and, consequently, that the gender relations represented by them reflect reality. Instead, I want to emphasize that we should not fall into the trap of believing in the realism of these stories simply because they are set in a world where the gendered rules of conduct, social boundaries, and the law seem to neatly fit those of the real world. Within their realistic settings, these stories represent a heteronormative gender regime that is not of flesh-and-blood characters but of stereotypes: this fictional world consists of wily, witty, and pretty women; rich and imbecilic men; good-looking and sexually potent lovers; and invisible slave girls acting as servants. However, this set of stereotypes is different from the stereotypes that Ottoman love poetry presents: the age-structured same-sex relationships, idealized young beloveds, and grief-stricken and poetic lovers are absent from the fictional world of prose in the example of women's wiles stories. What is interesting and needs to be further discussed is that these different genres were reproduced and circulated in similar circles. This reminds us of the significance of the genre and readership in determining gender representations; in other words, that each genre has its own characteristics.

Notes

1 For a more detailed discussion of the topic with examples, see N. İpek Hüner Cora, " 'The Story Has It': Prose, Gender and Space in the Early Modern Ottoman World" (PhD diss., University of Chicago, 2018). An early version of this chapter was presented at the conference, "Rethinking Genre in the Islamicate Middle East," September 6, 2019, and I am thankful to the presenters and audience for their feedback.

2 Walter G. Andrews and Mehmet Kalpaklı, *The Age of Beloveds: Love and the Beloved in Early-Modern Ottoman and European Culture and Society* (Durham, NC: Duke University Press, 2005). See also Selim S. Kuru, "Naming the Beloved in Ottoman Turkish Ghazal: The Case of Ishak Çelebi (D. 1537/8)," in *Ghazal as World Literature II: From a Literary Genre to a Great Tradition. The Ottoman Gazel in Context,* ed. Angela Neuwirth, Michael Hess, Judith Pfeiffer, and Börte Sagaster (Istanbul: Orient Institut, 2006), 163–73.

3 Khaled El-Rouayheb, *Before Homosexuality in the Arab-Islamic World, 1500–1800* (Chicago: University of Chicago Press, 2005).

4 On female poets of the Empire, see, e.g., Didem Havlioğlu, "On the Margins and Between the Lines: Ottoman Women Poets from the Fifteenth to the Twentieth Centuries," *Turkish Historical Review* 1 (2010): 25–54.

5 Didem Z. Havlioğlu, *Mihrî Hatun: Performance, Gender-Bending, and Subversion in Ottoman Intellectual History* (Syracuse, NY: Syracuse University Press, 2017).

6 On reading circles, see Tülün Değirmenci, "Bir Kitabı Kaç Kişi Okur? Osmanlı'da Okurlar ve Okuma Biçimleri Üzerine Bazı Gözlemler," *Tarih ve Toplum Yeni Yaklaşımlar* 13 (2011): 7–43.

7 An example of gendered readings of stories in *mesnevi* form is by Bahar Gökpınar, *Osmanlı Yazınında Erkeklik(ler) Kurgusu* (The Fiction of Masculinities in Ottoman Literature), which problematizes representations of manhood and masculinities in the early modern context using literary sources—a rather uncharted area. Bahar Gökpınar, *'Er Kişi Niyetine,' Osmanlı Yazınında Erkeklik(ler) Kurgusu, 17–18–19. Yüzyıl Metinlerinde Bitmeyen Dönüşüm* (Istanbul: Bilge Kültür Sanat, 2018).

8 Selim S. Kuru, "Sex in the Text: Deli Birader's Dâfi'ü 'l-gumûm ve Râfi'ü 'l-humûm and the Ottoman Literary Canon," *Middle Eastern Literatures* 10, no. 2 (2007): 157–74; Selim S. Kuru, "A Sixteenth-Century Scholar: Deli Birader and His Dāfiʿüʾl-Gumūm ve Rāfiʿüʾl-Humūm" (PhD diss., Harvard University, 2000).

165

N. İpek Hüner Cora

9 Dror Ze'evi, *Producing Desire: Changing Sexual Discourse in the Ottoman Middle East, 1500–1900* (Berkeley: University of California Press, 2006).

10 İrvin Cemil Schick, "Representation of Gender and Sexuality in Ottoman and Turkish Erotic Literature," *The Turkish Studies Association Journal* 28, no. 1–2 (2004): 81–103.

11 Helga Anetshofer, "Representations of Women, Gender and Sexuality: Humorous Depictions: The Ottoman Empire," *Ewic* (2007): 437.

12 Cinānī's prose story collection, *Bedāyiʿüʾl-āṣār*, has been made accessible by Osman Ünlü's with transcription and facsimile. Another story collection especially useful with regard to women's wiles literature is the story *Forty Viziers*, made accessible in transcription by Aziz Birinci: Cinānī, *Bedāyiʿüʾl-āṣār*, ed. Osman Ünlü (Cambridge, MA: Department of Near Eastern Languages and Civilizations, Harvard University, 2009); Aziz Birinci, "Kırk Vezir Hikâyeleri, İnceleme-Metin-Sözlük" (PhD diss., Istanbul University, 2012). Recently, Nagihan Gür has published a long story featuring a female protagonist. However, *Afîfe Hanım Sergüzeşti* is not a story of women's wiles but the story of a woman going through hardships. For the text and analysis, see Nagihan Gür, *Hikâyenin Hikâyesi: Osmanlı'da Bir Kadın Anlatısı. Afîfe Hanım Sergüzeşti* (Istanbul: Kitabevi, 2020).

13 There are different attempts to categorize prose stories in Ottoman Turkish. Scholars categorize the stories according to themes, origins, sources, and so on. For an overview of the possible categorization, see Hasan Kavruk, *Eski Türk Edebiyatında Mensûr Hikâyeler* (Istanbul: M.E.B., 1998), 12–14.

14 On wiles of women stories, see Margaret A. Mills, "The Gender of the Trick, Female Tricksters and Male Narrators," *Asian Folklore Studies* 60, no. 2 (2001): 237–58; Margaret A. Mills, "Whose Best Tricks? Makr-i Zan as a Topos in Persian Oral Literature," *Iranian Studies: The Uses of Guile: Literary and Historical Moments* 32, no. 2 (1999): 261–70; Margaret A. Mills, "Women's Tricks: Subordination and Subversion in Afghan Folktales," in *Thick Corpus, Organic Variation and Textuality in Oral Tradition*, ed. Lauri Honko (Helsinki: NNF, 2000): 453–87; Afsaneh Najmabadi, "Reading—and Enjoying—'Wiles of Women' Stories as a Feminist," *Iranian Studies* 32, no. 2 (1999): 203–22; David Selim Sayers, "The Wiles of Women in Ottoman and Azeri Texts" (PhD diss., Princeton University, 2014).

15 On male tricksters, see Barbara Babcock-Abrahams, "'A Tolerated Margin of Mess': The Trickster and His Tales Reconsidered," *Journal of the Folklore Institute* 11, no. 3 (1975): 159–60. On the uneven representations of the trickster in Western literatures and the female trickster in the Islamicate literary traditions, see Margaret A. Mills, "The Gender of the Trick, Female Tricksters and Male Narrators," *Asian Folklore Studies* 60 (2001): 237–58. Of course, the image of wily women is not limited to the Islamicate world. For a discussion of the topic, see, e.g., İrvin Cemil Schick, *The Erotic Margin: Sexuality and Spatiality in Alteritist Discourse* (London: Verso, 1999), 223–25.

16 See, e.g., Marinos Sariyannis, "'Neglected Trades': Glimpses into the 17th Century Istanbul Underworld," *Turcica* 38 (2006): 155–79.

17 Anonymous, *Menāqıb-ı Ḥamsīn* [MH], Topkapı Sarayı Müzesi Yazma Eserler Kütüphanesi (The Library of Topkapi Palace Museum) (Hazine Kitaplığı, 1279), 192a16–94a7.

18 *Ḥikāye-i mekr-i zenān*, in *Ḥikāyāt*, Anonymous, *Ḥikāyāt* (Ankara: Adnan Ötüken İl Halk, 1928), 06 HK 3208, 26a14–32a6.

19 *Ḥikāyet-i zen-i ḥīlekār bā ṣūfī-yi ṣadāqat-şiʿār*, in *Menāqıb-ı Ḥamsīn*, 183b10–185b2 and *ḥikāyet-i mekr-i zenān* in *Ḥikāyāt* 06 HK 3208, 12a12–7b1.

20 *Ḥikāyet-i mekr-i zenān*, in *Ḥikāyāt* 06 HK 3208, 35a2–39b8.

21 "*Evdeki qarıncadan ve dīvārdaki örümcekten qısqanur ve şaqınur idi.*" *Menāqıb-ı Ḥamsīn*, 187a7.

22 *Ḥikāyet-i mekr-i zenān,* in *Ḥikāyāt* 06 HK 3208, 20a1–26a14.

23 See, e.g., *Ḥikāyet-i mekr-i zenān,* in *Ḥikāyāt* 06 HK 3208, 35a2–39b8.

24 See Cinānī, *Bedāyiʿüʾl-āṣār*, story no. 1.

25 "*Evleriñ içi ʿavretleriñ ḥükmündedir ve ṭaşrası erleriñ taşarrufundadır,*" in *Ḥikāyāt* 06 HK 3208, 37a4–6.

26 *Ḥikāyet-i merd-i ḥīleger bā vālī-yi bī-ḥaber*, in *Menāqıb-ı Ḥamsīn*, 163b12–64b10.

27 *Ḥikāyet-i zen-i bī-amān bā ebleh-i nādān*, in *Menāqıb-ı Ḥamsīn*, 196b4–98a5.

28 See, e.g., the untitled story in *Menāqıb-ı Ḥamsīn*, 192a16–94a7 and "*Ḥikāyet-i zen-i ġarrā bā civān-[ı] bī-hemtā,*" in *Menāqıb-ı Ḥamsīn*, 193b7–94b14.

29 See, e.g., the couplet at the end of story no. 32 in Cinānī, *Bedāyiʿüʾl-āṣār*.

30 See, e.g., the description of the young and unexperienced beloved in *Ḥikāyet-i mekr-i zenān,* 06 HK 3208, 35a2–39b8.

31 See, e.g., *Ḥikāyet-i zen-i ḥammāl*, MH, 187a3–88b14 and *Fāḥişe ʿavretiñ biri zenpāresiniñ ḥānesine girüb erini qapuda bekletdügi* TDK A 142, 351a13–52a16.

166

32 Of course, there are exceptions. See, e.g., *Ḥikāyet-i duḫter bā muʿazzim-i bed-aḫter* MH 143b16–145a7. In this story, the premarital intercourse of the woman is a key motive in the story.

33 See, e.g., *Ḥikāyet-i qaṣṣāb bā ḥayyāṭ-ı pür şitāb,* MH, 128a10–129a17.

34 See, e.g., stories no. 6 and no. 7 in Cinānī, *Bedāyiʿü'l-āṣār.*

35 Remarkably, women of different ethnic and religious backgrounds seem rarely feature in the stories. (This observation relies on the assumption that in the narrative tradition, the default was the Muslim and other religions were remarked.) For a discussion of gender and age in Ottoman social life with reference to legal evidence, see Leslie Peirce, "Seniority, Sexuality and Social Order: The Vocabulary of Gender in Early Modern Ottoman Society," in *Women in the Ottoman Empire: Middle Eastern Women in the Early Modern Era,* ed. Madeline C. Zilfi (Leiden: Brill, 1997).

36 Examples include *Ḥikāye-i mekr-i zenān,* in *Ḥikāyāt* 06 HK 3208, 26a13–32a6 and *Ḥikāyet-i mekr-i zenān,* in *Ḥikāyāt* 06 HK 3208, 20a1–26a14.

37 Cinānī, *Bedāyiʿü'l-āṣār,* story no.1.

38 For different versions of the story, see *Bir zen-i mekkāre qāḍī ü'l-quḍātıñ ḫānesini soyduġu ḥikāye* in *untitled,* Türk Dil Kurumu El Yazması ve Nadir Eserler Kütüphanesi A 142, 313b1–316a2; Cinānī, *Bedāyiʿü'l-āṣār,* story no. 1; *Süheylī, Ve Min el-Nevādir,* 274–77.

39 *Ḥikāyet-i qaṣṣāb bā ḥayyāṭ-ı pür şitāb* in *Menāqıb-ı Ḥamsīn,* 128a10–29a17.

40 See *Ḥikāyet-i ʿayyārān bā dellāl-i nādān Ḥikāyet-i ʿayyārān bā dellāl-i nādān* in *Menāqıb-ı Ḥamsīn,* 148a7–49b4.

41 Cinānī, *Bedāyiʿü'l-āṣār,* story no. 47.

42 For a discussion of historical context in description of the erotic in the English context, see Ian Frederick Moulton, *Before Pornography: Erotic Writing in Early Modern England* (New York: Oxford University Press, 2000).

43 There are exceptions to this, but in my scattered sample, I have not encountered a same-sex intercourse that is consummated. For references to same-sex desires, see the first story in Cinānī's compilation as an example.

44 Literary debates and elaborations on the ideal sexual partner being male or female constitute another genre. See, e.g., Selim S. Kuru, "Sex in the Text" and İrvin Cemil Schick, "Tarihi Çok Eskiye Giden bir Tartışma Sevgilinin Makbulü Mahbûb mudur, Mahbûbe mi?," *Toplumsal Tarih* 314 (Şubat 2020): 36–41.

45 See, e.g., *Ḥikāyet-i mekr-i zenān,* in *Ḥikāyāt* 06 HK 3208, 35a2–39b8.

46 Naṣīr al-Dīn Ṭūsī, *Akhlāq-i Nāṣirī,* ed. Mujtabā Minuvī and ʿAlīriżā Ḥaydarī (Tehran: Khwārazmi, 1978), 219, for an English translation, see G. M. Wickens, trans., *The Nasirean Ethics* (London: George Allen & Unwin, 1964), 164, quoted by Merguerian and Najmabadi in "Zulaykha and Yusuf: Whose 'Best Story?,'" *International Journal of Middle East Studies* 29, no. 4 (1997). The authors also refer to modern readings with a similar attitude in "Zulaykha and Yusuf," 501.

47 For a discussion of "realism of representation," see Hayden White, "Introduction: Historical Fiction, Fictional History and Historical Reality," *Rethinking History* 9, no. 2–3 (2005): 149.

References

Andrews, Walter G., and Mehmet Kalpaklı. *The Age of Beloveds: Love and the Beloved in Early-Modern Ottoman and European Culture and Society.* Durham, NC: Duke University Press, 2005.

Anetshofer, Helga. "Representations of Women, Gender, and Sexuality: Humorous Depictions: The Ottoman Empire." *Ewic* (2007): 437–38.

Anonymous. *Menāqıb-ı Ḥamsīn [MH].* Topkapı Sarayı Müzesi Yazma Eserler Kütüphanesi (TSMK), Hazine Kitaplığı, 1279.

———. *Ḥikāyāt.* Ankara: Adnan Ötüken İl Halk Kütüphanesi, 1928.

———. "Untitled." *Türk Dil Kurumu El Yazması ve Nadir Eserler Kütüphanesi (TDK), A 142.* https://www.tdk.gov.tr/kutuphane/kutuphane-kutuphane/el-yazmalari-ve-nadir-eserler/.

Babcock-Abrahams, Barbara. "'A Tolerated Margin of Mess': The Trickster and His Tales Reconsidered." *Journal of the Folklore Institute* 11, no. 3 (1975): 159–60.

Birinci, Aziz. "Kırk Vezir Hikâyeleri, İnceleme-Metin-Sözlük." PhD diss., Istanbul University, 2012.

Cinānī. *Bedāyiʿü'l-āṣār.* Edited by Osman Ünlü. Cambridge: Department of Near Eastern Languages and Civilizations, Harvard University, 2009.

Değirmenci, Tülün. "Bir Kitabı Kaç Kişi Okur? Osmanlı'da Okurlar ve Okuma Biçimleri Üzerine Bazı Gözlemler." *Tarih ve Toplum Yeni Yaklaşımlar* 13 (2011): 7–43.

El-Rouayheb, Khaled. *Before Homosexuality in the Arab-Islamic World, 1500–1800*. Chicago: University of Chicago Press, 2009.

Gökpınar, Bahar. *"Er Kişi Niyetine," Osmanlı Yazınında Erkeklik(ler) Kurgusu, 17–18–19. Yüzyıl Metinlerinde Bitmeyen Dönüşüm*. Istanbul: Bilge Kültür Sanat, 2018.

Gür, Nagihan. *Hikâyenin Hikâyesi: Osmanlı'da Bir Kadın Anlatısı. Affe Hanım Sergüzeşti*. Istanbul: Kitabevi, 2020.

Havlioğlu, Didem. "On the Margins and Between the Lines: Ottoman Women Poets from the Fifteenth to the Twentieth Centuries." *Turkish Historical Review* 1 (2010): 25–54.

———. *Mihrî Hatun: Performance, Gender-Bending, and Subversion in Ottoman Intellectual History*. New York: Syracuse University Press, 2017.

Kavruk, Hasan. *Eski Türk Edebiyatında Mensûr Hikâyeler*. Istanbul: M.E.B., 1998.

Kuru, Selim S. "A Sixteenth-Century Scholar: Deli Birader and His Dāfi'ü'l-Gumūm ve Rāfi'ü'l-Humūm." PhD diss., Harvard University, 2000.

———. "Naming the Beloved in Ottoman Turkish Ghazal: The Case of Ishak Çelebi (D. 1537/8)." In *Ghazal as World Literature II: From a Literary Genre to a Great Tradition. The Ottoman Gazel in Context*, edited by Angela Neuwirth, Michael Hess, Judith Pfeiffer, and Börte Sagaster, 163–73. Istanbul: Orient Institut, 2006.

———. "Sex in the Text: Deli Birader's Dâfi'ü 'l-gumûm ve Râfi'ü 'l-humûm and the Ottoman Literary Canon." *Middle Eastern Literatures* 10, no. 2 (2007): 157–74.

Merguerian, Gayane Karen, and Afsanah Najmabadi. "Zulaykha and Yusuf: Whose 'Best Story'?" *International Journal of Middle East Studies* 29, no. 4 (1997): 485–508.

Mills, Margaret A. "Whose Best Tricks? Makr-i Zan as a Topos in Persian Oral Literature." *Iranian Studies: The Uses of Guile: Literary and Historical Moments* 32, no. 2 (1999): 261–70.

———. "Women's Tricks: Subordination and Subversion in Afghan Folktales." In *Thick Corpus, Organic Variation and Textuality in Oral Tradition*, edited by Lauri Honko, 453–87. Helsinki: NNF, 2000.

———. "The Gender of the Trick, Female Tricksters and Male Narrators." *Asian Folklore Studies* 60, no. 2 (2001): 237–58.

Moulton, Ian Frederick. *Before Pornography: Erotic Writing in Early Modern England*. New York: Oxford University Press, 2000.

Najmabadi, Afsaneh. "Reading—and Enjoying—'Wiles of Women' Stories as a Feminist." *Iranian Studies* 32, no. 2 (1999): 203–22.

Peirce, Leslie. "Seniority, Sexuality and Social Order: The Vocabulary of Gender in Early Modern Ottoman Society." In *Women in the Ottoman Empire: Middle Eastern Women in the Early Modern Era*, edited by Madeline C. Zilfi. Leiden: Brill, 1997.

Sariyannis, Marinos. "'Neglected Trades': Glimpses into the 17th Century Istanbul Underworld." *Turcica* 38 (2006): 155–79.

Sayers, David Selim. "The Wiles of Women in Ottoman and Azeri Texts." PhD diss., Princeton University, 2014.

Schick, İrvin Cemil. *The Erotic Margin: Sexuality and Spatiality in Alteritist Discourse*. London: Verso, 1999.

———. "Representation of Gender and Sexuality in Ottoman and Turkish Erotic Literature." *The Turkish Studies Association Journal* 28, no. 1–2 (2004): 81–103.

———. "Tarihi Çok Eskiye Giden bir Tartışma: Sevgilinin Makbulü Mahbûb mudur, Mahbûbe mi?" *Toplumsal Tarih* 314 (Şubat 2020): 36–41.

White, Hayden. "Introduction: Historical Fiction, Fictional History and Historical Reality." *Rethinking History* 9, no. 2–3 (2005): 149.

Ze'evi, Dror. *Producing Desire: Changing Sexual Discourse in the Ottoman Middle East, 1500–1900*. Berkeley: University of California Press, 2006.

14

TOWARDS A GYNOCRITICAL STUDY OF TURKISH FICTION

Contemporary Turkish Women's Literature (1950–1970)

Olcay Akyıldız

This chapter provides a critical discussion of some of the leading Turkish female fiction writers, including Nezihe Meriç (1924–2009), Leylâ Erbil (1931–2013), Sevim Burak (1931–1983), and Sevgi Soysal (1936–1976).[1] These authors challenged the established literary conventions of the period between 1950 and 1970 and were systematically marginalized by the dominant socialist realist criticism of the time. I retrospectively reexamine these women writers with a particular focus on their early texts within the critical discussions of gynocriticism. The primary objective of such a retrospective evaluation is to discuss women's literature through these writers from the perspective of literary history and within the context of discussions on the literary canon in Turkey. This chapter consequently aims to make a feminist claim about the necessity of reorganizing/rewriting literary historiography in Turkey by questioning the male-oriented social(ist) realist criticism that dominated the literary milieu for many years.

As shown throughout this chapter, each of these women writers is associated with modernist literature in different ways, understood literature with this sensibility, and was engaged in innovative literary pursuits through their texts. During this period between 1950 and 1970, women's writing in Turkey introduced a new dimension to literature not only through a break with mimetic representation but also by addressing gender issues in its content. The radical changes in form that each writer created by intervening in the established forms of expression through more innovative strategies of narration fundamentally transformed the nature of fiction in Turkey. In addition, these women writers created and centered more complex female protagonists with internal contradictions and ambiguities rather than the simple representations of shallow, quiet, secondary characters of the previous male literature.

In discussing these writers and their texts from a gynocritical perspective, this chapter aims to demonstrate the complexity of women's literature in Turkey both in terms of form and content. This literature did not merely object to and deconstruct masculine language, the male-dominated system of literature, and the conventional forms of narration; rather, it replaced it with new forms of fiction. For this analysis, gynocriticism provides a critical framework by expanding the historical study of women writers as a distinct literary tradition and developing new models based on the study of female experience in order to question and replace male models of literary creation, and so to "map the territory" left unexplored in earlier literary criticism, especially socialist literary criticism, in the case of Turkey. This new mapping will

DOI: 10.4324/9780429279270-19

provide a new framework for the literary environment under discussion, radically changing its topography. In this regard, the chapter relies especially on Elaine Showalter's conceptualization of *gynocriticism*, interested in the specificity of women's writings (gynotexts) and women's experiences by focusing on female subjectivity, female language, and female literary career. It combines this with attempts to construct a female framework for the analysis of literature and the term "feminine writing" (*l'ecriture féminine*), with a specific focus on Helen Cixous' "The Laugh of Medusa," in which she discussed a *genre* of literary writing that deviates from traditional masculine styles of writing, one which examines the relationship between the cultural and psychological inscription of the female body and female difference in language and text, thus including the writing of the body and sexuality.[2]

When one looks at the texts produced by Turkish women writers between 1950 and 1970, one sees how their narratives reflect the various characteristics that both Showalter and Cixous discuss in their theoretical conceptualizations.

Although this chapter does not claim to produce a new literary history, it does seek to demonstrate that women writers made an enormous intervention towards the existing system of literature, language, and forms of narration through their shared literary strategies, especially as of the 1960s. Despite their differences, writers from Nezihe Meriç to Sevgi Soysal and Sevim Burak to Leylâ Erbil created a paradigm shift in terms of content by positioning female characters at the center of their texts and problematizing the issues women are subjected to due to gender inequality, producing formally experimental works in the process. I maintain that beyond a merely aesthetic concern for literary autonomy and arbitrary linguistic acrobatics, this formal unorthodoxy was mostly a convenient literary device to engage with the complexity of the gender issues with which they were deeply concerned and also a challenge to the established male language and dominant understandings of literature.

Modernist texts can have more complex plots than mainstream realist literature and tend to be more desultory, obscure, and hard to read. However, when they are written by women, modernist texts have often been described as resorting to stream of consciousness and inner monologues to reflect a woman's inner world and inner voice; yet when we look at the variety of narrative strategies employed in such texts, we see that the fragmented projection of that which is internal is at the same time the manifestation of that which is social and external.[3] This chapter proposes a rereading in this context by looking at these writers' early texts, which have been largely marginalized, to show why these texts have been constitutive of their literary approaches and how socialist realist critics have missed this. Although I am aware of the contemporary critic's advantage of analyzing these texts with a retrospective perspective after having read the writer's later works and the subsequent critical approaches,[4] I also analyze mainstream criticism's blind spots, which interestingly form a consistent pattern. Therefore, I will also provide an overview of how these first books were received with a focus on specific critical texts written by Fethi Naci, Erdal Öz, Asım Bezirci, and Atilla Özkırımlı on Nezihe Meriç, Leylâ Erbil, Sevim Burak, and Sevgi Soysal, respectively.

Unorchestrated Noises of the Contemporary Short Story: Nezihe Meriç

Nezihe Meriç (1925–2009) began by writing short stories published in the journal *Seçilmiş Hikâyeler* [Selected Stories], and at a rather early stage in her career a special issue/dossier was prepared that focused on her.[5] It would be fitting to seek the first impetus of the women writers' movement—which took place in the 1960s and especially the 1970s, radically transforming Turkish literature—in the works of Nezihe Meriç. One might assume that Nezihe Meriç,

Towards a Gynocritical Study of Turkish Fiction

whom Jale Özata Dirlikyapan cites alongside Sait Faik and Vüs'at O. Bener as among the fore-runners of the storyteller generation of the 1950s,[6] wrote in a more conventional manner compared to writers such as Leylâ Erbil or Sevim Burak. However, one should not forget that she both precedes these writers generationally and also employed interior monologue and stream of consciousness in an extremely functional manner to strengthen her stories. The way she used those narrative techniques formed also her narrative strategy, through which she mimics the unorchestrated noise of the inner doubts, desires, and internalized voice of the social oppression of women. Reading her first three books *Bozbulanık* [Murky Affairs, 1953], *Topal Koşma* [Lame Running, 1956], and *Menekşeli Bilinç* [Violet Consciousness, 1965] reveals a panorama of urban women's increasing demands for freedom and individualization.

Meriç's stories are more slice-of-life snapshots with vague plot structures focusing on characterization rather than events. She depicts the female characters she places at the center of most of her stories in the kitchen, at home, in the neighborhood, in the street, usually alongside the distress they experience in confined spaces. The portrayal of inner worlds, relationships with the outside world, and boundaries of these female characters strictly besieged by gender norms and social expectations convey a feminist perspective in terms of its assessment of the social situation. Moreover, considering that almost invariably all the individuals who constitute the main characters of Sait Faik's stories, for instance, are male, Meriç generates a rupture not only by being a woman writer but also with her choice of characters. The women depicted in her stories are no longer templates labeled by the male gaze, instrumentalized objects of desire, or cursorily sketched characters. The reader instead views the world through the eyes of these female protagonists. Whether the stories are told in a female first-person narrative or through a third-person narrator, women are at the center of their own stories. Even if the narrated life or the plot does not accord them the freedom they need, Meriç's works create their own urban universe in an elaborate language with an autonomous view different from male literature.

In this early period, Meriç does not liberate all her female characters but depicts them realistically with their limited revolts and small tricks that symbolize their potential objection to their disadvantaged and vulnerable roles in society. As a result, she also portrays the reasons why these characters cannot become free all at once. This depiction also exposes the closely knit social structure, explicit and implicit social pressure, and networks that enclose those characters. Considering that the first steps of liberation should be sought in those tiny revolts, it is as if the stories of young Meriç are drawing up what one might actually call a covert feminist manifesto for those years. Moreover, even if the characters' revolts seem insubstantial to a present-day observer, the writer's defiance is substantial. By opening alternative behaviors and lifestyles up to discussion—such as sexual freedom or women or young girls' demands to live alone, which were not readily acceptable for the social life of the 1940s and 1950s—she opens cracks in the Law of the Father.[7] She wages war on fathers and uncles, and their envoys the aunts and neighbors—anyone evoking authority and gossip. While her characters risk bringing anger on themselves through their defiance, the writer is taking a risk as well. Young female characters advocating sexual freedom without suffering a calamity were a novelty in Turkish literature.[8] Meriç's stories, novels, and plays feature female characters who, despite social pressure, stand on their own two feet without getting married. On the one hand, she tells the stories of the women without a way out, whose movements are controlled by social pressure, and who work outside but enter the kitchen once they get home. Nevertheless, she also writes about a new generation that does not fit into these patterns.

In the story titled "Susuz VII" [Parched VII] in her book *Topal Koşma* (1956), the character puts up resistance, albeit silently, through her refusal to explain herself to her uncle about getting caught with her friend, a male lawyer wanted by the authorities, in the apartment in which she lives alone. However, the explanation is quite simple: the two young people are friends, the narrator of the story Meli and her neighbor Sofiya have looked after the man because he was sick and while he slept the two women stayed up all night. Meriç includes the same story almost verbatim in her novel *Korsan Çıkmazı* [Pirate's Impasse, 1961]. "Susuz VII" can be considered an early manifesto not only for its revolt against women's obligation to account for their behavior but also for its objection to marriage and its treatment of the issue of sexual freedom, as we see in the following quotation:

> Sexual matters generate derangements that wear one out both morally and materially. Today's girls are elevated mentally and emotionally and have become difficult to satisfy. . . . Thus, not to give a percentage but many of the marriages are marriages in order to lose [their] virginity. . . . One way or another they get married. If it doesn't work out, they break up. This changes their position from that of a single girl to a young widow. . . . So, you see, instead of losing their virginity by sleeping with someone they love, which is honest as per the laws of nature, in certain societies which as you say have names, titles, yes instead of doing that they do it via the signature of the registrar. As I do not appreciate that method, I slept with someone I love. And I do not intend to get married.[9]

Meli thinks these words and imagines having this sarcastic conversation with the son of her uncle who is sent to question her. As much as her refusal to explain herself, these sarcastic thoughts expose the gender codes of her family and society, and the hypocrisy of their understanding of morality. In this way, it makes these practices and expectations strange to the reader.

One of the early critics of Meriç's *Topal Koşma* was Erdal Öz. In 1956, in *Pazar Postası* he mentions the interrelatedness of the stories in the book but chooses to analyze and criticize the characters.[10] Meli, in particular, gets a good portion of the criticism by being labeled a character unable to compromise with herself. Leaving aside the question of how one would compromise with oneself, the more methodological objection to Öz's article is his harsh critique of the characters as if he is talking about real people. Meli, for him, is a cowardly, inconsistent character but not a single question is asked about how this character is represented in this fictional world or what the inner monologue of Meli implies or the narratological dynamics of that monologue. He is frustrated that Meli does not utter those words out loud without questioning the dynamics of the inner monologue and whether it would be realistic for a young woman to defend sexual freedom while confronting her family. Öz's critique is not about the literary text itself but about the fictional world which he analyses more like a sociologist than a literary critic. He seems to skip over Meriç's narratological trick. At the moment she puts those words in the story—be it as an audible dialogue or an inner monologue—she challenges the moral hypocrisy of a patriarchal society. But for Öz, this scene by being an imaginary dialogue only reveals Meli's hypocrisy. Vedat Günyol, on the contrary, in a later essay from 1957, grasps the trick: "Wouldn't you say Meli's blunt, wonderfully unyielding answers to imaginary questions—so deliberate in their excessiveness—are an emancipatory call to arms unlike any other?"[11]

I simultaneously agree and disagree with the assessment of Jale Özata Dirlikyapan, who compares Leylâ Erbil's and Nezihe Meriç's reviews in an article focusing on these writers' early periods. She analyses the way they each deal with femininity and asks if some portion of Meriç's positive reviews results from her being more conventional both with her female characters and form. Being more radical, Özata Dirlikyapan argues, Leylâ Erbil is either ignored or harshly criticized.[12] Even if that was correct—daughters or women writers are acceptable to the extent they obey the Law of the Father—it is important to state that Meriç was also quite assertive for the 1940s and 1950s. Describing Meriç as agreeable might cause us to oversee the way she calls out the conditions that force a woman to reconcile her desires with the patriarchal society's expectations. She discusses how family, relatives, or neighbors function as ideological apparatuses via gossip and rumor. As a whole, this system functions as a powerful tool for social control and reveals patriarchal expectations and limitations. So portraying a character thus torn between those pressures without any moral judgment, the way Meriç does, thus cannot easily be labeled as a compromise.

An Unorthodox Writer: Leylâ Erbil the Rebellious

Leylâ Erbil cuts a more unorthodox figure in the literary world as compared to Nezihe Meriç's so-called literary compromise. Despite the environment created by the 1950s generation's sense of literature,[13] it took time for Erbil's first two books to reach readers and gain recognition,[14] fundamentally because she wrote without adhering to anything previously established. Neither the syntax nor the semantic plane of her language, nor the punctuation or her narrative techniques, were congruent with the dominant practices of her time.[15] The notion of "disrupting the grammar of Turkish language" associated with Erbil's work from the very beginning results, in her later works, in an irregular, palimpsestic narrative surface—a narrative surface that resists the linearity and hegemonic language of history and instead incorporates everything that spills over, turns into excess, or is exiled or forced to disappear. The traces of this can be found in her first two books. This rupture from standard grammar is not an arbitrary play on aesthetics. As she tried to explain in numerous interviews, what she wanted to express and her forms of expression were the projections of the differently functioning minds which she was trying to convey or the violent events of the past that are erased from history. These can only appear and disappear through narrative cracks. In this context, she was not seeking to voice the ordinary but that which is outside the norm.

One can follow these pursuits in her later books as well but they can be said to have made a steady breakthrough in *Hallaç* [Carder, 1960] and *Gecede* [At Night, 1968], which challenge, in essence, not only the established language and official discourse of the history but also the existing patriarchal order. Inasmuch as the world of literature produced with this language is extremely masculine—which she explains in detail in her first novel *Tuhaf Bir Kadın* [A Strange Woman, 1971]—this masculine language cannot become her language. In an interview in 1997, Leylâ Erbil said:

> I watched, astounded, at how the language the woman writer falls into a language that has been the language of a history established and written by men, and how our entire mind takes on a biased form. Yes one uses her brain not her body while writing but the language we inherited was a patriarchal one which was woven by men and this language had no place for women.[16]

Thus we can deduce that even if at times she rejected this differentiation, she was from the very outset aware that the experience of the woman writer is completely different. Realizing that merely writing as a woman, placing female characters at the center of the story, or objecting to gender norms, customs, or the family as an institution—though significant—does not suffice for a radical deconstruction, Erbil disrupted the game, broke down language, and baffled the reader by dismantling established structures with the first stories she wrote. And this, of course, did not conform to the horizon of literary expectation on which the male-dominated canon focused. That is, rather than drawing a clearer picture and presenting social criticism like Nezihe Meriç or Adalet Ağaoğlu, Erbil also dared to not conform/compromise formally. As stated earlier, this kind of formal challenge was not appreciated by socialist realist critics. Atilla Özkırımlı, in his article on *Gecede*, tries to analyze Erbil's novel by reading it alongside the Turkish translation of Lukács' *The Meaning of Contemporary Realism* [1969]. He criticizes Erbil's stories for their distance from reality and for narrowing societal problems by focusing only on sexuality. Any objective reader could oppose this opinion only by listing the titles and topics of the short stories in the book. "Vapur" [Ferry], the surreal story of an Istanbul ferry going out of control, weaves in various palimpsestic histories of certain Istanbul neighborhoods. "Çekmece" [The Drawer] consists of letters a mechanist working on ships wrote to his wife during his trips. These letters were kept in a drawer with the newspaper clippings on the tragic ship accident in which the author of the letters also died. This kind of defamiliarizing use of language and new aesthetic inevitably elicited a critical reaction, even at the price of not being reviewed, just like the criticisms directed against Sevim Burak's first book.

The Politics of Fragmented and Visual Narrative: Sevim Burak

Sevim Burak began publishing her stories in the 1950s but did not collect the stories she wrote in her early youth that were published in the daily *Ulus*.[17] Her first book *Yanık Saraylar* [Burnt Palaces, 1965] is a collection of stories published in various journals later in the 1960s. Unlike the rapid recognition of Nezihe Meriç and Adalet Ağaoğlu, which may be explained by their acceptance of certain compromises in language and form, the misfortune or marginalization that befell Leylâ Erbil was also the case for Sevim Burak; the interest she generated fell far behind the statement she created in *Yanık Saraylar*. Her article in the journal *Yeni Dergi* in 1966 explains her literary approach and in a sense responds to the criticisms leveled against her, revealing how much thought she gave to her narration and her awareness of the dominant features of her writing. As opposed to the macro and superficial approach of literary critic Asım Bezirci[18]—who indirectly tells Burak how to write more correctly and beautifully—and the masculine form of critique he represents, Burak's microanalysis carefully reveals how the dynamics of her text function.[19] Asım Bezirci's 1965 review of *Yanık Saraylar* appeared to praise it even while criticizing it. More importantly, he misreads her work to such an extent that Sevim Burak seems to feel the need to explain herself.

If the only reference point for Sevim Burak's *Yanık Saraylar* were Bezirci's (mis)reading, the reader would not have a concrete understanding of Burak's approach. Or anyone who reads the short story "Sedef Kakmalı Ev" [Pearl Inlaid House, 1965] would be astonished to read his summary of the story claiming the character Nurperi Hanım's misfortune was being married to a rich but ugly old man. This erases Nurperi Hanım's entire traumatic past of being raised in that mansion against her will as a child. The reader could only follow the scattered and fragmented recollections that also allude to the repressed memoirs of a traumatic past. Through Bezirci's summarized distant reading, all the nuances of mimicking a fragmented, repressed memory through language fade away.

The critic Murat Belge also wrote a critique on Sevim Burak. However, Belge's main goal in this 1965 article was not to write a piece on *Yanık Saraylar* but to attack Asım Bezirci's critical methodology.[20] Even though it is impossible not to agree with Belge's critique of Bezirci, the form of classification which he regards as mere nonsense is far too problematic to be dismissed solely as such. Belge is referring to how Asım Bezirci, while describing a characteristic supposedly pertaining to Sevim Burak, compares—often incorrectly—these traits of expression always with other and mostly male writers. Bezirci does not make comparisons, but in losing sight of the subject of the article he is writing, he gets carried away by discussing the other writers he

Towards a Gynocritical Study of Turkish Fiction

has alluded to. As a consequence, this attitude not only overlooks the main concerns of *Yanık Saraylar* but is at the same time a concrete illustration of one of the main arguments raised in Belge's article: namely, the obscuring of women writers from the canon by the male-dominated approach of socialist realist criticism in particular. In *Yanık Saraylar*, Sevim Burak emerges with a very new and unsettling style of writing that cannot be analyzed by summarizing the themes of the stories as Bezirci does.

Sevim Burak's textual experiments ponder the possibilities of the literary representation of nonhuman beings and nonliving things.[21] The writers discussed in this chapter do not make innovations that repeat one another; however, they share the common trait of shaking the monolithic narratives of the symbolic order, and this is precisely why these writers should be considered together, as the existing narratives of the post-1950s literary milieu do not suffice to explain women writers' avant-garde breakthroughs. While Burak makes a completely unprecedented subject-object shift in her stories, which she accomplishes by virtually becoming the objects themselves, Erbil protests the punctuation marks for being insufficient for what she wants to tell. Even though each writer creates a similar effect, they have unique writing styles. In her 1966 article "Hikâye ya da İmge ya da Tansık" (Story or Image or Miracle), Burak argues that her stories cannot be captured through summaries or thematic inventories:

> For me, in order to reveal the Essence with utter simplicity, the Formal Effort must move forward. Therefore, the parts that seem formal are those where the Essence emerges most powerfully. Stories like "Yanık Saraylar" and "Büyük Kuş" [The Big Bird] are examples of this. Lines shifting under one another, their breaks—the use of capital letters, are nothing short of the effort to grasp the Essence.[22]

This detailed opposition and explanation indirectly criticize Bezirci's approach. The reputation of these stories and other books by Burak, which today have been used for many different readings ranging from feminist criticism to ecocriticism, has long been restored.[23]

Following this first book, Burak took a break from literature and did not publish again until the 1980s. Because we know from her letters to her son that she had ruminated at length on not being understood, we can find the explanation for why she started publishing books again after 1980 in the diversification of the predominant critical understanding of the 1970s in favor of modernist/postmodernist literature in the subsequent decade.

Subjectivity and Individualism in Sevgi Soysal

Similar to the way Leylâ Erbil's first two books were overlooked only to be discovered retrospectively, neither publishers nor critics could pin down the first two books by Sevgi Soysal in terms of genre and they had difficulty reaching readers. The characters of *Tutkulu Perçem* [Passionate Bangs, 1962], who even sense the apple blossoming right beside them and whose fragmented inner monologues and voices we read as they roam unseen through the crowds of the city, are like successors to Nezihe Meriç's urban female individuals.[24] But neither the subjectivities of these urban characters in *Tutkulu Perçem* nor the passionate antihero Tante Rosa's fragmented life story (in the eponymous novel from 1968) received the critical attention they deserved. On the contrary, these books were labeled the naïve texts of a period when the young Sevgi's consciousness was not sufficiently developed. From this perspective, her truly mature works were written following the coup of March 12, 1971, in the context of her political activism.[25]

Was it really the March 12th coup that made Soysal who she became, as critic Erdal Öz argues, or is this again an effort to silence the rebellious voice of a woman writer who disrupts the alignment? Even if there is no conscious effort at silencing, like many other things that did not fit the era's horizon of expectations, these texts were also brushed aside to odd corners. The March 12th coup did create changes in Soysal's themes—and perhaps her writing style—just like its effect on her life; however, the question of whether or not it was definitive for her fiction should be discussed through her books. To that end, one should take a closer look at *Tante Rosa* [Aunt Rosa], which became the cult book of a later generation, and her first book *Tutkulu Perçem*, to assess the dynamics of change and transformation within the historical context beyond simply establishing a political hierarchy between Soysal's later novels and previous work. One should read these texts, which we may in a sense deem constitutive for Soysal's literary output, without using a filter assessing the post–March 12th political novels as more successful using a political rather than aesthetic criterion. Atilla Özkırımlı, for instance, like many others, places Soysal's books in a certain positive development from individualism to socialism. Asserting that *Tutkulu Perçem* cannot be considered a promising debut, Özkırımlı criticizes the book's surrealistic images, hopeless and pessimistic narrative, and isolation from reality.[26] Later discussing *Tante Rosa*, Özkırımlı declared that he liked this book in places, but eventually came to the following conclusion: "The social dimension of reality was recognized, but the *woman* Sevgi [née] Sabuncu could not socialize the problem because she could not overcome her *femininity*."[27] The reason Özkırımlı criticizes both texts is that he thinks these texts do not deal with reality from a socialist perspective. In other words, although *Tante Rosa* is somewhat more "conscious" in this sense, the problem has not disappeared. In this problematic critical approach based on the author's gender, it is apparent that Özkırımlı is confined to the limits of orthodox left-wing literary criticism and sees the visibility of femininity/female identity in the literary text as an obstacle to it having a socialist perspective. Just like in the other texts criticized in this chapter, Özkırımlı has sacrificed both books to a crude understanding of socialist realism.

Many other studies[28] that define Soysal's literary output on a continuum extending from individualism to socialism are built on an open or covert hierarchy and harbor an approach locating the writer on a developmental axis. Therefore, by writing the story in reverse, I want to suggest that what made Sevgi Soysal who she was is present in the core of these first books. That is why her novels responding to the March 12th coup were written in that form; they were not purely political texts but rather quite layered and plural. Veysel Öztürk similarly credits Soysal's strong writerly self in *Tutkulu Perçem* for *Şafak*'s [Dawn] departure from the tedium of thesis novels as well as the depth brought to the novel by its central character Oya's faltering between her multiple identities with all her anxieties, fears, and inconsistencies.[29]

We find a similar claim in Funda Soysal's foreword to the new edition of *Tante Rosa*.[30] From a sound footing, the foreword discusses both *Tante Rosa*'s problematic and the social reasons behind the resistance it encountered when first published as a book in 1968. While claiming that *Tante Rosa* is the best introduction to Sevgi Soysal, Funda Soysal builds her argument on the representation of the issues of womanhood. This thematic observation is correct; however, the best way to start reading Soysal—not just content-wise but also in terms of her style—is in her own chronology: first *Tutkulu Perçem* and then *Tante Rosa*. This prepares the reader for the fragmented structure of the novel *Yürümek* [To Walk, 1970], the new understanding of realism in the writing style of *Yenişehir'de Bir Öğle Vakti* [Noontime in Yenişehir, 1973], which does not neglect the complex dynamics of that which is personal while narrating the social.[31]

The story "Tutkulu Perçem" harbors revolt already in its title. In the "passions" the female character has affixed to her bangs, or in the image created at the end of the story when she tears away her passions from her bangs and throws them into the manhole to mix with the sewage of the city, it is impossible not to remember Ottoman divan poetry's image of the lover who has hung their lovers to the lovelock and is obscured as an object of desire. Yet this woman narrator vagabonding about the streets of the city is trying to survive while being blamed and misunderstood by the crowd. She is not an object of desire but a subject who desires. Both looking at the world through her eyes and the fragmented state of that world were new for Turkish literature. A literary horizon able to recognize this novelty and audacity has yet to arise.

In this context, I think it is not a coincidence that the first person who gave *Tutkulu Perçem* its due and grasped its significance within Soysal's corpus was a female writer from another generation. In the foreword Sema Kaygusuz wrote for the reprint of *Tutkulu Perçem* in 2004, she concludes by saying, "even with the best of intentions, seeing *Tante Rosa* as the core of [Soysal's project] would be doing injustice to *Tutkulu Perçem*."[32] In this way, she shows that in this first book we can find the essence of Soysal's literary understanding which she deepened over the following years. Veysel Öztürk's article "*Tutkulu Perçem*' in Mikro Anlatıları" [Micro Narratives of *Tutkulu Perçem*] also retrospectively pays the necessary objective critical attention to the text and examines the relationship between the genre-specific characteristics and the language of the text.[33] Öztürk indicates that the transformation in Soysal's literature should not be evaluated with distinctions like "socialist" or "individualist" literature that disregard the autonomy of literature. Certainly, we must take into account the influence of the sociopolitical conditions after the 1970s, but even more essentially her later works appeared as a necessity of her individual approach. Another relevant issue Öztürk's article touches upon is her connection with existentialism. Showing that Soysal engaged with as much as distanced herself from existentialism, which in the 1960s was regarded as a common ground, Öztürk's reading takes into account the feminist critique of existentialism as well.[34]

Towards a Conclusion: A "Kitchen" of One's Own

One of the fundamental arguments constituting the framework of this chapter is that the socialist realist criticism dominant from the 1950s until the 1980s, not only with its political agenda but at the same time its aesthetic approach, has been one of the primary obstacles to analyzing and understanding the early texts of the writers studied here. This form of criticism defined not only these women writers but also the poetry of İkinci Yeni and other modernist writers of the Generation of the 1950s as aimless, apolitical, "existentialist," and at times meaningless. It stressed the comprehensibility and functionality of literature and its relationship with social issues. The writing of new literary histories that do not regard women simply as a supplement to these issues and includes the specific challenge of women writers will only be possible by retrospectively questioning the socialist realist critical approach. When the pursuit of the Social and the Political (written in capital letters) is the first criteria of literary criticism, many possibilities and fundamental issues of the literary text in question can be overlooked.

As late as the 1990s, Fethi Naci[35] was writing about Nezihe Meriç in a way that reflected this same attitude. His essay "Ey Nezihe Meriç! 'Gel Kurtul o Mutfağın Dar Hendesesinden'" [Nezihe Meriç! "Come Free Yourself from that Confined Space of the Kitchen"] focused on Meriç's short story collection *Bir Kara Derin Kuyu* [A Dark Deep Well, 1989]. Naci finds Meriç's statements on the social issues of the post-1980 era in her stories artificial. He criticizes her by saying, "The first condition of transforming the whines and plaints into a real opposition is to get out of the kitchen."[36] On one hand, this statement maintains that all reactionary governments want to imprison women in the kitchen; on the other hand, he claims that it is impossible to express social turmoil by narrating from the perspective of women imprisoned in the kitchen.

Intersecting with the main issues of this chapter, there are two fundamental problems with the argument of Naci. Firstly, depicting the post-1980 era is clearly not possible only by depicting grand social turmoil. Naci says one cannot see the outside from the kitchen. However, I insist that the inside of the house (private space) is as important as the outside (public) and how the street/outside looks from inside the house through the kitchen window is an important determinant. What is called the "outside" also determines the dynamics of the kitchens described. At the same time, not only in the case of *Bir Kara Derin Kuyu* but taking into account all of Meriç's books, objecting to the repetition of the kitchen as a setting in her work would mean misinterpreting it. Essentially, the central role of the "kitchen" in her stories indicates that Meriç realized much earlier that there is no separation between what is private and public. That is, through the metaphor of the kitchen she ends up recounting not only the liberation struggle of that first generation of women coded according to certain gender roles in those kitchens but at the same time the obstacles they encountered while daring to find the opportunity to write. Nezihe Meriç's stories are filled with the sound of the air coming from the kitchen, the heat of the grill, the scent of fried butter. In one story, a troubled mood is dispelled by going into the kitchen and frying peppers in another.[37] While writing of the compassion of the kitchen, the scent of the food, the peace of brewing tea, Meriç also recounts the allure of that whirlpool and the difficulty of taking leave from that fumy kitchen that beckons one inside. Rather than liberating a woman on the textual plane and unrealistically portraying her on the street, the first step is to demonstrate how very intricate those interior dynamics are. This is exactly what Meriç does. Contrary to Naci's thought, this revelation is political. Moreover, it is political with a literariness that never sidelines aesthetic concerns. My claim is that the achievements of women's literature draw their strength from this combination of ethics and aesthetics whether with a less bold challenge in terms of narrative techniques and the functioning of language, as in the case of Nezihe Meriç, or with a narrative style sharp and incongruous enough to dazzle the reader as if hit by a wall, as in Sevim Burak. What emerges can still be a bold statement, but this is exactly what the socialist critics fail to notice.

On that note, it is no coincidence that it is a feminist critic who has opened the kitchen door closed by Fethi Naci. In her article looking at Nezihe Meriç's bubbling saucepans, Neslihan Cangöz shows with a much more comprehensive reading, one can see that in Meriç's storytelling the kitchen is never merely a kitchen, nor are the meals just food.[38] In this reading, one that has parallels with my argument, Cangöz rereads the stories one by one, focusing on household objects and food, and also borrowing from Arendt, criticizes Fethi Naci, who mistakenly separated public and private. She demonstrates how his objection to the narration of these women's stories imprisoned in the kitchen constitutes a rather confining approach. She concludes her article by saying that these stories bring into the scope of literature a large sphere of life that had previously been ignored as if nonexistent. These stories look at the kitchen from the inside through the light of the stove instead of pontificating while looking in from the outside through the light of the streetlamp. Women calling out to one another from kitchen windows talking about what's going on outside, or women coming home from work and having to go straight into the kitchen, vividly lay bare the tension between the home and the outside world.

Is it meaningful to look closer at the early texts of these writers and ask new questions? After all, we are doing this retrospectively, at a time when the indisputable place of these writers in the literary canon is recognized. The central issue is that labeling these literary quests and breakthroughs—some of which took place at a very early age—with words like "inexperience," "carelessness," "existentialism," or "crippled by describing the states of womanhood" is also a result of the male, socialist realist critique. Therefore, looking at these texts from the present day together with their reception history precisely at the time of their writing signifies a feminist rereading both in terms of the texts and the history of literature. A closer look reveals that what is in question is not a recurrent story of breakthrough. Each writer intervened in the literary

Towards a Gynocritical Study of Turkish Fiction

tradition in different ways; however, the importance of these interventions was only understood years later. As Sevim Burak declares for her own fictional works, I argue that the women's literature discussed in this chapter reveals its main essence and content exactly at the moments where it displays its most unequivocal formal paradigm shifts with new strategies and narrative techniques.

Starting, almost without exception, at the outset of their literary careers, the women writers of the first two generations of the Republican period made and continued to make avant-garde breakthroughs. In a male world of publishing and criticism where being a woman writer was in itself a marginal act, these women narrated the portrait of the woman as a writer. At the same time, by defying established literary conventions, they wrote about the states of womanhood, the body, sexuality, and the effort to become an intellectual individual, which the other tried to discipline and curb using society's expectations. Through their female protagonists defined as society's other, these authors conveyed numerous socially excluded issues. They did this while employing modernist narrative techniques rendered possible by unreliable narrators marked by madness, senility, or delirium that used a fragmented language which at times disrupted the syntax. These texts, which in this sense may be considered together with Julia Kristeva's theory of the semiotic, created a language and a semiotic order that shakes and defies—sometimes openly, sometimes covertly—the rule of the symbolic order. Contrary to popular belief, the issues they problematized in their books were not only gender based. Through a feminist perspective, they wrote on many controversial subjects ranging from the official account of history to political events, from scarcely voiced massacres to the palimpsest-like history of urban space. Regardless of whether the issue at hand was gender, this feminist perspective enabled them to see that the discourses that exist as an extension of the patriarchal structure that begins in the nuclear family is a structural problem very much based on power relations. And they wrote with a language that aimed not only to expose but demolish these structures by deconstructing them, thus becoming "feminist killjoys" in the sense used by Sara Ahmed.[39]

Notes

1 In the 1950s and 1960s when these writers were publishing their short stories, another important woman writer, Adalet Ağaoğlu, began her literary career by writing drama (radio and stage plays) before penning novels in the 1970s. For more on her unique novel-writing approach with overlaps with elements of my argument, see Murat Gülsoy's chapter in this volume.

2 Starting with her article "Toward a Feminist Poetics" in 1979 to her book *A Jury of Her Peers: Celebrating American Women Writers from Anne Bradstreet to Annie Proulx* (New York: Vintage, 2009), Elaine Showalter has argued for the necessity of approaches focusing on the body of women's writing. Helen Cixous, "The Laugh of Medusa," *Signs* 1, no. 4 (Summer 1976), is more a manifest call for women to include their bodies in their body of writings. My main aim in this chapter is to focus on women's writing, not their representations in fiction or the critical reading of such representations. Therefore, a broader discussion on feminist literary criticism is not included. For two important studies carried out in Turkey on feminist literary criticism both in studies of single women writers and their feminist readings but also as a macro shift in theoretical studies, see Jale Parla, "Kadın Eleştirisi Neyi Gerçekleştirdi," in *Kadınlar Dile Düşünce: Edebiyatta Toplumsal Cinsiyet* (Istanbul: İletişim Yayınları, 2004); Sibel Irzık, "Öznenin Vefatından Sonra Kadın Olarak Okumak," in *Kadınlar Dile Düşünce: Edebiyatta Toplumsal Cinsiyet* (Istanbul: İletişim Yayınları, 2004), 35–56. Meanwhile, *Kadınlar Dile Düşünce: Edebiyatta Toplumsal Cinsiyet* (Istanbul: İletişim Yayınları, 2004), edited by Parla and Irzık, includes articles focused both on male writers' skewed gender representations and the literary production of the female subject. For another contribution to the field that throws a curveball by exploring how the texts of male writers (especially those like Ahmet Hamdi Tanpınar, Kemal Tahir, and Attila İlhan who are central in the canon) are crippled by their gender perspectives, see Sema Kaygusuz and Deniz Gündoğan İbrişim, eds., *Gaflet: Modern Türkçe Edebiyatın Cinsiyetçi Sinir Uçları* (Istanbul: Metis, 2019).

3 For an article suggesting a new approach to this topic, see Zeynep Uysal, "Yeni Bir Toplumsallığın Peşinde: Deneyimden Dünyaya Açılan Roman," *Notos* 67 (2017): 16–19.

4 All of the authors mentioned here received increasing interest from readers and critics/academics starting in the 2000s. Academic conferences, published proceedings, and edited volumes on the authors have begun to appear, and these writers also become the topic of dissertations. For the sake of space, I will not include a comprehensive bibliography but I want to name some of the main studies on each of the authors at relevant parts in the chapter. Here, I would like to mention two recent texts that use a similar approach to discuss women writers together in the periods of 1950–1970 and 1960–1990, respectively. Senem Timuroğlu designates the women's literature of the 1960s in particular as an early stage of the second-wave Turkish feminist movement by exploring the biographies and relationships of these authors. Beyhan Uygun Aytemiz gives a thematic overview of how women's public and private experiences have been represented in women's literature between the 1960s and 1990s. Aytemiz first covers Nezihe Meriç, Peride Celal, and Sevgi Soysal with their "first novels" as an early step in questioning patriarchal gender norms and family dynamics. Then she goes on to focus on the novels of Adalet Ağaoğlu, Leylâ Erbil, and Sevgi Soysal in 1970s. In line with these two articles, what I try to do here is propose a new approach to literary history by analyzing what women's literature has accomplished and the asymmetrical why this accomplishment went unseen by male critical discourse. In this sense, Timuroğlu, Aytemiz, and my work complete each other, perhaps forming the first steps of, as Timuroğlu says, giving a name to what happened in the periods we study: Feminist statements and a literary challenge both in form and content. Senem Timuroğlu, "Artık Adını Koyalım: Feminist Edebiyatımızın Köşe Taşları," *K24*, March 8, 2017, https://t24.com.tr/k24/yazi/feminist-edebiyatimizin-kose-taslari,1105; Beyhan Uygun Aytemiz, "Nezihe Meriç'ten Tezer Özlü'ye: 1960–1980'li Yıllar Edebiyatında Kadın," in *Feminizm*, ed. Feryal Saygılıgil and Nacide Berber (Istanbul: İletişim Yayınları, 2020), 731–52. I won't have a chance to discuss Duygu Çayırcıoğlu's 2022 book *Kadınca Bilmeyişlerin Sonu* fully, as it was published as the current volume was completed, but I find it important to mention the main argument in her book analyzing novels by women writers between 1960 and 1980. Çayırcıoğlu focuses on the feminist content of these novels and argues for the invisibility of the feminist movement in Turkey. Though this movement rose most intensely after the 1980s, in the previous two decades this was compensated for in literature. Therefore, the strong feminist statements of these novels are important for rethinking the history of the feminist movement in Turkey. This description of the absence of a strong feminist movement notwithstanding, I find it important that Çayırcıoğlu brings these novels together with a feminist focus. However, my main argument in this chapter differs from this perspective with an emphasis on how these writers not only dealt with certain feminist topics but also challenged the entire whole literary canon with their avant-garde formalistic rebellion.

5 "Nezihe Meriç Özel Sayısı," *Seçilmiş Hikâyeler*, May 1957. This special issue consists of eight short stories of Nezihe Meriç. Half of them were later published in her first book *Bozbulanık*, but the other half had to wait until 2011 when *Püf Noktası: İlk Öyküleri ve Yazıları*, a biography and five critical essays on her stories, was published by Yapı Kredi Yayınları in Istanbul.

6 Jale Özata Dirlikyapan, *Kabuğunu Kıran Hikâye: Türk Öykücülüğünde 1950 Kuşağı* (Istanbul: Metis, 2010), 87–105.

7 The Law of the Father is a term used by Jacques Lacan in which he further develops the Freudian concept of the Oedipus complex by differentiating between the real, imaginary, and symbolic Father. Here, I use the term to emphasize the structural continuation between the real father in the family and the symbolic Father of the social structure.

8 Previously, the female characters driven to ruin following a sexual experience had gone through with these transgressions—not in line with their own desires but typically by being tricked into it. Or if it was their own desire in question, then pursuing it resulted in becoming antagonists. Without going into a discussion on the female characters of male literature, for an article on whether or not Muazzez Tahsin and Kerime Nadir, the woman authors of the previous generation's popular novels, had a feminist statement to make, see Didem Ardalı Büyükarman, "*Aşkımın Mezarı*" yahut Popüler Edebiyatın Köşe Taşı Kadın Yazarlardan Feminist Söz Çıkar mı?" in *Feminizm*, ed. Feryal Saygılıgil and Nacide Berber (Istanbul: İletişim Yayınları, 2020), 766–74.

9 Nezihe Meriç, *Bütün Öyküleri I* (Istanbul: Yapı Kredi Yayınları, 2018), 160.

10 Erdal Öz, "Topal Koşma'nın Özü," *Pazar Postası*, August 19, 1956.

11 Quoted in Asım Bezirci, *Nezihe Meriç: Monografi* (Istanbul: Evrensel Basım Yayın, 1999), 113.

12 Jale Özata Dirlikyapan, *Öykünün Modernleşme Sürecinde İki Kadın Öykücü: Leyla Erbil ve Nezihe Meriç* (Eskişehir, Turkey: Bir Bilim Kategorisi Olarak "Kadın" Uluslararası Sempozyumu, Anadolu Üniversitesi Eğitim Fakültesi, April 29–May 2, 2008).

Towards a Gynocritical Study of Turkish Fiction

13 Some of Erbil's contemporaries with whom she is listed as a 1950s generation (50 kuşağı) writer include: Feyyaz Kayacan (1919–1993), Orhan Duru (1933–2009), Demir Özlü (1935–2021), and Ferit Edgü (1936–).

14 In this regard, it would be significant to compare the first edition of *Hallaç* with the additions Erbil made to its second edition, and the number of editions printed after Erbil was, in a sense, retrospectively discovered. Also significant is the fact that after the first publication of *Hallaç*, only two short articles were written about it. For a detailed analysis of the change in the perception of Erbil with growing number of publications and studies, see the Leylâ Erbil bibliography and the analysis of it: Esra Nur Akbulak and Olcay Akyıldız, "Leylâ Erbil Bibliyografyası Bize Ne Söyler? Leylâ Erbil Edebiyatına ve Alımlanışına Verilerle Bakmak" and "Leylâ Erbil Bibliyografyası," *Zemin* 1 (2021): 3–29, 30–69.

15 To date, Leylâ Erbil has been discussed mostly in the context of her rebelliousness in the use of language and of how she built her literature as a space of resistance. For a number of comprehensive studies on this subject, see Hilal Aydın, "Türk Edebiyatındaki Direnme Noktası: Leylâ Erbil," *Moment Dergi* 2, no. 2 (2015): 272–88; Ahmet Cemal, "Bir Direnme Eylemi Olarak Yazmak," in *Bir Tuhaf Kuştur, Gölgesi Zihin*, ed. Kaya Tokmakçıoğlu (Istanbul: Aylak Adam, 2013), 41–51; Süha Oğuzertem, "Kaybolmayan Yazar: Leylâ Erbil'in Özgünlüğü, Özgürlüğü," in *Leylâ Erbil'de Etik ve Estetik* (Istanbul: Kanat, 2007), 147, 179. I address Leylâ Erbil's act of resistance, even though she herself did not initially define it as such, as fundamentally a feminist act of resisting male literature. For an analysis of Leylâ Erbil's work as a form of feminist opposition, see Ürün Şen-Sönmez, "Bir Leylâ Erbil Portresi ya da Hiçbir Kavme Dâhil Olmayan Bir 'Öteki,'" in *Feminizm*, ed. Feryal Saygılıgil and Nacide Berber (Istanbul: İletişim Yayınları, 2020), 738–45.

16 Leylâ Erbil, "Ben Deliliğe Düşkün Bir Yazarım," *Düşler/Öyküler* 4 (May 1997): 6–35.

17 Bedia Koçakoğlu, *Büyük Günah: Bilinmeyen Öyküleriyle Sevim Burak* (Konya: Palet Yayınları, 2013).

18 Asım Bezirci, "Yanık Saraylar," *Yeni Dergi* 12–13 (October 1965), 251–59.

19 Alongside a speech she made on BBC, this article is virtually a reading key for *Yanık Saraylar*. This is not to say that Sevim Burak explains her stories, but while she speaks about the relationship of literature and reality, the intrinsic order of the text, and intuitional forms of writing, she warns the reader, as it were, about the chasm between the signifier and the signified.

20 For a more detailed article on how yet another Marxist critic tackles the understanding of socialist realist literature which caused modernist literature, avant-garde women's literature and even the İkinci Yeni (Second New Wave) poetry to be criticized in similar ways, see, Hasan Turgut, "Yeryüzünde Serseri ve Kaçak' Sevim Burak'ın Yanık Saraylar'ında Maduniyet," in *İkinci Bir Yaşam: Sevim Burak'ın Edebiyat Dünyası*, ed. Mustafa Demirtaş (Istanbul: Yapı Kredi Yayınları, 2018), 195–215, 322–25.

21 For an analysis in this context of *Ford Mach 1*, which is one of the most interesting examples of such a work, and was prepared for publication posthumous by Nilüfer Güngörmüş, see Selver Sezen Kutup, "Textual Network in Sevim Burak: The Nonhuman Beings of *Ford Mach I*" (MA thesis, Boğaziçi University, 2019).

22 Sevim Burak, "Hikâye ya da İmge ya da Tansık," *Kitap-lık* 71 (2004): 103–5.

23 For a critical analysis summarizing the previous readings, see Selver Sezen Kutup in note 21.

24 İpek Şahbenderoğlu analyses *Tutkulu Perçem* with a focus on the tension between the masculine city and the female characters. She criticizes the tendency to see an author's corpus as increasingly successful from beginning to end: "'Adamlar, Kadınlar ve Duvarlar': Eril Kentin Tepelerinde *Tutkulu Perçem*," in *"Ne Güzel Suçluyuz Hepimiz" Sevgi Soysal İçin Yazılar*, ed. Seval Şahin (Istanbul: İletişim, 2013), 37–60.

25 On the coup of March 12, 1971, and its effect on literature, see Çimen Günay-Erkol's chapter in this volume.

26 Atilla Özkırımlı, "*Tutkulu Perçem*'den *Şafak*'a Sevgi Soysal'ın Yazarlık Çizgisi," *Birikim* 23 (1977): 8.

27 Ibid., 9. Italics are mine. This essay was also republished in the edition of *Tante Rosa* published by Bilgi Yayınevi in 1980. This was replaced in the new edition İletişim Yayınları by Funda Soysal's introduction "*Tante Rosa*'dan Sevgi Soysal'a Yolculuk" is an example of the change in the critical approach to Sevgi Soysal. Sevgi Soysal, *Tante Rosa* (Istanbul: İletişim, 2010), 11–17. For an alternative reading of Sevgi Soysal's first two books, see Aydın Baran Gürpınar, "*Tutkulu Perçem ve Tante Rosa* ile Toplum Söylencesinin Feshi," *Varlık* 1306 (July 2016): 22–27. A similar approach making a hierarchical comparison between being a woman writer and a writer can be found in an article written after Soysal's death: Mehmet H. Doğan, "Sevgi Soysal'ın Ölümüyle Edebiyatımız Kendini Bilinçle Değiştirmeyi Başarmış Bir Yazarını Kaybetti," *Milliyet Sanat* 210 (1976). There Doğan sees the female, feminine, and I guess feminist emphasis of literature as a kind of handicap for being a good writer.

28 Priska Furrer, *Sevgi Soysal: Bireysellikten Toplumsallığa* (Istanbul: Papirüs, 2004). The book originates from Furrer's published MA thesis. Though we do not find an emphasis on individuality in the title,

Furrer's analysis in this study also sees a certain kind of development towards more social concerns. Priska Furrer, *Das erzählerische Werk der türkischen Autorin Sevgi Soysal* (Berlin: Klaus Schwarz Verlag, 1992).

29 Veysel Öztürk, "*Tutkulu Perçem*'in Mikro Anlatıları," in *İsyankâr Neşe: Sevgi Soysal Kitabı*, ed. Seval Şahin and İpek Şahbenderoğlu (Istanbul: İletişim, 2015), 51–64.

30 Funda Soysal, "*Tante Rosa*'dan Sevgi Soysal'a Yolculuk," in *Tante Rosa*, ed. Sevgi Soysal (Istanbul: İletişim, 2010), 11–17.

31 Egem Atik, "Sevgi Soysal'ın Romanlarında Özne ve İktidar" (PhD diss., Boğaziçi University, 2014).

32 Sema Kaygusuz, "Vuruş," in *Tutkulu Perçem* (Istanbul: İletişim, 2004), 7–14.

33 Veysel Öztürk, "*Tutkulu Perçem*'in Mikro Anlatıları," in *İsyankâr Neşe: Sevgi Soysal Kitabı*, ed. Seval Şahin and İpek Şahbenderoğlu (Istanbul: İletişim, 2015), 51–64 (ibid.).

34 This chapter cannot include a comprehensive bibliography of studies on these books, but for new queer perspectives on Sevgi Soysal's first two books, see Hülya Adak, "From l'ecriture Feminine to Queer Subjectivities: Sevgi Soysal, Emine Sevgi Özdamar and Perihan Mağden," *Journal of Middle East Women's Studies* 12, no. 1 (2016): 107–11; İpek Şahinler, "Tante Rosa ve Düş(üş) Kavramı, ya da Tante Rosa'nın 'Queer Düşüş Sanatı,'" *Kaos Q+* 8 (2019): 102–5; Nazan Maksudyan and Burcu Alkan, "Embracing Embodiedness, Desire and Failure: Women's Fluid Gender Performances in Sevgi Soysal's Oeuvre from the 1960s," *Journal of European Studies* 52, no. 2 (2022): 111–28.

35 Fethi Naci can be considered a representative of the aforementioned critical approach. With her play on names (Tacettin) in the story "Biz İki Sosyalist Erkek Eleştirmen" [Us, Two Socialist Male Critics], which she wrote in 1974 Leylâ Erbil also points at him. Leylâ Erbil, *Eski Sevgili* (Istanbul: Adam Yayıncılık, 1984), 83–98.

36 Fethi Naci, "Ey Nezihe Meriç! 'Gel Kurtul o Mutfağın Dar Hendesesinden,'" in *Roman ve Yaşam: Eleştiri Günlüğü III (1991–1992)* (Istanbul: Yapı Kredi Yayınları, 2002), 26–30.

37 I do not believe it is a coincidence that Meriç's first published short story "Bir Şey" is centered around the thoughts of a newlywed young woman in a freshly decorated kitchen while frying meatballs and potatoes. It is possible to find the first clues of her subsequent writings in this story where a woman loves yet questions the cozy kitchen in which she waits for her husband. Nezihe Meriç, "Bir Şey," in *Püf Noktası: İlk Öyküleri ve Yazıları* (Istanbul: Yapı Kredi Yayınları, 2011), 13–18.

38 Neslihan Cangöz, "Nezihe Meriç'in Fıkırdayan Tencereleri," *Birikim* 367 (November 2019): 62–67.

39 Sara Ahmed uses the term "killjoy" in her book *Living a Feminist Life* (Durham, NC: Duke University Press, 2017). A feminist killjoy is a person of any gender who not only feels uncomfortable with but *speaks out* against the patriarchal status quo in society. To be a killjoy is an action. In this case, the act of killing joy is done by writing, which I argue simultaneously creates an aesthetic joy.

References

Adak, Hülya. "From L'ecriture Feminine to Queer Subjectivities: Sevgi Soysal, Emine Sevgi Özdamar and Perihan Mağden." *Journal of Middle East Women's Studies* 12, no. 1 (2016): 107–11.

Ahmed, Sara. *Living a Feminist Life*. Durham, NC: Duke University Press, 2017.

Akbulak, Esra Nur, and Olcay Akyıldız. "Leylâ Erbil Bibliyografyası." *Zemin* 1 (2021): 30–69.

Akyıldız, Olcay, and Esra Nur Akbulak. "Leylâ Erbil Bibliyografyası Bize Ne Söyler? Leylâ Erbil Edebiyatına ve Alımlanışına Verilerle Bakmak." *Zemin* 1 (2021): 3–29.

Atik, Egem. "Sevgi Soysal'ın Romanlarında Özne ve İktidar." MA Thesis, Boğaziçi University, 2014.

Aydın, Hilal. "Türk Edebiyatındaki Direnme Noktası: Leylâ Erbil." *Moment Dergi* 2, no. 2 (2015): 272–88.

Aytemiz, Beyhan Uygun. "Nezihe Meriç'ten Tezer Özlü'ye: 1960–1980'li Yıllar Edebiyatında Kadın." In *Feminizm*, edited by Feryal Saygılıgil and Nacide Berber, 731–52. Istanbul: İletişim Yayınları, 2020.

Bezirci, Asım. "Yanık Saraylar." *Yeni Dergi* 12–13 (October 1965): 251–59.

——— *Nezihe Meriç: Monografi*. Istanbul: Evrensel Basım Yayın, 1999.

Burak, Sevim. *Yanık Saraylar*. Istanbul: Türkiye Basımevi, 1965.

———. "Hikâye ya da İmge ya da Tansık." *Kitap-lık* 71 (2004): 103–5.

Büyükarman, Didem Ardalı. "*Aşkımın Mezarı* yahut Popüler Edebiyatın Köşe Taşı Kadın Yazarlardan Feminist Söz Çıkar mı?" In *Feminizm*, edited by Feryal Saygılıgil and Nacide Berber, 766–74. Istanbul: İletişim Yayınları, 2020.

Cangöz, Neslihan. "Nezihe Meriç'in Fıkırdayan Tencereleri." *Birikim* 367 (November 2019): 62–67.

Çayırcıoğlu, Duygu. *Kadınca Bilmeyişlerin Sonu: 1960–1980 Döneminde Feminist Edebiyat*. Istanbul: İletişim, 2022.

Towards a Gynocritical Study of Turkish Fiction

Cemal, Ahmet. "Bir Direnme Eylemi Olarak Yazmak." In *Bir Tuhaf Kuştur, Gölgesi Zihin,* edited by Kaya Tokmakçıoğlu, 41–54. Istanbul: Aylak Adam, 2013.

Cixous, Helen. "The Laugh of Medusa." Translated by Paula Cohen and Keith Cohen. *Signs* 1, no. 4 (Summer 1976): 875–93.

Demirtaş, Mustafa. *İkinci Bir Yaşam: Sevim Burak'ın Edebiyat Dünyası.* Istanbul: Yapı Kredi Yayınları, 2018.

Dirlikyapan, Jale Özata. *Öykünün Modernleşme Sürecinde İki Kadın Öykücü: Leyla Erbil ve Nezihe Meriç.* Eskişehir, Turkey: Bir Bilim Kategorisi Olarak "Kadın" Uluslararası Sempozyumu, Anadolu Üniversitesi Eğitim Fakültesi, April 29–May 2, 2008.

———. *Kabuğunu Kıran Hikâye: Türk Öykücülüğünde 1950 Kuşağı.* Istanbul: Metis, 2010.

Doğan, Mehmet H. "Sevgi Soysal'ın Ölümüyle Edebiyatımız Kendini Bilinçle Değiştirmeyi Başarmış Bir Yazarını Kaybetti." *Milliyet Sanat* 210 (1976).

Erbil, Leylâ. *Hallaç.* Ankara: Dost, 1960.

———. *Gecede.* Istanbul: Asya Matbaası, 1968.

———. *Tuhaf Bir Kadın.* Istanbul: Habora, 1971.

———. "Biz İki Sosyalist Erkek Eleştirmen." In *Eski Sevgili,* 83–98. Istanbul: Adam Yayıncılık, 1984.

———. "Ben Deliliğe Düşkün Bir Yazarım." *Düşler/Öyküler* 4 (May 1997): 6–35.

———. *Eski Sevgili.* Istanbul: Adam Yayıncılık, 1984.

Furrer, Priska. *Das erzählerische Werk der türkischen Autorin Sevgi Soysal.* Berlin: Klaus Schwarz Verlag, 1992.

———. *Sevgi Soysal: Bireysellikten Toplumsallığa.* Istanbul: Papirüs, 2004.

Gürpınar, Aydın Baran. "*Tutkulu Perçem* ve *Tante Rosa* ile Toplum Söylencesinin Feshi." *Varlık* 1306 (2016): 22–27.

Irzık, Sibel. "Öznenin Vefatından Sonra Kadın Olarak Okumak." In *Kadınlar Dile Düşünce: Edebiyatta Toplumsal Cinsiyet,* edited by Sibel Irzık and Jale Parla, 35–56. Istanbul: İletişim Yayınları, 2004.

Irzık, Sibel, and Jale Parla, eds. *Kadınlar Dile Düşünce: Edebiyatta Toplumsal Cinsiyet.* Istanbul: İletişim Yayınları, 2004.

Kaygusuz, Sema. "Vuruş." In *Tutkulu Perçem,* 7–14. Istanbul: İletişim, 2004.

Kaygusuz, Sema, and Deniz Gündoğan İbrişim, eds. *Gaflet: Modern Türkçe Edebiyatın Cinsiyetçi Sinir Uçları.* Istanbul: Metis, 2019.

Koçakoğlu, Bedia. *Büyük Günah: Bilinmeyen Öyküleriyle Sevim Burak.* Konya: Palet Yayınları, 2013.

Kutup, Selver Sezen. "Textual Network in Sevim Burak: The Nonhuman Beings of *Ford Mach I.*" MA thesis, Boğaziçi University, 2019.

Maksudyan, Nazan, and Burcu Alkan. "Embracing Embodiedness, Desire and Failure: Women's Fluid Gender Performances in Sevgi Soysal's Oeuvre from the 1960s." *Journal of European Studies* 52, no. 2 (2022): 111–28.

Meriç, Nezihe. *Bozbulanık.* Ankara: Dost Yayınları, 1952.

———. *Topal Koşma.* Ankara: Seçilmiş Hikâyeler, 1956.

———. *Korsan Çıkmazı.* Ankara: Dost Yayınları, 1961.

———. *Menekşeli Bilinç.* Ankara: Dost Yayınları, 1965.

———. "Bir Şey." In *Püf Noktası: İlk Öyküleri ve Yazıları,* 13–18. Istanbul: Yapı Kredi Yayınları, 2011.

———. *Püf Noktası: İlk Öyküleri ve Yazıları.* Istanbul: Yapı Kredi Yayınları, 2011.

———. *Bütün Öyküleri I.* Istanbul: Yapı Kredi Yayınları, 2018.

Naci, Fethi. "Ey Nezihe Meriç! 'Gel Kurtul o Mutfağın Dar Hendesesinden.'" In *Roman ve Yaşam: Eleştiri Günlüğü III (1991–1992),* 26–30. Istanbul: Yapı Kredi Yayınları, 2002.

Oğuzertem, Süha. "Kaybolmayan Yazar: Leylâ Erbil'in Özgünlüğü, Özgürlüğü." In *Leylâ Erbil'de Etik ve Estetik,* 147–79. Istanbul: Kanat, 2007.

Öz, Erdal. "Topal Koşma'nın Özü." *Pazar Postası,* August 19, 1956.

Özkırımlı, Atilla. "*Tutkulu Perçem'*den *Şafak'*a Sevgi Soysal'ın Yazarlık Çizgisi." *Birikim* 23 (1977): 7–15.

Öztürk, Veysel. "*Tutkulu Perçem'*in Mikro Anlatıları." In *İsyankâr Neşe: Sevgi Soysal Kitabı,* edited by Seval Şahin, İpek Şahbenderoğlu, 51–64. Istanbul: İletişim, 2015.

Parla, Jale. "Kadın Eleştirisi Neyi Gerçekleştirdi." In *Kadınlar Dile Düşünce: Edebiyatta Toplumsal Cinsiyet.* Istanbul: İletişim Yayınları, 2004.

Şahbenderoğlu, İpek. "'Adamlar, Kadınlar ve Duvarlar': Eril Kentin Tepelerinde *Tutkulu Perçem.*" In *"Ne Güzel Suçluyuz Hepimiz" Sevgi Soysal İçin Yazılar,* edited by Seval Şahin, 37–60. Istanbul: İletişim, 2013.

Şahinler, İpek. "Tante Rosa ve Düş(üş) Kavramı, ya da Tante Rosa'nın 'Queer Düşüş Sanatı.'" *Kaos Q+* 8 (2019): 102–5.

Saygılıgil, Feryal, and Nacide Berber. *Feminizm.* Istanbul: İletişim Yayınları, 2020.

Şen-Sönmez, Ürün. "Bir Leylâ Erbil Portresi ya da Hiçbir Kavme Dâhil Olmayan Bir 'Öteki.'" In *Feminizm,* edited by Feryal Saygılıgil and Nacide Berber, 738–45. Istanbul: İletişim Yayınları, 2020.

Showalter, Elaine. *A Jury of Her Peers: Celebrating American Women Writers from Anne Bradstreet to Annie Proulx*. New York: Vintage, 2010.

———. "Toward a Feminist Poetics." In *Women Writing and Writing About Women*, edited by Mary Jacobus, 22–41. London & New York: Routledge, 2012. (First published 1979).

Soysal, Funda. "*Tante Rosa*'dan Sevgi Soysal'a Yolculuk." In *Tante Rosa*, edited by Sevgi Soysal, 11–17. Istanbul: İletişim, 2010.

Soysal, Sevgi. *Tante Rosa*. Ankara: Dost Yayınları, 1968.

———. *Tutkulu Perçem*. Ankara: Doğan Matbaası, 1962.

Timuroğlu, Senem. "Artık Adını Koyalım: Feminist Edebiyatımızın Köşe Taşları." *K24*, March 8, 2017. https://t24.com.tr/k24/yazi/feminist-edebiyatimizin-kose-taslari,1105.

Turgut, Hasan. "'Yeryüzünde Serseri ve Kaçak' Sevim Burak'ın Yanık Saraylar'ında Maduniyet." In *İkinci Bir Yaşam: Sevim Burak'ın Edebiyat Dünyası*, edited by Mustafa Demirtaş, 195–215. Istanbul: Yapı Kredi Yayınları, 2018.

Uysal, Zeynep. "Yeni Bir Toplumsallığın Peşinde: Deneyimden Dünyaya Açılan Roman." *Notos* 67 (2017): 16–19.

SECTION V

Linguistic Diversity

15

KARAMANLIDIKA LITERARY PRODUCTION IN THE MID-NINETEENTH CENTURY

Şehnaz Şişmanoğlu Şimşek

Up until the beginning of the twentieth century when various nation-states were founded on the empire's shrinking territories, the Ottoman Empire could be described as a multiethnic, multilingual, and multicultural society. One segment of this multicultural society was Turcophone Orthodox Christians of Anatolia, also known as Karamanlides or *Karamanli*,[1] living mostly in the interiors of Asia Minor in the wider Cappadocia region. The language of this community was Turkish and the written language was called Karamanlidika (*Karamanlıca* in Turkish), which was Turkish in Greek script.[2] Karamanlidika was one of many other hybrid languages in the empire—that is, languages and scripts intermingled in various combinations, such as Armeno-Turkish, Greek in the Arabic alphabet (Al-Jamiado), Greek in the Hebrew alphabet, and so on.[3] From the mid-nineteenth century onwards, newspapers and periodicals circulating in various languages and alphabets became one of the fundamental tools and arenas of expression of ideas as well as literary production,[4] especially due to serialized novels and short stories.[5] This was also relevant for the Turkophone Orthodox Christians of the empire. Literary activities of the community were bounded by a couple of historical and social developments in the mid-nineteenth century. As Stefo Benlisoy puts forward in one of his articles, due to the increased educational and professional opportunities emerging in the mid-nineteenth century, a local, non-cleric, intellectual stratum composed of professionals like lawyers, doctors, teachers, and even state officers had emerged among the Turkophone Orthodox Anatolians, who created for themselves tools of expressions such as the press.[6] In the same period, the fact that they were Turcophones started to be problematized and treated as an anomaly by the ecclesiastic and secular Greek leadership and so the identity of Anatolian Orthodox Christians was called into question. This was also due to Balkan nationalisms that introduced language as the most important "objective" criterion in determining nationhood.[7] Turcophony began to be associated with the name *Karamanli* and being "uncivilized," "uneducated," and "rude,"[8] which affected also the discourse on literary production. Throughout the nineteenth century, there was also a flow of immigration from Orthodox settlements of Cappadocia to places of economic opportunity like Istanbul and Izmir, where the newcomers continued to be in touch with the central Anatolian homeland and the local notables, especially with the help of the associations founded in large cities[9] that focused on the welfare and enlightenment of the remaining people in the hometowns. This strong tie between the urban centers and the hometowns in Cappadocia had a direct effect on the literary production in Karamanlidika in terms of the language and the circulation of the novels.

DOI: 10.4324/9780429279270-21

Karamanlidika Literary Production: First Efforts in Ottoman/ Turkish Literature

Karamanlidika book production shows parallels with the various literatures of the Ottoman Empire in different alphabets and languages.[10] This production, which started with religious publishing in certain centers in Ottoman and European regions such as Venice, Vienna, Istanbul, and Izmir, gained a secular dimension after the second half of the nineteenth century. The first printed work in Turkish with Greek characters was a translation of a declaration of the Orthodox faith by the Patriarch Gennadios Scholarios presented to Sultan Mehmet II, which was included in Martin Crusius' *Turcograecia* in Basel in 1584. As Richard Clogg mentions, this work was not intended for circulation among Turkish Orthodox communities but later was included in *Gülzar-ı İmanı Mesihi*, which is accepted as the first book printed and circulated among members of the Karamanlidika community in 1718. Thus, from the eighteenth to the nineteenth century, Karamanlidika printing was launched with the publishing of religious texts as can be seen in the Karamanlidika catalogues.[11] The aim of these religious books, which were generally catechisms, psalters, and vitae of saints, was to enlighten Turcophone Christians about their religion and teach the doctrine of the Orthodox Church, because they were not able to read in Greek. Secular book printing including popular books, grammar books, treatises on rhetoric, volumes concerning geography and history, and books on education. These began to appear in the second half of the nineteenth century and continued until the end of Karamanlidika book production.[12] It was the Karamanlidika press, namely newspapers and periodicals, which introduced a new genre, the novel, to the reading public, first through its serialized form. Johann Strauss in his article "Who Read What in the Ottoman Empire (19th–20th Centuries)?" gives a list of periodicals circulating in various languages of the empire (e.g., Turkish, Armenian, Greek, Bulgarian, Judeo-Spanish, and Arabic) but also Turkish written in the Armenian and Greek alphabets, which contained literary material including serialized novels.[13] Thus, giving a place to literary material in periodicals was a common feature of nineteenth-century journalism regardless of the ethnic community.

The newspaper *Anatoli*, founded by Evangelinos Misailidis (1820–1890) first in Izmir in 1843 and later in Istanbul in 1850,[14] was central in serializing novels mostly translated from French and Greek for its Turcophone Christian Orthodox readers. Misailidis was a pioneer in Karamanlidika press and book production. He was a journalist and publisher, as well as a fiction writer like his Muslim and non-Muslim counterparts of the period such as Ahmet Mithat, Hovsep Vartanyan, Ben Ghiat, and others. Born in Kula, a small town in Western Anatolia, he moved to Izmir, a multicultural port city on the western coast of Asia Minor, where he started to publish his first periodicals such as *Beşaret'ül Maşrik* (1845–1847) [Eastern Messenger], the monthly pictorial *Mekteb-ül Fünun-u Meşriki* (1849–1850) [School of Oriental Knowledge], and *Şark* (1849–1850) [Orient].[15] He settled in Istanbul in 1850 where he continued to publish *Anatoli* [Orient], in 1854 establishing his publishing house *Anatoli*, which would publish many of his books, journals, and newspapers such as *Mikra Asia* (1874–1875) [Asia Minor] and *Kukurikos* (1876–1881). Misailidis also invented the usage of dotted letters for the Greek alphabet in order to better present Turkish vowels.[16] In addition to being a writer, journalist, and publisher, together with his brothers he also translated French novels written by Xavier de Montépin and Eugène Sue. Of the 20 translated novels dating from this period, 14 were completed by the Misailidis family.[17]

Being one of the oldest and longest-running newspapers of the Ottoman Empire, *Anatoli* was one of the first mediums in Turkish that opened space for literary production from the first years of its circulation. The first narrative serialized in *Anatoli* was *Theagenes and Chariclea*, one of the oldest Greek romances, also known as *Aethiopica* by Heliodorus in 1851. This was followed by *Robinson Crusoe* in 1852, a "translation"[18] by Hadji Dimitrios, the son of Hadji Ephraim Daniiloglou. This was an earlier translation than the one published in Ottoman Turkish in 1864.[19] Being the most popular newspaper among the Turkish-speaking Orthodox communities, the serialized novels published in *Anatoli* between 1888 and 1899 give a general idea about the literary production and literary taste of the community.[20] The narratives chosen for serialization were mostly popular narratives that had been also serialized or published in various languages and scripts of the Ottoman press or publishing houses. The list of the serialized novels include titles such as *Pavlos ve Virginia* (1890) [Paul et Virginie] by Bernardin de Saint Pierre; *Çingane Kızı* (1892–1894) [La Gitane] by Xavier de Montépin; *Prenses Anzol*[21] (1891–1892) [Princess Anzol, trans. Ioannis Ioannidis]; *Paris Sırları* (1897) [Les Mysteres de Paris]; and *Serseri Yahudi* (1897) [Le Juif Errant] by Eugene Sue, the last two being Misailidis' "translations," "adaptations," or "rewritings."[22] Eugène Sue's *Mystères de Paris*, which was published in 1842 and 1843 in the *Journal des débats*, is also significant in literary history, having given birth to many derivative novels in many languages including G. Reynolds' *Mysteries of London* (1844–1848), Ned Buntline's *The Mysteries and Miseries of New York* (1848), and Camilo Castelo Branco's *Os Mistéros de Lisboa* (1854).[23] Accordingly, Epaminondas Kiriakides' *Beyoğlu Sırları* (1888–1889) [Mysteries of Beyoğlu], translated from Greek by Misailidis, appears in the newspaper following the subgenre-like series "mysteries of cities," which also gave birth to several Greek mystery novels in Istanbul in the nineteenth century.[24] Ahmet Mithat, the famous Ottoman writer, is the exception in the list with his three novels or short stories *Yeniçeriler*[25] (1890–1891) (The Janissaries); *Şeytan Kayası* (1891) (The Evil Rock); and *Diplomalı Kız* (1896) (The Girl With the Diploma/Degree) adapted by Ioannis Gavriilidis.

Not only in serialized form but in book formats, there were pioneering attempts in fiction in Karamanlidika. Though neglected for a long time in Turkish literary history, Evangelinos Misailidis, the founder of *Anatoli*, wrote one of the first Turkish novels, *Temaşa-i Dünya ve Cefakâr u Cefakeş* [Contemplation of the World and Tormentor and Tormented] (hereinafter *Temaşa-i Dünya*) and published in his own publishing house in 1871–1872. It was only by the 1980s that this novel was rediscovered in Turkey by the Turcologist Robert Anhegger and writer Vedat Günyol. The novel was a 1839 rewriting of the Greek novel *Polypathis* [The Man of Many Sufferings] by Grigoris Palailogos[26] (b. 1794 in Istanbul). Misailidis transformed Palailogos' text literally and ideologically by adding new chapters, characters, and experiences of the Turcophone Orthodox Christians. This makes the text a significant contribution to nineteenth-century practices of fiction writing that is worthy of analysis.[27] Misailidis did not mention Palailogos' name, either in the foreword of the novel or in his other writings. While in today's world this issue would likely stir up debates concerning issues of originality, conceptualizations of "originality," and faithfulness in "translations" of literary works, nineteenth-century practices preclude such an argument, as adaptations of works through "translation" was a common practice. It should also be noted that Misailidis, who was an Ottoman subject, may have been reluctant to refer to Palailogos' work, which was also an appraisal of the newly founded Greek state, at a time when Greek nationalist sentiment would not have been well received in Ottoman circles. A member of the Turcophone Anatolian Orthodox community, often treated as being an anomaly by the Grecophone Greek authorities from the second half of the nineteenth century onwards, Misailidis was stuck between Ottoman/Greek, Muslim, and Anatolian identities. The text moves between the ideology of the Greek Enlightenment, the social and linguistic Ottoman-Greek and Ottoman-Muslim traditions, and the Christian Orthodox religion.[28]

There are also Karamanlidika editions of Turkish folk stories like *Âşık Garîb*, *Kerem ile Aslı*, *Köroğlu*, and *Şâh İsmail*.[29] Semi-religious and semi-fictional texts such as *Hazine-i Ara-i*

Müstakime-i Mesihiye (Tameion Orthodoksias) (1860); *Gerosthatis* (1866) [The Old Man Sthathis]; *Genovefa Hikâyesi* (no date) [The Story of Genevieve]; *Küçücük Eleni* (1878) [Little Eleni]; and *İffetli ve İsmetli Martha* (1886) [The Virtuous Martha] can also be added to this corpus of fiction.

As one can depict from the list of narratives in *Anatoli*, as well as the other novels published in book form, it is obvious that the corpus of the Karamanlidika literary production is mostly characterized by "translated," "adapted," or "non-original" works, which made the corpus neglected for a long period. However, for nineteenth-century literary works in general, the idea of "originality" or "original work" is highly problematic. The polysystem theory of Itamar Even-Zohar is a useful theoretical tool for explaining the various writing practices of a writer/translator in a literary system in which translation is crucial. According to Even-Zohar, if a piece of translated literature occupies a central space in a literary system, the distinction between author and translator is obscured. Coping with the new material, the translator introduces new ideas, words, and ways of narrating that blur the borderline between an original creation and the translation.[30] This may also be one of the reasons for anonymity in some of the Karamanlidika texts—including Misailidis' admission of Palailogos' name in *Temaşa-i Dünya*. Just as Olga Borovaya suggests for Ladino texts,[31] in some cases the translator/adapter or rewriter thinks of him/herself as the co-creator of the text and obscures the "actual writer's" name.

Thus, whether serialized in newspapers or published as books, Karamanlidika literary production should be studied beyond the paradigm of originality—which is already problematic for nineteenth-century literature—taking into account writers' self-designation of texts as well as paratexts used in the publishing process.

Learning to Appreciate the Novel: An Anatolian at a European Table

In 1890, Ioannis Gavriilidis wrote the following in his foreword to his rewriting of Ahmet Mithat's *Yeniçeriler* (Janissaries) published in *Anatoli*: "One should read either history or novels, as we Anatolians are in short supply of education and teaching."[32] This was a very similar attitude and a common discourse among his nineteenth-century Muslim counterparts referred to as the Young Ottomans. This group—including Şinasi, Namık Kemal, Ziya Paşa, and Ali Suavi, to name but a few—was made up of intellectuals mostly from the civil bureaucracy and the Translation Bureau of the Porte, who were the first to introduce and discuss such Enlightenment ideas as rational thought, constitutional and parliamentarian government in the empire, citizenship, and critique, offering a synthesis between these ideas and Islam. In addition, they were the first organized group of the Turkish intelligentsia who used media of mass communication such as newspapers and journals to criticize the government and the Tanzimat regime. The other medium they used to make their voices heard in public was literature. Their literary production was a tool for introducing their reformist ideals to the reading public; that is why they stressed the didactic value of the new literature.

Gavriilidis was a member of a community whose Turcophony was considered an anomaly by the Grecophone Greek authorities from the second half of the nineteenth century. This was because the Greek language, along with religion, was the foundation of the ethno-religious identity of the *millet*.[33] Thus, due to their lack of knowledge of Greek and the fact that they were living in the interior of Asia Minor, Turkophone Orthodox Anatolians were generally perceived in an Orientalist light as ignorant, crude, narrow-minded, and in need of being civilized. Greek diplomatic notes concerning Asia Minor in the nineteenth century,[34] as well as the reports of the well-known association the Greek Philological Syllogos of Constantinople, attest to this negative perception of Turkophone Orthodox Anatolians.[35]

Thus, the utilitarian function of the novel was very much related to Turcophone Orthodox Christian identity, as well as the general tendency of the nineteenth century concerning the genre novel. *Anatoli* was a very influential medium in the Karamanlidika press that had granted itself the mission of enlightening its readers and participating modestly in the Westernization project. Thus, besides articles and news concerning politics in the empire and abroad, and writings concerning historical aspects of Anatolia, Anatoli contributed to the secularization process of the period with a permanent column giving a distinguished place to the serialized novels and short stories taken mostly from Western literature. If we take into account "angry attempts" towards the Western novel throughout the entire Orthodox Greek-speaking world, as discussed by Ioanna Petropoulou,[36] we can better appreciate the column reserved for novels in *Anatoli* and the positive reactions to them by Turcophone-Orthodox readers.

Gavriilidis continues his foreword drawing an analogy between appreciating a novel and enjoying a meal. He argues that someone from Kastamonu (a town in the Black Sea region) who is invited to a rich Western table cannot enjoy it due to his ignorance and being unfamiliar with the taste itself. It seems that for Gavriilidis, becoming a reader of the novel is like turning the key in a door opening onto European civilization, but before this, readers should first be initiated to the "new genre" through a narrative familiar to them, such as Ahmet Mithat's *Yeniçeriler*. Only in this way could someone from Anatolia appreciate a European taste.

It was no coincidence that Gavriilidis gave Kastamonu as an example. The readers of *Anatoli* as well as the readers of the novels were not only from Istanbul but the general readership was from Asia Minor. Readers' letters from cities such as Adana, Adapazarı, Bafra, Samsun, Ürgüp, Ünye, Şebinkarahisar, and Konya give an idea of how the newspaper circulated in different parts of Anatolia. Accordingly, charts demonstrating the agents of Anatoli in the provinces are another source indicating the subscribers' places of residence. Readers were mostly from İzmir, Bursa, Çarşamba, Ereğli, Mersin, Niğde, Adapazarı, and Lefke. As Evangelia Balta points out, these readers mostly belonged to

> a class of merchants and professional craftsmen who had migrated to the capital of the empire. . . . Now wealthy and of established economic and social status, they wished to be informed of what was going on inside the Ottoman empire as well as in the world at large, just as they also needed a platform to express themselves.[37]

However, initiation into the novel form was not a top-down project of the press but was also shaped by the feedback and the responses of the readers. Going back to the announcements and readers' letters, it is clear from these announcements that Turcophone Orthodox readers were interested and involved in the literary material of the newspaper; they were writing their complaints and appraisals about the serials and publications and in a way participating as actors in the publishing and circulation politics of the newspaper. The feedback of the readers was significant for the newspapers as they were also dominant economic actors for the circulation of the newspapers. One can frequently see notices in *Anatoli* calling and warning the readers to pay their fees on time. Even the names of the subscribers were sometimes published to embarrass them into making their payments.[38]

Local Notables, Readership in Asia Minor, and the Language Issue in the Mid-nineteenth Century

Readers were also the dominant financial supporters to have the serialized novels published in book format. It was a subscription system that made the publishing process possible; that is, the readers subscribed beforehand and sent fees to the publishing house. In *Anatoli*, one can see occasional notices or advertisements declaring that those who want to subscribe to a specific book should send their subscription fees to the Anatoli publishing house. One additional example from *Anatoli* is the call to readers to subscribe to the novel of Montépin,[39] warning them that future volumes of *Çingane Kızı* [*La Gitane*] will be impossible if subscribers from the provinces do not send their fees.[40]

Being the main sponsors of the novel, a list of the subscribers was published at the back of the novels, which is an interesting peculiarity of Karamanlidika publishing in the mid-nineteenth century. One can have an idea about the gender, residence, sometimes professions of Turcophone Orthodox readers from these lists, the number of which change from novel to novel. The lists are organized usually according to the names or location of the readers. These lists indicate that the readers of fiction were not just from urban centers like Istanbul and Izmir, but also from the interior of Anatolia. One example is *Ekmekçi Hatun* (1895) [*La Porteuse de Pain*] by Montépin, whose financial supporters were from Zincidere, Niğde, Kayseri, Endirlik, Germir, Talas, Tavlusun, İncesu, Nevşehir, Fertek, Ürgüp, and so on. Obviously, subscription to a novel does not necessarily make one a reader of it, whereas the act of subscribing alone or contributing to the publishing process of the novel appears as a prestigious or beneficial act in the Turcophone Orthodox community.

Apart from subscribers, local notables also sometimes undertook the costs of publication. This is indicated by a typical page in a Karamanlidika publication in which the work is dedicated to someone, mostly a local notable who is well known for his charitable activities in the Turcophone Orthodox community. Accordingly, we understand that it was prestigious to sponsor a book in a community that was looked down upon for its low level of education. A typical example is the novel *Temaşa-I Dünya*, each volume of which is dedicated to a notable. Dedications were sometimes followed with small paragraphs appraising and expressing gratitude to the notable for his philanthropic activities for the homeland (*vatan*) and community (*millet*).

The language politics of Karamanlidika literary production was also very much affected by the sociology of its readers. Though there were different approaches to the language articulated in various newspapers and periodicals in Karamanlidika, such as *Terakki, Aktis, Anatol Ahteri*, and *Areti*,[41] mainly the literary texts were written in quite simple and ordinary Turkish mostly devoid of Ottoman compounds derived from Arabic and Persian words, which is parallel to Karamanlidika book production in general in the nineteenth century. "Written in clear and simple Turkish" (*sade ve açık Türkçe ile yazılmıştır*) is a common phrase on the first pages of the books in Karamanlidika. In the foreword to *Yeniçeriler* (1890) [Janissaries], Gavriilidis writes about the difficulty of "narrating" the story because of the rhetoric of Ahmet Mithat, which was full of words with which Anatolians would hardly be familiar (though the writer is known for the simple Turkish of his novels). Amet Mithat declared that he wrote without rhetorical flourishes, but not in the vulgar Turkish of the Anatolians; rather, he used simple Turkish so that everybody could understand it. Johann Strauss names this simplicity in language as "revolutionary" and he points out that "despite the efforts by certain writers [Christian Turcophones] to make use of the devices of the lofty style of Ottoman Turkish (*izafet, atf-ı tefsir* etc.) these imitations hardly ever worked well." According to him, the explanation for this is "the lack of formal training among the Turcophone Christians in the two cultural languages of the Muslims, Arabic and Persian."[42] As Strauss mentions, formal teaching is one of the main language issues discussed in various newspapers and periodicals in Karamanlidika. Apart from the simplification of the language, other issues concerning language included the necessity of knowledge of Ottoman Turkish for Anatolians in order to be included in the state apparatus and the acquisition of Greek, which is described sometimes as the national language or a mother tongue.[43]

By Way of a Conclusion

For literary production in Karamanlidika, the main medium was the newspapers and periodicals This is more or less in accordance with the general mediums of literary productions in other literatures of the nineteenth-century Ottoman Empire. However, one of the peculiarities was that literature was also circulating in the interiors of Asia Minor and books were able to be published mainly through the financial support of readers, especially local notables who were the main sponsors of the newspapers as well as the books published. The reader lists at the back of each book show the readers by name and city of residence, which offers invaluable data for a literary historian. Accordingly, the readers also had a powerful effect on the language used in the literary productions and, in a way, were participating in the production process with their responses sent to the press.

Literary production was also related to the enlightenment project of Anatolian Orthodox Christians. Being looked down on and labeled as "uneducated" by the Greek elites gave Karamanlidika novels a didactic value to educate members of the community, which was a value shared also by their Muslim counterparts. The tension with the Greek elites was also echoed in the ideologically different pieces of literature of some Anatolian Christians, such as *Temaşa-i Dünya*.

Literary production in Karamanlidika, in our context novels and short stories, constitute a worthy part of the nineteenth-century corpus of Turkish narrative fiction in various aspects, though it is almost completely unknown in Turkish literary history. Though dominantly characterized by "adaptations/translations," approaching these texts with "beyond-binary" perspectives,[44] and incorporating various rewriting practices beyond original versus translation, will allow us to grasp various practices of text production in the nineteenth-century Ottoman context. Such an analysis will also provide the readers significant clues to understand the social and cultural aspects of a community that was an important constituent of the multicultural and multilingual Ottoman society.

Notes

1 It is problematic to use the term *"Karamanli"* for this community because it is used by the Greek elites in a pejorative sense. Thus, the term "Turkophone Orthodox Anatolians/Christians" will be used instead. See Foti Benlisoy and Stefo Benlisoy, "Reading the Identity of Karamanli Through the Pages of *Anatoli,*" in *Cries and Whispers in Karamanlidika Books: Proceedings of the First International Conference on Karamanlidika Studies (Nicosia 11th–13th September 2008)*, ed. Evangelia Balta and Matthias Kappler (Wiesbaden: Harrassowitz, 2010), 93–108. The community itself used the appellations such as "Anadolulu Hristiyan karındaşlarımız" ("our *Anatoli*an Christian brethren")," "Anadolu Hristiyanları" (Eastern Christians), "Anadolu[lu] Ortodoks Hristiyanlar (*Anatoli*an Orthodox Christians). See Evangelia Balta, "Gerçi Rum İsek de Rumca Bilmez Türkçe Söyleriz: The Adventure of an Identity of the Triptych: Vatan, Religion and Language," *Türk Kültürü İncelemeleri Dergisi* 8 (2003): 25–44.
2 According to Matthias Kappler, Karamanlidika texts are the graphic reflection of a relatively large number of spoken and written varieties. Kappler designates the first researcher to employ the term "Karamanli" for the language of the Turkophone Orthodox population as Georg Jacob in 1898. However, for Kappler, it is not adequate to use the term as an Anatolian "dialect" or "language" but rather one should concentrate "on the graphic-cultural side without overstressing a linguistic homogeneity" (126). For a critical analysis of terminology used for Turkish in Greek script, see Matthias Kappler, "Transcription Text, Regraphization, Variety?—Reflections on 'Karamanlidika,'" in *Spoken Ottoman in Mediator Texts*, ed. Eva Csato, Astrid Menz, and Fikret Turan (Wiesbaden: Harrassowitz Verlag, 2016), 119–28. Anatolian Orthodox Christians named this language as "Rumca hurufat ile lisan-ı Türkî" or "Rumiu'l-huruf, Türkiü'l-ibare," both of them meaning "Turkish in Greek script." Due to convenience, the term "Karamanlidika" will be used in this chapter, keeping in mind Kappler's critical stance.

3 Johann Strauss, "Who Read What in the Ottoman Empire (19th–20th Centuries)?," *Middle Eastern Literatures* 6, no. 1 (January 2003): 39–76; Evangelia Balta and Mehmet Ölmez, eds., *Between Religion and Language Turkish Speaking Christians, Jews and Greek Speaking Muslims and Catholics in the Ottoman Empire* (Istanbul: Eren Yayınları, 2011).

4 In this chapter, the use of "literary production" is limited to novels and short stories.

5 Şehnaz Şişmanoğlu Şimşek, "Karamanlidika Literary Production at the End of the 19th Century as Reflected in the Pages of *Anatoli*," in *Cultural Encounters in the Turkish-Speaking Communities of the Late Ottoman Empire*, ed. Evangelia Balta (Istanbul: Isis Press, 2014), 429–47.

6 Stefo Benlisoy, "'Another Newspaper in Our Language': Competition and Polemic in the Karamanlidika Press," in *Cultural Encounters in the Turkish-Speaking Communities of the Late Ottoman Empire*, ed. Evangelia Balta (Istanbul: Isis Press, 2014), 429–47.

7 Stefo Benlisoy, "Education in the Turcophone Orthodox Communities of Anatolia During the Nineteenth Century" (PhD diss., University of Boğaziçi, 2013), 417. See also Paschalis M. Kitromilidis, "'Imagined Communities' and the Origins of the National Question in the Balkans," *European History Quarterly* 19 (1989): 149–92.

8 Foti and Stefo Benlisoy, "'Karamanlılar,' 'Anadolu Ahalisi' ve 'Aşağı Tabakalar': Türkdilli Anadolu Ortodokslarında Kimlik Algısı," *Tarih ve Toplum Yeni Yaklaşımlar* 11, no. 251 (Autumn 2010): 7–22.

9 Gülen Göktürk, "Well-Preserved Boundaries: Faith and Co-Existence in the Late Ottoman Empire" (PhD diss., Middle East Technical University, 2013), 246.

10 Strauss, "Who Read What in the Ottoman Empire?"

11 Eugene Dallegio and Severien Salaville, *Karamanlidika Bibliographie Analytique des Ouvrages en Langue Turque Imprimés en Caractère Grecs*, vol. 3 (Athens: Institut Français d'Athènes, 1958–1974); Eugene Dallegio and Severien Salaville, eds., *Karamanlidika XXe siécle Bibliographie Analytique* (Athens: Centre D'Etudes D'Asie Mineure, 1987); Eugene Dallegio and Severien Salaville, eds., *Karamanlidika Nouvelles Additions et Compléments* (Athens: Centre D'Etudes D'Asie Mineure, 1997), 1.

12 Balta, "Gerçi Rum İsek de Rumca Bilmez Türkçe Söyleriz."

13 Strauss, "Who Read What in the Ottoman Empire?" 43.

14 For a detailed analysis of *Anatoli*, see Şehnaz Şişmanoğlu Şimşek, "The *Anatoli* Newspaper and the Heyday of the *Karamanli* Press," in *Cries and Whispers in Karamanlidika Books: Proceedings of the First International Conference on Karamanlidika Studies (Nicosia 11th–13th September 2008)*, ed. Evangelia Balta and Matthias Kappler (Wiesbaden: Harrassowitz, 2010), 201–8; Benlisoy and Benlisoy, "Reading the Identity of *Karamanli* through the pages of *Anatoli*," 93–108.

15 Evangelia Balta, "Karamanli Press Smyrna 1845—Athens 1926," in *Izzet Gündağ Kayaoğlu Hatıra Kitabı Makaleler*, ed. Oktay Belli, Yücel Dağlı, and M. Sinan Genim (Istanbul: Türkiye Anıt Çevre Turizm Değerlerini Koruma Vakfı, 2005), 27–33.

16 Ioannis Polivios, "Evangelinos Misailidis," *Terakki*, July 30, 1888.

17 Ioanna Petropoulou, "From West to East: The Translation Bridge. An Approach from a Western Perspective," in *Ways to Modernity in Greece and Turkey*, ed. Anna Frangoudaki and Çağlar Keyder (London: I. B. Tauris, 2007), 91–111. For an annotated list of the novels and serials see also Evangelia Balta, "Novels Published in Karamanlidika," in *Karamanlidika Legacies*, ed. Evangelia Balta (Istanbul: Isis Press, 2018), 49–80.

18 To name any given literary work as "translation" or "adaptation" in the nineteenth century is problematic and hierarchical in terms of creating a binary opposition between the target and the source text, one being "original," the other "non-original." Thus, in this chapter, I use the terms "translations/ adaptations" in quotations and prefer to use "rewriting" as a value-free term.

19 Bülent Berkol, "133 Yıl Önce Yunan Harfleri ile Türkçe (Karamanlıca) bir Robinson Crusoe Çevirisi," *Sosyoloji Konferansları 25* (Istanbul: İstanbul Üniversitesi Yayınları, 1986).

20 Şişmanoğlu Şimşek, "Karamanlidika Literary Production."

21 This is actually the novel *Le Morne au Diable*, see Balta, "Novels Published in Karamanlidika," 62.

22 For the exact dates and issues see Şişmanoğlu Şimşek, "Karamanlidika Literary Production," 446, reflected in the Pages of *Anatoli*.

23 Marie-Ève Thérenty analyses Sue's novel as "the first massive occurrence of cultural globalisation." See Marie-Ève Thérenty, "Mysterymania. Essor et limites de la globalisation culturelle au XIXe siècle," *Romantisme* 160, no. 2 (2013): 53–64.

24 Γεωργίας Γκότση [Georgia Gotsi], "Μεταφράσεις Μυθιστοριών Αποκρύφων και Συναφών Έργων [Translations of the Mystery Novels and the Serials], 1845–1900," *Antí* 641 (August 1997): 12–16.

25 For Ahmet Mithat's, *Yeniçeriler* see Ahmet Mithat, *Yeniçeriler* (Istanbul: Muharririn Zatına Mahsus Matbaa [the Writer's Own Publishing House], 1290 [1871]); Ahmet Mithat, *Yeniçeriler*, ed. Mustafa Nihat Özön (Istanbul: Remzi Kitabevi, 1942).

Karamanlidika Literary Production in the Mid-nineteenth Century

26 Grigoris Paleologos, *O Polipathis*, ed. Alki Angelou (Athens: Ermis, 1989).

27 Şehnaz Şişmanoğlu Şimşek, "Romanı 'İki Kilise Arasında Bînamaz' Kılmak: Karamanlıca Edebi Üretim, Evangelinos Misailidis ve Bir Yenidenyazım Örneği Olarak *Temaşa-i Dünya ve Cefakâr u Cefakeş*" (PhD diss., Boğaziçi University, 2014).

28 For a group of Ottoman Greek subjects mostly from Cappadocia who were inspired by Ottoman patriotism and supported the integrity of the Ottoman Empire rather than a Hellenic ideology, see V. K. Kechriotis, "On the Margins of National Historiography: The Greek İttihatçı Emmanouil Emmanouilidis: Opportunist or Ottoman Patriot," in *Untold Histories of the Middle East*, ed. A. Singer, C. K. Neumann, and S. A. Somel (London: Routledge, 2011), 124–42.

29 See M. Sabri Koz, "Türk Halk Hikâyelerinin Karamanlıca Baskıları Üzerine Karşılaştırmalı Bibliyografik Notlar," in *Cries and Whispers in Karamanlidika Books: Proceedings of the First International Conference on Karamanlidika Studies (Nicosia 11th–13th September 2008)*, ed. Evangelia Balta and Matthias Kappler (Wiesbaden: Harrassowitz, 2010), 241–54.

30 Itamar Even-Zohar, "The Position of Translated Literature Within the Literary Polysystem," *Poetics Today* 11, no. 1 (1990): 45–51.

31 See Olga Borovaya, *Modern Ladino Culture Press, Belles Lettres, and Theater in the Late Ottoman Empire* (Bloomington: Indiana University Press, 2012).

32 *Anatoli* 4272, December 13, 1890.

33 Though challenged by some historians, in the context of the Ottoman Empire, the term *millet* refers to "an autonomous self-governing religious community, each organized under its own laws and headed by a religious leader, who was responsible to the central government for the fulfillment of *millet* responsibilities and duties, particularly those of paying taxes and maintaining internal security." Encyclopedia Britannica, "Millet," online, www.britannica.com/topic/millet-religious-group. For various critiques of the *millet* theory, see Elif Bayraktar-Tellan, "The Patriarch and the Sultan: The Struggle for Authority and the Quest for Order in the Eighteenth-Century Ottoman Empire" (PhD diss., Bilkent University, 2011), 1–14.

34 Sia Anagnostopoulou, "Greek Diplomatic Authorities in *Anatolia*," in *Cries and Whispers in Karamanlidika Books: Proceedings of the First International Conference on Karamanlidika Studies (Nicosia 11th–13th September 2008)*, ed. Evangelia Balta and Matthias Kappler (Wiesbaden: Harrassowitz, 2010), 63–78.

35 Haris Exertzoglou, *Εθνική ταυτότητα στην Κωνσταντινούπολη τον 19ο αιώνα. Ο Ελληνικός Φιλολογικός Σύλλογος Κωνσταντινουπόλεως 1861–1912* (Ethnic Identity in the Constantinople of 19th Century, The Hellenic Literary Society of Constantinople 1861–1912) (Athens: Nefeli, 1996).

36 See Petropoulou, "From West to East," 95; Olga Borovaya writes about many rabbis "who harshly censured those who bought 'perverse books [referring to novels] written by liars, invented by non-Jews,' and those who 'wasted time on vanities and jokes.'" See Borovaya, *Modern Ladino Culture*, 139.

37 Balta, "Karamanli Press Smyrna 1845—Athens 1926," 28.

38 *Anatoli* 5426, March 11, 1889.

39 *Anatoli* 4375, July 8, 1891.

40 *Anatoli* 4945, February 17, 1895.

41 Şehnaz Şişmanoğlu Şimşek, "19. Yüzyıl Yunan Harfli Türkçe (Karamanlıca) Gazete ve Süreli Yayınlarda Dil Tartışmaları," *Hacettepe Üniversitesi Türkiyat Araştırmaları Dergisi* 31 (Autumn 2019): 29–56.

42 Johann Strauss, "Is Karamanli Literature Part of a 'Christian-Turkish (Turco-Christian) Literature'?" in *Cries and Whispers in Karamanlidika Books: Proceedings of the First International Conference on Karamanlidika Studies (Nicosia 11th–13th September 2008)*, ed. Evangelia Balta and Matthias Kappler (Wiesbaden: Harrassowitz, 2010), 191.

43 Şehnaz Şişmanoğlu Şimşek, "19. Yüzyıl Yunan Harfli Türkçe (Karamanlıca) Gazete ve Süreli Yayınlarda Dil Tartışmaları," 43–51.

44 Cemal Demircioğlu, "From Discourse to Practice: Rethinking 'Translation' (terceme) and Related Practices of Text Production in the Late Ottoman Literary Tradition" (PhD diss., Boğaziçi University, 2013), 335.

References

Ahmet Mithat. *Yeniçeriler*. Istanbul: Muharririn Zatına Mahsus Matbaa, 1290 [1871].

———. *Yeniçeriler*. Edited by Mustafa Nihat Özön. Istanbul: Remzi Kitabevi, 1942.

Anagnostopoulou, Sia. "Greek Diplomatic Authorities in Anatolia." In *Cries and Whispers in Karamanlidika Books: Proceedings of the First International Conference on Karamanlidika Studies (Nicosia 11th–13th September 2008)*, edited by Evangelia Balta and Matthias Kappler, 63–78. Wiesbaden: Harrassowitz, 2010.

Anatoli. 5426, March 11, 1889.

Anatoli. 4375, July 8, 1891.

Anatoli. 4945, February 17, 1895.

Balta, Evangelia. *Karamanlidika Additions (1584–1900) Bibliographie Analytique*. Athens: Centre D'Etudes D'Asie Mineure, 1987.

———. *Karamanlidika XXe siécle Bibliographie Analytique*. Athens: Centre D'Etudes D'Asie Mineure, 1987.

———. *Karamanlidika Nouvelles Additions et Compléments I*. Athens: Centre D'Etudes D'Asie Mineure, 1997.

———. "Gerçi Rum İsek de Rumca Bilmez Türkçe Söyleriz: The Adventure of an Identity of the Triptych: Vatan, Religion and Language." *Türk Kültürü İncelemeleri Dergisi* 8 (2003): 25–44.

———. "Karamanli Press Smyrna 1845—Athens 1926." In *Izzet Gündağ Kayaoğlu Hatıra Kitabı Makaleler*, edited by Oktay Belli, Yücel Dağlı, and M. Sinan Genim, 27–33. Istanbul: Türkiye Anıt Çevre Turizm Değerlerini Koruma Vakfı, 2005.

———. "Novels Published in Karamanlidika." In *Karamanlidika Legacies*, edited by Evangelia Balta, 49–80. Istanbul: Isis Press, 2018.

Balta, Evangelia, and Mehmet Ölmez, eds. *Between Religion and Language Turkish Speaking Christians, Jews and Greek Speaking Muslims and Catholics in the Ottoman Empire*. Istanbul: Eren Yayınları, 2011.

Bayraktar-Tellan, Elif. "The Patriarch and the Sultan: The Struggle For Authority and the Quest for Order in the Eighteenth-Century Ottoman Empire." PhD diss., Bilkent University, 2011.

Benlisoy, Foti, and Stefo Benlisoy. "'Karamanlılar,' 'Anadolu Ahalisi' ve 'Aşağı Tabakalar': Türkdilli Anadolu Ortodokslarında Kimlik Algısı." *Tarih ve Toplum Yeni Yaklaşımlar* 11, no. 251 (Autumn 2010): 7–22.

———. "Reading the Identity of Karamanli Through the Pages of Anatoli." In *Cries and Whispers in Karamanlidika Books: Proceedings of the First International Conference on Karamanlidika Studies (Nicosia 11th–13th September 2008)*, edited by Evangelia Balta ve Matthias Kappler, 93–108. Wiesbaden: Harrassowitz, 2010.

Benlisoy, Stefo. "Education in the Turcophone Orthodox Communities of Anatolia During the Nineteenth Century." PhD diss., University of Boğaziçi, 2013.

———. "'Another Newspaper in Our Language': Competition and Polemic in the Karamanlidika Press." In *Cultural Encounters in the Turkish-Speaking Communities of the Late Ottoman Empire*, edited by Evangelia Balta, 429–47. Istanbul: Isis Press, 2014.

Borovaya, Olga. *Modern Ladino Culture Press, Belles Lettres, and Theater in the Late Ottoman Empire*. Bloomington: Indiana University Press, 2012.

Bülent Berkol. "133 Yıl Önce Yunan Harfleri ile Türkçe (Karamanlıca) bir Robinson Crusoe Çevirisi." In *Sosyoloji Konferansları 25*. Istanbul: İstanbul Üniversitesi Yayınları, 1986.

Dallegio, Eugene, and Severien Salaville. *Karamanlidika Bibliographie Analytique des Ouvrages en Langue Turque Imprimés en Caractére Grecs*, vol. 3. Athens: Institut Français d'Athènes, 1958–1974.

———. *Karamanlidika XXe siécle Bibliographie Analytique*. Athens: Centre D'Etudes D'Asie Mineure, 1987.

———. *Karamanlidika Nouvelles Additions et Compléments*, vol. 1. Athens: Centre D'Etudes D'Asie Mineure, 1997.

Demircioğlu, Cemal. "From Discourse to Practice: Rethinking 'Translation' (terceme) and Related Practices of Text Production in the Late Ottoman Literary Tradition." PhD diss., Boğaziçi University, 2013.

Even-Zohar, Itamar. "The Position of Translated Literature Within the Literary Polysystem." *Poetics Today* 11, no. 1 (1990): 45–51.

Exertzoglou, Haris. *Εθνική ταυτότητα στην Κωνσταντινούπολη τον 19ο αιώνα. Ο Ελληνικός Φιλολογικός Σύλλογος Κωνσταντινουπόλεως 1861–1912* (Ethnic Identity in the Constantinople of 19th Century, The Hellenic Literary Society of Constantinople 1861–1912). Athens: Nefeli, 1996.

Göktürk, Gülen. "Well-Preserved Boundaries: Faith and Co-Existence in the Late Ottoman Empire." PhD diss., Middle East Technical University, 2013.

Gotsi, Georgia. "*Μεταφράσεις Μυθιστοριών Αποκρύφων και Συναφών Έργων* 1845–1900 (Translations of the Mystery Novels and the Serials 1845–1900)." *Antí* 641 (August 1997): 12–16.

Kappler, Matthias. "Transcription Text, Regraphization, Variety?—Reflections on 'Karamanlidika.'" In *Spoken Ottoman in Mediator Texts*, edited by Eva Csato, Astrid Menz, and Fikret Turan, 119–28. Wiesbaden: Harrassowitz Verlag, 2016.

Kechriotis, V. K. "On the Margins of National Historiography: The Greek İttihatçı Emmanouil Emmanouilidis: Opportunist or Ottoman Patriot." In *Untold Histories of the Middle East*, edited by A. Singer, C. K. Neumann, and S. A. Somel, 124–42. London: Routledge, 2011.

Kitromilidis, Paschalis M. "'Imagined Communities' and the Origins of the National Question in the Balkans." *European History Quarterly* 19 (1989): 149–92.

Koz, Sabri M. "Türk Halk Hikâyelerinin Karamanlıca Baskıları Üzerine Karşılaştırmalı Bibliyografik Notlar." In *Cries and Whispers in Karamanlidika Books: Proceedings of the First International Conference on Karamanlidika Studies (Nicosia 11th–13th September 2008)*, edited by Evangelia Balta and Matthias Kappler, 241–54. Wiesbaden: Harrassowitz, 2010.

Paleologos, Grigoris. *O Polipathis*. Edited by Alki Angelou. Athens: Ermis, 1989.

Petropoulou, Ioanna. "From West to East: The Translation Bridge. An Approach from a Western Perspective." In *Ways to Modernity in Greece and Turkey*, edited by Anna Frangoudaki and Çağlar Keyder, 91–111. London: I. B. Tauris, 2007.

Polivios, Ioannis. "Evangelinos Misailidis." *Terakki*, July 30, 1888.

Şişmanoğlu Şimşek, Şehnaz. "The Anatoli Newspaper and the Heyday of the Karamanli Press." In *Cries and Whispers in Karamanlidika Books: Proceedings of the First International Conference on Karamanlidika Studies (Nicosia 11th–13th September 2008)*, edited by Evangelia Balta and Matthias Kappler, 201–8. Wiesbaden: Harrassowitz, 2010.

———. "Karamanlidika Literary Production at the End of the 19th Century as Reflected in the Pages of Anatoli." In *Cultural Encounters in the Turkish-Speaking Communities of the Late Ottoman Empire*, edited by Evangelia Balta, 429–47. Istanbul: Isis Press, 2014.

———. "Romanı 'İki Kilise Arasında Bînamaz' Kılmak: Karamanlıca Edebi Üretim, Evangelinos Misailidis ve Bir Yenidenyazım Örneği Olarak *Temaşa-i Dünya ve Cefakâr u Cefakeş*." PhD diss., Boğaziçi University, 2014.

———. "19. Yüzyıl Yunan Harfli Türkçe (Karamanlıca) Gazete ve Süreli Yayınlarda Dil Tartışmaları." *Hacettepe Üniversitesi Türkiyat Araştırmaları Dergisi* 31 (Autumn 2019): 29–56.

Strauss, Johann. "Who Read What in the Ottoman Empire (19th–20th centuries)?" *Middle Eastern Literatures* 6, no. 1 (January 2003): 39–76.

———. "Is Karamanli Literature Part of a 'Christian-Turkish (Turco-Christian) Literature'?" In *Cries and Whispers in Karamanlidika Books: Proceedings of the First International Conference on Karamanlidika Studies (Nicosia 11th–13th September 2008)*, edited by Evangelia Balta and Matthias Kappler, 11–13. Wiesbaden: Harrassowitz, 2010.

Thérenty, Marie-Ève. "Mysterymania. Essor et limites de la globalisation culturelle au XIXe siècle." *Romantisme* 160, no. 2 (2013): 53–64.

16

COMPARATIVE GLIMPSE OF THE EARLY STEPS OF NOVELISTIC IMAGINATION IN TURKISH

Armeno-Turkish Novels of the 1850s and 1860s

Murat Cankara

Werner Sollors, in his introduction to *The Multilingual Anthology of American Literature* (2000) edited with Marc Shell, begins with an apparently simple yet long-forgotten and equally thought-provoking question: What is American literature?[1] He emphasizes that the purpose of this collection, running almost 800 pages, was "to make visible the most glaring blind spot in American letters." Being "the first of its kind," it made available "selections from a vast body of literature that has remained hidden" so as to "challenge the pervasive 'English-only' approach to American studies."[2] Sollors pointed out that there were more than 120,000 titles written in languages ranging from Native American ones to Arabic at Harvard University's libraries alone. The irony, for Sollors, is that even

> at the peak of the postwar efforts to "Americanize" the nation in an English mold, American multilingualism was still being taken very seriously as a subject of study, whereas our own age of multiculturalism has tended to ignore language as a factor in American literary and cultural diversity.[3]

The Multilingual Anthology of American Literature was a political statement made on the eve of 9/11. Yet it also still raises significant questions in broader contexts such as the definition of literatures in multiethnic, multireligious, multilingual, imperial, or even non-territorial spaces: What is, say, Jewish, Canadian, or Ottoman/Turkish literature? How are we to define them and set or question the boundaries of their literary canons?

Unfortunately, a multilingual anthology of Ottoman/Turkish literature is yet to be edited. The most significant challenge to the "Turkish-only" approach dominating Ottoman/Turkish literary historiography has been posed by a comprehensive collection of articles published in 2014.[4] This unsurpassed and comprehensive volume containing a wide range of articles on literatures produced within the Ottoman Empire in Arabic, Armenian, Bulgarian, Greek, and so on must now inspire new and more in-depth analyses, as well as translations from these

198

DOI: 10.4324/9780429279270-22

languages into Turkish, so that the canon can be revised and expanded in an appropriate way. However, one particular problem with the Ottoman/Turkish case which does not seem to appear in the American one is the relative prevalence of writing Turkish using the native scripts of specific communities, especially among Turcophone Armenians and Greeks. The "Turkish only" approach in Ottoman/Turkish literary historiography, then, is susceptible to criticism not only because it excludes the other languages of the empire but also because it has been unwilling, almost until the turn of the twenty-first century, to acknowledge the existence of and/or to incorporate literature produced in the Turkish language using non-Arabic scripts such as the Armenian or Greek. In other words, literature produced in Turkish in the Ottoman Empire is far from having been fully exploited by literary historiography as yet.

The aim of this chapter is to introduce and contextualize three Armeno-Turkish novels published around the mid-nineteenth century: *Akabi Hikâyesi* by Hovsep Vartanyan [Akabi's Story, 1851]; *Karnig, Gülünya ve Dikran'in Dehşetlü Vefatleri* by Hovhannes H. Balıkçıyan [Karnig, Gülünya and Dikran's Horrible Deaths, 1863]; and *Bir Sefil Zevce* by Hovsep Maruş [A Miserable Wife, 1868].[5] The rationale for this choice is quite simple: All three texts, written by Ottoman Armenians in the Turkish language using the Armenian script, were printed before the publication of the "first Turkish novel" that modern Turkish literary scholarship has hitherto acknowledged. In other words, they provide a good opportunity to muse over the following: (1) How did the Turkish language meet with the novel as a genre? (2) What are the similarities and differences between these pioneering examples and those that follow, written by Muslim/Turkish authors, and that have come to form the Turkish literary canon? (3) In a broader context, what could all these tell us about literature produced in a multireligious, multiethnic, and multilingual space such as the Ottoman Empire? What is Ottoman literature, after all? Skipping an in-depth historiographical critique and the question of encounters between Ottoman Armenian and Muslim/Turkish authors, this chapter introduces readers to the authors and plots of these novels to place them in a sociohistorical context and, eventually, to propose tentative but hopefully thought-provoking answers to these questions.

Love and Politics: The Novelistic Quest for Social/Religious Unification

Akabi Hikâyesi [Akabi's Story] (hereinafter *AS*) was the first novel written in the Turkish language. It was published anonymously in Istanbul in 1851, but today we know that it was written by Hovsep Vartanyan (1816–1879).[6] Vartanyan was born in Istanbul. Having received his elementary education there, he was sent to the Mekhitarist Monastery in Vienna. Upon his return to the Ottoman capital, he first began to teach at one of the well-known Armenian high schools of the time and then worked as a translator in the Ottoman navy, where he worked his way up to the position of chief translator. He was also appointed an associate member of the Ottoman Academy of Sciences (*Encümen-i Dâniş*) and a member of the Council of Judicial Ordinances (*Dîvan-ı Ahkâm-ı Adliye*). Throughout his career, Vartanyan not only held important offices for the Ottoman government and receive the title Pasha, but also assumed important responsibilities for the Catholic Armenian community of the empire. He would, however, opt for a civil career and publish books in Armeno-Turkish, Turkish written in Armenian script, as well as Armenian.[7]

For the purposes of this chapter, a very short account of Mekhitarists is necessary in order to establish a sociopolitical context not only for *AS* but also Armeno-Turkish publications in general. This is instrumental for understanding early Armeno-Turkish novels published in the Ottoman Empire not only because Vartanyan himself was a graduate of the Mekhitarist

Monastery in Vienna and an industrious servant of the Catholic Armenian community in the empire, but also because the communal conflicts lying at the heart of the three novels mentioned below are by no means independent from the confessional tension that played a central role in eighteenth- and nineteenth-century Western Armenian history.

Abbot Mekhitar (1676–1749) was born in Sebastia (Sivas in modern Turkey). Having embraced Catholicism in 1695, he founded his religious order in 1701 and settled down with his followers on the island of San Lazzaro in Venice where, from 1717 onwards, they

> became preeminent publishers and printers of Armenian books . . . and played a pivotal role in launching a "renaissance" of Armenian culture during that same period. They were pioneers in compiling and publishing grammars, dictionaries, books of history, geographical treatises, and other works.[8]

A significant portion of Mekhitarist publications was in Turkish, though. Indeed, the first book published by the order was a grammar of vernacular Armenian (1727), in Turkish using Armenian letters, written by Mekhitar himself. Overall, Mekhitarists, be it with their intense publishing activity or the schools they established across Europe as well as in major cities of the empire such as Istanbul and Smyrna, have come to be associated with a cultural awakening (*zartonk*), a renaissance so to speak, in the modern historiography of the Armenian nation. One thing needs to be mentioned here, though. Even though Abbot Mekhitar became a Catholic, "he rejected the excessive Latinization practices advocated by other Catholic converts and preachers. Until the end of his life Mekhitar, and subsequently his followers, remained both 'good Catholics' and 'good Armenians.'"[9] That is to say, not only with their resistance against the excessive interventions of the Vatican but also with their extensive intellectual production on Armenian history, geography, and literature, Mekhitar and the graduates of the schools established by his order played a pivotal role in the development of a modern national identity. It is for this reason that Mekhitarists, be it as authors or as actors in the communal struggles they took part in (such as the exile of Catholic Armenians by the Armenian Patriarchate, the promulgation of the Armenian Constitution, and the debates around the Latinization of Armenian Catholic church), will be indispensable for understanding the three novels taken up in this chapter.

It is within this context that Hovsep Vartanyan penned *AS*, the story of a thwarted love between Hagop (a Catholic Armenian) and Akabi (an Orthodox/Apostolic Armenian). The story is set in Istanbul, roughly between 1846 and 1847. The main plot is simple: Akabi and Hagop, both from well-to-do families in their respective communities, fall in love at first sight. Yet religious prejudice is so strong between these two confessions that authorities—be it familial or religious—tremble before the possibility of a marriage between these young lovers and are ready to hatch any plot to thwart it.

The story goes back to 1828, the year Catholic Armenians in Istanbul were exiled to Ankara by the Armenian Patriarchate. Akabi's mother, Anna, was a Catholic Armenian. Boghos had become Catholic, probably in order to marry her, and therefore had not only fallen out with his brother Baghdasar, a zealous Orthodox, but also incurred the wrath of the patriarchate which, in turn, had proclaimed him a traitor. Anna and Boghos manage to get married with the help of a French translator, but Boghos is forced to flee the country. Eventually, they attract animosity from both communities and Boghos abducts Akabi, then only an infant, in order to raise her as a good Orthodox. Meanwhile, Catholic Armenians are persecuted and their exile to Ankara turns out to be a catastrophe for the community.

So far we learn from Anna's narration to Akabi, who had never seen her father and was not aware of whose daughter she really was. The plot of *AS*, on the other hand, begins with the

Comparative Glimpse of the Early Steps of Novelistic Imagination in Turkish

year 1846, when Akabi and Hagop see each other for the first time and are instantaneously love-struck. The social rift that destroyed Boghos and Anna's lives is still present, though. Throughout the novel, the animosity between the camps is occasionally emphasized. So the remainder of the novel, even after two decades, is more like a repetition of poor Anna and Boghos' story. The "bad news" that Akabi and Hagop had fallen in love spread quickly around the two communities and the elderly, together with the ecclesiastical authorities, respond immediately and angrily. Hagop's father, Vichen Agha, rushes to consult Fasidian, a Catholic priest who is portrayed as evil in the novel, and they decide to do anything they can to remove this threat that would obviously set a bad example for the community's youth. What is noteworthy in their dialogue is that they equate the lovers' getting together with the unification of the Catholic and Orthodox Armenian communities, which, in Fasidian's own words, they had been struggling to keep apart for so long. Vichen Agha agrees: "No, no, this thing cannot begin, my son."[10] The other party is no less uncompromising; Akabi's despotic uncle Baghdasar, before beginning his terrible stream of threats, asks her: "How come you fell in love with Hagop, knowing that I loathe Catholics?"[11]

Unfortunately, in the end, those who strongly object to a possible marriage between Akabi and Hagop win. In a climactic scene reminiscent of Shakespeare's *Romeo and Juliet*, Akabi mistakes Hagop for those chasing her out and drinks the poison she brought along. She dies after a sad, short conversation with her lover; and her lover, Hagop, out of his grief, dies 21 days later.

Even though *AS* is built upon the animosity between Catholic and Orthodox Armenians, it is in fact the fanaticism of communal authorities, be they ecclesiastical or otherwise, that causes destruction for the young lovers. The real problem, in other words, is fanatical priests and notables who benefit from keeping the two communities apart, rather than religion itself. Indeed, it is emphasized in the novel that, for the zealous, a marriage between Akabi and Hagop would mean the unification of the two churches. Moreover, it should be noted that the author, a Catholic himself, does not refrain from portraying misbehaviors, or even a wicked priest, in the Catholic community either. Rupenig, a dear friend to Hagop, apes European manners, has a very conservative stance on women, never questions authorities, and disapproves of any contact with the Orthodox, except for commerce. As for Fasidian, the Catholic priest, a mentor to Hagop's father and the main plotter against the lovers, he warns Rupenig by saying that he will burn in hell if he listens to Hagop, arguing that Catholic and Orthodox Armenians are the same nation and that they should love each other as the Bible orders.

No wonder, then, Hovsep Vartanyan, a graduate of the Mekhitarist monastery in Vienna, did not put his name on *AS*. As a Mekhitarist, national identity mattered for him, which is why he was against the Latinizing efforts of Vatican. He must have foreseen how his novel would infuriate Catholic authorities. His prudence was eventually proved right and the novel was immediately banned by the Holy See on the grounds that "it discredited the Holy Faith."[12] Long forgotten by critics and excluded from literary histories, it was not translated into Eastern Armenian, one of the two standard forms of the Armenian language and the one used in Armenia, until 1953.[13] As the very first novel written in the Turkish language, it was transliterated into the Latin alphabet and published in Turkey only as late as 1991.[14] It was only around the 2000s, when concepts such as "multiculturalism," "hybridity," and so on were setting the trends in Western academic circles, that it became an object of scholarly interest.[15]

Another thwarted love story in which politics was highly involved, *Karnig, Gülünya ve Dikran'ın Dehşetlü Vefatleri* [Karnig, Gülünya, and Dikran's Horrible Deaths] (hereinafter *KGD*), was published in 1863, again in Istanbul. Very little is known about the author, Hovhannes H. Balıkçıyan (1833–1898). Born in Caesarea (Kayseri, in modern Turkey), he wrote poetry, in Turkish, using the pen name "Lütfi," worked as a lawyer, published at least two Armeno-Turkish periodicals, and passed away in Cairo,[16] where he possibly took refuge after the large-scale pogroms against Armenians across eastern Anatolia in the mid-1890s. The obstacle between the lovers in *KGD* is not confession but the Armenian Constitution of 1863, around which the empire's Armenian community was, once again, divided into two camps. As Hagop Barsoumian writes:

> The constitutionalists, known as *lusavoreal* [the enlightened], represented the young, educated generation, which was imbued with progressive, democratic principles and doctrines. In the opposing camp was the group of traditionalists and conservatives, composed of the sarraf-amiras and their adherent, called *xavareal* [obscurantists]. The conflict between these two antagonistic groups was not only political, it was also cultural, economic and social.[17]

Published the same year when the constitution was promulgated, *KGD* clearly reflects this communal rift. The novel opens with the narrator's short account of a heated argument, apparently between a father and his daughter, in an apartment in Beyoğlu. The neighborhood is alarmed by this fierce argument to the extent that some of the youth remain on guard in the street even after the father's shouting comes to an end, and all is quiet for the rest of the night. At dawn, a young and beautiful girl accompanied by an old lady leaves the apartment quietly: Gülünya, the young protagonist, and her nanny head towards the Armenian graveyard nearby where almost one-third of the novel will take place. Gülünya wants to end to her life by drinking poison by one of the tombs. It is the tomb of Gülünya's late lover, Karnig, for whose death her father was responsible. As the story unfolds, we learn that there was a political tension between Karnig and Ghugas, Gülünya's father. The late Karnig, educated in Europe and thus, from the narrator's perspective, a representative of the enlightened class of Young Armenians, was an enthusiastic supporter of the Armenian Constitution, whereas Ghugas Agha was an active member of the conservative group that was against it because it would curb their power over the Armenian community and thus represented a severe blow to their traditional authority. The latter had attacked the former, both verbally and physically, in public, in a meeting on communal matters, which had ended abruptly and dramatically because Karnig had felt obliged to defend the constitution against Ghugas' stream of invective. Karnig killed himself after this unfortunate event, and Gülünya had decided to do the same. Just as she is about to drink the poison, a young man intervenes who admits that he had been following them for a while. This young man, Dikran, engages in a long conversation with Gülünya in order to talk her out of suicide. During this conversation, which functions as exposition, it turns out that Dikran and Karnig were dear friends. In the end, Dikran asks Gülünya if she could love him instead of his late friend. Her response is quite unexpected, at least for readers of modern romance: "But I beg you, tell me your name, and your family, and are you for the constitution or not, let me know that as well."[18] Dikran's answer is equally bizarre. After telling his name, family, and occupation, he ends his words saying that "just like late Karnig, I am one of those who sacrifice their lives for the constitution."

As the title suggests, the rest of *KGD* describes how this time the love between Gülünya and Dikran is thwarted. Ghugas, extremely rageful against the young and educated generation struggling for power and say in communal affairs, plots against the lovers and sets his daughter up with one Arabian Harutiun, apparently a worthless drunkard with no other qualities than being "old school." Having realized the future waiting for her, Gülünya manages to drink the poison she put away for the sake of a possibility of a life with Dikran. Her mother Pupul and nanny Mariam are devastated. Dikran dies out of his grief in a couple of days. Ghugas, however, shows no sign of regret, not even of sadness. Being a representative of those resisting the redistribution of power in the Armenian community of the mid-nineteenth-century Ottoman Empire, his hatred for the young and educated pro-reformists culminate not only in the deaths of the three protagonists whose names are given in the title of the novel, but also in the destruction of his family.

The third and last Armeno-Turkish novel to be mentioned here, *Bir Sefil Zevce* [A Miserable Wife] (hereinafter *MW*), was published in Istanbul in 1868.[19] There is no information available on its author, Hovsep Maruş, which suggests that it might be a pen name.[20] The novel sets off with a gripping prologue. One night in 1852, an elderly woman, a madwoman, and a guard are taking care of an infant girl in a two-story wooden house in Karasubazar, Crimea. Two villains set the house on fire in order to kidnap the infant, but the madwoman resists. Meanwhile, the chief of police of the district receives a letter from a reputable friend in Petersburg kindly asking him to protect these people who came from Istanbul two months ago and are in great danger at the moment. The police act quickly and the infant, together with the women and the guard, is saved. The woman and the infant are safely sent to Petersburg, the madwoman to a mental institution, and the guard to Istanbul. The narrator ends the prologue by saying that one must go back to Istanbul in order to give the gist of the story. Hence, the flashback and the story begins in one of the famous opera houses of mid-nineteenth-century Istanbul, namely Naum Theatre. The reader is told it is three years before the Crimean War (1853–1856) and the Ottoman Empire is ruled by Sultan Abdülmecid (r. 1839–1861). This means the action must take place between 1850 and 1852. A famous European opera singer is starring in Bellini's *La Straniera* [The Foreign Woman][21] and the theatre is very crowded. A young man, Muhib Sebuh, is among those waiting for the performance to start, and while he is skimming over the audience with his opera glasses, he notices a beautiful young girl, Vartug, in one of the boxes. As the story unfolds, we learn that Sebouh is the son of a wealthy Armenian merchant who had emigrated from the Ottoman Empire long ago. Vartug, originally an Armenian from Istanbul, had been adopted and raised by a rich Russian aristocrat after being rescued from a shipwreck. Apparently unaware that they had been destined to meet each other, they had both come to the empire's capital to start new lives.

The scene in which Sebuh and Vartug speak to each other for the first time is quite interesting in terms of the relationship between love and politics in Armeno-Turkish novels emphasized here. After describing how their eyes met for the first time in the opera in the first chapter, the narrator begins the second by recounting how the Catholic Armenian community suffered from a bitter conflict at the time, that is the 1850s. The root cause of the conflict, according to the narrator, was a society that was established with the name Hamazkyats Ingerutyun (National Society).[22] Even though its aim was to educate girls and promote knowledge, the majority had objected to it by saying that the organization had a secret agenda, the reader is told. In fact, the community is torn apart and even members of the same family become enemies, with commerce and marriages between the parties reduced to a minimum.

What is noteworthy here is that the narrator claims objectivity, underlining that the real purpose is to describe the events without telling the reader who is right. However, the narrative implies quite the opposite. That is, evil is represented by the opponents of the National Society, whereas the angelic hero of the novel, Muhib Sebuh, as mentioned above, attends the meetings of this society that divided the community. After the meeting that night, Sebouh comes across Vartug, who does not seem to know where to go in the dark and deserted streets of downtown Istanbul, namely Beyoğlu. Out of despair, she goes over to Sebouh and his companions to ask if one of their manservants could accompany her home. Realizing that she is the wife of a notorious enemy of the society, the meeting of which they had just left, the companions refuse to help her. Sebouh, however, recognizes Vartug and offers to walk her home himself. This walk under the rain, presumably the first of its kind in fiction written in Turkish, is when the novel's protagonists are struck by love. As the story progresses, however, it turns out that Vartug, as the adopted daughter of a wealthy Russian gentleman, had left Petersburg for Istanbul in order to settle down and is, in fact, married. Her husband Mardiros Agha, because of whom Sebouh's companions refused to help her, is the archenemy of the National Society that Sebouh supports. Throughout the novel, Vartug's husband is portrayed as pure evil. Addicted to gambling and drinking, he is ready to do anything to seize his wife's wealth and pay off his enormous debts. As an evil *sarraf* (banker), representative of a conservative and decaying social structure, he is the counter-image of Sebouh, the angelic hero who is a representative of the progressive merchant class. In the end, Mardiros goes so far as to condone his wife's extramarital affair with Sebouh, waits until they have a baby, and plans to kill Vartug and usurp the fortune the baby would inherit. This baby is the one the reader was introduced to as it slept in its cradle at the beginning of the novel. Eventually, Sebouh fails to get Vartug out of this murderous plot. Yet the baby is saved and adopted by Vartug's Russian protector. Mardiros is unable to get a penny, and Sebouh leaves for Paris. Meanwhile, Vartug's family in Istanbul, whom she had lost years ago and just found, are devastated once again.

Conclusion

The story of the novel, as we know it today in the Turkish language, seems to have begun with a ban in an extremely polarized society. *Akabi's Story*, the first novel published in the Turkish language, was the product of and response to a community divided along religious lines. The authorities were quick take action against this romantic love story. The above-mentioned three novels by Armenian authors, published in Turkish using Armenian letters between 1851 and 1868 in Istanbul, are obviously quite inviting for students of modern literary theory. There is, to begin with, the question of cultural encounter in an ethnically, religiously, and linguistically diverse empire. Even though a considerable number of Muslim/Turkish intellectuals at the time knew the Armenian alphabet, there is no evidence that any of them read these novels besides *AS*.[23] Interestingly, there is only a single reference to the Muslim/Turkish population of the empire in these Armeno-Turkish novels. They take place entirely in an Armenian setting. What they share with the larger Ottoman world, on the other hand, is a vast topic yet to be explored by scholars. Concepts such as "minor literature," "national allegory," "hybridity," and "digraphia" are also promising in terms of early Armeno-Turkish novels.[24] It is, of course, impossible to delve into the depths of any single one of these within the scope and limits of a handbook.

To conclude, I would like to point out a significant difference between early Turkish novels published in the Armenian and Arabic alphabets. Authors of novels in the Ottoman Empire in the second half of the nineteenth century—be they Armenian, Greek, or Muslim/Turkish—seem to have been inspired by/interested in more or less the same literary figures, trends, and even specific works in Europe.[25] In other words, they appropriated similar texts and techniques to convey the messages they thought were vital for their society. Broadly speaking, that European Romanticism set their standards by the mid-nineteenth century has been acknowledged with almost no exception.[26] There is, however, a significant contrast between the appropriation of European Romanticism by early Armenian and Muslim/Turkish authors writing in Turkish, each in their own alphabets. I argue that the novels in these two groups, both distant and close, offer an opportunity to observe Romanticism's "fabulously contradictory character, its nature as *coincidentia oppositorum*," as Michael Löwy and Robert Sayre named it; according to them,

Romantics could be "simultaneously (or alternately) revolutionary and counterrevolutionary, individualistic and communitarian, cosmopolitan and nationalistic."[27] Once we agree on the double nature of Romanticism, at the expense of sweeping generalizations, we can argue that Armeno-Turkish novels' authors appropriated "revolutionary" and "progressive" Romanticism, whereas Muslim/Turkish authors have preferred to appropriate its "conservative" aspects.[28] In all three novels mentioned here, the narrative voice explicitly sides with the well-educated, anti-authoritarian, pro-change youth: those who read novels or newspapers; those who know languages other than Turkish or Armenian; those who question the authorities, traditions of the community, or simply their elders are all good and beautiful. The villains, in contrast, hate those who read or are educated, and cannot even speak their own language properly, let alone a foreign one. They have close ties with the Sublime Porte, get furious about any kind of demand for change in the order of the community, drink, gamble, beat their wives or children, say unbearable things about women, and, moreover, are very ugly. The mothers, in all three novels, are either missing or fail to intervene between the patriarchal authority and their children. The canonical Turkish novels, in contrast, foregrounded Romanticism's fear and/or revolt against modernity. Whereas religious intolerance and a communal strife due to the redistribution of power were the major cause of the young lovers' miseries in Armeno-Turkish novels, early Muslim/Turkish authors were more interested in a culturally alienated individual or segment of the community, the dangers of a public life where man and woman could get together, and the perils of excessive consumption or adopting European manners.[29] Unlike *MW*, where the protagonists had an extramarital affair and were far from being condemned for it, in early Turkish novels in the Arabic alphabet love and desire were presented as things that had to be suppressed. Within this context, questioning patriarchal authority was unacceptable. Indeed, one scholar has discussed the birth of the Turkish novel in terms of missing fathers and their sons who lost their ways.[30]

In short, European Romanticism seems to have had distinct impacts on the Armenian and Muslim/Turkish pioneers of the novel. One reason for this is obviously the time difference between the two groups of novels. The early Armeno-Turkish texts mentioned here were published in 1850s and 1860s, and the ones in the Arabic alphabet in 1870s and 1880s. That the religious roots of Romanticism—that is, the theme of religious tolerance and the use of miserable love stories in order to convey strong politico-religious messages—were obviously relevant for Armenian authors who wrote in Turkish could have been another reason, taking into account the sociopolitical context for the Ottoman-Armenian community of the time, as mentioned above. *Atala* (1801) by François-Auguste-René Chateaubriand (1768–1848), one of the founding texts of French Romanticism, must have struck them with its main theme. In fact, this is the book Hagop promises to bring for Akabi when they meet for the first time and would later discuss. Apparently, this religious, Christian to be precise, background meant nothing for Muslim/Turkish authors. Even though Ahmet Mithat (1844–1912), undeniably the most prolific and arguably influential author of his time, instrumentalized religious, mainly Christian, stereotypes to political ends in his novels, Muslim/Turkish authors were generally more interested in the male hero's misery caused by the lack/loss of father/authority and an uncontrolled cultural change accompanying it. One can observe a similar distinction in the Armenian and Muslim/Turkish readings of *Les Aventures de Télémaque* (1699) by François de Salignac de la Mothe-Fénelon (1651–1715), arguably a pre-romantic text and predecessor of romantic novel. The first, adopting a perspective from below, seems to have foregrounded themes such as love for the homeland, resistance against barbaric invasions, and the persecution of a people, whereas the latter interpretation saw it instead as a guide for rulers.[31] In a broader context, then, such a comparative approaches raises questions about how literary texts are appropriated in imperial settings where the languages and alphabets of various nations intermingle, thus reminding us how national literary historiographies based on a single language, and a script thought to be innately associated with it, smooth out the true complexity.

Notes

1 Marc Shell and Werner Sollors, eds., *The Multilingual Anthology of American Literature: A Reader of Original Texts with English Translations* (New York: New York University Press, 2000).

2 Ibid., 4.

3 Ibid., 2.

4 Fatih Altuğ and Mehmet Fatih Uslu, eds., *Tanzimat ve Edebiyat: Osmanlı İstanbulu'nda Modern Edebi Kültür* (Istanbul: İş Bankası Kültür Yayınları, 2014).

5 For an up-to-date account on Armeno-Turkish writing in general, see Bedross Der Matossian, "The Armeno-Turkish (Hayatar T'rk'eren) Language in the 19th Century: Marking and Crossing Ethno-Religious Boundaries," *Intellectual History of the Islamicate World* (January 2019): 67–100.

6 For a detailed account on the novel's authorship, see Murat Cankara, "Reading Akabi (Re-)Writing History: On the Questions of Currency and Interpretation of Armeno-Turkish Fiction," in *Cultural Encounters in the Turkish-Speaking Communities of the Late Ottoman Empire*, ed. Evangelia Balta (Istanbul: ISIS Press, 2014), 53–75.

7 Kevork Pamukciyan, *Biyografileriyle Ermeniler* (Istanbul: Aras Yayıncılık, 2003), 373–74; Ohannes Kılıçdağı, "Sahmanatragan Jshmardutinner (The Constitutional Truths)," in *Discourses of Collective Identity in Central and Southeast Europe (1770–1945): Texts and Commentaries (Modernism—Representations of National Culture)*, ed. Ahmet Ersoy, Maciej Górny, and Vangelis Kechriotis, vol. 2–3 (Budapest: Central European University Press, 2006), 333–42.

8 Sebouh D. Aslanian, "'Prepared in the Language of the Hagarites': Abbot Mkhitar's 1727 Armeno-Turkish Grammar of Modern Western Armenian," *Journal of the Society for Armenian Studies* 25 (2016): 54. See also Sebouh D. Aslanian, "Port Cities and Printers: Reflections on Early Modern Global Armenian Print Culture," *Book History* 17 (2014): 51–93.

9 Razmik Panossian, *The Armenians: From Kings and Priests to Merchants and Commissars* (London: Hurst, 2006), 102.

10 Hovsep Vartanyan, *Akabi Hikyayesi*, ed. Andreas Tietze (Istanbul: Eren Yayınları, 1991), 82.

11 Ibid., 131.

12 For a detailed account, see Cankara, "Reading Akabi," 63–65.

13 Hovsep Vartanyan, *Akabii Badmutyun*, trans. Garnig Sdepanyan (Yerevan: Gitut'yunneri Akademiayi Hratarakch'ut'yun, 1953).

14 Vartanyan, *Akabi Hikyayesi*.

15 Apart from the linguists' quite justifiable interest in Armeno-Turkish as a phenomenon (Andreas Tietze, who transliterated *AS* into the Latin alphabet, to name one), Laurent Mignon was probably the foremost promoter of these texts in Turkish literary circles with his preliminary writing in the early 2000s and the dissertations he supervised in the following decade. For an early example, see Laurent Mignon, "Tanzimat Dönemi Romanına Bir Önsöz: Vartan Paşa'nın *Akabi Hikâyesi*," *Hece*, no. 65–67 (2002): 538–43.

16 Pamukciyan, *Biyografileriyle Ermeniler*, 294.

17 Hagop Barsoumian, "The Dual Role of the Armenian Amira Class Within the Ottoman Government and the Armenian Millet (1750–1850)," in *Christians and Jews in the Ottoman Empire: The Functioning of a Plural Society*, ed. Benjamin Braude and Bernard Lewis, vol. 1 (The Central Lands) (New York: Holmes & Meier, 1982), 180.

18 Hovhannes H. Balıkçıyan, *Karnig, Gülünya ve Dikran'in Dehşetlü Vefatleri* (Istanbul: Minasyan Matbaahanesi, 1863), 69.

19 For a short account on the novel from the perspective of its woman protagonist, see Murat Cankara, "Türkçe Romanın Emekleme Yıllarında Bir Kadın Kahraman: *Bir Sefil Zevce*'nin Vartug'u," *Roman Kahramanları*, no. 19 (December 2014): 6–11.

20 It is possible to infer from the text that the author is a Catholic Armenian.

21 In fact, this opera was staged in Naum Theatre during the season 1852–1853. Emre Aracı, *Naum Tiyatrosu: 19. Yüzyıl İstanbulu'nun İtalyan Operası* (Istanbul: Yapı Kredi Yayınları, 2010), 202.

Comparative Glimpse of the Early Steps of Novelistic Imagination in Turkish

22 A few words are necessary on the National Society around which the two main characters of *MW*, Sebouh and Mardiros, are contrasted. This society was established in 1846 by graduates of Mekhitarist schools and advocated the national unity of the Armenian community, which was divided along confessional lines. One major debate within the mid-nineteenth-century Catholic Armenian community in the Ottoman Empire was the issue of control by the Holy See. The leading figure that strove for the Vatican's control over the community was Cardinal Andon Hasunian (1809–1894). The community was divided into two camps and graduates of Mekhitarist schools led the anti-Hasunist campaign, which "demanded a say in running the affairs of the community," as well as an undivided Armenian nation. Indeed there is at least one scholar who argues that the above-mentioned Catholic priest Fasidian who hatched the plot against Akabi and Hagop in *AS* was based on Cardinal Hasunian himself. Moreover, the decision by the Holy See to condemn *AS* seems to have been the result of a report written by him to the Vatican. For more on these issues, see Kevork Bardakjian, *A Reference Guide to Modern Armenian Literature, 1500–1920: With an Introductory History* (Detroit, MI: Wayne State University Press, 2000), 124–25. For a detailed account on the banning of *AS*, see Cankara, "Reading Akabi."

23 For a detailed account, see Murat Cankara, "Rethinking Ottoman Cross-Cultural Encounters: Turks and the Armenian Alphabet," *Middle Eastern Studies* 51, no. 1 (January 2, 2015): 1–16.

24 For two examples, see Murat Cankara, "Empire and Novel: Placing Armeno-Turkish Novels in Ottoman/Turkish Literary Historiography" (PhD diss., İhsan Doğramacı Bilkent University, 2011), 394–408; Murat Cankara, "Armeno-Turkish Writing and the Question of Hybridity," in *An Armenian Mediterranean: Words and Worlds in Motion*, ed. Kathryn Babayan and Michael Pifer (Cham: Palgrave Macmillan, 2018), 173–91.

25 For a rich account from readers' perspective, see Johann Strauss, "Who Read What in the Ottoman Empire (19th–20th Centuries)?" *Arabic Middle Eastern Literatures* 6, no. 1 (2003): 39–76.

26 James Etmekjian, *The French Influence on the Western Armenian Renaissance, 1843–1915* (New York: Twayne, 1964), 195, 214; Vahé Oshagan, "Modern Armenian Literature and Intellectual History from 1700 to 1915," in *The Armenian People from Ancient to Modern Times*, ed. Richard G. Hovannisian, vol. 2 (Foreign Dominion to Statehood: The Fifteenth Century to the Twentieth Century) (London: Macmillan Press, 1997), 158–60.

27 Michael Löwy and Robert Sayre, *Romanticism Against the Tide of Modernity*, trans. Catherine Porter (London: Duke University Press, 2001), 1.

28 Even though Namık Kemal (1840–1888) and Şemseddin Sami (1850–1904) should also be noted as examples, Ahmet Mithat Efendi (1844–1912), with his massive production and strong influence, is the representative of the early Muslim/Turkish novelist par excellence.

29 Aping European manners is touched upon in *AS*, as well, but it is not presented as the real threat to the order of society.

30 Jale Parla, *Babalar ve Oğullar: Tanzimat Romanının Epistemolojik Temelleri* (Istanbul: İletişim Yayınları, 1989).

31 For the Armenian reading of the text, see Alain Lautel, "La diffusion de la littérature occidentale en Arménie à travers un example caractéristique: Le 'Télémaque' de Fénelon," *Revue de littérature comparée* 61 (April 1987): 209–16; for a comparison between Armenian and Muslim/Turkish readings of the text, see Murat Cankara, "Empire and Novel," 366–79.

References

Altuğ, Fatih, and Mehmet Fatih Uslu, eds. *Tanzimat ve Edebiyat: Osmanlı İstanbulu'nda Modern Edebi Kültür.* Istanbul: İş Bankası Kültür Yayınları, 2014.

Aracı, Emre. *Naum Tiyatrosu: 19. Yüzyıl İstanbulu'nun İtalyan Operası.* Istanbul: Yapı Kredi Yayınları, 2010.

Arslan, Nihayet. "Chateaubriand'ın Romanlarının İlk Çevirileri ve Atala Uyarlaması." MA diss., Ankara University, 1995.

Aslanian, Sebouh D. "Port Cities and Printers: Reflections on Early Modern Global Armenian Print Culture." *Book History* 17 (2014): 51–93.

———. "'Prepared in the Language of the Hagarites': Abbot Mkhitar's 1727 Armeno-Turkish Grammar of Modern Western Armenian." *Journal of the Society for Armenian Studies* 25 (2016): 54–86.

Balıkçıyan, Hovhannes H. *Karnig, Gülünya ve Dikran'in Dehşetlü Vefatleri.* Istanbul: Minasyan Matbaahanesi, 1863.

Bardakjian, Kevork. *A Reference Guide to Modern Armenian Literature, 1500–1920: With an Introductory History*. Detroit, MI: Wayne State University Press, 2000.

Barsoumian, Hagop. "The Dual Role of the Armenian Amira Class within the Ottoman Government and the Armenian Millet (1750–1850)." In *Christians and Jews in The Ottoman Empire: The Functioning of a Plural Society*, edited by Benjamin Braude and Bernard Lewis, vol. 1 (The Central Lands), 171–84. New York: Holmes & Meier, 1982.

Cankara, Murat. "Empire and Novel: Placing Armeno-Turkish Novels in Ottoman/Turkish Literary Historiography." PhD diss., Ihsan Doğramacı Bilkent University, 2011.

———. "Reading Akabi, (Re-)Writing History: On the Questions of Currency and Interpretation of Armeno-Turkish Fiction." In *Cultural Encounters in the Turkish-Speaking Communities of the Late Ottoman Empire*, edited by Evangelia Balta, 53–75. Istanbul: The ISIS Press, 2014.

———. "Türkçe Romanın Emekleme Yıllarında Bir Kadın Kahraman: *Bir Sefil Zevce*'nin Vartug'u." *Roman Kahramanları*, no. 19 (December 2014): 6–11.

———. "Rethinking Ottoman Cross-Cultural Encounters: Turks and the Armenian Alphabet." *Middle Eastern Studies* 51, no. 1 (January 2, 2015): 1–16.

———. "Armeno-Turkish Writing and the Question of Hybridity." In *An Armenian Mediterranean: Words and Worlds in Motion*, edited by Kathryn Babayan and Michael Pifer, 173–91. Cham: Palgrave Macmillan, 2018.

Der Matossian, Bedross. "The Armeno-Turkish (Hayatar T'rk'eren) Language in the 19th Century: Marking and Crossing Ethno-Religious Boundaries." *Intellectual History of the Islamicate World* 8, no. 1 (2019): 67–100.

Etmekjian, James. *The French Influence on the Western Armenian Renaissance, 1843–1915*. New York: Twayne, 1964.

Kılıçdağı, Ohannes. "Sahmanatragan Jshmardutinner (The Constitutional Truths)." In *Discourses of Collective Identity in Central and Southeast Europe (1770–1945): Texts and Commentaries (Modernism—Representations of National Culture)*, edited by Ahmet Ersoy, Maciej Górny, and Vangelis Kechriotis, 333–42. Budapest: Central European University Press, 2006.

Lautel, Alain. "La diffusion de la littérature occidentale en Arménie à travers un example caractéristique: Le 'Télémaque' de Fénelon." *Revue de littérature comparée* 61 (April 1987): 209–16.

Löwy, Michael, and Robert Sayre. *Romanticism Against the Tide of Modernity*. Translated by Catherine Porter. Durham, NC: Duke University Press, 2001.

Mignon, Laurent. "Tanzimat Dönemi Romanına Bir Önsöz: Vartan Paşa'nın Akabi Hikâyesi." *Hece*, no. 65–67 (2002): 538–43.

Oshagan, Vahé. "Modern Armenian Literature and Intellectual History from 1700 to 1915." In *The Armenian People from Ancient to Modern Times*, edited by Richard G. Hovannisian, vol. 2 (Foreign Dominion to Statehood: The Fifteenth Century to the Twentieth Century), 139–74. London: Macmillan Press, 1997.

Pamukciyan, Kevork. *Biyografileriyle Ermeniler*. Istanbul: Aras Yayıncılık, 2003.

Panossian, Razmik. *The Armenians: From Kings and Priests to Merchants and Commissars*. London: Hurst, 2006.

Parla, Jale. *Babalar ve Oğullar: Tanzimat Romanının Epistemolojik Temelleri*. Istanbul: İletişim Yayınları, 1989.

Shell, Marc, and Werner Sollors, eds. *The Multilingual Anthology of American Literature: A Reader of Original Texts with English Translations*. New York: New York University Press, 2000.

Strauss, Johann. "Who Read What in the Ottoman Empire (19th–20th Centuries)?" *Arabic Middle Eastern Literatures* 6, no. 1 (2003): 39–76.

Vartanyan, Hovsep. *Akabii Badmutyun*. Translated by Garnig Sdepanyan. Yerevan: Gitut'yunneri Akademiayi Hratarakch'ut'yun, 1953.

———. *Akabi Hikyayesi*. Edited by Andreas Tietze. Istanbul: Eren Yayınları, 1991.

17

MAKING THE "OTHER" YOUR OWN

The Challenge of Modern Kurdish Literature Regarding Kurdish Voices in Turkish

Suat Baran and Ömer Faruk Yekdeş

The national narrative of Turkish literary history has moved in parallel with Turkish national historiography from the Tanzimat period onward, during which the meaning and origin of "Turkish" has been recast accordingly. The transition from imperial power to nation-state arguably engendered an exploration of the questions "Who is Turkish?" and/or "What is Turkish?" alongside the ethnic remnants of the Ottoman Empire. On the one hand, the hegemonic religious identity, Sunni Islam, swept away the non-Muslim communities within the structure of the new state; on the other hand, it led the other Muslim groups to be thoroughly assimilated and become Turkified. This is how the new ethnic state handled its non-Turkish citizens within the political and social sphere of Turkish nationalism; additionally, such a dramatic ethnic alteration left marks in the literary sphere. Non-Turkish authors become either an exotic subject deserving of scrutiny or deprived of their non-Turkish linguistic, cultural, or ethnic origins.[1] This chapter studies Kurds and their history, yet is always situated in parallel to Turkish literature and its readership.

As a socially and politically recognized fact, after the collapse of the Ottoman Empire, the most populous and autochthonous non-Turkic population of the Turkish Republic has been Kurds. Surrounded by other dominant nations and compared to that of its neighbors, Kurdish literature has been the latest to bloom with its own nationalistic discourse claiming to be distinct in terms of linguistic difference. However, until the rise of modern Kurdish literature, many of those born to a Kurdish-speaking cultural milieu have mostly adopted the languages of the nations they were born into as their literary language. This situation has led to hot debates on the nature of Kurdish literature and the classification of Kurdish-born authors. Therefore, regarding the difficulties Kurdish literature encounters, those who are ethnically Kurdish but write in Turkish have been targeted quite heavily both in political and literary spheres. More precisely, it is not feasible to suggest that Kurds living under the sovereignty of different nations form a single and united literature. Due to the constitutional difficulties and lack of means of communication, Kurdish literature has developed in a fragmented way. Thus, Kurdish literature in each country has gone through a process of interaction with and reaction against the dominant national literatures of those countries. Consequently, the Kurmanji/Kurdish literature created by Kurds in Turkey has become a branch at the periphery of Turkish literature but growing through ideological and aesthetic reactions against it.

DOI: 10.4324/9780429279270-23

209

Within a highly politicized environment, Kurds are arguably in an arduous position regarding their language of writing, whether it will be their own language or the one that they are forced to learn and use through mandatory public education, in which there is no place for Kurdish. Thus, writing in Kurdish is never simply an act of writing but always turns into a political "signifier."[2] To some extent, literati writing in Kurdish are even considered a part of Turkish readership and authorship in terms of the social and political map of Turkey and Turkish literature.[3] Under such circumstances, the transition to Kurdish takes place after a self-learning process, occurring as a preference under which political-ideological discussions tend to become unavoidable. In terms of these preferences, there have been fierce debates between Kurdish authors writing in Turkish and Kurdish authors writing in Kurdish, which have sometimes led to serious accusations from both sides. For instance, in 2007, when İlhami Sidar—an author previously writing in Turkish and lately both in Kurdish and Turkish—sent a letter to the Turkish linguist and columnist Necmiye Alpay, he subsequently received harsh responses from Kurdish intellectuals and readers because of his standing between the two literary languages. As a consequence, this sparked an intense debate between the two sides that created a more visible platform to trace the basic arguments about identity and the sense of belonging created through language. In her defense of İlhami Sidar in a column, Necmiye Alpay enumerated some renowned writers who wrote in a language different than their ethnic one, such as Kafka, Joyce, Yeats, Conrad, and Yaşar Kemal. Additionally, Alpay said that according to Sidar, when Kurdish writers are literarily and politically forced to write with their weak Kurdish, they also limit Kurdish literature to their "stuttering Kurdish."[4] This criticism undermining the linguistic ground of Kurdish literature, however, has led to the wrath of Kurdish authors to such an extent that İlhami Sidar had to apologize and say that he had been misunderstood.[5]

In stark contrast, scrutinizing the stance of Kurdish writers who refuse to write in Turkish will crystallize the issue. One such author, Remezan Alan, reviews the ethnic Turkish-Kurdish relationship within the frame of colonialism in his essay titled "A Refutation of Being Minor." There he claims that writing in Turkish or/and Kurdish points to the major-minor dichotomy already created between Turkish and Kurdish. Due to the political integration and assimilation carried out against Kurds since 1918, which has reached the level of linguicide, Alan highlights the fact that relinquishing Kurdish in favor of Turkish would also mean desisting from all national claims. For this reason, he powerfully addresses the desire and necessity of "making Kurdish a major language."[6] Regarding the refutation of being minor which he views within a political context, Alan considers writing in Kurdish as, above all, an anti-colonial response to devaluation, belittling, assimilation, and destruction at the hands of the "other."[7] This sort of resistance emphasizes the role of the mother tongue in claiming a national literature.

Another scholar who draws the borders of Kurdish literature based on linguistic politics is Haşim Ahmedzade. Noting the obstacles to describing the boundaries of Kurdish literature, he notes that not having a nation-state makes it almost impossible for Kurdish literature to be regarded as a national literature. Further, he asserts that without taking into consideration national and geographical characteristics, it would be a problematic approach to regard a literature as a national one. On the other hand, he, too, considers Kurdish as something that can be used to define writers' identities and also as a marker to draw the borders of Kurdish literature. As Kurds live under the sovereignty of different nation-states, face assimilation practices, and remain isolated from each other, language is regarded as a primary criterion to create bonds between all members of the Kurdish nation.[8] In a word, Kurdish literature should only include works written in Kurdish, not the other way around.[9] Simultaneously, several writers and critics of modern Kurdish literature (e.g., Mehmed Uzun, Firat Ceweri, Ehmed Huseynî) approach the classification of those writing in languages other than Kurdish differently.[10] Not surprisingly, they end up including these writers as part of Kurdish literature only based on their ethnic identity despite the non-Kurdish language in which they produce their works. Mehmed Uzun, the renowned Kurdish novelist, asserts that as long as the topic of the work is related to Kurdish land and Kurdish culture, despite the use of another language, they all should be included in modern Kurdish literature.[11] This form of argumentation has been strongly backed up by others and led to lengthy discussions about the criteria of membership in the field of Kurdish literature. In categorizing the field in this way, they include those writing in other languages (mostly in neighboring languages, i.e., Turkish, Persian, and Arabic) but by consistently emphasizing their Kurdishness and claiming strong bonds to Kurdish intellectual and literary history.

As Kurdish people have been suppressed not only territorially but also linguistically and culturally, the emergence of modern Kurdish literature has encountered several difficulties. These include the lack of educated readership, marketing, and most importantly the numerous Kurdish writers producing in other languages. At this juncture, when the written language becomes the oppressor's, the critiques of the Kurdish literary scholars can become harsher against those regarded as members of "other's" literature. In this case, the writers of Kurdish origins such as Yaşar Kemal, Suzan Samancı, Yavuz Ekinci, Murat Özyaşar, Burhan Sönmez, and so on have been classified as voices of a "minor literature"—a term first proposed by Deleuze and Guattari—or, to express it differently, exclusively within the borders of Turkish literature. Yet their ethnic origin has always been considered an important sign depicting the content of their artistic work, either by themselves or by literary scholars. Thus, this situation arguably positions them in between the blurred borders of Kurdish and Turkish literatures. At this point, this vague and contradictory classification leaves space for further discussion and urges us to find alternative routes to include them in whichever literature to which they want to belong. One of these alternative routes, in our case, is the literary translation of their works. As a result, their translation into Kurdish relieves the conundrum they find themselves in and creates new spaces for a stronger sense of identity for both languages. In this chapter, we scrutinize how the translation of Kurdish writers into Turkish reveals the discomfort of identity they face or, to put it differently, how a "minor literature" of another national literature (Turkish) can turn into another national literature (Kurdish) via translation, that is shifting from a "small literature" to what Pascale Casanova calls a "great" one.

Translation as a Literary-Political Agenda

In the case of Kurds and their literature, it is evident that the aesthetic space is necessarily embedded into a political frame as a fact imposed by historical conditions. In other words, the matter is not only the role of ideology, as a Marxist term constructing aesthetics, but also the instrumentalization of literature for the sake of politics, the evaluation of literature as a political fact distant from aesthetics. Concerning Kurdish authors in Turkey, the major-minor dichotomy cannot be debated merely as an aesthetic approach. In particular, within the space of Kurdish literature, the matter gives rise to an inevitable discussion in the context of national literature. Therefore, as seen in the debate between Remezan Alan and İlhami Sidar, the problem signals the issue of which literature they belong to or want to belong to.

In our view, several parameters serve to determine the Kurdish authorial habitus. The most basic parameter is the statelessness of Kurds and the fact that they live under the sovereignty of different nation-states. This has led to the use of divergent vernaculars and scripts. Accordingly, Kurds have several fragmented literary traditions with restricted communication among themselves. These conditions have made it almost impossible to define Kurdish literature within the framework of a nation-state or relate it to a geographical region. Consequently, language, as another parameter, comes to represent the essential signifier of Kurdish literature and highlights the borderline that shapes the frames of Kurdish national literature.

Writers producing in languages other than the official language cannot always be regarded as part of "a minor literature" but rather of a literature produced by a minority with the language of the majority, as stressed by Deleuze and Guattari.[12] Yet Kurdish writers, for instance, have not only produced literary texts in Turkish but also in other languages of the states they inhabit. That is to say, Kurds have produced numerous minor literatures in many languages, such as Turkish, Arabic, Persian, Armenian, and Russian. Hence, writers not writing in Kurdish are articulated within those sovereign nation-states using the literary language they have acquired. However, taking into account the readership they address and the literary tradition with which they are in communication, the Kurdish readership, too, is multilingual and in touch with the Kurdish literary space as occurs with Kurdish writers. To clarify, when it comes to writers producing in Turkish, they can be found drifting in between the Kurdish and Turkish literary spaces. Speaking theoretically, the distinction between "great" and "small" literature from Pascale Casanova's *The World Republic of Letters* is paramount in making the subject more tangible and transparent. Defining world-literary space and drawing attention to the clash between the oldest and the best endowed "great national literary spaces" and more recently appearing, impoverished "small literary spaces,"[13] Casanova states that the sites of great literature have the advantages of determining the aesthetic values. According to her, there are two main approaches in the conflict between these literary spaces: one is *assimilation*, "integration with a dominant literary space through a dilution or erasing of original differences," and the other is *differentiation*, "which is to say the assertion of difference, typically on the basis of a claim to national identity."[14] Speaking within the Turkish context and considering the historical accumulation and opportunities provided by the nation-state, it is evident that the Turkish literary space is a great literary space compared to the Kurdish one. Putting it differently, the linguistic preference of Kurdish writers in Turkey signals their choice between a great literary space and a small one. However, in the case of Turkey, Casanova's binary terms do not suffice to define the space. This is because Kurdish writers writing in Turkish have not been thoroughly assimilated into Turkish literature; in contrast, they have developed contact between the two literary spaces by strongly marking their national identity. The most significant factor that makes this ground of contact feasible is the fact that Kurdish readers have been primarily reading them in Turkish due to the strict ban on state education in minority languages in Turkey. Furthermore, this is also an issue about the accessibility for Kurdish readers of a literary text produced in Turkish. Such texts do bring forth the recognition of the writers at the periphery of Kurdish literature. To put it differently, the works of the writers in question become meaningful when they are promoted and sold on online Kurdish bookstores or in places known as Kurdish bookstores in the Turkish metropoles.

The second factor providing the ground of communication between two spaces is the topic of this chapter: translations from Turkish to Kurdish. This sort of translation has three significant functions. The first is that the practice of translation carries those regarded as within a minor context within Turkish literature into the major space of Kurdish literature. So the translation practice from Turkish into Kurdish aims to consider those writers a part of Kurdish literature. Therefore, this practice, via the ethnic and cultural codes of the writers, has the purpose of reincorporating Kurdish writers who have been annexed and assimilated with the means of the nation-state. The second point is that the translation practice creates a transition between two spaces. One is the great literary space with all the tools provided to it by the state apparatus, legally recognized within the borders of a state with an official language and literary institutions based on a national commonsense and allegedly owned by the state. The other one is Kurdish literature, the small literary space existing on the scale of resistance with restricted opportunities as a result of constantly prohibitive measures taken by the state. With translation practice within the great literary space, the writers published by the leading publishers and granted the prestigious literary prizes of this greater space are incorporated into the small literary space, which thus broadens its scope. The last and third function is marketing. Taking into consideration the capacity of Kurdish literary marketing, those writing in languages other than Kurdish can help attract more attention from readers to notice how Kurdish literature is traditionally rich, divergent, and dispersed all around the world, even though some of those works translated were not produced originally in Kurdish. Therefore, by prioritizing the Kurdish publishing market and revealing the difficulties Kurdish literature has suffered from, translation creates a sense of homecoming not only for writers but also for readers, who up to that point have only seen those writers published in Turkish. As will be seen with the grouping of the works translated into Kurdish, marketing concerns, to some extent, can become superior to the sense of identity when paratextual materials (i.e., back covers of related works) are under scrutiny.

The Conundrum of Kurdish Writers and Some Proposals

Modern Kurdish novelist and essayist Mehmed Uzun is one person who has investigated the content of contemporary Kurdish literature and the suffering of those writing outside Kurdish. In one of his interviews, Uzun addresses the bilingual characteristic of Kurdish people and suggests that swaying between divergent languages and cultures, they should experience this bilingualism as a way of readily moving back and forth from one language to the other. For him, if Kurds, who already have a very limited intelligentsia, fail to preserve their Kurdish and surrender to other languages and cultures, they may lose their intellectuals and gifted members in exilic ghettos.[15] He continually refers to the inequality the Kurdish language faces and how few works its literary archive contains.[16] While trying to balance out the languages he knows for literary production, he underlines the crucial function of literary translation to bind Kurdish literature to the dominant literature. Here, he specifically refers to the significance of building bridges between Kurdish and Turkish literature. Still, his formula is quite uncommon: "[Translation] would crucially function as a bridge between Kurdish and Turkish cultures. However, we are still unable to transfer Kurds' writing in Turkish into Kurdish and Kurds' writing in Kurdish into Turkish."[17] Here is his formula, the counterpart of the other side of the works to be translated is not Turks writing in Turkish but Kurds writing in Turkish, which explains the necessity of translation between Turkish and Kurdish literature only to transfer the other Kurds not writing in their native tongue.[18] In his opinion, as long as a writer claims an identity bond to his or her Kurdishness, albeit with the use of a language other than his native one, we cannot deny his or her sense of belonging and access to Kurdish literature.[19] Therefore, Uzun can readily include Kurds (such as Hicri Özgören) writing in a non-Kurdish language (in this case, Turkish) into his anthology of Kurdish literature, as does Firat Cewerî in his *Short Story Anthology of Kurdish* (with the inclusion of Suzan Samancı). This is because the milieux of these writers have been shaped thoroughly by Kurdish history, culture, language, and traditions, which is a song of "a full Kurdish spirit." According to Uzun, no Turkish poet can write the verses of Ahmed Arif, nor can a Turkish writer from Istanbul produce works similar to Yaşar Kemal's. Therefore, "we should not exclude those writers of ours," he argues. Here the function of translation, as a constructive proposal, intervenes. Uzun claims that as such writers cannot be forced to write in Kurdish, because they cannot, which reflects a real fact, the only thing that remains is to translate them into Kurdish. "This would bring richness. There would be communication and dialogue. Besides, why shouldn't they publish bilingual books?"[20]

On the other hand, reflecting on the subject Ramazan Kaya highlights the negative implications of colonization that create such a large gap between Kurds writing in Kurdish and Kurds writing in non-Kurdish languages, by which he acknowledges the fact that this kind of "preference" never emerges simply from free will.[21] Additionally, Clémence Scalbert Yücel shows strong bonds between Kurdish and other neighboring literatures in the form of the literary *microcosmos* and *macrocosmos*. These two world systems are interrelated and "to understand the progress, the work system and possible autonomization, it is necessary to define the features of that *macrocosmos* in which it has flourished and developed."[22] As claimed and supported by others, the diglossic characteristic of Kurds plays a crucial role in their sense of belonging and identity.[23] Yücel's interpretation shows that Kurdish and Turkish literatures have an unavoidable, dichotomous, and interwoven relationship, and she foresees that it will constantly shape their future, as well.

Back Covers as a Means of Unveiling the Purpose of Translation Practice

To pinpoint the reasons behind which books to choose for translation into Kurdish, the back covers would be used as the primary data. However, to reveal the differences between the materials translated into Kurdish, it would be more prudent to select divergent translated works with different backgrounds. To be more specific, within the framework of this chapter, in total, six translated works have been chosen and placed in three groups. Group 1 consists of two works by authors of Kurdish origin but writing in Turkish (Suzan Samancı, Yavuz Ekinci). Group 2 consists of two authors of non-Kurdish origin writing in Turkish but with a Kurdish geographical background (Mıgırdiç Margosyan, Murathan Mungan). Group 3 is composed of authors of Turkish origin writing in Turkish (Orhan Pamuk, Vedat Türkali). This selection aims at demonstrating how marketing concerns and writers' identity issues can form the central ground of translation process. Comparing the three groups, it will become more apparent how the publishing world treats them differently.

The two back covers of the first group are of writers of Kurdish origin writing in Turkish and linguistically placed within the boundaries of Turkish literature. Originally born in Diyarbakır, Suzan Samancı's translated short story collection *Bajarê Mirinê* (The City of Death) has this quotation on the back cover:

> The sun set down behind the mountains. I wish I could reach those mountains! Right now, the birds are playing with each other. Oh, my dear son, how much I missed your face! The lovely Tigris knows how I love and suffer; we tell our sorrows to each other, pray together, and sometimes I send you my greetings, I don't know, but do you hear the voice?

In addition to the quotation, the back cover introduces the author in this way: "With these short stories, Suzan Samancı did not want 'the silence and stuttering to move through those soundless cries and fade away.'" As can be clearly seen, the sign of linguistic difficulty and "forced" or volunteered silence is strongly implied both in the quotation and in the introduction of the author. However, the quotation displays the geographical signifier of Kurdistan shown in the Turkish language in a way that readers can identify instantly.[24]

The second author in the first group is Yavuz Ekinci, born in the Kurdish city of Batman, who has several novels and short story collections published in Turkish. The back cover of the book discussed here is of *Erdên Bihuştê Yên Wenda* (The Lost Lands of Paradise):[25]

> I wrote this novel because when the world of fairy tales of villages like Mişrîta, built amidst the uniformed mountains, were evacuated with the invasion of military officers,

Making the "Other" Your Own

I just wanted to hear how all those people, like fragile pomegranate seeds, were scattered in the streets of cities and how they had been destroyed there. . . .

I wrote this novel because I wanted to make visible the memory of geography and its preserved plaque through the story of the family of Almast and Ehmed. . . .

When I wrote the novel *Erdên Bihuştê Yên Wenda*, just two sayings were ringing in my ears: the first is from Ibn-Khaldun, "Geography is fate," and the other one is from Hannibal, "Either we find a way or we open a way."

Both silencing and the importance of geography are revealed here. That is, Kurdistan exists in Kurdish oral and written history but is officially denied and nonexistent in official Turkish accounts. In these two books from Group 1, what we see besides the geographical signifiers is the problematizing and highlighting of silence itself, a means of proving the nonexistence of the Kurdish language, not spoken or heard. This point is actively addressed on both of the back covers of these works by writers of Kurdish origin.

Considering Group 2, writers not of Kurdish origin but from a Kurdish geographical background, we see that due to geographical and spatial bounds, the Kurdish publishing market has shown increasing interest in them, which has ended with them being translated into Kurdish. The author we will analyze first is Mıgirdiç Margosyan, born in Diyarbakır, like Suzan Samancı, but of the Armenian-Christian heritage of the region. There is only one quotation on the back cover of the book *Li Ba Me Li Wan Deran* (In Our Lands In Those Lands):

I talked about our lands and those lands in my book. I told them what I did and how I lived, everything as it was. You can say that I never touched any type or names of people, [but] left them as they had been. Many of those people, those sisters, those uncles, either from [the] paternal or maternal sides, have passed away to the other World. Even if they are few, I wanted their names, their memories to live in these lines, in this book."[26]

"Our lands" or "those lands" as mentioned here signals a geographical unity, which has no name and cannot be addressed directly. However, in the Turkish original edition, this place is called *Gavur Mahallesi* (the district of giaour or infidels), whereas in the Kurdish edition, published at the end of the 1990s, the original Kurdish name *Xançepek*, or *Taxa Filla* (a district located in historical Diyarbakır) is not used in the title. This ambiguity complies perfectly with the image of Kurdistan in people's minds during the 1990s in Turkey: a region without a name, a region whose "real name" would be dangerous when uttered.

Born in Mardin to an Arabic- and Turkish-speaking family, the writer Murathan Mungan has closer bonds to the Kurdish community than Margosyan in terms of culture. Here, in addition to the cultural elements of the Kurdish majority-region, the role of the same religion, Islam, has a crucial impact on his works among the Kurdish readership. To show this impact, his memoirs-autobiography will be used as a source. The back cover of *Cinên Pereyan* (Money Djinns) reads:[27]

Money Djinns, an autobiographical book, consists of ten texts. Murathan Mungan no doubt has written this in Turkish, but if the readers who know both Turkish and Kurdish compare the Kurdish edition with the Turkish one, they will see the soul of the book is Kurdish and the real taste of these texts have become more evident in Kurdish. This is not only thanks to the skill of Murathan Mungan but also to the success of Felat Dilgeş, who translated this book. This work is a great pleasure for readers who enjoy taste, theme, and plot in accordance with setting.

Though not Kurdish but writing about Kurdish territory from within the Turkish literary milieu and addressing an "imagined" sensitive Kurdish readership, whatever Mungan writes has to do with Kurdish literary and cultural history, which locates him in a rather special position not only in the eyes of Kurdish publishers but also in that of the Kurdish readership.

The last and third group comprises authors of solely Turkish origin and writing in Turkish. The first author we will analyze is Istanbul-born Orhan Pamuk. His first work translated into Kurdish was *Navê Min Sor E* (My Name is Red) in 2002. The back cover of the book has the verbatim quotation: "The thought that my book would be read by Kurdish readers makes me blissful, that they are tied to their language as ornaments on their traditional chests."[28] Interestingly, whatever is translated from Turkish into the Kurdish-Kurmanji dialect, as discussed in this chapter, boasts about the beauty of the Kurdish language or national territory in relation to its "suppressed history and reality." So even the translation of Pamuk (as an author linguistically and culturally unassociated with Kurdish) focuses on the fact of how beautiful it is to read Pamuk in Kurdish. The indirect statement to Kurdish readers is that reading him in Kurdish might be greater than reading him in Turkish. In our view, one response to cultural and linguistic decay has led to—along with a delusional sense of language—an exaggerated confidence in the linguistic beauty of Kurdish in relation to Turkish. This can be regarded as compensation for the belittling and abandonment of the mother tongue.

The second author from this third group is the leftist Turkish novelist Vedat Türkali. His renowned and canonic 1974 novel, *Rojekê Bi Tena Serê Xwe* (One Day All Alone), which portrays the left-wing social tendencies and strikes of the period leading up to 1960, was translated into Kurdish in 2017. The back cover reads:[29]

> Thanks to his long-term experience in the film industry and great capability to shoot and capture images, Vedat Türkali created the characters of this novel. The characters are people who reveal the social suffering and disease of the sovereignty of the Turkish Republic of that era as reflected through a mirror. *One Day All Alone* is a miracle. The scenes before us tell that—whatever reasons lie behind it—whatever we cannot see or can see is incomplete. Yet he completes them. We are always reminded of the people around us. The things that happened to us, the things that had made us suffer. After reading *One Day All Alone*, we look at people with different eyes . . . at people's hearts, at their faces . . . people not only in Cağaloğlu, Tahtakale, Şişli, and Beyoğlu, but also at people like Kenan in the Smugglers Market, The Burnt Market, Xançepek [The Giaour District], and in the groups and communities of Kurdistan, as well. Those who had gone through hard times were all alone and spoke to themselves. . . . Thanks to the translation of Tehsîn Baravî, the book [that] has a language with Kurdish flavor, an opus magnum of world literature, has become a part of Kurdish literature.

Here, the geographical atmosphere of Türkali's novel, even if it is not included in the plot, is extended to Kurdistan. We saw a similar thing with Pamuk's *My Name is Red*, which has a plot independent of the Kurdish language and territory, yet on the back cover of the Kurdish edition, Pamuk's statement on the Kurdish language and his emphasis on its vitality for Kurds are strongly highlighted. The emphasis here on language and territory makes these two translations appear to be part of a similar group as the previous two translations in Group 2. Yet there is an overt difference here. The linguistic emphasis on Pamuk's translation has nothing to do with the content of the book and is written solely to allure the Kurdish readership. Türkali's novel's setting is imaginarily extended to Kurdish territory for the book's marketing and promotion. This territorial reference has nothing to do with the territorial testimony present in Samancı,

Ekinci, and Margosyan's fiction. As previously mentioned, when we consider translation practices from Turkish into Kurdish, two motives outweigh the other possible ones. The first is incorporating ethnically Kurdish but linguistically Turkish authors into Kurdish literature. The other one is marketing the Kurdish publishing industry. While analyzing Group 3, it is clear that though they, too, are translated from Turkish, the way the books are promoted is more neutral and distant compared to the previous groups. These writers are chosen for translation because they are regarded as high quality in Turkish literature. On the other hand, the works of Groups 1 and 2 are treated differently, as the stress is on Kurdish geography and national identity. To put it differently, analyzing Group 3 was necessary in order to highlight this difference. That is, taking into account the literary quality of a book—separate from the linguistic, cultural, or territorial references it might include—this promotional strategy regards translation as an endorsement for a surviving language that has faced heavy assimilation practices.

Is Kurdish Translation Necessary for Readers in Turkish?

Translation has a straightforward purpose: to transmit a text to a reader who cannot read it in the source language. However, regarding translations from Turkish into Kurdish, it is noticeable that some other motives are present. There are presumably no Kurdish readers who cannot read in Turkish except for a small portion of readers who have a religious-madrasah education, read Kurdish solely in Arabic script, have a limited interest in the Kurdish based on the classics, and do not follow contemporary literary events. At this point, the project of translating a source text into Kurdish for a readership who can read in Turkish seems to derive from other motivations. Throughout this chapter, we have stressed that these reasons basically rely on the issues of national identity and marketing. Consequently, it is possible to claim that these translation practices have progressed in line with the goal of creating a national language and literature for the Kurdish public. In this study, an investigation of the back covers of several translations supports this argument about the national approach. We have observed that all six books are prompted with an emphasis based on language and territory. The linguistic and territorial emphasis on the translations of the writers of Kurdish origin, Samancı and Ekinci, are mostly related to the subject matter, which deals with both language and geography simultaneously in a melting pot. The writers of Group 2, although not of Kurdish origins, have been included to some extent in Kurdish space. With Margosyan, the experience correlates with the territory in which he grew up. Yet in Mungan's works, the claim is based on the idea that the text has found its true and ultimate voice in Kurdish. In this way, these two writers are included in the Kurdish national space. In these examples, the reason for their inclusion in Kurdish literature is not related to ethnic origin but territory and culture.

Considering the translations of Kurdish writers or others incorporated for the cultural and territorial elements in their works, it is clear that translations from Turkish into Kurdish go beyond a straightforward practice of translation. However, this kind of translation done for a specific purpose seems to have become an act of including and incorporating these writers into the realm of Kurdish literature. Translations into Kurdish also contribute to the enrichment of literary texts available in the Kurdish language. Thus by providing examples of "good" literature, translations may open the path to the production of more literary works directly in the Kurdish language. Yet this act of translation between Turkish and Kurdish literature also highlights the heavily "blurred borders of Kurdish literature," as pointed out by Clémence Scalbert Yücel.[30] Since the assimilation practices in literary milieux have led to a great amount of deprivation whether either personal or collective, writing in Turkish has, as one might expect, enriched Turkish literature both in content and in language. Signs of this enrichment and "being at limbo" can be traced in the works of Yaşar Kemal, Murathan Mungan, Ahmed Arif, Seyidhan Kömürcü, and the like. Such writing practices have simultaneously blurred the borders between Kurdish and Turkish literature and created a potentially pluralistic literary space placing cultural, ideological and aesthetic interactions, and the territory itself at the center, instead of imposing a literature based on a single linguistic and ethnic identity. Thus translating such authors and poets into Kurdish would be expected to enrich Kurdish literature not only in language but also in content.

Notes

1 Laurent Mignon, "Bir Varmış, Bir Yokmuş: Kanon, Edebiyat Tarihi ve Azınlıklar Üzerine Notlar," in *Ana Metne Taşınan Dipnotlar: Türk Edebiyatı ve Kültürlerarasılık Üzerine Yazılar* (Istanbul: İletişim, 2009), 121–32; Servet Erdem and Ömer Faruk Yekdeş, "Bölücü Bir Edebiyat mı Bölünmüş Bir Edebiyat mı: Geç Osmanlı Dönemi Kürt Edebiyat(lar)ı," in *Tanzimat ve Edebiyat: Osmanlı İstanbul'unda Modern Edebî Kültür*, ed. Mehmet Fatih Uslu and Fatih Altuğ (Istanbul: Türkiye İş Bankası Kültür Yayınları, 2014), 327–58.

2 In the introduction of his book *Bendname*, to explain his own act of writing relying on Ehmedê Xanî's verses, Remezan Alan characterizes writing in Kurdish as *"xodreste"* (autodidactic) distinguishing it from the writing tradition in other languages of religion, culture, and administration in the region such as Arabic, Persian, and Kurdish. Remezan Alan, "Pêşgotin," in *Bendname: Li Ser Ruhê Edebiyatekê* (Istanbul: Peywend, 2013), 7–9.

3 Clémence Scalbert Yücel, "Languages and the Definition of Literature: The Blurred Borders of Kurdish Literature in Contemporary Turkey," *Middle Eastern Literatures* 14, no. 2 (2011): 171–84; Clémence Scalbert Yücel, "Emergence and Equivocal Autonomization of a Kurdish Literary Field," *Nationalities Papers: The Journal of Nationalism and Ethnicity* 40, no. 3 (2012): 357–72.

4 Necmiye Alpay, "Dil Meseleleri," *Radikal*, March 16, 2007, accessed March 18, 2022, https://groups.google.com/g/diwanxane/c/e0Bj5_EaUec?pli=1.

5 Remezan Alan, "Reddiyeya Mînoriyekê," in *Bendname: Li Ser Ruhê Edebiyatekê* (Istanbul: Peywend, 2013), 59–76.

6 Ibid., 70.

7 Ibid., 71.

8 Haşim Ahmedzade, *Ulus ve Roman: Fars ve Kürt Anlatısal Söylemi Üzerine Bir Çalışma*, trans. Azad Zana Gündoğan (Istanbul: Perî Yayınları, 2004), 160.

9 Ibid., 167.

10 Firat Cewerî, *Huner û Edebiyat* (Stockholm: Nûdem, 2006), 71–101.

11 Mehmed Uzun, *Destpêka Edebiyata Kurdî* (Ankara: Beybûn, 1992), 91–96.

12 Gilles Deleuze and Félix Guattari, *Kafka: Toward a Minor Literature*, trans. Dana Polan (Minneapolis: University of Minnesota Press, 1986), 16.

13 Pascale Casanova, *The World Republic of Letters*, trans. M.B. DeBevoise (Cambridge, MA: Harvard University Press, 2004), 83.

14 Ibid., 179.

15 Mehmed Uzun, *Bir Dil Yaratmak*, ed. Ali Biçer (Istanbul: Belge Yayınları, 1997), 12.

16 Ibid., 15.

17 Ibid.

18 Ibid., 16.

19 Ibid., 93–94.

20 Ibid., 143.

21 Ramazan Kaya, "Tercüme Edilen Dünyaların Edebiyatı," *Kırıksaat* 2 (2020): 27–28.

22 Clémence Scalbert Yücel, *Kürt Edebiyatının Anatomisi*, trans. Yeraz Der Garabedyan (Istanbul: Ayrıntı Yayınları, 2018), 18.

23 Ibid., 19.

24 Suzan Samancı, *Bajarê Mirinê*, trans. Songül Keskin (Istanbul: Avesta, 1996).

25 Yavuz Ekinci, *Erdên Bihuştê Yên Wenda*, trans. Kawa Nemir (Istanbul: Doğan Kitap, 2013).

26 Mıgırdiç Margosyan, *Li Ba Me Li Wan Deran*, trans. Rûken Bağdu Keskin (Istanbul: Avesta, 1999).

27 Murathan Mungan, *Cinên Pereyan*, trans. Felat Dilgeş (Istanbul: Doz, 2008).

28 Orhan Pamuk, *Navê min Sor E*, trans. Mustafa Aydoğan (Istanbul: Doz, 2002).

29 Vedat Türkali, *Rojekê bi Tena Serê Xwe*, trans. Tehsîn Baravî (Diyarbakır: Lîs, 2017).

30 Yücel, "Languages and the Definition of Literature," 171–84.

References

Ahmedzade, Haşim. *Ulus ve Roman: Fars ve Kürt Anlatısal Söylemi Üzerine Bir Çalışma*. Translated by Azad Zana Gündoğan. Istanbul: Perî Yayınları, 2004.

Alan, Remezan. "Pêşgotin." In *Bendname: Li Ser Ruhê Edebiyatekê*, 7–9. Istanbul: Peywend, 2013.

Alan, Remezan. "Reddiyeya Mînoriyekê." In *Bendname: Li Ser Ruhê Edebiyatekê*, 59–76. Istanbul: Peywend, 2013.

Casanova, Pascale. *The World Republic of Letters*. Translated by M. B. DeBevoise. Cambridge, MA: Harvard University Press, 2004.

Cewerî, Firat. *Huner û Edebiyat*, 71–101. Stockholm: Nûdem, 2006.

Deleuze, Gilles, and Félix Guattari. *Kafka: Toward a Minor Literature*. Translated by Dana Polan. Minneapolis: University of Minnesota Press, 1986.

Ekinci, Yavuz. *Erdên Bihuştê Yên Wenda*. Translated by Kawa Nemir. Istanbul: Doğan Kitap, 2013.

Erdem, Servet, and Ömer Faruk Yekdeş. "Bölücü Bir Edebiyat mı Bölünmüş Bir Edebiyat mı: Geç Osmanlı Dönemi Kürt Edebiyat(lar)ı." In *Tanzimat ve Edebiyat: Osmanlı İstanbul'unda Modern Edebî Kültür*, edited by Mehmet Fatih Uslu and Fatih Altuğ, 327–58. Istanbul: Türkiye İş Bankası Kültür Yayınları, 2014.

Kaya, Ramazan. "Tercüme Edilen Dünyaların Edebiyatı." *Kırıksaat* 2 (2020): 22–35.

Margosyan, Mıgırdiç. *Li Ba Me Li Wan Deran*. Translated by Rûken Bağdu Keskin. Istanbul: Avesta, 1999.

Mignon, Laurent. "Bir Varmış, Bir Yokmuş: Kanon, Edebiyat Tarihi ve Azınlıklar Üzerine Notlar." In *Ana Metne Taşınan Dipnotlar: Türk Edebiyatı ve Kültürlerarasılık Üzerine Yazılar*, 121–32. Istanbul: İletişim, 2009.

Mungan, Murathan. *Cinên Pereyan*. Translated by Felat Dilgeş. Istanbul: Doz, 2008.

Pamuk, Orhan. *Navê Min Sor E*. Translated by Mustafa Aydoğan. Istanbul: Doz, 2002.

Samancı, Suzan. *Bajarê Mirinê*. Translated by Söngül Keskin. Istanbul: Avesta, 1996.

Türkali, Vedat. *Rojekê bi Tena Serê Xwe*. Translated by Tehsîn Baravî. Diyarbakır: Lîs, 2017.

Uzun, Mehmed. *Bir Dil Yaratmak*. Edited by Ali Biçer. Istanbul: Belge Yayınları, 1997.

Uzun, Mehmed. *Destpêka Edebiyata Kurdî*. Ankara: Beybûn, 1992.

Yücel, Clémence Scalbert. *Kürt Edebiyatının Anatomisi*. Translated by Yeraz Der Garabedyan. Istanbul: Ayrıntı Yayınları, 2018.

Yücel, Clémence Scalbert. "Languages and the Definition of Literature: The Blurred Borders of Kurdish Literature in Contemporary Turkey." *Middle Eastern Literatures* 14, no. 2 (2011): 171–84.

Yücel, Clémence Scalbert. "Emergence and Equivocal Autonomization of a Kurdish Literary Field in Turkey." *Nationalities Papers: The Journal of Nationalism and Ethnicity* 40, no. 3 (2012): 357–72.

SECTION VI

National Identity

18

NATIONAL LITERARY HISTORIOGRAPHY IN TURKEY

Mehmet Fuat Köprülü and His Legacy

Halim Kara

This chapter investigates the development of national literary historiography within the framework of Ottoman literary modernity, the nation-building process, and its persistence in modern literary studies in Turkey. Drawing on the notion of a "national model" of literary history writing, it examines the institutionalization of the concept of national literary historiography by Mehmet Fuat Köprülü, the leading literary historian in the early twentieth-century period of transition from the Ottoman Empire to the Turkish nation-state. Accordingly, this chapter explores the emergence of the concept of modern literary history based on the idea of linear time and progress, showing how the modern concept of literary history was imported from Western Europe, indigenized, and transformed into Turkey's first national literary history by Köprülü. The chapter argues that the nationalization process in Turkish literary historiography occurred gradually through a productive engagement and negotiation with European models and the premodern local biographical collections of poets, or *şair(ler) tezkireleri*, the dominant form of literary history in the Ottoman Empire. It contends that writing in the early twentieth century, Köprülü systematically developed the primary formulations of national literary historiography based upon a shared Turkish ethnicity, language, culture, and literature with ancient origins rooted in Central Asia. His notion of national literary history during the nation-building period became the norm for subsequent literary histories and still predominates in contemporary literary historiography in Turkey today.

Towards Narrative Literary Historiography

The nineteenth-century encounter between Ottomans and Europeans generated profound social, political, and cultural changes in Ottoman society. Regarding literature, this encounter with Europe and its subsequent social, political, and cultural consequences compelled Ottoman Turkish authors to abandon producing works in the old forms, thus interrupting the traditional practices of writing. However, the encounter in turn also created new possibilities for artistic creativity for the innovative literati who sought to revitalize and renew literature to replace previous forms of writing, which they considered, insufficient, obsolete, and long overdue for change in the age of modernity. Literary modernity became an inevitable process for the majority of writers who felt the urgency to produce new works different from those of the old and traditional, which they considered obsolete in the age of modernity. Accordingly, they

DOI: 10.4324/9780429279270-25

223

attempted to transform previous forms of writing and used them for the purpose of the new. This marked a paradigm shift in Ottoman Turkish literature, which became a primary form of Ottoman society's social and cultural transformation.

It was in this context that the first modern narrative histories[1] began to be produced in the Ottoman Empire. This was because modern literati approached the concept of literary history as a novel form of writing about the history of literature with the intention of inventing replacements for the *şair tezkireleri* form, or the biographical collections of the poets of Ottoman literature.[2] They began to write narrative accounts of Ottoman Turkish literature based on the idea of historical progress and a conceptualization of time as linear. In subsequent years in the late Ottoman and early Republican eras, this led to the domestication of modern narrative literary history and its gradual transformation into a nationally oriented literary history. In writing their narrative literary histories, these historians attempted to create a cohesive and progressive narrative that linked literature and society, connecting the literature of the past to the present and future. In addition, they wrote critical introductions addressing the question of what constituted modern literary history, and how it differed from the *tezkire*s of the past. These new Ottoman literary historians arranged their works based on the premise of historical progress and cohesive narration, thus leading to the specialization and academic growth of modern literary historiography as a discipline.

The first example of the *Tarih-i Edebiyat-ı Osmaniye* (History of Ottoman Literature) in the modern era was published in 1888.[3] Written by Abdülhalim Memduh (1866–1905), it is the first comprehensive book under the umbrella of a literary history in Ottoman Turkish literature for which *şair tezkireleri*, or the biographical collections of poets, had been the major form of literary history for centuries. This first book on literary history in a modern sense is vital in showing us the author's attempt to familiarize a modern form of literary history writing and open the way for its practice in the Ottoman cultural context. One had to wait 20 years for the publication of new comprehensive literary histories in Ottoman Turkish after Abdülhalim Memduh's first narrative history in 1888.

The years between 1910 and 1914 were highly productive in the numbers of new narrative literary histories as five new studies came out in quick succession.[4] This was also a time when literary historians were more analytically concerned with the key question of what modern literary history as an academic discipline was and how it differed from the old-fashioned *tezkire*s. This was due in part to the history of Ottoman literature becoming a separate object of study at the newly founded Faculty of Arts at Istanbul University. Seeking to free literary studies both from the *tezkire* tradition of the past and semi-academic activity, these modern literary historians devoted their energies to the formation of the discipline of scholarly literary history based on "scientific criticism" and "positivism." Such concerns resulted in a continuing engagement with both the *tezkire* tradition and modern literary history based on scientific methodology, derived from both premodern *tezkire*s as historical sources and European authors as models to follow. This contributed to the construction of a hybrid narrative in their literary histories that demanded a new form of literary history, which they thought more appropriate and useful for a modern society.

In addition to shaping the primary principles of modern literary history in Turkish literature, this period was decisive in the invention of a national literary history based on Turkish ethnicity, culture, and language. This was because modern literary histories produced during this period were used as contested domains by literary historians through which Ottoman Turkish and Turkish identities were constantly negotiated, displaying ambivalence in the meanings and limits of Ottoman Turkish literature. Despite acknowledging a connection with the Turks outside the Ottoman Empire, some modern literary histories published their works under the name of *tarih-ı edebiyat-ı osmaniye* (Ottoman literary history), separating the Ottoman literary tradition from that of Turks outside the Ottoman Empire. Mehmet Fuat Köprülü (1890–1966),[5] also known as Köprülüzade Mehmed Fuad, radically changed this conceptualization by using the term "Turkish literature" for what had formerly been known as "Ottoman literature" and by producing scholarly works on the history and literature of the Turks, eventually becoming the founder of modern Turkish literary studies. His scholarly research and publications in the 1910s and the 1920s incorporated the history, culture, language, and literature of the entire Turkic people into the organic component of nationally defined literary history. Köprülü, therefore, played the most significant role in transforming modern narrative literary historiography that began to be practiced in the nineteenth century into a national literary history model in the age of transition from the Ottoman Empire to the Turkish nation-state in the early twentieth.

Refashioning National Literary History Writing

The publication of Köprülü's seminal article "Türk Edebiyatı Tarihinde Usul" (Method in Turkish Literary History) in December 1913 was perhaps the most important event in modern literary historiography in Turkey. This article, which Köprülü wrote at the age of 23, played a decisive role in institutionalizing modern literary historiography and its rapid nationalization in Turkey. After the publication of the article, he was appointed as a professor of Turkish literature at the University of Istanbul with the help of Ziya Gökalp (1876–1924), the theorist of modern Turkish nationalism. For the first time in modern literary history writing, a literary historian used the wording "history of Turkish literature" instead of the "history of Ottoman literature," showing his intention to generate a narrative based on a shared Turkish literature and culture.

Köprülü's article explores the primary tenets of modern literary historiography and problems facing a history of Turkish literature by critically engaging with various European philosophers and historians, the premodern *tezkire* tradition and its inapplicability to the present, and the failure of earlier modern literary history to formulate a "scientific" method for the study of Turkish literature as a whole. In addition to the emphasis on the concept of modern literary history and its scientifically defined methods, the key concern of this article is the definition of Turkish literature as a national literature, how and where it originated, and its development over centuries. According to Köprülü, "The history of the literature of a nation, with respect to describing its intellectual and sensory life in the past, is one aspect of its cultural history, that is, the general history of a nation."[6] Köprülü thus aimed to shape a concept of literary history narrating the coherent and continuous development of a nation's history through its masterpieces with its own particular genealogy and historical transformations over the course of history. The considerable emphasis on the close relationship between a society and its literary culture shows his desire to expand the scope of Ottoman Turkish literature to include all literary and cultural products of Turks in the world:

> A good historian of literature could present fairly clearly the extent of the relationship of the transformations that the Turkish spirit has undergone with the literature of Turkish society if he could do a rigorous analysis of Turkish literature, beginning with its still very obscure origins.[7]

In narrating the survey of Turkish literature based on a teleological account of the past, Köprülü thus advocated a concept of literary history shaped around the primacy of Turkish ethnicity, culture, language, and literature. He thus aimed to replace the idea of Ottoman Turkish literature as the literature produced in the Ottoman Empire with the concept of a literature that signifies a sense of Turkish national consciousness, eventually leading to a nation-state with the demise of the Ottoman Empire in the early 1920s. His stress on the singularity of national culture and his mission to invent a specific national literature for it explicitly manifests itself in his definition of Turkish literature as "a life of well-defined and continuous growth and development for at least seven centuries and which is very worthy of note with respect to showing the intellectual and cultural life of a great and heroic nation."[8] For this reason, he underlines the kind of literary history that is necessary:

> A history of Turkish literature that fully meets our national needs should be based on the latest scientific methods and be a synthetic work that is the product of lengthy and rigorous analyses. Such a work, which would completely and clearly bring to life not only the poetry of the Turks but also all their intellectual and cultural manifestations over the centuries, would be not only a national monument but also a human and scientific monument.[9]

Similarly, as a literary historian, Köprülü was preoccupied with the shaping of a systematized literary history in producing a comprehensive and scholarly study of the formation and development of Turkish national literature through which the reader is also invited to witness the invention of a modern Turkish nation.

The taxonomy of Turkish literature separated in this article, mentioned above as "Türk Edebiyatı Tarihinde Usul" (Method in Turkish Literary History), for the first time into two distinctive oral and written traditions contributes to his efforts to invent a national literary historiography. Köprülü asserts that, especially starting in the fifteenth century, literary productions became completely separate from the ordinary masses and took the form of court (*divan*) literature for a very restricted class due to foreign influences (meaning Persian and Arabic) beginning in the fifteenth century. Köprülü's remarks on Ottoman classical literature shows how he viewed the differentiation between the popular culture and the elite culture central to the study of Turkish literature, thus clearly rejecting the idea of a literary history based upon the writing of the ruling class or the learned elite generally associated with Ottoman classical literature. With this he, in fact, instigated a paradigm shift in modern literary historiography that evolves through the creativity of the ordinary masses. He specifically points to the importance of the oral literary texts of the mystic poets of Anatolia,[10] who he claims had been marginalized by both the Ottoman classical tradition and earlier modern literary historians in the invention of a national literary history during a time in which folk literature was viewed as a vital source of inspiration and component of nation-formation. The division of popular and elite culture highlights the practice of mystic oral literature as an important means of expression for common Turkish-speaking people, especially during the formative years of the Ottoman Empire, by showing that there was another literary tradition composed in a language and style that appealed to popular taste alongside elite literature, which relied heavily on forms and themes from foreign cultures. Like many of his contemporaries, Köprülü sought not only to generate a "scientific" method for the study of Turkish literature as a unified whole, but also to shed light upon the "true" characteristics of it as a national literature, how and where it originated, and its historical transformation over centuries, thus contributing to the construction of a shared sense of national identity among the Turks based on a common ethnic, cultural, linguistic, and literary heritage.

This attempt by Köprülü to institutionalize a literary history for the emerging modern Turkish nation reminds us of the "national model of literary history" conceptualized by Hutcheon in her comparative discussion of the relationship between the writing of literary history and identity politics. Speaking of the rise of nation-states and writing about the past, especially the

National Literary Historiography in Turkey

emergence of narrative literary history as an academic field in the nineteenth century, Hutcheon argues:

> The versions of the story of the past that the present tells have always been associated with questions of cultural authority and thus with politics, especially with some kind of "identity" politics. Since the nineteenth century the identity has been national, and so the accounts of the history of the nation's literature have played a significant role in the formation of certain national self-imaginings.[11]

Similar to Hutcheon's views on national literary histories, in this article Köprülü, who has essentially dominated modern Turkish literary historiography until today, sought not only to shape modern literary history as an academic field but also to trace the history of Turkish literature through scholarly studies of oral and written texts to their ancient origins in Central Asia.

Köprülü's study of Turkish literature in "Türk Edebiyatı Tarihinde Usul" therefore constitutes a milestone in the nationalization of literary historiography in Turkey. It was profoundly important not only in outlining his future studies on the concept of modern literary history as a scientific discipline and the history of Turkish literature but also showing his transformation of literary historiography into a national project for imagining a modern Turkish nation and creating an appropriate but scientifically sound history of literature for it. Köprülü was able to trace the history of Turkish literature through oral and written texts to its ancient origins in Central Asia, making the writing of literary history not only an academic but also an ideological one through creating a cohesive continuous narrative structure based upon shared experience, language, culture, ethnicity, and civilization. Köprülü demanded a social history of Turkish literature beyond the aesthetic and formal elements of texts by assembling research that articulated the broad context of the newly emerging Turkish nation's literature, thereby gaining canonical status in modern Turkish literary studies.

Köprülü's concept of literary history based on a teleological literary-historical narrative and centered around a shared Turkish language, culture, ethnicity, and literature found its first expressions in his next literary history: *Yeni Osmanlı Tarih-I Edebiyatı* (the New History of Ottoman Literature), published in 1914. Co-authored by Mehmet Fuat Köprülü himself and Şahabettin Süleyman (1885–1921), the author of an earlier history of Ottoman literature, this new book constitutes the most critical engagement of early Ottoman Turkish modern literary historians with both the traditional *tezkire* form and European concepts of literary histories. A manifestation of this is the 60-page methodological introduction providing an outline of primary premises and the goals of the kind of modern literary history the authors strived to conceptualize. The exploration of the following questions and topics offers important insights into our understanding of the authors' objects and expectations: the notion of literature and its formation in relation to other fine arts; the lack of scientific approach in the *tezkire* tradition; the persistence of the *tezkire* tradition in earlier modern literary histories of Ottoman Turkish; the early formation of various literary genres in societies (e.g., myths, legends, songs, folktales, and epics); the physiological, psychological, and biological forces of the formation of literature; the question of literary periodization based on scientific criteria; the link between text and its author; the question of a text's influence on the subsequent texts; the formal and external elements of literary texts; and the influence of economic, societal, environmental and political conditions on literature. This illustrates how, within such a short period, these authors' engagement with the concept of modern literary history intensified.

In addition, this work contains the most detailed, scholarly, and refined accounts of the history, culture, language, and literatures of the Turks during the pre–Ottoman era up to that point. Close attention is paid to the oral folk literatures of the Turks such as legends, epics, folk tales, songs, and romances. In doing so, the authors construct a narrative in which they clearly identify their ethnic selves with the entire Turkic peoples, referred to in the book with the plural pronoun "we," thereby forming a connection between Ottoman Turkey and Turkistan through their self-identification. In addition, one chapter of the work is entirely devoted to the narrative survey of the history, language, literature, and civilization of the Seljuk Turks in general along with the rise of Anatolian Turkish as a literary language between the thirteenth and fourteenth centuries. This section was indeed written to prove that Ottoman Turkish language and literature was a continuation of the former, as exemplified in the works of Sultan Veled (1226–1312) and Yunus Emre (1240–1321), who formally and thematically formed the basis for the development of literary cultures, both written and oral traditions, during the Ottoman period.[12] For this reason, like the earlier modern literary histories, despite confining its scope to the narrative account of Ottoman literature and taking its name after the ruling dynasty, the *Yeni Osmanlı Tarih-i Edebiyatı*, for the first time, approached Ottoman literature as a branch of literature of the entire Turks, rather than a separate literary tradition, opening a path for the nationalization of modern literary historiography in the late Ottoman Empire. Accordingly, this national narrative based upon a shared tradition of the Turks includes entire oral and written texts of the Turkic people from ancient times, the first written Turkic text (the Orkhon Inscriptions); various religious texts in the Uyghur language and the *Kutadgu Bilig* composed in Middle Turkic; different historical personalities like Timurlane (1336–1405), Hüseyin Baykara (1470–1506), and poets like Ali Şher Nevai of Central Asia (1441–1501); and cities like Samarkand and Bukhara representing the Turks' great contribution to eastern civilizations.

This approach demonstrates that through a connection between Ottoman Turks and other Turkic peoples, the authors basically attempted to construct a literary history designed along the lines of teleological narratives of progress and evolution, conceptualized as a national model of literary history by Hutcheon. This is apparent in their definition of literary history and its task:

> Literary history is to explore and analyze a nation's or period's entire artistic creations both in terms of their forms and content in order to comprehend the spirit of that particular nation and period, their societal developments and numerous intellectual transformations.[13]

Thus, "just as a national literature was seen to develop over time, increasing in quality, power, and authority, so too the nation itself matures from its founding moment to the telos of its political apotheosis."[14] In short, Köprülü ve Şahabettin Süleyman's book is profoundly important in two respects to the writing of modern Turkish literary history during this time: It first characterized the evolution and localization of modern literary history writing as a scientific discipline in replacing the *tezkire* tradition, which basically became an irrelevant practice for modern historians to follow in the early twentieth century. It also marked the transformation from an Ottoman-oriented literary culture to a nationally defined literary history in the late Ottoman Empire in order to include the Turkic peoples, as we call them today, from Central Asia to the Balkans. In so doing, *Yeni Osmanlı Tarih-i Edebiyatı*, along with Köprülü's article on the method of Turkish literary history, constituted the methodological and thematic foundations for the modern literary histories based upon a shared Turkish culture and literature that followed.

Köprülü's next scholarly work on literary history, *Türk Edebiyatı Tarihi* (The History of Turkish Literature) published in 1920, thoroughly institutionalized his politically conscious scholarly project of inventing a national literary history based on the geographic and cultural extension of the Ottoman literary tradition with the inclusion of the culture and history of the entire

Turkic people into his narrative structure. The book was extensively revised by the author and republished in 1925. Since then it has been republished numerous times and used as a textbook for teaching the history of Turkish literature at universities in Turkey, providing the methodological, thematic, taxonomic, and discursive framework for the subsequent literary histories produced in Turkey up to today. Köprülü essentially built his book on the expansion of his earlier studies on the notion of literary history and its application to the history of Turkish literature. For example, "Türk Edebiyatının Menşei" (The Origins of Turkish Literature), published in 1915, exposes the primary problems of the oldest forms of Turkish literature expressed in primitive songs, the lyrics of ancient Turkish poets known as *baksi* or *ozan*.[15] Here with an "emphasis on the importance of origins and its assumption of continuous development," Köprülü's concept of literary history was intended to establish a parallel between the inevitable progress of the nation and that of its literature.[16]

In his probably most famous and internationally circulated book, titled *Türk Edebiyatında İlk Mutasavvıflar* (Early Mystics in Turkish Literature), first published in 1919, Köprülü intended to show the literary evolution of the Turkish nation by establishing a cultural, linguistic and social connection between Anatolia and Central Asia. He fundamentally maintained this same argument in his studies of Turkish culture, civilization, history, and literary history. In his own words,

> in order to understand the [Turkish] national spirit and taste in Muslim Turkish literature, the period most worthy of study is that of the great mystics who spoke to the masses using the popular language and meter and whose works have endured for centuries.[17]

In this case, two mystical poets, Ahmet Yasawi (1093–1166) of Central Asia and Yunus Emre of Central Anatolia, played a profound role in his attempt to underline the cultural and literary continuity between Central Asia and Anatolia. He argued that popular sufi/mystic and folk poetry produced by these poets was a significant element in the distinctive national characters of the Turks, whose noble cultural heritage had been too long undermined, first by the dominance of Persian and later European influences. He rationalized his argument by showing poetic, linguistic, thematic, stylistic, and discursive similarities in the poetry of Ahmed Yasawi and Yunus Emre. Köprülü especially insisted on the influence of Ahmed Yasawi in the development of Turkish literature in Anatolia in the thirteenth century. He underlined the direct influence of Ahmet Yasawi's sufi poetry on that of Yunus Emre in order to invent a cultural linkage between Central Asia and Anatolia. This thesis constituted the foundation of his entire scholarship and other modern studies on the history of Turkish literature. Although some scholars, like Devin Deweese, have argued that there was no direct connection between Ahmet Yasawi and Yunus Emre,[18] Köprülü's argument still dominates contemporary Turkish literary studies in Turkey.

Based on his earlier studies on the subject, Köprülü's *Türk Edebiyatı Tarihi* describes the emergence and development of Turkish literature in its historical, social, economic, and cultural contexts from ancient times in Central Asia (Central Mongolia) to the fourteenth century in Anatolia. In the introduction of the book, Köprülü argues that, as one of the most important branches of general history, literary history undertakes to describe the moral and spiritual life of a nation as an index of the evolution of thought and spirit that that nation has experienced over a period of centuries. He further asserts that "literary history consists of the past and present, reflecting the nation's intellectual development as well as its national genius, which reflect national pride and its unique characteristics as well as its great contributions to world civilization and culture."[19] Köprülü shaped his history of Turkish literature "premised on ethnic and linguistic singularity," as Hutcheon argues with respect to the formation of a national model of literary history more generally.[20] He thus constructed a narrative that described a Turkish nation and imagined a literature for it at the same time by creating a developmental and teleological narrative model directly related to the specific "end" or telos of cultural rationalization in a similar way to what took place during the formation of nation-states around the world.[21]

Accordingly, in the introduction to the book, Köprülü divides the history of Turkish literature into three broad periods for the first time based on the civilizational encounters of the Turks over centuries: Turkish literature before Islam, Turkish literature under the influence of Islamic civilization (the eleventh century to the mid-nineteenth), and Turkish literature under the influence of European civilization (the mid-nineteenth century to the present). This literary periodization reflected Köprülü's search for a historical account of Turkish literature as a single, continuous, and unique narrative. Therefore, both structurally and thematically, Köprülü's national model is expressed in evolutionary metaphors of organic growth extending from primitive times to the present and following the encounters of Turks with two major (Islamic and European) civilizations that profoundly changed the way they have practiced literature. We fundamentally witness a story of the nationalization process of the Turkish nation over centuries. Köprülü's formulation of a Turkish literary history based on a total and singular past between Central Asia and Anatolia became absolute truth in modern Turkish literary history writing. In the decades following his works, Turkish literary historians continued to write narrative accounts of Turkey's literature based on his premises and arguments.

Consolidating National Literary Historiography

Two striking examples of such modern literary histories were published right after Köprülü's book in the early 1920s. The first of these literary histories is İbrahim Necmi Dilmen's (1887–1945) *Tarih-I Edebiyat Dersleri* (Lectures on Literary History) published in 1922. In the preface, the author states that his book is about the history of Ottoman Turkish literature, which he taught in different schools for years, contributing to the consolidation of modern narrative literary history as an academic discipline in Turkey. He further points out he aims to "investigate Turkish literature, especially its trends in Turkey" by also considering "the impact of the literatures of the Turks reigning in other places on the products of ancient Turkish literature."[22] Although he does not directly refer to Köprülü's theoretical and methodological works on the concept of literary history in general and on the history of Turkish literature in particular, Dilmen shapes a model of literary history informed by a common Turkish cultural and literary past, echoing Köprülü's previously discussed assumptions and formulations.

Another history of Turkish literature exemplifying the consolidation of Köprülü's model of national literary history is İsmail Habip Sevük's (1892–1954) *Türk Teceddüt Edebiyatı Tarihi* (History of Turkish New Literature) published by the Ministry of Education in 1925 after the foundation of the Republic of Turkey in 1923. Although the focal point of the book is the historical survey of the new (*teceddüt*) Turkish literature, the writer, who taught the history of Turkish literature in high schools for years, constructs his long introductory chapter entirely on the narrative structure of a typical national literary history. Before examining the encounter between the Ottoman Turks and Europeans and this encounter's formative consequences in shaping modern literature, Sevük deals with such topics and questions as the origins of Turkish literature, the classifications of Turkish literature into folk (*halk*) and high (*yüksek zümre*) traditions, the unity of these two literatures in terms of their origins, the importance of oral folk literature and its various genres, the encounter with Europe and resulting changes in way of life, the shortcomings and virtues of Ottoman classical literature, and the influence of French literature on Ottoman Turkish literature. These topics and the ways Sevük deals with them are directly related to Köprülü's preoccupations and efforts to shape a national literary history for the emerging Turkish nation. In this respect, his division of the new Turkish literature into three major literary periods (the Tanzimat, Servet-i Fünun, and national literature movement) best illustrates his objective in writing his literary history. Such categorization of the new Turkish literature in fact characterizes the three most recent phases of nationalization of Turkish society and culture that started with this contact. Sevük argues that in creative response to this encounter with Europe and its social, political, and cultural consequences, the Ottoman modernizing intelligentsia began to appropriate and incorporate European modes, models, and forms such as the modern novel, plays, and essays in order to replace the old literature which, according to him, became "the literature of a decaying civilization."[23] It is apparent that Sevük, who wrote his book while a literature teacher in the new capital Ankara, produced his history of recent Turkish literature to explore the constitutive impact of modernity in the making of modern Turkey through the writing of its recent literary past within the context of Ottoman Turkish modernity. This shows how Sevük approached the process of nationalization in society and literature as a natural outcome of modernity that started with the Ottomans' integration into the global, modern world and completed with the foundation of the Republic of Turkey as a nation-state in 1923.

The publication of Nihat Sami Banarlı's *Resimli Türk Edebiyatı Tarihi* (The Illustrated History of Turkish Literature) in 1948 permanently enshrined Köprülü's notion as the singular form of literary historiography in Turkey. In his preface, Banarlı states that rather than bringing about new information, his book aimed to provide a comprehensive historical account of Turkish literature from its origins in Central Asia by drawing on Köprülü's in-depth and extensive research on the subject. Banarlı's history of Turkish literature was later republished by the Turkish Ministry of National Education several times and is taught regularly in the departments of Turkish Language and Literature at universities. This clearly manifests how Köprülü's formulation of a national literary history based on the primacy of Turkish ethnicity and culture has dominated the writing of literary historiography since its creation in the early twentieth century due to the fact that Turkish literary historians have continued to reproduce the basic assumptions of this constitutive period in respect to their narrative structure, content, and periodization.

Conclusion: The Legacy of Köprülü's National Literary Historiography in Turkey

The nineteenth-century encounter of the Ottomans with Europeans radically changed not only the way the Ottomans wrote literature but also the way they wrote about it. Modern literary history writing separated from traditional biographical collections of poets was, in fact, a result of the Ottoman response to this encounter and the political, social, and cultural consequences that brought the Ottoman Empire into global modernity. It was in this context that Ottoman literary historians demanded new ways of thinking, analyzing, and writing about literature based upon modern premises and produced the first examples of literary histories in the modern sense. Initially, they constructed their literary histories based upon modern Ottoman identity, later transforming it into a national model of literary history during a time of transition from empire to nation-state in the early twentieth century. This occurred through its internal transformation in response to the social, political, and cultural transformations and a negotiation with both European models and traditional biographical writing. Even today, although refined and transformed, national-oriented literary history fashioned during the period of nation-building in the early twentieth century continues to dominate contemporary literary history writing in Turkey, essentially repeating the basic formulations, methods, ideas, arguments, and taxonomies. Therefore, every time historians produce new histories of Turkish literature they reimagine, reconstruct, and refashion the modern Turkish nation at the same time.

The ideological commitment to the national model has basically resulted in the exclusion and marginalization of authors and texts that have potentially challenged or "failed" to meet the predominant paradigms and premises of the Turkish national model of literary history. For example, a number of modern literary texts produced in Turkish in Armenian and Greek scripts in the Tanzimat period have been denied inclusion to the canon of Turkish literary history simply because their writers were non-Turkish or non-Muslim.[24] Similarly, Ottoman classical literature closely associated with the courtly milieu and Persian literary culture was marginalized for failing to express national character or spirit for a long time; only recently has such attitude partially changed.

Indeed, the dominance of this national model manifests itself in an interesting and ironic way in Turkish contemporary literary history writing on Turkic societies after the collapse of the Soviet Union. Several major scholarly works have been published to offer a narrative literary history of Turkic literatures over centuries from Central Asia to the Balkans. Following Köprülü's formulations of national literary history, these new histories still approach different contemporary Turkic literatures as the products of a single nation. The basic assumption in these studies is that although great internal and external historical and political events over the centuries have made Turkic people widespread geographically, they are indeed ethnically, linguistically, and culturally a homogeneous community without taking into consideration the literary, historical, social, and political changes that have taken place across cultures and literatures of these societies over time. A good example of the persistence of the Turkish national literary history produced in the early twentieth century is the series *Türk Dünyası Edebiyat Tarihi* (The Literary History of the Turkic World) published between 2001 and 2007. The book was edited by a commission and contributed to by a wide variety of literary historians from different contemporary Turkic societies in order to explore the shared literary history of the 200 million Turks around the world. In so doing, it seeks to show the historical accomplishments of the Turks as a united society and their great contribution to world civilization through 2,000 years of cultural tradition because, according to the editor, literary texts are the most "solid sources" that show the shared experiences of contemporary Turkic societies. Generally speaking, this literary history is basically an expanded rewriting of Köprülü's *History of Turkish Literature* published in 1920 in terms of its concept of national literary history and its scope.

Today in Turkey, there are many writers who publish in Turkish yet emphasize their own ethnic and religious identities different from the Turkish majority and represent more complex cultures, worldviews, and values despite a common nationality, challenging the traditional national model of literary history based on the strict premises of the nation-making process. As Hutcheon argues in her discussion of the persistence of the national model and the problems it causes in contemporary literary studies across cultures, we live today in a world that is very different in economic, social, and cultural terms from the one that saw the rise of the nation-states and experienced the political and social crisis of the early twentieth century. Our globalized twenty-first-century world has created a complex context that is ethnically and culturally diverse. An emphasis on a common language, ethnicity, and culture in the twenty-first century has little meaning or correspondence to the study of the literary history of a nation even within a single country. This illustrates that when contemporary Turkish literary historians write the literary history of contemporary Turkic peoples, they in fact reimagine and rewrite the literary history of modern Turkey based on the premises, nationalist discourses, and assumptions of the nation-building period in Turkey in the early twentieth century. They attempt to

National Literary Historiography in Turkey

underline a culturally, ethnically, and linguistically shared past among a unified population and reinforce Turkey's place at the center of the Turkic world, advocating for Turkey as its leader.

Finally, literary studies have gone through phases of theoretical and methodological transformations in the past century, radically changing the ways we examine literary texts. Contemporary literary studies today share little resemblance with the literary, scientific, and intellectual paradigms of the late nineteenth and early twentieth centuries, during which most national models of literary histories were created worldwide. Historians of literature embed conventions and discourse, value judgments, and periodization of traditional narrative literary histories in their work. Yet one must not forget the fact that challenging and coming to terms with them is also part of the writing of literary history. Engaging with conventional modes of narrative national literary history is different from allowing these established norms to dominate the assumptions, narratives, and premises of today's literary history writing. Only by writing new literary histories shaped around more flexible, dynamic, and heterogeneous frameworks can we go beyond inventories of literary studies composed of stereotypical literary figures and trends fitting within the very narrow boundaries of a national Turkish literature. These new histories will allow us to better comprehend the nature of Turkish national literature's place in world literature and its relationship with other national literatures around the world.

Notes

1 Around the same period, the first examples of modern literary histories based on a cohesive and unified narrative began to be produced in Western literatures. See, e.g., David Perkins, *Is Literary History Possible?* (Baltimore: Johns Hopkins University Press, 1992), 29–53.

2 For different scholarly examination of the biographies of poets in Ottoman literature, see Walter Andrews, "The Tezkere-i Şu'ara of Latifi as a Source for the Critical Evaluation of Ottoman Poetry" (PhD diss., University of Michigan, 1970); Mustafa İsen, *Şair Tezkireleri* (Ankara: Grafiker, 2002); Filiz Kılıç, "Edebiyat Tarihimizin Vazgeçilmez Kaynakları: Şair Tezkireleri," *Türkiye Araştırmaları Literatür Dergisi* 5, no. 10 (2007): 543–64; and J. S. Stewart-Robinson, "The Ottoman Biographies of Poets," *Journal of Near Eastern Studies* 24, no. 1–2 (1965): 57–74.

3 Abdülhalim Memduh, *Tarih-i Edebiyat-ı Osmaniye* (Istanbul: Ohennes Matbaası, 1306 [1888]).

4 Comprehensive histories of Ottoman Turkish literature based upon progressive narrative published during this period include the following: Şahabettin Süleyman, *Tarih-i Edebiyat-ı Osmaniye* (Istanbul: Ohennes Matbaası, 1910); Reşat Faik, *Tarih-i Edebiyat-ı Osmaniye* (Istanbul: Ohennes Matbaası, 1911); Ali Ekrem, *Tarih-i Edebiyat-ı Osmaniye* (Istanbul: Ohennes Matbaası, 1912); Köprülüzade Mehmed Fuad [later known as Mehmet Fuat Köprülü] and Şahabettin Süleyman, *Yeni Osmanlı Tarih-i Edebiyatı: Menşelerden Nevşehirli İbrahim Paşa Sadaretine Kadar*, vol. 2 (Istanbul: Ohennes Matbaası, 1332 [1914]).

5 For Köprülü's life and scholarly work, see Ömer Faruk Akün, "Mehmed Fuad Köprülü," *TDV İslâm Ansiklopedisi*, accessed May 26, 2021, https://islamansiklopedisi.org.tr/mehmed-fuad-koprulu; Nuran Tezcan, "Fuat Köprülü'nün Türk Edebiyatı Tarihi Üzerine," in Yahya Kemal Taştan, ed. *Mehmet Fuat Köprülü* (Ankara: TC Kültür ve Turizm Bakanlığı, 2012), 93–118; Yahya Kemal Taştan, "Mehmed Fuad Köprülü, Hayatı," in *Türk Edebiyatı Dersleri* (Istanbul: Alfa, 2014), 9–176.

6 Mehmet Fuat Köprülü, "Method in Turkish Literary History," trans. Gary Leiser, *Middle Eastern Literatures* 11, no. 1 (2008): 55. This important article, originally published in the Ottoman Turkish journal *Bilig* in 1913, was later translated into English as "Method in Turkish Literary History," by Gary Leiser. See Köprülü, "Method in Turkish Literary History," 53–84. Unless otherwise noted, all citations used in this chapter are from this translation.

7 Ibid., 65.

8 Ibid., 67.

9 Ibid.

10 For more on these mystic oral poets, see Zeynep Oktay Uslu's chapter on Yunus Emre in this volume.

11 Linda Hutcheon, "Rethinking the National Model," in *Rethinking Literary History: A Dialogue on Theory*, ed. Linda Hutcheon and Mario Valdes (Oxford: Oxford University Press, 2002), 4.

12 Köprülü and Şahabettin Süleyman, *Yeni Osmanlı Tarih-i Edebiyatı*, 113.

Halim Kara

13 Ibid., 8.
14 Ibid., 7.
15 An impressive list of Köprülü's scholarly articles on various origins, genres, issues, authors, traditions, and periods of Turkish literature in the 1910s and 1920s can be found in Akün, Taştan, Tezcan's articles on Mehmet Fuat Köprülü's life and scholarly work. See note 5.
16 Linda Hutcheon, "Interventionist Literary Histories: Nostalgic, Pragmatic, or Utopian?" *MLQ: Modern Language Quarterly* 59, no. 4 (December 1998): 404.
17 Mehmet Fuat Köprülü, *Early Mystics in Turkish Literature*, trans. Gary Leiser and Robert Dankoff (London: Routledge, 2006), LII.
18 Devin Deweese, "Foreword," In *Early Mystics in Turkish Literature*, trans. Gary Leiser and Robert Dankoff (London: Routledge, 2006), viii–xxvii.
19 Mehmet Fuat Köprülü, *Türk Edebiyatı Tarihi* (Istanbul: Ötüken Neşriyat, 1981), 1.
20 Hutcheon, "Rethinking the National Model," 3.
21 Ibid., 5.
22 İbrahim Necmi [Dilmen], *Tarih-i Edebiyat Dersleri*, vol. 2 (Istanbul: Matbaa-i Âmire, 1922), 5.
23 İsmail Habip Sevük, *Türk Teceddüt Edebiyatı Tarih* (Istanbul Matba-i Âmire, 1924), 687.
24 See Murat Cankara's chapter in this volume.

References

Abdülhalim Memduh. *Tarih-i Edebiyat-ı Osmaniye*. Istanbul: Ohennes Matbaası, 1306 [1888].
Andrews, Walter. "The Tezkere-i Şu'ara of Latifi as a Source for the Critical Evaluation of Ottoman Poetry." PhD diss., University of Michigan, 1970.
Banarlı, N. Sami. *Resimli Türk Edebiyatı Tarihi: Destanlar Devrinden Zamanımıza Kadar*. Istanbul: Yedigün Neşriyatı, 1948.
DeWeese, Devin. "Foreword." In *Early Mystics in Turkish Literature*, edited by Mehmed Fuad Köprülü and translated by Gary Leiser and Robert Dankoff, VIII–XXVII. London: Routledge, 2006.
Dilmen, İbrahim Necmi. *Tarih-i Edebiyat Dersleri*, vol. 2. Istanbul: Matbaa-i Âmire, 1922.
Faik Reşat. *Tarih-i Edebiyat-ı Osmaniye*. Istanbul: Zarafet Matbaası, 1911.
Hutcheon, Linda. "Interventionist Literary Histories: Nostalgic, Pragmatic, or Utopian?" *MLQ: Modern Language Quarterly* 59, no. 4 (December 1998): 402–17.
———. "Rethinking the National Model." In *Rethinking Literary History: A Dialogue on Theory*, edited by Linda Hutcheon and Mario Valdes, 3–49. Oxford: Oxford University Press, 2002.
İsen, Mustafa. *Şair Tezkireleri*. Ankara: Grafiker, 2002.
Kılıç, Filiz. "Edebiyat Tarihimizin Vazgeçilmez Kaynakları: Şair Tezkireleri." *Türkiye Araştırmaları Literatür Dergisi* 5, no. 10 (2007): 543–64.
Köprülü, Mehmet Fuat. *Türk Edebiyatı Tarihi*. Istanbul: Ötüken Neşriyat, 1981.
———. "Türk Edebiyatının Menşei." In *Edebiyat Araştırmaları 1*, 49–130. Istanbul: Ötüken Neşriyat, 1981 [MTM, no: 4, Eylül-Teşrinievvel, 1331/1913].
———. "Türk Edebiyatı Tarihinde Usul." In *Edebiyat Araştırmaları 1*, 3–47. Istanbul: Ötüken Yayınları, 1989.
———. *Early Mystics in Turkish Literature*. Translated by Gary Leiser and Robert Dankoff. London: Routledge, 2006.
———. "Method in Turkish Literary History." Translated by Gary Leiser. *Middle Eastern Literatures* 11, no. 1 (2008): 53–84.
———. *Türk Edebiyatında İlk Mutasavvıflar*. Istanbul: Alfa Yayınları, 2018.
Köprülü, Mehmet Fuat, and Şahabeddin Süleyman. *Yeni Osmanlı Tarih-i Edebiyatı: Menşelerden Nevşehirli İbrahim Paşa Sadaretine Kadar*. Istanbul: Şirket-i Mürettibiye Matbaası, 1332 [1914].
Mehmed Hayreddin. *Tarih-i Edebiyat Dersleri*. Konya: Vilâyet Matbaası, 1330 [1913].
Perkins, David. *Is Literary History Possible?* Baltimore: Johns Hopkins University Press, 1992.
Sevük, İsmail Habip. *Türk Teceddüt Edebiyatı Tarih*. Istanbul Matba-i Âmire, 1924.
Stewart-Robinson, J. S. "The Ottoman Biographies of Poets." *Journal of Near Eastern Studies* 24, no. 1–2 (1965): 57–74.
Tural, Sadık. (Ed.). *Türk Dünyası Edebiyatı Tarihi*, vol. 9. Ankara: Atatürk Kültür Merkezi Yayınları, 2008–2013.

19

THEATRE AS A PROPAGANDA TOOL FROM THE LATE OTTOMAN EMPIRE TO THE 1930s

Esra Dicle

Introduction

Art, as part of society's superstructure, which includes theatre, can play an important role in creating social consensus in a way that fosters the dominant ideology. This consensus, which can be described as, to use Gramsci's terms, "the ideological consent of the masses,"[1] is the acknowledgment of a general structure consisting of the dominant value judgments, prevailing moral qualifications, or any other measures of social relations used by the broad masses. A play can be based on a form of discourse producing and reinforcing this homogenous structure in parallel with the dominant ideology while also containing impulses that contribute to the dissolution of this shared compromise. For this reason, dominant ideologies firstly control and direct theatre by integrating it into their mechanisms and, second, seek ways to fully utilize the power of the theatre to inspire.

The history of using theatre as a means of religious and political propaganda has developed nearly in parallel with the history of humanity. However, this subject falls outside the aim of this chapter, which is to examine the relationship of theatre to dominant ideologies and oppositional ideas stemming from various political positions in the Ottoman Empire and Turkey specifically, where a modern understanding of theatre developed starting in the Tanzimat period (1839–1876). Theatre during the Tanzimat served to educate and shape society through new values. With the declaration of Second Constitution in 1908, theatre turned into a type of public sphere where different and conflicting political ideas were expressed. Theatre became like a dais on which certain essential behaviors, discourses, and symbols were produced to raise the political consciousness of the public. As a consequence of never-ending wars, nationalistic rhetoric began to surround the stage.

The most important aim of Kemalist modernization after the establishment of the Turkish Republic was to construct a new Turkish identity based on Western norms. In order to achieve this aim, the modern nation-state used the power of the arts in particular. Music, painting, architecture, sculpture, and theatre became effective tools to instill national identity and consciousness. The one-party state in Turkey centralized these activities within the Halkevleri (Public Houses), which had economic, bureaucratic, and administrative relations with the Cumhuriyet Halk Partisi (Republican People's Party, or CHP). Between 1932 and 1944 in

DOI: 10.4324/9780429279270-26

235

particular, more than a hundred plays were staged in the Halkevleri in order to generate a new type of citizen that would meet the needs of the state.

However, responding to the activities of the Halkevleri, some writers (such as Yakup Kadri, Nâzım Hikmet, and Halide Edip) who had a variety of conflicts with the principles of the modern nation-state also expressed their criticisms by means of the theatre. In this way, the art of the theatre in Turkey, from the Tanzimat to the Republican period, was a kind of propaganda tool in the battle between the dominant powers and oppositional ideologies.

The Theatre as a Moral Institution

The modernization process that began in the Tanzimat period is regarded also as a beginning point for the modern Turkish theatre. In the nineteenth-century Ottoman Empire, both the palace and intellectuals became interested in the genre of the play. Although the palace was unable to establish a multilingual imperial theatre, probably because it thought that a bilingual theatre formed with plays in the Turkish and Armenian languages would adequately respond to this need, Hagop Vartovyan was granted a ten-year "monopoly for staging dramas, tragedies, comedies and vaudevilles in Turkish."[2] Immediately following this patent, together with a high imperial order (*ferman-ı âli*), Muslims were permitted to go to theatre[3] and, therefore, theatre became central in the social and cultural life of the city for the first time. The new intellectuals that emerged after the sultanate began to share more of its power with Bab-ı Ali—that is, with the state bureaucracy—explored theatre as a means of teaching ideas, engaging in politics, and shaping the people's morals and even educating them.[4] In Ottoman-Turkish theatre, for a long period, the theatre's foremost duty was to contribute to a project of social change. In other words, theatre as an art was seen as an effective tool of the ideology of Westernization. In this period, an intense period of producing original plays—especially for the melodrama, comedy, and historical drama genres—developed with such figures as Şinasi, Namık Kemal, Ahmet Mithat, Manastırlı Mehmet Rıfat, and Ali Haydar Bey. Meanwhile, Osmanlı Tiyatro Edebi Heyeti (the Literary Delegation for Ottoman Theatre) was pioneered by such figures as Namık Kemal, Ali Bey, and Şemseddin Sami. It was established with the central ideals of

> resolving the articulation problem of Armenian actors and actresses, which was regarded as the most prominent problem of the theatre in Turkish; enrichment of the literature of theatre through plays translated from European languages; the correction of past translations and adaptations that had been superficially made; and the improvement of national theatre literature through the composition of as many plays as possible.[5]

In this way, Muslim intellectuals began to reform and discipline society through theatre. The palace began to directly interfere with theatrical activities with practices like the ban of plays such as Namık Kemal's *Vatan Yahut Silistre* [Homeland or Silistre, 1872] and Ahmet Mithat Efendi's *Çerkez Özdenleri* [*Circassian Nobles*, 1884] or *Çengi* [1885]. The palace also ordered the presence of a censor and an inspector in each theatre house, the demolition of Gedikpaşa Theatre, and a ban on plays not staged in the Turkish language in Üsküdar, Kadıköy, and so on. Therefore, it can be seen that theatre was not accepted as an autonomous art and political authority's interest in theatre developed with a strong motivation of control, regulation, politicization, and nationalization.

Theatre and the Politicization of the Public Sphere During the Second Constitutional Period

With the declaration of the Second Constitution, theatre contributed to the expansion of the public sphere. Plays were being staged within a relatively free atmosphere but were still under the guard of the ruling İttihat ve Terakki (Union and Progress Party), princes, pashas, and ministers. However, it was ensured that the audience would develop a close interest in the stage not because of the plays but also thanks to the national anthems, speeches, and conferences. Theatre became an area in which the symbols and messages required for the political mobilization of the masses were generated. In this period, plays with historical and documentary attributes were more frequently staged. The Young Turk revolution and the constitution were celebrated with enthusiasm. Hundreds of hastily composed plays were launched. Many of them began with a statement about the inauguration of parliament, the anniversary of the Ottoman state's foundation. On some occasions, theatre soirees were organized to collect donations for building schools, to collect aid for the navy or army, and for victims of disasters such as fire, earthquake, and floods. The plays were sometimes organized by the center or branches of İttihat ve Terakki and thus were staged under the protection of diplomats such as the Prince Abdülmecit Efendi, Reşat Efendi, or Iranian Ambassador Rıza Han, and statesmen such as the Minister of Education Recaizâde Ekrem. Intellectuals such as Ahmet Mithat Efendi and Halit Ziya sometimes gave speeches before the plays, or Tevfik Fikret's poems like "*Sis*" [Fog] or the text of Mithat Pasha's defense were read.[6]

The establishment of a national theatre in the Ottoman Empire can be reconsidered through the example of Comédie-Française in 1909, while figures like Cenap Şehabettin, Hüseyin Cahit, Hüseyin Rahmi, Mehmet Rauf, and Ali Kemal were included in the literary delegation of the organization of Ottoman Stage presided over by Recaizâde Mahmut Ekrem. Though it did not last long and was disbanded after the March 31st incident,[7] the committee did similar work as the previous delegation and sought solutions for several issues, such as finding female actors, writing domestic plays, improving actors' Turkish articulation, and so on.[8]

The steps taken during the Tanzimat and Constitutional periods to ensure the institutionalization, organization, control, and management of the theatre, its politicization, and the government's education of its people through the theatre and incorporating them into political engagements—all this continued after the declaration of the Turkish Republic in 1923 and the establishment of a new modern nation-state.

Citizenship Education in the Modern Nation-State Through Theatre

The 1930s was a period in Turkey when the modern and nationalist nature of the new republic was reflected in numerous areas, from sports to arts, architecture to education, language to history, the organization of daily life both in the private and public spheres, and to rural life. As a consequence of political, economic, and social changes such as the worldwide economic crisis during the first half of the 1930s, the unexpected support of the Serbest Cumhuriyet Fırkası (Liberal Republican Party) established on Atatürk's orders by the CHP leadership as a controlled opposition party, Kemalism began to place importance on adapting and organizing its program in the area of civil society as a way to ensure the resonance and reinforcement of its ideology in the arena of civil society. For this reason, the party organization initiated widespread political training of the masses and the official development of Kemalist ideology.

Kemalist discourse began structuring society with institutions that began operating in the early 1930s, such as the Turkish Language Institution, Turkish Historical Society, Faculty of

Language and History-Geography, People's Houses. These institutions helped the state begin its controlled transformation of society in line with its principles. One of the most prominent centers for this societal project carried out in the political, academic, and cultural arena was the People's Houses, which began with 14 branches simultaneously opened in 1932 and which operated in nine areas, including the branches of language/history and literature, theatre, sports, library sciences and publishing, rural affairs, museum and exhibitions, and art and social aid. By 1950, the number of People's Houses had reached 478 as the state sought to ensure that they spread across Anatolia. Between 1932 and 1940, the People's Houses had their peak period both in terms of number and activities. Throughout this period, 12,350 theatre plays were staged in the People's Houses.[9]

The aim and philosophy behind the establishment of People's Houses was explained by Atatürk:

> The nation should be organized in the form of masses of people who are conscious, who have understanding and love towards each other and who are committed to the ideal. It is not sufficient to have the most profound means of learning and the most professional armies of teachers. We shall not neglect to nurture the people, to transform them into a mass, or the regulation of efforts for the people. And this shall be achieved by the People's Houses.[10]

The People's Houses, the majority of which had branches centered on culture and the arts, were directly bound to the CHP, and the instructions that determined the activities, aims, and procedures of these branches were formed in parallel to the ideology of single-party rule. The Minister of National Education of the period, Dr. Reşit Galip, explained the characteristics of the plays to be staged at the People's Houses as follows:

> On the stages of the People's Houses, only plays that defend the national theses will be staged. Our subjects will take their sources from general Turkish history as well as the many phases of national struggle that represent perpetual pride and honor for the nation, the good morals and high virtues of the Turk, and the endless material and spiritual power within the soul of the Turk.[11]

The plays that were approved began touring the People's Houses to be put on stage. The number of people who viewed these plays was counted and their success was measured based on the number of people reached. For example, Reşit Galip had the following opinion about Faruk Nafiz Çamlıbel's play *Akın* [*Influx*, 1932]:

> Our experience after the staging of *Akın*, seen by 6,000 people within five days when it was staged in Ankara, reveals that so far and probably for a long time in the future, and most particularly for today, theatre is the best and most beneficial means of publication in our country.[12]

To reach this goal, the state ordered new plays to be written in support of Kemalism's project to train the desired citizen (*makbul vatandaş*). Plays were to be staged at schools within the framework of the educational reform enacted by the young Republic. This included productions such as Reşat Nuri's *Vergi Hırsızı* [Tax Thief, 1933]; Aka Gündüz's *Gazi Çocukları İçin* [For the Ghazi Children, 1933]; Burhan Cahit's *Gavur İmam* [Giaour İmam, 1933]; Nihat Sami's *Kızıl Çağlayan* [Red Waterfall, 1933)]; Vedat Nedim's *29 Birinci Teşrin* [October 29, 1933];

and Vasfi Mahir's *On İnkılap* [The Ten Revolutions, 1933]. All of these had themes such as national morality in education, national consciousness, national ideals, and discipline, as well as the necessity to struggle with all kinds of social elements that are enemies of the Republic of Turkey's existence.

In addition, within the scope of the ten-year anniversary celebrations of the Republic, several plays were commissioned that embodied national consciousness and the core concepts of nationalism. In many plays—including Yaşar Nabi's *İnkılap Çocukları* [The Revolution's Children, 1932]; Halit Fahri's *On Yılın Destanı* [The Epic of Ten Years, 1938]; Aka Gündüz's *Mavi Yıldırım* [Blue Lightning, 1933]; Faruk Nafiz Çamlıbel's *Kahraman* [Hero, 1932]; and Nahit Sırrı's *Sönmeyen Ateş* [The Fire That Doesn't Burn Out, 1938]—the nation-state structure was rendered with mentions of the reforms the young Republic enacted throughout its first decade. In the plays that were used as tools of propaganda in this period, the content was dominated by themes of reform and independence. These emphasized the independence movement sustained by the whole nation; the major glories that were achieved with the merging of a militaristic nation with a militaristic leader; the position of the armed forces in the structure of the young Republic and its reputation among the people; the motivation necessary in order to achieve the targeted economic, cultural, and civilized reforms; and the role and duties of each individual and each segment of the nation—each student, teacher, peasant, intellectual, artist, and sportsperson.

One of the most significant phases in the construction of the nation-state was official historiography, which allowed for the creation of a powerful and rooted past. In this period, the historical narrative explained in detail how the development of Turkish identity and Turkish history had been prevented during the Ottoman period, the misrepresentation of Turkish history in foreign sources, the motherland of Turks and how they came to Anatolia, Turks' relations with other cultures and civilizations throughout history, and their language and basic characteristics. This essentialist national identity discourse was also created and supported through plays like Faruk Nafiz's *Akın, Özyurt* [Homeland, 1932]; Yaşar Nabi's *Mete* (1933); Muharrem Gürses' *Köroğlu* (1945); Hakkı Günal's *Bozkurt* (1934); İbrahim Tarık Çakmak's *Bozkurt* (1935); Ali Kazanoğlu's *Alp Aslan* (1948); Behçet Kemal's *Attila*; Naci Tanseli's *Attila*; and M. Kemal Ergenekon's *Attila* (1935). In their basic themes, these plays emphasized the deep-rooted history of a warrior and raider nation full of victories, the leader, country, and flag: all these shaped the discourse that aimed at removing the Ottoman Empire and connecting with the Turks' Central Asian roots.

In the plays with the theme of peasantism (*köycülük*)—which was the basis of the economic, cultural, and political policies of Kemalism—rural life was used to express the national spirit and the essence and ideal of the nation. The idea that the development and independence of the country depended on the development of the villages was highlighted in plays including Vehbi Cem Aşkun's *Atatürk Köyünde Uçak Günü* [A Flight Day in the Village of Atatürk, 1936]; Ercüment Lav's *Karagöz Stepte* [Karagöz on the Steppe, 1940]; Faruk Nafiz Çamlıbel's *Ateş* [Fire, 1939]; and Hüsamettin Işın's *Atatürk'e İlk Kurban* [The First Victim for Atatürk, 1935]. These plays contained such themes as the establishment of healthy communication and solidarity between the villages and cities, the organization of the villages, the education of villagers, the improvement in the efficiency of agriculture and animal breeding, and the coordination of the necessary steps to industrialize.

The Stage of the "Other": How About the Opposing Voices?

The plays written during the period of the People's Houses and used as an effective tool for the spread of official ideology did not represent a first in the history of Turkish theatre. As previously mentioned, starting from the Tanzimat, in parallel with the diversification of political ideologies in the Second Constitutional Period, plays became the most effective weapon for both the rulers and the opposition. With the foundation of the Republic, theatre was under the control and supervision of the ruling party both structurally and directly. However, with the modern nation-state, theatre was also produced (on the political, economic, and aesthetic levels) with an oppositional energy as well through the works of some figures who were openly or implicitly part of the opposition.

The play *Sağanak* [Downpour],[13] written in 1929 by Yakup Kadri Karaosmanoğlu—who was among the most prominent figures of the national independence movement and the Republican establishment with his novels and stories and later tenure as a member of parliament during the period of single-party rule—is one of the most significant plays of the author for being a text containing some of his open and implicit criticism of the official ideology of the modern nation-state. The play deals with the impacts of the process of rapid reform and change after the foundation of the Republic within the framework of nation-motherland/family home parallelism and the conflict of the old and new. What is interesting about the play is that it contains not only the conflict between the Ottoman Empire and the Republic and between the tradition and modernization but also the conflict—although implicitly—between the Kurdish movement and the nation-state through the characters Lütfi and Eşref, who are stepsiblings with the same father.

The patriarch of the house, Afif Molla, is a character alienated by the objects surrounding him and troubled by the new type of household that took shape so rapidly after the Republic. Living in a house in which the material and spiritual elements that preserved the former order were turned upside down and where the "kiblah is now in another direction,"[14] the family hierarchy deteriorates and the house began to be ruled not by Afif Molla but by the younger son Eşref and the wife of the older son, Belkıs Hanım. The older son of the house, Lütfi, likens the chaotic state of the house to the "state of the homeland,"[15] and showing the hat in his hand, he says, "Being contemporary, this has become a heavy necessity for us."[16] For this reason, he rejects even facing off with his brother Eşref, a famed and reputable author who defends the reforms of the Republic and who Lütfi holds responsible for whatever is going on. In turn, Eşref blames his stepbrother, although he has not yet clearly declared his position, for "turning their father's house into the den of some clandestine societies and the mass of reactionaries."[17] Thus, the conflict between these two stepbrothers, "one of whom is differently raised and the other also differently raised,"[18] is powerfully portrayed.

As the play progresses, Lütfi's motivation and the ideas behind his struggle are revealed. When he and his friends from the society are planning to struggle against the government, it is revealed that the name of the society is Tarikat-ı Felahiye (Sect for Salvation), and it is mentioned that the detentions and prosecutions at the İstiklal Mahkemeleri (Independence Tribunals) against the members of this sect are ongoing and that some of the people from this sect were sent to "Elaziz" (Elazığ). All of these are reminiscent of the 1925 Kurdish Uprising and the process related to the Takrir-i Sükûn Kanunu (Law on the Maintenance of Order) and to the Independence Tribunals. Elazığ is also a city that was temporarily seized by Kurds.[19] Therefore, it is implied that Lütfi is a member of a Kurdish secret society and the differing political attributes of the stepbrothers become more evident. At this point, Afif Molla stands both against Eşref and the struggle in which Lütfi is involved. Considering that Turks and Kurds were the two major identities within the Muslim subjects of the Ottoman Empire, it is understandable that Afif Molla, who is Ottomanist-traditionalist-conservative, does not openly support one side in this fraternal conflict and seeks a way to settle their differences. Afif Molla underlines the

Theatre as a Propaganda Tool From the Late Ottoman Empire to the 1930s

unifying attribute of the idea of the Ummah and therefore thinks a clash based on differences of ethnic identity is meaningless.

In an environment of conflict between opposing poles throughout the text, we do not witness the weight of the narrative shifting towards either character's side. The discourse of the text is not based on an open good-evil struggle. Representing the Republican ideology and "the regiment of a revolutionary generation,"[20] Eşref is an intellectual and revolutionary "who hears some grunts, murmurs instead of sounds of appreciation and encouragement around him while he endeavors alone to save the homeland from darkness,"[21] and he is represented as an idealist character. In contrast, Lütfi, his opposite, is depicted as someone who struggles boldly on behalf of his beliefs and ideals and who is willing to die for the sake of them. Eşref looks for ways to save his half-brother from execution, despite the values he believes in and at the cost of sacrificing them. Therefore, as these parties clash with one another, rather than a clash between right and wrong, good and evil, or old and new, the play portrays the reality of a house/family/country whose idealistic and living integrity has degenerated and which has reached the brink of disintegration. At the end of the play, the fruitlessness of the calls for dialogue and agreement are demonstrated through the disintegration of the family after the news of the execution of Lütfi, Eşref's decision to leave home, Belkıs' loss of her mind, and the illness of Afif Molla. The play, written in 1929, seems to have been written as a kind of call for self-criticism and calm, at a time when the state's ethnic policies and the rebellions of the Kurdish tribes still affected the course of events after the 1925 Kurdish Rebellion. It is necessary to link this with the play's being banned and taken off the stage after four performances.

After the mild criticism of the modern nation-state's ethnic policies, the criticism directed at the state's economic policies came from the political left. In the 1930s, subjects such as class relations, conditions of production, and poverty, which started to form the content of stories and novels that analyzed society with a socialist perspective on the basis of economic relations, were also deftly handled in the poetry and theatrical works of Nâzım Hikmet. He wrote his important play, *Kafatası* [Skull] in 1932, to be staged at Darülbedayi upon the request of theatre actor, director, and producer Muhsin Ertuğrul, who he got to know during his days in Moscow.

Kafatası is the story of a doctor and medical researcher who is about to develop a cure for tuberculosis to save his daughter and humanity but who is stopped by capitalists who have invested in sanatoriums. The doctor first loses his daughter, then his reputation, and finally his mind and his life. In the play, there is a crowded cast consisting of journalists, invitees, vendors, circus employees, police officers, as well as the primary characters. Some of these characters are the Journalist, Publisher, Concierge Woman, Broker, Prostitute, Stranger, Officer, Governor, and Guardian, all with names that indicate their jobs and therefore their position in society. The characters with actual names include Doctor Dalbanezo, who is working on a serum to cure tuberculosis. He believes "science is the work of expertise and expertise does not widen but it deepens."[22] He is blind to anything beyond his work expertise, making him clever and honest but lacking in consciousness. Pedro understands well how the capitalist economic system functions and continuously endeavors to demonstrate to the doctor "the relationship between the science of economics and the science of medicine."[23] Then there are the representations of capitalism's exploitation and tyranny: Vilyam, the President of the Administrative Council of Combined Tuberculosis Sanatoriums Trust of Dolaryanda; Paolina, the Chief Medical Doctor of Sanatoriums; and Freyman, the President of the Administrative Committee of Post Combined Newspapers Trust, who creates realities according to the needs of the capitalist class. In addition, in the second part of the play, there are such characters as the Man in a Frock, the Art Trader, the Oil Baron, the Spiritualist, the Poet, those who attend the fake "former patients cured at sanatoriums ball," and characters who reveal the social-moral degeneration, hypocrisy, opportunism, and self-interest of scientists, business people, and artists.

The doctor is forced to delay the production of the tuberculosis vaccine for six months and treat cows and oxen on the farm of Paolina and Vilyams, paying his debts while trying to heal his daughter on her deathbed and replicate this dose for all people. Although he responds to this agreement by saying "I am not a veterinarian,"[24] he is forced out of the lab that he works in when he runs out of funds. As he secretly continues his work on the vaccine on the farm, he is caught by Paolina and Vilyams and first imprisoned and, when released for having lost his mind, is later sent to work in a circus by a member of the Society for Fighting Vagabondism and Helping the Poor. The Doctor eventually dies and after his death, even his skull is sold in exchange for money.

The play exposes the links between the economic system, which is part of the base according to Marxist thought, with science, the arts, and media as part of its superstructure. In this way, the play offers a powerful criticism of the bourgeois state and ethics. For this very reason, it was banned on its third day on the stage, although it had been previously approved by the censors, on the pretext that veterinarians were insulted with the Doctor's line, "I am not a veterinarian."

Another critique came from Halide Edib, who was one of the most prominent figures in the struggle for national independence and also who lived abroad until Atatürk's death because of the problems she had with him shortly after the declaration of the Republic. She criticized the cultural politics of the modernization movement, in which the radical reforms made the modern nation-state implemented damaged the spirit, spiritual values, identity, and cultural heritage of Anatolia. She expressed this critique in her play *Maske ve Ruh* (Mask and Soul),[25] written in 1937–1938 and published in 1945 but never staged.

The play opens in the fourteenth century with Nasreddin Hodja's[26] death and his return to the world and to his own tomb as a spirit to get his donkey Bozoğlan. In the meantime, there is a scene between Tamburlaine and Ibn Khaldun framed as a historical dialogue between the two figures where they discuss power, authority, and ruling. Tamburlaine gives the portrait of a leader who prefers to rule rather than serve, who thinks that the greatest virtue is power, and believes the world should be ruled according to the will of one person under one system, making occupation and war necessary to achieve this as the will of the god. The writer depicts the city of Akşehir in the fourteenth century and again exposes how an authoritarian-oppressive approach to leadership and ruling establishes a system of uniformity through war.

The part of the play set in twenty-first-century Akşehir discusses the Republican period. The dome of Nasreddin Hodja's tomb is described as painted pink. Its columns are painted in yellow and it is covered with posters. There is a tea garden built in a Cubist architectural style.[27] In the yard of the tomb, a primary school teacher is teaching children, reading Nâzım Hikmet's poem "I Want to Turn into a Machine." The wife of the Governor of Akşehir, Remziye, is a character who believes that in order for the modern age to start, "One must be as practical so as to remove from sight not only the old useless buildings but also the outdated old people."[28] She supports the ban on gypsies dancing and being visible on the streets, she tries to spread jazz music, makes fun of those who drink *rakı* because she regards whiskey as an indicator of being civilized, and argues that the soul is "an organ whose existence is not needed just like appendicitis."[29] Through her, Halide Edib criticizes the interventions of the ruling party into daily life, habits, and culture in a prohibitory, supervisory, and exclusionist manner.

In the twenty-first century, the prime minister, Timur, whose aim is to "establish a powerful state machine based on science and technique, remote from personal and arbitrary influences."[30] Timur is annoyed with being likened to Tamburlaine and says that it is no longer the time to rule the world by force claiming that the world can only be peaceful, happy, and motivated through uniformity. He is positioned in the play as a character to criticize totalitarian regimes and especially the Kemalist one-man regime. At the end of the play, in order to achieve a "revolution of the soul," the twenty-first-century spirits of Shakespeare and Nasreddin Hodja land from Middle Heaven on the surface of the earth. Turkish Embassy Chief of London, Nasır Cebe, and the journalist, Şeyk, defend the soul and argue that the specter or the dream of the West, or whatever it is, has begun to shape the East, whereas the thing that we call the soul "is something peculiar to the soil [or] the climate and even when it is forced upon these, if it takes root, the soul takes shape according to the climate."[31] Against the despotic leader, Timur, Şeyk defends the diversity and richness of cultures and identities. According to Şeyk, "the real skill . . . is to catch up with the harmony of differences. This skill is not killing the souls of people and regarding them as puppets whose strings are controlled by the state machine.[32]

In her articles in the newspaper *Akşam* during the Second World War, Halide Edib strongly criticized the German, Italian, and Russian regimes that tried to uniformize the world and erase the freedom of the individual. For her, the loss of balance between the soul and matter made the West the center of a totalitarian-authoritarian regime, a soulless, unmanned civilization. The East had been captured by despotic rulers and then by the West because it could not establish the proper balance between matter and spirit. Therefore, the modernization process for Halide Edib means a loss of identity and culture. In the play, the subject of the loss of balance between the material and the soul is a way to express her rather alternative ideas regarding belief, metaphysics, originality, creativity, and so on in order to criticize the Republican era for its political authoritarianism and loss of soul—and therefore of identity—as well as for being under the influence of Western materialism.

Ideology Never Leaves the Stage

Since the Tanzimat, theatre has played an important propaganda function and a key role in the education of society in line with the needs of official ideology. The transition took place from a multilingual, multi-identity empire to a modern nation-state while the institution of the theatre was shaped in line with national goals. In the 1930s, during the institutionalization of Kemalism, the theatre, with the organizations and activities carried out especially within the People's Houses, became a very important tool for determining the culture-art environment of the period, shaping the public sphere in line with the needs of the government and ensuring state-public integration. Nevertheless, figures such as Nâzım Hikmet, Yakup Kadri, and Halide Edib, who experienced different conflicts with different dimensions of the economic, cultural, and ethnic policies of the modern nation-state, also chose to express their criticisms within the possibilities of the theatre. These plays, created with the energy of dissent, were directly or indirectly exposed to the state's control over the theatre in the 1930s. The plays of Nâzım Hikmet and Yakup Kadri were banned after a few shows, while Halide Edib's play could only be published in 1945. However, these plays and figures paved the way for art that criticized the Ottoman-Republic modernization projects and their consequences, especially after 1950.

Notes

1 For detailed information about the subject, see Antonio Gramsci, *Hapishane Defterleri* (Istanbul: Dorlion Yayınevi, 2014).
2 Metin And, *100 Soruda Türk Tiyatrosu Tarihi* (Istanbul: Gerçek Yayınevi, 1970), 127.
3 Gıyasettin Altuntaş, *Tanzimatta Tiyatro Edebiyatı Tarihi* (Ankara: Akçağ Yayınları, 2002), 18.
4 Mehmet Fatih Uslu, *Çatışma ve Müzakere, Osmanlı'da Türkçe ve Ermenice Dramatik Edebiyat* (Istanbul: İletişim Yayınları, 2014), 60–61.

5 Fırat Güllü, *Vartovyan Kumpanyası ve Yeni Osmanlılar: Osmanlıya Has Çokkültürlü Bir Politik Tiyatro Girişimi* (Istanbul: BGST Yayınları, 2008), 96.

6 Metin And, *Meşrutiyet Döneminde Türk Tiyatrosu* (Ankara: Türkiye İş Bankası Kültür Yayınları, 1971), 22–23. Mithat Pasha was exiled to Taif and kill ed there after being tried by a court during the reign of Sultan Abdülhamit, following the dethronement of Sultan Abdülaziz and his suspicious death, during which he was the head of the Council of State (Şûra-yı Devlet Reisliği).

7 The March 31st incident was a notable uprising and coup attempt against the government in Istanbul after the proclamation of the second constitutional monarchy.

8 And, *100 Soruda Türk Tiyatrosu Tarihi,* 224.

9 Sefa Şimşek, *Bir İdeolojik Seferberlik Deneyimi—Halkevleri (1932–1951)* (Istanbul: Boğaziçi Üniversitesi Yayınevi, 2002), 61.

10 Adem Kara, *Halkevleri* (Ankara: 24 Saat Yayıncılık, 2006), 35.

11 Şimşek, *Bir İdeolojik Seferberlik Deneyimi,* 190.

12 Arzu Öztürkmen, *Türkiye'de Folklor ve Milliyetçilik* (Istanbul: İletişim Yayınları, 1998), 94.

13 Yakup Kadri Karaosmanoğlu, "Sağanak," in *Tiyatro Eserleri* (Istanbul: İletişim Yayınları, 2011), 39–96.

14 Ibid., 43.

15 Ibid.

16 Ibid., 45.

17 Ibid., 50.

18 Ibid., 49.

19 Nilgün Firidinlioğlu, "Sağanak," *Istanbul Üniversitesi Edebiyat Fakültesi, Tiyatro Eleştirmenliği ve Dramaturji Bölüm Dergisi* 10 (2007): 69.

20 Karaosmanoğlu, "Sağanak," 91.

21 Ibid., 77.

22 Nâzım Hikmet, "Kafatası," in *Oyunlar 1* (Istanbul: Yapı Kredi Yayınları, 2018), 33–90.

23 Ibid., 41.

24 Ibid., 51.

25 Halide Edib Adıvar, *Maske ve Ruh* (Istanbul: Atlas Kitabevi, 1968).

26 Nasreddin Hodja is a legendary figure and comic hero who lived around the Hortu and Akşehir area during the Anatolian Selçuk state.

27 Halide Edib thought that Cubism represents German art and architecture, so it is "beautiful despite its sadness." But such an understanding of art and architecture did not fit the Turkish spirit. İnci Enginün states that in *Tatarcık,* the Cubic Palas, which a nouveau riche figure built by following the fashion of the period, was used to create a funny effect in the novel. İnci Enginün, *Halide Edib Adıvar'ın Eserlerinde Doğu ve Batı Meselesi* (Ankara: Millî Eğitim Bakanlığı, 1995), 465.

28 Adıvar, *Maske ve Ruh,* 85.

29 Ibid., 90.

30 Ibid., 102.

31 Ibid., 83.

32 Ibid., 102.

References

Adıvar, Halide Edib. *Maske ve Ruh.* Istanbul: Atlas Kitabevi, 1968.

And, Metin. *100 Soruda Türk Tiyatrosu Tarihi.* Istanbul: Gerçek Yayınevi, 1970.

———. *Meşrutiyet Döneminde Türk Tiyatrosu.* Ankara: Türkiye İş Bankası Kültür Yayınları, 1971.

———. *Osmanlı Tiyatrosu.* Ankara: Dost Kitabevi, 1999.

Altuntaş, Gıyasettin. *Tanzimatta Tiyatro Edebiyatı Tarihi.* Ankara: Akçağ Yayınları, 2002.

Aşkun, Vehbi Cem. *Atatürk Köyünde Uçak Günü.* Ankara: Ulus Basımevi, 1936.

Banarlı, Nihat Sami. *Kızıl Çağlayan.* Istanbul: Devlet Matbaası, 1933.

Çağlar, Behçet Kemal. *Attila.* Ankara: Ulus Basımevi, 1935.

Çamlıbel, Faruk Nafiz. *Akın.* Ankara: Ankara Halkevi Yayınları, 1932.

———. *Özyurt.* Ankara: Hakimiyeti Milliye Matbaası, 1932.

———. *Kahraman.* Istanbul: Cumhuriyet Kütüphanesi, 1933.

———. *Ateş.* Istanbul: Ahmet Sait Basımevi, 1939.

Enginün, İnci. *Halide Edib Adıvar'ın Eserlerinde Doğu ve Batı Meselesi.* Ankara: Millî Eğitim Bakanlığı, 1995.

Ergenekon, Kemal, M. *Attila*. np, 1935.

Firidinlioğlu, Nilgün. "Sağanak." *Istanbul Üniversitesi Edebiyat Fakültesi, Tiyatro Eleştirmenliği ve Dramaturji Bölüm Dergisi* 10 (2007): 62–76.

Gramsci, Antonio. *Hapishane Defterleri*. Istanbul: Dorlion Yayınevi, 2014.

Güllü, Fırat. *Vartovyan, Kumpanyası ve Yeni Osmanlılar: Osmanlıya Has Çokkültürlü Bir Politik Tiyatro Girişimi*. Istanbul: Bgst Yayınları, 2008.

Günal, Hakkı. *Bozkurt*. Zonguldak: Bingöl Matbaası, 1941.

Gündüz, Aka. *Gazi Çocukları İçin*. Istanbul: Milli İktisat ve Tasarruf Cemiyeti, 1933.

———. *Mavi Yıldırım*. Ankara: CHF Temsil Neşriyatı, 1934.

Güntekin, Reşat Nuri. *Vergi Hırsızı*. Istanbul: Devlet Matbaası, 1933.

Gürses, Muharrem. *Köroğlu*. Istanbul: np, 1945.

İbrahim, Tarık. *Bozkurt*. Istanbul: Remzi Kitabevi, 1935.

Işın, Hüsamettin. *Atatürk'e İlk Kurban*. Istanbul: Bozkurt Matbaası, 1935.

Kara, Adem. *Halkevleri*. Ankara: 24 Saat Yayıncılık, 2006.

Karaosmanoğlu, Yakup Kadri. "Sağanak." In *Tiyatro Eserleri*, 39–96. Istanbul: İletişim Yayınları, 2011.

Kazanoğlu, Ali. *Alp Aslan*. Istanbul: Remzi Kitabevi, 1948.

Kısakürek, Necip Fazıl. *Tohum*. Istanbul: Büyük Doğu Yayınları, 1997.

Kocatürk, Vasfi Mahir. *On İnkılap*. Istanbul: Muallim Ahmet Halit Kütüphanesi, 1933.

Lav, Ercüment. *Karagöz Stepte*. Ankara: Ankara Ulusal Matbaası, 1940.

Morkaya, Burhan Cahit. *Gavur İmam*. Istanbul: Devlet Matbaası, 1933.

Nayır, Yaşar Nabi. *İnkılap Çocukları*. Ankara: CHF Kitabıumumiliği, 1933.

———. *Mete*. Ankara: Varlık Yayınları, 1933.

Nâzım Hikmet. "Kafatası." In *Oyunlar 1*, 33–90. Istanbul: Yapı Kredi Yayınları, 2018.

Örik, Nahit Sırrı. *Sönmeyen Ateş*. Istanbul: İkbal Kitabevi, 1938.

Ozansoy, Halit Fahri. *On Yılın Destanı*. Istanbul: Kanaat Kütüphanesi, 1933.

Öztürkmen, Arzu. *Türkiye'de Folklor ve Milliyetçilik*. Istanbul: İletişim Yayınları, 1998.

Şimşek, Sefa. *Bir İdeolojik Seferberlik Deneyimi—Halkevleri (1932–1951)*. Istanbul: Boğaziçi Üniversitesi Yayınevi, 2002.

Tanseli, Naci. *Attila*. Ankara: Ülkü Basımevi, 1948.

Tör, Vedat Nedim. *29 Birinci Teşrin*. Ankara: Türkiye Cumhuriyeti Maarif Vekaleti Yayınları, 1933.

Uslu, Mehmet Fatih. *Çatışma ve Müzakere, Osmanlı'da Türkçe ve Ermenice Dramatik Edebiyat*. Istanbul: İletişim Yayınları, 2014.

20

IMAGINING THE NATION FROM THE STREET

Nationalism, Daily Life, and Emotions in the Short Stories of Ömer Seyfettin

Erol Köroğlu

Whenever we hear Ömer Seyfettin's name, we think of the late Ottoman period in Turkish nationalism and the related National Literature movement (*Millî Edebiyat Akımı*). One of the bedside books of every researcher who studies the literature or literary culture of this period is Ruşen Eşref Ünaydın's *Diyorlar Ki* [They Say], published in late 1918. Ruşen Eşref's interviews with 19 leading literary figures of the period in late 1917 and the first months of 1918 are indispensable sources for understanding the time's literary positionings. In these interviews, we can observe the past of Turkish literature, the moment that was molded by World War I, and how each writer positions themselves against each other at that moment. There was a war going on that caused all kinds of material deprivation, and the pressure of the Committee of Union and Progress (CUP) war government was felt politically, especially in the cultural field.

For this reason, the reader of these works can sense that all the literary writers were trying to speak without touching on dangerous subjects, those related to the government's policies, but still inevitably engage in political polemics with each other over literary matters. The most discussed and indirectly contested issue was the National Literature movement, which proceeded under the supervision of Ziya Gökalp, who tried to establish cultural hegemony with the support of the political authorities. However, the movement had not yet produced very successful literary texts. The issue was more visible in terms of technical aspects, such as the use of plain language or syllabic meter in poetry instead of the traditional *aruz* meter. However, the central aspect that led to the literary conflict was the Turkish nationalism behind the movement. All the writers included in *Diyorlar Ki* deal with Ruşen Eşref's questions about the history of literature from this perspective and evaluate the literary sphere based on their proximity to or distance from this ideology.

There were some vaguely opposed camps, but it is impossible to divide them into Turkish nationalists and anti-nationalists. The situation was complicated and this complexity stems from the sociopolitical and historical context of 1917–1918. Speaking with Ruşen Eşref, these literary figures became the cultural actors of a "nation formation process" that began before 1908 and continued until the 1940s. There is a "national movement" that cannot be limited to Turkish nationalism and encompasses various positions. Literary writers and other cultural actors strove to envision and construct the nation, whether they were nationalists or not.

246

DOI: 10.4324/9780429279270-27

I use the concepts of the nation formation process and national movement here on borrowing from Miroslav Hroch, one of the leading names in nationalism studies.[1] In his study, Hroch draws attention to a three-phase development, comparatively examining the national movements originating from Europe. Accordingly, in the initial phase of this development, a reservoir is created by researching linguistic, historical, and cultural areas that will constitute the nation. In the second phase, an activist group of intellectuals launch a movement of "patriotic agitation" based on this reservoir and bring society into national consciousness. In the third phase, the new society, now possessing a developed national consciousness, has become a civil society with its institutions. In this framing, we can evaluate the late Ottoman period dating back to 1908 as the first phase of the Turkish nation formation process, the second phase between 1908 and 1923, and the third one from 1923 to 1940. However, this periodization is problematic due to specific historical conditions. The actors in the national movement in the period between 1908 and 1923 were unable to inherit a sufficient reservoir from the period that preceded them. While they practiced patriotic agitation towards society in line with the Turkish nationalism that emerged from the 1910s, they also tried to produce the national cultural material on which such patriotic agitation would be based.[2]

Imagining the Nation and the National Identity Formation Program

National cultural material, patriotic agitation, the nation formation process: these are the elements of a spectrum of national identity production that does not progress in a uniform and harmonious manner and continues with conflicts and changes from moment to moment. National identity production requires the imagining of the nation. The word "imagination" here does not mean unreal, false, or invented. The imagining of the nation is based on factual and real conditions. However, it is inevitable to use imagination to reach a national society and a nation-state based on these conditions. Benedict Anderson, another prominent figure in nationalism studies, expresses this situation in his famous book *Imagined Communities*: "It [the nation] is an imagined political community—and imagined as both inherently limited and sovereign."[3]

According to Anderson, the nation is "imagined" because even the members of the smallest nations cannot recognize everyone who is a member of that nation. However, they always keep in their minds the existence of a total. The nation is limited because even the largest nation recognizes that there are nations outside it and does not consider all of humanity a part of itself. In its history, the nation is sovereign because nationalism, coordinated with modernity, attributes the authority of freedom not to God or the dynasty but to itself, or rather to the nation-state that represents it. Finally, according to Anderson, the nation is a community because, despite the relations of inequality and exploitation that never disappear, it has at its forefront the design of a "deep, horizontal comradeship" involving all members.[4]

At this point, much work will be left to the writers in the national movement to ensure that society imagines itself as a nation, recognizes its borders, reaches awareness of sovereignty, and feeds this consciousness with the comforting confidence of being included in a community. To understand the nature of this work, let us now return to *Diyorlar Ki*. Ruşen Eşref speaks to Refik Halit, who at the time has been in exile in Anatolia for nearly five years and recently returned to Istanbul. Refik Halit is an anti-Unionist, but with his "homeland stories" (*memleket hikâyeleri*) in particular, which he wrote while in exile, he drew the attention of Ziya Gökalp, the leading ideologue of the CUP. Gökalp and his close associate Ömer Seyfettin, the short story writer, thought that Refik Halit used Turkish in a very mature manner, in the direction targeted by the National Literature movement they led. Therefore, they ensured that he was forgiven and comes to Istanbul. Refik Halit, who was an anti-nationalist in the context of Unionism but also a genuinely national writer, replies to Ruşen Eşref's question, "How can [we] perfect our literature?" in the following way:

> We have found the language, now we will get to know the people and we will engage with the people without becoming vulgar. We need a Russian literature. In other words, a literature that participates in the suffering of the people, feels their needs, shapes our ambitions.[5]

With these words, Refik Halit points to some preconditions for perfecting a national literature. There is a people, and in order to develop literature, it is necessary to learn about this people and act according to its needs. There is also a model such as Russian literature that can be taken as an example. However, it is necessary to emphasize the difficulty and complexity of this program, which Refik Halit expresses simply and with ease. Because the goal is not to describe national identity but to create it, the people will not be told, "This is who you are," but rather, "If you start from these conditions and act like this, you can be this or that." Therefore, literature that seeks to construct national identity has to deal with a dynamic field of becoming, not a static field of being. Tim Edensor, who examines the issue of national identity in popular culture and daily life, expresses this situation as follows:

> Crucially then, national identity, like other identities, is about using resources of history, language and culture in the process of becoming rather than being: not "who we are" or "where we came from," so much as what we might become.[6]

Therefore, there is an unstable field of national identity that is always reestablished according to social, material, temporal, and spatial contexts. "Fluidity," here, does not mean inconsistency but something that will have to be reproduced continuously to form a stable nation. As Renan said, the continued existence of the nation depends on "a daily plebiscite."[7] The way people say, "Yes" every day to becoming a nation is by being convinced that they are a nation and believing that the imagination of the nation will continue in the future. The program Refik Halit mentioned targeted exactly this. Today, when we consider the appearance of National Literature or Turkish nationalism in literature more broadly, we first think of Mehmet Emin Yurdakul's heroic poems or fictional works that praise Turkishness through history or the epic. However, these are just the tip of the iceberg. The works written in the style mentioned by Refik Halit do not bring nationalism to mind at first glance. Rather, they focus on the daily lives of the lower sections of the society and try to capture national identity in its becoming. Ordinary people and daily life are needed in order to imagine the nation coming into being. At that exact point, we see that nationalism and a specific literary realism become intertwined.

A Literary Realism Specific to Nationalism

Erich Auerbach, in his comprehensive and classic *Mimesis*, which examines the representation of reality in Western literature, evaluates the introduction of ordinary people and everyday life into literature as follows:

> The serious treatment of everyday reality, the rise of more extensive and socially inferior human groups to the position of subject matter for problematic-existential representation, on the one hand; on the other, the embedding of random persons and events in

the general course of contemporary history, the fluid historical background—these, we believe, are the foundations of modern realism, and it is natural that the broad and elastic form of the novel should increasingly impose itself for a rendering comprising so many elements.[8]

Auerbach makes this comment not in the context of nationalism but the realist novel in nineteenth-century France. However, in belated national movements such as Turkish nationalism from the beginning of the twentieth century, ordinary people and daily life would be handled with a specific purpose and specific literary realism. Realism in Turkish literature emerged with the prose of the Servet-i Fünun literary movement. It led to two masterpieces in the hands of the novelist Halit Ziya Uşaklıgil: *Mai ve Siyah* [The Blue and the Black] (1897) and *Aşk-ı Memnu* [Forbidden Love] (1899). Nationalist writers such as Refik Halit or Ömer Seyfettin willingly expressed their debt to the prose of *Servet-i Fünun* in their interviews with Ruşen Eşref.

Then what makes Refik Halit and Ömer Seyfettin's realism different from and specific compared to the realist writers that came before them? The answer to this question lies in the matter of narrative voice. The narrator type who dominated the first fictional texts produced by the pioneers of Turkish literature—such as Namık Kemal, Ahmet Mithat, and Nabizade Nazım after 1870—was the intrusive third-person, heterodiegetic narrator. In these authors' narratives, we see that the narrator directly intervenes in the text, explicitly settling into the text to educate the reader through a dialogue with the narratee.[9]

However, especially starting with Halit Ziya Uşaklıgil, we come across the omniscient third-person heterodiegetic narrator (i.e., the narrator type of realist fiction). This narrator does not appear in the narrative and does not comment but is omnipresent. The narrator shows us the actions and speeches of the characters and what goes on in their minds. Because this kind of narrator does not manifest itself openly, its power to guide the reader is higher. The readers get the illusion that what they are reading is happening in real life, right in front of them— and the more powerful this illusion of reality, the greater our persuasion of the realist writer's ideological agenda.

The specificity of the realism seen in writers like Refik Halit and Ömer Seyfettin stems from their intention to capture national identity as it develops and convince society to become a nation. Therefore, their realism is more pragmatic than that of Halit Ziya and is based on goals that are not purely artistic. While they represent ordinary people's lives, they construct the imagined community pointed out by Anderson. Those who read the ordinary stories of these ordinary people will be able to envision their limited and sovereign communities more concretely, as well as undergo an emotional education for this community and their fellow citizens thanks to the covert guidance of the omniscient narrator.

We see a clear example of this process in the story "Yatık Emine" [Emine the Loose] written by Refik Halit in Istanbul in 1919. The story takes place in a town that is a two-day journey away from Ankara but not visited by many people due to the unfavorable location and climate. The difficult living conditions are reflected in the characters of those living there. One day, a prostitute known as Yatık Emine is driven to this town from the city center. Throughout the story, we watch the various torments inflicted by the townspeople on Emine, a poor and very young woman. At the end of the story, Emine will starve. Throughout this painful story, the omniscient narrator tells what is happening without interfering with anything. While doing this, he sometimes gives summaries and makes objective comments. Sometimes he shows us the dialogues of the characters or what goes through their minds.

Nevertheless, at only one point in the narrative does he abandon his cold-blooded attitude and express without restraint what we (the reader) desire for Emine. In this passage, Emine begs in front of the police station due to hunger, but the ruthless commissioner does not care. When a police officer decides to give her a penny, the commissioner intervenes hastily and stops him. The narrator is no longer be able to stand at this point:

> Emine's hand was left idle. An unbearable jolt of life had this woman shut to the ground once, then a long, heavy chain, each ring of which was made of a different form of hardship and folding, wrapped around her body, dragging her to pieces. It was a tangible chain, not a spiritual one. This was not an analogy; it was the truth. How deeply she had endured everything. However, she had not come across such malice until now. She turned her eyes and looked at the commissioner for a long time, with a look carrying the undigested pain of fifteen years of bad luck. Then, again, without saying a word, *she left the courtyard undaunted, still not willing to rebel against this guy who one should have jumped like a hungry wolf and bit and smashed.*[10]

This passage is a deviation from the realist author's usage of the omniscient narrator. A realistic writer must maintain the allegedly objective attitude seen in the remainder of the story. However, the emotional judgment that emerges with this deviation also contains the main message that the narrator conveys to the reader. It is not a mistake in the author's intention, only a slight technical deviation. Because the author treats this town as a pre-national community, explaining the ruthlessness of the townspeople by their distance from the ability of "imagining the nation as a limited and sovereign community." That is to say, it invites readers into a positive "national imagination" through an example that can be seen at any time in Anatolia, which is negative but at the same time has not yet started to become a nation. Forming a negative community within the boundaries of the town and its townspeople's interdependence, they will teach the nation's members who will read the story how not to be.

Ömer Seyfettin and Ways of Expanding the National Imagination

There are other examples similar to "Yatık Emine" among Ömer Seyfettin's stories, especially those written during the Armistice period.[11] Especially "Zeytin Ekmek" [Olive and Bread],[12] which was published in the *Yeni Dünya* [New World] daily on July 3, 1919, recalls "Yatık Emine" in terms of the development of the subject and events. This heartbreaking story about the deprivation experienced during the war years and this poverty forcing young and beautiful women to choose between prostitution or starvation is one of the most impressive literary products regarding the Ottoman civilian home front during World War I. The protagonist of the story is a beautiful young woman named Naciye. Naciye's husband, a bricklayer, is employed in labor battalions and brings a half *okka*[13] of olives and *vesika* [state-distributed] bread to his wife every week. Naciye has eaten nothing but this for the four years of war. One day, she meets her childhood friend Sabire and Füsun, another young woman. We learn that these two women are top-level prostitutes, and they deceive Naciye with the promise of giving her a lavish banquet and then selling her to a rich young man. Naciye, who endured this situation only to eat a hot plate of food, runs away from this house by crying when she finds only a bowl of black olives and a slice of state-distributed bread because it is late at night. At the end of the story, Naciye lies down by the sea, unable to even find the strength to commit suicide. Although the end of the story is uncertain, the reader assumes she will die there of hunger or cold.

On the other hand, Ömer Seyfettin differed significantly from Refik Halit in a certain respect. While Refik Halit wrote Chekhov-esque short stories presenting slices of life, Ömer Seyfettin wrote Maupassant-style short stories based on surprise and estrangement, necessarily

Imagining the Nation From the Street

and generally containing humorous surprises. Ömer Seyfettin's method of estrangement is sometimes so excessive that a nihilistic humor emerges. The reader laughs at the end of the story. However, they might assume that his stories are about ordinary people, especially the bullies and rooks. Known as "*kabadayıs*" and "*kulhanbeys*" in Turkish (two terms used for a sort of mafia-like, tough guys in Turkish), they were not mainly concerned with historical and political events, had no emotional education in terms of the national imagination, and aim nothing but sarcastic humor. Should we assert that these short stories by Ömer Seyfettin do not fall within the scope of national imagination but were written negatively and only for humor? I will argue the opposite and say that stories, too, remain within the limits of the nationalist imagination. In saying this, I will concentrate on a few of the author's stories.

First of all, let us look at the stories "Çakmak" [The Lighter],[14] published on November 15, 1917, and "Külâh" [The Conical Hat],[15] published on February 24–27, 1917. I deal with these two stories, both published in the newspaper *Vakit*, because their protagonists are Balkan emigrants. In "Çakmak," we see the meeting of Mıstık and İboş, two Macedonian immigrants and fellow townspeople, in Anatolia. These two friends, farmers rather than artisans, make a living by cart driving and porterage. They sit by a stream and chat, remembering the beauty of their life in Macedonia and expressing their dissatisfaction with Anatolia. According to them, there is little work in Anatolia, the water and the weather are bad, and the people are liars and cheaters. While getting up after this long chat, İboş realizes that his lighter has disappeared, and he blames Mıstık. However, Mıstık denies this accusation. As a result, they find themselves in court, where Mıstık, who swears by the Qur'an that he did not take the lighter, wins the case. However, while leaving court, when the judge asks Mıstık to pay a court fee of ten cents, Mıstık throws the lighter in the face of İboş, saying, "I cannot pay ten cents for something worth one and a half cents."

We come across another Mıstık in the short story "Külâh," but this one is a Bulgarian immigrant. Mıstık, who always lived along the border, was made an immigrant four times due to the Balkan War and the World War I border arrangements, eventually crossed to Anatolia and became a traveling horse trader. He buys poor-quality animals cheaply and sells them using various tricks. His only rival in this business is an Anatolian colleague known as the Mullah (*Molla*). In the end, Mıstık becomes partners with the Mullah, but he always has it in his mind to deceive him. In the meantime, we also learn that the Mullah is from Kayseri, but Mıstık does not really know "where and what is Kayseri."[16] As a matter of fact, due to this ignorance, he will be defrauded by the Mullah, caught trying to steal a donkey painted in white, and thrown into prison.

Before moving on to Ömer Seyfettin's other stories in this style and especially those about the Istanbul tough guys, we need to ask: Where is the nationalism or the national imagination in "Çakmak" and "Külâh"? In these stories, is there a positive emotional education similar to "Yatık Emine" or "Zeytin Ekmek"? Naturally, there is not. We can say that the narrators in these stories approach the characters with antipathy, not sympathy. The omniscient narrator conveys what is happening very objectively and mostly through dialogue. However, in descriptive or summative passages outside of dialogue, we encounter an immensely hostile, judgmental gaze. For example, a short excerpt from "Külâh" well illustrates the narrator's antipathetic approach: "Mıstık raised his *dirty, weak* hand to his *sparse, yellow* mustache. His glowing eyes could not find a place to look. He *squinted* his *colorless* lips and smiled."[17]

However, despite the narrator's negative attitude, the national imagination is subtly represented in Ömer Seyfettin's two stories. First, the reader is helped to grasp the territory associated with the national imagination despite the strange humor in these stories. The stories were published in 1917 and the recent past leading up to that date was a period of turmoil. Borders narrowed as people had to migrate from their homelands and gather in Anatolia. These people, disconnected from their old lives and the environment they knew, were in the process of adapting to the new environment. This explains, for example, why Mıstık does not know where and what Kayseri is. For this reason, as well, Mıstık and İboş unrealistically praise everything in their lost homeland and find everything in Anatolia wrong. However, after all this disorderliness, the nation to which all the Mıstıks of the region belong will be formed in these lands.

These stories perform another essential function to educate the reader in nationalism. These immigrants, who came from the Balkans as lumpen proletarians, are elements that have not yet been included in the nation's imagination. Therefore, introducing these characters, who stand threshold of "self" and "other," to "us" with humor, albeit a strange humor, alleviates concerns about the formation of "us" in the mind of the reader. At this point, we seek assistance from the concept of "liminality" by the American political theorist Anne Norton. According to Norton, while a nation envisions itself, it keeps some of its members at the threshold, either territorially, intellectually, or structurally. Bandits, bedouins, and cowboys are territorial examples; madmen, traitors, and bohemians are intellectual; and the poor, women, and ethnic minorities are examples of structural liminality. Norton interprets their place on the threshold of the national imagination as follows:

> The recognition of liminality provides for the differentiation of self and other, subject and object, by establishing a triadic relation: the self, an object of likeness, and an object of difference. Liminars serve as mirrors for nations. At once other and like, they provide the occasion for the nation to constitute itself in reflection upon its identity. Their likeness permits contemplation and recognition, their difference the abstraction of those ideal traits that will henceforth define the nation.[18]

In line with the concept of liminality, the characters in these stories are at the threshold in terms of both territorial because they are immigrants, and structurally, because they are poor. On the one hand, they are members of the future nation because they speak Turkish and are ethnically Turkish. On the other hand, they are different because they come from a region that is no longer included in the state's borders; they are not producers and are simply closer to the culture of the other. Above all, they have moral weaknesses and problems with the law. However, despite all the inconvenience they cause, they also have some positive qualities: they are cunning and naïve, have as-yet unfixed energy, and are fun. Based on these positive features that the author sees or imagines in them, they can be made to belong to "us" by eliminating the harmful aspects and withdrawing into the limits of the law, thus contributing to our imaginary community.

The Strategy of "Traitstripping" and Capturing National Identity as Becoming

Anne Norton discusses a strategy employed by those at the threshold of national imagination. This strategy, "traitstripping," has three stages. In the first stage, a particular trait or collection of traits is defined as belonging to a particular liminal group. In the second stage, another group, closer to the center but still deprived of the existing structures, makes these traits their own. In the third stage, the system prevents the original carriers from applying or exhibiting these traits. Norton gives the North American Indians' situation in the formation of the United States as an example of this strategy. First, the natives are defined by violence, independence, and free will. Then, during the colonial, revolution, and civil war periods of US history, white Americans, such as soldiers or politicians, appropriate these traits and identify with the natives. In the last stage, the indigenous people are prevented from exhibiting or applying these characteristics due to state intervention.[19]

Immigrants' positive characteristics in the stories of Ömer Seyfettin are also be presented in this way. As a result, after they are forced to obey the law, their cunning, energy, and modes of entertainment will be made to belong to all of Anatolia but they themselves will be prevented from exhibiting the negative characteristics associated with these traits. Thus, they are assimilated by sharing these characteristics with the whole nation.

This strategy works more easily in Ömer Seyfettin's stories about the Istanbul tough guys. Let us take the short story "Düşünme Zamanı" [Time to Think],[20] published in the *Yeni Mecmua* on January 17, 1918. This story's protagonists are Badik [Duckling] Ahmet and Ödlek [Coward] Murat, two tough guys. Both of them became famous during the reign of Abdülhamit II. However, when the gendarmerie was reorganized with the declaration of the Ottoman Empire as a constitutional monarchy in 1908, they were no longer able to ply their trade. Ultimately, the narrator will take the side of the established order, just like his readers. These tough guys, who commit crimes like the mafia of other countries but without the same level of organization, exhibit negative traits with their illegal demeanor, gambling, lumpiness, and "*racon*" [swagger]. However, they are hungry because the law has them under pressure; they cannot find a means of subsistence in the new regime and have not eaten for days. Eventually, on Badik Ahmet's initiative, they enter a restaurant, fill their stomachs, and just sit there since they have no money.

In "Hatiften Bir Seda . . ." [Hearing a Divine Voice . . .],[21] published in *Yeni Mecmua* on March 7, 1918, we see Hacı İmadeddin Efendi—who has given up worldly affairs and dedicated himself to worship—and his drunk, nasty, gambling, rascal son Bad Tahsin. İmadeddin Efendi, who is basically an angel, rejected his naughty son when he was a child and kicked him out of the family home. Bad Tahsin is now impatiently waiting for his father's death and his inheritance to live it up in Beyoğlu. Bad Tahsin's dreams come true when he least expects them and in the strangest of ways. While İmadeddin Efendi is praying one night after deciding to shut himself up in the garden for a religious retreat, the drunk Tahsin ends up in front of his father's house and starts screaming, "Fly, oh blessed one, fly!" İmadeddin Efendi perceives this as a message from Allah that his end has come and leaps from the window, crashing to the ground. Thus, his entire inheritance is left to Tahsin and the residents of the neighborhood remember İmadeddin Efendi, who they assume committed suicide, with hatred.

The final story of Ömer Seyfettin that I will take up here is "Kerâmet" [The Miracle],[22] published in *Yeni Dünya* on July 17, 1919. In this concise story, we witness a large fire in a poor neighborhood in Istanbul. The locals believe that the rapidly advancing fire will stop when it reaches a saint's mausoleum in the neighborhood. However, the concerns of Çiroz [Skinny] Ahmet, the tough guy of the neighborhood, are entirely different. Fire times are the best times for looting and theft, but Çiroz Ahmet knows how poor the neighborhood is. However, in the mausoleum there are two candlesticks for ten liras each, two prayer rugs that can be sold for five liras, and two manuscripts that can be sold for ten liras. Çiroz, who enters the tomb without being noticed by anyone, knows he will have difficulty taking these heavy items out without anyone seeing. Therefore, he enters into the person's sarcophagus in the shrine, leaves the door, and passes in front of everyone. The locals who see the walking tomb do not realize what is going on and believe that the saint has come to life and escaped.

In both "Hatiften Bir Seda" and "Keramet," Ömer Seyfettin mocks the prevalent religious beliefs of the people which prevent the national imagination from spreading. In both stories, those who are religious are deceived by highly immoral and materialist tough guys who are not even remotely connected to religion. Thus, Ömer Seyfettin ostensibly ridicules the people's religious superstitions in these stories and tries to influence his readers in this way. However, it is no coincidence that the characters in both these two short stories and in "Düşünme Zamanı" are tough guys. These parasites, which are unacceptable in terms of law and morality, do not add anything to the social order with their existence but still exhibit positive characteristics with their materiality, quick and practical intelligence, and their energies that have not yet been channeled in a positive direction, just as with the Balkan refugees. Portraying them in literature will help bring readers to adopt the national imagination and separate off their positive traits so they can be spread throughout the nation. Besides, discussing these tough guys in these stories, people who frighten and disturb people while walking on the streets, will help reduce the fear they cause. They will be perceived in their real dimensions and, thus, they will pass from the liminal threshold, as Norton describes, to ordinary citizenship by law.

The surprising, strange, and thought-provoking elements of humor seen in almost all of Ömer Seyfettin's short stories allow daily life to be treated with its naked realities and utilitarianism towards an ideal. Ömer Seyfettin draws the unthinkable elements of the imaginary community to the limits of the national imagination, even in his stories distant from themes of nationalism. From this point of view, we can say that there is complete harmony in Ömer Seyfettin's storytelling and ideology. He was the most comprehensive and skilled practitioner of the program that Refik Halit expressed to Ruşen Eşref. His literary output succeeded in capturing and literalizing a national identity still in a state of becoming based on the most unimaginable, fluid elements.

Notes

1 See Miroslav Hroch, *Social Preconditions of National Revival in Europe* (New York: Columbia University Press, 1985).

2 For a detailed discussion, see Erol Köroğlu, *Türk Edebiyatı ve Birinci Dünya Savaşı (1914–1918): Propagandadan Millî Kimlik İnşasına* (Istanbul: İletişim, 2004); Erol Köroğlu, *Ottoman Propaganda and Turkish Identity: Turkish Literature During World War I* (London: I. B. Tauris, 2007).

3 Benedict Anderson, *Imagined Communities: Reflections on the Origin and Spread of Nationalism*, revised ed. (London: Verso, 1991), 6.

4 Ibid., 6–7.

5 "Biz lisanı bulduk, şimdi halkı öğreneceğiz ve adileşmeden kendimizi halkla meşgul edeceğiz. Bize bir Rus edebiyatı lâzım. Yani halkın acılarına iştirak eden, ihtiyaçlarını duyan, emellerimize şekil veren bir edebiyat . . ." Ruşen Eşref Ünaydın, *Bütün Eserleri Röportajlar I: Diyorlar Ki*, ed. Necat Birinci and Nuri Sağlam (Ankara: Türk Dil Kurumu Yayınları, 2002), 169 (my translation).

6 Tim Edensor, *National Identity, Popular Culture and Everyday Life* (Oxford: Berg, 2002), 24.

7 Ibid., 29.

8 Erich Auerbach, *Mimesis: The Representation of Reality in Western Literature* (Princeton, NJ: Princeton University Press, 1953), 491.

9 For a discussion of narrative voice in early novelist Ahmet Mithat, see Nüket Esen, "The Narrator and the Narratee in Ahmet Mithat," *Edebiyat, Journal of Middle Eastern Literatures* 13, no. 2 (2003): 139–46.

10 "Emine'nin uzattığı el boşta kaldı. Hayatın dayanılmaz bir sarsıntısı bu kadını bir defa yere kapatmış, sonra her halkası başka biçim sıkıntı ve katlanıştan yapılma bir uzun, ağır zincir vücuduna dolanarak onu yaralıya, bereliye sürüklemiş, paramparça etmişti. Bu, manevi değil âdeta elle tutulur bir zincirdi. Bu, benzetme değil, işin doğrusuydu. O her şeye ne derin bir boyun eğişle katlanmıştı. Fakat bu kadar hayınlığa şimdiye dek rasgelmemişti. Gözlerini çevirdi, içinden on beş senelik uğursuzlukların hazmedilmemiş acısı taşan bir bakışla komiseri uzun uzun süzdü. Sonra gene bir şey demeden, *aç bir kurt gibi üstüne atılıp ısırması, parçalaması gereken bu herife karşı hâlâ isyan etme isteği duymadan* salına salına hükûmet avlusundan çıkıp gitti." Refik Halit Karay, *Memleket Hikâyeleri*, ed. Ender Karay (Istanbul: İnkılap, 1986), 32 (my translation and emphasis).

11 The period after World War I started with the Mudros Armistice of October 30, 1918.

12 Ömer Seyfettin, "Zeytin Ekmek," in *Bütün Eserleri: Hikâyeler 3*, ed. Hülya Argunşah (Istanbul: Dergâh, 1999), 272–89.

Imagining the Nation From the Street

13 *Oka* or *okka* is an Ottoman measure of mass equal to 1.2829 kg.

14 Ömer Seyfettin, "Çakmak," in *Bütün Eserleri: Hikâyeler 2*, ed. Hülya Argunşah (Istanbul: Dergâh, 1999), 135–40.

15 Ömer Seyfettin, "Külâh," in *Bütün Eserleri: Hikâyeler 2*, ed. Hülya Argunşah (Istanbul: Dergâh, 1999), 259–67.

16 Ibid., 262. People from Kayseri are famous for their commercial and entrepreneurial skills.

17 "Mıstık *kirli zayıf* elini *seyrek sarı* bıyıklarına kaldırdı. Çakır gözleri bakacak yer bulamadı. *Renksiz dudaklarını kısarak* gülümsedi." Ömer Seyfettin, "Külâh," 261 (my translation and emphasis).

18 Anne Norton, *Reflections on Political Identity* (Baltimore: Johns Hopkins University Press, 1988), 54.

19 Ibid., 90.

20 Ömer Seyfettin, "Düşünme Zamanı," in *Bütün Eserleri: Hikâyeler 2*, ed. Hülya Argunşah (Istanbul: Dergâh, 1999), 214–25.

21 Ömer Seyfettin, "Hatiften Bir Seda . . .," in *Bütün Eserleri: Hikâyeler 2*, ed. Hülya Argunşah (Istanbul: Dergâh, 1999), 268–73.

22 Ömer Seyfettin, "Keramet," in *Bütün Eserleri: Hikâyeler 3*, ed. Hülya Argunşah (Istanbul: Dergâh, 1999), 294–96.

References

Anderson, Benedict. *Imagined Communities: Reflections on the Origin and Spread of Nationalism*, revised ed. London: Verso, 1991.

Auerbach, Erich. *Mimesis: The Representation of Reality in Western Literature*. Princeton, NJ: Princeton University Press, 1953.

Edensor, Tim. *National Identity, Popular Culture and Everyday Life*. Oxford: Berg, 2002.

Esen, Nüket. "The Narrator and the Narratee in Ahmet Mithat." *Edebiyat, Journal of Middle Eastern Literatures* 13, no. 2 (2003): 139–46.

Hroch, Miroslav. *Social Preconditions of National Revival in Europe*. New York: Columbia University Press, 1985.

Karay, Refik Halit. *Memleket Hikâyeleri*. Edited by Ender Karay. Istanbul: İnkılap, 1986.

Köroğlu, Erol. *Türk Edebiyatı ve Birinci Dünya Savaşı (1914–1918): Propagandadan Millî Kimlik İnşasına*. Istanbul: İletişim, 2004.

———. *Ottoman Propaganda and Turkish Identity: Turkish Literature During World War I*. London: I. B. Tauris, 2007.

Norton, Anne. *Reflections on Political Identity*. Baltimore: Johns Hopkins University Press, 1988.

Ömer Seyfettin. "Çakmak." In *Bütün Eserleri: Hikâyeler 2*, edited by Hülya Argunşah, 135–40. Istanbul: Dergâh, 1999.

———. "Düşünme Zamanı." In *Bütün Eserleri: Hikâyeler 2*, edited by Hülya Argunşah, 214–25. Istanbul: Dergâh, 1999.

———. "Hatiften Bir Seda . . ." In *Bütün Eserleri: Hikâyeler 2*, edited by Hülya Argunşah, 268–73. Istanbul: Dergâh, 1999.

———. "Keramet." in *Bütün Eserleri: Hikâyeler 3*, edited by Hülya Argunşah, 294–96. Istanbul: Dergâh, 1999.

———. "Külâh." In *Bütün Eserleri: Hikâyeler 2*, edited by Hülya Argunşah, 259–67. Istanbul: Dergâh, 1999.

———. "Zeytin Ekmek." In *Bütün Eserleri: Hikâyeler 3*, edited by Hülya Argunşah, 272–89. Istanbul: Dergâh, 1999.

Ünaydın, Ruşen Eşref. *Bütün Eserleri Röportajlar I: Diyorlar Ki*. Edited by Necat Birinci and Nuri Sağlam. Ankara: Türk Dil Kurumu Yayınları, 2002.

21

TRANSLATED HUMANISM AND THE MAKING OF MODERN TURKEY

Fırat Oruç

When Mustafa Kemal Atatürk, the founder of modern Turkey, died in 1938, he left a personal library of more than 4,000 books, many with extensive notes and marginalia. For a politician with a military background, Atatürk had an unusual library. Except for a negligible portion, his library consisted of a solid collection in a range of humanistic fields: history, literature, religion, linguistics, philology, and archeology. A marginal note that he jotted down in Alfred Fouillée's *Psychologie du people français* (1898) seems to reveal precisely what he was searching for in these texts: "National soul—religion, philosophy, literature."[1] The library of "the chief teacher and author," as Atatürk was hailed by the new nation, had another peculiar feature: It contained very few Turkish works. Those present were mainly official annals, statistical volumes, law, and regulation books published by the Turkish government. Atatürk drew on multiple sources in shaping the discourse of the Turkish revolution: Gustave le Bon's crowd psychology, Colmar von der Goltz's "nation-in-arms," Leone Caetani's Orientalist history of Islam, David Léon Cahun's and Hermann Feodor Kvergić's philology on the origins of world languages, Émile Durkheim's civic religion, Jean-Jacques Rousseau's social contract, Léon Bourgeois' and Alfred Fouillée's cooperative solidarism, Eugène Pittard's racial anthropology, and H. G. Wells' and James Churchward's cosmographic history.[2] In fact, Atatürk's library reflects the intriguing paradox at the heart of the making of modern Turkey: The nation-making project depended almost entirely on translation and foreign books. One could argue that no postimperial state experienced this paradox of solidifying national culture through an imported canon more acutely than Turkey. This situation encapsulates the foundational predicament of a ruling elite that wanted to discard traditional sources of self and identity markers[3] but found itself dependent on a foreign, translated repertoire for its cultural institutions.

With the collapse of the Ottoman Empire in the early twentieth century and the founding of the Republic in 1923, a new ruling class of military-civilian bureaucrats and official intellectuals came to power in Turkey. Under the leadership of Atatürk, they embarked on a series of radical modernization reforms aimed at leaving the country's Ottoman and Islamic past permanently behind. In less than a decade following the declaration of the Republic, the new ruling class launched a series of foundational reforms that reflected Kemalism's restlessness to skip multiple stages of modernization and secularization in a heroic leap. Acting in a rushed tempo to create a new society and country out of the ashes of the Ottoman Empire, they envisioned a total revolution in all possible aspects of life to initiate a genuine "Turkish awakening."

256

DOI: 10.4324/9780429279270-28

Translated Humanism and the Making of Modern Turkey

The driving force behind these reforms was the institution of an officially sanctioned, new national culture that the elite believed was necessary to save Turkey from its state of purgatory between East and West, past and present, tradition and modernity. A dominant majority of Turkish intellectuals (who also occupied key bureaucratic positions in the state apparatus) ardently supported the Kemalist reform program as a movement of self-discovery through a new unified, holistic, and organized national culture. An authentic Turkish Renaissance, they claimed, would reawaken the national spirit from centuries-old lethargy. However, they soon had to confront a tremendously vexing question: What would the content and source of this culture be? They found an intriguing and paradoxical answer: the path to creating a Turkish national culture was the European humanist canon. They believed that by translating and re-creating the humanistic corpus of Western thought and literature not simply in form but in spirit, understanding, and worldview, Turkey would find its true cultural identity. If Turkish cultural modernization emanated from the fantasy of instituting a new national ontology freed of death, translation promised a new life.[4] To this end, they endorsed translatability in all forms, including the transliteration of the Ottoman script into a new phonetic-based Turkish written in the Roman alphabet, the replacement of Arabic and Persian loanwords with Turkish equivalents, the transfer of European scholarship and institutions for the modernization of education, and the translation of world literary classics under a massive state-sponsored program.

The Turkish cultural elite of the 1930s and 1940s embraced a certain notion of world literature in order to formulate a programmatic response to the crisis of national culture that emerged during the formative decades of the Turkish Republic. Although they employed various Turkish equivalents for the term "world literature"—*dünya edebiyatı, cihan edebiyatı, ecnebi edebiyatı, tercüme edebiyatı*—they ultimately conceived of it as a regime of translating, reading, adopting, and circulating the European canonical works as reference culture. As source culture, the European humanist tradition would function not only as a normative canonical standard, a higher authority, and an iconic signifier but also as "a cultural superego that could be drawn on for one's own justification."[5] To put it in bolder terms, the Turkish national imaginary was formed in the mirror of translation. As a nation in its infancy, Turkey would discover its unified, whole image of the self in that mirror. Perhaps none other than Hasan Ali Yücel, the chief bureaucratic architect of the humanist project in Turkey, could express how his generation saw the relationship between nation and translation:

> National feelings are nurtured by human knowledge. Those who are incognizant of the world cannot know themselves. When you want to know what you look like, you look at the mirror. One the most important mirrors [for knowing the self] is translation.[6]

In addition to its psychically restorative function, translation would also serve as a dual-pronged strategy for modernization and nationalization, and as a necessary apprenticeship in the course of fulfilling Turkey's ambitions of becoming the pioneering country of a new twentieth-century humanism.

To note, this was not the first time in the history of Turkish modernization that the state had been directly involved in translation. During the Ottoman Empire, the state had established a series of translation institutions, including the Tercüme Odası (1822), Encümen-i Daniş (1851), Tercüme Cemiyeti (1865), Daire-i İlmiye (1869), Telif ve Tercüme Dairesi (1879), and Telif ve Tercüme Heyeti (1912). These state-run initiatives were predicated on the notion that in order to implement successful modernization reforms, intellectual openness to "the outside" (i.e., Europe) was necessary.[7] Similarly, the translation program of the new Turkish Republic was designed by the cultural bureaucratic elite and oriented towards Europe. Yet the Republican program presented a clear break with its predecessors in one particular aspect: It drew its repertoire from the canon of Western literary and philosophical humanism. The Kemalist elite invested fervently on translated humanism as a key constituent of instituting a new national culture in Turkey because they regarded it to be perfectly compatible with the ideological pillars, the "six arrows," of the Turkish cultural revolution: namely, Republicanism, nationalism, populism, laicism, statism, and revolutionism.[8] But what historical factors led to this unusual coexistence of an extensive practice of translation with a passionately articulated Turkish nationalism?

A Turkish Renaissance

Although the new republic was filled with a euphoric sense of excitement of independence, sovereignty, self-determination, and emancipation, the physical destruction of a long war and the psychological trauma of defeat had left the country in utter devastation. As a firsthand witness, Yakup Kadri Karaosmanoğlu, one of the most influential novelists of the early Republican period, would remember these turbulent years as follows: "We opened our eyes to the world in the hour of a catastrophe. We were like castaways saying their last prayers on a sinking ship: *Hosanna, Hosanna!* [Save us!]."[9] On the occasion of the opening of the Grand National Assembly in 1923, Atatürk reiterated the same sentiment through different imagery: "In its current condition, the homeland appears as nothing but a territory of black soil devoid of any sign of life and civilization."[10] The country was in need of reconstruction and revival in every aspect. Atatürk was adamant that the new Turkish state had to be built upon new foundations different from the historical institutions that preceded it. In the same speech that he delivered in the national assembly, he cautioned the emergent ruling class:

> Gentlemen! The grand idea that emancipated the leading nations of the world is the relentless enemy of those who set their hopes on fusty institutions and decayed ways of governance. Austria, Germany, Russia, and even the most conservative civilization in the world, China, were toppled in front of our eyes by the crushing blows of that grand idea. Therefore, gentlemen, our new state is the manifestation of that grand and omnipotent idea dominating the world.[11]

The "great and omnipotent idea" was none other than a westernized, secular and modern nation-state that would not only exorcise the specters of the old for once and all but also ensure national survival and territorial sovereignty.

Turkey followed a particular pattern of nationalism. For Gellner, if nationalism basically referred to the marriage of state ("groom") and culture ("bride"), then "the paths to this blessed marriage" took different forms, "according to the availability and condition of the partners."[12] To use Gellner's allegory, in the Turkish case, the groom (in the form of a consolidated state elite) was present; yet he was not so much in love with the bride. The groom felt superior to Anatolian Turks and certainly hated the "reactionary" elements they inherited from the ancien régime. Furthermore, although Turkey's declared intent was to adopt a "Western style" of modernity, this was carried out in a "fundamentalist" and "scripturalist" method with very little tolerance for ambiguity or indeterminacy.[13] "The Kemalist ulama"—Gellner's epithet for the Republican elite—envisioned the world in terms of a perpetual struggle between life, reason, reality, will, and action on the one hand, and decadence, decline, stagnation, feudalism, and superstition on the other. In this Manichean framework, the good forces came from the West, the bad ones from the rest. This "puritanical" consecration of Western civilization could be best exemplified in the following "sermon" by none other than Atatürk himself:

> It is futile to try to resist the thunderous advance of civilization, for it has no pity on those who are ignorant or rebellious. The sublime force of civilization pierces mountains, crosses the skies, enlightens and explores everything from the smallest particle of dust to stars. . . . When faced with this, those nations who try to follow the superstitions of the Middle Ages are condemned to be destroyed or at least to become enslaved and debased. . . . Civilization is such a fire that it burns and destroys those who ignore it.[14]

The "Empire to Republic" generation of the Turkish intelligentsia which, like the owl of Minerva, appeared "between the dark night of the Ottoman Empire and the dusk of the Turkish Republic" was in close agreement with the leader.[15] This generation, as represented by key figures such as Celal Nuri İleri claimed that the Turkish nation had to recover immediately from "the spiritual malaise caused by the way of thinking that prevailed for thousands of years."[16] Although they argued that the Turkish nation was young and energetic with strong will and ambition, Turkey also had an impoverished past. Due to the historical influence of Persian-Arabic cultures, "the creative character of the Turkish spirit" was too emasculated to enjoy a respectable status in the world. What was to be done in the absence of a past to which the nation could refer? What would be the source of reference for renewal? The answer for this generation was clear and simple: Europe. "The West," Celal Nuri wrote, "has a richer past than ours, whereas we inherited merely a handful of Islamic conceptions."[17] Ancient Greece and Rome, medieval Christianity, and early modern Renaissance coalesced and created a synthesis that shaped all facets of modern Western culture. In Celal Nuri's opinion, European languages, arts, and aesthetics were powerful because they had strong roots. "If we are to live as a free, independent, developed, and progressive nation," he cautioned, "we have to benefit from this accumulated wealth. Just as Peter the Great's Russia and Mutsuhito's Japan bid farewell to the past and accepted Europe's superior methods in their entirety, so too we must borrow them to the letter."[18] The West would provide Turkey with the new cultural capital it needed to achieve its national Renaissance. In their conception, "rebirth" meant Turkey's "resurrection from death" (*Türk basülbadelmevti*) and the recipe for warding off the threat of annihilation was to adopt "a civilizationist state nationalism" (İnsel 2001:21). The creation of a new Turkish state and society, in other words, was conceived as a modernizing and civilizing project on the basis of reconciling nationalism and Westernism. In this formula, nationalization, modernization, westernization, secularization, progress, and civilization correlated with one another.

For the Turkish intelligentsia, renaissance was conceived as a deliberate solution for changing Turkey's civilizational identity in order to secure a respectable status in the modern, secular nation-state system. They also believed that by adopting a Western identity, Turkey would be able to continue its hegemonic leadership among other Muslim nations. Mehmet İzzet—a translator of Neo-Kantian idealist philosophy and author of *Milliyet Nazariyeleri ve Millî Hayat* ("Theories of Nationalism and National Life," 1924)—stated this conviction explicitly: "History is preparing us for a new dominant role in the intellectual and moral development of the Eastern nations. We have to prove that we deserve to take on this honorable role."[19] But for Mehmet İzzet and his generation, in a somewhat paradoxical way, the key prerequisite for donning that role was to sever ties with the Muslim Orient. This separation, they thought, would allow Turkey "to be like Europe." In this vision of "mimetic modernity,"[20] Turkey would not only emulate the West but also *represent* it. More strikingly, through this identification with Europe, Turkey would perform a civilizing mission in the East. As Halil Nimetullah Öztürk, author of *İnkılâbın Felsefesi* ("The Philosophy of the Revolution," 1928) and translator of Henri Bergson, wrote: "The Turkish cultural revolution carrie[d] the *human* responsibility to serve as a source of knowledge and civilization for the Eastern nations."[21] Young Turkey would translate, study, absorb, and "master" the West not only for itself but for the entire Orient. As a translating mediator, it would close the gap between backward East and advanced West. Needless to say, the Kemalist cultural elite did not signal any discomfort with the implicit hierarchical logic embedded in their argument, which assumed some nations to be backward and some advanced. What mattered was Turkey's inclusion in the second category.

In a way, the Kemalists were rejecting the pattern that Partha Chatterjee has identified as the synthetic formula of national identity based on a miraculous reconciliation of "the superior material qualities of Western cultures with the spiritual greatness of the East."[22] The cultural elite of the Kemalist era was convinced that the post-Ottoman political and cultural identity that synthesized Turkish, Muslim, and Western elements together was flawed. In their eyes, Ottoman modernizing reformers had wasted a century in the name of creating a composite society nurtured by confusing hybrid values, which amounted to nothing but delaying the Turkish cultural awakening. Now it was time to rectify that historical error.

The first step in Kemalist monism was to posit European modernity as the authentic form of Turkishness. From that perspective, culture (Turkish) and civilization (European) constituted a "natural" and "essential" unity.[23] Thus, Europe was not external to the national self. As one of the later apologists of Kemalism would say, "the West was a means of unearthing the Turk's forgotten or repudiated inborn civilized traits."[24] The Kemalists argued that they were not adopting *one* civilization among others but the *totality* of all previous civilizations. Europe, therefore, was not a particular civilization among others but the incarnation of the universal. This slippery move between the universal and the particular offered the Kemalists strategic leverage in addressing the question of why Turkey needed to follow Europe: The Geist of human civilization in modern times manifested itself in the West. Yet let us keep in mind that beneath this seemingly comfortable solution was the bitter acknowledgment of defeat, as stated by most strikingly by Burhan Asaf, one of the first official Turkish intellectuals to ask the question of "How to arrive at humanism?": "The creator of the victorious civilization is the victorious culture, and the source of this culture is one and singular: Renaissance—Hellenism—Humanism on a Greco-Latin axis."[25]

The Humanist Canon and Cultural Revolution

The institutional, intellectual, and political history of humanist translation in Turkey was inseparably linked to this complex set of national expectations as well as anxieties around the emergence of modern Turkey. As cultural critic Orhan Koçak points out, "the cultural policies of the Republic were determined by a deep anxiety and by the psychological, intellectual and institutional defense mechanisms to cope with it. At the source of this anxiety, we find the feeling of historical belatedness."[26] Turkey's attraction to humanism certainly emerged as a symptom of this mood of belatedness. In one of the earlier formulations of the humanist project in Turkey, Yakup Kadri Karaosmanoğlu wrote:

> Although we are entering a period of renaissance, we may feel melancholic and sorrowful in the face of the fact that Western nations went through this period successfully

Translated Humanism and the Making of Modern Turkey

three centuries ago and accordingly, surpassed us considerably in this felicitous movement of civilization.[27]

While acknowledging the issue of time lag, he also argued that there was no reason to fall into despair:

> There may actually be some advantages of this belatedness. One of the advantages is that the path that we aspire to take is already paved and prepared by our predecessors. In order to save ourselves from the darkness of the Medieval Ages, we do not have to go through (like they did) a long and fervent period of hesitation and confusion, wandering and fluttering unnecessarily in all directions. In some respect, the first pioneers of the great path of progress and development have also labored for us. . . . They are collectively called "humanists," or "*insaniyatçı*" in our new language.[28]

In Yakup Kadri's passionate description, the humanists were like genies, tapping on the classical fountains of elixir—Homer, Sophocles, Aeschylus, Pindar, Virgil, Horace, Euripides, Seneca, and Lucretius—to bring forth a miraculous rebirth. What made the West a triumphant civilization, he argued, was classical humanist education. If the humanist canon embodied all the cultural values that created the West, then going directly, quickly, and systematically to the origins would compensate for the historical delay. Although the Ottoman intellectual engagement with European culture and literature remained superficial, fragmented, incoherent, incomplete, and undisciplined, Yakup Kadri argued, Turkey could reach a deep understanding of Europe in a short time through its humanist roots. Humanism would make Turkey "European in essence," not merely "Europeanized in appearance." Humanism not only played a key discursive role in overcoming the civilization and culture dichotomy outlined above but also gave a seemingly universal face to Westernization. From that perspective, becoming Western meant joining the progressive advancement of the human intellect and world civilization that began with Greece.

Along with this universalizing consecration of European humanist culture, Turkish intellectual circles of the 1930s and 1940s advocated the creation of a Turkish-specific version of humanism (*Türk hümanizması*). This discourse was based on a peculiar equation between nationalism and humanism, as expressed in its most tautological form by Burhan Asaf:

> The twentieth century is not an era in which nations that fail to accomplish their humanism can survive as a nation. This point should have been clear to us [Turkish] intellectuals since the Tanzimat. A powerful nation is powerful thanks to constructing a powerful nationalism on the basis of a powerful humanist education and learning.[29]

Turkish humanism emerged as a paradigm of self-discovery and cultural renaissance that would place Turkey in a respected position in the presumed historical progress of world civilization. Its advocates intended to shift the center of gravity of modern Turkish national identity to the Mediterranean (as opposed to the Central Asian "steppes" or the "deserts" of Persia and Arabia) and envisioned Turkey as the most qualified country to rise as the center of a new humanism in the twentieth century.

For the Turkish intelligentsia, one key area for demonstrating a country's high status in the universal humanist civilization was literature. Great literature made a great nation. To this end, in tandem with the discourse of national humanism, the Turkish intellectuals of the period invented a new concept of literature for Turkey called the "literature of the revolution" (*inkılap edebiyatı*). This formulation of a new literature had to do with their perception of national prestige in the global scene. They measured prestige by the number of universally consecrated writers that a nation boasted in the international literary order. Only literatures with strong national qualities could enter world literary space and put their own distinguished color on literary forms, genres, and conventions. Weaker national literatures, therefore, had to strive for occupying the highest possible ladder in the hierarchy. In the view of the Turkish cultural elite, it was due to the lack of a historically strong national essence that Turkish literature was too weak to attain a respected status in the international literary system. Turkish literature remained invisible, for the Turks had failed to add a genius to the internationally consecrated company of the Scandinavian Ibsen, the Russian Gorky, or the Indian Tagore. The culprit, once again, was the "Oriental" direction of pre-Republican Turkey, which, under the damaging influence of Persian and Arabic literature, produced a "degenerative" and "imitative" literature. The hybridization of Turkish literature with those literatures resulted in nothing but "a handful of tedious love tales, individualistic passions, [and] lifeless objects."[30] The old aesthetic regime not only delayed nationalization but also increased Turkey's distance from the European literary center.

What was the solution? The Kemalists were adamant that the literature that the Turkish cultural revolution envisioned would not arise from the debris of Ottoman literature. There was hardly anything that the old literature could offer. The latter, they argued, was too obsolete and incomprehensible to exist in modern literary culture and was far removed from the spirit of the Republican regime. The cultural elite did not find much hope in folk literature either. The latter could at best provide some motifs or flavors, but was still "too primitive to match the standards of modern world literature."[31] According to this positivist approach to literary modernization, Turkish folk literature needed its Herder and Grimm Brothers first. They also dismissed the Turkish literature of the late Ottoman period, which modeled itself after nineteenth-century French literature, for being "cosmopolitan, passive, decadent, hybrid, and colonial."[32] Turkish literature was in crisis and this crisis could be overcome by adopting a new form of classicism based on rational, universal, and secular principles. Even Ziya Gökalp, a great advocate of Turkish folk literature, would argue that

> the masterpieces of classical literature are the best models for a new national literature. Without first digesting all the aesthetic nutrition from the classics, Turkish literature should not approach other literary movements. Young nations need a literature that celebrates ideals and heroisms, and classical literatures are perfect for fulfilling this purpose.[33]

Apprenticeship in humanist classicism, which Ziya Gökalp defined as "our period of gaining competence in the museum of European masterpieces," would teach Turkish writers and artists how to express their feelings and sensations (the raw material of creative labor) with reason, balance, and discipline. Humanism, therefore, would lay the foundation for the institution of a new literary culture and "a style of national life" in Republican Turkey.[34]

While exceedingly critical of Arabic and Persian as obsolete and non-modern, the Kemalist elite saw enormous advantages in the fact that Greek and Latin literatures were based on "dead" languages. Both languages not only had a rich reservoir of words and styles to express the human condition but also became crystallized and free from any change in form and meaning. The literature of new Turkish would reach a much more advanced stage by opening itself up to Greek and Latin, just as contemporary national literatures of Europe did earlier. Thanks to classical sources, modern European languages had risen to become "producers of the highest literatures of the world."[35] Yet it was also clear that the creation of a new national canon in Turkish that could meet expectations would not happen overnight. Until Turkey could generate its own canon that would serve as reference for becoming idealist, committed, and enlightened citizens of the new republic, the vacuum had to be filled with translated texts of the humanist canon.

In addition to its generative and legitimating role in the visions for Turkish history, literature, and language, translated humanism was used to shape Kemalist reforms in the areas of higher education and civic pedagogy, too. The Kemalists envisioned humanistic studies in the new university as a way to close the gap between what they saw as Ottoman scholastic backwardness and modern knowledge. To this end, during the interwar period, the Turkish state invited German humanist scholars who lost their academic posts after the rise of Nazism—including Erich Auerbach and Leo Spitzer, the "founding fathers" of comparative literature—to establish language and literature departments at Istanbul and Ankara universities in line with the methods of modern European philology.[36]

The institution of humanistic studies at the university overlapped with the implementation of a colossal state translation program called "Translations from World Literature" (*Dünya Edebiyatından Tercümeler*). World literature functioned as an ideological state apparatus in the cultural agenda of the Turkish cultural elite. The state positioned itself both as an agent of translation and a direct intervener in the circulation of translated texts among citizen-readers. Notwithstanding its elitist discourse, Kemalist culture planning had a strongly populist character. As the following quotation from Hüseyin Avni Başman—a pedagogue and translator of John Dewey's treatise *The School and Society* (*Mektep ve Cemiyet*, 1929)—would reveal, their notion of populism was formulated in terms of an internal civilizing mission and as the sum of sacrifices that the elite was willing to make for their compatriots: "To work for the people until there is not a single Turkish peasant whom we have not saved, enlightened with the light of civilization, and endowed with [a decent] human life."[37]

Under the strange slogan of "for the people, in spite of the people," the Kemalists claimed that in order to save the masses from the oppressive influence and dominance of conservative forces ("internal enemies"), compulsory cultural transformation was necessary. Idealizing culture as the potent power that would enable the nation's transition from backward material conditions to the advanced material life of contemporary civilization, the Kemalist cultural elite envisioned themselves as an army of revolutionary and forward-looking pioneers committed to "a crusade against ignorance," the root of all "evil." The philistines (*kültürsüz adamlar*) not only lacked character and morals but also posed a threat to the nation. The state had to mobilize all its sources to transform these minds that for centuries had become "prisoners of old superstitious beliefs and dogmas." Civic pedagogy, therefore, was particularly urgent for a country such as Turkey, whose majority population was still living in rural conditions. To "convert" from a peasant dependent on God's grace to an enlightened individual under the guidance of the state, the Turkish citizen needed "the cultural knowledge that would enable them to discover their intellectual and spiritual capabilities."[38] Convinced that the European Renaissance took place thanks to culture, not economic factors, they measured the success of the Turkish revolution by the extent to which culture could penetrate into Anatolia.[39]

It is not, of course, surprising to find some dose of populist enlightenment mission in any nation-state project. However, Kemalism was arguably unique in terms of ascribing translated humanism a central role in the education and cultivation of "acceptable" citizens.[40] The interest in humanist classics was strongly tied to the state's desire for an organized program of *paideia* to raise and cultivate ideal members of the polis. The humanist canon offered them the artillery they needed to attack all the undesirable elements from the national body and to raise the Turkish nation as "an advanced cultured member of the family of humanity." Individuals trained in classical humanist education (*klasik terbiye*) would be equipped with reason, knowledge, and will to resist instincts, temptations, and other imprudence that led to religious fanaticism and archaic practices. The pedagogic function of the humanist canon in Turkey culminated in the implementation of the translation program by the Ministry of Education's Translation Bureau. The state played a regulatory and supervisory role not only in the construction of the world literature canon in Turkey but also facilitated its dissemination through cultural institutions such as the People's Houses, People's Reading-Rooms, and the Village Institutes, which were conceived as channels of introducing the principles of Kemalism, on the one hand and Western cultural forms and practices on the other. In addition to being affordable and educational, the Translations from World Literature series was also a safe way of controlling what people read. In particular, the cultural bureaucratic elite believed that by "feeling and living" the texts of the Western canon at the subjective level, the reader-citizens would go through the desired cultural internalization and transformation.

Conclusion

Did translated humanism offer a viable solution to Turkey's cultural quest? Did the solutions, practices, and dissemination tactics proposed by the cultural elite lead to stable solutions and effective outcomes? It might best to approach these questions in the light of a keen insight about the concept of culture planning by none other than the scholar who introduced it to translation studies, Itamar Even-Zohar:

> We are too often tempted, for the sake of elegance of description, to accept neatly finalized states. In matters of culture planning, as with all matters of culture analysis, neat states are only temporary, and even then, visible at only some sector of the overall network of relations we call "society" or "culture." Accordingly, at the very moment when a given enterprise, the implementation of a certain repertoire fought for by dedicated individuals, has reached its peak, it may already be on its way towards disintegration and irrelevance for the emerging new circumstances, those which would call for another, different repertoire.[41]

This is precisely what happened with the political purge of the humanist faction of the Turkish intellectual establishment at the end of World War II. Under the pressures of the new geopolitical realities, Turkey had to shift from a single-party regime to a multiparty system. In an unexpected turn of events, the humanist translation project became a convenient target for new incumbent power groups to attack the former cultural elite and after the 1950s, it gradually began to lose its hegemonic status in Turkey's cultural politics. Although the legacy of state-sponsored humanism may have had fair success in generating a certain nexus of literary production that suited the purposes of both the new state and its cultural elite, it could never escape lingering questions about its authenticity and derivativeness.

As a study of how a certain vision of the power of translation played an operative role in the making of modern Turkey, this chapter aims to disrupt the assumption, common among scholars, that humanist world literature was a normative ideal that primarily served cosmopolitan and transnational aspirations in the face of the political and cultural upheavals during the turbulent decades of the twentieth century. If anything, the institutional, intellectual, and political history of the Turkish case tells us that humanist world literature itself was already caught up in the tensions between nationalism and transnationalism, universalism and particularism, religious and secular, modern and traditional. The making of world literature during the making of modern Turkey must serve as an important reminder for us to examine more carefully the historical role of translation in the contested processes of nation-building in non-western societies, the relationship between humanistic studies and cultural reforms, and the impact of the state in the production of literary capital.

Notes

1 Quoted in Şükrü Hanioğlu, *Atatürk: An Intellectual Biography* (Princeton, NJ: Princeton University Press, 2011), 155.
2 Recep Cengiz, ed., *Atatürk'ün Okuduğu Kitaplar* (Ankara: Anıtkabir Derneği Yayınları, 2001).
3 Şerif Mardin, "Projects as Methodology: Some Thoughts on Modern Turkish Social Science," in *Rethinking Modernity and National Identity in Turkey*, ed. Sibel Bozdoğan and Reşat Kasaba (Seattle: University of Washington Press, 1997), 64–80.
4 Nergis Ertürk, *Grammatology and Literary Modernity in Turkey* (New York: Oxford University Press, 2011), 72.
5 Wiebke Denecke, *Classical World Literatures: Sino-Japanese and Greco-Roman Comparisons* (Oxford: Oxford University Press, 2014), 4.
6 Hasan Ali Yücel, *Kültür Üzerine Düşünceler* (Ankara: Türkiye İş Bankası Yayınları, 1974), 221–22.
7 Taceddin Kayaoğlu, *Türkiye'de Tercüme Müesseseleri* (Istanbul: Kitabevi, 1998).
8 Erik J. Zürcher, *Turkey: A Modern History* (London: I. B. Tauris, 2013), 176–205.
9 Yakup Kadri Karaosmanoğlu, *Atatürk: Biyografik Tahlil Denemesi* (Istanbul: İletişim Yayınları, 2014), 29.
10 *TBMM Zabıt Ceridesi,* term II, vol. 1 (Ankara: Türkiye Büyük Millet Meclisi, 1923), 36, http://hdl.handle.net/11543/1677.
11 Ibid.
12 Ernest Gellner, "The Turkish Option in Comparative Perspective," in *Rethinking Modernity and National Identity in Turkey*, ed. Sibel Bozdoğan and Reşat Kasaba (Seattle: University of Washington Press, 1997), 240.
13 Reşat Kasaba, "Kemalist Certainties and Modern Ambiguities," in *Rethinking Modernity and National Identity in Turkey*, ed. Sibel Bozdoğan and Reşat Kasaba (Seattle: University of Washington Press, 1997), 27.
14 Quoted in ibid., 26.
15 Murat Belge, "Mustafa Kemal ve Kemalizm," in *Modern Türkiye'de Siyasi Düşünce: Kemalizm*, ed. Ahmet İnsel (Istanbul: İletişim Yayınları, 2001), 29.
16 Celal Nuri İleri, "Milletin Tecdidi," in *Atatürk Devri Fikir Hayatı*, ed. Mehmet Kaplan et al., vol. I (Ankara: Kültür Bakanlığı Yayınları, 1992), 52.
17 Ibid., 53.
18 Ibid.
19 M. İzzet, "Türk'ün Rolü," *Hayat* 2, no. 50 (1927): 463–64.
20 Bryan S. Turner, *Weber and Islam* (London: Routledge, 1998), 163.
21 Halil Nimetullah Öztürk, "Türk İnkılabının Şümulü," *Milli Mecmua* 9, no. 99 (1927): 1590–91.
22 Partha Chatterjee, *Nationalist Thought and the Colonial World: A Derivative Discourse* (London: Zed Books, 1993), 51.
23 Tanıl Bora, "İnşa Döneminde Türk Milli Kimliği," *Toplum ve Bilim* 71 (1996): 168–92; Ayşe Kadıoğlu, "The Paradox of Turkish Nationalism and the Construction of Official Identity," *Middle Eastern Studies* 32, no. 2 (1996): 177–93.
24 Tarık Zafer Tunaya, *Türkiye'nin Siyasi Hayatında Batılılaşma Hareketleri* (Istanbul: Yedigün Matbaası, 1960), 112.
25 Burhan Asaf, "Hümanizm'e nasıl gidebiliriz?" *Ulus*, December 20, 1938.
26 Orhan Koçak, "1920'lerden 1970'lere Kültür Politikaları," in *Modern Türkiye'de Siyasi Düşünce: Kemalizm*, ed. Ahmet İnsel (Istanbul: İletişim Yayınları, 2001), 371.
27 Yakup Kadri Karaosmanoğlu, "Avrupakârî, Avrupaî," *Hâkimiyet-i Milliye*, July 1, 1924.
28 Ibid.
29 Burhan Asaf, "İnsan ve Kültür: Milliyetçilikte Realizm ve Rasyonalizm," *Ulus*, December 15, 1938.
30 Kâzım Nami Duru, "İnkılap Edebiyatı," *Ülkü* 3, no. 13 (1934): 52–53.
31 Hasan Ali Yücel, *Pazartesi Konuşmaları* (Istanbul: Remzi Kitabevi, 1937), 83.
32 Yakup Kadri Karaosmanoğlu, "Edebiyat Buhranına Dair," *Kadro* 1, no. 8 (1932): 27.
33 Ziya Gökalp, *Türkçülüğün Esasları* (Istanbul: Ötüken Neşriyat, 2015), 112.

34 Yakup Kadri Karaosmanoğlu, "Ham Madde ve Halkla Sanatkar," *Kadro* 1, no. 3 (1932): 17.
35 Kâzım Nami Duru, "Humanisma," *Ülkü* 3, no. 17 (1934): 333.
36 Fırat Oruç, "Rewriting the Legacy of the Turkish Exile of Comparative Literature: Nationalism and Philology in Turkey, 1933–1946," *Journal of World Literature* 3, no. 3 (2018): 334–53.
37 Hüseyin Avni Başman, "Halka Doğru," *Hayat* 1, no. 25 (1927): 481–82.
38 Nusret Kemal Köymen, "Köycülük Programına Giriş," *Ülkü* 5, no. 26 (1935): 139.
39 Necip Ali Küçüka, "Kültür ve Medeniyet," *Ülkü* 1, no. 3 (1933): 244–45.
40 Füsun Üstel, *"Makbul Vatandaş" ın Peşinde: II. Meşrutiyet'ten Bugüne Türkiye'de Vatandaş Eğitimi* (Istanbul: İletişim Yayınlar, 2011), 175.
41 Itamar Even-Zohar, "Culture Planning, Cohesion, and the Making and Maintenance of Entities," in *Beyond Descriptive Translation Studies: Investigations in Homage to Gideon Toury*, ed. Pym et al. (Philadelphia: John Benjamins, 2008), 288.

References

Asaf, Burhan. "Hümanizm'e nasıl gidebiliriz?" *Ulus*, December 20, 1938.
———. "İnsan ve Kültür: Milliyetçilikte Realizm ve Rasyonalizm." *Ulus*, December 15, 1938.
Başman, Hüseyin Avni. "Halka Doğru." *Hayat* 1, no. 25 (1927): 481–82.
Belge, Murat. "Mustafa Kemal ve Kemalizm." In *Modern Türkiye'de Siyasi Düşünce: Kemalizm*, edited by Ahmet İnsel, 29–43. Istanbul: İletişim Yayınları, 2001.
Bora, Tanıl. "İnşa Döneminde Türk Milli Kimliği." *Toplum ve Bilim* 71 (1996): 168–92.
Cengiz, Recep, ed. *Atatürk'ün Okuduğu Kitaplar*. Ankara: Anıtkabir Derneği Yayınları, 2001.
Chatterjee, Partha. *Nationalist Thought and the Colonial World: A Derivative Discourse*. London: Zed Books, 1993.
Denecke, Wiebke. *Classical World Literatures: Sino-Japanese and Greco-Roman Comparisons*. Oxford: Oxford University Press, 2014.
Duru, Kâzım Nami. "Humanisma." *Ülkü* 3, no. 17 (1934): 332–36.
———. "İnkılap Edebiyatı." *Ülkü* 3, no. 13 (1934): 46–53.
Ertürk, Nergis. *Grammatology and Literary Modernity in Turkey*. New York: Oxford University Press, 2011.
Even-Zohar, Itamar. "Culture Planning, Cohesion, and the Making and Maintenance of Entities." In *Beyond Descriptive Translation Studies: Investigations in Homage to Gideon Toury*, edited by A. Pym et al., 277–92. Philadelphia: John Benjamins, 2008.
Gellner, Ernest. "The Turkish Option in Comparative Perspective." In *Rethinking Modernity and National Identity in Turkey*, edited by Sibel Bozdoğan and Resat Kasaba, 233–44. Seattle: University of Washington Press, 1997.
Gökalp, Ziya. *Türkçülüğün Esasları*. Istanbul: Ötüken Neşriyat, 2015.
Hanioğlu, Şükrü. *Atatürk: An Intellectual Biography*. Princeton, NJ: Princeton University Press, 2011.
İleri, Celal Nuri. "Milletin Tecdidi." In *Atatürk Devri Fikir Hayatı*, edited by Mehmet Kaplan et al., vol. I, 52–57. Ankara: Kültür Bakanlığı Yayınları, 1992.
İnsel, Ahmet. "Giriş." In *Modern Türkiye'de Siyasi Düşünce: Kemalizm*, edited by Ahmet İnsel, 17–28. Istanbul: İletişim Yayınları, 2001.
İzzet, M. "Türk'ün Rolü." *Hayat* 2, no. 50 (1927): 463–64.
Kadıoğlu, Ayşe. "The Paradox of Turkish Nationalism and the Construction of Official Identity." *Middle Eastern Studies* 32, no. 2 (1996): 177–93.
Karaosmanoğlu, Yakup Kadri. "Avrupakârî, Avrupaî." *Hâkimiyet-i Milliye*, July 1, 1924.
———. "Edebiyat Buhranına Dair." *Kadro* 1, no. 8 (1932): 27–29.
———. "Ham Madde ve Halkla Sanatkar." *Kadro* 1, no. 3 (1932): 17–18.
———. *Atatürk: Biyografik Tahlil Denemesi*. Istanbul: İletişim Yayınları, 2014.
Kasaba, Resat. "Kemalist Certainties and Modern Ambiguities." In *Rethinking Modernity and National Identity in Turkey*, edited by Sibel Bozdoğan and Resat Kasaba, 15–36. Seattle: University of Washington Press, 1997.
Kayaoğlu, Taceddin. *Türkiye'de Tercüme Müesseseleri*. Istanbul: Kitabevi, 1998.
Koçak, Orhan. "1920 'lerden 1970' lere Kültür Politikaları." In *Modern Türkiye'de Siyasi Düşünce: Kemalizm*, edited by Ahmet İnsel, 370–81. Istanbul: İletişim Yayınları, 2001.
Köymen, Nusret Kemal. "Köycülük Programına Giriş." *Ülkü* 5, no. 26 (1935): 132–41.
Küçüka, Necip Ali. "Kültür ve Medeniyet." *Ülkü* 1, no. 3 (1933): 244–45.

Mardin, Şerif. "Projects as Methodology: Some Thoughts on Modern Turkish Social Science." In *Rethinking Modernity and National Identity in Turkey*, edited by Sibel Bozdoğan and Resat Kasaba, 64–80. Seattle: University of Washington Press, 1997.

Oruç, Fırat. "Rewriting the Legacy of the Turkish Exile of Comparative Literature: Nationalism and Philology in Turkey, 1933–1946." *Journal of World Literature* 3, no. 3 (2018): 334–53.

Öztü±k, Halil Nimetullah. "Türk İnkılabının Şümulü." *Milli Mecmua* 9, no. 99 (1927): 1590–91.

TBMM Zabıt Ceridesi, term II, vol. 1. Ankara: Türkiye Büyük Millet Meclisi, 1923. http://hdl.handle.net/11543/1677.

Tunaya, Tarık Zafer. *Türkiye'nin Siyasi Hayatında Batılılaşma Hareketleri*. Istanbul: Yedigün Matbaası, 1960.

Turner, Bryan S. *Weber and Islam*. London: Routledge, 1998.

Üstel, Füsun. *"Makbul Vatandaş" ın Peşinde: II. Meşrutiyet'ten Bugüne Türkiye'de Vatandaş Eğitimi*. Istanbul: İletişim Yayınlar, 2011.

Yücel, Hasan Ali. *Pazartesi Konuşmaları*. Istanbul: Remzi Kitabevi, 1937.

———. *Kültür Üzerine Düşünceler*. Ankara: Türkiye İş Bankası Yayınları, 1974.

Zürcher, Erik J. *Turkey: A Modern History*. London: I.B. Tauris, 2013.

SECTION VII

Literary Modernisms

22

ENVISIONING THE MODERN INDIVIDUAL IN LATE NINETEENTH-CENTURY OTTOMAN-TURKISH FICTION

Zeynep Uysal

The avant-garde literary movement known as "Servet-i Fünun" (The Wealth of Sciences) or "Edebiyat-ı Cedide" (The New Literature) appeared in the late nineteenth century in an environment that regarded literature as a political and social instrument to advocate modernization in the Ottoman Empire. Rejecting the socially oriented understanding of literature, the leading literary figures of the Servet-i Fünun literary movement, who gathered around the weekly magazine also titled *Servet-i Fünun*, radically changed the intellectual and cultural repertoire of literary creation by implementing extensive thematic and formal innovations both in poetry and fiction that had started with the previous generation of modernizing Ottoman intelligentsia in the mid-nineteenth century after the Ottoman encounter with modern Europe and its subsequent consequences created a major paradigm shift in Ottoman society, including in its literature.[1] The fear of lagging behind the new technological and scientific developments in the "civilized" world compelled the modernizing Ottoman intelligentsia to implement a series of rapid economic, political, and cultural modernization policies in the empire. In accordance with this, they also used the new means of communication—including newspapers, magazines, and literature—as effective tools to appropriate European modernity in the empire.[2] In contrast to these first modernizers, the following generation of literati, known as the *Servet-i Fünuncular*, regarded literature as an autonomous space and began to produce literature for literature's sake. In so doing, they refused the instrumentalization of literature to express social and political issues. Rather, they produced texts that explored the complex experiences of modernity and the predicaments of modern individuals in Ottoman society.

This chapter discusses how Ottoman individual experiences of modernity were imagined and the ways modernity constructed the individuals in two different yet intertwined mediums: the novel and the aforementioned weekly periodical published in the late nineteenth century. I will show how these cultural mediums imagine the modern individual in seemingly paradoxical ways inherent to the complexities and contradictions of modernity. I will contend that they were resemblances and differences between the content of the periodical and that of the novels serialized there. While *Servet-i Fünun* itself envisioned an ideal individual who possessed the willpower to change the world based on the idea of modern progress, the novels serialized in this very same magazine presented troubled characters whose desire constantly transgresses the limits of the social contract. This disconnect springs from the magazine's notion of an individual

DOI: 10.4324/9780429279270-30

271

based upon rationality and romantic progress, whereas the novels had the concept of an individual whose cravings are not formed by reason or morality. To demonstrate this, I will compare the nonliterary content of the journal with the novels of Halit Ziya Uşaklıgil, the leading writer of the movement.

The Nonfictional World of the *Servet-i Fünun* Journal

As a popular cultural medium to which Halit Ziya Uşaklıgil and other literary figures of the period actively contributed, the weekly *Servet-i Fünun* followed the illustrated format of French journals, especially *L'Illustration* or the English journal *Graphics*, and exhibited various features of contemporary Ottoman periodicals, such as *Malumat* and *Mektep*, that were published in the empire's capital Istanbul during the same years. Illustration was the most striking and distinguishing characteristic of this format used by major periodicals across Europe.[3] *Servet-i Fünun* had a very wide variety of coverage from science to the arts: Accompanied by illustrations, criticisms, poems, and serialized and translated novels, this periodical published news, reports, and articles providing views on the week's events, along with commentaries, information, and stories from Istanbul, other Ottoman provinces, and the rest of the world. The material published in *Servet-i Fünun* on these locations reveals how *Servet-i Fünun* intellectuals attempted to link their literary and cultural production with other geographies around the world.[4] The reflection of this attitude, which encompassed the empire and the world through the wide range of knowledge, is evident in the *ifade* (editorial note) in the first issue of the year 1896. Written by the owner Ahmet İhsan to demonstrate the policy change in the journal with the appointment of Tevfik Fikret as the editor-in-chief of the literary section in 1896, the editorial note, titled "Teşekkür ve İfade (Acknowledgment and Statement)," informs the reader about the new coverage and purpose of the journal. In particular, it singles out the two major purposes of the magazine: to publish local and international current news and pictures, including "Oriental landscapes," as well as original fiction and poetry in Ottoman Turkish.[5] As seen in this editorial note, from 1896 onwards the magazine clearly began to include equally news and photographs both from Ottoman provinces and the world. This notion of journalism also reveals how they transformed the perception of time and space through experiencing the opportunities and potentials of modernity. Mahmut Sadık, one of the prominent journalists in *Servet-i Fünun*, pointed out that the whole world had become smaller than a country, a city, or even a neighborhood for a meticulous individual thanks to knowledge as a product of discoveries, expedition, and scientific inquiry. In the following lines, he emphasizes the velocity of hearing about and knowing about an incident that happened on the other side of the globe thanks to telegraph cables. He then gives an example of how the Ottomans learned about the news of a war between Spain and the United States around Cuba right after it began. Due to travel on trains and modern ships, the newspapers published in Europe and the United States arrived in the Ottoman Empire within a few days and the Ottomans learned details about other societies. He briefly emphasizes that people meet each other, are informed about events around the world, and have started to travel more around the world thanks to the new means of transportation and communication.[6] As seen in his arguments, individuals inevitably associated differently with the world in an environment created by the rapid increase in communication and the spread of information.

This manifests how the *Servet-i Fünun* magazine sought to imagine an ideal individual based fundamentally on the values of Enlightenment rationality and urbanity in the changing Ottoman society. The detailed news articles on discoveries and expeditions printed in the journal informed the reader about new developments in the world. One of the foremost scientific expedition narratives was the series of articles about the Norwegian explorer Dr. Fridtjof Nansen's

Envisioning the Modern Individual in Late Nineteenth-Century Ottoman-Turkish Fiction

Arctic journey. This journey was welcomed in the pages of the magazine with great fascination and curiosity thanks to the writer of the series, Mahmut Sadık, who celebrated the courage and eagerness of the explorer's journey to the North Pole.[7] The article describes that before Nansen, there were many unsuccessful attempts to reach the pole before he eventually made the inaccessible destination accessible and realized an impossible desire:

> The Pole. Yes. To the Pole. . . . *Servet-i Fünun* keeps up with the rest of our city's periodicals in giving the details about Doctor Nansens's exotic and crucial expedition, during which he has been walking on the path to the frozen and unknown lands, holding a vigorous fire of passion and curiosity as many other science admirers and dreamers could only walk step by step at the risk of their lives.[8]

In these and the following sentences, Mahmut Sadık expresses his admiration for the traveler Nansen, who achieved his dreams for humanity and his respect for the man's courage and grandiosity.

In a similar way, in the 320th issue of *Servet-i Fünun*, Tevfik Fikret, the leading poet of Servet-i Fünun literary period, published a poem with exactly the same title: "Kutba Doğru" (To The Pole). The poem praises Nansen's heroic courage to reach his goal in the name of humanity, as well as his journey full of suffering and tribulation that promised only scientific glory. In particular, the poem stresses that human beings are not born for comfort and must go after their dreams in order to reach the meaning of life, finding a close connection between the importance of progress in civilization and a modern Prometheus, symbolized by Nansen's accomplishment of discovering the North Pole.[9]

The concept of individuality as an agent/subject in power, as defined in Mahmut Sadık's articles and Tevfik Fikret's poem through the description of Nansen's voyage, is seen concurrently both in popular scientific articles and fiction published in *Servet-i Fünun*. On the one hand, these texts depict the work and struggle of individuals for progress and civilization; on the other hand, they portray the will and courage of the modern subject in pursuing their grand desires and goals. In this respect, the North Pole journey is a significant example of the journal's editorial policy, which juxtaposed science and art in a manner similar to its many European contemporaries. It also envisioned a world intertwined with literature, art, current news, and popularized science in order to be accessible to the imagined reader. In doing this, *Servet-i Fünun* tried to show the vastness of the world in which they lived at the turn of the century Ottoman society while also building a model for a new individuality and proper citizenship based upon a modern understanding of time and space.

This new kind of individual or reader who was able to access far distant knowledge, travel, dream of other lives and places was to be a subject or agent following scientific exploration and participating in the cultural and artistic events of the time; they were expected to go beyond the limited space because of their curiosity about the world. These modern subjects were exposed to various yet superficial stacks of information, thus becoming a part of modern progress through their own minds. The journal aimed to show the vastness of the world by taking the reader or individuals outside of their small world and triggering their curiosity and desires through the romanticized stories of the nineteenth-century expeditions—such as the journey to the North Pole—and great scientific inventions—including the X-ray, photograph, microbe, and electricity—that made unseen visible at the turn of the century. Their promised world was full of endless riches and brand-new magical inventions. Especially the writings and photographs of scientific/technological inventions published in the journal (e.g., the electrical vehicle, electrical sea tram, cinematography, the newly invented tram without horses, telegram, radiograph, wheeled steamer, winged bicycle, winged balloon, bicycled sled, submarine boat, artificial organ) reflect the vision of these cultural figures and their fascination by the human will to create.[10] This outlook demonstrates a transformation from a religious- or divine-oriented world to a secular one through the scientific vision that refashioned the world humans inhabit. It also presents their changing perception of time concretized as linear time rather natural.

This curious individual/citizen was also imagined as an agent capable of filling their living space with modern daily living practices. The writings in the journal illustrate not only the aforementioned worldview but also the individual's private space displaying all aspects of modern urban life. In this regard, for example, one of the longest-running series in *Servet-i Fünun*, "Istanbul Mail," attempted to provide weekly guidance about the capital city's daily life.[11] It reported news about weather conditions, current cultural and artistic events, the status of the city's architectural and constructional developments, and complaints and critiques about urban infrastructure written in a conversational mode by Ahmet İhsan himself, the owner and the editor-in-chief of the magazine. Resembling the "Paris Mail" in its contemporary magazine *L'Illustration*, "Istanbul Mail" addressed itself to citizens living in the nineteenth-century capital of the Ottoman Empire to remind them of the quotidian details of modern individuals in such a way that provoked the reader's desires and curiosity. Ahmet İhsan wrote the entries attracting the attention of urban individuals, such as weekly culture and entertainment events in the city, famous troupes, actors/actresses coming from Europe, coach trips on the promenade, crowded avenues and boulevards, and Ramadan festivities. The conversational tone and subjective position of the narrator in this series indicated the personal perspective of the author. At the same time, it functioned as the guidance for urban life in Ottoman society.[12] As seen in these examples, *Servet-i Fünun* envisioned a new man (typically gendered as male) whose desire and curiosity would pave the way for progress and civilized society through scientific exploration and developments. This modern subject would also live in a modern city where s/he spent daily life sharing common cultural and joyful practices of public space as a consequence of recent urbanization.

The Fictional World of Halit Ziya Uşaklıgil

The imagined individual that appeared in the nonfictional writings in the weekly journal can be also seen in the fictional works serialized there. However, these fictional individuals were constructed in much more complex and multilayered ways than they were imagined in the nonfictional material. The fiction of Halit Ziya, the most prominent writer of the period, played a significant role in showing the distinction between the nonfictional and fictional imagination. He published many of his short stories and three novels first as serials which were juxtaposed with this nonfictional world of the periodical. At first glance, his portrayal of characters' worlds seems completely coherent within the vision of the nonfiction medium. Yet when one looks more closely, his fictional texts narrate the disillusionment of the individual whose desires and ambitions are prevented from being realized by their very social and consistent inner conflicts. This is because *Servet-i Fünun* celebrated infinite progress based upon modern rationality and scientific development while the fictional world presented there fundamentally explored the boundaries of the individual whose desires ensure progress yet are limited by the social contract. In other words, although this horizon shown in the magazine—everyday life habits, the possibilities offered by technology—constitutes the context of fiction, and the world of objects surrounding the individual belongs to this modern world, the individual cannot self-actualize within this fictional world.

Envisioning the Modern Individual in Late Nineteenth-Century Ottoman-Turkish Fiction

The novels of Halit Ziya describe the boundaries of desires, inevitable (self-)destruction, and the desolation of individuals who initially possess a plenitude of hope with infinite dreams and wide-open horizons. They then drift into bad subjectivity when they come across the barriers and invisible rules of the social contract. Halit Ziya accomplished this portrayal of conflict by creating a novelistic style and generic form that both took into account the cultural agenda of his own social environment and appropriated contemporary western literary understandings. From the beginning of his literary career, he questioned the literary conventions of his age. In fact, he wrote a book to advocate realism in contrast with romanticism as an established literary trend of the period. Halit Ziya put forth fundamentally similar arguments to promote literary realism in the Ottoman context in accordance with his European contemporaries. Among these arguments, one is particularly significant to my discussion. He argues that literature, in particular the novel, must understand and fictionalize human beings, the individual and his/her inner world, capacity of feeling, and the motivations for their actions while emphasizing the importance of the realist novel as a genre for narrating the human condition and people's complex inner struggles.[13]

Accordingly, Halit Ziya specifically produced fictional narratives describing and disclosing in detail the modern Ottoman individual's complicated experiences. His characters are always portrayed as desiring individuals. They make choices in life and make their own decisions in accordance with their strong desires. They, therefore, become the agents of their own acts. In turn, this agency makes them an actor/actress in their tragic life stories. The novels published before Halit Ziya's, such as *Felatun Bey ve Rakım Efendi* (1875), *Henüz On Yedi Yaşında* (1881), and *İntibah* (1876), portrayed immoral characters and ridiculed those whose desire or curiosity contradicts proper and moral protagonists. However, from his first novels onwards Halit Ziya criticized and challenged the novels of Ahmet Mithat and Namık Kemal to transform ridiculed or immoral stereotypes into characters who think, desire, and ask through their agency.

In addition, the changing role of the narrator focalizing the character was used by Halit Ziya to describe an individual's story whereas the omniscient narrators of the earlier novels openly revealed their thoughts and feelings in order to impose their worldview on the reader. Halit Ziya's narrative perspective was used to disclose the conflicting inner world of the characters, their perceptions and point of view formed by impressions of reality, not the visible outside world. Not only the position of the narrator but also his persistent quest for an aesthetic literary language differentiated him and his generation from the former generation who prioritized simple language for social use. Halit Ziya's works, like other Servet-i Fünun writers, reflect the dark side of human lives, sorrows, and agonies whereas the journal's nonfictional world mostly narrated success stories through explorations, expeditions, scientific inventions, and models for modern humanity within an idealized environment as the new reality.

Producing texts in the context of the fin de siècle, for Halit Ziya truth was not only a thing seen or grasped by the senses but rather generated by art; thus, art recreates nature and truth according to the artist's subjective thoughts and feelings. In this respect, the approach of Halit Ziya's fiction springs from Flaubert's phrase "There is no truth. There are ways of seeing."[14] Halit Ziya shows the different ways of seeing and modes of perception through the character's gaze and unveils the hidden meanings of objects and things that make up the world of his protagonists. He also reflects the impressions of the scientific gaze and wonder for the world evident in *Servet-i Fünun* onto objects that represent the desires of the characters in his novelistic world.

His fictional characters are examples of the nineteenth century's desiring individuals. In *How Novels Think*, Nancy Armstrong discusses the experiences of fictional individuals in the eighteenth- and nineteenth-century British novel. She writes, "A character had to harbor an acute dissatisfaction with his or her assigned position in the social world and feel compelled to find a better one" in order to become the protagonist of a novel.[15] This means that severe uneasiness is the determinant for the protagonist to long for a new life. In other words, uneasiness brings with it acute desires. Armstrong emphasizes the unwillingness "to adjust the subject completely to the social world into which he or she was born" as a characteristic feature of eighteenth-century novels.[16] In a similar way, the characters of Halit Ziya's novels were primarily captured by this very desire along with a similar feeling of dissatisfaction and restlessness.

Halit Ziya describes a romantic protagonist, Ahmet Cemil, who possesses elevated desires in his novel, *Mai ve Siyah* (Blue and Black) first serialized in *Servet-i Fünun* in 1896.[17] For literary critics, the novel offers a few key concepts, such as romantic disillusionment, *Künstlerroman*, and the Faustian pattern. In this respect, the novel's depiction of Ahmet Cemil's individual desire to live all kinds of human experiences is particularly important in showing its extensive use of the Faustian pattern associated with hunger for knowledge and progress. Cemil, as a Faustian young man, desires both "the good things in life"—such as money, fame, and glory—and human experience in all its complexity. At the beginning of the novel, under a starry night, he dreams of being a famous and well-known poet as he listens to French musician Emile Waldteufel's waltz "Rain of Diamonds" (1879). The third-person narrator relates his passionate desire to "being captivated by elevated things," that is, material gain and knowledge. When he looks at the blue skies, "he could not find any measure for the high position he envisioned."[18] Just like Goethe's Faust, he wants a "full capacity for feeling."[19] He also desires to express or translate this deep feeling to create a literary language and to search for a new vocabulary that has not yet been employed.[20] As Peter Brooks argues, the practice of writing the world or the representation of the world in language, by its very nature, is useless.[21] Similarly, in *Mai ve Siyah*, Cemil is obsessed with searching for a new language, new words, and brand-new images. This language is supposed to be a medium to express the Faustian passion and feelings that he also possesses. However, language is never sufficient to express himself, showing how his feelings are indeed beyond expression.

Ahmet Cemil, like Faust, builds a world of his own created by books and thoughts far from the actual world in which he does not wish to live. On the other hand, he does his best to struggle for his desires and to work hard, thereby compensating for the loss of his father who was the sole provider of the family. Therefore, even if he does not like the actual world, he tries to survive within this reality and yet still becomes an agent of his own actions and choices. When we look at his envisioned poem at the beginning of the novel, we see a sort of symbolic imagination of life. This is the life of a human being constructed on a tension between joyful beginnings and sorrowful endings, as symbolized by the colors blue and black. He wishes to represent a kind of life in his poem with a new language. In fact, he writes the poem and accomplishes this dream successfully in the textual world. On the other hand, his actions in the actual world are destined to fail in accordance with his imagination of life for human beings in the poem. He lives his own life as his poem; in fact, his life reflects and copies his work, so his text becomes his own life, as Halit Ziya underlines with the phrase "life imitates the work."[22]

The second aspect of Ahmet Cemil that transforms him into a Faustian man/bad subject is a very desire to have a printing house and printing press. He signs an agreement with a merciless capitalist Vehbi Bey, the owner of the printing house. Ahmet Cemil becomes a partner of the printing house in return for an arranged marriage between Vehbi Bey and his sister İkbal, and he receives the printing press in exchange for pledging his family home. His main motivation to broker this deal seems to be to make money because Ahmet Cemil wants to employ capital as a means to reach his desires. The lack of money stemming from the loss of his father as a provider both triggers and obstructs his desires. This lack motivates him to act, therefore becoming an agent for his own action. This Faustian act of mortgaging his family house in order to buy a

Envisioning the Modern Individual in Late Nineteenth-Century Ottoman-Turkish Fiction

printing press is crucial since the printing press is a symbol of a new world that will allow him to circulate his writings, conveying his works to new worlds and reaching all kinds of knowledge. He is impressed by the machine both as a technological object and as capital for his desires. He is fascinated by the noise of the machine, which is described as a huge, monstrous creature with its crashing and clattering. Consequently, his fascination includes both fear and adoration. After all, the most impressive aspect of the printing press is its quick access to the rest of the world, knowledge, and power.[23] His fascination with it as a technological object and his awareness of being connected to the rest of the world through it recalls the characteristics attributed to the desiring individual imagined in *Servet-i Fünun*. Considering all the opportunities it provides, he decides to accept Vehbi Bey's offer. Ahmet Cemil leaves behind his past and his family relations for the sake of realizing his desires. However, unlike the nonfictional world, the fictional one shows that the character willing to pay the price pays a higher price than he imagines because of the complexity of life. At the end of the novel, he loses everything, including both the objects of desire and his sister İkbal, who is mistreated by her husband.

Ahmet Cemil's elevated desires and the price he pays to realize them to some extent resembles the form of desiring and imagining embodied in Nansen's journey to the North Pole. However, apart from the reality Nansen represents, as I mentioned before, Cemil's self-fashioned reality through his perception is a reality of a world imagined in his artwork. In accordance with this romantic vision, his life will end in darkness due to being a bad subject unable to adjust his desires to society's norms and expectations.

Halit Ziya's other protagonists, Bihter and Ömer Behiç of the two novels *Aşk-ı Memnu* (Forbidden Love) and *Kırık Hayatlar* (Broken Lives), which were also serialized in *Servet-i Fünun*, share some common features with Ahmet Cemil. As stated above, they are the agents of their own acts and this agency makes them bad subjects according to the society in which they live. In Halit Ziya's novels, characters are always on the edge of bad subjectivity, as conceptualized by Armstrong. Their common theme is the individual desire for property, possessions, money, and reputation along with the desire for love which usually violates the social and sexual contract. Individual desires trigger the protagonists to realize themselves. However, according to society, individuals should ultimately adjust their desires to the social world and turn themselves into proper citizens. In contrast, the kinds of transgressive individuals/protagonists Armstrong identifies as bad subjects fail to adjust their desires to society's conventions.[24] In Halit Ziya's novels, particularly in *Aşk-ı Memnu* and *Kırık Hayatlar*, the protagonists' intense desires and passions eventually bring their self-destruction and desolation as well as the destruction of the sacred family home, the primary site of the social contract. Morality, as the protector of both the social contract and the family, was impotent in the face of desires in Halit Ziya's novelistic world. In contrast to the hopeful world envisioned by *Servet-i Fünun* journal, as described in the first part of this chapter, Halit Ziya's fictional world describes the limits and transgression of modern individual's desires as well as the notion of progress.

In *Aşk-ı Memnu*, serialized from 1899 to 1900 in *Servet-i Fünun*, Halit Ziya focused on a tragic story of a nineteenth-century middle-class Ottoman woman, Bihter as a bad subject whose irresistible desires keep her from being a decent individual.[25] Even if the forbidden love or adultery engenders the backbone of the plot, the story as a whole, focuses on how her desires destroy both the individual and the family. Bihter is married to an older man, Adnan Bey, who lives in a mansion with his two young children and his nephew, Behlül. In the course of the novel, Bihter starts to experience a passionate love or/and sexual desire through her affair with Behlül. After confessing to the affair, she kills herself and consequently destroys the entire family.

Aşk-ı Memnu's characters are all but isolated in a nineteenth-century Ottoman mansion on the Bosporus. Their living style, daily life habits, and notions of fashion are predictably harmonious with the nineteenth-century urban life presented in *Servet-i Fünun*. Especially women's superior position in Istanbul's pleasure life is emphasized through their elegance and their fashionable dresses. The third-person narrator comments on their taste in the following way:

> Such delicious and exceptional taste ruled everything, from the most sacrosanct garments to the veils across their faces, the color of their gloves, the embroidery on their handkerchiefs; that by their simplicity they reduced the most carefully chosen adornments to banality. When they were seen, it was impossible that their beauty go unnoticed—only the causes for the appearance of such a result escaped detection. Here, pale, ash-grey gloves with black embroidery from Pygmalion, here half boots in kid leather from Au Lion D'or, and sheets of black satin like everyone else's from Lion. But by the air of beauty that breathed at the heart of their elegance, these little things that looked like everyone else's were swathed in luxury, and taken from being coarse and turned into the objects of another world. What could not be *imitated was not what they wore, but their way of wearing.*[26]

With these lines, we come across not only modes of fashion but also clues about urban life in Istanbul as a landscape for contemporary individuals' bourgeois habits of shopping. The emphasis of the passage shows that "fashion is the imitation of a given example and satisfies the demand for social adaptation," to use Georg Simmel's words. But fashion oscillates between uniformity and differentiation as an effort to combine the "tendency towards social equalization with the desire for individual differentiation and change."[27] As imitators, these women perform the social need for equalization; at the same time, they want to be different, to be seen uniquely with their bodies through their mode of wearing stylish clothing. As self-fashioning individuals, they evoke nineteenth-century dandies' need to see and to be seen. This emphasis on fashion and self-exhibition in the novel also recalls the fashion pages of *Servet-i Fünun*, which featured illustrations of fashionable women in European style. These were some of the few pages presumably addressed to women in the magazine that overall treated men as its interlocutors.[28]

In accordance with the role of fashion and the world of commodities, the protagonist Bihter's desires first appeared as material ones. She was keen on the ostentatious objects, furniture, and clothes that were supposed to be secured with marriage:

> But marriage to Adnan Bey meant one of the largest residences on the Bosphorus; the house in which, as one passed by, chandeliers, heavy curtains, carved Louis XV walnut chairs, lamps with large lampshades, and gilded desks and stools could be discerned through the window, and in the boathouse, a canoe, and the mahogany boat, covered with their clean white sheets. Then as this residence rose before Bihter's eyes with all the richness of her dreams, fabrics, laces, colors, jewels, and pearls were sprinkled over it, a rain composed of *all those longed-for things that were madly loved but could not be bought*, rained and filled her eyes.[29]

The narrator, focalizing Bihter, displays her determined ambition and passion that are directed with a desire for beautiful objects. Instead of sexuality or love, in these lines we feel the intense pleasure she gains by possessing these objects and having their glamor surround her body. The main focus is on the intensity of her desires, her "tireless enthusiasm" for these objects instead of the objects in themselves. She is also the agent of her all desires: fondness for possessions as well as deciding to marry, forbidden love, and eventually suicide. She is the agent of her acts and choices which bring her into bad subjectivity.

Envisioning the Modern Individual in Late Nineteenth-Century Ottoman-Turkish Fiction

After her marriage to the older Adnan Bey, Bihter gradually begins to feel a lack of love, the pressure of her body's unrealized desires and passions in this splendid mansion full of things that were used to be "madly loved but could not be bought."[30] Her desire for things gradually turns into carnal desire, for a sexuality shaped by the will to possess, resembling her former desire for possessions.

> Love, she wanted to love. That was all she lacked in life; but love was all. To love, yes, all happiness could only be gained through it. A small, sordid, bare room, an iron bedstead, white curtains, two cane chairs, a chamber for loving composed of just these. But to love, my god! She wanted to love, she would be content in a feverish, mad affair. Now in the riches of this splendid room, she felt as though she had been buried alive in a tomb of black marble. She could not breathe, she was suffocating; she wanted to escape this grave, to live, to love.[31]

In this passage, the deepest desires and the intimacy of the individual is exposed as a projection of the privacy of a middle-class woman stuck in a life ruled over by the social and sexual contract. Throughout the novel, the tension continues between Bihter's incommensurable need to love and be loved and the lifestyle of a decent subject. Eventually, lack brings bad subjectivity. This privation appears in her vision of a mirror shattered in two pieces, two Bihters projecting her gaze into her body and soul, into her deepest desires.

> Yes, she loved this body. Now there was an attachment, an enchantment in her heart for this body. This body was hers, she was looking at it with a slight smile. In the mirror, this white picture, thin, indistinct, seemed to be separated from its ground by an airy blue line, a fine blue halo that opened around her, and in which she swelled and took on a corporeality. Leaving its panel, it was moving towards Bihter—the other Bihter. There, the two Bihters, in the tremblings of a kiss that burned the lungs, that brought to light all suppressed passions, in an embrace that created and destroyed, appeared as two bodies ready to throw themselves into each other's arms. Now in the frostiness of this mirror, she looked upon this lovely vision that came from the green horizons of a deep cave, painted with shades of translucent aquamarine, from the point of view of a man who wanted to own her.[32]

In this first and unique scene from a Turkish novel, particularly one written by a male writer, the woman protagonist nakedly looks at herself, her divided self, her twin's body, her inner world, thus both perceiving each part of her body and embracing its desires with a "narcissistic gaze," in the words of Nurdan Gürbilek.[33] The desire for her own body will soon merge with the desire to be seen, admired, and loved by someone else—the desire to see her admired body as the desire of the other—and will eventually fall into Behlül's arms. Bihter violates the social and sexual contract first and foremost with this confrontation in the mirror and her act of adultery is actualized as a consequence of this affection.

Finally, Halit Ziya repeated the pattern of disillusionment and desolateness of destructively desiring individuals in *Kırık Hayatlar* with a male protagonist who resembles Bihter to a certain extent. Ömer Behiç is a self-made man who has meticulously built his own life through his career as a doctor. He has bought an upper-middle-class house filled with desired objects and furniture to live in with his happy family, to which he passionately committed himself. As such, he seems the fictional embodiment of the modern individual envisioned by the *Servet-i Fünun* magazine. Ömer Behiç also rigidly longed for a moral society and world. He imagines his dream house as a solid rock protecting his family and its inner life from the outside, public space, as a secluded area to let him live his own privacy. From the very beginning of the novel, it implies concerns about the misery, hazardousness, and disillusionment that could leak from the public space into the house where they live their separate lives. Here, too, adultery becomes the embodiment of this concern, transgression of the border between the private and public, crackling of the solid rock of the house and opening it up to be defenseless in the face of all the storms of the world. Accordingly, the adultery narrative is not only the story of a moral collapse or breakdown but rather one of the impossibility of such a moral norm in both private and public spaces when desiring individuals conflict with the social contract.

The fact that the world outside the home is presented as a disgusting one of poverty, immorality, disease, and suffering for afflicted and sorrowful human beings reveals Ömer Behiç's imagination of a moral, sterile, aesthetic, and healthy life—that is, his bourgeois elitism, positivism, and rationalist idealism. At the same time, this imagination points out how the modern individual shaped by all these ideals stands on a slippery ground. Thus, despite the magazine's approach glorifying public space and inviting individuals to participate more in urban life, the fictional world of *Kırık Hayatlar* shows the dangers of these spaces, the individual weaknesses and inner darkness that, so the fear goes, can be triggered by the world outside the home.

Another aspect of the novel worth emphasizing is the protagonist's relationship with science and medicine. In addition to the evils penetrating the house from the outside world, the main character, who cannot find a cure for his daughter's illness even though he is a doctor, feels helpless in the face of the complexity and uncertainty of life. The inability of science to explain life, people, and diseases is excessively emphasized. The inability of man to cope with the difficulties of life and its cruelties, the incomprehensibility of the human spirit and the failure of science to cure illnesses, inevitably point to the deadlocks of the modern individual and the loss of safety in the world created by Halit Ziya. This creates doubt and ambiguity about the existence of absolute truth. The fictional characters serialized in *Servet-i Fünun* appear as lonely and desolate individuals in contrast to the magazine's imagination of an individual fascinated by science and excited to mingle with urban life.

Conclusion

The first Ottoman modernizing generation insisted on both the social function of literature and its communicational contract, producing texts easily comprehensible for the common reader. However, at the turn of the century when the Servet-i Fünun writers began to produce works that rejected the socially oriented idea of literature, they were sharply criticized by Ahmet Mithat, one of the leading authors of the previous generation. Ahmet Mithat accused this new generation of modern writers of being decadent because of their extensive use of figurative language and images he considered bizarre and artificial. In addition, the literature they produced portrayed individuals displaying ontological predicaments and psychological conflicts not easily overcome. Servet-i Fünun writers and poets argued that they need this new language to express themselves, their emotions and inner conflicts in their response to these accusations.[34] These literary figures were not only criticized by their contemporaries but also by later Republican literary historians who emphasized the social function of literature.[35] These figures criticized Servet-i Fünun writer for being alienated from society, extremely Westernized, overly individualistic, nonlocal/national, and escapist, therefore inaccessible to the common reader. However, as this analysis of Halit Ziya's novels shows, although the leading writers and poets of the Servet-i Fünun literary school portrayed a complex world and created multilayered characters, they were not disconnected or alienated from their society. Halit Ziya published novels representing a modern individual who desires and pursues his/her desires as a manifestation of the complex experience of modernity in the Ottoman Empire at the end of the nineteenth century. This demonstrates that, contrary to the dominant narrative in Turkish literary historiography on the Servet-i Fünun literary movement, their works were not indeed alienated and escapist as they imagined themselves as a part of a wider global modernity. Indeed, they produced texts describing the confusing experience of Ottoman modernity and revealing thematic and stylistic parallels with other contemporary authors across the globe. Thus, their literary texts are closely associated with the common "structure of feeling" or "structure of experience," of the world period, as discussed by Raymond Williams. With these terms, Williams refers to the shared "characteristic elements of impulse, restraint, and tone; specifically, affective elements of consciousness and relationships" that display "special relevance to art and literature."[36] Similar to what Williams discusses, the Servet-i Fünun generation conveyed these "affective elements of consciousness" in their fictional and nonfictional works.

Nevertheless, as examined throughout this chapter, while they shared a common structure of feeling, the Servet-i Fünun writers reflected conflicted aspects of modernity in the fictional and nonfictional world in the juxtaposing pages of the pages of their weekly magazine. Readers who were bombarded with rapid information thanks to current news and enthusiastic stories of science and expeditions in the journal were also invited to stop and think about the characters in serialized fiction to explore the complex inner world and to face their own subjectivity through them. In this respect, Halit Ziya handles the individual's attitude towards the world full of excitement, his/her desires and wonders grown out of his/her inner world without boundaries. Then he goes on to narrate the fragmentation of the characters who cannot orientate his/her desires in the right direction as shown by the social contract. Therefore, the attitude of the literary text moves away from the Romantic potential of infinitely imagining the future, as reflected from the nonfictional pages of *Servet-i Fünun*. While the magazine invites the reader to discover the endless possibilities of the world, Halit Ziya's reader explores the limited or unlimited desires of modern individuals. In other words, fiction exposes the mood of uneasiness and insufficiency hidden behind the tempting nonfictional pages of the magazine. The reason for the brutal realism of the fiction versus the Romantic outlook of nonfiction is twofold: The modern human condition that creates the modern individual who cannot actualize the endless possibilities adorned in the success stories imagined for her/him. This condition was appropriated and localized as the unfulfilled Ottoman individual against the more distant "Western" or global success story in this geography in the late nineteenth century.

Notes

1 For detailed information and the pages of *Servet-i Fünun*, see as the database of the TÜBİTAK project "Osmanlı Kültür Tarihinde Servet-i Fünun Dergisi" (Servet-i Fünun Magazine in Ottoman Cultural History), 2019, www.servetifunundergisi.com.

2 For nineteenth-century Ottoman Turkish modernization and literature, see Talat Halman, *A Millennium of Turkish Literature: A Concise History* (Syracuse, NY: Syracuse University Press, 2011); Robert Finn, *The Early Turkish Novel: 1872–1900* (Istanbul: Isis Press, 1984); Ahmet Evin, *Origins and Development of The Turkish Novel* (Minneapolis: Bibliotheca Islamica, 1983); Zeynep Uysal, "The Development Towards a Turkish National Literature: Becoming Modern and/or Remaining Oneself," in *Dragomanen*, ed. Birgit N. Schlyter (Istanbul: The Swedish Research Institute, 2008).

3 Josiah Conder's observation from 1811 about British periodicals can also be applied to the case of Ottoman nineteenth-century periodicals: "Reviews are a substitute for all other kinds of reading—a new and royal road to knowledge" and "periodicals were proliferating, rapidly increasing in popularity, and becoming a major sector in the market for print." Sally Shuttleworth and Geoffrey Canto, eds., *Science Serialized, Representation of the Sciences in Nineteenth-Century Periodicals* (Cambridge, MA:

MIT Press, 2004), 1. Similarly, in the late nineteenth-century Ottoman intellectual world, periodicals, particularly illustrated ones, were becoming increasingly popular. *Servet-i Fünun* was first and foremost among these illustrative magazines. In his article investigating "late nineteenth-century Ottoman illustrated journals as a key site for the articulation of new, popular, and visualized forms of historical knowledge and sensibility in the imperial domain," Ahmet Ersoy also underlined that these "journals were . . . both a manifest sign and a powerful agent of the global culture of modernity." For a detailed discussion of *Servet-i Fünun* as an illustrated journal see, Ahmet A. Ersoy, "Ottomans and the Kodak Galaxy: Archiving Everyday Life and Historical Space in Ottoman Illustrated Journals," *History of Photography* 40, no. 3 (2016): 330.

4 The existing research on modern Ottoman literature has fundamentally overlooked the diverse cultural, intellectual, and scientific content of *Servet-i Fünun*, contributing to a simplistic, essentialist, and narrow litero-centric understanding in Turkish literary studies. See Kenan Akyüz, *Modern Türk Edebiyatının Ana Çizgileri 1860–1923* (Istanbul: İnkılap Yayınları, 1994); İnci Enginün, *Yeni Türk Edebiyatı: Tanzimat'tan Cumhuriyet'e (1839–1923)* (Istanbul: Dergâh Yayınları, 2006); Orhan Okay, *Batılılaşma Devri Türk Edebiyatı* (Istanbul: Dergâh Yayınları, 2010); İsmail Parlatır, *Servet-i Fünun Edebiyatı* (Ankara: Akçağ Yayınları, 2006).

5 Ahmet İhsan [Tokgöz], "Teşekkür ve İfade," *Servet-i Fünun* 10, no. 255 (January 19, 1311 [1896]): 3.

6 Mahmut Sadık, "Musahabe-i Fenniye," *Servet-i Fünun* 15, no. 382 (June 25, 1314 [1898]): 274–78.

7 Mahmut Sadık, "Kutba Doğru," *Servet-i Fünun* 13, no. 318 (April 3, 1313 [1897]): 89–92.

8 Translated by Veysel Öztürk. Mahmut Sadık, "Kutba Doğru," 89.

9 Tevfik Fikret, "Kutba Doğru," *Servet-i Fünun* 13, no. 320 (April 17, 1313 [1897]): 119. Both Fikret's poetic hero and Mahmut Sadık's historical figure Nansen are Romantic individuals according to the concept of Romantic science, which refers to the expedition full of dangers taken alone. See for the details of the concept: Richard Holmes, *The Age of Wonder: How the Romantic Generation Discovered the Beauty and Terror of Science* (New York: Vintage Books, 2010), 6.

10 See the database www.servetifunundergisi.com/kategori/fen/icat-kesif/.

11 See the database www.servetifunundergisi.com/kategori/guncel-haber/istanbuldan-haber/.

12 Besides local urban life, detailed travel writing—such as in the correspondence of writers who convey their experiences in foreign cities, such as in the city journal (*şehir günlükleri*) genre—also focalize the unique critical gaze of the subject/agent who looks around with curiosity and narrativizes individual experience, thus visualizing them for the reader through photographs, photographic images, and scenes. For example, in a travel narrative titled "From Haydarpaşa to Konya," Ahmet İhsan narrates his own observations and experiences around the cities he visited while also providing details about lifestyle, daily experiences, and buildings and architecture in the provinces of the Ottoman Empire. Ahmet İhsan [Tokgöz], "Osmanlı Demiryolu Hattında Haydarpaşa'dan Konya'ya Bir Cevelan," *Servet-i Fünun* 12, no. 296 (October 13, 1312 [1896]): 146–47; also see www.servetifunundergisi.com/kategori/guncel-haber/vilayattan-haber/page/2/.

13 Halit Ziya Uşaklıgil, *Hikaye*, ed. Nur Gürani Arslan (Istanbul: Yapı Kredi Yayınları, 1998), 20.

14 John Rignall, *Realist Fiction and the Strolling Spectator* (London: Routledge, 1992), 82.

15 Nancy Armstrong, *How Novels Think: The Limits of British Individualism from 1719–1900* (New York: Columbia University Press, 1989), 4.

16 Ibid., 5.

17 Uşşakizade Halit Ziya [Uşaklıgil], "Servet-i Fünun'un Romanı: Mai ve Siyah," *Servet-i Fünun* 11, no. 273 (May 23, 1312 [1896]): 206.

18 Halit Ziya Uşaklıgil, *Mai ve Siyah* (Istanbul: Özgür Yayınları, 2009), 39.

19 See Marshall Berman, *All That Is Solid Melts into Air: The Experience of Modernity* (New York: Verso, 1983), 39; Johann Wolfgang von Goethe, *Faust: A Tragedy in Two Parts,* trans. Thomas Wayne (New York: Algora, 2016), 42.

20 "It is such a language that . . . it will articulate all our sorrows, joys, thoughts, all kinds of delicacies of that heart, a thousand depths of ideas, excitements, and furies; a language that will dive into the sad colors of sunset with us and think, a language that will weep with a mourning with our souls. . . . We want a language that will have those tunes, those colors, those depths. Let it roar with the storms, let it roll with the waves, let it be shaken by the winds; then let a consumptive girl fall on the side of the bed, cry, bend over a child's cradle, smile, hide in the hopeful eye of a young person. A language . . . Oh! I'm talking nonsense, you'll think, a language that is fully human." Uşaklıgil, *Mai ve Siyah*, 23 (translation is mine).

Envisioning the Modern Individual in Late Nineteenth-Century Ottoman-Turkish Fiction

21 Peter Brooks, *Realist Vision* (London: Yale University Press, 2005), 65.
22 See, Zeynep Uysal, *Metruk Ev: Halit Ziya Romanında Modern Osmanlı Bireyi* (Istanbul: İletişim Yayınları, 2014), 215–57.
23 Uşaklıgil, *Mai ve Siyah*, 243.
24 Armstrong discusses how the notion of the social contract from Rousseau turned into a sexual contract in Victorian domestic fiction as a genre in which the social contract was implicitly hidden in sexual relations. For women, sexuality is legitimized by marriage and paves the way for a virtuous life. See Nancy Armstrong, *Desire and Domestic Fiction: A Political History of the Novel* (New York: Oxford University Press, 1989), 38.
25 Uşşakizade Halit Ziya [Uşaklıgil], "Yeni Romanımız: Aşk-ı Memnu," *Servet-i Fünun* 16, no. 413 (Ocak 28, 1314 [1899]): 366.
26 Translated by Eva Deverell, "Forbidden Love by Halit Ziya Uşaklıgil," www.eadeverell.com/forreaders/forbidden-love/#c1.
27 Georg Simmel, *On Individuality and Social Forms* (Chicago: University of Chicago Press, 1971), 296–97.
28 At the same time, the novels serialized in the magazine seemed to include women among their implied readers.
29 Deverell, "Forbidden Love."
30 Ibid.
31 Ibid.
32 Ibid.
33 Nurdan Gürbilek, *Kör Ayna, Kayıp Şark* (Istanbul: Metis Yayınları, 2004), 144–45. See also Uysal, *Metruk Ev*, 155–57.
34 This argument was called the "Dekadanlar Tartışması" (Decadent Argument). For more detail, see Uysal, *Metruk Ev*, 37–51.
35 Niyazi Berkes, *Türkiye'de Çağdaşlaşma* (Ankara: Bilgi Yayınevi, 1978); Niyazi Berkes, *The Development of Secularism in Turkey* (Montreal: McGill University Press, 1964).
36 "Yet we are also defining a social experience which is still in process, often indeed not yet recognized as social but taken to be private, idiosyncratic, and even isolating, but which in analysis . . . has its emergent, connecting, and dominant characteristics." Raymond Williams, "Structure of Feeling," in *Marxism and Literature* (Oxford: Oxford University Press, 1977), 132–33.

References

Akyüz, Kenan. *Modern Türk Edebiyatının Ana Çizgileri 1860–1923*. Istanbul: İnkılap Yayınları, 1994.
Armstrong, Nancy. *Desire and Domestic Fiction: A Political History of the Novel*. New York: Oxford University Press, 1989.
———. *How Novels Think: The Limits of British Individualism from 1719–1900*. New York: Columbia University Press, 1989.
Berkes, Niyazi. *The Development of Secularism in Turkey*. Montreal: McGill University Press, 1964.
———. *Türkiye'de Çağdaşlaşma*. Ankara: Bilgi Yayınevi, 1978.
Berman, Marshall. *All That Is Solid Melts into Air: The Experience of Modernity*. New York: Verso, 1983.
Brooks, Peter. *Realist Vision*. London: Yale University Press, 2005.
Enginün, İnci. *Yeni Türk Edebiyatı: Tanzimat'tan Cumhuriyet'e (1839–1923)*. Istanbul: Dergâh Yayınları, 2006.
Ersoy, Ahmet A. "Ottomans and the Kodak Galaxy: Archiving Everyday Life and Historical Space in Ottoman Illustrated Journals." *History of Photography* 40, no. 3 (2016): 330–57.
Evin, Ahmet. *Origins and Development of The Turkish Novel*. Minneapolis: Bibliotheca Islamica, 1983.
Finn, Robert. *The Early Turkish Novel: 1872–1900*. Istanbul: Isis Press, 1984.
Goethe, Johann Wolfgang von. *Faust: A Tragedy in Two Parts*. Translated by Thomas Wayne. New York: Algora, 2016.
Gürbilek, Nurdan. *Kör Ayna, Kayıp Şark*. Istanbul: Metis Yayınları, 2004.
Halman, Talat. *A Millennium of Turkish Literature: A Concise History*. Syracuse, NY: Syracuse University Press, 2011.
Holmes, Richard. *The Age of Wonder: How the Romantic Generation Discovered the Beauty and Terror of Science*. New York: Vintage Books, 2010.
Mahmut, Sadık. "Kutba Doğru." *Servet-i Fünun* 13, no. 318 (April 3, 1313 [1897]): 89–92.
———. "Musahabe-i Fenniye." *Servet-i Fünun* 15, no. 382 (June 25, 1314 [1898]): 274–78.

Okay, Orhan. *Batılılaşma Devri Türk Edebiyatı*. Istanbul: Dergâh Yayınları, 2010.

"Osmanlı Kültür Tarihinde Servet-i Fünun Dergisi (Servet-i Fünun Magazine in Ottoman Cultural History)." TÜBİTAK Project Database, 2019. www.servetifunundergisi.com.

Parlatır, İsmail. *Servet-i Fünun Edebiyatı*. Ankara: Akçağ Yayınları, 2006.

Rignall, John. *Realist Fiction and the Strolling Spectator*. London: Routledge, 1992.

Shuttleworth, Sally, and Geoffrey Canto, eds. *Science Serialized, Representation of the Sciences in Nineteenth-Century Periodicals*. Cambridge: MIT Press, 2004.

Simmel, Georg. *On Individuality and Social Forms*. Chicago: University of Chicago Press, 1971.

Tevfik Fikret. "Kutba Doğru." *Servet-i Fünun* 13, no. 320 (April 17, 1313 [1897]): 119.

Tokgöz, Ahmet İhsan. "Teşekkür ve İfade." *Servet-i Fünun* 10, no. 255 (January 19, 1311 [1896]): 3.

———. "Osmanlı Demiryolu Hattında Haydarpaşa'dan Konya'ya Bir Cevelan." *Servet-i Fünun* 12, no. 296 (October 13, 1312 [1896]): 146–47.

Uşaklıgil, [Uşşakizade] Halit Ziya. "Servet-i Fünun'un Romanı: Mai ve Siyah." *Servet-i Fünun* 11, no. 273 (May 23, 1312 [1896]): 206.

———. "Yeni Romanımız: Aşk-ı Memnu." *Servet-i Fünun* 16, no. 413 (Ocak 28, 1314 [1899]): 366.

———. *Hikaye*. Edited by Nur Gürani Arslan. Istanbul: Yapı Kredi Yayınları, 1998.

———. *Mai ve Siyah*. Istanbul: Özgür Yayınları, 2009.

———. "Forbidden Love by Halit Ziya Uşaklıgil." Translated by Eva Deverell. *Aşk-ı Memnu*. www.eadeverell.com/forreaders/forbidden-love/#c1.

Uysal, Zeynep. "The Development Towards a Turkish National Literature: Becoming Modern and/or Remaining Oneself." In *Dragomanen*, edited by Birgit N. Schlyter. Istanbul: The Swedish Research Institute, 2008.

———. *Metruk Ev: Halit Ziya Romanında Modern Osmanlı Bireyi*. Istanbul: İletişim Yayınları, 2014.

Williams, Raymond. "Structure of Feeling." In *Marxism and Literature*. Oxford: Oxford University Press, 1977.

23

"WE, TOO, ARE EASTERN"

Nâzım Hikmet's Futurist and Anti-colonial Modernity

Kenan Behzat Sharpe

This chapter focuses on the Turkish poet Nâzım Hikmet Ran (1902–1963). It explores how his communist and anti-colonial political commitments helped him forge an alternative vision of what it meant to be modern, one that challenged the pro-Western and capitalist orientation of the young Turkish state. Nâzım (as he is affectionately known in Turkey) had an eventful life that spanned the end of the Ottoman Empire and the formation of the Turkish Republic. At 19, he left school in Istanbul to join the nationalist independence movement in Anatolia. On the way, he was exposed to communist ideas and in 1921 made his way to the Soviet Union, spending over half of the decade in Moscow. There he studied Marxism-Leninism, met other young revolutionaries from across the world, and participated in the Soviet avant-garde artistic currents of the era. Back in Turkey, the poet faced near-constant repression. From 1929 until his final arrest in 1938, he was tried with various charges calculated to silence him. Able to command crowds with his powerful reading voice and uniquely demotic poetic style, Nâzım posed a threat to the authorities. In 1938 a military judge threw the book at Nâzım, sentencing him to 15 years for inciting the military to revolt with his poetry. An international campaign to free the poet was coordinated by Pablo Neruda, Simone de Beauvoir, Jean-Paul Sartre, Paul Robeson, and Pablo Picasso. In 1950 he was finally released but fled to the Soviet Union upon further harassment by the authorities. As he settled in Moscow he was stripped of Turkish citizenship. He was never able to return home but spent the rest of his life circling the globe, traveling everywhere from Cuba to Tashkent as a spokesman for the revolution. He died of a heart attack in Moscow at the age of 61, leaving behind a massive collection of poems, plays, and essays in Turkish and translated into the world's major languages.

In the national context, Nâzım is seen as an important modernizer of Turkish-language poetry. He popularized free-verse poetry in the country, attempting to "demolish the idols" represented by the previous generation of poets. By the time of his death in 1963, he had produced a rich and diverse body of work that would transform the literary scene in Turkey—once censorship against his writings was lifted in the mid-1960s.[1] Despite the large shadow cast by his work, Nâzım's place within the history of Turkish poetry's modernization remains ambiguous. For example, the poet Oktay Rifat echoes a common emphasis on temporal lag in describing this history:

> Since the middle of the nineteenth century our poetry has been struggling to Westernize, all the while doing nothing more than following Western poetry sixty, seventy

DOI: 10.4324/9780429279270-31

years behind. . . . In saying this, I am not taking into account Nâzım Hikmet. For he is an altogether separate starting point in our poetic tradition.[2]

What makes Nâzım unique was his unanxious contemporaneity with the dominant literary trends of the age. He not only kept abreast of the European avant-garde, but as early as the 1920s he was producing Futurist poetry contemporaneously with writers in the Soviet Union and beyond. In Moscow, he met Vladimir Mayakovsky, whose Futurism pushed Nâzım to focus on the everyday and the new rather than aesthetic refinement and tradition. As Mayakovsky argued in 1918: "We do not need a dead mausoleum of art where dead works are worshiped, but a living *factory of the human spirit*—in the streets, in the tramways, in the factories, workshops and workers' homes."[3] Nâzım was also influenced by Constructivism, befriending theatrical producer Vsevolod Meyerhold in Moscow. The latter's theatrical experiments gave Nâzım methods for de-naturalizing his work, portraying constant motion, and treating the poem as "a product of an industrial order like a car, aeroplane, and such like."[4]

Thus, the fact of residing in Moscow and seeing the political and artistic revolution firsthand was a key factor in Nâzım's rejection of the anxiety of belatedness that frequently characterized Turkish letters. Yet Nâzım's outlier position within Turkish literature should not cause us to see him as separate from that tradition. This chapter argues that Nâzım's synchronicity vis-à-vis modern European literature and his relevance to Turkish literature and history are not at odds. Admittedly, Nâzım's early work was deeply influenced by Futurism and Constructivism. However, an overemphasis on the question of influence makes it all too easy to see Nâzım as a passive recipient of foreign themes. What is crucial is how he adapted these themes to the Turkish context.

This chapter uses Nâzım's early and most obviously Futurist poetry as a limit case; these poems show how even his work that most clearly bears the traces of experiences in Moscow is also deeply engaged with the Turkish context. These youthful poems are not considered among his best works. The poet described his early style as a bombastic "orchestra of wind instruments," as compared to his more mature lyrical and epic poems.[5] Some of the poems analyzed here remained unpublished in his lifetime. Yet they are helpful literary and historical documents, revealing Nâzım's alternative conception of what it means to be modern. This conception involves both a Futurist celebration of the latest advances in science and technology, as symbolized by the modern metropolis, and a decoupling of this advancement from Europe.[6] In Nâzım's communist, anti-colonial vision of modernity, it was the "East" (including the Soviet Union) that was the vanguard of history. And, for Nâzım, Turkey should properly be seen as "Eastern."

The question of Nâzım's modernism reveals his double position as both a member of a global artistic vanguard and a poet deeply engaged with conditions in Turkey. For example, he was a typical Futurist in his poetic love affair with speed, machines, and the paraphernalia of modern life. As Mayakovsky expressed it in the 1913 lecture "The Achievements of Futurism": "Telephones, airplanes, expresses, elevators, rotating machines, sidewalks, factory chimneys, stone colossi, soot, and smoke—these are the elements of beauty in the new urban landscape."[7] Nâzım's early poems are full of the flotsam and jetsam of the modern city; he preferred the urban to the rural, the mechanical to the natural, the functional to the beautiful. He was, of course, not the only Turkish poet to explore modern life, though his approach was unique. Nâzım's celebratory attitude sets him apart from contemporaries like Necip Fazıl Kısakürek, who wrote about the city in a more pessimistic manner. In the poems "Sidewalks," "Hotel Rooms," and "Chimneys," written in the 1920s and 1930s, Necip Fazıl laments the loneliness and alienation of the urban individual. In this sense, poets like Necip Fazıl (who become an influential Islamist and anti-communist figure by the 1950s) represent a current of "conservative modernism" that looks on modernity and technology (as well as rationalism and Enlightenment thinking) with both fascination and deep suspicion.[8] For left-wing Futurists like Nâzım, in contrast, modern life and technology were a source of optimism. He embraced urban life as a hammer for destroying the drowsiness of the past and tradition.

Yet Nâzım's interest in automobiles, machines, and radios as symbols of the new was not an imitation of foreign writers in European countries who enjoyed these objects in abundance. Rather, this interest was directly related to the sparsity of this technology—both in the Soviet Union and in Turkey. In this sense, Nâzım's modernism bears a family resemblance to what Marshall Berman calls the "modernism of underdevelopment."[9] Berman discovered this "distinctively weird form of modernism" through readings of nineteenth-century Russian literature. He argues that it also characterizes the early Soviet Union as well as the "Third World" (including, in this outdated Cold War classification, Turkey):

> In relatively backward countries, where the process of modernization has not yet come into its own, modernism, where it develops, takes on a fantastic character, because it is forced to nourish itself not on social reality but on fantasies, mirages, dreams.[10]

In other words, the hypermodernity of Futurist literature, for example, is paradoxically linked to a reality of economic backwardness. This literature is "forced to build on fantasies and dreams of modernity" rather than the real thing, which helps to explain its overexcited and often "shrill, uncouth" tone.[11] Nâzım's early poems contain paeans to electrification and fantasies of becoming a human machine. This attitude must be seen in relation to the modernism of underdevelopment's "extravagant attempts to take on . . . the whole burden of history" through force of will, just as the Turkish Republic rushed to modernize in the 1920s and 1930s.[12]

Just as Nâzım was not the only Turkish poet to write about the modern city, he was not the only one to explore science and technology. From at the least the time of Ziya Paşa's famous 1870 ghazel ("*Diyar-ı küfrü gezdim . . .*") comparing the political advancement of the "infidel lands" to the "ruins" on the "lands of Islam," literature in Turkish had registered the underdevelopment of the Ottoman Empire—but always in comparison with Western Europe.[13] This approach took a more technological focus in the poetry of Tevfik Fikret, who in his 1911 collection *Halûk'un Defteri* rousingly argued that science and development needed to be delivered to the empire by the youth: "Whatever you find, don't let it go: Art, science. . . . They're all needed here, all beneficial / Embrace the light and bring it to us in abundance."[14] This demand was rather literal in Tevfik Fikret's case; he sent his son Halûk to Glasgow to study electrical engineering. For Tevfik Fikret, progress, rationalism, and technology needed to be learned from the "West." This is not the case for Nâzım. He associates Europe with a doomed colonialism and identifies the "East" as the motor of history. For the many communist and anti-colonial intellectuals from Asia, Africa, and Latin America who were Nâzım's contemporaries and friends, it was precisely the underdevelopment of the East that made this geography the vanguard of humanity. Just as Marx and Engels argued that the bourgeois produced its own "grave-diggers" in the form of the proletariat, Nâzım's poetry described the exploited and impoverished peoples of what today is called the Global South as the grave-diggers of European colonialism.

With poems set in locations such as Shanghai, Kolkata, and Addis Ababa, Nâzım frequently depicts airplanes, cinemas, and electrical plants—as well as in the slums of colonial cities like Manchester, Rome, and Paris. Even when these early poems say nothing about Turkey, they intervene in national debates by uncoupling the conception of modernity from the bourgeois Western model that, for modernizers in both the late Ottoman Empire and early Turkish Republic, had provided the "ego-ideal" for projects of economic-social-cultural reform.[15] As Fırat Oruç writes, the young Republic sought to "translate, study, absorb, and 'master' the West not only for itself but for the entire Orient. As a translating mediator, it would close the gap between backward East and advanced West."[16] Nâzım rejected this sense of inferiority vis-à-vis Europe or condescension towards the "orient," aligning Turkey not with an idealized West but with the colonial and semi-colonial masses in the tri-continent (Asia, Africa, and Latin America). This "wretched of the earth," precisely because of their underdevelopment, would be the vanguard transforming human history.

Nâzım's portrayal of the East as the pinnacle of modernity can be seen in his 1929 work *Jokond ile Si-Ya-U*. This narrative poem describes a fantastical love story between Leonardo da Vinci's painting the *Mona Lisa* and a Chinese university student in Paris, Si-Ya-U.[17] The action begins in Paris, where Si-Ya-U frequently visits the *Mona Lisa* at the Louvre. Yet when Si-Ya-U is deported back to China for his political activities in France, the *Mona Lisa*—who has fallen in love with him—decides that she must break out of the museum and find him in Shanghai. So begins a rollicking caper that stretches from Paris, across Africa, and over to the Indian Ocean, Singapore, Australia, Madagascar, and finally China. The *Mona Lisa* first decides to flee France when she hears news on the radio about an uprising in China:

NEWS FROM THE PARIS WIRELESS

Voices race through the air
      Like fiery greyhounds.
The wireless in the Eiffel Tower calls out:

    HALLO
        HALLO
           HALLO

    PARIS
        PARIS
           PARIS . . .

"WE, TOO, are Eastern—this voice is for me.
My ears are receivers, too.
I, too, must listen to Eiffel."
News from China
        News from China

        News from China
The dragon that came down from the Kaf Mountains has spread his wings
Across the golden skies of the Chinese homeland."[18]

In this short segment, Nâzım brings together both Futurist and proto–Third Worldist themes. The setting is the Eiffel Tower, that ultimate symbol of bourgeois modernity, but the news coming in is about the fate of the Chinese communists, events that affect the entire world. The speaker here, a machine-like human whose ears are receivers, realizes that they too are an "Eastern" (*şarklı*). On one level, this refers to the *Mona Lisa*, who after traveling to colonial Shanghai and discovering that her love has been killed in the 1927 massacre of communists, decides to carry on Si-Ya-U's legacy; she becomes a traitor to European empire (and European art) by slitting a British officer's throat.[19] Yet the message "We, too, are Eastern" is also meant for the ears of peasants and workers in Turkey—and across the world. In the internationalist vision of Nâzım's early poetry, Turkey will be truly modern when it aligns itself with the East against European capitalism and colonialism.

Across Asia, Africa, and Latin America, the Soviet Union was a source of exhilaration for intellectuals and revolutionaries in the 1920s and 1930s due to its stance against colonialism and imperialism. The Communist International was the only political organization in Europe "to declare the equality of the races and to officially embrace anti-imperialism."[20] This was part of a conscious Soviet policy of winning over international allies—especially among its "ex-Ottoman neighbors" in West Asia.[21] By late 1920, after failed uprisings in Germany and Hungary, it was clear that Europe had no easy path to revolution.[22] The Soviet leadership thought that the best strategy for weakening the European powers was to target the colonies through which they gained their wealth. At the Second Congress of the Comintern in 1920, Lenin announced the Soviet Eastern Policy, which prioritized building solidarity with nationalist movements and recruiting Asian (and specifically Muslim) communists.[23] To this end, the Congress of the Peoples of the East was convened in Baku in September 1920. The summons for the conference addressed itself directly to the "Peasants of Anatolia" and denounced the fact that "the English, Italian and French governments have kept Constantinople under the fire of their guns."[24] The peoples of the Ottoman Empire had become, in Lenin's rhetoric, part of "advanced Asia," as compared to "backward Europe."[25] And it was Asia that would imminently liberate Europe and the world. This dialectic transformation of Asia's economic backwardness into political advancedness inspired tri-continental intellectuals like Nâzım. They wrote their nations into the political—and aesthetic—vanguard of the world.

Overcoming Underdevelopment by Becoming a Machine

Before becoming a communist, Nâzım Hikmet was sympathetic to anti-colonialist nationalism. These currents gained strength in the Ottoman Empire after it was split up between the Allied powers after World War I. As a patriotic youth, Nâzım watched with horror as British, French, Italian, and Greek forces occupied Istanbul. In 1921, he dropped out of school and fled Istanbul to join the independence movement. On the way to Ankara he met a group of Turkish students who had been expelled from Germany after the Spartacist uprising. In 1922, by way of Georgia, Nâzım and his friend Vâ-Nû (Vâlâ Nureddin) settled in Moscow. Nâzım studied for two years at the Communist University of the Toilers of the East (KUTV), where he read Marx, studied Russian, and soaked up the frenetic energy of the Soviet Union's early days.

The revolutionary fervor of those times transformed both the form and content of Nâzım's poetry. Since childhood, he had employed the classic forms and symbols of Ottoman poetry. However, he soon found both classical metrical prosody (aruz) and folk-style syllabic meter (hece vezni) to be inadequate for portraying the events occurring before his eyes. Nâzım recounted witnessing throngs of starving peasants crowding around the train as he traveled to Moscow from Tbilisi in 1922. He wanted to write a poem about the experience but found that traditional poetic forms were unsuitable to the content. Vâ-Nû recounts how Nâzım stormed about their building at the KUTV unsatisfied with his early drafts. Finally, he burst into the room shouting "Enough of the old-style verse forms and rhyme!"[26] He brought out a sheet of paper featuring what would become the most influential early example of free verse in Turkish poetry:

> *Not a few*
>> not five or ten
>>> the thirty million
>>>> **starving**
>>>> are ours!*[27]*

"The Pupils of the Starving," later published in Nâzım's first collection *835 Satır* (1932), made liberal use of enjambment, bold and italic fonts, and variable text sizes. These typographical innovations allowed the poet to play with scale and perspective in a manner suitable for portraying a mass event like a famine. "The Pupils of the Starving" is often given as an example of the influence of Futurism on Nâzım's poetry in the early 1920s.[28] Yet what Nâzım found in Soviet Futurism was determined by what he was already searching for: modern poetic forms and content suitable for the modern world he was witnessing. These were then filtered through his own, highly idiosyncratic poetic persona and adapted to be relevant for conditions in Turkey.

It is worth looking at one of Nâzım's most obviously Futurist-inspired poems of the period for what it reveals about both the economically "backward" but politically "advanced" East. Radically, the 1921 poem "Makinalaşmak" (To Become a Machine), opens not with words but the onomatopoetic clanking and whirring of machinery:

> trrrrum,
> 			trrrrum,
> 					trrrrum!
> trak tiki tak!
> I want to become
> 			a machine!
>
> . . .
>
> I will certainly find a solution for this
> and will only be happy
> on the day I place a turbine in my stomach
> And affix twin propellers to my tail![29]

This poem reveals a search for human perfectibility through machinery. It is inspired by what Susan Buck-Morss calls the early Soviet "cult of the machine."[30] This cult emerged out of frustration with underdevelopment, appearing at a time when Soviet industrial capacity had been crippled by war. Mass casualties had caused an extreme decrease in the factory workforce. In 1920, the Soviet government founded a Central Institute of Labor to research efficiency. Yet this practical emphasis on industry also had a "utopian surplus."[31] Aleksei Gastev, director of the Central Institute of Labor, was also a poet. He dreamed of "creating one world brain in place of millions of brains" through the creation of what Buck-Morss glosses as "a new human sensorium of electric nerves, brain machines, and cinema eyes."[32] Thus, in a time of weakened industrial capacity, the Soviet "cult of the human-as-machine" served a wish-fulfillment function for industrial development that would outpace Europe.

Turkey, of course, experienced a similar hunger for development after World War I and its War of Independence (1919–1923). One of the first priorities of the new Turkish state was rapidly increasing production and improving the weak industrial base. Nâzım's machines poetically internalized these ambitions, as clarified by the unpublished sequel poem "Makinalaşmak 2." The 1923 poem begins with the speaker imagining a state of advanced technology from his own rather undeveloped position, thereby creating an allegory of international inequality:

> I live in a four-story wooden house
> My room is on the fourth floor.

"We, Too, Are Eastern"

> Across from my window are apartment blocks, 20 stories of reinforced concrete.
> At every moment 20 elevators glide
> from foundation to roof
> roof to foundation.
> Whereas I,
> a man who wants to
> place a turbine in my stomach
> and affix twin propellers to my tail,
> every night
> I climb 80 steps of wooden stairs.
> With each step my animosity for the bosses
> rising in the elevators increases 100-fold.
> Yet I'm still optimistic.
> I believe in socialism.
> The machines will be ours.
> And I will become
> a machine . . .
> Yet until that time
> to soothe my great desire
> every morning
> down the banisters of 80 steps of stairs
> Buzzzzz . . . .
> I slide . . .
> The doorkeeper woman
> says of me, "He's lost his mind."
> She doesn't know—nitwit!
> that I want to
> become a machine . . .[33]

The poem's speaker contrasts the humble wooden house he resides in to massive, state-of-the-art apartment blocks with futuristic elevators. He dreams of attaching turbines to his body and is fascinated by the speed and power represented by these gliding compartments. On the subjective level, the poem transforms frustration with underdevelopment into a stubborn joy: short of being able to actually add a propeller to his tail, the speaker runs up and down the stairs in a makeshift approximation of machine movements. It is as if he can usher in the machine age through enthusiasm alone.

Yet the poem also has a strong social and geopolitical component. The speaker despises the rich who enjoy the actual fruits of modern technology: "the bosses." But when socialism comes, "The machines will be ours." The animosity against the owners of the elevators in "Makinalaşmak 2" can be read both as class resentment within a single country and anger at the global unevenness of industrial development. The Russian Revolution, the political event that seemed to herald a new age, occurred in one of the most economically unadvanced countries in Europe. The Bolshevik leadership was uncomfortable with this "temporal paradox"[34] and increasingly defined economic modernization itself as revolution. Turkey shared this emphasis on speed-up and development. It too was an insufficiently industrialized country that sought to "reach the level of contemporary civilization" (in Mustafa Kemal Atatürk's famous phrase). On the level of policy, this meant economic planning modeled on the Soviet Union's five-year plans.

In Nâzım's poetry, machines—or, more precisely, their absence—become a symbol of Turkey's industrial ambitions. As Hasan Bülent Kahraman writes:

> Machines, industry, and other things occupying an important position in Nâzım's episteme have their source in this [economic] situation. When he returned to Turkey [from the Soviet Union] he saw something interesting. Turkey, too, had undergone a revolution, though not a socialist one. Turkey, too—if for different reasons—had the same goal as the Soviets: to industrialize.[35]

It is in this context of massive psychic investment in industrialization, versus the stubborn fact of underdevelopment, that made machines a powerful object of compensatory fantasy in Nâzım's early poetry. The East will not only produce more machines than capitalist Europe: its citizens themselves will become mechanized.

The East as Vanguard

It is clear that theme of development/underdevelopment in Nâzım's mechanization poems can be easily applied both to the Soviet and the Turkish context. In fact, the two locations are often treated as interchangeable in his poetry, with the Soviet Union becoming something of an honorary Eastern nation. Nâzım's poem "Farewell"—written "while leaving the USSR in 1924," as the epigraph notes—reveals what socialist intellectuals in Turkey and throughout the tri-continent saw in the Soviet Union: a model for leaping out of prehistory and into the future.

> Russia,
> with the love of a schoolchild preparing for an exam,
> Russia reciting the ABCs of communism!
> Hey, land that stuck out its nose first
> from the window of our age's prehistory!
> Hey, barefoot
>   and running
>   country where Mercedes motors pass!
> We saw everything along with you, sharing the same pillow,
> your dreams filled with armies of tractors!
> Like a radio forming a bridge from
> aeroplane to aeroplane we heard it,
> the love for electricity
> beating in your veins! . . .[36]

The Soviet Union is shown as a model for the entire world. It started off with the enthusiasm of a "schoolchild" but is now racing towards the future, even if barefoot. The "we" watching the Soviet experience from outside identifies intimately with its struggle, sharing the "same pillow" and the same dreams. The mention of radios, airplanes, and electricity shows the emotional charge carried by industrialization. As John Berger writes, for communist artists in this period "the idea of industrialization had acquired lyrical power, for it seemed to offer a way of avoiding, instead of suffering and enduring, a whole phase of history."[37] For Nâzım, returning to Turkey from Moscow, what he brought home was this dream of an alternative route to modernity, one which incorporates the advanced technology of capitalism but eschews its inequalities. For the "we" of this poem—who are not just from Turkey but the entire underdeveloped or colonized world—the Soviet example offers an instruction manual for catapulting into a new age.

In this sense, Nâzım's poems must be seen within the context of anti-imperialism and anti-colonialism. This is the other lesson that people in Asia, Africa, and Latin America extracted from the Soviet example. The 1925 poem "Piyer Loti" shows how Nâzım's Marxist education taught him to see Turkey's geopolitical position in new terms, particularly in terms of its potential allies. The poem denounces the French naval officer and famous nineteenth-century Orientalist novelist Pierre Loti and then calls for revolution in Turkey and across Asia.

> *"Submission!*
> *Fatalism!*
> *Lattice-work, caravanserai*
>   *fountains!*
> *A sultan dancing on a silver tray!*
> . . .
>
> This is the Orient the French poet sees!
> This is
>   the Orient
> in the books
> printed at the rate of 1,000,000 a minute![38]

Against these orientalist visions of opulence and faith that tantalize European readers, the poem's speaker defines the east in more material terms:

> The east
> land where naked
>   slaves
>   drop dead starving!
> Land that is the common property
> Of all except for the easterner![39]

The poverty described here is not eternal but historically specific: a direct result of colonial exploitation and intentional underdevelopment. The East is "a wheat granary / filled to the brim! / Europe's granary!" The poem then mentions British, American, and French imperialism from Turkey and India to China. As the Easterners wake up to the fact of their exploitation, they fight back: "the year of the east's liberation is ahead of us / waving a bloody handkerchief."[40] Yet the East is not alone in its struggle. The poem addresses the "sans-culottes" of Europe: "we give you our hands / embrace us." Nâzım builds on rhetoric that describes colonized people as the igniting force for revolution among the European working classes. For example, according to Tartar Bolshevik Mirsaid Sultan-Galiev, "The East is a revolutionary cauldron capable of putting a revolutionary torch to all of Western Europe."[41] In other words, the underdevelopment of the East is the key to its position as liberator.

Nâzım's poetic output from this period makes more sense when we zoom out from the Turkish context. There is the example of the left-wing Tamil poet Sabramania Bharati, who wrote about the "New Russia" where "no slaves exist now."[42] Then there is modernist Mexican poet

Manuel Maples Arce, who in 1924 wrote *City: Bolshevik Super-Poem in Five Cantos* describing how "Russia's lungs / blow the wind / of social revolution toward us."[43] From Chile to Greece, poets were articulating the relevance of the 1917 revolution for their own contexts.[44] Nâzım did the same for Turkey but never lost sight of the rest of the world. His poems about China, India, and Ethiopia implicitly argue that Turkey shares something fundamental with these contexts.

In three long narrative poems, Nâzım went on to explore this theme of the East as vanguard. Besides *Jokond ile Si-Ya-U* (1929), there is *Benerci Kendini Niçin Öldürdü?* (1932) and *Taranta Babu'ya Mektuplar* (1935). *Benerci* centers on the colonial metropolis of Kolkata and solidarity between the oppressed. In the epistolary poem *Taranta Babu'ya Mektuplar*, an anti-fascist Italian friend of Nâzım's translates letters written by an Ethiopian art student in Rome to his wife back home on the eve of the Mussolini's invasion. The letters incorporate news clippings, telegrams, and photographs to provide an internationalist, anti-racist critique of fascism. Though the action in these three epic poems is far afield from Turkey, they implicitly link the capitalist, colonial world-system to conditions at home, while also providing the author with plausible deniability when taken to court.[45] Using allegory and displacement (as well as the poet himself as a character traveling between Istanbul, Shanghai, and Bengal), these poems offer a different conceptualization of Turkey's place in the world's balance of power, one quite different than the official Kemalist narrative. They suggest that Turkey's natural allies are not in the West but the East, where prehistory will be brought to an end and the next, most advanced, stage of humanity will begin.

Conclusion

More than Futurist influence or the fact of living in Moscow, it was Nâzım's internationalist political commitments that allowed him to frame a specifically "Eastern" vision of modernity. This set him apart from fellow Turkish poets who treated modern technology as a product of Europe (like Tevfik Fikret). For others, modern life was a source of pessimism and anomie (Necip Fazıl and the conservative modernists), or the city was simply politically neutral backdrop for a colloquial poetry of the urban everyman (Orhan Veli). While taking the side of the East, Nâzım's poetry also steered clear of chauvinist nationalism or Islamism. He created what Nergis Ertürk calls a "non-identitarian form of revolutionary collectivism."[46] His work claimed Ethiopian farmers, Chinese laborers, and Indian anti-colonial fighters as allies.

Interestingly, it was before Nâzım left for the Soviet Union that he first developed this notion of Turkey as part of the "advanced East." While in Ankara in 1921, he planned a literary journal called "Asia" with the help of some Turkish Spartacists. At the time, Nâzım described the project to Ziya Gökalp, an influential Turkist ideologue whose idea of importing "civilization" (technology) for the West while preserving national "culture" (art and traditions) influenced a generation of Turkish nationalists. According to Vâ-Nû's account, Gökalp told Nâzım that putting out a journal called "Asia" would mean "erecting a conception of Asianness against Europeanness. I don't see this as acceptable. Turks must be European."[47] For Nâzım, this was exactly the problem. The future would be Eastern.

With his "unique intuition," as Vâ-Nû describes it, Nâzım was developing a vision of the East that would not come to fruition until decades later, as in the famous Bandung Conference of 1955 and the Asia-Africa conferences of the Cold War period. Gül Bilge Han describes the poet's late "tricontinental poetics of solidarity" that grew out of his experiences meeting other writers in Havana, Tashkent, Dar es Salaam, and beyond.[48] In the poem "To Asian and African Writers," written in 1962, Nâzım says: "never mind my blond hair / I am an Asian / never mind my blue eyes / I am an African."[49] In this way, Nâzım's approach radically clashed with the dominant pro-Western orientation of Turkey.[50] This was certainly a bold position after Turkey joined NATO in 1952, but in the pro-Western climate of the 1920s Republic, it was even more radical. And in our own day—as Eurasianist factions in Turkey's government cozy up with Russia or China or Islamists and nationalists show intermittent solidarity (when the geopolitical conjuncture is suitable) with Azerbaijanis, Palestinians, or Uyghurs based on religious or ethnic identity—it is worth looking back at Nâzım's alternative vision. For him, being modern (both in politics and art) and being Eastern were not a contradiction.

Notes

1 For Nâzım's posthumous reception and influence in Turkey, see Yalçın Armağan, "Nâzım Hikmet, İkinci Yeni'ye Tokat Attı mı?" in *Şiir Dünyadan İbaret: Nazım Hikmet Üzerine Yeni Çalışmalar*, ed. Olcay Akyıldız and Murat Gülsoy (Istanbul: Boğaziçi University Press, 2019), 218–36; Kenan Behzat Sharpe, "Gerçekçilik ve Kavgacılık: Nâzım Hikmet'in 1960'lar Türkiye Sosyalist Şairleri İçin Önemi," in *Şiir Dünyadan İbaret: Nazım Hikmet Üzerine Yeni Çalışmalar*, ed. Olcay Akyıldız and Murat Gülsoy (Istanbul: Boğaziçi University Press, 2019), 179–217.
2 Orhan Koçak, "'Our Master, the Novice': On the Catastrophic Births of Modern Turkish Poetry." *South Atlantic Quarterly* 102, no. 2–3 (Spring–Summer 2003): 577.
3 Camilla Gray, *The Great Experiment: Russian Art, 1863–1922* (London: Thames & Hudson, 1962), 216.
4 Eugene Lunn, *Marxism & Modernism: An Historical Study of Lukács, Brecht, Benjamin, and Adorno* (Berkeley: University of California Press, 1982), 53.
5 Saime Göksu and Edward Timms, *Romantic Communist: The Life and Work of Nazım Hikmet* (London: Hurst, 1999), 129.
6 For Europe as the locus of technological modernity in the imagination of the Ottoman Empire, see Zeynep Uysal's chapter in this volume.
7 Anna Lawton, "Russian and Italian Futurist Manifestoes," *Slavic and East European Journal* 20, no. 4 (1976): 408.
8 For more on "conservative modernism" in Turkey, see Nergis Ertürk, "Modernism Disfigured: Turkish Literature and the 'Other West,'" in *The Oxford Handbook of Global Modernisms*, ed. Mark Wollaeger and Matt Eatough (Oxford: Oxford University Press, 2012), 530–42.
9 Marshall Berman, *All That Is Solid Melts into Air: The Experience of Modernity* (New York: Penguin, 1998), 193.
10 Ibid., 236.
11 Ibid., 232.
12 Ibid.
13 Ataol Behramoğlu, *Büyük Türk Şiiri Antolojisi*, vol. 1 (Istanbul: Sosyal Yayınlar, 2001), 30.
14 Tevfik Fikret, *Rübab-ı Şikeste ve Tevfik Fikret'in Diğer Bütün Eserleri* (Istanbul: İnkilap ve Aka Yayınları, 1985), 69.
15 Koçak, "'Our Master, the Novice,'" 582.
16 See Fırat Oruç's chapter in this volume.
17 The character Si-Ya-U is based on the Chinese student Emi Siao, whom Nâzım befriended at the University for the Toilers of the East in Moscow. For more on Emi's life and the international atmosphere at KUTV, see Elizabeth McGuire, *Red at Heart: How Chinese Communists Fell in Love with the Russian Revolution* (Oxford: Oxford University Press, 2018).
18 Nâzım Hikmet, *Poems of Nâzım Hikmet*, trans. Randy Blasing and Mutlu Konuk (New York: Persea Books, 2002), 12.
19 For a longer account of this poem's historical background, see Alice Xiang, "Re-Worlding the *Mona Lisa*: Nâzım Hikmet's Modernist Diplomacy," *Journal of Modern Literature* 41, no. 2 (Winter 2018): 1–22.
20 Marc Matera and Susan Kingsley Kent, *The Global 1930s: The International Decade* (Abingdon: Routledge, 2017), 9.
21 James H. Meyer, "Children of Trans-Empire: Nâzım Hikmet and the First Generation of Turkish Students at Moscow's Communist University of the East," *Journal of the Ottoman and Turkish Studies Association* 5, no. 2 (Fall 2016): 211.
22 Bülent Gökay, *Soviet Eastern Policy and Turkey, 1920–1991: Soviet Foreign Policy, Turkey and Communism* (New York: Penguin, 2006), 7.

23 Meyer, "Children of Trans-Empire," 200.

24 Gökay, *Soviet Eastern Policy*, 21.

25 Vijay Prashad, *Red Star Over the Third World* (London: Pluto Press, 2017), 17.

26 Vâ-Nû, *Bu Dünyadan Nâzım Geçti* (Ankara: Cem Yayınları, 1975), 260.

27 Nâzım Hikmet, *Bütün Şiirleri* (Istanbul: Yapı Kredi Yayınları, 2015), 40.

28 It was seeing one of Mayakovsky's poems in a newspaper that inspired him to play with new styles of free-verse. Göksu and Timms, *Romantic Communist*, 38.

29 Nâzım Hikmet, *Bütün Şiirleri*, 38–39.

30 Susan Buck-Morss, *Dreamworld and Catastrophe: The Passing of Mass Utopia in East and West* (Cambridge, MA: MIT Press, 2002), 105.

31 Ibid.

32 Ibid.

33 Nâzım Hikmet, *Bütün Şiirleri*, 2034.

34 Buck-Morss, *Dreamworld and Catastrophe*, 58.

35 Hasan Bülent Kahraman, *Türk Şiiri, Modernizm, Şiir* (Ankara: Büke Yayınları, 2000), 45.

36 Nâzım Hikmet, *Bütün Şiirleri*, 2075.

37 John Berger, *Art and Revolution: Ernst Neizvestny and the Role of the Artist in the USSR* (New York: Vintage Books, 1997), 44.

38 Nâzım Hikmet, *Bütün Şiirleri*, 35.

39 Ibid.

40 Ibid., 37.

41 Gökay, *Soviet Eastern Policy*, 20.

42 Prashad, *Red Star Over the Third World*, 39.

43 Ibid., 45.

44 For a comparison of Nâzım's poetry with the work of the international communist poets Langston Hughes, Pablo Neruda, Yannis Ritsos, and Muriel Rukeyser, see Kenan Behzat Sharpe, "Radical Moderns/Poetry International: Nâzım Hikmet, Langston Hughes, Pablo Neruda, Muriel Rukeyser," in *Back to the 30s? Crisis, Repetition and Transition in the 20th and 21st Centuries*, ed. Susan Falls et al. (London: Palgrave Macmillan, 2020), 257–75.

45 Göksu and Timms, *Romantic Communist*, 184.

46 Nergis Ertürk, *Grammatology and Literary Modernity in Turkey* (Oxford: Oxford University Press, 2011), 162.

47 Vâ-Nû, *Bu Dünyadan Nâzım Geçti*, 160.

48 Gül Bilge Han, "Nazım Hikmet's Afro-Asian Solidarities," *Safundi* 19, no. 3 (August 2018): 287.

49 Ibid., 296.

50 The United States asked Turkey to send representatives to the Bandung Conference in 1955 but initially balked at joining a "meeting of the colored races" because this was "a status from which Turkish statesman believed they were exempt." Begüm Adalet, *Hotels and Highways: The Construction of Modernization Theory in Cold War Turkey* (Palo Alto, CA: Stanford University Press, 2018), 6.

References

Adalet, Begüm. *Hotels and Highways: The Construction of Modernization Theory in Cold War Turkey*. Palo Alto, CA: Stanford University Press, 2018.

Armağan, Yalçın. "Nâzım Hikmet, İkinci Yeni'ye Tokat Attı mı?" In *Şiir Dünyadan İbaret: Nazım Hikmet Üzerine Yeni Çalışmalar*, edited by Olcay Akyıldız and Murat Gülsoy, 218–36. Istanbul: Boğaziçi University Press, 2019.

Behramoğlu, Ataol. *Büyük Türk Şiiri Antolojisi*, vol. 1. Istanbul: Sosyal Yayınlar, 2001.

Berger, John. *Art and Revolution: Ernst Neizvestny and the Role of the Artist in the USSR*. New York: Vintage Books, 1997.

Berman, Marshall. *All That Is Solid Melts into Air: The Experience of Modernity*. New York: Penguin, 1998.

Buck-Morss, Susan. *Dreamworld and Catastrophe: The Passing of Mass Utopia in East and West*. Cambridge: The MIT Press, 2002.

Ertürk, Nergis. *Grammatology and Literary Modernity in Turkey*. Oxford: Oxford University Press, 2011.

———. "Modernism Disfigured: Turkish Literature and the 'Other West.'" In *The Oxford Handbook of Global Modernisms*, edited by Mark Wollaeger and Matt Eatough, 530–42. Oxford: Oxford University Press, 2012.

Gökay, Bülent. *Soviet Eastern Policy and Turkey, 1920–1991: Soviet Foreign Policy, Turkey and Communism*. New York: Penguin, 2006.

Göksu, Saime, and Edward Timms. *Romantic Communist: The Life and Work of Nazım Hikmet*. London: Hurst, 1999.

Gray, Camilla. *The Great Experiment: Russian Art, 1863–1922*. London: Thames & Hudson, 1962.

Han, Gül Bilge. "Nazım Hikmet's Afro-Asian Solidarities." *Safundi* 19, no. 3 (August 2018): 284–305.

Kahraman, Hasan Bülent. *Türk Şiiri, Modernizm, Şiir*. Ankara: Büke Yayınları, 2000.

Koçak, Orhan. "'Our Master, the Novice': On the Catastrophic Births of Modern Turkish Poetry." *South Atlantic Quarterly* 102, no. 2–3 (Spring–Summer 2003): 567–98.

Lawton, Anna. "Russian and Italian Futurist Manifestoes." *The Slavic and East European Journal* 20, no. 4 (1976): 405–20.

Lunn, Eugene. *Marxism & Modernism: An Historical Study of Lukács, Brecht, Benjamin, and Adorno*. Berkeley: University of California Press, 1982.

Matera, Marc, and Susan Kingsley Kent. *The Global 1930s: The International Decade*. Abingdon: Routledge, 2017.

McGuire, Elizabeth. *Red at Heart: How Chinese Communists Fell in Love with the Russian Revolution*. Oxford: Oxford University Press, 2018.

Meyer, James H. "Children of Trans-Empire: Nâzım Hikmet and the First Generation of Turkish Students at Moscow's Communist University of the East." *Journal of the Ottoman and Turkish Studies Association* 5, no. 2 (Fall 2016): 195–218.

Nâzım Hikmet. *Poems of Nâzım Hikmet*. Translated by Randy Blasing and Mutlu Konuk. New York: Persea Books, 2002.

———. *Bütün Şiirleri*. Istanbul: Yapı Kredi Yayınları, 2015.

Prashad, Vijay. *Red Star Over the Third World*. London: Pluto Press, 2017.

Sharpe, Kenan Behzat. "Gerçekçilik ve Kavgacılık: Nâzım Hikmet' in 1960 'lar Türkiye Sosyalist Şairleri İçin Önemi." In *Şiir Dünyadan İbaret: Nazım Hikmet Üzerine Yeni Çalışmalar*, edited by Olcay Akyıldız and Murat Gülsoy, 179–217. Istanbul: Boğaziçi University Press, 2019.

———. "Radical Moderns/Poetry International: Nâzım Hikmet, Langston Hughes, Pablo Neruda, Muriel Rukeyser." In *Back to the 30s? Crisis, Repetition and Transition in the 20th and 21st Centuries*, edited by Susan Falls et al., 257–75. London: Palgrave Macmillan, 2020.

Tevfik Fikret. *Rübab-ı Şikeste ve Tevfik Fikret'in Diğer Bütün Eserleri*. Istanbul: İnkilap ve Aka Yayınları, 1985.

Vâ-Nû. *Bu Dünyadan Nâzım Geçti*. Ankara: Cem Yayınları, 1975.

Xiang, Alice. "Re-Worlding the Mona Lisa: Nâzım Hikmet's Modernist Diplomacy." *Journal of Modern Literature* 41, no. 2 (Winter 2018): 1–22.

24

THE EMERGENCE AND THE END OF AN ENDEMIC GENRE IN TURKISH LITERATURE

The Case of the Village Novel in a Comparative Context

Erkan Irmak

The emergence of the Turkish novel is a popular subject field among literary critics in Turkey, and there is a prolific and ongoing discussion on the ontological and epistemological nature of the birth of the first novels.[1] Because the foundation of modern Turkish literature is dated to 1850s, it is not wrong to claim—like any other late or less novelized literatures—that the first novels and the first modernization movements of the Ottoman Empire were tightly intertwined.[2] In this regard, Turkish novels and Turkish modernization efforts share a common fate, in terms of their initial concerns and desires. On the other hand, when it comes to subgenres of the Turkish novel, the very same field begins to become barren. Although the first steps of the leftist or socialist realist novel tradition of Turkish literature date back to the early Republican era and has had a large audience since then, the origin, history, and evolution of this subgenre has been rarely studied.[3] Village novels of Turkish literature—as a branch of leftist novels—are in this respect an even more neglected subject. When critics do pay attention to them, it is mostly considered through prejudices and clichés. Therefore, in this chapter, my goal is to point out the main features of Turkish village novels and determine the conditions of their historical appearance, success, and ultimate extinction from the literary scene. To achieve this, I will first describe and fact-check the well-known yet poorly studied characteristics of village novels. Besides defining the position of the village novels, I will reread some of the main arguments of literary critics and assess the validity of their perspectives. Then, through a detour of village novels, I will discuss how the ambiguity of this genre is interpreted in some other literatures and try to compare Turkish village novels with their counterparts. Third, to understand the unique historical background and philosophy of these novels, I will briefly introduce the Village Institutes of the 1940s, how these schools helped (and caused) village notes to come into being, and how these village notes eventually evolved into village novels. Finally, I will interpret the way village novels were received by the leftist writers and the literary community of the period (1950–1980) and the reasons for the different receptions that emerged over time.

298

DOI: 10.4324/9780429279270-32

"Emergence and End of an Endemic Genre in Turkish Literature"

Defining the Turkish Village Novel

The first question that comes to mind in terms of Turkish village novels is, as might be expected, related to a basic definition: What is the village novel? Although the question is valid and fundamental, the existing answers are both limited and mostly tautological. Unfortunately, apart from a few exceptional examples, almost everyone who writes about the "village novel" has evaluated this genre based on only one criterion: If the events in a novel take place in the village, it should be called a "village novel."[4]

For example, Ramazan Kaplan's work *Cumhuriyet Dönemi Türk Romanında Köy* [Village in Turkish Novel in the Republican Period], which we can consider the most important and foundational text in village novel criticism, was published in 1988. For a long period, this study remained the most comprehensive study conducted on the subject. Therefore, it is possible to claim that almost everyone who wrote about the subject referred to Kaplan, that the periodization and descriptions he made became the norm, and that this work lies at the root of the field's boundaries and mythology.

Indeed, Kaplan is also aware of the pioneering role of his book and writes the following in his preface:

> This study has arisen from the need to save a literary movement that has been influential in the Turkish novel for a long time and caused controversy with one-sided studies that have been unable exceed the boundaries of an article and to deal with it within the framework of scientific principles. And up until today, in Turkey, there has not been scientific research examining how village issues are handled in the novels.[5]

As can be understood from the title of his book, Kaplan determines the texts he will examine based on the setting of the events. In other words, the village novel is categorized as a novel set in the village, as has always been done. As a matter of fact, Kaplan also states in his preface that he made his definition according to the current assumptions:

> In this study, novels published between 1923–1980 and commonly known as "village novels" were evaluated in terms of their subjects. These novels, whose subject is in the village and whose characters are peasants, focus on the problems of the villagers [but] have been studied *without any selection*.[6]

However, when the location of a novel's plot is used as the one and only criterion to describe village novels, it is impossible to interpret these texts historically, sociologically, or literarily. Therefore, describing all these texts as village novels, which differ from each other in many respects and were written over a span of almost 150 years, reveals contradictions rather than simplicity and creates clichés rather than arguments.

Another important issue with the studies on village novels is the insistence on the isolation of the texts from their authors and the periods in which they were written. The main goal of Kaplan and many other researchers is to distinguish the novels from each other at various periodic intervals, group them in terms of their subject matter, gather these groups within subcategories, and present a list of contents based on these criteria.

Berna Moran, one of the prominent critics of the Turkish novel, also uses a similar method and tries to frame the village novels with five basic content characteristics. According to Moran, village novels (1) are action oriented, not dependent on analysis; (2) are built on the opposition of famine versus abundance; (3) are formed by the victim-rebel duality, with main characters turning from the first to the second; (4) treat the village as one of the main focus points; and (5) accordingly, emphasize the contrast between village-town/city.[7] The problem frequently seen in these pioneering works is the confusion between the content and the space, the characters, and the plot when describing village novels. This situation also constitutes the source of a tautology that became inextricable in the following years.

For example, Orhan Kemal's novel *Bereketli Topraklar Üzerinde* (1953) is considered a village novel in all these critical works despite only a few pages of the novel actually taking place in the village. The main concern of the text is to explain the social relations that were rearranged after working conditions changed in the city due to capitalism and urbanization in the Çukurova region of Turkey. Reşat Nuri Güntekin's *Çalıkuşu* (1922, revised edition 1937) and *Yeşil Gece* (1928), and Yakup Kadri Karaosmanoğlu's *Yaban* (1932) also took the village as their main setting in certain chapters, but for many critics, rightly, these novels deal not with peasants but the issues of the city dwellers who encounter the villagers. And if all these novels were to be named under a single genre, it would be much more appropriate and convincing to call them "urban novels." Yet, this confusion (and contradiction) is not unique to Turkish literature. When examples from world literature are examined, the prevalence and complexity of the problem can be understood more clearly.

Village Novels in Other Literatures

Undoubtedly, Turkish is not the only language in the world that produces literary texts focused on the village. Likewise, these novels also differ from each other in many aspects, such as history, content, intention, and formal features. For example, when we examine English literature, we see that the terms "rustic novel," "rural novel," "regional novel," and "pastoral novel" are also used in addition to "village novel." Yet this variation in naming does not mean that the genre is better defined but that the problem is more extensive.

For instance, even if the term "regional novel" is used for novels set in the countryside, this adjective alone does not mean it necessarily takes place in the provinces. Likewise, the "region" itself is not necessarily limited to a small region or village.[8] It may be possible to consider Yaşar Kemal's books "regional" due to their setting in the Taurus Mountains or Çukurova, for example, and many of Orhan Pamuk's novels could be included in the same genre as they focus on Istanbul.

"Pastoral novels," on the other hand, are directly related to the concept of the "pastoral," which has a much broader historical background and a very strict definition. The purpose of these texts is to symbolically describe, interpret, or discuss certain religious, moral, and philosophical teachings or knowledge.[9]

The "rural/rustic novel" appears, however, to most approximate the vague definition that comes to mind when the village novel is mentioned. The most distinctive feature shared by these two terms, which can be used interchangeably, is that the expression "rural/rustic" is sometimes also used for town-sized settlements. Another situation where the rural/rustic novel diverges from village novels is that the latter appear in literatures where a peasant population is predominant. Therefore, the expression "village novel" is more common in countries with a "village/peasant problem" (such as Turkey), while "rural/rustic novels" are mostly encountered in regions where the peasantry, in the traditional sense, has disappeared. The heroes of rural/rustic novels are also different from village novels. These characters are either the old town dwellers who consciously choose to live in the countryside, the people who travel there, or the rural dwellers who live in the countryside but have access to and benefit more or less from the opportunities the city possesses, as a result of the country's general level of development.[10] Yet these minor distinctions also become intertwined in scholars' interpretations, and it becomes impossible to define each novel's specific genre. Moreover, even if all the present determinations were valid, it would not be possible to get rid of the oddity of comparing a nineteenth-century French rustic novel with a twentieth-century Nigerian village novel, since the question of periodization as a basis for definition remains unanswered.

Therefore, the village novel genre seems to be a dust cloud that needs to be considered in terms of literary history and is far from being defined yet. In that case, giving up the naming efforts and dealing with the content, authorial intention, and historical background in novels set in the village may be a better step towards gaining an idea about these texts in general.

As mentioned above, in order for village novels to become widespread in a certain period, as in Turkish literature, some positive or negative developments regarding villages and peasants can be expected to occur in the region in question. In this context, before looking more closely at the unique side of the village novel in Turkish literature, it may be helpful to look at other "village novels" that appeared in regions that experienced similar rapid social transformations in the last two centuries.

For example, George Nyamndi argues that when evaluating village novels the main emphasis should be put on space. Because the distinctiveness of these novels is related to the setting of events, the village, what makes them special is that they record notable life experiences in village life.[11] According to Nyamndi,

> The village novel in West Africa belongs to the mainstream of cultural awakening to which political independence gave rise. Its genesis and developments are therefore intimately bound with the historical circumstances which went into the making of present-day Africa.[12]

In Egypt, too, another country that has undergone rapid and radical transformations in politics, society, economics, religion, and culture since the nineteenth century, many novels have been written about villages and peasants. Samah Selim, at the very beginning of his study of the village imagination in the novels written in Egypt between 1880 and 1985, states: "In the twentieth century, the Egyptian peasantry . . . came to dominate the social discourse and political ideology of the modern Egyptian nation-state, and the *fellah* suddenly emerged as a potent emblem of national identity."[13] He adds,

> the village novel also reflects issues related to the sociology of culture in the modern Egyptian context. The problem of social identity in both a personal and a political sense is repeatedly articulated in the novel through the trope of the "clash" between the country and the city as it is lived by individuals and by entire communities.[14]

In her book on Russian "village prose," Kathleen F. Parthé also states that the primary concern of these texts is the return of the ex-peasants to their lands, albeit for a short time.[15] This return also allows the hero to regain his own past. The dominant emotion in return narratives is melancholy. The source of this melancholy is both the sadness of moving away from one's roots, the realization that those left behind are no longer there, and the gradual disappearance of village life itself. Some of the other themes Parthé draws attention to are the stories of "becoming rootlessness," in which those who have left their villages are told "childhood" memories from the protagonist who also is away from his village.[16] Therefore, it is possible to treat these texts as nostalgic stories about the village or peasants, as well as a lament about the village life, which is gradually disappearing due to industrialization. Parthé writes,

> The basic characterization of Village Prose could be expanded from one theme (*tema*) to a collective thematics (*tematika*) that encompassed the rural/urban split, criticism of government policy in the countryside, the revival of Russian national and religious sentiment, a search for national values, a concern for the environment, and a nostalgia generated by the loss of traditional rural life.[17]

The distinctive similarities in all three (non-western) examples and their commonalities with village novels in Turkish literature are also striking. First of all, in the literatures of these three regions, the concern that a rapidly dissolving peasantry will lead to the loss of traditional cultural values comes to the fore. In connection with this, it is understood that the first place where societies entering the process of nationalization turn their attention while building a national identity is the village. In this context, it can be said that the leftist "village-themed" novels (e.g., in the books of Orhan Kemal, Yaşar Kemal, and Kemal Tahir) in Turkish literature are not distant from these examples. But one important difference in the context of the other literary examples is that even if the origins of the authors are rural, their minds are shaped by a modernist, abstract education (unlike the authors of the Turkish "village novels" who all graduated from the Village Institutes, which will be explained in the next section). Moreover, writing texts about the village is not an inevitable end, but a choice for them. And many of the Turkish village novelists have written not only about the village but also about the life of the city dwellers. All these parallels reveal that examples of Turkish leftist literature, despite some differences, have many similarities with other non-western, late, or less novelized literatures. In this respect, it can be claimed that village novels in western and non-western literatures have emerged with different origins and intentions. On the other hand, some of the decisions made to solve the "village problem" in the early Republican era in Turkey caused a new form of village novels to emerge. To understand the reasons behind this mutation in the genre, we need to focus on the Village Institutes and the unique experiences of their students.

The Village Institutes

Like many other nation-states founded in the first half of the twentieth century, Turkey is closely related to the village/peasant problem. From the 1920s onwards, the question of what the village and the villagers are, and what they should be, led to many long-standing debates.[18] Discussions were caught between a romantic discourse claiming that the essence of the nation could only be found in the village and an elitist view that the village must be trained and recruited to the regime as soon as possible. These approaches were finally transformed into a concrete and common dream in 1940 with the Village Institutes. However, the life of the Village Institutes was much shorter than expected and the results were distant from what was initially hoped.[19] This project—perhaps because of the infinity of its horizon, as it was expected to unite the villagers with the regime to break the hegemony of religion over the village and increase economic efficiency in the rural areas—was first slowed down after less than ten years and then completely abolished by its founders.

However, there were important differences between the state's rural development plans and the opinions of the graduates of the Institutes. As a matter of fact, many young people among the graduates would quickly break from what was expected of them. The first serious and visible example of these efforts in the field of literature was Mahmut Makal's "village notes" called

Bizim Köy [*Our Village*], published in 1950. *Bizim Köy* consists of the memories of a peasant boy between the ages of 13 and 17 who left his home for the first time to go to school. The book generally depicts what Makal experienced in his village in Central Anatolia, where he returned as a teacher after the training he received at the İvriz Village Institute. The problems addressed by Makal and the way he deals with them quickly lead to his rise on the literary scene. The first edition of the book, published in January 1950, reached its fourth edition by April of the same year.[20] Makal's *Bizim Köy* and the newborn "village note" genre was so influential that it was translated into many foreign languages and gave rise to many heated debates in the country. Moreover, many other graduates of the Institutes who followed Makal and his monumental book began to publish their own village notes one after the other during the 1950s and 1960s.[21]

In *Bizim Köy*, peasants, who had previously appeared in novels only when described by "urban" writers, were depicted for the first time by an author who describes what he saw himself as a villager. This new, insider view of the village quickly spread to other Village Institute graduates after its first example with Makal. This effect continued and evolved until 1980 and gave rise to a "village literature" specific to Turkish literature. Yaşar Nabi Nayır, one of the most important publishers and influential authorities of cultural life in the period, emphasized the importance of Makal's book in his preface to *Bizim Köy*:

> It seems to me that the bitter truth of a Central Anatolian village is expressed for the first time in all its nakedness in this book, despite some things having been written before about the situation of our villages. However, these were either economic and social studies or observations by the intellectuals who had visited the village. Yet this book is the testimony of a peasant child who was born in a village and lives in the village. This is the reason for its great value.[22]

Although its life and success did not last very long, the village notes genre managed to transfer its genetic code to the next generation, causing the emergence of another endemic genre in Turkish literature: the village novel. In other words, while village notes represented the first moment of a writer from the village emerging, village novels were the products of these writers' efforts to re-distinguish themselves in the literary environment. Thus, the graduates of the Village Institutes, who created the "village notes" genre first and transformed it into village novels, became some of the most dominant figures of the literary scene from the late 1950s until the early 1980s.

Despite some stylistic differences and ideological nuances, it is quite possible to claim that the primary aim of village novelists was not *how* the text is narrated, but *what* is told, unlike the village-themed novels written by leftist authors. In this respect, *Bizim Köy* can be considered as a "mine for themes" used for all subsequent village novels. Whether it is a village note or a village novel, we see that the themes mentioned in *Bizim Köy* were reused in almost all of the books written afterward. Undoubtedly, each author adds his own colors to the villages created through literature, but the organic link between the novels remains extremely strong and visible. However, it should also be remembered that the novels about the village, whose numbers increased rapidly after the 1950s, were not written only by authors who graduated from the Village Institutes. And this fact leads us to a new problem: the question of how "village novels" and "village-themed" novels can be meaningfully distinguished from each other.

The Rise and the Fall of Turkish Village Novels

A relatively thin and mostly neglected book, *Beş Romancı Tartışıyor*[23] [Five Novelists Debate], published in 1960, can be useful to solve this issue of distinguishing village novels from village-themed novels. *Beş Romancı Tartışıyor* contains records of a panel discussion that brought together the most important names of the period from the village novel and village literature in Turkish more generally. In this slim book, it is possible to read the ideas of Mahmut Makal, Fakir Baykurt, Talip Apaydın, Kemal Tahir, and Orhan Kemal on the question of what the village novel is. While the first three names graduated from the Village Institutes, the last two received their education in modern, urban institutions. It is quite surprising to see the degree of difference in almost every subject between authors who graduated from Village Institutes and those who did not. These differences offer an opportunity to further define the village novel as a genre and how they are different from simply village-themed novels. In fact, this differentiation is so evident that it can be easily said that the village novelists' opinions about rural life follow a completely separate line (philosophically, sociologically, ideologically, and even epistemologically) from authors such as Yaşar Kemal, Orhan Kemal, and Kemal Tahir, who were the most famous leftist and socialist realist novelists of the time (also known as the "Üç Kemaller" or "Three Kemals"). In the works of graduates of the Village Institutes, the "village" turns into a singular, withdrawn, closed, isolated, invariable, and often ahistorical (if not anachronistic) scene that serves as the setting for a mostly repetitive story; in others, the village usually functions as a tool which helps authors to convey their ideological or sociological determinations or to motivate the reader to act for the cause.

As a result of this fundamental and irreversible split in modes of thinking, graduates of the Village Institutes, who were welcomed with great pleasure by socialist realists throughout the 1950s and 1960s in the leftist cultural milieu, faced increasingly intense criticism by the 1970s. Their literary, educational, or theoretical defects that were formerly welcomed with sympathy eventually become the cause of their exclusion from leftist cultural scene. In other words, Institute graduates were put in a defensive position and forced to show why their writings were still relevant in the 1970s. One of the reasons behind this harsh reception is that the effects of internal migration in Turkey began to become increasingly intense in the 1970s and the problems of the working class strongly entered Turkish society's political agenda for the first time. Socialist realists, of course, transformed the locations of their texts from rural areas and villages to cities, factories, and slum neighborhoods without confronting any literary difficulty. In parallel with these new settings, they renewed their subjects, characters, and ideological positions. However, it was not possible to realize the same transformation in village novelists' texts for several reasons. First of all, the village that these novelists described in their works had never served functions such as building ideological allegories or embodying a political agenda the way socialist realists' novels did. Secondly, there is no description or recipe for a social transformation in the texts of village novelists. Last, as Fakir Baykurt pointed out in *Beş Romancı Tartışıyor*, it was not a choice but a necessity for the graduates of Institutes to describe the village in their books.[24]

The acceleration in objections to the village novelists was sparked by the radical change in rural-urban demographics, the increase in working-class demands, the desire in the cultural milieu to give more and more attention to describing political and the individual issues, and the fact that the village began to draw less attention. As a result, the leading village novelists such as Fakir Baykurt and Talip Apaydın tried to harmonize two things that were difficult to reconcile: the village and the city or villagers and workers.

To attempt this reconciliation, the village novelists first followed the footsteps of the villagers who formed the backbone of their writings and who had to migrate to the city in increasing numbers over the years. This was depicted in novels either by villagers who travel to the cities to solve their problems or by looking closer at the new lives of former peasants who moved to urban areas for work. In both scenarios, however, there is not a meaningful interaction or dialogue between villagers and city dwellers. The peasants preserve their old habits, their ways of thinking,

"Emergence and End of an Endemic Genre in Turkish Literature"

their traditional family relations, and of course their daily routines. In other words, although they encountered the possibilities of urban life, modernity cannot change them. More precisely, village novelists have difficulties analyzing this transition and transferring or adapting it to their books.

Criticisms raised against village novelists during the 1970s concentrate especially on their lack of conceptual thinking and political theory as well as their overuse of the same templates in their texts.[25] In order to invalidate these claims, graduates of the Village Institutes tried to develop another solution: they introduced urban ideas to their villagers and forced them to gain political consciousness without leaving rural life. As might be expected, this attempt was condemned to fail. Since it is impossible to reestablish the polyphonic nature of the city in the village, in the end the works of village novelists gave rise to even more criticism.

Conclusion

In the end, village novels, which started to be written starting at the end of the 1950s, stood out primarily for their handling of the subjects. On the one hand, writers trained in the Village Institutes, reflected oral narratives, the traditional social structure, and the premodern lifestyle in their village novels. On the other hand, they carried the Enlightenment doctrine of the Village Institutes into their texts. This determination also makes clear the peculiarities of the genre and distinguishes it from other leftist or socialist realist novels set in the village. After the 1970s, political, social, and historical conditions made it necessary and inevitable for village novelists to replace and redefine their works as part of a bigger and more dominant genre: socialist realist novels. However, this unification made the stitch marks of the village novels even more visible, thus weakening their content: the village novelists trying to fulfill the requirements of socialist realist literature at the cost of losing their self-identity. All these factors, combined with the regression of socialist realism in the face of a more modernist/postmodernist literature after 1980, completely eradicated the genre of village literature and the village novel. The village novel appeared in a specific period and under specific conditions in Turkey and, after leaving a powerful influence, left the stage once it completed its unique role in the history of Turkish literature. In the end, while an endemic subgenre of Turkish literature, the village novel went extinct and the ongoing epidemic of the global novel continues to evolve both in Turkish novels and the depiction of the village in literature.

Author's Note

The arguments expressed in this chapter are based on my dissertation, completed at Boğaziçi University, and my book published in 2018. Erkan Irmak, *Eski Köye Yeni Roman—Köy Romanının Tarihi, Kökeni ve Sonu (1950–1980)* (Istanbul: İletişim Yayınları, 2018).

Notes

1 Among many others who write about the birth of the novel in Turkish, see in particular Azade Seyhan, *Tales of Crossed Destinies—The Modern Turkish Novel in a Comparative Context* (New York: Modern Language Association, 2008); Berna Moran, *Türk Romanına Eleştirel Bir Bakış—Ahmet Mithat'tan Ahmet Hamdi Tanpınar'a* (Istanbul: İletişim Yayınları, 2005 [1983]); Ahmet Ö. Evin, *Origins and Development of the Turkish Novel* (Minneapolis: Bibliotheca Islamica, 1983); Nurdan Gürbilek, *Kör Ayna, Kayıp Şark—Edebiyat ve Endişe* (Istanbul: Metis Yayınları, 2004); Jale Parla, *Babalar ve Oğullar—Tanzimat Romanının Epistemolojik Temelleri* (Istanbul: İletişim Yayınları, 1990).

2 For more information about Turkish modernization movements in the nineteenth century, see Eric Jan Zürcher, *Turkey: A Modern History* (London: I. B. Tauris, 1994); Feroz Ahmad, *The Making of*

Modern Turkey (London: Routledge, 1993); Niyazi Berkes, *Türkiye'de Çağdaşlaşma* (Istanbul: Yapı Kredi Yayınları, 2002); Bernard Lewis, *The Emergence of Modern Turkey* (Oxford: Oxford University Press, 2002).

3 For a pioneering study about socialist realist movements in Turkish literature, see Ahmet Oktay, *Toplumcu Gerçekçiliğin Kaynakları* (Istanbul: Bilim Felsefe Sanat Yayınları, 1986).

4 For one of the oldest examples of this phenomenon, see Gündüz Akıncı, *Türk Romanında Köye Doğru* (Ankara: Türk Tarih Kurumu Basımevi, 1961), 15.

5 Ramazan Kaplan, *Cumhuriyet Dönemi Türk Romanında Köy* (Ankara: Kültür ve Turizm Bakanlığı Yayınları, 1988), vi. Unless otherwise stated, all translations in this chapter are mine.

6 Kaplan, *Cumhuriyet Dönemi Türk Romanında Köy*, v (emphasis added).

7 Moran, *Türk Romanına Eleştirel Bir Bakış*, 315–18.

8 K.D.M. Snell, "The Regional Novel: Themes for Interdisciplinary Research," in *The Regional Novel in Britain and Ireland, 1800–1990*, ed. K.D.M. Snell (Cambridge: Cambridge University Press, 1998), 1–53.

9 See, e.g., J. A. Cuddon, *The Penguin Dictionary of Literary Terms and Literary Theory* (London: Penguin Books, 1999), 644–49; Amedeu Solé-Leris, *The Spanish Pastoral Novel* (Boston: Twayne, 1980); Michael Squires, *The Pastoral Novel—Studies in George Eliot, Thomas Hardy, and D. H. Lawrence* (Charlottesville: University of Virginia Press, 1974).

10 See, e.g., W. J. Keith, *Regions of the Imagination: The Development of British Rural Fiction* (Toronto: University of Toronto Press, 1988); Marc Storey, *Rural Fictions, Urban Realities—A Geography of Gilded Age American Literature* (Oxford: Oxford University Press, 2013); Michael H. Parkinson, *The Rural Novel—Jeremias Gotthelf, Thomas Hardy, C. F. Ramuz* (Bern: Peter Lang, 1984); V. D. Katamble, *The Rural Novel in Indian English* (Jaipur: Shruti, 2008).

11 George Nyamndi, *The West African Village Novel with Particular Reference to Elechi Amadi's "The Concubine"* (Bern: Peter Lang, 1982), 1.

12 Ibid., 2. For more information on the West African village novel, see Emmanuel Obiechina, *Culture, Tradition and Society in the West African Novel* (Cambridge: Cambridge University Press, 1975); Joanna Sullivan, "Redefining the Novel in Africa," *Research in African Literatures* 37, no. 4 (2006): 177–88; Taiwo Adetunji Osinubi, "Slavery, Death, and the Village: Localizing Imperatives of Nigerian Writing," *University of Toronto Quarterly* 84, no. 4 (2015): 131–52; Wendy Griswold, "Transformation of Genre in Nigerian Fiction: The Case of the Village Novel," in *Empirical Approaches to Literature and Aesthetics*, ed. Roger J. Kreuz and Mary Sue MacNealy (Norwood, NJ: Ablex, 1996), 573–82.

13 Samah Selim, *The Novel and the Rural Imaginary in Egypt, 1880–1985* (New York: Routledge Curzon, 2004), 1.

14 Ibid., 3.

15 Kathleen F. Parthé, *Russian Village Prose: The Radiant Past* (Princeton, NJ: Princeton University Press, 1992), 19.

16 Ibid., 19–21.

17 Ibid., 3.

18 For more information about the peasants and peasantry in Turkey, see Asım Karaömerlioğlu, *Orada Bir Köy Var Uzakta—Erken Cumhuriyet Döneminde Köycü Söylem* (Istanbul: İletişim Yayınları, 2011); Metin Çınar, *Anadoluculuk ve Tek Parti CHP'de Sağ Kanat* (Istanbul: İletişim Yayınları, 2013); Sinan Yıldırmaz, "From 'Imaginary' to 'Real': A Social History of the Peasantry in Turkey (1945–1960)" (PhD diss., Boğaziçi University, 2009).

19 The literature on the Village Institutes is vast yet mostly descriptive and ideologically positioned. Fay Kirby's study is one of the best examples to understand the nature and history of the Village Institutes: Fay Kirby, *Türkiye'de Köy Enstitüleri*, trans. Niyazi Berkes (Istanbul: Tarihçi Kitabevi, 2010). For a critical approach to these schools and literature, see Asım M. Karaömeroğlu, "The Village Institutes Experience in Turkey," *British Journal of Middle Eastern Studies* 25, no. 1 (1998): 47–73.

20 A. Rıza Atay and Sami N. Özerdim, eds., *Varlık Yayınları Bibliyografyası* (Istanbul: Varlık Yayınları, 1968), 10–15.

21 Authors, titles and dates of these village notes are: Talip Apaydın-*Bozkırda Günler* (1952); Mahmut Makal-*Köyümden* (1952), *Memleketin Sahipleri* (1954), *Kuru Sevda* (1957), *Köye Gidenler* (1959), and *Kalkınma Masalı* (1960); Mehmet Başaran-*Çarığımı Yitirdiğim Tarla* (1955), *Aç Harmanı* (1962), and *Zeytin Ülkesi* (1964); Mahmut Yağmur-*Dertler Pazarı* (1957); Selâhattin Şimşek-*Hakkâri Dedikleri* (1960); Hayrettin Uysal-*Yollar Çamur* (1960); İbrahim Kuyumcu-*Bir Avuç Toprak İçin* (1960); Behzat Ay-*Başkanın Ankara Dönüşü* (1961).

"Emergence and End of an Endemic Genre in Turkish Literature"

22 Yaşar Nabi Nayır, "Birkaç Söz," in *Bizim Köy* (Istanbul: Varlık Yayınları, 1950), 4.
23 Fakir Baykurt, Kemal Tahir, and Mahmut Makal, *Beş Romancı Tartışıyor* (Istanbul: Düşün Yayınları, 1960).
24 Ibid., 8.
25 See, e.g., Attilâ İlhan, "Bırakın Allah Aşkına!" in *Nesin Vakfi Edebiyat Yıllığı 1976* (Istanbul: Tekin Yayınevi, 1976), 346–48.

References

Ahmad, Feroz. *The Making of Modern Turkey*. London: Routledge, 1993.

Akıncı, Gündüz. *Türk Romanında Köye Doğru*. Ankara: Türk Tarih Kurumu Basımevi, 1961.

Atay, A. Rıza, and Sami N. Özerdim, eds. *Varlık Yayınları Bibliyografyası*. Istanbul: Varlık Yayınları, 1968.

Berkes, Niyazi. *Türkiye'de Çağdaşlaşma*. Istanbul: Yapı Kredi Yayınları, 2002.

Çınar, Metin. *Anadoluculuk ve Tek Parti CHP'de Sağ Kanat*. Istanbul: İletişim Yayınları, 2013.

Cuddon, J. A. *The Penguin Dictionary of Literary Terms and Literary Theory*. London: Penguin Books, 1999.

Evin, Ahmet Ö. *Origins and Development of the Turkish Novel*. Minneapolis: Bibliotheca Islamica, 1983.

Fakir, Baykurt, Kemal Tahir, and Mahmut Makal. *Beş Romancı Tartışıyor*. Istanbul: Düşün Yayınları, 1960.

Griswold, Wendy. "Transformation of Genre in Nigerian Fiction: The Case of the Village Novel." In *Empirical Approaches to Literature and Aesthetics*, edited by Roger J. Kreuz and Mary Sue MacNealy, 573–82. Norwood, NJ: Ablex, 1996.

Gürbilek, Nurdan. *Kör Ayna, Kayıp Şark—Edebiyat ve Endişe*. Istanbul: Metis Yayınları, 2004.

İlhan, Attilâ. "Bırakın Allah Aşkına!" In *Nesin Vakfi Edebiyat Yıllığı 1976*, 346–48. Istanbul: Tekin Yayınevi, 1976.

Irmak, Erkan. *Eski Köye Yeni Roman—Köy Romanının Tarihi, Kökeni ve Sonu (1950–1980)*. Istanbul: İletişim Yayınları, 2018.

Kaplan, Ramazan. *Cumhuriyet Dönemi Türk Romanında Köy*. Ankara: Kültür ve Turizm Bakanlığı Yayınları, 1988.

Karaömeroğlu, Asım M. "The Village Institutes Experience in Turkey." *British Journal of Middle Eastern Studies* 25, no. 1 (1998): 47–73.

———M. *Orada Bir Köy Var Uzakta—Erken Cumhuriyet Döneminde Köycü Söylem*. Istanbul: İletişim Yayınları, 2011.

Katamble, V.D. *The Rural Novel in Indian English*. Jaipur: Shruti, 2008.

Keith, W.J. *Regions of the Imagination: The Development of British Rural Fiction*. Toronto: University of Toronto Press, 1988.

Kirby, Fay. *Türkiye'de Köy Enstitüleri*. Translated by Niyazi Berkes. Istanbul: Tarihçi Kitabevi, 2010.

Lewis, Bernard. *The Emergence of Modern Turkey*. New York: Oxford University Press, 2002.

Moran, Berna. *Türk Romanına Eleştirel Bir Bakış—Ahmet Mithat'tan Ahmet Hamdi Tanpınar'a*. Istanbul: İletişim Yayınları, 2005 [1983].

Nayır, Yaşar Nabi. "Birkaç Söz." In *Bizim Köy*, 3–5. Istanbul: Varlık Yayınları, 1950.

Nyamndi, George. *The West African Village Novel with Particular Reference to Elechi Amadi's "The Concubine."* Bern: Peter Lang, 1982.

Obiechina, Emmanuel. *Culture, Tradition and Society in the West African Novel*. Cambridge: Cambridge University Press, 1975.

Oktay, Ahmet. *Toplumcu Gerçekçiliğin Kaynakları*. Istanbul: Bilim Felsefe Sanat Yayınları, 1986.

Osinubi, Taiwo Adetunji. "Slavery, Death, and the Village: Localizing Imperatives of Nigerian Writing." *University of Toronto Quarterly* 84, no. 4 (2015): 131–52.

Parkinson, Michael H. *The Rural Novel—Jeremias Gotthelf, Thomas Hardy, C. F. Ramuz*. Bern: Peter Lang, 1984.

Parla, Jale. *Babalar ve Oğullar—Tanzimat Romanının Epistemolojik Temelleri*. Istanbul: İletişim Yayınları, 1990.

Parthé, Kathleen F. *Russian Village Prose: The Radiant Past*. Princeton, NJ: Princeton University Press, 1992.

Selim, Samah. *The Novel and the Rural Imaginary in Egypt, 1880–1985*. New York: Routledge Curzon, 2004.

Seyhan, Azade. *Tales of Crossed Destinies—The Modern Turkish Novel in a Comparative Context*. New York: MLA, 2008.

Snell, K.D.M. "The Regional Novel: Themes for Interdisciplinary Research." In *The Regional Novel in Britain and Ireland, 1800–1990*, edited by K.D.M. Snell, 1–53. Cambridge: Cambridge University Press, 1998.

Solé-Leris, Amedeu. *The Spanish Pastoral Novel.* Boston: Twayne, 1980.

Squires, Michael. *The Pastoral Novel—Studies in George Eliot, Thomas Hardy, and D. H. Lawrence.* Charlottesville: University of Virginia Press, 1974.

Storey, Marc. *Rural Fictions, Urban Realities—A Geography of Gilded Age American Literature.* Oxford: Oxford University Press, 2013.

Sullivan, Joanna. "Redefining the Novel in Africa." *Research in African Literatures* 37, no. 4 (2006): 177–88.

Yıldırmaz, Sinan. "From 'Imaginary' to 'Real': A Social History of the Peasantry in Turkey (1945–1960)." PhD diss., Boğaziçi University, 2009.

Zürcher, Eric Jan. *Turkey: A Modern History.* London: I. B. Tauris, 1994.

25

POETIC URBANISM IN TURKISH MODERNIST POETRY

Dramatic Monologue in the Second New Wave

Veysel Öztürk

The 1950s marked a modernist turn in Turkish literature with the production of a number of works both in prose and poetry that displayed a search for new themes and forms of expression in literature. This modernist turn first began to take shape in the 1940s and consolidated itself in the 1950s with the publication of literary works that sought artistic experimentation. These works are characterized by individualism, alienation, formalism, irony, and a direct break with mimetic representation. In addition to fiction, Turkish poetry experienced a similar modernist paradigm shift that continues to shape today's poetic production. In addition to the aforementioned type of fictional texts, a number of poetry collections with modernist characteristics were published one after another in the second half of the 1950s: Turgut Uyar's *Dünyanın En Güzel Arabistanı* (The Most Beautiful Arabia in the World, 1959); Edip Cansever's *Yerçekimli Karanfil* (The Gravitational Carnation, 1957), *Umutsuzlar Parkı* (The Park of the Despairing, 1958), and Petrol (1959); Cemal Süreya's *Üvercinka* (1958); Ece Ayhan's *Kınar Hanımın Denizleri* (Kınar Hanım's Oceans, 1959); Sezai Karakoç's *Körfez* (The Bay, 1959); Ülkü Tamer's *Soğuk Otların Altında* (Under the Cold Weeds, 1959); and İlhan Berk's *Galile Denizi* (The Sea of Galilee, 1958). It is precisely for this reason that literary critic Orhan Koçak has characterized this period as one of an "explosion" in the production of modernist poetry.[1] Interestingly enough, this was not the result of a predetermined poetic movement. None of the poets was cognizant of each other's experimental poems being written published in different magazines at the same time as they were writing the early poems which would be later collected in their first books. This modernist turn in Turkish literature was a result of a social, political, economic, and cultural transformation in Turkey during the 1950s.

Among these developments, urbanism played the most determinant role in the search for new forms of writing thus creating, so to speak, a poetics of urbanism. The prose writings of these modernist poets about poetry during this period show that they were in urgent need of a new narrative mode against the insufficiency of conventional poetic devices in representing the confusion, shock, and alienation brought by urban transformation. Dramatic poetry emerged as an efficacious form at this point and the Second New Wave poets utilized its potential remarkably. Edip Cansever (1928–1986) and Turgut Uyar (1928–1985) were the leading poets among other Second New Wave (İkinci Yeni) poets employing dramatic form and monologue

DOI: 10.4324/9780429279270-33

309

extensively in their poetry. In this chapter, I will discuss how dramatic poetry became instrumental to represent the modern experiences of alienation and isolation of the fragmented self as a result of urbanization in the dramatic poems of Edip Cansever and Turgut Uyar.

Generally speaking, literary historians have argued that the First World War, which shook the foundations of modern civilization, resulted in major social, economic, and political shifts that ultimately led to a modernist turn in artistic production. More specifically, radical changes in urban habitats had a defining influence on shaping modernist art and literature. Julia E. Daniel argues that modern artists "felt the need to address the 'problem' cities presented to both the overwhelmed psyche of the individual on the sidewalk and the increasingly fragmented modern populace as a whole."[2] Daniel pays particular attention to Georg Simmel's claim in his well-known essay, "The Metropolis and Mental Life," originally published in 1903, in which he discusses how a deep alienation became inevitable with the experience of displacement and the loss of identity brought by urbanization. The ultimate protective response to the material culture of urbanism was "dissociation, a blasé attitude that put the city dweller at risk of deep alienation."[3] The loss of belief in order and meaning, the disintegration of old values, and the rise of material culture in a highly urbanized environment all urged the poets to seek a new language and form to express this new reality.

Yet the Turkish public was experiencing a completely different transformation during this urbanization process that shaped modernist tendencies in the arts, especially in the West. The First World War was nothing but the traumatic end of the Ottoman Empire, which set the conditions for a struggle for independence. The War of National Independence between 1919 and 1922 paved the way for a new republic that strictly designed cultural life based on the ethos and nationalist discourse of the modern nation-state. Literature, which was effectively used as a means for the nation-building project, played an important role in this designation. This socially motivated approach rejected the idea of autonomous and individualistic literature. Embracing modernity, Turkey did not provide an environment of skepticism about its values, such as democracy, rationalism, progress, and secularism. Thus, the modernizing narrative of the nationalist elite was rarely challenged in literature during the early years of the Turkish Republic. This only happened in the 1940s by a few writers, like Ahmet Hamdi Tanpınar (1901–1962) and Nâzım Hikmet Ran (1902–1963). Yet their critique of modernity never became a widespread current as it remained a personal endeavor, especially in comparison to the widespread practice of modernist literature of the 1950s under discussion. During this period, Turkey also witnessed a genuine transition from a traditional society to a more urbanizing society due to the urbanizing policies under the newly elected Democrat Party, a moderately right-wing political party with a populist and liberal ideology. Urbanization especially became evident in the two metropolitan cities: Istanbul, the old capital of the empire, and Ankara, the new capital of the Republic. In the nationalist discourse of the early Republican period, Istanbul was represented as "the symbolic vestige of decadent Ottoman cosmopolitanism" and was marginalized "not only economically but culturally."[4] Following the Second World War, Istanbul once again emerged as "the growth pole in the inflationary expansion of the economy" due to Turkey's "changing international alliances and shifting patterns of integration into world markets."[5] Turkey's state-sponsored import-substitution industrialization model guaranteed "the continuous expansion of the internal consumer market," which was "accompanied by redistributive measures and a populist discourse, aiming to mobilize and incorporate a larger proportion of the population into product and labor markets" in big cities.[6] The population of Istanbul exploded between 1950 and 1960 roughly from 1 million to 1.8 million due to work opportunities created by new industries in which poor immigrants became the dominant element in the city. The population of Ankara reached beyond 1 million in 1960, tripling in ten years. This rapid growth triggered a fundamentally profit-oriented urban development. This was a sudden new reality in big cities that caught the artists unprepared who did not know how to handle this dramatic transformation in daily life as well as in art. Turgut Uyar (1928–1985), one of the leading figures of the Second New Wave poetry, describes the shock and thrill of encountering the new urban transformation in the following way:

> One may ask what happened at that moment and an imminent change in poetry became inevitable. In addition to the liveliness and specific necessities of poetry, one must pay attention to the policies of the Democrat Party that led to the explosion of money in daily life that triggered a change and dissolution of values. I, personally, experienced a profound shock and felt an urgent need for a reckoning when I returned to Ankara from Terme as a military officer.[7]

In another essay he makes a similar point:

> Experience of how the environment changed around me has pushed me to write the poetry I wrote. Sudden urbanization, an encounter with neon lights, big hotels, the conditions that inform a number of new developments were keeping me away from being an Orhan Veli-style poet.[8]

Uyar's observations illustrate how the modernist turn in poetry was a direct response to the massive urbanization process of the 1950s in Turkey. He appears to welcome the opportunity provided by this urbanization to describe new themes and forms of expression in poetry. Therefore, a cultural crisis for Uyar and his generation became a means of new poetic experimentation and creative opportunity. For this reason, he underlines that in this new environment, producing poetry following the style of Orhan Veli (1914–1950), a representative of the Garip Movement, a group of young poets promoted simple language and rejection of figures of speech as a reaction to classical poetry, is outdated. The conditions the Garip Movement had built on had nothing to do with the recent urban development that the Second New Wave witnessed. Although "Orhan Veli-style poetry" employed the theme of alienation to some degree, it was far from showing the inner depth of the subject Turgut Uyar's generation aspired to reflect.

The Second Wave New poets crafted alternative solutions to represent personal responses to the change in daily life in the big cities beginning of the 1950s in Turkey. In order to do this, these poets extensively used dramatic monologue as a means of creating a narrator, a dramatic persona separated from themselves in narrating his/her experiences in an urban setting. This form of narration makes use of this device one of the defining characteristics of this modernist poetry. Unlike the lyrical poetry that retained its popularity in the Second New Wave, these were long dramatic poems in which the narrators almost always become estranged from the outer world, isolated and disoriented. The narrator expresses his/her solitude in the form of dramatic monologue where the narrator speaks to himself/herself so as to reveal certain thoughts and feelings to the reader.

So what did these poets expect from dramatic poetry, or the dramatic monologue in particular, in the first place? The first answer is the change in these poets' attitudes towards the voice in poetry. The lyric "I," a Romantic invention above all things, is designed to express personal feelings that require a coherent voice, thus jeopardizing the effective representation of the disunified self. When the Second New Wave poets sought to give a voice to a disunified and solipsistic self shaped by an alienating setting, dramatic poetry appeared as the most appropriate medium for this poetic diction. For this reason, it is not surprising to see that in almost all of their dramatic poems, the Second New Wave poets gave a voice to a narrator with a fragmented self under the pressure of social conventions. In addition, dramatic poetry provides a literary strategy to avoid the problem of impersonality found in lyric poetry. The new reality brought by urbanization and consumerism had an effect upon not only a certain class or the poet himself but every individual in the fast-changing city to a different extent. Thus, the new mode of poetry was supposed to be personal, but not so personal that it would make the reader think that the feeling of alienation in the poem was only unique to the poet. Aware of this new situation, the poets of the Second New Wave employed dramatic monologue in order to express their sincere thoughts and emotions yet they represented these emotions and thoughts as the experiences of the poetic narrator while they were, in fact, naturally their own emotions. This poetic voice in dramatic poetry, just like in prose fiction, enables the poet to impersonalize the feelings of alienation and isolation whereas the reader easily internalizes these very emotions and thus is immersed in the poem.

Edip Cansever (1928–1986), a leading poet who employed the dramatic monologue, wrote an article titled "Şiiri Bölmek" ("To Divide Poetry") in 1963 in order to emphasize the importance of this usage in modernist poetry. He argues that the urban dwellers wear different masks in performing different roles in their daily routines, ultimately leading to the loss of their personality. To Cansever, this is the sheer reality of modern life. Therefore, human beings "are bewildered in choosing whether to escape or submit to a series of dead-ends. We ceaselessly fluctuate in non-dimensional, meaningless, and tormenting life."[9] However, both in terms of its themes and forms of writing, the established poetry failed to produce poems appropriate to the spirit of the changing time. That is why Cansever insists that the poet needs to employ a "divided poetry" in order to represent a "divided self":

> So, if we want to convey the "I," which has been losing its privilege and identity through a constant splitting again and again, we will finally have to turn to dramatic poetry. Because we are actually experiencing a horrible drama.[10]

Cansever's thoughts on Turkey's recent urbanization summarize the poets' search for the language and form of poetry suitable for the changing life of the 1950s. It was this modernist attitude towards life that essentially enabled the poets to generate modernist poetry of the world which already found the dramatic narrative mode as an answer to the problem of impersonality inherited from Romantics. The modernist Anglo-American poetry provided the major textual source for the turning point in Turkish poetry by the Second New Wave poets. As argued by Ahmet Oktay, this caused an orientation change in Turkish poetry inspired by French models starting the nineteenth century.[11] The Anglo-American interrelation is clearly evident in Edip Cansever's profound interest in T. S. Eliot's poetry despite the fact that Cansever did not know English. It appears that Cansever read both T. S. Eliot's poetry and writing on poetry alongside other twentieth-century modernist poets in Turkish translation. Eliot is the most referenced poet in Cansever's own writings about poetry, which shows his particular interest in the Eliotian objective correlative and dramatic monologue. Whereas the former attribute is evident in his image-making mostly in his lyric poems, the latter appears to play an inspirational role in his dramatic poems.

The earliest example of dramatic poetry in Cansever date back to 1958's *Umutsuzlar Parkı* (The Park of the Despairing); which consists of four long poems in which the poet concerns himself with objective correlative rather than dramatic monologue.[12] His dramatic poetry, however, took a new shape in the 1960s and became the most distinctive feature of his poetics. Starting with *Tragedyalar* (Tragedies) published in 1964, Cansever began to compose books consisting of one single poem in the form of dramatic monologue. From then on, Cansever's technique in his long poems closely coincided with Eliot's well-known modernist poem *The Love Song of J. Alfred Prufrock*. Dramatic monologue, incomplete dialogues, and thoughts that characterize his dramatic technique are effectively used in his poetry collections of *Tragedyalar*, Çağrılmayan Yakup (Uninvited Yakup, 1966), Ben Ruhi Bey Nasılım (How Am I Ruhi Bey, 1976), and Bezik Oynayan Kadınlar (Women Playing Bezique, 1982). They all consist of one long poem similar to *Prufrock*. Cansever's solipsist characters in these collections are always "chosen from the public life of Istanbul, and mostly from the most marginal sections of the society" lost in daily routine and representing "the fragmentation and self-contradiction of modern man."[13] The form, a dramatic mode most often using dramatic monologue as the basic poetic device, is deliberately chosen to represent a certain content: the modern urban individual's dilemma in a contemporary metropolitan city.

A striking example of these poems is *How Am I Ruhi Bey*, which expresses the gloomy sentiments of a troubled modern individual in a rapidly changing modern city. The main character in the poem speaks to himself in the form of dramatic monologue, sometimes through stream of consciousness, and wanders in Istanbul interacting with other people in suspended dialogues. The central feelings in this space are displacement, disengagement, boredom, dullness, and isolation rising from fast-paced transformations in the modern urban landscape. The poem depicts Ruhi Bey's daily routines in the streets, pubs, and brothels through his vivid account of his urban surroundings:

> Have you ever seen how water is burned within the salt
> I saw that lifelong groaning
> Slight inside of big gardens
> In some of the flower pots
> I saw it, but
> A geranium, maybe, raised me
> As if someone shook me awake while sleeping
>
> Me, who
> Is it a ghost of a child within a woman
> A ghost of a woman within a child
> Or, just a ghost?
>
> So, what is it
> A silence of flour spilled on the ground[14]

Cansever in these lines employs impersonality in order to objectify the speaking "I." The first-person narrator observes himself from outside and calls himself "silence of flour spilled on the ground." The voice appears to be concerned with a state of mind, being disoriented. The poet uses striking imagery to starkly reveal the anguish and feelings of isolation. This mode of writing is supported with an ungrammatical syntax causing obscurity and opaqueness in meaning. Such manner of narration continues for the first four parts of the poem, enumerated in Roman numbers. The form of representation is suddenly changed in the fifth part when the narrator, the speaking voice Ruhi Bey, appears in the first stanza addressing himself: "I, Ruhi Bey, the one who is how I am / how am I."[15] Ruhi Bey speaks freely through his consciousness which is emblematic of Cansever's dramatic monologues that directly project his narrator's mind to the reader. This form of expression expects the reader to identify himself/herself with Ruhi Bey's narration by embodying his discomfort and existential crisis. A lack of communication appears to be the distinctive feature of the dialogues in this part. Ruhi Bey is surrounded by other individuals on the surface, but they never hold a meaningful conversation:

How would you be, Ruhi Bey
You are early today too, Ruhi Bey
Are you having beer along with wine, Ruhi Bey
Early in the morning, Ruhi Bey
This time of the night, Ruhi Bey
In the morning and night, Ruhi Bey
Would you like to have a cigarette, Ruhi Bey
Let's light it, Ruhi Bey, let's light it
Don't you get cold like that Ruhi Bey
. . .
So, how are you then, Ruhi Bey
– I am fine, I am fine.
. . .
Keep in touch with you, Ruhi Bey
I don't have time, I don't have time
Ruhi Bey, just keep in touch
I don't have time to see anyone
Ruhi Bey!
– Not even to myself, not even to myself[16]

Although in these cited lines the narration revolves around a single character, Cansever does not employ a single voice but divides it into "different narrative voices, namely his drawing near the form of a dramatic poem, enabl[ing] him to represent this divided man properly," as Dirlikyapan has pointed out.[17] After the first six parts of the poem in which Ruhi Bey speaks in the form of dramatic monologue, many other narrators—a flower lady, a waiter in the pub, the boss of the pub, a fur repairman, an undertaker—begin to speak about him. These characters resemble him: They depict their boring routines briefly in each part. This boredom and dullness become a defining atmosphere in the poem which proves it is not peculiar to Ruhi Bey but the general lives of urban people. They tell what they know about Ruhi Bey and speak to him, whereas he is always preoccupied with himself and rarely talks back to them. They assemble a chorus at the end of the poem, speaking in the form of a plural third-person pronoun that transforms the poem into a classical tragedy and enhances the dramatic setting. Interaction with the other is never fulfilled, as poetic diction is always interrupted throughout the poem. Alongside these characters in the present tense of the poem, Ruhi Bey remembers some events and people from his past. For example, he recalls his wedding night in which he failed to have sexual intercourse with his wife because of his earlier trauma. When he was young, he was forced to have sexual intercourse by his stepmother. As an adult, whenever he has sexual intercourse, he remembers this traumatic experience with a hidden pleasure and a deep feeling of guilt simultaneously.

In addition to this poem, Edip Cansever employs dramatic monologue as the sole narrative mode in his 1982 work *Women Playing Bezique*. This collection of poetry contains four

Poetic Urbanism in Turkish Modernist Poetry

narratives: "Epistles to Hilmi Bey," "Cemal's Interior Monologues," "From Seniha's Diary," and "What Esther Says." Each poem has different narrators living in the same house. Three women and a boy respectively speak in dramatic monologues, sometime in the forms of diary entries and letters. They do not directly speak to each other. What they know and think about each other is only heard through monologues that substantiate a lack of communication and alienation as the primary theme of the book. A lack of communication and alienation are always enhanced with the presence of other characters. Cansever's narrators are physically surrounded by other people and appear to interact with each other one way or another. However, the crowd does not help the desolation of the main characters but becomes one of the causes of his/her isolation. For instance, in "Epistles to Hilmi Bey," the narrator is a woman named Cemile who addresses Hilmi Bey—whom the narrative leaves ambiguous on purpose, whether he is a real man from Cemile's past or just a vision of her imagination. Cemile perceives herself as "an enormous hole," revealing her desolation and alienation:

> See this rain, this balcony, me
> This begonia, aloneness
> These drops of water, on my forehead, on my arms
> This city born of my death
> I'm flowing nowhere, only oozing into myself
> By me, I mean an enormous hole
> In the chair, in the mirror's reflection
> A hole! In the sofa, the kitchen, my bed
> As if I'm looking at life upside down[18]

Cemile does not remember her past precisely and invents a new one including an imaginative character, Hilmi Bey. This imaginative character seems the only addressee but considering the other narratives' revelation that the letters were never sent, the poem is a soliloquy in which Cemile speaks to herself to reveal her thoughts and emotions to the reader. These examples show that dramatic monologue enables Edip Cansever to portray an urban individual's point of view about himself/herself and surroundings. He accomplished this by blending a loose interior monologue with another effective literary tool of modernist literature: stream of consciousness. The voices of his narrators are ambiguous and interrupted, showing the fragmented modern self in a changing urban city trapped in a monotonous life.

In his collection of poetry *Uninvited Yakup* published in 1966, Cansever explores the theme of alienation through the means of dramatic monologue. Similar to *How Am I Ruhi Bey* and in *Women Playing Bezique*, a long poem in this collection uses the dramatic monologue to problematize the emotional disassociation and isolation of an individual in a modern urban environment. Cansever himself remarked that "the prevailing reality in *Uninvited Yakup* is alienation from start to end." The poem represents a character named Yakup who symbolizes, as Cansever commented, "a person who is marginalized, belittled and estranged by his society. For this reason, he appears as a type who is alienated to society, humans, and himself."[19] Accordingly, throughout the poem, Yakup reveals his confusion about his self-identity, his disoriented perception of himself, and alienation from himself and society in these repeated lines: "I don't know": "I don't know / I don't know, I don't know / I, Yusuf, did I say Yusuf? No, Yakup / I get confused sometimes."[20] The narrator's confusion about his identity is not only expressed in his words but displayed through the change of voice. In some lines in the poem, his first-person narrative voice appears to be replaced by the voice of the third-person singular narrator.

However, the whole poem makes it clear that the voice is not someone else's but Yakup's own voice from the very beginning to end:

> I come from seeing the frogs
> Said, Yakup. Told this, three times himself
> They were sitting on a table
> I come from there.[21]

This change in voice emphasizes Yakup's confusion, split personality, and dissociation from himself and society. His relationship with his selfhood and others rests ultimately on a lack of communication and alienation. He repeatedly says that nobody called him:

> I, Yakup, an ordinary form of every calling
> I haven't been called yet
> Nobody called out to me like "Yakup!"
> Yakup!
> No one called me so that I could turn back and look
> And I could drop out dead and rotten water out of me
> I could throw worn-out papers in my pockets
> Then I could wash myself.[22]

Yakup reduces his entire existence into a single act: being uninvited or uncalled. As if he is called, he will become someone else, maybe a complete self. Being uncalled, on the other hand, represents his true self, fragmented and alienated in an urbanized city.

Turgut Uyar (1927–1985) is another prolific poet of the Second New Wave who employed dramatic monologue in his poetry. His early poems use rhyme, and the meaning is easily grasped. Beginning from the second half of the 1950s, he abandons clear diction. He employs modernist devices extensively in 1959's *The Most Beautiful Arabia of the World*, which is widely acknowledged as one of the most prominent texts of the Second New Wave. There, Uyar replaces the persevering and diligent countrymen of the earlier books with a crowd of idle onlookers of the city. Accordingly, the hopeful atmosphere of the early poems is replaced with a gloomy one. Like Cansever, Uyar's main concern during this period was to impersonalize the poetic diction. Initially, his linguistic "solution" to "the problem" was the voice of plural first-person instead of singular first-person:

> I was thinking there was an issue in poetry that I believed I had to deal with for a long time, I found it recently, kept it waiting to make sure of its authenticity: To liberate the poetry from the single point of view of "I." At least in terms of the form, the expression. That's why I hadn't been writing for a while. Whatever I think, how I think, singular first-person came to my mind. Then I solved it. I nourish the first-person plural and speak with it. Maybe I can get rid of that selfish singular. I do not discredit it, though. I wore it off. It would eventually bring "I" to the dead end. I'm on the edge of that predicament.[23]

Uyar's comments illustrate how he consciously rejected the use of the first-person singular pronouns in his poetry due to the dominance of the lyrical "I." The first-person plural pronoun "we" provided additional opportunities for him to represent alienated urban individuals and helped him distance his own voice while producing poetry. The "we" reminds the reader that the overlap of the speaker and the poet should not be taken for granted, a feature that the contemporary reader of Turkish poetry in the 1950s was not accustomed to. The first poem for which Uyar used this mode of expression was "Night with Deer" in his collection *The Most Beautiful Arabia of the World*.

> But nothing was frightening there
> Only everything was made of nylon
> And when we died, we died in thousands against the sun
> But before we found the night with deer
> We were all afraid like children[24]

A sudden negative beginning in the opening line with the word "but" or "yet" (*halbuki*) implies the poem begins in the middle of the narration. The obscurity of time and surroundings enhances the gloomy atmosphere depicted here. The poem never reveals clearly who the speaking "we" is exactly and this remains unclear throughout the poem. Yet it implies that "we" impersonates silent crowds of people trapped and vanished in the halls of history: "First we dug into the earth / And vanished / From gladiators and the cogs of wild machines / From giant cities / Staying hidden and fighting / We saved the night with deer."[25] The poem itself, in this respect, is a dystopian vision of humanity where urbanization is represented with the concrete images of "nylon" and "asphalt." These industrial images strikingly symbolize the last phase of the alienation of a human to his/her own nature. The image of the "night with deer" manifests a romantic revelation that would "redeem" the anonymous "us" from time, the time of the industrial age. "Night with Deer" compensates the darkness of "gladiators and the cogs of wild machines" with its wildness and greenness in "far off forests": "You should all know the night with deer / In far off forests wild and green / Sun sinking slowly over the asphalt road / Redeeming us all from time."[26] Uyar puts forward the "we" as the narrator instead of the lyrical "I," but "Night with Deer" ends up with a first-person pronoun: "And I lean forward to kiss myself on the cheek." This isolated last line, in fact, demonstrates the impossibility of "we" regarding the theme of the poem. No matter how much the subject strives to be part of "we," s/he is destined to be alone where even an action requiring reciprocity, like kissing, is done on one's own.

Aside from "Night with Deer" and a few lyric poems, the larger portion of *The Most Beautiful Arabia of the World* represents the accounts of an alienated character, Yekta of Akçaburgaz. Consisting of episodes that are not always interrelated, this fragmented section of the book encompasses multiple narrators. The first part tells of Yekta's defense against an immoral offense he appears to have committed. He was invited to the house of a married couple, Sinan and Gülbeyaz. He had a sexual relationship with Gülbeyaz, but Sinan caught the couple and brought them into the court. The narrative begins after Yekta hears the court verdict. The poem is told in a dramatic monologue that Yekta speaks to himself to justify his betrayal of Sinan. In the next episode, Yekta is married to a woman named Hümeyra this time and their marriage suffers from a monotonous life. Dissatisfied with his unhappy marriage, Yekta nurtures sexual desire for his sister-in-law, Hümeyra's sister, Azra. Even though Yekta presents it as a love story, in fact the source of these desires come from his dissatisfaction with life. Thus, Azra is nothing more than a desired object to get rid of his boredom and anxiety. In the end, he seduces Azra, betrays his wife, and marches off, finally leaving both Hümeyra and Azra behind. Throughout the poem, Yekta does not appear persuasive since he tells his story from his own perspective. Since the poem establishes Yekta as an unreliable narrator, the reader is never sure whether he is telling the truth or not. The dramatic monologue here thus serves for Uyar to create an inconsistent and ambiguous narrative that represents troubled, isolated, alienated, vulnerable, contradictory, and libidinous characters.

Uyar's long poems with dramatic monologues enable him to elaborate on the chaotic psychology of the character in depth. His obscure style presenting events allusively confuses and demands much from the reader to discover what happened and why, also functioning as a means for the reader's appreciation of his poetic creation. The reader is invited to the realm of disconnected images and thoughts enhanced by ungrammatical language signifying the stream of consciousness. The poem asks its reader to identify with the narrator's self-scrutiny. At some point in the poem, Yekta finds himself isolated and lost amid the crowd, becoming nothing but a number:

> We are gas consumers in the city
> My subscriber number is 44741, I don't know the others'
> We buy papers and read, bread and eat
> We pay on the first day of the month.[27]

Being nothing but a number symbolizes Yekta's absolute alienation from his own self-identity. Feeling an external pressure to comply with the unwritten rules of daily life, like paying bills, creates a sense of mechanized life. This new order destroys the sense of individual uniqueness so much so that the modern subject ultimately loses her/his inner unity. A constant feeling of horror and a sense of entrapment are inevitable outcomes when the city becomes a monster with a dreadful roar that preys on the modern subject, as represented by Yekta: "The roar of the city was behind me, I used to suspect / Sometimes I used to suspect as such, then / Horrors and sweats lean against me."[28] The poem impersonally dramatizes the tragedy of the modern subject in the personality of Yekta, who rejects coming to terms with the bewildering environment of the contemporary city.

As seen in this poem of Uyar, the success of the Second New Wave was to combine stylistic novelty with the power of representing modern subjects overwhelmed by the routines of modern urban life. Orhan Koçak points out that these poets saw a potential in the allusiveness of language to represent this new subjectivity shaped by a modern experience of the city.[29] The stylistic novelty and the use of allusive language permitted the Second New Wave poets to represent the most intimate inner thoughts and complex experiences of the alienated urban individuals in their poetry. In Uyar's poem, Yekta's attempt at self-justification does not eradicate his sense of guilt completely. This creates tension in the reader between sympathy and judgment. Uyar's poem does not demand his readers view reality from the perspective of an immoral character. He problematizes the distinction between moral and immoral by showing such moral distinctions as ambiguous and relative. This ambiguous and inconsistent narration is supported by another narrative in the poem where Yekta is depicted as a character trapped in a love triangle. Unlike the earlier episode, here it is his wife Adile, not Yekta, who commits adultery. This complex content, the ambiguous attitude towards moral values in the three sub-narratives, is consistent with the form of the poem as a whole, which ends without clear closure thereby leaving its themes and problems unresolved. This is not peculiar to Uyar's poem but is one of the most defining characteristic functions of the dramatic monologue evident in Second New Wave poetry which attempted to represent the naked experiences of the alienated individuals of modern urban settings without providing a resolution.

Conclusion

Starting in the 1950s, almost all of the modernist poets of the Second New Wave shared the same technique of representing the sense of alienation in poetry through new poetic abstractions and techniques. This caused them to be harshly criticized as being "elitist, individualist, and detached from the people, their lives and language" by some poets and critics in the highly politicized atmosphere in Turkey after the 1960 military coup.[30] However, when one thinks of the close connection between alienation and urbanism, one clearly sees poetry with the theme of alienation is a political act itself. This is indeed evident in the Second New Wave poetry's relevance with one of the recent political upheavals in Turkey, the Gezi Park protests of 2013 in Turkey. The nationwide protests broke out against the government after an urban plan was announced to rebuild the Ottoman-era Taksim Military Barracks on the site of Taksim Gezi Park, one of the remaining green sites in the Istanbul city center, in June 2013. As E. Atilla Aytekin effectively argues, poetry left its mark on these protests because poetic "verses were written down on walls as graffiti, put up as signs, posted as tweets or Facebook status updates or simply recited in spaces of protest." That these verses fundamentally belong to the Second New Wave poets, "not socialist realist poets," clearly underscores the Second New Wave poetry's revolutionary relevance to society and politics as "an aesthetic political act" in the twenty-first century.[31]

The verses of the Second New Wave poets on walls and on social media during the Gezi protests were mostly single lines quoted from the short lyric poems of the poets. For example, "We may both rejoice, let's look at the sky" by Turgut Uyar became one of the most shared lines among the protesters. Thematically, this shows that the revolutionary characteristics of their poems are still valid today. However, as discussed throughout this study, poets like Edip Cansever and Turgut Uyar took a further step in radically changing poetic form by employing dramatic monologues. A new experience of urban life needed a radical remaking of forms and techniques in representing this new reality and dramatic monologue was the most effective poetic device to respond to this new poetic challenge. Although these dramatic poems are not many in number compared to the lyrical poems produced by the Second New Wave poets, they became their most characteristic works which are still widely read in Turkey.

Notes

1 Orhan Koçak, "Melih Cevdet Anday: After the Second New," trans. Victoria Holbrook, *Red Thread Journal* 2 (2010), http://red-thread.org/en/melih-cevdet-anday-after-the-second-new/.
2 Julia E. Daniel, *Urbanism: A Companion to Modernist Poetry*, ed. David E. Chinitz and Gail McDonald (Oxford: Wiley-Blackwell, 2014), 24.
3 Ibid., 25.
4 Ayşe Öncü and Çağlar Keyder, *Istanbul and the Concept of World Cities* (Istanbul: Window, 1993), 15.
5 Ibid.
6 Ibid., 16–17.
7 Tomris Uyar and Seyyid Nezir, eds., "Turgut Uyar ile Şiirden Hayata," in *Sonsuz ve Öbürü*, interviewed Atilla Özkırımlı (Istanbul: Broy, 1985), 93.
8 Turgut Uyar, "Turgut Uyar: Hangi Soruyu, Niye," in *Sonsuz ve Öbürü*, ed. Tomris Uyar and Seyyid Nezir (Istanbul: Broy, 1985), 107.
9 Edip Cansever, *Şiiri Şiirle Ölçmek*, ed. Devrim Dirlikyapan (Istanbul: Yapı Kredi Yayınları, 2012), 127.
10 Ibid.
11 Ahmet Oktay, "Şairin Kanı," in *Gül Dönüyor Avucumda* (Istanbul: Adam, 1994), 239.
12 Devrim Dirlikyapan, *Ölümü Gömdüm, Geliyorum: Edip Cansever Şiirinde Varolma Biçimleri* (Istanbul: Metis, 2013), 43.

Veysel Öztürk

13 Devrim Dirlikyapan, "Phoenix'in Devrimi: Edip Cansever'de Dramatik Monolog" (PhD diss., Bilkent University, 2007), iv.
14 All translations are mine unless otherwise stated. Edip Cansever, *Sonrası Kalır II: Bütün Şiirleri* (Istanbul: Yapı Kredi Yayınları, 2011), 17–18.
15 Ibid., 31.
16 Ibid., 36–37.
17 Dirlikyapan, *Phoneix'in Devrimi*, iv.
18 George Messo, ed. and trans., *Ikinci Yeni The Turkish Avant-Garde* (Exeter: Shearsman Books, 2009), 91.
19 Cansever, *Şiiri Şiirle Ölçmek*, 269.
20 Edip Cansever, *Yerçekimli Karanfil: Toplu Şiirleri I* (Istanbul: Adam, 2002), 221.
21 Ibid., 227.
22 Ibid., 221.
23 Turgut Uyar, "Şiir Günlüğü," in *Arz-ı Hal ve Sonrası* (Istanbul: Can Yayınları, 1999), 166.
24 Messo, *Ikinci Yeni*, 143.
25 Ibid.
26 Ibid.
27 Turgut Uyar, *Büyük Saat* (Istanbul: Yapı Kredi Yayınları, 2011), 151.
28 Ibid., 144.
29 Koçak, "Melih Cevdet Anday."
30 E. Atilla Aytekin, "A 'Magic and Poetic' Moment of Dissensus: Aesthetics and Politics in the June 2013 (Gezi Park) Protests in Turkey," *Space and Culture* 20 (2017): 201.
31 Ibid., 202.

References

Aytekin, E. Attila. "A 'Magic and Poetic' Moment of Dissensus: Aesthetics and Politics in the June 2013 (Gezi Park) Protests in Turkey." *Space and Culture* 20 (2017): 191–208.
Bezirci, Asım. *Ikinci Yeni Olayı*. Istanbul: Evrensel, 2005.
Cansever, Edip. *Yerçekimli Karanfil: Toplu Şiirleri I*. Istanbul: Adam, 1999.
———. *Şiiri Şiirle Ölçmek*. Edited by Devrim Dirlikyapan. Istanbul: Yapı Kredi Yayınları, 2012.
———. *Sonrası Kalır II: Bütün Şiirleri*. Istanbul: Yapı Kredi Yayınları, 2015.
Daniel, Julia E. *Urbanism: A Companion to Modernist Poetry*. Edited by David E. Chinitz and Gail McDonald. Oxford: Wiley-Blackwell, 2014.
Dirlikyapan, Devrim. "Phoneix'in Devrimi: Edip Cansever'de Dramatik Monolog." PhD diss., Bilkent University, 2007.
———. *Ölümü Gömdüm, Geliyorum: Edip Cansever Şiirinde Varolma Biçimleri*. Istanbul: Metis Yayınları, 2013.
İlhan, Attilâ. *Ikinci Yeni Savaşı*. Istanbul: Türkiye İş Bankası, 2004.
Koçak, Orhan. "Melih Cevdet Anday: After the Second New." Translated by Victoria Holbrook. *Red Thread Journal* 2 (2010). Accessed January 28, 2021. http://red-thread.org/en/melih-cevdet-anday-after-the-second-new/.
Messo, George, ed. and trans. *Ikinci Yeni: The Turkish Avant-Garde*. Exeter: Shearsman Books, 2015.
Oktay, Ahmet. "Şairin Kanı." In *Gül Dönüyor Avucumda*. Istanbul: Adam, 1994.
Öncü, Ayşe, and Keyder Çağlar. *Istanbul and the Concept of World Cities*. Istanbul: Window, 1993.
Uyar, Tomris, and Seyyit Nedir, eds. *Sonsuz ve Öbürü*, Istanbul: Broy, 1985.
Uyar, Turgut. *Arz-ı Hal ve Sonrası*. Istanbul: Can, 1999.
———. *Büyük Saat*. Istanbul: Yapı Kredi Yayınları, 2011.

26

LAUGHTER IN THE DARK

The Modernist Avant-Garde Path in Turkish Literature

Murat Gülsoy

The history of Turkish literature is intertwined with the modernization of Turkey since the 1839 Tanzimat reforms of the Ottoman Empire. This yields a fruitful research area for literary critics and social scientists. The Turkish novel played a double role in the modernization period: first of all, novels were used as a popular medium for presenting new Western ideas, scientific developments, and especially new ways of life. Second, post-Tanzimat writers were criticized as being decadents and lost souls alienated from their own cultural beliefs and ideas at the dawn of the new national Republic. This ambiguous image of Turkish fiction reflects public opinion towards the Westernization/modernization of Turkey from the very beginning of this transformation.

A rough division of post-Republican Turkish literature into periods brings out 1940 as a turning point. Literature prior to this date was considered "national literature," or literature in the service of building a national identity, whereas post-1940s literature which extends into the mid-1960s is "social realist" or "socialist realist" literature.[1] The post-1960s, by contrast, is too diverse to be easily classified, such as Göknar has noted in including feminists, existentialists, post-Kemalists, and Neo-Ottomans. This classification is based on social and political developments, since the prominent Turkish writers and critics defined all literary activities as a function of politics, that is, as an instrument used for "educating" the people or "criticizing" the system. The writer was also seen as a public intellectual with various political responsibilities. Novels were expected to be the reflection of the writers' worldview, and their reception by the public and the state authorities was indeed consonant with this. Writers who contributed to mainstream literature usually applied realist narrative strategies. Modernist avant-garde attempts[2] were marginalized and ignored by representatives of the established cultural elite. My purpose in this chapter is to discuss authors and works that employed modernist narrative forms and avant-garde fictional strategies, even though they were not marked as modernists in their time, and to point out their deep-rooted influence in the creation of today's Turkish literature. Nâzım Hikmet, who was known as a communist activist poet; Ahmet Hamdi Tanpınar, who was mainly influenced by French Romantics and English modernists; Haldun Taner, who took up German modernism; and Leyla Erbil, who tried to synthesize Freudian and Marxist points of view: All will be discussed to investigate their contribution to Turkish literature because of their growing influence on contemporary literature. These writers are usually classified under different titles, genres, and schools of literature. However, I will try to show their common modernist roots.

DOI: 10.4324/9780429279270-34

"Romantic Communist": The First Transnational Experience in Turkish Literature

Nâzım Hikmet was the first writer and poet of the Turkish language to gain international recognition.[3] Starting with his early works, he went to the extremes of modernist experimentalism and carefully considered how to go about this, constructing his poetics highly consciously and meticulously. Nevertheless, his political affiliation and the resulting repression overshadowed his modernist avant-gardism, leading him to be considered under the general rubric of socialist/opposition literature. A closer look into the author's poems, plays, novels, screenplays, and essays will reveal them to be stunning first examples of the avant-garde aspiration in Turkish literature.

Nâzım Hikmet's first epic, *Jokond ile Si-Ya-U* (Jokond and Si-Ya-U), in which he experimented with different narrative styles, amazed readers when it was published in 1929 and further secured the poet's deserved fame that came with his first collection *835 Satır* (835 Lines). The distinguishing feature of this book is the use of a collage-like structure made up of various narrative styles. It was plot based and at times screenplay-like, which was different from his previous poems but would often be seen in his later works. Radio dialogues, sound effects, and descriptions reminiscent of film scenes impart the spirit of the time in this astoundingly dynamic narrative. Modernism was at its height across the world in the 1920s when the book was written. As the quest for the new that was central to modernism became manifest in experiments in form, the new possibilities opened up by technology had transformative (and sometimes disruptive) effects on art. With this narrative poem, Nâzım Hikmet shows that he was positively receptive to these influences. *Jokond and Si-Ya-U* is a story of love, journey, and revolutionary struggle that begins in Paris and ends in China. Nâzım Hikmet narrates the story like the parody of a thriller film, simultaneously mocking the imperialist perspective of American cinema. The overarching discourse of the work is a universal attitude encompassing the entire world. Considering that Turkish poetry and the novel had so far been constrained to its own national territory, producing a self-admiring sense of locality, Nâzım Hikmet's contribution becomes even more significant. He owes this universal discourse to the ideal of communism with which he mostly identified. As is well known, communism's ultimate promise is an international utopia built with universal concepts that supersede localities. Nâzım Hikmet was closely aligned with the internationalist communist thought thanks to his education at KUTV[4] in his youth and his revolutionary experience in Moscow. His unique poetics is the fruit of this intellectual background and the experimentalism of avant-garde literature.

In *Jokond and Si-Ya-U*, Nâzım Hikmet touches upon two important points as he tells the story of Marxist revolutionaries who bring together distant parts of the world. First, he discusses what painting and art in general should be in the twentieth century, questioning the concept of museums that display works by old masters and have no significance other than being tourist attractions. He also refers to Picasso's cubism to imply that the old idols must be shattered in order to progress. In fact, in the years after this poem, he launched a campaign called "Demolish the Idols" (in the journal *Resimli Ay* in June and July 1929) and engaged in avant-garde modernist action that would disenchant the public with the established Turkish poets. The second point in *Jokond and Si-Ya-U* is the transnational attitude he brings to the East-West conflict that serves as the backbone of Turkish literature. The lead character of the story, Si-Ya-U, is Chinese. Consequently, the issue is no longer "us versus them" but "exploited countries versus imperialist countries." The poem juxtaposes the Easterner's fascination with Western art and culture and his disappointment at realizing the destruction brought upon his country by the enormous wars and an exploitation machine devised by Western societies. Nâzım Hikmet succeeds in stepping outside the intricate love-hate relationship of the Turkish intelligentsia with modernization,

Laughter in the Dark

an endeavor that had been going on for nearly a century at the time, and he owes this to his Marxist education as well as his modernist avant-garde attitude.[5] Compared to his contemporaries, he writes from a perfectly contemporaneous position and does not feel belated in any way. Like other works by Nâzım Hikmet, *Jokond and Si-Ya-U* is not limited to a local audience in its appeal. Its subject and narrative strategies open it to a global audience.

Nâzım Hikmet's modernist quest would become more intense after this book and culminate in his masterpiece, *Memleketimden İnsan Manzaraları* (Human Landscapes from My Country). This epic work of thousands of lines has multiple narrative strategies spanning from poetry, drama, film, and epic. He began writing this work in 1939 and finished it sometime in 1945, but due to his banned status in Turkey the book could only be published in the 1960s, reaching the Turkish reader after considerable delay. It is interesting to consider how Turkish literature would have been influenced by this work and how it would have shaped the future had he been able to publish this work when it was actually completed. The "landscapes" described in the book are revolutionary in all aspects; they are the product and manifestation of an experimental quest. Nâzım Hikmet says that he benefited from poetry's brevity and the possibilities that drama and film provide.[6] However, a study of the book's narrative style was postponed because of its radical criticism of Turkey in the Republican era. *Human Landscapes from My Country* tells the truths that had been kept hidden from the Turkish landscape until that time: It was a stark depiction of how not much had improved for the oppressed masses under the new regime. It is such a radical argument that it overshadows the book's stylistic experiments and its new take on literature. The foundation of the new Turkish state was a project of modernization that expected its writers and poets to disseminate its founding discourse rather than criticize it; what needed to be criticized was the defunct Ottoman era and old culture. Because he defied the establishment, Nâzım Hikmet's works were suppressed and he was rendered an outcast. In this way, the author who best understood the spirit and aesthetics of the time was cut out of Turkish literature. The attempts were successful to a certain extent. His books were printed in Turkey only in the 1960s, after his death, and it would take until the 2000s for school textbooks to make any mention of him. Nâzım Hikmet's influence on Turkish literature can be a topic of research in its own right.[7]

A Godless Mystic

Another author who was influenced by the romanticist and modernist movements in Western literature and created his unique style is Ahmet Hamdi Tanpınar. As a poet, storywriter, and novelist, Tanpınar's reception in Turkey has shifted dramatically over the years. He was once associated with Ottoman nostalgia for writing his masterpiece *Huzur* (*A Mind at Peace*, 1949) and was branded "conservative" because he criticized the Republican single-party period in his ironic novel *Saatleri Ayarlama Enstitüsü* (The Time Regulation Institute, 1962). When he was revisited in the 1990s by a new generation of critics, they found the allegations baseless and misleading.[8] To understand Tanpınar, one must look into his early works. Published in 1943, *Abdullah Efendinin Rüyaları* (The Dreams of Abdullah Efendi) is Tanpınar's first printed book and contains his artistic creative motives in a nutshell.[9] It is the story of a nighttime journey embellished with surreal elements in which Abdullah Efendi roams the city amid themes of doppelgängers, sexuality, solitude, insanity, and obsession. There are plenty of thematic similarities and surreal elements to argue that Tanpınar was inspired by Gérard de Nerval's *Aurélia* (1855) for this story. *Aurélia* is also the story of a night journey where hallucinations, nightmares, and illusions are intertwined. Of course, in Nerval's case, his mental breakdowns, hospitalization, and experiences in an asylum feed the story. The terrifying secrets of his inner world become apparent with the powerful introspection of a madman. Nerval has had a profound effect in

Turkish literature.[10] Tanpınar's *The Dreams of Abdullah Efendi* was based on Nerval's work and reinterpreted through Tanpınar's own quest for existence. While the "grief of lost love" causes alienation from reality in Nerval, "impossible love" in Tanpınar leads to a so-called profound comprehension of reality. Throughout his journey, the secrets behind ordinary life are revealed to Abdullah Efendi. The love for a woman who is so sublime that she has or will descend from the stars creates this transcendental experience for him. This theme will be further taken up to become one of the leitmotifs of his prominent works.

In *The Dreams of Abdullah Efendi*, Tanpınar problematizes the dichotomy between psychological and fantastical experience, as his popular nineteenth-century predecessors did. In Nerval's *Aurelia*, this dichotomy becomes manifest in a scene of nightmare and insanity, while Stevenson's 1886 *Dr. Jekyll and Mr. Hyde*, as well as Oscar Wilde's 1891 *The Picture of Dorian Gray*, feature dichotomy as a central element of discussing the good and evil parts of the self. The scene where Abdullah Efendi's self begins to split both bears traces of this tradition but goes beyond it. For instance, contrary to Nerval's insanity-infused mysticism, Tanpınar's proposition is clearer: "Abdullah was a great mystic. A godless mystic."[11]

Nerval's *Aurelia* was the logbook of the throes of a troubled mind. Tanpınar acts like a researcher who reads this book of insanity and experiments with this insanity on himself through writing. The classical theme of good and evil coexisting in a single mind is one of the main elements of Tanpınar's fiction, and it serves as a starting point for a series of dichotomies arising from various cultural, historical, and sociological issues. In every piece of writing, he describes various aspects of the dichotomy rooted in the modernization and Europeanization of Turkey; his characters are stuck between past and present, east and west, Ottoman and Republican. Thus, he built a distinctive style of fiction by problematizing this dichotomy on the psychological, cultural, and ontological levels. Abdullah Efendi's surreal experience shows the modern individual's nightmarish inquiries of living in that period in Turkey. *The Dreams of Abdullah Efendi* is not only a remarkable example of Tanpınar's aesthetics but also one of the most unique and dark masterpieces of Turkish literature.

Does Rainfall in Şişhane Induce a Storm in Brazil?

Starting in the second half of the nineteenth century, Turkish intellectuals who studied in Europe, mostly Paris, brought their influences back to Turkey. However, authors in the early twentieth century traveled to different countries and brought back different influences which resulted in transformations unlike those that occurred before. For example, closer ties between Germany and Turkey in the 1930s, and authors who studied there as a result, had new things to offer. Among them, Haldun Taner has a unique place.

Haldun Taner was educated in Heidelberg and Vienna. He had a major impact on cultural life in Turkey with the plays and cabarets he composed. Modernist innovativeness infuses all aspects of his works. His 1953 story, *Şişhane'ye Yağmur Yağıyordu* (Rain was Falling on Şişhane), describes the events that occur after a tired old horse neighs while pulling a garbage cart along the busy Şişhane street of Istanbul. The neighing causes an accident, which prevents a tradesman from phoning a coffee company in Brazil and causes him to lose the contract, which changes someone else's life in Hamburg. In this way, a simple accident that occurs somewhere in Istanbul triggers a series of events spreading all over the world. The story illustrates that in a global world, anything we do and any choice we take has the power to affect many other people, situations, and events all across the world. The story won an international award held by the *New York Herald Tribune* with a meaningful message: We live in such a world that the neighing of a horse in Istanbul can change the world in Brazil or Hamburg. Considering that the dominant genre

Laughter in the Dark

in Turkish literature at the time was the village novel[12] and social realism, Haldun Taner's work cannot be viewed as part of the canon. What Taner did is investigate the defining and powerful role of storytelling on the construction of reality. His best example would be his *Ayışığında Çalışkur* (Çalışkur Under the Moonlight)—the literal meaning of "Çalışkur" in Turkish being "Work-and-Build"—a highly experimental piece published in 1954.

The story consists of two main chapters and "commentaries" at the end of each chapter. In the first chapter, a story that takes place in a bourgeois apartment called Çalışkur is told from the divine perspective. A young couple from a poor neighborhood is watching the moon near the Çalışkur Apartment, dreaming of a happy future. Meanwhile, the residents of the apartment building are in the grips of vice. Everyone is at varying degrees of moral turpitude: from a man cheating on his wife with her sister, a corrupt businessman, a doctor performing illegal abortions, a young man playing the audio recording of him making love to his girlfriend for his friends, to an old pedophile and pervert to a concierge's wife who secretly sleeps with the night watchman. In contrast, the couple outside is poor and of good character. The man is a worker who is deeply in love with his girlfriend, whom he plans to marry soon. At the end of the story, the watchman arrests the young couple, the only characters depicted as morally sound in the story, for public indecency because they are sitting in a public area while holding hands. He takes them to the police station under the disapproving stares of the Çalışkur Apartment residents, who have conveniently forgotten about their depravities and play the morality police.

Until this point, the story is a somewhat schematic satire of hypocritical morality as upheld in the world of bourgeois values. We realize that we are in an experimental narrative as we begin to read the commentary that follows the story. Written from different perspectives, these letters, criticisms, and reports create new layers of reality, showing how each text may be read differently and how the reality of a text is reconstructed by readers, thus emphasizing the fact that the story we have just read is such a text. Although the commentaries are heteroglossic discourse parodies, they are so well written that they gain a reality of their own. The most notable criticism is a report that recommends the revision of the severe criticism of the bourgeois class in order for the text to be considered for radio theater. After the commentary, a new chapter starts. This is the "revised and amended" version of the first text. The revised text goes along with the criticisms submitted in the commentary. To make it easier for the reader to track the changes, the two versions are given on alternating pages. The left page contains the "original" text, while the right side has the "revised" version. Added words are printed in boldface for better visibility to the reader. Since the leading criticism is the author being classist and an enemy of wealth, the new version has all moral attitudes reversed: the wealthy residents of Çalışkur Apartments (and its concierge and watchman) are depicted as moralistic individuals with incorruptible character, while the young couple from a poor neighborhood border on the dark and criminal. Since other criticisms are also applied verbatim, the revised text is a pleasure in itself: It shows the monstrosity that baseless criticism will create if fulfilled. *Çalışkur Under the Moonlight* leads the reader to contemplate the possibilities of fiction while also compelling them to think how the discourse and art produced by political powers are adept at concealing unseemly issues. Reading such texts really does dispel the magic of fiction. At this point, we must remember the answer Vicki Mahaffey gave to the question of why we should read challenging modernist texts.[13] The problematic of the modernist avant-garde often challenged the spheres of government discourse and revealed the uncanny sides of language. Haldun Taner creates a complex, multilayered novelistic structure in *Çalışkur Under the Moonlight*, using metafiction as the main strategy. His irony and black humor serve as sharp critical tools, thus the text both entertains and undermines the ideological discourse of the time. It also presents an alternative way of being critical by using playful tools of narration rather than applying conventional realist techniques as his predecessors did.

Murat Gülsoy

A Strange Woman

Although social realism was dominant in Turkish literature in the 1950s and 1960s, new generations of authors also emerged, causing modernist undercurrents in poetry, novel, and short story to be strongly felt. At first there were singular examples, often viewed as petty bourgeois whining to be deliberately avoided, but these writers became more visible in the 1970s and became the precursors of the wave of postmodernism that would emerge from 1980 onwards. One spectacular example is Leylâ Erbil, who started publishing in the early 1960s and came to be one of the most prominent representatives of the modernist avant-garde in Turkish literature until her last book in 2013.

Through stylistic experiments, violating boundaries between genres, taking irony and stream of consciousness to extremes, Erbil's works created a textual analysis of the conflict between the personal and the social and historical. She never avoided current politics and history; to the contrary, she openly invited them into her works. Her books went from being simple media for the conveyance of her stories and instead were loaded with functions never seen before. For example, she added notes about her research into the murder of Mustafa Suphi and friends in each new edition of her *Tuhaf Bir Kadın* (A Strange Woman), originally published in 1971. A character in the "Father" chapter of the novel, called Skipper Ahmet, wonders who killed Mustafa Suphi and his friends. The subject is a central issue in that chapter of the novel, which even includes references to historical documents. The actual Mustafa Suphi and friends were founders of the Community Party of Turkey in Soviet Azerbaijan who were invited to Turkey in 1921. However, the military was unable to provide adequate protection and the group encountered hostilities in Kars and Erzurum. Since reaching Ankara did not seem a viable option, they were sent back to the Soviet Union on a boat. The boat sunk on the way, killing Mustafa Suphi and his 14 comrades. Erbil considers this the first political assassination that would be covered up by the state or, even if not covered up, allowed to remain unsolved due to the invisible protection by some state actors. Erbil did not limit the issue to a character or a story in the novel; she wrote a new preface for each edition to keep the Mustafa Suphi incident from disappearing into the dark pages of history. These prefaces become part of the book and create a new layer of narrative. She built complex architectural structures using different layers of narratives.

Leylâ Erbil created her fiction along a line extending from documentary to the surreal. A typical example of this is the story titled "Vapur" (The Boat) in her 1968 collection *Gecede* (At Night): An Istanbul ferry goes out of control and roams the Bosporus on its own as the people watch this event unfold either as an entertaining spectacle or in the headiness of rising against authority. As she describes this surreal situation in a realist atmosphere, she provides documentary information about the neighborhoods and landmark houses along the Bosporus, as well as the history of the ferry company. Erbil's narrative is not only based on the experiences of the characters or their role in the dramatic plot but also on their interactions with the historical. The fictional dimension transcends itself and intersects with the real world, becoming an extension of the intellectual and social identities of Leylâ Erbil. Another difference between her and her social realist contemporaries was her conception of time and space. The historical events she discussed were not limited to the Republican period, as her works mainly set in Istanbul deal with its Ottoman, Byzantine, and Roman periods and its Turkish, Greek, Armenian, Jewish, Levantine communities with historical personalities as an integral and inseparable part of the city's *topos*. As she reveals the historical layers of the real world within the multi-structure of her text, the experimental nature of the language she uses gives visibility to the inner layers of the characters, thus exploring the unconscious. The practice of exploration covers the mental crises of the characters in their childhood, youth, or adulthood and evolves into something indefinitely intricate with the involvement of the historical and social almost as a violent, destructive force. Thus the intellectual activity becomes a genuine instrument in the mental struggle of the individual. Thinking, saying, writing—or the inability to think, say, or write—are vital forces in Erbil's work, just as sexuality shapes a person with the desires and fears it provokes. In one of her later works, *Kalan* (The Remaining) from 2011, she places the biblical story of Abraham in the center and discusses it using Kierkegaard's arguments and with an enthusiasm that borders on schizoid ravings; the multilayered structure is there again, so while the characters are victims of history, they also discuss the nature of belief with references to Marx, Adorno, Foucault, Bakhtin, Wittgenstein, Sartre, and other modern thinkers in opposition to Kierkegaard: the social is placed as a force of obstruction against the existence of the individual. Erbil was not a philosopher, but she managed to portray philosophical discussions as the experience of a consciousness in literature. This has made the reception of her works difficult. She attempts to reveal the inner worlds, consciousness, and unconscious fears of individuals while also battling with the state, patriarchy, and the canonic repression and competition caused by male critics. Her life and her work fuse and become one integrated magnum opus.

Other Strange Women and Men

As the modernist undercurrent became pronounced in Turkish literature, topics like the loneliness of the individual, their estrangement from the world they live in, and the powerlessness of the individual against society gained prominence in fiction. Starting in the 1960s and continuing until the 1980s, authors like Sevim Burak, Vüsat O. Bener, Hulki Aktunç, Feyyaz Kayacan, Bilge Karasu, Adalet Ağaoğlu, and Yusuf Atılgan pushed the boundaries of the novel and short story genres, included different genres in their works, and explored human conditions like sexuality, insanity, loneliness, and estrangement within their quest for form. The narrative strategies frequently used by these authors are irony, multiple voices, and fragmental structures. However, each had a pursuit of their own and a highly subjective, personal style. For example, Sevim Burak deconstructs language through an experimental stream of consciousness, while Hulki Aktunç uses folkloric elements, slang, or subculture jargon as possibilities in his works. Meanwhile, Bilge Karasu resorts to mythology, surreal motifs, and genres like the gothic or dystopia. Bilge Karasu's masterpiece, the novel *Gece* (The Night), is a dystopian narrative of the violent social conflict and rising fascism in 1970s Turkey.[14] One may claim that the dystopian, metafictive, experimental, and complicated narrative in *Night* is the result of severe governmental repression, but this may not be the only reason. The reason might be the author's modernist reflex, which leads him to the search for a new language to describe fascism and the failure of social struggle.

Zeynep Uysal discusses the social aspects of the modernist path that I attempt to trace in this chapter.[15] Discussing canonical authors such as Adalet Ağaoğlu, Oğuz Atay, Latife Tekin and Orhan Pamuk, who have emerged as figureheads of different quests from 1980 onwards, Uysal argues that modernist pursuits focused on an individual who was defined in a new social sphere saying "the novel in Turkish always has something to say about the social even when it is at its most individualistic."[16] Indeed, these authors were aware of the link between experimenting with new ways of crafting fiction and redefining existing ideological engagements. That was the main premise of modernist movement and it became crystal clear in the last quarter of the twentieth century in Turkish literature. These writers developed a form of fiction focusing on the individual under the deforming and reshaping power of social and political discourse. The protagonists of these new novels were far from being role models; quite the opposite, they are antiheroes who struggle with ethical and existential dilemmas. One of the most important antiheroes is Zebercet from Yusuf Atılgan's 1973 novel *Anayurt Oteli* (Motherland Hotel). The novel has an old mansion at its center. The collapse of a mansion and/or a big family is a metaphor for the Ottoman Empire in Turkish literature of the early twentieth century. Atılgan continues this convention but with a new perspective: It is not a collapse but rather a transformation. The mansion was converted into a hotel after the proclamation of the Republic. The hotel is run by Zebercet, who is implied because he is the bastard son of the mansion's owners. Zebercet's depression, nearly schizophrenic ravings, and absurd existence that reworks aspects of Camus' *The Stranger* turn into an allegory for disappointment with the results of Republican modernization. The interesting aspect of the novel is that it makes a highly political statement while entirely focusing on personal experience. Yusuf Atılgan deals in particular with the sexual and mental disintegration of a male individual oppressed by the social and historical forces, and he did this more overtly than Ahmet Hamdi Tanpınar. This is the new dimension that is contributed by the modernists to Turkish literature. A similar form of mental breakdown and depression is seen in Adalet Ağaoğlu's novel *Ölmeye Yatmak* (Lying Down to Die), published in 1973. Aysel, a woman and academic, seeks refuge in a hotel room and lies down to die to solve the crisis of her life. The novel flows along Aysel's stream of consciousness; as the story oscillates between the past and the present, the clash of the Republican project with traditional culture is told from the perspective of a woman who has struggled with her sexual desires and the ideological climate that shapes women. The irony is more intense than in Ağaoğlu's other novels.

A New Foreword

The 1970s were a time when novels and short stories stemming from a variety of literary pursuits were published. The 1970 novel that drew the most attention was *Tutunamayanlar* (The Disconnected), notable for its desire to "write itself a new foreword"[17] and its rebellion against the existing literary tradition, canon, and familiar ways of writing, just like Nâzım Hikmet's "demolishing the idols" movement in the late 1920s. Furthermore, its author, Oğuz Atay, was an engineer. He was not just any engineer, of course: He had worked for leftist culture magazines for years, read European literature, and had dared to publicly say that he found the existing literary tradition in Turkey inadequate. He openly referred to James Joyce, Virginia Woolf, Vladimir Nabokov, and Franz Kafka as his influences; he made extensive use of techniques like stream of consciousness, parody, pastiche, and intertextuality, and he wrote about the lives of the well-educated, urban-dwelling petty bourgeoisie at a time when literature was more interested in employing sociological analyses to criticize the feudal system in rural areas or dealing with the issues of migrating to the city; finally, instead of writing novels that contributed to social awakening through "positive protagonists" like the social realists, the dominant force in literature at the time, he used a Bakhtin-like, carnivalesque style to write about antiheroes discussing Kafkaesque dilemmas or existential issues.[18] Moreover, the key issue with these characters was disappointment and the frustration caused by the inability of the modernization project to deliver, on both the universal and local levels. As an engineer and scientist, Oğuz Atay never turned his back on scientific thought but was also aware of the issues that were the bane of modernity. This was the source of the cynical attitude that permeated his works. The borderline manic-depressive or even schizophrenic state of his characters was amplified with the frustration of being in a country in which the modernization attempts had not succeeded. In his books, Atay was, like his contemporaries Ağaoğlu and Erbil, strongly critical of the constructed Turkish identity and Turkish intellectuals' deficiencies. The promise of the modern Turkish Republic was to create a homogeneous nation-state while strictly adhering to the enlightenment project. The hope was that Turkey would

Laughter in the Dark

develop along the scientific path and become wealthy and "civilized" like the European nations. But by the 1970s, the landscape was dominated by corruption and superciliousness that Atay did not hesitate to admit. Turkey, as depicted by Atay, was impoverished and orphaned in every sense. And *The Disconnected*, with its ironic narrative and cyclic structure, is not a guide that shows the right path for the reader but a book that confuses the reader's mind and soul, forcing them to question everything. Each statement in the novel is refuted or voided by another statement, which serves to present crucial issues to the reader. It is laughter in the dark, made by a madman. Although the laughter would leave deep traces in his contemporaries and especially the generations that succeeded him, Atay died too early to see his indelible mark on Turkish literature.

The Path From Breaking Idols to Writing One's Own Foreword

Although they may have been representatives of vastly different eras and literary schools, the authors mentioned in this chapter created modernist avant-garde conventions that helped Turkish literature expand the boundaries of fiction and enabled it to challenge the tradition and the ongoing ideological discourse. Interestingly, they were influenced by Western authors and thinkers more than their national predecessors and created an original modernist path to investigate the new possibilities of political and critical literature. They produced multilayered texts, did not avoid experimenting with different genres, and aimed to break down the canonical works of their times. Their writing praxis illustrated that a world constructed by language could be deconstructed or reconstructed in an alternate way, also using language. Their bold formal quest began with rebelling against the literary canon and paved the way to the construction of a new literature. This is also reflective of the pains associated with the emergence of the modern individual in Turkey. They do not use the novel as an instrument to interpret and/or reflect on historical and social events but by placing centrally philosophical matters in their fiction they point out the deeper structures behind visible facts. Their perspective of history and geography is as multilayered as the structure of their literary texts; they avoid the constraints of homogenizing Turkish nationalism or Ottoman nostalgia. Their new multilayered, polyphonic perspective redefines issues such as Westernization as a central theme of Turkish literature from the Tanzimat to the 1950s, gender equality, enlightenment, and the repressed existence of different identities. One must note Orhan Pamuk's *Kara Kitap* (The Black Book), published in 1990, as one of the best syntheses of the outputs of this new perspective: it transposes individual existential issues with social problems to create a multidimensional novelistic architecture.

Although avant-garde attempts ranging from "demolishing the idols" to "writing one's own foreword" may have caused these authors to be misunderstood or misconstrued during their lifetimes and productive years, their efforts created the strongest undercurrent contributing to the diversity of the Turkish literary environment and brings the transformative power of modernism into the present day.

Notes

1 For a detailed classification of literary periods of Turkish literature from the Tanzimat to 2000s, see Erdağ Göknar, "The Novel in Turkish: Narrative Tradition to Nobel Prize," in *The Cambridge History of Turkey*, ed. Reşat Kasaba (Cambridge: Cambridge University Press, 2008), 472–503.
2 Modernist literature is a movement that emerged by the end of the nineteenth century, as approaches like realism, romanticism, and naturalism reached their limits, and literature started to reflect on itself, which led to the beginning of an era during which narrative styles and structures became the key issue. See James Fletcher and Malcolm Bradbury, "The Introverted Novel," in *Modernism: A Guide to European Literature 1890–1930* (New York: Penguin Books, 1992).

3 For a detailed biography, see Saime Göksu and Edward Timms, *Romantic Communist: The Life and Work of Nâzım Hikmet* (London: Hurst, 1999).

4 KUTV, the Communist University of the Toilers of the East, was an institution that ran from 1921 to 1938, where young people from Eastern countries were educated in a Marxist perspective.

5 For another discussion about Nazım Hikmet's modernism, see Kenan Behzat Sharpe's chapter in this volume.

6 Nazım Hikmet, *Kemal Tahir'e Mapusaneden Mektuplar* (Istanbul: Adam Yayınları, 1975), 105.

7 See, Murat Gülsoy and Zeynep Uysal, "Günümüz Türk Şairlerinde Nâzım Hikmet Etkisi, Bir Sözlü Tarih Projesi," in *Şiir Dünyadan İbaret: Nâzım Hikmet Üzerine Yeni Çalışmalar*, ed. Olcay Akyıldız and Murat Gülsoy (Istanbul: Boğaziçi University, 2019), 237–323.

8 Süha Oğuzertem, "Fictions of Narcissism: Metaphysical and Psychosexual Conflicts in the Stories of Ahmet Hamdi Tanpinar," *Turkish Studies Association Bulletin* 14, no. 2 (1990): 223–33.

9 Ahmet Hamdi Tanpınar, *Abdullah Efendinin Rüyaları* (Istanbul: Halit Kitabevi, 1943).

10 Erdoğan Alkan provides comparative examples to how Nerval has influenced prominent writers and poets in Turkish literature. See Erdoğan Alkan, *Düş Gezgini* (Ankara: Broy Yayınları, 1994).

11 Ibid., 32.

12 For more on the village novel, see Erkan Irmak's chapter in this volume.

13 In *Modernist Literature Challenging Fictions*, Vicki Mahaffey argues that a realist story told by an omniscient narrator (or at least one more knowledgeable than both the reader and the characters) relegates the reader to passivity, even relieves them of the responsibility to interpret the story, which in turn makes it easier to unconditionally submit to authority. Contrarily, "difficult" modernist fiction challenges the reality illusion of the reader and makes her more resistive to the ideological effect of the system. Vicki Mahaffey, *Modernist Literature Challenging Fictions* (New York: Wiley-Blackwell, 2007).

14 Although the novel was written in the late 1970s, it was only published in 1985.

15 See Zeynep Uysal, "Yeni Bir Toplumsallığın Peşinde: Deneyimden Dünyaya Açılan Roman," *Notos* (December 2017): 32–40.

16 Ibid., 32.

17 Oğuz Atay, *Tutunamayanlar* (Istanbul: İletişim Yayınları, 1972), 541.

18 For a more detailed study on Oğuz Atay's literature, see Meltem Gürle, *Carnivalizing the Turkish Novel, Oğuz Atay's Dialogue with the Canon in the Disconnected* (Bern: Peter Lang, 2012).

References

Alkan, Erdoğan. *Düş Gezgini*. Istanbul: Broy Yayınları, 1994.

Fletcher, James, and Bradbury Malcolm, "The Introverted Novel." In *Modernism: A Guide to European Literature 1890–1930*, 394–415. New York: Penguin Books, 1992.

Göknar, Erdağ. "The Novel in Turkish: Narrative Tradition to Nobel Prize." In *The Cambridge History of Turkey*, edited by Reşat Kasaba, 472–503. Cambridge: Cambridge University Press, 2008.

Göksu, Saime, and Edward Timms. *Romantic Communist: The Life and Work of Nâzım Hikmet*. London: Hurst, 1999.

Gülsoy, Murat, and Zeynep Uysal. "Günümüz Türk Şairlerinde Nâzım Hikmet Etkisi, Bir Sözlü Tarih Projesi." In *Şiir Dünyadan İbaret Nâzım Hikmet Üzerine Yeni Çalışmalar*, edited by Olcay Akyıldız ve Murat Gülsoy, 237–323. Istanbul: Boğaziçi University, 2019.

Gürle, Meltem. *Carnivalizing the Turkish Novel, Oğuz Atay's Dialogue with the Canon in the Disconnected*. Bern: Peter Lang, 2012.

Mahaffey, Vicki. *Modernist Literature Challenging Fictions*. New York: Wiley-Blackwell, 2007.

Oğuzertem, Süha. "Fictions of Narcissism: Metaphysical and Psychosexual Conflicts in the Stories of Ahmet Hamdi Tanpinar." *Turkish Studies Association Bulletin* 14, no. 2 (1990): 223–33.

Tanpınar, Ahmet Hamdi. *Abdullah Efendinin Rüyaları*. Istanbul: Halit Kitabevi, 1943.

Uysal, Zeynep. "Yeni Bir Toplumsallığın Peşinde: Deneyimden Dünyaya Açılan Roman." *Notos* (December 2017): 32–40.

SECTION VIII

Political Turmoils and Traumas

27

THE *AUFHEBUNG* OF TRAUMATIC MEMORY

Literary Responses to Military Coups in Turkey and Çetin Altan's *Büyük Gözaltı*

Çimen Günay-Erkol

Turkey's military coups are reflected in literature in a variety of complementary and contrasting ways. It is important to think back on these reflections because there are specific caveats added to the official history by literature, most of which are ignored or left unnoticed in the age of amnesia, and visiting such caveats is necessary to confront the memories of the military coups critically. Literature, in a sublime confidence, accommodates what is often left unsaid about coups in history or documents of memory, such as autobiographies and other texts. Disguised as fiction, the most dramatic pains in the history of Turkish military coups can become visible while insecurities about the past are opened for discussion. Most research on military coups take political and economic analyses as their explicit focus; to study the post-coup atmosphere, scholars tend to prefer autobiographies and oral history documents. It is a pity that novels come only as an afterthought, as there is a rich variety of witness narrations in the post-coup literature of Turkey, the algorithms of which still await further research.

Literature bears witness to things beyond immediate recognition and can reach a deeper understanding of the historical "facts" of military coups. In this chapter, I intend to show that fiction should be a vital part of regenerative attempts at looking back at history because it gives us the chance to talk about the dialectical *Aufhebung* of traumatic memory, the somehow problematic urge to preserve and integrate memories in an effort to annul or surpass them. I give an overview of post-coup novels in Turkey and summarize the history of the three successful and two abortive interventions in the 20-year period between 1960 and 1980, and for closer examination, move to Çetin Altan's *Büyük Gözaltı* (Extreme Surveillance, 1972), a side product of the 1971 military coup, in which a traumatic post-coup prison experience is claimed and transformed into a creative moment of *Aufhebung*.

Post-coup literature in Turkey was stuck in a process of *Aufhebung*, whereby traumatic memory is negated, sometimes annulled but also preserved.[1] In his *Sites of the Uncanny* in a discussion of prosthetic sites of Holocaust memory, Eric Kligerman details Hegel's use of *Aufhebung* in his *Phenomenology of Spirit* as follows:

> The verb *aufheben* has four possible meanings: 1) to lift up, 2) to seize 3) to preserve, and 4) to cancel or annul something. Hegel employs all four senses of the word in his closing section to describe how something can be held onto and preserved but at the

DOI: 10.4324/9780429279270-36

333

same time annulled. He is describing the process of transformation in which Spirit integrates its previous stages of development into a synthetic unity and moves toward self-consciousness. According to Hegel, one stage of consciousness is elevated into the next stage, but only through the negation of the former. While *Aufhebung* involves the presence of memory (*Erinnerung*) and the preservation on what is past, something is cancelled out as well. The presentation (*Vorstellung*) or image (*Bild*) of Spirit is transformed (*aufgehoben*) into an absolute knowing (*absolute Wissen*), and this process of *Aufhebung* is behind Hegel's concept of the development of world history.[2]

Aufhebung is also a multidimensional process in the context of the "coup history" hidden within the post-coup novels. Despite the fact that all post-coup novels in Turkey are preoccupied with mourning, recording, and historicizing, they do not have a singular agenda or a singular layer of historical witnessing. The act of historical witnessing depends on a selection of certain events or emotional states. Some writers acknowledge the military mentality as the norm of the collective consciousness in Turkey while others resist this. Some prefer victim-blaming, while others turn to actors of power instead. Though some novels introduce an abstract discussion of power, others provide selective documentary scenes from Turkish history. Memory in these novels is an interaction of several forces and ideologies, of horror and affection. It is a never-ending process and a powerful tool for the reconstruction of identity.

The memory debate in Turkish coup novels exceeds the coup in question as a singular event and grows into a wider discussion of power within the history of Turkish modernization. This gives post-coup novels a peculiar multidimensionality. Not only ideological and political polarities but also ethnic, religious, and gender frictions buried in Turkish history are evoked and analyzed. Post-generational trauma is negotiated and the discussion on trauma gets displaced from its "inexpressibility"[3] towards its visibility through "everyday forms of traumatizing violence."[4] Instead of treating trauma as an "unclaimed experience" following Cathy Caruth's foundational line of discussion from within trauma theory, recent transnational trends that discuss and challenge this approach try to make visible "the creative and political" instead of the "pathological and negative" in texts about trauma.[5] Turkish post-coup novels likewise undermine the centralized Western theory and tradition with their approach to trauma.

Continuity and Change in Post-Coup Novels

The first military coup on May 27, 1960, in Turkey was against the Justice Party (Adalet Partisi [AP]) government and resulted in the execution of the country's first elected prime minister, Adnan Menderes, with two of his ministers on September 16–17, 1961.[6] Two abortive coup attempts by Colonel Talat Aydemir took place in 1962 and 1963, and unrest in military cadres continued in the 1960s.[7] Aydemir obtained a pardon after his first attempt but faced the death penalty after the second. During the Turkish 1968, the idea of pursuing political change towards socialism by military force became a popular option in some left-wing circles.[8] At the height of Turkey's 1968, when student movements and protests of the unions accelerated, there was a powerful appeal to the state authorities for liberation, in concert with the general tendency in Europe. A left-wing junta (later known as the Madanoğlu junta) was uncovered on March 9, 1971, with its coup plan. The members were forced into retirement. The second military intervention followed three days later, on March 12, 1971. This time, the military did not assume direct power but urged for a technocratic government while exercising power behind the scenes. Turkey became a site of torture under the military regime from 1971 to 1973, for leftists overwhelmingly.[9] The third coup, a direct intervention into politics, which was considered a

The Aufhebung *of Traumatic Memory*

CIA-assisted overthrow, took place on September 12, 1980. The military outlawed all political parties and passed numerous laws drastically affecting the socioeconomical and political structures.[10] Turkey's integration into the global market economy gained a new momentum with the coup d'état of 1980. The assumed role of the military as the guardian of Turkey's democracy continued after the elections in 1983.[11]

Several people who were lay "witnesses" of the first coup in Turkey were targeted by the military and turned into "victims" of the second and the third ones. This inserted a powerful discussion of alienation and "moral injury"[12] to the post-coup novels of the post-1970s and post-1980s which, with a diversification of popular narrative techniques, created innovative methods to address structures of subjectivity. The urge to revisit the first intervention in 1960 in literature was a side product of the overwhelmingly leftist perspective of the trauma context of the post-1970s novels. It is clear that the coup in 1960 was recognized as a game changer, but writers did not prefer to go into the traumatic details of the coup in 1960s.[13] Novels that deal with the first military intervention in Turkey as a traumatic event were written during the "memory boom" of the 1990s, almost 30 years after the actual events.[14] This is partly because the higher casualties of the second (1971) and the third (1980) coups created the trauma context in literature and fashioned the public memory. Several novels published in the 1990s opened the 1960s to political debate and underlined the victimization of Prime Minister Adnan Menderes.[15]

The ten-year period between 1960 and 1970 was a period of turmoil, with student uprisings, riots of the workers, and economic backlashes in Turkey. On the streets, there were paramilitary right- and left-wing armed men torn into ideological subgroups based on their particular camps.[16] Left-wing intellectuals were targeted by the military after the 1971 coup, and this initiated a witness literature in response. Several novels filled with traumatic prison memories arrived immediately after the detained intellectuals published their (semi-)autobiographical works. Some of these novels carry graphic details of mistreatment and torture, but their strength is not limited to their documentary features.[17] These initial novels successfully hit a nerve with the self-criticism of their leftist protagonists, who questioned the success of the socialist movement within the strongly traditional Turkish society.

The discussion was further diffused from the military coup itself to personal dimensions of power relations in friendships and families in this self-criticism. In addition to documentarist prison novels, several other examples focused on fabricated stories about student movements or dealt with oppression in the daily practices of society.[18] In the second half of the 1970s, a comparative witness memory in literature became a more visible trend, giving rise to novels that compare and contrast socialist resistance in the specific conditions of 1971 with its European counterparts, anti-communist compeers, or previous movements in earlier phases of Turkish history.[19]

The victim-blaming rhetoric of the anti-communist novels proves the harshness of the "memory war" between the revolutionary and the anti-communist camps of the 1970s. In 1979, on the eve of the third and most devastating coup, several writers were looking critically at turning points in Turkish history, such as ideological factionalism, political assassination attempts, the Korean War, and so on while questioning the rationale of revolutionary violence as an option to resist endless asymmetric wars.[20]

When the third coup arrived in 1980, both the socialist and the anti-communist camps found themselves targeted; as if with a reversal of Carl von Clausewitz's famous dictum, the state considered politics a "continuation of war by other means" and did not tolerate any political activism. To give the impression of a "fair" treatment of "crimes," all ideological movements were brought under control, while a controversial "Turkish-Islamic synthesis" was developed as the political mainstream.[21] Casualties of the third coup were very high. Novels touching upon the realities of the military prisons could only be published after 1987, while plenty of novels in the meantime foregrounded the need to rethink the alienation felt in the post-coup atmosphere and revealed the fears and demolished relationships of a traumatized society.

The literary post-coup output of 1980s is widespread, miscellaneous, and multi-centered.[22] In the second half of the 1980s, prison experiences prevailed in literature. Writers used trauma as a productive venue and published novels as an act of resistance to the authoritarian military regime and the extinction of memory forced by it.[23] While some examples of this subgroup are limited exclusively to the victimization caused by the coup, in other works trauma regenerates itself as the victimized personas try to start a new life when they get out of prison. As the history behind "fair" treatment of "crimes" was revealed in 1990s, accounts by anti-communist victims of torture with similar motifs of power and violence arrived.[24]

While the post-coup ethos of "remembering" was a dominant trend in literature in the 1990s, the Turkish political headlines were not free of tensions between the military and elected leaders. A boom of historical novels emerged in the 1990s with the aim of going back in history to the golden ages of Ottoman times in order to enrich the discussion and interpretations of Turkey's contemporary problems. The "social theory" hidden in some such novels was intended as a diagnosis of current problems and, in this vein, military coups remained a focus of attention as the task of remembering brought the task of critically working through the country's collective traumas. However, when the so-called postmodern coup took place in 1997 and forced Turkey's Islamist prime minister to resign, it did not initiate an act of interpellation in literature at all, as most of the writers were still preoccupied with the memories of the previous coups.[25]

What kept most writers of the period on the track of Cold War anxieties (and thus made them attached to the 1971 and 1980 coups as defining themes) instead of focusing on the anti-democratic attacks on elected politicians during their own period was the heavier toll of the previous coups and the ongoing clash between the two antagonistic political projects. The distance of Islamist writers to the novel as a genre, friction between the Turkish left and Islam, and leftist intellectuals' view of religion as a unifying thread between Islamists and anti-communists: These all influenced the self-imposed silence in novels that prevented the postmodern coup from being registered in literature.[26]

In the literature of the 2000s, the work of several writers continued to revolve around the problem of solidarity in the neoliberal society and revisited memories of the coup.[27] The depoliticization of society after 1980 became a popular theme. The generation of '78 (the generation that experienced the 1980 coup as activists) and their political resistance has been revisited by many contemporary writers.[28] Recurring military coups has meant that younger generations in Turkey are being born into an already traumatized political culture. Further interventions against Islamist governments by the military in 1997 and 2007, and the abortive coup in 2016, have not yet been represented in literature in any depth, but they legitimately bring the concept of intergenerational trauma to the discussion.

Aufhebung of the Coup Memory in Turkey and *Büyük Gözaltı*

As a corpus, post-coup novels in Turkish literature show an awareness that the subjectivity of a person is always addressed, negated, and disputed by other subjects, but a limited number of them invite a dialectical and multidirectional way of thinking through subjectivity in depth. Instead, several works include often single-handed analyses of events, with these novels failing to exceed the dualistic patterns forced by stereotypical ideological thinking.[29] Still, the coexistence of conflicting memories of the coups in literature as a whole indeed shows that "trauma is never simply one's own."[30] Several novels with (auto)biographical overtones offer counterhegemonic insights into the coup atmosphere. These, in particular, can be regarded as texts of narrative recoveries.[31] Such texts provide a powerful survival strategy against trauma, which offer subject positions that claim sociopolitical agency in line with the theory of witnessing developed by Shoshana Felman and Dori Laub.[32] Çetin Altan's *Büyük Gözaltı* is one such example.

Büyük Gözaltı details the trauma of a political prisoner. Altan was himself a member of parliament from the Workers' Party of Turkey (TİP) when he was taken into custody immediately after the armed forces came to power in 1971.[33] He published *Büyük Gözaltı* following his release from prison in 1972, and the French edition of the novel was published by the prestigious publisher Flammarion three years later in 1975. In prison, the protagonist of *Büyük Gözaltı* becomes the overseer of his acts, memories, and motives, allowing Altan to perform *Aufhebung* over traumatic memories, which becomes an important center of gravity in the novel.

Laub and Felman's theory of witnessing reminds us that when no one dares to listen, the subject becomes an "inner witness" to be addressed.[34] This is the case in *Büyük Gözaltı*. The novel is based on the monologues of the protagonist stuck in a prison cell. He sometimes creates addressable others using what psychiatrist Dori Laub calls "inner witness[es]" and turn his monologues into dialogues. Dead relatives, friends, family, and colleagues happen to become visitors of the prison cell, creating the impression of being heard by others. Observing people in post-coup Turkey as victims of trauma, with an enormous loss of power and lack of agency, Altan turns his attention to dramatic objectification, oppression, and the discrimination of individuals via politics and other social contexts.

Being under surveillance serves as a leitmotiv in this novel, but Altan suggests that this is not a case limited to the post-coup atmosphere or the confines of the prison cell. The protagonist reveals how as a man born and raised in Turkey, he felt under constant surveillance during his entire life. He recalls being monitored by his family members during his childhood and youth, and by the society at large in his performances of masculinity in his formative years. This is the framework by which Altan turns the traumatic prison memories of the protagonist into a trigger to access the memories of his life before prison. For example, the protagonist's fear of being sexually tortured by the guards in prison gets connected to his childhood fears of circumcision, since his traumatic state connects both events as mandatory rites of passages that should be passed through in order to reach a strong and durable masculinity.

Mistreatment of the protagonist as a young boy at his boarding school, as a young man trying to build his masculinity, and finally as a political prisoner who fails to rationalize the physical violence targeting him makes the memory war among competing versions of surveillance and trauma more visible. Altan paves the way forward to resilience through this multidimensional trauma narrative. His call includes open identification with the position of the victim, a targeting of every individual born into the pressures of the predominantly traditional Turkish society, and attempts to build a therapeutic form of criticism within the post-coup atmosphere. The projection of the protagonist's memories of circumcision to his fear of sexual torture helps Altan to catch a dramatic climax which serves as the process of *Aufhebung* in this novel. His memories about circumcision make it clear that memory is shaped as much by the present as by the past and can be rearranged. Altan attempts to negate and surpass past traumas through the present ones, and the present ones by questioning the confines of the cell. The protagonist painfully recognizes that there has always been surveillance and pressure in his life. Hence he begins to think that being in prison always carries ways to resist the prison mentality within. This is where he starts building his positive power.

Büyük Gözaltı shows that family, school, and social norms are all part of an oppressive system, but resistance is always an option and none of those authorities can triumph as long as people intervene into their traumatic memories to revise, alter, and mute them. While historicizing traumatic memories of the coup, Altan attempts to restore the subjectivity of the victims in order to help them move beyond trauma. He elaborates on the traumas of his protagonist as regenerative experiences instead of a finite problem. As a trendsetter of the post-coup novels built on witnessing and testimony in the 1970s, Altan's *Büyük Gözaltı* grows into a criticism of the witnessing culture, in as much as it turns into a surveillance culture that weakens the democratic sphere in Turkey. His look at post-coup trauma connects the traumas caused by military rule to the daily reality of people in Turkey, who live under the militaristic mentality of institutions such as patriarchal families and despotic boarding schools. Altan successfully shows that getting stuck in a process of *Aufhebung* is the reality of the post-coup period, but that traumatic memories of the coup can produce survivors, instead of victims and witnesses, if remembering becomes a process of reevaluation and active creation instead of reproduction.

Notes

1 Only a small group of the post-coup novels have attracted attention outside of Turkey and been translated into other European languages. Çetin Altan, *Étroite Surveillance* (Paris: Flammarion, 1975), originally published as *Büyük Gözaltı* (Ankara: Bilgi Yayınevi, 1972); Erdal Öz, *Je Bend Gewond* (Amsterdam: Ambo, 1988), originally published as *Yaralısın* (Istanbul: Cem Yayınevi, 1974); Bilge Karasu, *Night* (Baton Rouge: Louisiana State University Press, 1994) originally published as *Gece* (Istanbul: İletişim Yayınları, 1985); Feyza Hepçilingirler, *As the Red Carnation Fades* (Rudgwick, UK: Milet, 2015), originally published as *Kırmızı Karanfil Ne Renk Solar?* (Istanbul: Simavi Yayınları, 1993); Adalet Ağaoğlu, *Curfew* (Austin: University of Texas Press, 1997), originally published as *Üç Beş Kişi* (Istanbul: Remzi Kitabevi, 1984); Sevgi Soysal, *Noontime in Yenişehir* (Rudwick, UK: Milet, 2016), originally published as *Yenişehir'de Bir Öğle Vakti* (Ankara: Bilgi Yayınevi, 1973). While Altan's and Karasu's novels operate in an abstract time/setting with little reference, if any at all, to Turkey, others such as Öz's, Hepçilingirler's, Ağaoğlu's and Soysal's question political activism under authoritarian rule, document prison life with minute details (some coming from the real-life experiences of the writers) and celebrate the resilience of political activism.
2 Eric Kligerman, *Sites of the Uncanny: Paul Celan, Specularity and the Visual Arts* (Berlin: de Gruyter, 2007), 20–21.
3 Shoshana Felman and Dori Laub, eds., *Testimony: Crises of Witnessing in Literature, Psychoanalysis, and History* (New York: Routledge, 1992); Cathy Caruth, *Unclaimed Experience: Trauma, Narrative and History* (Baltimore: Johns Hopkins University Press), 1996; Geoffrey H. Hartman, "On Traumatic Knowledge and Literary Studies," *New Literary History* 26, no. 3 (1995): 537–63.
4 Michael Rothberg, "Decolonizing Trauma Studies: A Response," *Studies in the Novel* 40, no. 1–2, Postcolonial Trauma Novels (Spring–Summer 2008): 226. In 2005, Leylâ Erbil made visible the persistence of coup mentality in contemporary political struggles of Turkey in her novella *Üç Başlı Ejderha* (The Three-Headed Dragon; Istanbul: Türkiye İş Bankası Kültür Yayınları, 2012) by addressing some of the black holes in Turkish history such as the "disappearance" of the arrested from military prisons, the political pressures on the Saturday Mothers who have insisted on searching for their disappeared sons and relatives, and the death of Alevis in the Maraş massacres of 1978. Her literary witnessing to post-coup history gets dissolved in a more generalized witnessing to the history of Turkey; in *Üç Başlı Ejderha*, what permeates the text is no longer an event-based witnessing that prioritizes the aftermath of the military's coming to power, but rather a psycho-political treatment of the post-coup trauma as the norm in Turkish history and the founding feature of the current climate of the 2000s under civilian control. Uğur Çalışkan explores the witnessing in Erbil's late works under the title "traumatic poetics" in his unpublished MA manuscript. See Uğur Çalışkan, "Travmatik Poetika: Leylâ Erbil'in Son Metinlerinde Tanıklık ve Ufukları (Traumatic Poetics: Witnessing and Its Horizons in Leylâ Erbil's Last Texts)" (MA thesis, Boğaziçi University, 2018).
5 Stef Craps, *Postcolonial Witnessing: Trauma Out of Bonds* (Basingstoke: Palgrave Macmillan, 2012), 127.
6 See Mogens Pelt, *Military Intervention and a Crisis of Democracy in Turkey: The Menderes Era and Its Demise* (London: I. B. Tauris, 2014, 1); Ömer Aslan, *The United States and Military Coups in Turkey and Pakistan: Between Conspiracy and Reality* (New York: Palgrave Macmillan, 2018), 107.
7 See William Hale, "Challenge, Accommodation and Crisis: 1961–1971," in *Turkish Politics and the Military* (New York: Routledge, 1994), 153–83.

The Aufhebung *of Traumatic Memory*

8 See Özgür Mutlu Ulus, *The Army and the Radical Left in Turkey: Military Coups, Socialist Revolution and Kemalism* (London: I. B. Tauris, 2020).

9 See Igor P. Lipovsky, *The Socialist Movement in Turkey, 1960–1980* (Leiden: Brill, 1992).

10 See Elifcan Karacan, *Remembering the 1980 Turkish Military Coup d'État: Memory, Violence, and Trauma* (Wiesbaden: Springer, 2016).

11 On February 28, 1997, a memorandum by the military on the grounds of rising religious extremism in the country caused the resignation of the first Islamist prime minister Necmettin Erbakan. This was later dubbed "the postmodern coup." On January 1998, Erbakan's Welfare Party (Refah Partisi [RP]) was closed by the constitutional court. See Banu Eligür, *The Mobilization of Political Islam in Turkey* (Cambridge: Cambridge University Press, 2010), 220–34. On April 27, 2007, in the "midnight memorandum" (or e-memo) prepared by the then-chief of general staff, the military announced immediate concern over the parliamentary deadlock on whether the presidential nominee's spouse should be able to wear an Islamic headscarf, putting the elections under the shadow of a coup. On July 15, 2016, another abortive attempt to topple the government took place. See Nikos Christofis, ed., *Erdoğan's 'New' Turkey: Attempted Coup d'état and the Acceleration of Political Crisis* (New York: Routledge, 2019); Feride Çiçekoğlu and Ömer Turan, eds., *The Dubious Case of a Failed Coup: Militarism, Masculinities, and 15 July in Turkey* (New York: Palgrave Macmillan, 2019). The government declared a state of emergency as of July 20 and kept extending it. Turkey experienced presidential and parliamentary elections under the state of emergency on June 24, 2018.

12 Joshua Pederson, "Moral Injury in Literature," *Narrative* 28, no. 1 (January 2020): 43–61.

13 Samim Kocagöz's *İzmir'in İçinde* in 1973, Attilâ İlhan's *Bıçağın Ucu* in 1973, and Vedat Türkali's *Bir Gün Tek Başına* in 1974 deal with the 1960s, revolving around the political polarization of the society. Both *Bıçağın Ucu* and *Bir Gün Tek Başına* come to an end on the exact date of the coup, on May 27, 1960. Kocagöz's *İzmir'in İçinde* in 1973 details how the intimate relationship of a young couple is troubled because of their extremely polarized family ties to the Democrat Party, on the bride's side, and to the military cadres that supported coup, on the groom's side.

14 In terms of their literary outputs, the first coup in 1960 is rather premature, and the third coup in 1980 lacks the collectivity in response maintained by the 1971 coup. Intellectuals under the pressure of the Adnan Menderes government in the 1950s widely regarded the 1960 military coup as a "libertarian" one. The new constitution introduced immediately after the 1960 coup with a wide range of civil liberties and social rights helped the army gain support from the society. After the 1980 coup, the military regime was so harsh that resistance to the military measures became almost impossible. Hence literary responses to the third coup arrived with a greater time gap than they had after the second intervention. Works built on the memories of the September 12th coup are widespread in the post-1980s and exhibit diversity in form and literary techniques.

15 Sevinç Çokum's *Karanlığa Direnen Yıldız* (1996), Yılmaz Karakoyunlu's *Yorgun Mayıs Kısrakları* (2004), and Nilüfer Kuyaş' *Yeni Baştan* (2007) revolve around the disintegration of the society along ideological lines, with added witness accounts from the Yassıada trials, which handed down the death sentence for Prime Minister Adnan Menderes. Popular romances that follow Menderes' romantic relationship with Ayhan Aydan, such as İsa Yılmaz's *Ben Bu Adamı Sevdim* (2012) and Melike İlgün's *Bir Başvekil Sevdim* (2013) also attempt to advocate for a fragile human persona hidden behind the stiff political image of Menderes.

16 Melih Cevdet Anday in *Gizli Emir* (1970) foresaw that another military coup was coming a year ahead of the intervention. In his novel, alienated intellectuals discuss the overwhelming political tension in society and weigh the probability of a second coup in Turkey.

17 Çetin Altan's *Büyük Gözaltı* (1974) and *Bir Avuç Gökyüzü* (1974), Öz's *Yaralısın* (1974), and Soysal's *Şafak* (1975) are primary examples of such accounts.

18 Füruzan's *Kırk Yedi'liler*, Tarık Dursun K.'s *Gün Döndü*, and Melih Cevdet Anday's *İsa'nın Güncesi*, all of which were published in 1974, build on the horrors of military control over society to comment on the shortcomings of being trapped in a politically polarized and alienating society.

19 Pınar Kür's *Yarın Yarın* (1976) makes a sketchy comparison of Istanbul with Paris in terms of the student movements and critically discusses how to develop a politically motivated radicalism in the post-coup society. Emine Işınsu's *Sancı* (1975) and Sevinç Çokum's *Zor* (1977) provide victimization stories from the other camp, alluding to the pains of the anti-communist youth.

20 Novels published in 1979 such as Tarık Buğra's *Gençliğim Eyvah*, Demir Özlü's *Bir Küçükburjuva'nın Gençlik Yılları*, Ayla Kutlu's *Kaçış*, and Adalet Ağaoğlu's *Bir Düğün Gecesi* revealed the rising tensions in society as a whole, as members of the same family and close friends had found themselves on the

opposite sides of the political fight. In 1979, Mehmet Eroğlu's climactic novel *Issızlığın Ortası* shared the Milliyet novel prize with Turkey's Nobel laureate Orhan Pamuk's *Cevdet Bey ve Oğulları*, but none of the publishers in Turkey could offer Eroğlu's political novel a contract in the wake of the pressures of the third coup.

21 See Yıldız Atasoy, *Islam's Marriage with Neoliberalism: State Transformation in Turkey* (London: Palgrave Macmillan, 2009); Gavin D. Brockett, *How Happy to Call Oneself a Turk: Provincial Newspapers and the Negotiation of a Muslim National Identity* (Austin: University of Texas Press, 2011).

22 Inaugural novels are Ahmet Altan's *Dört Mevsim Sonbahar* (1982) and Orhan Pamuk's *Sessiz Ev* (1983). In his *Gece* (written in the 1970s but published in 1985), Bilge Karasu underwent the burden of working through and interpreting the psychopathology of the post-coup society. *Gece* is an abstract work inspired by the alienation felt in a society under institutionalized fascism and violence, and with the implied inability of restoration it frames, it positioned literature on a double gesture of remembrance and forgetting.

23 A. Kadir Konuk's *Gün Dirildi* (1987) and *Çözülme* (1988), Kaan Arsanoğlu's *Devrimciler* (1988) and *Kimlik* (1989), and Feride Çiçekoğlu's *Uçurtmayı Vurmasınlar* (1989) revolve around the maltreatment experienced in and out of prisons and discuss the political rifts around traumatic moments. Halil Genç's *Koyabilmek Adını* (1988) and Hüseyin Şimşek's *Ayrımı Bol Bir Yol* (1988) focus on torture and hunger strikes in the prisons.

24 M. Naci Bostancı's *Seksenler: Işığın Gölgesi* (1996) is one of the early examples of this subgroup.

25 Gürsel Korat's *Ay Şarkısı* (1997) and Timur Ertekin's *Şamanın Üç Soygunu* (1999) detail the prison experiences of young men during the second military coup; Tahir Abacı's *İkinci Adım* (1999) revolves around the neglect of the law as the founding principle of this period; Cem Selcen's *1578* (1999) and Erendiz Atasü's *Gençliğin O Yakıcı Mevsimi* (1999) turn to the atmosphere before the third coup to discuss the political radicalism and personal relations woven around it. The atmosphere that prepared the coup of February 28, 1997, can be seen in Mehmet Efe's *Mızraksız İlmihal* (1993) and Halime Toros' *Halkaların Ezgisi* (1997). Yıldız Ramazanoğlu's *İkna Odası* (2008) and Sibel Eraslan's *Saklı Kitap* (2013) also deal with the political pressures targeting the Islamists. It was with novels such as Ahmet Kekeç's *Yağmurdan Sonra* (1999) that the politically tense atmosphere of the postmodern coup appeared as a visible theme in detail.

26 Orhan Pamuk ended this silence with his *Kar* in 2002, which consists of an elegant account of military power in the everyday lives of ordinary people and suggests a lineage of victims of the postmodern coup with victims of the previous coups, with a collectivist gaze. On this novel, see Erdağ Göknar's chapter in this volume.

27 Mehmet Eroğlu's *Yüz: 1981* (2000) details the abrupt transformation of Turkey under the violent rise of capitalism. The collapse of friendships under military dictatorships and the generational trauma of the coups is revisited in novels such as Metin Celâl's *Ne Güzel Çocuklardık Biz* (2000), Yiğit Bener's *Eksik Taşlar* (2001), Atilla Keskin's *Dostluk* (2001), and Osman Akınhay's *Gün Ağırmasa* (2002). In a harsh negotiation of Turkish political history, power, and masculinity, Murat Uyurkulak connected the memories of the military coups to each other in his 2002 novel *Tol* around the metaphorical father-son relationship he had created between two strangers that became confidants during a train journey. Zülfü Livaneli in his dystopic novel *Son Ada* (2008) discussed the totalitarian society created by the September 12th coup, and Şebnem İşigüzel in her *Resmigeçit* (2008) presented a vivid picture of Turkey's political history around the coups. Irmak Zileli's *Eşik* (2011) returned to the theme of intergenerational trauma and discussed how the military coups caused trembles in the younger generations of the family. Eren Aysan's *Silsile* (2020) is another recent example in which a young female academic studying abroad struggles with coup memories of her family's past.

28 Some examples are Süheyla Acar's *Yağmurun Yedi Yüzü* (2004), Ayşegül Devecioğlu's *Kuş Diline Öykünen* (2004), Atilla Keskin's *Çiçekler Susunca* (2006), Mine Söğüt's *Şahbaz'ın Harikulâde Yılı 1979* (2007), and Şöhret Baltaş' *Koşarken Yavaşlar Gibi* (2007). Pamuk Yıldız's *O Hep Aklımda* (2010) brings autobiographical details of torture into a powerful discussion with hegemony. Victim testimonies from the right wing such as Misli Baydoğan's *Hatırla Beni* (2012) and Adnan Şenel's *Elma ve Bıçak* (2013) were also published.

29 Inspired by Michael Rothberg's work on multidirectional memory, which suggests that there exists a "companionship" instead of "competition" among memories of different camps, Deniz Şenol-Sert and I examined the interaction between conflicting coup memories, using a dataset of novels created as part of the project *Memory and Witnessing in Literary Studies: Literature and Military Coups in Turkey* (2014–2017, TÜBİTAK 114K137), which covered 137 novels written between 1960 and 2015, with

The Aufhebung *of Traumatic Memory*

both explicit and implicit accounts of the military coups and related events. Çimen Günay-Erkol and Deniz Şenol-Sert, "From Competitive to Multidirectional Memory: A Literary Tool for Comparison," *Turkish Studies* 19, no. 1 (2018): 118–38.

30 Cathy Caruth, *Unclaimed Experience: Trauma, Narrative and History* (Baltimore: Johns Hopkins University Press, 1996), 24.

31 In my book *Broken Masculinities*, I argued that novels written after the military coup of March 12, 1971, which "broke" the rise of Turkish socialism, constitute a subgenre in which the discussion on power boils down to a discussion on masculinity as the founding element of the problem. Writers comment on masculinity as both the root cause of the problem (of the misuse of power) and the integral solution to resist it. This gendered perspective is a side product of Turkey's 1968, during which men were the leading figures of almost all of the social movements and were involved in violent skirmishes in the streets. By all means, the attempt to retain "masculinity" uncovers the "underlying truth" of the resistance to militarized power in Turkey. The insistence on masculinity as a trope in the post–March 12th literature is because the courage to resist the military regime is believed to require an equally powerful "image of masculinity," which only by showing an equally destructive masculinity can put an end to domination and oppression. Çimen Günay-Erkol, *Broken Masculinities: Solitude, Alienation, and Frustration in Turkish Literature after 1970* (Budapest: Central European University Press, 2016).

32 Shoshana Felman and Dori Laub, eds., *Testimony: Crises of Witnessing in Literature, Psychoanalysis, and History* (New York: Routledge, 1992).

33 Seval Şahin and Didem Ardalı Büyükarman, "Çetin Altan," in *Dictionary of Literary Biography 379*, ed. Burcu Alkan and Çimen Günay-Erkol (Farmington Hills, MI: GALE Cengage), 3–15.

34 See Dori Laub, "An Event Without a Witness: Truth, Testimony, and Survival," in *Testimony: Crises of Witnessing in Literature, Psychoanalysis, and History*, ed. Shoshana Felman and Dori Laub (New York: Routledge, 1992), 85.

References

Altan, Çetin. *Büyük Gözaltı*. Ankara: Bilgi Yayınevi, 1972.

———. *Étroite Surveillance*. Paris: Flammarion, 1975.

Aslan, Ömer. "May 27 Coup and the US Role." In *The United States and Military Coups in Turkey and Pakistan: Between Conspiracy and Reality*, 107–9. New York: Palgrave, 2018.

Çalışkan, Uğur. "Travmatik Poetika: Leylâ Erbil'in Son Metinlerinde Tanıklık ve Ufukları (Traumatic Poetics: Witnessing and Its Horizons in Leylâ Erbil's Last Texts)." MA thesis, Boğaziçi University, 2018.

Caruth, Cathy. *Trauma: Explorations in Memory*. Baltimore: Johns Hopkins University Press, 1995.

———. *Unclaimed Experience: Trauma, Narrative and History*. Baltimore: Johns Hopkins University Press, 1996.

Christofis, Nikos, ed. *Erdoğan's 'New' Turkey: Attempted Coup d'état and the Acceleration of Political Crisis*. New York: Routledge, 2019.

Çiçekoğlu, Feride, and Ömer Turan, eds. *The Dubious Case of a Failed Coup: Militarism, Masculinities, and 15 July in Turkey*. New York: Palgrave Macmillan, 2019.

Craps, Stef. *Postcolonial Witnessing: Trauma Out of Bonds*. Basingstoke: Palgrave Macmillan, 2012.

Eligür, Banu. "The Soft Intervention of 1997 and the Islamist Social Movement." In *The Mobilization of Political Islam in Turkey*, 214–75. Cambridge: Cambridge University Press, 2010.

Felman, Shoshana, and Dori Laub. *Testimony: Crises of Witnessing in Literature, Psychoanalysis, and History*. New York: Routledge, 1992.

Günay-Erkol, Çimen. *Broken Masculinities: Solitude, Alienation, and Frustration in Turkish Literature After 1970*. Budapest: Central European University Press, 2016.

Günay-Erkol, Çimen, and Deniz Şenol-Sert. "From Competitive to Multidirectional Memory: A Literary Tool for Comparison." *Turkish Studies* 19, no. 1 (2018): 118–38.

Hale, William. "Challenge, Accommodation and Crisis: 1961–1971." In *Turkish Politics and the Military*, 153–83. New York: Routledge, 1994.

Hartman, Geoffrey H. "On Traumatic Knowledge and Literary Studies." *New Literary History* 26, no. 3 (1995): 537–63.

Karacan, Elifcan. "The Military Take Another Turn: The September 12th Coup." In *Remembering the 1980 Turkish Military Coup d'État: Memory, Violence, and Trauma*, 81–85. Wiesbaden: Springer, 2016.

Kligerman, Eric. *Sites of the Uncanny: Paul Celan, Specularity and the Visual Arts*. Berlin: de Gruyter, 2007.

Laub, Dori. "An Event Without a Witness: Truth, Testimony, and Survival." In *Testimony: Crises of Witnessing in Literature, Psychoanalysis, and History*, edited by Shoshana Felman and Dori Laub, 75–92. New York: Routledge, 1992.

Lipovsky, Igor P. *The Socialist Movement in Turkey, 1960–1980*. Leiden: Brill, 1992.

Pederson, Joshua. "Moral Injury in Literature." *Narrative* 28, no. 1 (2020): 43–61.

Pelt, Mogens. *Military Intervention and a Crisis of Democracy in Turkey: The Menderes Era and Its Demise*. London: I.B. Tauris, 2014.

Rothberg, Michael. "Decolonizing Trauma Studies: A Response." *Studies in the Novel* 40, no. 1–2, Postcolonial Trauma Novels (Spring–Summer 2008): 224–34.

Şahin, Seval, and Didem Ardalı Büyükarman. "Çetin Altan." In *Dictionary of Literary Biography 379*, edited by Burcu Alkan and Çimen Günay-Erkol, 3–15. Farmington Hills: GALE Cengage, 2017.

Ulus, Özgür Mutlu. *The Army and the Radical Left in Turkey: Military Coups, Socialist Revolution and Kemalism*. London: I.B. Tauris, 2020.

28

INTELLIGENTSIA NARRATIVES OF THE 1970s TURKISH NOVEL

Burcu Alkan

The massive, 900-page *A History of Russian Literature* by Andrew Kahn et al. ends with an entire chapter titled "Intelligentsia Narratives" in which the writers trace, from the twentieth century onwards, the theme of "the intelligentsia self-consciously thinking about its own mission and history."[1] It is, of course, not uncommon for writers to depict intellectual types in their works, and examples of this are abundant in any world literary tradition. The concept of the intellectual bears an innate self-reflexivity that renders such depictions to be expected. In fact, the very act of depicting an intellectual character is an intellectual pursuit in itself that points to the writer's perception and conceptualization of intellectuality. However, when such thematic typology becomes so prevalent that it requires special mention, the existence of a literary phenomenon needs to be acknowledged.

The degree of prevalence of such a phenomenon is linked to the politics of and literature in a given cultural tradition and some traditions are more susceptible to it than others. For instance, in contexts where the relationship between literature and society is rather direct and that literature's reality as an artistic, aesthetic artifact is somewhat secondary, there tends to be major appearances of intellectual types in literary works, especially in novelistic representations with their ample narrative space. In their case, Kahn et al. explain such a specific choice of a social type in Russian literature deserving its own chapter by maintaining that "[b]oth the intelligentsia and literature were (and still are) perceived in Russian culture as vehicles of social modernization and, at the same time, of moral consciousness."[2]

Not unlike its Russian counterpart, Turkish literature is one of those traditions in which a prevalence of intelligentsia narratives can be traced through the modern era.[3] The very existence of the Turkish novel attests to the relationship between literature and the intellectual and the manifestation of both in literary format. The emergence of the novel genre in Turkish literature was not only an outcome of the country's general drive to modernize but also a key tool in its realization. The "wrong" kind of westernization, an idea central to the conflict-ridden transformation that the country was going through, was essentially the main theme in this initial period of the Turkish novel. Novelists focused on the contrasts between "western" morals (or from their viewpoint, lack thereof) and advancements of various kinds and their "native" counterparts in a drive to "educate" the people in western ways while advocating against the loss of their own values and mores.[4]

DOI: 10.4324/9780429279270-37

343

Although there are no plausible representations in these "wrong westernization" novels, the kernel of an intellectual type can be discerned in the form of negation. The snobbish, half-learned "(wrong) westernized" characters, such as Bihruz Bey in Recaizâde Mahmud Ekrem's *Araba Sevdası* (The Carriage Affair, 1898) with his French learning, bear qualities of certain premature expectations from potential learned types. Such earlier characters are, of course, rough caricatures depicted for didactic purposes, and thus they can at best be deemed negated prototypes.

However, later in the early Republican era the east-west contrast is maintained in a related form and becomes manifest in the conflict between the urban, modern culture and the Anatolian, rural tradition in its various formulations. In Yakup Kadri Karaosmanoğlu's *Yaban* (The Stranger, 1932), for instance, the learned, modern man (i.e., the intellectual type) Ahmet Celâl is a veteran military officer who retires to a village. He is alienated from the local people and they mistrust him for being an outsider, a *yaban*. His narrative is an earlier example of one of the most prominent patterns in the representation of the intellectual in Turkish novels: the unbridgeable gap between the intelligentsia and the common people, and in this particular case the rural folk.

The second half of the twentieth century follows suit with its variations on intelligentsia narratives that match the social and political milieus of the works. A notable example is Peyami Safa's *Matmazel Noraliya'nın Koltuğu* (The Armchair of Mademoiselle Noralia, 1949). The protagonist of this novel studies medicine and western philosophy and is depicted as suffering from internal turmoil, a form of existential crisis. Not unlike his predecessors shaped by the Tanzimat ideology, the protagonist is presented as an intellectual type who is lost in the materialist ideas of the western world. Having turned his back on his native culture's spiritual traditions, he ends up becoming a lost soul. As a student torn between the polar values of the east and the west as represented in the narrative and in search of answers in between, he interacts with both an older understanding of intellectuality with links to a form of spiritual knowledge and points to the currency of the secular ones that prevail in modern times.

About 15 years later, Attilâ İlhan employs what will later become his signature Freudo-Marxist approach in the depiction of his idealist journalist, Mahmud Ersoy in *Kurtlar Sofrası* (Dining with the Wolves, 1963) as a part of his broader critique of the intelligentsia. His protagonist is a politically involved intellectual type who seeks the truth and desires the best for his country. He is such a strong character that even in his death he effects change on other people both directly and by proxy. Mahmud Ersoy is a precursor to İlhan's later intellectual typology and the narrative of *Kurtlar Sofrası* evolves towards the establishment of an entire interlinked novelistic world. Following this novel, İlhan creates his series, "Aynanın İçindekiler" (Those in the Mirror) in a fashion that replicates Émile Zola's Rougon-Macquart series with a network of characters related to one another through various social and filial ties. In his ambitious seven-novel set with additional connecting works, the novelist creates a range of intellectual types that evolve through the historical narrative of Turkey in an overarching chronological structure.

While the examples of the patterns in the portrayal of the intellectual through the decades can be multiplied, the above brief outline with its representative cases clearly points to the aforementioned self-reflexivity of writers depicting intellectual types. Elsewhere, I have formulated such self-reflexivity along the lines of an interconnection between "writers as intellectuals" and "writers' intellectuals."[5] While acknowledging the difficulties of pinning down such a complex concept and instead, specifying its perception in a particular moment in history, I highlighted its mise en abyme formulation in the modern novelistic tradition. Novelists as intellectuals, in their drive for social change, depict intellectual types (including writer-characters) who strive for social change.[6]

In line with the trajectory outlined above, the intellectual figures of the Turkish novel of the 1970s maintain a typology of learned people who embrace social critique, public engagement, and progressive transformation in their respective ways. However, they are also mostly distanced from the people whose circumstances they seek to change for the better. They are a mixture of revolutionaries and students; writers, artists, and journalists; and teachers and military officers who are from different generations but are interlinked with one another through the historical continuity of the nation's foundation and transformation.

In this context, the 1970s is not just another decade in the historical portrait of the intellectual but a key period that presents the convergence of vital transformative forces. Wedged between two coups (1960 and 1980), shaped by the radicalism of the 1960s, and marked by its own military intervention, the 1970s was arguably the most political decade of the Turkish novel. On May 27, 1960, the military seized control of the government in Turkey, and following the coup, the self-appointed National Unity Committee invited academics to draw up a new constitution. As Feroz Ahmad notes, such intellectual involvement transformed the coup into a kind of an "institutional revolution."[7] This new constitution provided many civil liberties, social rights, and political regulations. It became, as Behice Boran (a leading name of the Turkish left) called it, a "turning point" in the political life of Turkey.[8] It was not perfect, but it opened the way for leftist ideas to be introduced into the public sphere and leftist politics to achieve a legitimate foothold in the country. The revolutionaries of the 1960s benefited greatly from the relatively liberal and progressive environment that the new constitution engendered. However, as political tension and economic instability increased, the military intervened once again in 1971. The 1970s were equally tense and troubled years yet also highly productive in their literary output until another military intervention on September 12, 1980, put a definitive end to it all.[9]

The Turkish novel of the 1970s thus was the outcome of extraordinary circumstances. It bears the idealistic enthusiasm and the spirit of resistance of the 1960s, as well as the immediate, yet to some extent unprocessed reactions to the trauma of the 1970s. The highly politicized and socially oriented novels of the decade are mostly by writers who were themselves intellectuals involved in the decade's commotion and who depict kindred characters. Consequently, the historical continuity that defines their novels results in the presentation of a complex picture of the conflicting ideologies and competing ideals of the different but interlinked intellectual types and offers portrayals of key historical processes that lead to and reach beyond the 1971 intervention.[10]

Perhaps most representative examples of conflicting ideologies and competing ideals among the different generations of intelligentsia in modern Turkey appear in Füruzan's *Kırk Yedi'liler* (Generation of '47, 1974). As its title suggests, it is populated with the generation of '47—those who were born in 1947 or thereabouts and who came of age politically as university students in the 1960s. It tells the story of the student revolutionaries, the ways in which they united in a shared ideal despite their differences in attitude and background, and how they selflessly sacrificed themselves resisting against a force much greater than them. They were the young intellectuals of a new generation that were both familiar with leftist literature and contributed to their movement with the experiences of their diverse backgrounds.

Kırk Yedi'liler is a highly emotive text that unfolds in three separate but interconnected narrative strands. The protagonist Emine is one of the previously described students, and her characterization links the different generations depicted in the novel. She reminisces about her friends who were tortured, persecuted, and prosecuted. Her clashes with her mother, Nüveyre, who is a teacher of the early Republican era and who represent the conflicts in their perceptions of progress and social change. Her memories of her childhood in an Anatolian town embellished by the details of the folk culture present a romanticized, albeit naïve alternative against the rough and rigid values of her mother. Each representative character manifests their generational potential in terms of intellectual typology and bears some form of knowledge along the lines of cultural values and societal change.[11]

The novel begins with Emine at home, broken by the horrific torture she has endured and everything else that has happened to her and her friends. In her attempts at coming to terms with such intense trauma, she remembers how her young and idealistic friends, "who were trying to defend and collect so much beauty and justice," were crushed.[12] Eleven students, including Emine, are portrayed individually, rendering the novel multivocal but also somewhat crowded. They are from different backgrounds: poor students from rural Anatolian families like Kadir, those from the middle classes like Emine, and others from affluent urban classes like Melek. They argue for different revolutionary theories and practices for social change. Kaya is trained as a guerrilla. Cemşit believes in progress through science and technology. Seyhan is an aesthete. These students also represent the geographical dispersion of the economic classes in the country from the eastern to the western lands, rural and urban. As such, their collective movement presents a unity in difference along the lines of class relationships. That they are all depicted through their personal stories adds to their idealization and they stand out as a new generation of well-read, thoughtful, and progressive people joined in solidarity. With their ideals for a better world, desire for the knowledge to realize social change, and courage to take action, Füruzan's "generation of '47" belongs to a revolutionary intellectual category in global history.

While the idealized portrayal of the generation reaches out for a social unity beyond class divisions, it is also built upon rather naïve presumptions on the protagonist's side. Marked by her memories of her childhood in Erzurum, a highly romanticized premodern rural lifestyle underlies Emine's understanding of social relationships. Her initial sense of justice, compassion, and solidarity develop as a result of her relationship with the villagers and against her mother's condescending attitude towards them. In particular, the old woman, Leylim Nine (Granny Leylim), who sometimes looks after the children, is accentuated as a representative figure of care, affection, and kinship: the values Emine lacks in her family but finds among her friends.

Leylim Nine is a relic of another age. She tells stories to the children, passing on to them the knowledge of long-gone times and faraway places. Her magical world becomes a hopeful and cordial alternative to the rigid and distant reality of Emine's own home. Her tales present a timeless kind of knowledge, and she signifies an intellectual type based on wisdom and collective memory. Leylim Nine as an intellectual figure is not a conventional choice; however, being a storyteller, she falls together with the other, modern formulations of the type in terms of the perception of knowledge, its transformation, and its function within society. In *Illuminations*, Walter Benjamin maintains that the "communicability of experience" expressed in "counsel" fuses into "the fabric of real life" as "wisdom," which is one of the most essential aspects of storytelling, "the epic side of truth."[13] In that sense, Leylim Nine's case as an intellectual type precedes intellect.

The premodern configuration of Leylim Nine's portrayal is key to the criticism of the early Republican generation in the narrative. Both the idealization of the students of 1968 and the romanticization of the premodern rural life in Erzurum come at the expense of the generation between them, that is, the modernizing early Republicans. The national modernization project of the new state was maintained by its representatives, such as the teachers, military officers, and bureaucrats who were sent from the urban centers to the rural villages for, what Deniz Kandiyoti calls, a "civilizing mission . . . the struggle of science and enlightenment against ignorance and obscurantism."[14] In *Kırk Yedi'liler*, Emine's parents, the members of the nation's "education army" represent the Republican modernizing elites, and through them, the national modernization project of the Republic is criticized.

Intelligentsia Narratives of the 1970s Turkish Novel

Emine's mother, Nüveyre is particularly vilified in the narrative through both her harsh portrayal and the opinions of her victimized daughter. According to Nüveyre, the uneducated peasants "don't develop but stay as they are," and people like herself are there to "teach and educate them" so "they can learn how people should behave."[15] Her civilizing mission is based on an infantilizing perception of the local folk, and she is often disdainful and discriminatory. As such, Nüveyre's highly charged negative depiction follows the historical pattern of the intelligentsia being disconnected from the common people. Such disconnection is maintained along the lines of a hierarchy that is often based on the modern intellectual types' self-assumed superiority over the rural and poorer public. In that sense, the early Republican modernizing intellectuals continue the elitist pattern of the earlier westernizing Ottoman intelligentsia.

The early Republican intelligentsia is a continuation of the Ottoman westernizing elites and their modernization project is a development on their efforts aligned with new national parameters. There are indeed many problems with such a forceful top-to-bottom understanding of social and institutional change. However, the reality was probably a lot more complex and complicated and the people involved were much more idealistic and oftentimes selfless than the way Nüveyre is depicted in *Kırk Yedi'liler*. Notwithstanding the common elitism of the Republican intellectual, many works also show their selfless idealism and genuine desire for a better Turkey. Moreover, in addition to facing many material challenges, these early Republican intellectuals faced their own crises as they struggled to understand and realize the enormous transformation that they were meant to lead while they were themselves fashioning a new sense of self.

Adalet Ağaoğlu's novel, *Ölmeye Yatmak* (Lying Down to Die, 1973) portrays these combined problems of the modern Republican intellectual's self-fashioning and their roles in the establishment of the new social values. She depicts characters from different classes, some of whom are expected to join the ranks of the intelligentsia the new Turkey needs. Similar to Füruzan's approach, the different classes of the characters in Ağaoğlu's novel determine the levels of their access to opportunities for social change and their understanding of what it entails. Not unlike Emine, *Ölmeye Yatmak*'s protagonist Aysel is different from some of her peers. However, contrary to Emine's experience, her difference is due to *not* belonging to the privileged classes of the modernizing elites. As a result, she has a rougher initiation into the intelligentsia and is burdened by a constant sense of insecurity, a fervent drive to achieve, and self-doubt all her life.

Aysel's narrative begins with a scene that is suggestive of her having chosen to die in a hotel room. Through her memories and the narrative flashbacks, her social, familial, and academic circumstances are presented, as well as her fears, worries, and doubts. Becoming the ideal modern woman of the newly founded Republic and a proud member of the educated citizens in the path laid out by the founder of the country underlie her position as the typical Republican intellectual. Yet, long before she faces the challenges of being a member of the intelligentsia with responsibilities of realizing social change, she first has to engage in her own battle to achieve that status against all the disadvantages of coming from a provincial family.

An intertwined generational conflict similar to the one in *Kırk Yedi'liler* is presented through Aysel's relationship with her father, but this time the focus is on the formation of the Republican intellectual. Her father is a conservative man who is not happy about the new values advocated at the school, and he allows Aysel to attend only because the state elites—teachers, administrators, bureaucrats—are influential in their small town. Moreover, he is a small trader; therefore, like most of her classmates, Aysel does not have the material means to realize the modern lifestyle that is promoted by her teachers. The material circumstances and social values represented by the modernized elites are both alien to and mainly unattainable for the townsfolk, and Aysel's desire to become an ideal citizen and an intellectual like her teachers exposes the clashes between them.

Early in the novel, the graduation ceremony with its misguided idealism and awkward incompatibilities becomes a telling metaphor for both Aysel's personal experiences on her path to become the desirable modern citizen and those of her country through the national modernization project. That those experiences are inextricably enmeshed is epitomized in Aysel's "lady civil servant of the city" sketch. Her teachers decide that for this role she should wear "a silken [robe] tailored according to the fashion. On her shoulders, a coat with fur collar. On her head, a hat according to the fashion. In her hand, a lady's purse. Silk socks and heeled shoes."[16] These directions are given regardless of whether she can afford to achieve that representative look. Aysel's improvised outfit and provincial hairstyle fail to match these expectations, and she feels humiliated. As the significance of such a minor ceremony is blown out of proportion to represent the values dear to the early Republican intelligentsia, Aysel's perception of them is invested with the dissonance between ideas and practices. Similar to Emine, even though she does not initially comprehend the repercussions of such discord between the Republican ideals and their application by the intelligentsia, they become central to what kind of an intellectual she will develop into later.

Ağaoğlu not only depicts the birth pangs of the modern Republican intellectual but also exposes the key problem of the national modernization project that creates that model. Its idealistic aspirations aside, the national modernization movement is an ideological "project." It was embarked upon by the state elites to be expanded in the provinces through their representatives (i.e., the Republican intellectuals). Concurrently, the modern Republican intellectual is shaped by the conflicts resulting from the lack of material realities that engender the idea of the modern. They are fundamentally an outcome of what happens when those ideas of the modern are imported and employed top to bottom without similar material conditions.

Despite the enormous challenges, Aysel still wants to develop into the ideal intellectual figure she envisions. She manages to continue her education and becomes an academic. Yet, she pays its price with traumatic experiences, guilt-driven torment, confusion about ideological contradictions, and doubts and disillusionments that lead her to the hotel room. Becoming a questioning intellectual and moving beyond the parameters of the acceptable Republican model result in her alienation from the community to which she belongs.[17]

In her two sequel novels, Ağaoğlu returns to some of the critical issues regarding the idea of the intellectual as the country's ideological alliances and class relations shift. In *Bir Düğün Gecesi* (A Wedding Night, 1979), in which Aysel is not present directly but is a reference point in the background for the characters, Ağaoğlu depicts the middle class, disillusioned intellectual types. In *Hayır. . .* (No. . ., 1987) she portrays Aysel resolutely questioning what it means to be an intellectual, what responsibilities it entails, and the failure of her generation to fulfill them. Aysel's journey takes her from the Republican intellectual to a new model: a critical and independent mind despite the challenges and bleak prospects. At the end of the novel, in her final study on "Suicides of Intellectuals and the Future's Resistance," she writes, "Preserving our independent identities under any and every circumstance depends on this single and final word that can be uttered only through deed: No. . . ."[18]

Another writer of the period Attilâ İlhan, who was briefly mentioned earlier, also recognizes the generational class relations, the conflicting ideologies and the competing ideals, and the transformation of the intellectual types within Turkey's historical continuity. In fact, this historical continuity is crucial to his critical thinking to the extent that he creates an expansive novelistic world to portray their integrated composition. With his "Aynanın İçindekiler" series, he endeavors to capture that continuity by interlinking the novels and their temporal settings from the late Ottoman era onwards through the various characters that reappear in different works. That many of these characters bear traits that qualify them as intellectuals allows for a complex portrait of the intelligentsia's varying nature and position in modern Turkish history.

The novels in the "Aynanın İçindekiler" series were published between 1973 and 2006, but the narrative timeline reaches further back to some critical moments in Turkish history, namely, the coup of May 27, 1960, the Korean War, the Second World War, the national independence movement and war, and the Young Turk revolution. *Bıçağın Ucu* (The Tip of the Knife, 1973) is set in 1960; *Sırtlan Payı* (The Share of the Hyena, 1974) is set in 1919 and 1960; and *Yaraya Tuz Basmak* (Rubbing Salt into the Wound, 1978) is set in 1950–1955 and 1960. *Dersaadet'te Sabah Ezanları* (Morning Prayers in Dersaadet, 1981) is set in 1909 and 1919–1920. *O Karanlıkta Biz* (Us in that Darkness, 1988) is set in 1940–1942. *Allahın Süngüleri* (The Bayonets of Allah, 2002) is set in 1920, with the founder of Turkey—at the time Mustafa Kemal Pasha—as the protagonist. *Gazi Paşa* (Ghazi Pasha, 2006) is set in 1921–1922 and continues that narrative.

Considering the central place the 1960 coup has in the political and intellectual life of the country, that it serves as an ending point of the overarching narrative from different perspectives is not surprising. In fact, it is the intellectual instigator of the series, as the first three novels—all written in the 1970s—share the decade as a key temporal reference. Moreover, the novelist pitches the coup against other military acts to expose the decline in the military's revolutionary potential as a result of authoritarian political interests. In this context, İlhan does not choose the teacher as the model for his Republican intellectual but the military officer who is fundamental to the foundation of the country and is a key part of its historical continuity. Through the interconnected narratives of the various novels, he highlights the legacy of the military as a force for change (for better or worse) that is particular to the Turkish situation.[19]

The protagonist of *Yaraya Tuz Basmak*, Demir is the model for the military officer as a potential intellectual figure in the series. He is an officer active in the execution of the 1960 coup, but at the beginning of the novel, set in 1950, he is portrayed as a young lieutenant fighting in the Korean War. As the question "Where is Korea?" resonates among the soldiers and Demir fears for their safety, his first doubts about the government's war ideology begin to take shape.[20] However, the definitive transformation comes later with the new kind of inquisitive intellectual understanding he acquires from Ümid, who appears in İlhan's novelistic realm for the first time in the previously mentioned *Kurtlar Sofrası*. In this work, which does not belong to the series but is its progenitor, Ümid is a young, well-educated woman from a wealthy family. She falls in love with an idealist journalist, Mahmud Ersoy, but they constantly clash because she lacks interest in the country's affairs. However, when Mahmud is murdered, Ümid changes, and it is this new Ümid who Demir meets in *Yaraya Tuz Basmak*. By 1960, she is a critical intellectual type, a journalist like Mahmud, and instigates similar transformations in others.

Like many intellectual types of the era, Ümid upholds the military's ability to take action. Her position (which is essentially that of Mahmud) is Republican in that she argues within the parameters of Mustafa Kemal's national revolution. According to her, the government, which has grown authoritarian and undemocratic under the guise of democracy, should be purged:

> The military is the indispensable force of the purge because the working classes are not self-aware, they are not organized; the peasants are still enslaved by customs and traditions. How Mustafa Kemal did it should be studied: Did he not appoint the military and the intelligentsia as guides and mobilize the people? That is the prescription.[21]

This prescription charts the military's position among the intelligentsia of a particular Republican type. In essence, the general perception is that the officers are well-educated men of action who have the best interest of their country at heart. Still, Demir has his doubts, and he realizes after his conversations with Ümid, as well as through what he has himself read in recent years, that "no revolutionary movement can succeed without the people." However, when decisions regarding the country are left to them, they elect conservative authoritarians.[22]

Shaped by the national independence movement, the military's revolutionary role is important in İlhan's ideological world, and he is particularly critical of the untapped intellectual potential of the military cadres. He portrays many military characters in his various novels to critique the problem of "the man of action" lacking in intellectual drives and thus having lost his revolutionary edge. He endorses and promotes the fusion of revolutionary ideas and intellectual acuity, both of which are qualities that he idealizes in Atatürk and his generation. The lineage between the military generations that connects Demir to a tradition is already present in the earlier work, *Sırtlan Payı*, in which Demir meets Ferid, a veteran of the independence war.

Sırtlan Payı is set shortly after the 1960 coup and begins with the moment Colonel Ferid has a heart attack. During his flashbacks, one of the things he remembers is the lack of enthusiasm among the public for the "revolution" and the presidency of Cemal Gürsel, who is a veteran like himself. For Colonel Ferid and his generation, the 1960 coup and Gürsel's presidency share a genealogy with the national revolution. In the words of Ahmet Ziya, another key intellectual figure of the series, "the generation of the Colonel is entirely one of action: from 1908 to 1919, they never stopped,"[23] and in *Yaraya Tuz Basmak*, Ferid is depicted as scolding Demir in his frustration with the military cadres' lack of action against the growing authoritarianism of the government. The interconnection between Demir and Ferid as such presents the historical continuity between military types, political ideas, and intellectual priorities that underlie the transformation of the nation. Unlike the other works discussed in this chapter, the generational relationship between them is depicted as not one of polarized conflict but an organic progress of a particular mode of revolutionary thinking.

As one of "the men of action" who has spent his whole life fighting to realize the revolutionary ideals in which he believes, Ferid's "heart" attack is rather symbolic. However, İlhan's valorization of the military's revolutionary potential does not mean that he was supportive of military interventions. On the contrary, he was critical of the 1960 coup for lacking in programs to convey the fundamental ideas of progress to the public in order to prevent undemocratic abuses of democracy. Ahmet Ziya's criticism of the military intervention in *Sırtlan Payı* haunts Colonel Ferid: "It won't do, no, my dear Colonel, this is no revolution at all, by god, it's merely a coup that a handful of officers somehow pulled off. Besides it appears to be without a plan or a program."[24] Still, although the idea of the military as a potential intellectual model is counterintuitive, in the Turkish context it is not unusual because since the late Ottoman era both the education of the officers and their drive for social change enabled them to fulfill certain elemental expectations that define the intelligentsia.

This chapter has underscored İlhan's particular use of the military character as a modern, Republican intellectual with his generational interconnections within the historical continuity of the nation. However, there are many other intellectual types in his multivolume series, including artists, actors, writers, teachers, officers, and bureaucrats in the Greek, Jewish, and Turkish communities, and mainly from the middle classes. It would not be possible to do justice to such a broad typology with its diverse set of characters in this short piece, but it could be concluded that the novelist had a very strong ideological perspective along the lines of a nationalized left, shaped by a great admiration for Atatürk.[25] In his detailed typology, perhaps except for the idealist journalist Mahmud Ersoy of *Kurtlar Sofrası* and the "revolutionary socialist" engineer Ahmet Ziya of *O Karanlıkta Biz*, he is very critical of his intellectual types, most of whom do not live up to his standards, including the left-oriented ones.

The portrayal of the intellectual in the novels of the 1970s is not limited to those discussed in this chapter, which has focused on the specific generational relationships between intellectual models. Many writers depict characters within a broad intellectual typology based on level of education, professional practices, inclinations for critical thinking, and desire to change society for the better. For instance, in *Karartma Geceleri* (Blackout Nights, 1974), social realist novelist Rıfat Ilgaz depicts a poet/teacher Mustafa who is being pursued by the police due to his "leftist" poems. Vedat Türkali wrote several novels with intellectual characters in the 1980s, but his first one published in 1974, *Bir Gün Tek Başına* (One Day on Your Own) portrays a bookseller, Kenan, as a failed and timid former political activist. Sevgi Soysal, in her acclaimed novel *Şafak* (The Dawn, 1975), depicts a political exile, Oya, who is picked up at a police raid and interrogated with several others in her narrative of a single night. Examples of intelligentsia narratives with many different formulations can be multiplied for not only the 1970s but also the entirety of modern Turkish literary history. Their quantity and diversity say plenty about the place of literature in the intellectual world of the country while also attesting to the undeniable presence of the intelligentsia narrative as a literary phenomenon.

The representation of the intellectual in the 1970s reveals a significant moment in modern Turkish history. As I argue in *Promethean Encounters*, the left-inclined novels of the period are preoccupied with the conflicts between the modernizing Republicans and the populations expected to be modernized, as well as the student activists of the 1960s who are critical of their modernization project. In this chapter, I maintain that such antagonistic encounters of differing ideological perspectives expose an ideational world where ideals compete and ideologies conflict but are not necessarily too distant from one another. The 1970s is a significant culmination point of an almost century-long historical continuity whereby its novelistic realm provides a platform for valuable discussions and critique.

Notes

1 Andrew Khan, Mark Lipovetsky, Irina Reyfman, and Stephanie Sandler, *A History of Russian Literature* (Oxford: Oxford University Press, 2018), 739.
2 Ibid.
3 Russian and Turkish examples are particularly relatable along the lines of the intelligentsia and their narratives. Murat Belge draws parallels between the intellectuals of the Ottoman and Russian Empires due to their proximity to the "west" but not being quite "western" enough. According to him, such ambiguous proximity defines the ideological pitfalls of the intellectuals of the two nations; see Murat Belge, "Osmanlı'da ve Rusya'da Aydınlar," in *Türk Aydını ve Kimlik Sorunu*, ed. Sabahattin Şen (Istanbul: Bağlam, 1995), 123–32.
4 Beginning with the *Tanzimat* (1839), the various reform movements that shaped the end of the nineteenth century in the Ottoman Empire recognized the shifting power structures and systemic changes that enabled them. It thus aimed at the adaptation of "western" institutions and modes of thinking to compensate for their negative impact on the Ottoman Empire. While the necessity for certain kinds of social and cultural changes were acknowledged and pursued, a radical transformation was out of the question and a synthesis of western structures with Ottoman values (with the latter having precedence) were desired. See Erik Jan Zürcher, *Turkey: A Modern History* (London: I.B. Tauris, 2007) for a detailed context.
5 Burcu Alkan, "Spatial Experiences of the Intellectual: Exile, Isolation and Imprisonment in *Bread and Wine* and *Karartma Geceleri*," *Journal of European Studies* 49, no. 1 (2019): 18–30.
6 Ibid., 21.
7 Feroz Ahmad, *The Making of Modern Turkey* (London: Routledge, 1993), 127.
8 From Boran's interview in exile with Stefka Pirvanova of the Sofia Radio in 1985, http://behiceboran. net/index.php/boran-kendini-anlatiyor/.
9 Uğur Çalışkan and Çimen Günay-Erkol provide an overview of the "coup literature" in Turkey, in "Bellekten Beklentiler: Eleştirinin Darbe Romanlarına Tanıklığı," *Monograf, Edebiyat Eleştirisi Dergisi* 5 (2016): 10–35.

10 This chapter aims to present an overarching framework of the said intellectual types. I have written in-depth analyses of such novelistic representations previously in *Promethean Encounters* (2018) and "Spatial Experiences" (2019).

11 The definition of the intellectual, of course, is crucial to any discussion on the concept. In fact, the transformation of the concept in the Turkish context is represented in the changing terminology from "*münevver*" to "*aydın*" to "*entelektüel.*" It would be difficult to go into the complexities of definitions in this chapter, but suffice it to say that the three terms present the Ottoman, Republican, and Western approaches, respectively. Since this chapter explores the self-reflexivity of the writers as intellectuals and writers' intellectuals, the idea of the intellectual as represented in the works and the significance of such narrative choices determine the definitions used.

12 Füruzan, *Kırk Yedi'liler* (Istanbul: YKY, 2002), 206.

13 Walter Benjamin, *Illuminations*, trans. Harry Zorn (London: Pimlico, 1999), 86.

14 Deniz Kandiyoti, "Gendering the Modern: On Missing Dimensions in the Study of Turkish Modernity," in *Rethinking Modernity and National Identity in Turkey*, ed. Sibel Bozdoğan and Reşat Kasaba (Seattle: University of Washington Press, 1997), 122.

15 Füruzan, *Kırk Yedi'liler*, 16.

16 Adalet Ağaoğlu, *Ölmeye Yatmak* (Istanbul: YKY, 1994), 18.

17 Sibel Irzık's "Allegorical Lives: The Public and the Private in the Modern Turkish Novel" is an insightful reading of novelistic characters' having to become representations of ideas larger than themselves, such as Aysel in *Ölmeye Yatmak*, in *South Atlantic Quarterly* 102, no. 2–3 (2003): 551–66.

18 Adalet Ağaoğlu, *Hayır . . .* (Istanbul: Everest, 2014), 293.

19 For a concise summary of the role of the military in Turkish politics, see Feroz Ahmad, "Introduction: Turkey, a Military Society?" in *The Making of Modern Turkey* (London: Routledge, 1993).

20 Turkey's involvement in the Korean War was the result of a fresh membership to NATO and the decision to send troops to Korea was taken illegally by the president of the time, Adnan Menderes, without the approval of the parliament. In the novel, like all the other novels in the series, historical details as such are included at the beginning and the end of the sections.

21 Attilâ İlhan, *Yaraya Tuz Basmak* (Ankara: Bilgi, 1995), 203.

22 Ibid., 243.

23 Attilâ İlhan, *Sırtlan Payı* (Ankara: Bilgi), 226.

24 Ibid., 23.

25 For a more detailed study on characterization and culture in the "Aynanın İçindekiler" series, see Gönülden Esemenli Söker, *Attilâ İlhan'da Kültür Sorunsalı* (Ankara: Bilgi, 2002).

References

Ağaoğlu, Adalet. *Ölmeye Yatmak*. Istanbul: YKY, 1994.

———. *Hayır. . . .* Istanbul: Everest, 2014.

Ahmad, Feroz. *The Making of Modern Turkey*. London: Routledge, 1993.

Alkan, Burcu. *Promethean Encounters: Representation of the Intellectual in the Modern Turkish Novel of the 1970s*. Wiesbaden: Harrassowitz Verlag, 2018.

———. "Spatial Experiences of the Intellectual: Exile, Isolation and Imprisonment in *Bread and Wine* and *Karartma Geceleri*." *Journal of European Studies* 49, no. 1 (2019): 18–30.

Belge, Murat. "Osmanlı'da ve Rusya'da Aydınlar." In *Türk Aydını ve Kimlik Sorunu*, edited by Sabahattin Şen, 123–32. Istanbul: Bağlam, 1995.

Benjamin, Walter. *Illuminations*. Translated by Harry Zorn. London: Pimlico, 1999.

Boran, Behice. "Interview with Stefka Pirvanova." *Behice Boran Website*, 1985. Accessed October 22, 2019. http://behiceboran.net/index.php/boran-kendini-anlatiyor/.

Çalışkan, Uğur, and Çimen Günay-Erkol. "Bellekten Beklentiler: Eleştirinin Darbe Romanlarına Tanıklığı." *Monograf Edebiyat Eleştirisi Dergisi* 5 (2016): 10–35.

Esemenli Söker, Gönülden. *Attilâ İlhan'da Kültür Sorunsalı*. Ankara: Bilgi, 2002.

Füruzan. *Kırk Yedi'liler*. Istanbul: YKY, 2002.

İlhan, Attilâ. *Sırtlan Payı*. Ankara: Bilgi, 1992.

———. *Yaraya Tuz Basmak*. Ankara: Bilgi, 1995.

Irzık, Sibel. "Allegorical Lives: The Public and the Private in the Modern Turkish Novel." *South Atlantic Quarterly* 102, no. 2–3 (2003): 551–66.

Kandiyoti, Deniz. "Gendering the Modern: On Missing Dimensions in the Study of Turkish Modernity." In *Rethinking Modernity and National Identity in Turkey*, Sibel Bozdoğan and Reşat Kasaba, 113–32. Seattle: University of Washington Press, 1997.

Khan, Andrew, Mark Lipovetsky, Irina Reyfman, and Stephanie Sandler. *A History of Russian Literature*. Oxford: Oxford University Press, 2018.

Said, Edward. *Representations of the Intellectual: The 1993 Reith Lectures*. New York: Vintage, 1996.

Zürcher, Erik Jan. *Turkey: A Modern History*. London: I. B. Tauris, 2017.

29

THE GRAMMAR OF CONSPIRACY IN ORHAN PAMUK'S *SNOW*

Erdağ Göknar

"Truths"

Could a Turkish novel about conspiracism help us better understand Turkey's political transition from the 1997 soft coup to the 2016 failed coup? Books on conspiracy theories constitute a popular genre in Turkey. Purporting to uncover historical and geopolitical "truths," these works are often characterized by counterfactual history, paranoia, scapegoating, gaslighting, and not infrequent antisemitism. While conspiratorial narratives have a literary structure with protagonists, antagonists, mysteries, crimes, conflicts, dramatic ironies, and morals, contemporary Turkish literature also self-consciously engages the logic of conspiracism as a plot device.[1] Though conspiracy theories might be considered political whodunits, detective stories indexed to broad political or ideological conflicts, conspiracism seeks a deeper, secret story in the superficial objects and signs that surround us. Often the details, people, texts, and dates of conspiratorial discourse are verifiable facts. What establishes their skewed logic is their fictional emplotment, which usually implicates some named or unnamed totalizing force such as the "deep state" (*derin devlet*) or Islamism (often denigrated as *irtica*, or "regression"). Conspiracism, functioning at the intersection of fact and fiction, curates representations of the real.

Whereas world literature has long had a fascination with conspiracies, from Euripides' *Bacchae* to Dan Brown's *The Da Vinci Code*, tropes of conspiracy shape many of Orhan Pamuk's novels, which engage and parody this popular mode of political melodrama and (dis)information. The protagonists of conspiracy novels are often journalists or amateur investigators (like Ka or "Orhan" in *Snow*), who find themselves inadvertently pulling on a small thread that unravels a vast conspiracy implicating a group, the government, or the state. What might be termed the "grammar of conspiracy" in Pamuk's fiction functions on the level of form and content. Pamuk relies on narrative techniques such as multiple genres, pastiche, and intertextuality, as well as plot devices such as doubles, absent texts, and self-reflexive themes of literary production to structure his metafictional novels. Pamuk's characters, especially in *Snow*, frequently believe in or act on ideologically "constructed" truths.

Conspiracism, as recent geopolitical events have shown, can manifest as both a cause and symptom of authoritarianism, and Pamuk's postmodern critique of the Turkish political field hints at Turkey's authoritarian, post–truth political present.[2] Broadly, scholars trace either a pathologizing approach to conspiracy (e.g., Hofstadter's "paranoid style") or a cultural one

354

DOI: 10.4324/9780429279270-38

The Grammar of Conspiracy in Orhan Pamuk's Snow

that treats them as attempts to understand social and political reality (e.g., Jameson's "cognitive map"). Recent books on Turkish conspiracism, including De Medeiros (2018), Karaosmanoğlu (2019), and Gürpınar (2020), have done the important work of historicizing conspiracy as an interdisciplinary field of analysis. But in this context, the intersection of literature, state power, and conspiracism has not been fully analyzed.

Pamuk's novel *Snow* dramatizes aspects of conspiracy, repeatedly tracing links between conspiratorial discourse and political violence. Pamuk's fiction presents conspiracism as a genuine cognitive attempt to understand the world that his characters inhabit while also treating conspiracy as the misapprehension of a situation in an ironic or satirical vein. Like mysteries or detective stories, conspiracies are structured around political imaginaries based on disparate clues with the expectation that a "truth" or hidden "plot" will be uncovered. By extension, the reader of *Snow* is placed in the position of being an arbiter of truth in distinguishing representation from reality, fact from fantasy, and finally, in producing a superseding interpretive account that deconstructs or debunks the conspiracism presented in the plot.

The relationship between disinformation and authoritarianism is significant to understanding the function of conspiracies. Conspiracy theories are predicated on fictions that explain complex, confusing, rapidly changing, and threatening events and make them legible. As such, conspiracies weave parable-like accounts of defeat or victimhood and redemption. The theories, which make the distinction between facts and fiction porous, cannot be proven or disproven. Conspiratorial thought also functions to enfranchise the disenfranchised through narrative reframings that re-sequence and reinterpret established historical facts. Though conspiracy theories do reveal truths, they are not truths per se. That is, conspiracism exercises the function of "truth" in knowledge formation. Pamuk's novels seem to construct conspiratorial narratives in their plots while deconstructing them through their metafictional structure. Explaining the hold of conspiratorial thought as a political problem, Pamuk states:

> I mock the naïve, primitive, vulgar and uncultured paranoia that is widespread in our society because I don't find it insightful. How? You see, in my novels; I wrote about it in *The Silent House*; in *The New Life* there were characters like this. The old leftists in *The Black Book* were this way. You know, paranoia along the line of "Clinton and Yeltsin have come to an agreement, and together with the Pope and the Italian prime minister they're going to divide Turkey. . . ." In the past, I'd mention this in my novels for the sake of satire, but now our newspaper editorials talk about this stuff in all seriousness. . . . In our country, the culture of paranoia is extremely rich.[3]

This chapter situates this culture of paranoia, or conspiracism, as a theme and as a postmodern literary device in Pamuk's novels. Two international contexts, one geopolitical and one literary, augment the relevance of this analysis. First, in contexts of rising authoritarianism in Turkey and elsewhere, the role of conspiracy in geopolitics has taken on a renewed significance that makes *Snow*, first published in 2002, even more relevant and revelatory in our present moment of authoritarianism. Second, the analysis emphasizes a connection, through structures of conspiracism, to modern and postmodern authors of world literature such as Conrad, Kafka, Borges, Orwell, DeLillo, Pynchon, Eco, Calvino, and others.[4]

İrtica ("Regression")

In dramatizing conspiratorial thought, *Snow* self-consciously depicts Turkish engagements with transnational ideologies such as Marxism, ethnic nationalism (Turkish and Kurdish), and

Islamism. The novel is informed by actual historical events that left their mark on Turkish politics in the 1990s; namely, (1) the 1995 election of the Islamist Refah Party to parliament and its rule in a coalition government fueling secularist fears of "*irtica*" or Islamist opposition; (2) the 1996 Susurluk scandal that established a concrete link between the mafia, members of parliament, and paramilitary groups, thus giving rise to rumors of a "deep state" operating outside the law; (3) the 1997 Sincan affair, in which tanks were sent out as a warning to the ruling government after a pro-Palestinian play in the town of Sincan; (4) the subsequent 1997 "postmodern coup" during which demands by the military led to Refah leader and Prime Minister Erbakan's resignation; (5) the 1998 closing of the Refah Party by the constitutional court for anti-secular activities; and (6) the 1999 Merve Kavakçı affair, in which an elected female parliamentarian for the Fazilet Party (formed after Refah was closed) attempted to take her oath of office wearing a headcovering, or hijab. These events, among others, point to the transformation of the place of secularism and Islamism in social spaces and in the public sphere of 1990s Turkey, marking a shift away from received understandings of them as a strict binary opposition. This cultural and political shift is captured in multiple ways throughout *Snow*, and is first alluded to early in the novel when Ka, a left-leaning secularist, is suddenly described by the narrator ("Orhan") as having "felt God inside him."[5] Ka's personal acknowledgement of the divine runs corollary to the ideological rise of Islamist politics.

Pamuk describes *Snow* as his first and last "political novel." This is ironic in that all of his novels exhibit a politics of form that intervenes in official Republican historiography to manifest a political argument in favor of liberal humanism. *Snow* is neither more nor less political than the rest of Pamuk's novels but is a consistent representation of Pamuk's political engagement through literature, or literary modernity as politics.[6] The meta-fictional and meta-historical position that is established in Pamuk's fiction allows the narrator (and reader) to weigh and consider, assess and judge, and finally learn from characters whose words and deeds are informed by conspiratorial thought that is often divorced from "the real." The incongruity between representation and reality in the public sphere, Pamuk's work argues, has dire consequences.

Absent Text

Pamuk's sustained narrative engagement with conspiracies and coups finds its fullest development in *Snow*. Characters in the novel occupy ideologically informed conspiratorial positions, and the dramatization of the Republican "coup" becomes what can only be called political theater, melodrama, or even farce.[7] *Snow* takes the small town of Kars as a microcosm for the nation. The central character, a poet named "Ka," is a secular Republican intellectual, a leftist exile from Istanbul bourgeois circles living in exile in Frankfurt, having fled Turkey after the 1980 military coup that quashed the left. Ka takes an assignment as an investigative journalist for the secularist daily *Cumhuriyet* (The Republic) to cover upcoming elections and a spate of suicides by young, conservative women. In the genre of conspiracy fiction, Ka could be described as a "subject who seeks to know." The novel follows Ka to the remote Anatolian town of Kars near the Armenian border, where soon after his arrival, the performance of an early Republican didactic play that promotes the unveiling of women as a gesture of modernity erupts into a bizarre military coup. In Kars, Ka also gets mixed up in political intrigues that pit leftists, Islamists, Kurds, and nationalists against one another. The task of reporting gets overtaken by his pursuit of his love interest, İpek, and his return to poetry writing, in which poems come to him in inspirational-prophetic revelations. Ka's newfound poetic inspiration coincides with consciousness of the divine, an experience that is an allegory for the rise of Islamist politics in 1990s Turkish secular society. Upcoming local elections in Kars reveal that the conservative Refah

Party stands to win.[8] To complicate matters, there has been a spate of suicides by young veiled women who have been pressured to remove their veils in state schools by the dictates of Ankara.

Though representing the intelligentsia, Ka is a weak, indefinite character. He is "abbreviated" in name and in character, literally and figuratively. He serves as a narrative vehicle that exposes the reader to the political conspiracies swirling through Kars. In the plot, Ka becomes torn by his associations with various competing factions. Evoking Kafka's protagonist "K.," Ka is subject to various cultural logics and the authority of competing political forces, the consequences of which he does not fully understand. In the surreal world of conspiracy and coup, characters misread the politics represented in theater, newspapers, and television as reality.

In Kars, Ka writes a revelatory collection of 19 poems (also titled *Snow*) that the novel withholds from the reader. This functions as an "absent text," a postmodern literary device that furthers the plot as references to an unspecified and indeterminate book develop and deepen the drama. Pamuk's novels overwrite the absent text in the plot with a superseding account of the same name. When arrested, Ka divulges the hideout of a leader of the Islamist resistance, Blue, and is forced to flee Turkey. *Snow* choreographs the narrative strategies associated with postmodern parody as an indictment of political coups fueled by conspiracy. The result is a multigenre novel that reveals the precarity of life in a landscape where reality and its representation are intentionally blurred by the ruling class and the media for the accumulation or maintenance of political power.

Once Ka arrives in Kars, a leftist-secular theater troupe helps instigate a coup with military support to forestall the eventuality of a Refah Party political victory. The coup emerges as the cooperative effort of a small cabal including Colonel Osman Nuri Colak (representing the military), Z Demirkol (representing the "deep state"), and Sunay Zaim (a figurehead actor who was once in contention for dramatizing Atatürk). This group is pitted against the growing political enfranchisement of Islamists represented by the Refah Party, the students of the religious high school (*imam-hatip*), and Blue, the figure of militant Islamist resistance. As with many of the characters, Blue describes himself as having vacillated in life between atheism and Islam. Echoing Ka's own past, he says he was a Marxist-leaning poet in his youth. Later, he was influenced by revolutionary and Islamist thinkers such as Ayatollah Khomeini, Frantz Fanon, Sayyid Qutub, and Ali Shariati, and apparently fought in Chechnya and Bosnia. He is furthermore Ka's rival in his affections for İpek.

Snow is also a satirical novel full of in-jokes, parodies, puns, and send-ups of Republican Turkey.[9] Things are not what they seem in Kars. The veiled Kadife and the secular İpek are daughters of the leftist Turgut Bey. Both sisters have had illicit affairs with the Islamist terrorist Blue, who is also involved with their veiled friend, Hande. All the characters are compromised figures. Ka's infatuation with İpek is also colored by his jealousy of Blue. Love and politics intersect as Blue is murdered by secularists tipped off by Ka, who is murdered by Blue's Islamist followers. Every ideological position is exposed for conspiratorial excesses that lead to political violence. Finally, *Snow* mounts a critique of the naïve liberal humanism of an intellectual like Ka, blind to the consequences and contingencies of class, ideology, and state power.

Hidden Symmetry

Establishing the novel's metafictional framework, "Orhan"—representing a subject who knows in contrast to Ka—is the savvy liberal humanist author figure and "detective" who pieces Ka's story together. "Orhan" states that his novel has an aim: to unveil the hidden symmetries that determine Ka's life.[10] These hidden symmetries have to do with mirrored "conspiracies" of secularism and Islamism, which have structural affinities in the mirrored characters and plot.

"Orhan" learns that Ka was guilty of revealing the whereabouts of the Islamist militant Blue to the coup authorities. Orhan's novel, *Snow*, is a satire and a tragedy; his homage to Ka is also an indictment of a character caught in the machinery of Republican politics. The figure of the Republican author-intellectual is a target of Pamuk's critical parody. Nevertheless, as a Republican intellectual and global novelist, "Orhan" is the one vested with the authority to present an alternative and redemptive version of Turkish (literary) modernity in the neoliberal context of early 2000s Turkey.

Coups

In modern Turkish history, conspiracy is directly linked to the disruption of civilian politics through military coups. Whereas the Turkish military was instrumental in establishing the Republic of Turkey in 1923, the Cold War coups of 1960, 1971, and 1980 were contestations over the founding Kemalist legacy along a left-right ideological axis. The 1997 "postmodern coup" responded to the rise of Islamist politics and was prefigured by a vast secular conspiracy under the trope of *irtica*, or religious (Islamist) revival, articulated by the secularist top brass and politicians and trumpeted in the mainstream media.[11] This coup was significant in revealing how conspiracism, with the help of a pliant judiciary and co-opted media, could be articulated to target and destroy political opposition. In contrast, a counterconspiracy began to gradually emerge that identified a hitherto unknown political actor: the "deep state," a nonelected national security apparatus that restricted or controlled the civilian government.[12] Conspiratorial narratives built around *irtica* or the deep state (such as in the "Ergenekon" and "Sledgehammer" trials) resulted in authoritarian turns that significantly affected the trajectory of Turkish politics.[13] The 2016 failed coup was another intervention that led to violent consequences, one in which a competing Islamist group, the Gülen Hizmet movement, attempted to overthrow the AKP.[14]

In *Snow*, the coup emerges as a symptom of secular Republican conspiratorial thought. It is triggered by a paranoid mode that reads Islamist and ethnic Kurdish political representation as a threat to the secular Kemalist state. Part of the dramatic irony of *Snow* rests in the fact that Ka survives the actual 1980 coup and its aftermath, but he meets his end in the wake of Sunay Zaim's theatrical coup. In other words, *Snow* argues, the representational, symbolic, and discursive force of the "coup" is a form of state power on par with actual military power.

The State Versus Allah

Early in *Snow*, the chapter "I Hope I'm Not Taking Too Much of Your Time" dramatizes the violent potential of secular versus Islamist conspiracism. The exchange between Nuri Yılmaz (director of the State Institute of Education) and his murderer (who is a representative of the Freedom Fighters for Islamic Justice, sent to kill the director for his atheism and his enforcement of the veiling ban) establishes two dominant conspiratorial logics, one secularist, the other Islamist:

Islamist assassin:	"How can you reconcile Allah's command with this decision to ban covered girls from the classroom?"
Secularist Nuri Yilmaz:	"We live in a secular state. It's the secular state that has banned covered girls, from schools as well as classrooms."
Islamist:	"Can a law imposed by the state cancel out Allah's law?"
Secularist:	"In a secular state these matters are separate." . . .
Islamist:	"My question is this, sir. Does the word *secular* mean *godless*?"

Secularist:	"No."
Islamist:	"In that case, how can you explain why the state is banning so many girls from the classroom in the name of secularism, when all they are doing is obeying the laws of their religion?"[15]

The irreconcilable positions are presented in a strain of black humor that exposes the internal consistency and logic of ideological thought that becomes an excuse for political violence. For example, the director presents the conspiratorial logic of the Islamophobic secular position:

Secularist: "Of course, the real question is how much suffering we've caused our women-folk by turning headscarves into symbols and using women as pawns in a political game. . . . Has it ever occurred to you that foreign powers might be behind all this? Don't you see how they might have politicized the headscarf issue so they can turn Turkey into a weak and divided nation?"[16]

In keeping with conspiratorial mapping and Pamuk's parody of it, the director mentions the invisible hand of "foreign powers" and their ultimate goal: weakening and dividing the Turkish nation-state.[17] Pamuk maintains his approach, this time by focusing on the conspiratorial logic of the Islamist position that also identifies a "secret plan." The director is forced by his murderer to read his own death sentence, as prepared by the Freedom Fighters for Islamic Justice, which reveals the logic of Islamicist conspiracy: "I, Professor Nuri Yılmaz, am an atheist. . . . I confess to being a pawn in a secret plan to strip the Muslims of the secular Turkish Republic of their religion and their honor and thereby to turn them into slaves of the West."[18] Both perspectives focus on persecution, respectively, of the nation (or *millet*) and of the community of believers (or *ümmet*). Nevertheless, in terms of discourse, they are remarkably similar in presenting the embattled position of a victimized group against a shadowy enemy with hidden resources and aims of disenfranchisement and dispossession. The zero-sum logic of conspiracy pits victims against perpetrators in the fantasy of self-determination. In exchanges such as this, Pamuk reveals that nationalism and secular modernity are susceptible to conspiratorial thought to such a degree that "Turkishness" itself could be described as a discursive formation predicated on articulations of political conspiracy.

The Media

By tracing conspiracies, Pamuk provides a cultural map of 1990s Turkish identity politics. In Ka's meeting with Blue, we are informed of yet another level of conspiracy, which reinterprets the murder of the director of the Institute of Education. Blue states,

But of course the whole thing is a state plot. First they [the secularists] used this poor director to enforce their cruel measures, and then they incited some madman to kill him so as to pin the blame on the Muslims.[19]

The conspiracy theorist becomes a figure of revelatory insight. Thus emerges the hermeneutic position of conspiracy and counterconspiracy that Pamuk first described in *The New Life*. This is an endless spiral of circular reasoning in which either a disenfranchised group attempts to secure the upper hand or those in power attempt to maintain their hold through discursive means.

The idea of conspiratorial thought as a discursive force with epistemological and ontological effect is furthered through one of Pamuk's literary twists in *Snow*. In Kars, the local newspaper, the nationalist *Border City Gazette*, in a kind of journalistic determinism, prints accounts of events that have yet to occur, events which transpire as they have been represented textually. In explaining this discursive construction of reality, Serdar Bey states:

> There are those who despise us for writing the news before it happens. They fear us not because we are journalists, but because we can predict the future; you should see how amazed they are when things turn out exactly as we've written them. And quite a few things do happen only because we've written them up first. This is what modern journalism is all about. I know you won't want to stand in the way of our being modern.[20]

Here, maintaining or attaining secular modernity becomes an alibi for the abuse of power. Pamuk identifies the collusion between state power and the media as a target of critique in this passage. The introduction of such anti-realism into the novel sets up a causal inversion between representation and reality that is representative of the cultural logic of Kars as a microcosm of the nation. The causal link between state-sponsored authoritarianism (and modern "enlightenment") and popular media is one that Pamuk's work exposes, questions, and subverts.

Traitor to the Nation

In *Snow*, characters adopt and negotiate unstable and somewhat contradictory ideological positions. Turgut Bey is a character who espouses the logic of conspiracy from a traditional leftist perspective. After the news of the director of the Institute of Education's assassination by a religious extremist, Turgut Bey states:

> The Islamists have embarked on a cleanup operation. They're taking care of us [leftists] one by one. If you want to save your skin, I would advise you to increase your faith in Allah at the earliest opportunity. It won't be long, I fear, before a moderate belief in God will be insufficient to save the skin of an old atheist.[21]

Political violence emerges as an outcome of conspiracy and as a soft force of "conversion." Later, as Ka is trying to convince Turgut Bey to sign the farcical joint declaration to the West (together with an Islamist and a Kurdish nationalist) at the ironically named Hotel Asia (so he can also arrange a tryst with İpek), Turgut Bey states:

> Speaking as the Communist modernizing secularist democratic patriot I now am, what should I put first, the enlightenment or the will of the people? If I believe first and foremost in the European enlightenment, I am obliged to see the Islamists as my enemies and support this military coup. If, however, my first commitment is to the will of the people—if, in other words, I've become an unadulterated democrat—I have no choice but to go ahead and sign that statement.[22]

The political landscape of the novel reveals that social reality is predicated on constructions of conspiratorial discourse. With no mutually intelligible common political language, there is little hope that the national "coup" can be explained to the "West." Theatrical impresario Sunay Zaim summarizes the Islamist conspiracy from the secular perspective as follows (with no awareness of the colonial cast of his position):

> Atatürk had no time for bird-brained fantasists; he had people like you [Ka] swinging from ropes from the very first day. . . . No one who's even slightly westernized can

The Grammar of Conspiracy in Orhan Pamuk's Snow

breathe free in this country unless they have a secular army protecting them. . . . If we don't let the army and the state deal with these dangerous fanatics, we'll end up back in the Middle Ages, sliding into anarchy, traveling the doomed path already traveled by so many tribal nations in Asia and the Middle East.[23]

Pamuk's dramatization and personification of the logic of conspiracy as a device that furthers the metafictional plot is evident through such passages. *Snow* argues that the popular legitimacy of such conspiracies becomes problematic when backed by the vested interests of state (and/or military) power. Ka, for his part, is also the object of ideological discourse that politicizes him as a conspiratorial subject. One of the religious high school students in Kars, Necip, states, "Everyone in Kars is very curious to know why you've come here. They think you're on a secret mission or else you've been sent here by the Western powers."[24] Ka, ultimately, does get pulled into the conspiracy of the military coup, which, in the end, results in his appropriation by the coup plotters and, later, in his assassination. The slanderous article printed in the *Border City Gazette* summarizes Ka's precarious position, as he is made into a target of national wrath and vigilante justice by the media:

Many readers have telephoned our offices to express their regret about [Ka,] this godless imitation-European's decision to stir up dissent in our city in these troubled times. They have voiced particular concern about the way in which he has wandered the shantytowns, knocking on the doors of the most wretched dwellings to incite rebellion against our state and indeed, even in our own presence, vainly attempting to stick his tongue out at our country and even at the great Atatürk, Father of our Republic. The youth of Kars know how to deal with blasphemers who deny Allah and the Prophet Muhammad (SAS)![25]

The religious tones of the passage echo the Sunni nationalist position of the newspaper. Ka's denigration as a "traitor" (*vatan haini*) is remarkably similar to that of Pamuk himself, who was charged with "insulting Turkishness" in 2005 and also became the target of death threats for his discussion of the Armenian genocide.

Political Theater

Snow is structured around two theatrical performances: *My Fatherland or My Headscarf* and *A Tragedy in Kars*. The troupe that performs these plays is described as being "Brechtian and Bahktinian," emphasizing the leftist, didactic function of the performances. The first play is an updated version of the "enlightenment masterpiece" *My Fatherland or My Scarf*. This new local adaptation uses the word "*türban*" instead of "*çarşaf*," in acknowledgment that the traditional scarf has now become the dissident symbol of political Islam or, from the secular perspective, *irtica*. It is, in some respects, a drama of "state feminism," a didactic play representing the secular and gendered values of the cultural revolution.[26] In the play, a veiled villager removes her traditional veil (or *çarşaf*) and declares her freedom with the help of soldiers of the Republic who protect her from the patriarchal wrath of religious zealots. The intended meaning is congruent with secular conversion to modernity as the feminine subject of modernity is unveiled and scripted into Republican ideology as a symbol of progress. Performed in Kars 60 years later, however, the play loses its didactic Kemalist message and is stripped of its moral and message entirely:

Most of the locals in the National Theater were shocked and confused by the first scene. . . . And as they watched this mysterious covered woman wandering up and down the stage, it was not immediately clear that she was meant to be sad: Many in the audience saw her as proud, almost arrogant. . . . When the woman made her grand gesture of independence, launching herself into enlightenment as she removed her scarf, the audience was at first terrified. Even the most westernized secularists in the hall were frightened by the sight of their own dreams coming true. . . . Having expected a bespectacled village girl, pure-hearted, bright-faced, and studious, to emerge from beneath the scarf, they were utterly discomfited to see it was the lewd belly dancer Funda Eser instead. Was this to say that only whores and fools take off their headscarves? If so, it was precisely what the Islamists had been saying all along.[27]

Unclear about how to read and interpret the play, the audience is confounded. The chaos resolves in favor of the secular nationalists and the coup, led by a rogue faction of the "deep state" headed by Z Demirkol, who has joined forces with Sunay Zaim and the theater troupe. The play is presented along with a series of other skits, poems, songs, and acts. The reaction of the audience recasts the secular play into a parodic melodrama that verges on camp in places. This symbolic representation of the Kemalist cultural revolution both contains Islamophobic and orientalist conspiratorial thought while it conceals, in this staging, the military violence of an actual coup. *My Fatherland or My Headscarf* is a play in which a woman, torn between the cultural logics of religion and the state, embraces state modernity with the "encouragement" of military force. As such, the play espouses a secularist catharsis.

Catharsis

From Ka's perspective, the "coup" is described through positive affect. Ironically, in the wake of the theatrical coup staged by Sunay Zaim and Z Demirkol, in the midst of tanks, gunshots, and roundups, Ka is nonplussed and filled with serenity: "His whole mind was fixed on the beauty of the silent night. . . . He was mightily thankful to be present in this silent and forgotten country, now filling him with poems."[28] Indeed, the coup brings with it an ironic sense of mystical inspiration, insight, and transformation. Ka's poem "The Night of the Revolution" reflects the intersection of secularism, revolution, and the sacred:

> The new poem . . . portrayed the bed, the hotel in which he lay, and the snowy city of Kars as a single divine unity. . . . It began with his childhood memories of other coups, when the whole family would wake up to sit around the radio, listening to military marches; it went on to describe the holiday meals they'd had together.[29]

By assigning this poem to the Memory axis of his snowflake, Ka recasts the coup as a legacy of the past that is full of warm feelings of family, nation, and "divine unity" (*vahit*). Ka sleeps a restful night. The distorted interpretation of military violence is justified by the logic of conspiracy, coup, and Republican nationalism.

Immediately in the wake of the coup, Ka is filled with pleasant nostalgia:

> The peacefulness in the empty street took Ka back to the curfews of his childhood and his youth . . . all Ka wanted was to go outside and play in the empty streets. As a child he'd loved those martial-law days like holidays, when his aunts, his uncles, and his neighbors would come together in a common cause. . . . They felt happier and more secure during military coups. . . . Ka remembered how the grown-ups in his life would congratulate each other after military coups, in much the same way that they congratulated one another during the old religious holidays.[30]

The conflation of the coup and the celebration of Muslim holidays provides insight into the cultural logic of Kars as a microcosm of the Republic. In its implementation of a new order, the coup is sacralized as a ritual act of the incarnation of national secular modernity. It is sacred in its evocation of the self-determination of the Muslim nation secularized as "Turks" after the fall of the Ottoman Empire. Later Ka thinks, "A small part of him was secretly relieved that the military had taken charge and the country wasn't bending to the will of the Islamists."[31] In the wake of the coup, the city is described blithely as follows:

> When he [Ka] returned to the enchanted white street to see swarms of joyous children throwing snowballs, he forgot all his fears. . . . No one seemed to be complaining about the coup; instead, the mood was much as he [Ka] remembered from the coups of his childhood: There was a sense of new beginnings and of a change from the vexing routines of everyday life.[32]

The coup, in other words, is a complex of transformative political power, affect, and nostalgia. This transformation is also imbued with mystical and quasi-religious overtones. Pamuk first represents the Turkish military coup as a political yet redemptive event in *The Black Book*, in which the journalist Celal's secret messages, embedded into his columns, variously indicate social revolution, the coming of the Messiah, and Judgment Day. The apocalyptic and the revolutionary are thus wedded in the trope of the impending coup, which delivers dramatic catharsis.

Un/veiling

A second melodramatic performance, *A Tragedy in Kars*, which occurs at the end of the novel, serves as a counterpoint and sequel to *My Fatherland or My Headscarf*. As with the first performance, this one also merges political representation with melodrama. The second play is described as a blood feud that ends in suicide (influenced by Thomas Kyd's *The Spanish Tragedy*). In its adaptation to Kars and Turkey, the blood feud is centered on Kadife and whether or not to veil; the actress Funda Eser will play her secular rival. The play is improvised and unscripted, pitting important figures of secular Republicanism against one another: the authoritarian coup leader/leftist revolutionary (Sunay Zaim), the Republican woman (Funda Eser), and her "nemesis," the veiled political Islamist (Kadife). Intended to make a secular, didactic statement, the series of mini-skits leading up to the "removing of the veil" climax is described as follows:

> Though he [Sunay Zaim] was a rich and enlightened member of the ruling elite, Sunay's character enjoyed dancing and joking with the poorest villagers and, indeed, engaged them in erudite discussion of the meaning of life, as well as regaling them with scenes from Shakespeare, Victor Hugo, and Brecht. . . . As one outburst followed another, it grew harder to imagine that they conformed to any logic at all.[33]

The performances conjure an existentialist "theater of the absurd" performance that incorporates comedy and Vaudeville mixed with horror or tragedy, characters caught in hopeless situations forced to engage in repetitive or meaningless actions, clichéd dialogue, wordplay, nonsense, and either a parody or dismissal of dramatic realism.

The play intends to frame Kadife for a stage murder that becomes real. As such, the play represents liberation from the confines of secular authoritarian rule. The secular state (represented by Sunay Zaim) attempts to have the "political Islamist" (Kadife) remove her veil, shoot him (and unwittingly take the rap for his murder), and perhaps even kill herself. All of the themes raised earlier in the novel of secularism—veiling, political Islam, women/gender, modernity, and representation—are rearticulated in this scene. As with the first play, in the sequel, a woman (this time Kadife) removes her head covering. Immediately afterward, she fires a stage prop gun whose chamber is supposedly empty. The gun, given to her by Sunay Zaim, ends up killing him when she fires it. Through his suicide disguised as murder, Zaim willingly sacrifices himself for a national imaginary in which public displays of Muslim practice have no place. Again, Pamuk underscores the fact that political theater carries real force in the world of Turkish politics. Zaim's final theatrical gesture is an attempt to frame her for his death/suicide. While questioning realist representations, the death, as previously reported in the *Border City Gazette*, affirms the discursive force of the secular word in print. Arrested for murder, Kadife is later released after serving a short prison term. Kadife, the heroine of this melodrama, has exercised her own agency, symbolically ending the political "theater" of the coup. At the same time that Sunay Zaim is killed, so too is Blue, an event that maintains (and undoes) the secular-religious symmetry of the plot, arguably liberating Kadife.

Conspiracy as a Literary Episteme

Coup and conspiracy are dominant tropes in *Snow* that appear in a mode of satire and demonstrate the development of Pamuk's work as a vehicle of political critique. Over time, the historically grounded representations of revolution/coup that appeared in his early novels serve as the subject of satire in his mature fiction. The logic of Middle Eastern national self-determination presented in *Cevdet Bey and Sons* has devolved into Middle Eastern conspiracy. Concomitant to these developments, the text and the author are presented through mystical and redemptive processes; for example, the moment of poetic inspiration in *Snow* is revealed as mystical experience of the divine.

Pamuk's literary modernity as an author who introduces innovations into Turkish literature also serves as a running commentary and critique of secular modernity. Tracing the 16-year rule of the Islamic-leaning AKP reveals that its politicians engage in an everyday variety of coercive cultural production by articulating, amplifying, and disseminating conspiracy theories. These amount to emotionally charged narrative interpretations of current events whose truth, if not fully in question, is indeterminate. Simply put, this ritual of political storytelling functions to protect and maintain the party's political and economic vested interests. Along with other processes, among the long-term outcomes as witnessed in Turkey, are the collapse of the balance of powers, the attack against pluralism, the co-opting of the media, the rise of a single party dominating the state, and the creation of a democratic façade for an illiberal, authoritarian government. Rather than simply dismissing conspiracy theories, this chapter reads the literary episteme of *Snow* as a means of rethinking conspiracism as a discursive practice at the intersection of political power and culture. In this way, the novel helps us address an overarching question: What has been the function of the conspiracies that have guided Turkey's transition from a secular "military democracy" to an Islamist illiberal democracy from the 1997 coup to the present?[34]

Snow was published a year after the AKP came to power, and in this regard, the novel not only exposes the conspiratorial political landscape of 1990s Turkey but forecasts the future foibles of Turkish politics as well, including the conspiratorial discourses around the 2016 failed coup. In Turkey's AKP era, we have witnessed the emergence of something beyond the fictions of political representation: namely, the rise of conspiracism as a political melodrama with authoritarian turns, which *Snow* dramatizes as an object lesson.

Notes

1 Conspiracy narratives in Turkish literature can be traced to early Republican fiction and the intersection of nationalism and the novel in which powerful outside forces were intent on "enslaving Turks and dividing Turkey." Turkish modernist and postmodernist novels by popular authors such as Ahmet Hamdi Tanpınar, Oğuz Atay, Adalet Ağaoğlu, Orhan Pamuk, İhsan Anar Oktay, Hasan Ali Toptaş, and others engage conspiratorial situations and plots. Furthermore, the influence of international modern and postmodern novel translations into Turkish of authors such as Dostoyevsky, Borges, Kafka, Pynchon, Eco, Auster, DeLillo, Bolaño, and others have also influenced the use of structures of conspiracism as devices in contemporary Turkish fiction.

2 In this regard, however, Pamuk's novels tend towards a leftist academic postmodernism that embraces modern liberal humanism in opposition to the post-truth authoritarianism of politicians like Erdoğan and Trump.

3 Orhan Pamuk, *Öteki Renkler: Seçme Yazılar ve Bir Hikaye* (Istanbul: İletişim, 1999), 80–81.

4 For more on the literature of conspiracism, see Adrian S. Wisnicki, *Conspiracy, Revolution, and Terrorism from Victorian Fiction to the Modern Novel* (New York: Routledge, 2008).

5 Orhan Pamuk, *Snow* (New York: Knopf, 2004), 19.

6 For more on the intersection of literary modernity and politics in Pamuk's work, see Erdağ Göknar, *Orhan Pamuk, Secularism and Blasphemy: The Politics of the Turkish Novel* (London: Routledge, 2013).

7 For more on political melodramas of conspiracy in Turkey, see Erdağ Göknar, "The AKP's Rhetoric of Rule in Turkey: Political Melodramas of Conspiracy from 'Ergenekon' to 'Mastermind,'" in *Oxford Handbook of Turkish Politics*, ed. Güneş Murat Tezcür (Oxford: Oxford University Press, 2020).

8 The Turkish version of the novel uses "Refah Partisi," whereas the English translation uses "Prosperity Party." The standard translation is "Welfare Party."

9 See Sibel Erol, "Reading Orhan Pamuk's *Snow* as Parody: Difference as Sameness," *Comparative Critical Studies* 4, no. 3 (2007): 403–32.

10 Pamuk, *Snow*, 87.

11 On April 29, 1997, the Turkish General Staff announced that priority would be given to combating internal threats from, primarily, Islamist activism (denigrated as "*irtica*") and, secondarily, Kurdish separatism. İrtica replaced Kurdish insurgency as the primary security threat to the state. Ironically, the AKP has continued state violence against Kurds, as well as against a narrowed Islamist activism in the form of the Gülen movement.

12 A few years ago, viral discussions around the deep state began in earnest in the US media and have continued into the present (with former President Trump referring to the US State Department as the "Deep State Department"). Most early commentaries were focused first on identifying the origin of the concept, which was traced to Turkey.

13 One of the cases brought against the secular-military alliance was based on unsubstantiated evidence in a 2009 document titled an "Action Plan to Counter Religious Reaction/*İrtica*" that supposedly openly targeted the AKP and the Gülen movement. See Saban Kardas, "Turkish General Staff Accused of Seeking to Undermine the Government," *Eurasia Daily Monitor* article mirrored on the website of the Jamestown Foundation Global Research and Analysis, June 15, 2009, https://jamestown.org/program/turkish-general-staff-accused-of-seeking-to-undermine-the-government/. See also Gareth Jenkins, "Ergenekon, Sledgehammer, and the Politics of Turkish Justice: Conspiracies and Coincidences," *Middle East Review of International Affairs: MERIA* 15, no. 2 (2011): 1–9.

14 See Berk Esen and Sebnem Gumuscu, "Turkey: How the Coup Failed," *Journal of Democracy* 28, no. 1 (2017): 59–73.

15 Pamuk, *Snow*, 40.

16 Ibid., 43.

17 For more on the "Sèvres Syndrome," see Michelangelo Guida, "The Sèvres Syndrome and '*Komplo*' Theories in the Islamist and Secular Press," *Turkish Studies* 9, no. 1 (February 8, 2008): 37–52.

18 Pamuk, *Snow*, 46.

19 Ibid., 76.

20 Ibid., 29.

21 Ibid., 131.

22 Ibid., 242.

23 Ibid., 203.

24 Ibid., 136.

25 Ibid., 295.
26 For more on the history of feminism in Turkey, see Sema Kaygusuz, "Eros and Thanatos at the Restaurant," in *The Passenger: Turkey* (Milan: Iperborea 2021), 90–107.
27 Pamuk, *Snow*, 47–48.
28 Ibid., 166.
29 Ibid., 167.
30 Ibid., 173.
31 Ibid., 181.
32 Ibid., 217.
33 Ibid., 392.
34 For more on discursive constructions of Turkey as a military democracy, see Ayşegül Altınay, *The Myth of a Military-Nation* (London: Palgrave Macmillan, 2006).

References

Altınay, Ayşegül. *The Myth of a Military-Nation*. London: Palgrave Macmillan, 2006.

Baer, Marc David. "An Enemy Old and New: The Dönme, Anti-Semitism, and Conspiracy Theories in the Ottoman Empire and Turkish Republic." *Jewish Quarterly Review* 103, no. 4 (2013): 523–55.

Bardakçı, Mehmet. "Coup Plots and the Transformation of Civil-Military Relations in Turkey Under AKP Rule." *Turkish Studies* 14, no. 3 (2013): 411–28.

Cizre-Sakallıoğlu, Ümit, and Menderes Çınar. "Turkey 2002: Kemalism, Islamism, and Politics in the Light of the February 28 Process." *The South Atlantic Quarterly* 102, no. 2 (2003): 309–32. www.muse.jhu.edu/article/43706.

de Medeiros, Julian. *Conspiracy Theory in Turkey: Politics and Protest in the Age of 'Post-Truth.'* London: I. B. Tauris, 2018.

Erol, Sibel. "Reading Orhan Pamuk's *Snow* as Parody: Difference as Sameness." *Comparative Critical Studies* 4, no. 3 (2007): 403–32.

Ertürk, Nergis. "Those Outside the Scene: *Snow* in the World Republic of Letters." *New Literary History* 41, no. 3 (2010): 633–51. www.muse.jhu.edu/article/408302.

Esen, Berk, and Sebnem Gümüşçü. "Turkey: How the Coup Failed." *Journal of Democracy* 28, no. 1 (2017): 59–73.

Göknar, Erdağ. *Orhan Pamuk, Secularism and Blasphemy: The Politics of the Turkish Novel*. London: Routledge, 2013.

Gürpınar, Doğan. *Conspiracy Theories in Turkey: Conspiracy Nation*. New York: Routledge, 2020.

Hofstadter, Richard. *The Paranoid Style in American Politics*. New York: Knopf, 1965.

Jameson, Frederic. "Cognitive Mapping." In *Marxism and the Interpretation of Culture*, edited by C. Nelson and L. Grossberg, 347–60. Champaign: University of Illinois, 1988.

Karaosmanoğlu, Kerem. *Komplo Teorileri: Disiplinlerarası bir Giriş*. Istanbul: İletişim, 2019.

———. "The Discourse of *Üstakıl*: A Search for Hegemony in the Turkish Media." *Southeast European and Black Sea Studies* 21, no. 1 (2021): 77–99.

Kaygusuz, Sema. "Eros and Thanatos at the Restaurant." In *The Passenger: Turkey*, 90–107. Milan: Iperborea, 2021.

Pamuk, Orhan. *Öteki Renkler: Seçme Yazılar ve Bir Hikaye*. Istanbul: İletişim, 1999.

———. *Snow*. New York: Knopf, 2004.

Pipes, Daniel. *Hidden Hand: Middle East Fears of Conspiracy*. New York: St Martin's Griffin, 1998.

Santesso, Esra Mirze. "Silence, Secularism, and Fundamentalism in *Snow*." In *Global Perspectives on Orhan Pamuk: Existentialism and Politics*, edited by Mehnaz M. Afridi and David M. Buyze, 125–40. New York: Palgrave Macmillan, 2012.

Wisnicki, Adrian S. *Conspiracy, Revolution, and Terrorism from Victorian Fiction to the Modern Novel*. New York: Routledge, 2008.

TIMELINE

Date	Turkish Literature	World Literature and Culture	Turkish History and Politics	World History and Politics
				"4000 BCE: Egyptian Hieroglyphs"
				3400 BCE: Cuneiform Script, Earliest Writing System
				3500 BCE: Invention of the wheel in Mesopotamia
				3200 BCE: Invention of writing in Mesopotamia
				3000 BCE: Founding of the first Sumerian cities in Mesopotamia
				"2500 BCE: The Epic of Gilgamesh, 1st Great Work of Literature"
				1754 BCE: Code of Hammurabi, Babylonian Law Code, 1901
				"1600 BCE– 1180 BCE: Hittite Empire, Turkey"
				1274 BCE: Battle of Kadesh, Between Egyptian and Hittiti Empire
				1194 BCE – 1184: The Trojan War, Troy
				"900 BCE – 500 BCE: The Torah, The First Five Books of the Bible"
				800 BCE: *The Iliad*, by Homer
				"800 BCE: *Ramayana*, Sanskrit Epic"
				800 BCE: *Mahabharata*, Sanskrit Epic
				"800 BCE: *The Odyssey*, by Homer"
				776 BCE– 393: First Olympic Games
				442 BCE: *Antigone*, Sophocles
				440 BCE: *The Histories*, Herodotus
				334 BCE: Alexander the Great of Macedon marches through Anatolia on his way to India

(*Continued*)

Timeline

Date	Turkish Literature	World Literature and Culture	Turkish History and Politics	World History and Politics
	732: The Köl Tigin inscription			
	735: The Bilge Kagan inscription			121–180: Marcus Aurelius, 16th Roman Emperor
	800: Irk Bitig			"600: The Adventures of Beowulf"
				632: The Holy Koran, The Qur'an

Timeline

Date	Turkish Literature	World Literature and Culture	Turkish History and Politics	World History and Politics
1000				
1001				
1002				
1003				
1004				The library and university Dar Al-Hekma is founded in Egypt under the Fatimids
1005				
1006				
1007				
1008		The Leningrad Codex		
1009				
1010		*Shahnameh (The Book of Kings)* by Ferdowsi		
1011				
1012				
1013				
1014				
1015				
1016				
1017				
1018				
1019				
1020				
1021		*The Tale of Genji* by Murasaki Shikibu		*The Book of Optics* by Ibn al-Haytham
1022		Translation of the *Mahabharata* into Telugu and the first work of Telugu literature by Nannaya Bhattaraka		
1023				*Hayy ibn Yaqdhan* by Ibn Sina (Avicenna)
1024				

(*Continued*)

Timeline

Date	Turkish Literature	World Literature and Culture	Turkish History and Politics	World History and Politics
1025				*The Canon of Medicine* by Ibn Sina (Avicenna)
1026				
1027				*The Book of Healing* by Ibn Sina (Avicenna)
1028				
1029				
1030				
1031				
1032				
1033				
1034				
1035				
1036				
1037				
1038			Seljuk Empire was founded	
1039				
1040				
1041				
1042				
1043				
1044				
1045				
1046				
1047				
1048				
1049				
1050				
1051				
1052				
1053				
1054				
1055				
1056				
1057				
1058				
1059				
1060				
1061				
1062				
1063				
1064				
1065				
1066				
1067				
1068				

(*Continued*)

Timeline

Date	Turkish Literature	World Literature and Culture	Turkish History and Politics	World History and Politics
1069	*Kutadgu Bilig (The Wisdom Which Brings Good Fortune)* by Yusuf Khass Hajib			
1070				
1071			The battle of Manzikert	
1072	*The Divan-ı Lugat al-Türk (Compendium of the languages of the Turks)* by Mahmud Kashgari			
1073				
1074				
1075				
1076				
1077				
1078				
1079				
1080				
1081				
1082				
1083				
1084				
1085				
1086				
1087				
1088				
1089				
1090				
1091				
1092				
1093				
1094				
1095				
1096		University of Oxford in England holds its first lectures		
1097				
1098				
1099				

(*Continued*)

Timeline

Date	Turkish Literature	World Literature and Culture	Turkish History and Politics	World History and Politics
1100	Atabetü'l Hakayık by Edip Ahmet Yükneki			
1101				
1102				
1103				
1104				
1105				
1106				
1107				
1108				
1109				
1110				
1111				
1112				
1113				
1114				
1115				
1116				
1117				
1118				
1119				
1120				
1121		Kelileh ve Dimneh, translation of the Panchatantra by Abu'l Ma'ali Nasr Allah Munshi		
1122				
1123				
1124				
1125				
1126				
1127				
1128				
1129				
1130				
1131				
1132				
1133				
1134				
1135				
1136				
1137				
1138				

(*Continued*)

Timeline

Date	Turkish Literature	World Literature and Culture	Turkish History and Politics	World History and Politics
1139				
1140				
1141				
1142				
1143				
1144				
1145				
1146				
1147				
1148				
1149				
1150				
1151				
1152				
1153				
1154				
1155				
1156				
1157				
1158				
1159				
1160				
1161				
1162				
1163				
1164				
1165				
1166				
1167				
1168				
1169				
1170				
1171				
1172				
1173				
1174				
1175				
1176			Battle of Myriokephalon	
1177				
1178				
1179				
1180				
1181				
1182				
1183				

(Continued)

Timeline

Date	Turkish Literature	World Literature and Culture	Turkish History and Politics	World History and Politics
1184				
1185				
1186				
1187				
1188				
1189				
1190				
1191				
1192		Layla and Majnun by Nizami Ganjavi		
1193				
1194		Eskandar-nameh by Nizami Ganjavi		
1195				
1196				
1197				
1198				
1199				

Timeline

Date	Turkish Literature	World Literature and Culture	Turkish History and Politics	World History and Politics
1200				
1201				
1202				*Liber Abaci* by Fibonacci
1203				
1204				
1205				
1206				Mongol Empire was established by Genghis Khan
1207				
1208				
1209				
1210				
1211				
1212				
1213				
1214				
1215		*Dîvân-ı Şems-i Tebrîzî* by Mevlânâ Celâleddîn-i Rûmî		Magna Carta Libertatum
1216				
1217				
1218				
1219				
1220				
1221				
1222				
1223				
1224				
1225				
1226				
1227				
1228				
1229				
1230				
1231				
1232				
1233	*Kıssa-i Yusûf* by Ali			
1234				
1235				
1236				
1237				
1238				
1239				
1240				
1241				

(*Continued*)

Timeline

Date	Turkish Literature	World Literature and Culture	Turkish History and Politics	World History and Politics
1242				
1243				
1244				
1245				
1246				
1247				
1248				
1249				
1250				
1251				
1252				
1253				
1254				
1255				
1256				
1257				
1258				
1259				
1260				
1261				
1262				
1263				
1264				
1265				
1266				
1267				
1268				
1269				
1270				
1271				
1272				
1273			*Mesnevî* by Mevlânâ Celâleddîn-i Rûmî	
1274				
1275				
1276				
1277	*Dîvân -ı Turkî* by Sultan Veled. The declaration of Turkish as the official language by the edict of Mehmet I of Karaman.			

(Continued)

Timeline

Date	Turkish Literature	World Literature and Culture	Turkish History and Politics	World History and Politics
1278				
1279				
1280				
1281				
1282				
1283				
1284				
1285				
1286				
1287				
1288				
1289				
1290			The reign of Osman I	
1291				
1292				
1293				
1294				
1295				
1296				
1297				
1298				Wooden movable type printing invented by Chinese governmental minister Wang Zhen
1299			The Ottoman Empire was founded	

Timeline

Date	Turkish Literature	World Literature and Culture	Turkish History and Politics	World History and Politics
1300				
1301	Feleknâme by Gülşehrî			
1302				
1303	Risâletü'n-Nushiyye by Yunus Emre			
1304				
1305				
1306	Dîvân by Yunus Emre			
1307				
1308		Divine Comedy by Dante		
1309				
1310	Mantıku't-Tayr by Gülşehrî			
1311				
1312				
1313				
1314				
1315				
1316				
1317				
1318				
1319				
1320				
1321				
1322				
1323				
1324				
1325				
1326			The death of Osman Ghazi and Orhan Ghazi's accession to the throne	
1327				
1328				
1329				
1330	Garibnâme by Âşık Paşa			
1331			The establishment of the first Ottoman medrese in Iznik by Orhan Gazi	
1332				

(Continued)

Timeline

Date	Turkish Literature	World Literature and Culture	Turkish History and Politics	World History and Politics
1333				
1334				
1335			Independence of Anatolian beyliks	
1336				
1337				The beginning of the Hundred Years' War between France and England
1338				
1339				
1340				
1341				The beginning of the plague epidemic in Asia
1342				
1343				
1344				
1345				
1346			Orhan Ghazi's marriage with Kantakuzenos' daughter and alliance with Byzantine Empire	
1347				
1348				
1349				
1350	*Süheyl ü Nevbahâr* by Hoca Mesud			
1351				
1352				
1353				
1354				
1355				
1356				
1357				
1358	*Menâkıbü'l-Kudsiyye* by Elvan Çelebi			
1359				
1360				
1361	*Cemşîd ü Hurşîd* by Selman-ı Sâvecî		Murat I's capture of Edirne. Edirne becomes the capital of the Ottomans	

(*Continued*)

379

Timeline

Date	Turkish Literature	World Literature and Culture	Turkish History and Politics	World History and Politics
1362			The death of Orhan Ghazi and Murat I's accession to the throne	
1363				
1364				
1365	*Yûsuf u Züleyhâ* by Darîr			
1366	*Hüsrev ü Şîrîn* by Fahrî		Pope's declaration of a Crusade against the Ottomans	
1367				
1368		*Dîvân* by Hafez-i Shirazî		
1369				
1370		*Dîvân* by Jahan Malek Hatun		
1371				
1372				
1373			Balkan States and Byzantine Empire recognize Ottoman sovereignty	
1374				
1375				
1376				
1377				
1378				
1379				
1380				
1381				
1382				
1383				
1384				
1385	*Hurşîdnâme* by Şeyhoğlu			
1386				
1387				
1388				
1389	*İskendernâme* by Ahmedî		The battle of Kosovo Death of Murat I and Reign of Bayezit I	

(Continued)

Timeline

Date	Turkish Literature	World Literature and Culture	Turkish History and Politics	World History and Politics
1390		*The Canterbury Tales* by Geoffrey Chaucer		
1391				
1392				
1393	*Dîvân* by Kadı Burhanettin			
1394				
1395				
1396			The arrival of the Crusaders in the Balkans	
1397				
1398				
1399				

Timeline

Date	Turkish Literature	World Literature and Culture	Turkish History and Politics	World History and Politics
1400			The construction of the Great Mosque in Bursa by Bayezid I The construction of the first Ottoman Darü'ş-şifa by Yıldırım Bayezid	
1401				
1402			The battle of Ankara and Yıldırım Bayezid's captivity Ottoman Interregnum (1402-1413)	
1403	Cemşid ü Hurşîd by Ahmedî	The Yongle Encyclopedia is written in China		
1404	Nesimî's execution in Aleppo			
1405				
1406	Çengnâme by Ahmed-i Da'î			
1407				
1408				
1409	Vesîletü'n-Necât by Süleyman Çelebi			
1410				
1411	Gül ü Nevrûz by Lutfî		The accession of Mehmed I to the throne	
1412				
1413				
1414				
1415				
1416			Sheikh Bedreddin- The Dervish Rebellion	
1417				

(Continued)

Timeline

Date	Turkish Literature	World Literature and Culture	Turkish History and Politics	World History and Politics
1418				
1419				
1420				
1421			The death of Çelebi Mehmed and Murad II's accession to the throne	
1422				
1423				
1424				
1425				
1426				
1427				
1428				
1429				
1430				
1431				Jeanne d'Arc's trial and execution
1432				
1433				
1434				
1435				
1436	*Târîh-i Âl-i Selçuk* by Yazıcıoğlu Ali			
1437	*Mecmû'atü'n-Nezâ'ir* by Ömer bin Mezcîd			
1438				
1439				
1440				
1441				
1442				
1443				
1444			The abdication of Murat II and Mehmed II's accession to the throne	
1445			The abdication of Mehmed II Second reign of Murad II	
1446	*Gazavât-ı Sultan Murad* by Gelibolulu Zaîfî			
1447				

(*Continued*)

Timeline

Date	Turkish Literature	World Literature and Culture	Turkish History and Politics	World History and Politics
1448			The second Battle of Kosovo	
1449	*Kitâb-ı Muhammediyye* by Yazıcıoğlu Mehmed			
1450				Johannes Gutenberg established the movable type printing press in Mainz as a commercial enterprise
1451			Murad II's death and Mehmed II's accession to the throne for the second time	
1452				
1453			Mehmed II takes Istanbul Conversion of Hagia Sophia into a mosque	The end of the Hundred Years' War
1454				
1455				Johannes Gutenberg completed the printing of the Gutenberg Bible, the first large book printed in movable type
1456				
1457				
1458				
1459				
1460				
1461				
1462				
1463				
1464				
1465				
1466				
1467				
1468			The establishment of Topkapı Palace in Istanbul by Mehmed II	
1469				
1470				
1471				
1472				
1473				

(*Continued*)

Timeline

Date	Turkish Literature	World Literature and Culture	Turkish History and Politics	World History and Politics
1474				
1475				
1476				
1477				
1478	*Leylâ vü Mecnûn* by Edirneli Şahidî	The first book printed in Oxford Canterbury Tales by William Caxton		
1479				
1480				
1481			The death of Mehmed II and Ascension of Bayezid II to the throne	
1482			Cem Sultan's defeat, his defection to Rhodes	
1483	*Vilayetnâme-i Otman Baba* by Küçük Abdal/ Otman Baba			
1484	*Tevârih-i Âl-i Osman* by Âşık Paşazade			
1485				
1486			The establishment of the first state hospital to treat with music (Edirne, Bayezid II Şifahanesi)	
1487				
1488				
1489	*Şem u Pervâne (The Candle and Moth)* by Fehmî			
1490	*Fetihnâme-i Sultan Mehmed* by Kıvamî			Chinese scholar Hua Sui invents bronze-metal movable type printing in China

(*Continued*)

Timeline

Date	Turkish Literature	World Literature and Culture	Turkish History and Politics	World History and Politics
1491	*Mecâlisü'n-Nefâis* by Ali Şir Nevayî			
	Yûsuf u Züleyhâ by Hamdullah Hamdi			
1492				Christopher Columbus landed in America
1493	*Hevesnâme* by Tâcîzâde Cafer Çelebi			
1494				
1495				
1496				
1497			The arrival of the first Russian ambassador in Istanbul	
1498				
1499				

Timeline

Date	Turkish Literature	World Literature and Culture	Turkish History and Politics	World History and Politics
1500	*Leylâ vü Mecnûn* by Hamdullah Hamdi			
1501	*Dîvân* by Mihrî Hatun			
1502	*Hüsrev ü Şîrîn* by Ahmed-i Rıdvan	Aldine Press editions appear of Dante's Divine Comedy, Herodotus' Histories and Sophocles	Peace with Venice Ismail founded the Safavid Dynasty in Iran	
1503				
1504				
1505				Martin Luther enters the monastery of St. Augustine and the Reformation begins
1506		Leonardo da Vinci completes the Mona Lisa		
1507				The first recorded epidemic of smallpox in the New World on the island of Hispaniola
1508				
1509				
1510				
1511				
1512	*Leylâ vü Mecnûn* by Celilî	Michelangelo paints the Sistine Chapel ceiling	Bayezid II's abdication and Selim I's accession to the thron	Commentariolus by Copernicus
1513				
1514				
1515				
1516		*Utopia* by Thomas More	Egypt Expedition and the Battle of Marj Dabiq	
1517		*Dîvân* by Aisha al-Bauniyye	The battle of Ridaniya and the capture of Cairo Piri Reis presented the first world map to Yavuz Sultan Selim in Egypt	
1518				The dancing plague of 1518 begins in Strasbourg

(*Continued*)

Timeline

Date	Turkish Literature	World Literature and Culture	Turkish History and Politics	World History and Politics
1519				
1520			Death of Selim I and Süleyman I's accession to the throne	
1521	Ferhâd u Şîrîn by Bursalı Lâmi		Conquest of Belgrade Piri Reis's preparation of his work called Kitab-ı Bahriye	
1522		Luther Bible is published		
1523				The cacao bean was introduced to Spain by Hernán Cortés
1524	Hüsn ü Dîl by Lâmi'î			
1525			The arrival of the first French ambassador in Istanbul	
1526			Battle of Mohács	The Mughal Empire was founded
1527				Protestant Reformation begins in Sweden
1528			Pîrî Reis presenting his second world map to Süleyman I	
1529			Siege of Vienna, recapture of Budin, Barbarossa Hayreddin Pasha's landing in Marseille	
1530				
1531				
1532	Selâmân ü Ebsâl by Lâmi'î	The Prince by Machiavelli		The Church of England separated from the Roman Catholic Church and recognized King Henry VIII as the head of the Church
1533		The censors of the Collège de Sorbonne condemn François Rabelais' Pantagruel		

(Continued)

Timeline

Date	Turkish Literature	World Literature and Culture	Turkish History and Politics	World History and Politics
1534		Cambridge University Press was granted a royal charter by King Henry VIII of England to publish "all kinds of books"		
1535				
1536	*Leylâ vü Mecnûn* by Fuzulî			
1537				
1538	*Heşt Bihişt* by Sehî Bey			
1539				
1540	*Gencîne-i Râz* by Taşlıcalı Yahyâ			
1541				
1542				
1543				De revolutionibus orbium coelestium (On the Revolutions of the Celestial Spheres) by Nicolaus Copernicus
1544	*Gülşen-i Esrâr* by Şahidî			
1545				
1546	*Tezkiretü'ş-Şu'arâ and Tabsıratü'n-Nüzamâ* by Latifî			
1547				
1548				
1549	*Bahrü'l Maârif* by Gelibolulu Mustafa Sürûrî			
1550			The establishment of the Süleymaniye Complex	
1551				
1552				
1553	*Gül ü Bülbül* by Kara Fazlî			

(Continued)

Timeline

Date	Turkish Literature	World Literature and Culture	Turkish History and Politics	World History and Politics
1554				
1555				
1556	Tercüme-i Bîh-i Çînî by Mahfî Gîlânî			
1557				
1558				
1559				
1560				
1561				
1562				
1563				
1564	Ahlâk-i Âlâî by Kınâlızade Ali Efendi			
1565				
1566			The last campaign of Suleiman I: Battle of Szigetvár The death of Suleiman I and Selim II's accession to the throne	
1567				
1568	Meşâriü'ş-Şuarâ by Âşık Çelebi			
1569				
1570				
1571				
1572				
1573				
1574	Münşeâtü's-Selâtîn by Feridun Bey		The death of Selim II and Murad III's accession to the throne	
1575			Selimiye Mosque was founded in Edirne by Mimar Sinan for Selim II	

(Continued)

Timeline

Date	Turkish Literature	World Literature and Culture	Turkish History and Politics	World History and Politics
1576				
1577			Takiyüddin continued his observations at the partially completed Daru'r-Rasadü'l-Cedid (Istanbul Observatory)	
1578	*Riyâzü'l-Cinân'* by Cinânî			
1579	*Nakş-ı Hayâl* by Azerî İbrahim Çelebi			
1580		*Les Essais (The Essays)* by Montaigne		
1581				
1582				
1583				
1584				
1585				
1586	*Tezkiretü'ş-Şuarâ* by Hasan Çelebi			
1587				
1588				
1589				
1590				
1591				
1592				
1593	*Gülşen-i Şuarâ* by Ahdî			
1594				
1595			Murad III's death and Mehmet III's accession to the throne	
1596				

(*Continued*)

Timeline

Date	Turkish Literature	World Literature and Culture	Turkish History and Politics	World History and Politics
1597	*Tezkire-i Şuarâ* by Beyanî	*Essays* by Francis Bacon		
		Romeo and Juliet by William Shakespeare		
1598	,	*Henry IV, Part 1* and *Love's Labor's Lost* by William Shakespeare		
1599				

Timeline

Date	Turkish Literature	World Literature and Culture	Turkish History and Politics	World History, Science and Politics
1600		*Henry IV, Part 2, The Merchant of Venice, Henry V, A Midsummer Night's Dream, and Much Ado About Nothing* by William Shakespeare		
1601		*Twelfth Night* byWilliam Shakespeare		
1602				
1603	*Saki-name* by Riyazi	*Measure for Measure, Othello, Macbeth* by William Shakespeare.	The death of Mehmed III and the accession of Ahmed I to the throne	
1604		*Hamlet* by William Shakespeare		
1605		*King Lear* by William Shakespeare *Don Quixote de la Mancha (Part 1)* by Miguel de Cervantes Saavedra.		
1606			Treaty of Zitvatorok	
1607				
1608	*Habnâme* by Veysî			Invention of the telescope
1609				*Astronomia nova* by Johannes Kepler
1610				
1611				
1612				
1613			Prohibition of alcohol in the Ottoman Empire	
1614				
1615		*Don Quixote de la Mancha (Part 2)* by Miguel de Cervantes Saavedra.		

(*Continued*)

Timeline

Date	Turkish Literature	World Literature and Culture	Turkish History and Politics	World History, Science and Politics
1616			Completion of the construction of the Blue Mosque in Istanbul	
1617	*Âlem-nüma* by Nev'izade Atai			
1618			The deposition of Mustafa I and	
			Osman II's accession to the throne	
1619				Johannes Kepler: third law of planetary motion
1620		*Novum Organum* by Francis Bacon		
1621				
1622			The murder of Osman II and	
			The accession of Mustafa I to the throne	
1623	*Bülbüliye* by Ömer Fuâdî		The dethronement of Mustafa I and	
	Menâkıb-ı İbrâhim-i Gülşenî by Muhyî-i Gülşenî		Murad IV ascends the throne	
1624				
1625				
1626	*Heft-han* by Atayi			
1627	*Selim-name* by Cevrî	*New Atlantis* by Sir Francis Bacon		
1628				
1629				
1630				
1631				
1632	*Nihalistan* by Nergisî			

(*Continued*)

Timeline

Date	Turkish Literature	World Literature and Culture	Turkish History and Politics	World History, Science and Politics
1633			The Great Fire of Istanbul Closure of coffee houses in Istanbul Tobacco ban	
1634				
1635	Nef'i's execution			
1636				
1637				
1638				
1639				Russia's access to the Pacific Ocean
1640	*Letters of Dream* by Asiye Hatun	*Meditations on First Philosophy* by Descartes	Murad IV's death and Ibrahim I's accession to the throne	
1641				
1642				
1643				
1644		*Principles of Philosophy* by Descartes		
1645				
1646				
1647				
1648			Ibrahim's dethronement and Accession of Mehmed IV to the throne	
1649				
1650				
1651		*Leviathan* by Thomas Hobbes		
1652				
1653				
1654	*Gamze vü Dil* by Simşekzâde Feyzî			
1655				
1656	*Mizānü'l-hakk fi ihtiyari'l-hakk* by Katib Çelebi	Velazquez, in *Las Meninas*, paints himself painting the king and queen of Spain	The beginning of the Köprülüler era	Robert Hooke discovers the cell Huygens built the first pendulum managed to make the clock

(*Continued*)

Timeline

Date	Turkish Literature	World Literature and Culture	Turkish History and Politics	World History, Science and Politics
1657		*Comical History of the States and Empires of the Moon* by Cyrano de Bergerac.		
1658	*Teşrifatü'ş Şu'ara* by Edirneli Güfti			
1659				
1660	*Zafer-name* by Güftî		The Great Fire of Istanbul	
1661				
1662		*L'école des femmes* by Molière		
1663				
1664		*Tartuffe* by Molière		
1665				
1666				*De Arte Combinatoria (On the Art of Combination)* by Gottfried Leibniz
1667		*Paradise Lost* by John Milton		
1668				
1669				
1670		*Le Bourgeois gentilhomme* by Molière.		
1671	*Fetih-name-i Kamaniçe* by Nabi			
1672		*Les Femmes Savantes* by Molière.		
1673				
1674		*Nouveaux contes* by Jean de la Fontaine		
1675	*Sur-name* by Nâbi			
1676				
1677		*Phèdre* by Jean Racine		
		Ethics by Baruch Spinoza		

(Continued)

Timeline

Date	Turkish Literature	World Literature and Culture	Turkish History and Politics	World History, Science and Politics
1678		*La Princesse de Clèves* by Madame de La Fayette		
		The Pilgrim's Progress by John Bunyan		
1679				
1680				
1681				
1682				
1683			Siege of Vienna by the Ottomans	
			Siege of Vienna II, loss of Esztergon	
1684		Poems by Aphra Behn		
1685				
1686				
1687			The deposition of Mehmed IV and The accession of Suleiman II to the throne	*Philosophiae Naturalis Principia Mathematica* by Isaac Newton
			Battle of Mohàcs	
1688				
1689		*An Essay Concerning Human Understanding* by John Locke		
1690				
1691			The accession of Ahmed II to the throne	
1692				
1693				
1694				
1695		.	Death of Ahmed II The accession of Mustafa II to the throne	
1696		.		

(*Continued*)

Timeline

Date	Turkish Literature	World Literature and Culture	Turkish History and Politics	World History, Science and Politics
1697		*Histoires ou contes du temps passé (Stories or Tales from Past Times)* by Charles Perrault		
1698				
1699		*Les Aventures de Télémaque (The Adventures of Telemachus)* by François Fénelon	Treaty of Karlowitz	

Timeline

Date	Turkish Literature	World Literature and Culture	Turkish History and Politics	World History and Politics
1700	*Hayriyye* by Nabi		Treaty of Constantinople	
1701				
1702				
1703			The Edirne Incident The dethronement of Mustafa II the accession of Ahmed III to the throne. The introduction of gold coins with "tughra"	Founding of the city of St. Petersburg
1704		*The Storm* by Daniel Defoe *New Essays on Human Understanding* by Gottfried Wilhelm Leibniz		
1705				
1706				
1707				*Arithmetica Universalis* by Isaac Newton. Unification of England and Scotland
1708				
1709			Baltaci Mehmet Pasha became grand vizier	
1710				
1711		*An Essay on Criticism* by Alexander Pope	The Prut Victory against Russia and the Treaty of Prut	
1712				
1713			Treaty of Adrianople (Edirne)	
1714				
1715				
1716				
1717				
1718		*Oedipus* by Voltaire was performed	Treaty of Passarowitz Beginning of the Tulip Period	
1719		*Robinson Crusoe* by Daniel Defoe		
1720	*Surnâme-i Vehbi* by Levni			
1721			Çelebi Mehmed Efendi's departure to France on an embassy mission	

(Continued)

Timeline

Date	Turkish Literature	World Literature and Culture	Turkish History and Politics	World History and Politics
1722				
1723				The fall of the Safavid State
1724				
1725				
1726		*Gulliver's Travels* by Jonathan Swift		
1727				
1728				
1729	The first printing press in Turkish by Ibrahim Muteferrika			Stephen Gray found a way to transmit electricity
1730	The Orkhon monuments were first introduced to the world by the Swedish officer Strahlenberg		Patrona Halil Rebellion Mahmud I's accession to the throne End of the Tulip period	
1731				
1732				
1733				
1734				
1735			Ottoman-Austrian-Russian Wars	
1736	*Divân* by Nedim			
1737				
1738				
1739		*Treatise of Human Nature* by David Hume	Treaty of Belgrade	
1740				
1741				
1742				
1743				
1744				
1745				
1746				
1747				
1748				

(*Continued*)

Timeline

Date	Turkish Literature	World Literature and Culture	Turkish History and Politics	World History and Politics
1749		*The History of Tom Jones, a Foundling* by Henry Fielding		
1750				
1751			The first Western work on Ottoman music (Charles Fonton's *Essaî*)	
1752				
1753				
1754			The death of Mahmud I and the accession of Osman III to the throne	
1755			Opening of Nuruosmaniye Mosque	
1756				
1757			The death of Osman III The accession of Mustafa III to the throne	
1758				
1759		*Candide* by Voltaire		
1760				
1761				
1762		*The Social Contract, Émile* by Rousseau		
1763		*Letters* by Lady Mary Montagu		James Watt invented the steam engine
1764		*The Castle of Otranto* by Horace Walpole		
1765				
1766				
1767		*Tristram Shandy* by Laurence Sterne		
1768			Beginning of the Ottoman-Russian War	James Cook begins explorations in the Pacific Ocean
1769				
1770				
1771				
1772				

(*Continued*)

Timeline

Date	Turkish Literature	World Literature and Culture	Turkish History and Politics	World History and Politics
1773			Establishment of the Mühendishane-i Bahr-i Hümâyun	
1774			Death of Mustafa III the accession of Abdülhamit I to the throne Treaty of Küçük Kaynarca Ottoman Sultans officially adopted the title of the caliph	
1775				
1776				
1777				
1778				
1779				
1780				
1781		*Critique of Pure Reason* by Immanuel Kant		
1782	*Hüsn ü Aşk (Beauty and Love)* by Şeyh Gâlip	*The Robbers* by Friedrich Schiller		
1783	*Adab-ı Zurefa* by Râmiz *Nuhbetü'l Asar fi Feva'idi'l-Eş'ar* by Mustafa Safvet *Tuhfe-i Vehbî* by Sünbülzade Vehbi			
1784				
1785		*120 Days of Sodom* by Marquis de Sade *Groundwork of the Metaphysic of Morals* by Immanuel Kant		
1786				
1787			Declaration of the Ottoman-Russian War	
1788				

(*Continued*)

Timeline

Date	Turkish Literature	World Literature and Culture	Turkish History and Politics	World History and Politics
1789		*Songs of Innocence* by William Blake	The death of Abdülhamid I and the accession of Selim III to the throne	French Revolution Following the 1789 French Revolution, "Declaration of the Rights of the Man and of the Citizen" was published to protect human rights. George Washington becomes the first president of the United States.
1790	*Tezkire-i Şuarâ* by Silahdarzâde Mehmet Emin		The openning of the first official Armenian school in Kumkapı	
1791	*Lütfiyye-i Vehbî* by Sünbülzâde Vehbi *Cân u Cânân* by Refi-i Âmidi	*Justine* by Marquis de Sade	The end of the last war between Austria and the Ottoman Empire	
1792		*A Vindication of the Rights of Woman* by Mary Wollstonecraft	Treaty of Jassy	
1793		*Songs of Experience* by William Blake		
1794		*The Mysteries of Udolpho* by Ann Radcliffe		
1795		*Wilhelm Meister's Apprenticeship* by Goethe *The Mysteries of Udolpho* by Ann Radcliffe	The first newspaper *Le Bulletin de Nouvelles* published in Istanbul, by the French embassy The opening of the Mühendishane-i Berr-i Hümâyun, the first foreign band at the Ottoman court (sent by Napoleon to Selim III)	

(*Continued*)

403

Timeline

Date	Turkish Literature	World Literature and Culture	Turkish History and Politics	World History and Politics
1796	*Tezkire-i Şu'ara-yı Mevleviyye* by Esrar Dede	*Jacques the Fatalist and his Master* by Denis Diderot		Edward Jenner produced smallpox vaccine
	Muhayyelat-ı Aziz Efendi by Aziz Ali Efendi			
1797	*Mir'at-ı Şi'r* by Enderunlu Akif Bey		The establishment of permanent Ottoman embassies in Paris, Vienna and Berlin	
1798				
1799				

Timeline

Date	Turkish Literature	World Literature and Culture	Turkish History and Politics	World History and Politics
1800				
1801		*Atala* by François-René de Chateaubriand		
1802				
1803				
1804		*William Tell* by Friedrich Schiller		
1805				
1806				
1807		*Tales from Shakespeare* by Charles Lamb and Mary Lamb	The first coup d'etat: Kabakçı Mustafa	
1808		*Faust Part One* by Goethe	The murder of Selim and second coup d'etat	
			Mahmud II's accession to the throne	
			Alemdar Vakası	
			Sekban-ı Cedid established	
			Charter of Alliance (Sened-i İttifak)	
1809		*Elective Affinities* by Johann Wolfgang von Goethe		
1810		*Zastrozzi and St. Irvyne* by Percy Bysshe Shelley		
1811		*Sense and Sensibility* by Jane Austen		
		Childe Harold's Pilgrimage by Lord Byron		
1812		*Grimms' Fairy Tales* by The Brother Grimm	Serbian independence	
1813		*Pride and Prejudice* by Jane Austen		

(*Continued*)

Timeline

Date	Turkish Literature	World Literature and Culture	Turkish History and Politics	World History and Politics
1814		*Mansfield Park* by Jane Austen		
		Waverley by Sir Walter Scott		
1815		*Emma* by Jane Austen		
1816		*The Sandman* by E. T. A. Hoffmann		
		Alastor by Percy Bysshe Shelley		
1817		*Persuasion* and *Northanger Abbey* by Jane Austen		The first cholera pandemic
1818		*Frankenstein* by Mary Shelley		
		Ozymandias by Percy Bysshe Shelley		
		In The World as Will and Idea by A. Schopenhauer		
1819		*Ivanhoe* by Walter Scott		
1820		*Ruslan and Ludmila* by Alexander Pushkin		
1821		*Confessions of an English Opium Eater* by Thomas De Quincey		
1822	The Translation Office was founded	*The Vision of Judgment* by Lord Byron		
		On Love by Stendhal		
1823		*The Fountain of Bakhchisaray* by Alexander Pushkin		
1824		*Ninth Symphony* by Beethoven		
1825	*Mihnet-Keşan* by İzzet Molla	*Boris Godunov* by Pushkin		

(*Continued*)

Timeline

Date	Turkish Literature	World Literature and Culture	Turkish History and Politics	World History and Politics
1826			Abolition of the Janissary army	French physicist Joseph Niepce took the first photograph in history
			Asakir-i Mansure-i Muhammediyye established	
			The Ottomans' possession of a British steamship.	
1827		*Cromwell* by Victor Hugo	The defeat of the Ottoman navy against Britain, France and Russia	
		Armance by Stendhal		
			Ottoman students were sent to France 3 or the first time	
1828				
1829			The independence of Greece	The second cholera pandemic
1830		*The Red and the Black* by Stendhal		
1831	*Takvim-i Vekayi (first official newspaper) was pubslihed*	*The Hunchback of Notre-Dame* by Victor Hugo		Michael Faraday invented the electric dynamo
1832		*Eugene Onegin* by Alexander Pushkin		
1833		*Evenings on a Farm Near Dikanka* by Nikolai Gogol		Slavery abolished in British Empire
		Indiana and *Valentine* by George Sand		
		Gamiani by Alfred de Musset		
		Eugénie Grandet by Honoré de Balzac		
1834		*Le Père Goriot* (*Father Goriot*) by Balzac		

(*Continued*)

Timeline

Date	Turkish Literature	World Literature and Culture	Turkish History and Politics	World History and Politics
1835		*The Lily of the Valley* by Balzac		
1836		*Taras Bulba* by Gogol *The Government Inspector* by Nikolay Gogol		Samuel Colt patents his rapid-fire revolver
		The Captain's Daughter by Pushkin		
		Nature by Ralph Waldo Emerson		
1837				
1838		*Oliver Twist* by Charles Dickens		Samual Morse invented morse code
1839	*Bahar-ı Efkar* by İzzet Molla	*The Charterhouse of Parma* by Stendhal *Polypathis (The Man of Many Sufferings)* by Grigoris Palailogos	Death of Mahmud II Proclamation of the Edict of Gülhane (Tanzimât Fermânı) Sultan Abdülmecid's accession to the throne	Charles Darwin by *The Voyage of the Beagle* Kirkpatrick Macmillan invented a bicycle The New York Philharmonic established
1840		*The Arabian Nights* by Edward William Lane *Tales of the Grotesque and Arabesque* by Edgar Allan Poe	The opening of foreign post offices	
1841		"The Murders in the Rue Morgue" by Edgar Allan Poe		
1842		*The Overcoat, Dead Souls* and *Diary of a Madman* by Nikolay Gogol		

(*Continued*)

Timeline

Date	Turkish Literature	World Literature and Culture	Turkish History and Politics	World History and Politics
1843	*Münşeat-ı Elhac Akif Efendi* by Akif Pasha	*A Christmas Carol* by Charles Dickens *Frygt og Bæven: Dialectisk Lyrik* by Kierkegaard *The Flying Dutchman* by Richard Wagner		
1844	Naum Theatre was established	*The Three Musketeers, The Count of Monte Cristo* by Alexandre Dumas *Le Juif Errant (The Wandering Jew)* by Eugène Sue		
1845	*Divân* by Leyla Hanım			
1846			Mixed Muslim-Christian commercial courts established Mustafa Reşit Pasha's first Grand Vizierate	
1847		*Wuthering Heights* by Emily Bronte *Jane Eyre* by Charlotte Bronte	Testing the telegraph at Beylerbeyi Palace The first piano recital in Istanbul (Liszt plays Donizetti's Mecidiye March for Abdülmecid)	
1848	*Seyahatnâme* by Evliya Çelebi	*The Vicomte of Bragelonne: Ten Years Later* by Alexandre Dumas *The Tenant of Wildfell Hall* by Anne Brontë	Official recognition of the Protestant Armenian community and church The opening of Darü'l-Muallimin in Istanbul Launching of the first Ottoman-made iron steamer	Nationalist uprisings in Poland and Hungary Revolutions of 1848 The second French Empire *The Communist Manifesto* by Marx and Engels
1849		*Annabel Lee* by Edgar Allan Poe	*Ceride-i Havadis* pubslihed by Winston Churchill	

(*Continued*)

409

Timeline

Date	Turkish Literature	World Literature and Culture	Turkish History and Politics	World History and Politics
1850		*David Copperfield* by Charles Dickens		
		The Black Tulip by Alexandre Dumas		
1851	Hovsep Vartanyan's novel *Akabi Hikayesi* (*The Story of Akabî*) in Turkish with Armenian letters published	*The House of the Seven Gables* by Nathaniel Hawthorne *Système de politique positive* by Auguste Comte	Encümen-i Daniş established	
	The newspaper *Anatoli* by Evangelinos Misailidis	*Moby Dick* by Herman Melville		
1852	*Muhayyelat-ı Aziz Efendi* by Ali Aziz Efendi			The third cholera pandemic
1853		*Villette* by Charlotte Bronte *The Heir of Redclyffe* by Charlotte Mary Yonge *Bartleby* and *the Scrivener* by Herman Melville	Crimean War Construction of the Dolmabahçe Palace in Istanbul by Abdülmecid I.	
1854			Siege of Sevastopol	1854 Japan-US Treaty France and Great Britain declare war on Russia
1855		*Leaves of Grass* by Walt Whitman *Aurélia* by Gérard de Nerval	Abolition of the "jizya" levied on non-Muslims The establishment of the Şehremanet in Istanbul (the beginning of modern municipal administrations) The introduction of the telegraph in the Ottoman Empire	

(*Continued*)

Timeline

Date	Turkish Literature	World Literature and Culture	Turkish History and Politics	World History and Politics
1856			The establishment of the Bank-i Osmani	
			Proclamation of the Edict of Reform	
			Paris Peace Treaty was signed	
			Dolmabahçe Palace was built	
1857		*Madam Bovary* by Gustav Flaubert		
		Les Fleurs du mal by Charles Baudelaire		
		The Professor by Charlotte Brontë		
1858	*Tercüme-i Manzume* published by Şinasi			
1859	*Fransız Lisânından Nazmen Tercüme Eylediğim Bazı Eş'âr* by Şinasi	*A Tale of Two Cities* by Charles Dickens		*Origin of Species by Means of Natural Selection* by C. Darwin
	Muhaverat-ı Hikemiye by Münif Pasha	*Oblamov* by Ivan Goncharov		
		On Liberty by John Stuart Mill		
1860	*Tercüman-ı Ahvâl* published by Şinasi, Ağah Efendi	*The Mill on the Floss* by George Eliot		
	Şair Evlenmesi by Şinasi			
1861	The Encümen-i Şuara Group, which included Ziya Pasha and Namık Kemal, started to organize meetings	*Humiliated and Insulted* by Fyodor Dostoevsky	The death of Abdülmecid	The American Civil War began
		Great Expectations by Charles Dickens	The accession of Sultan Abdüllaziz to the throne	The Kingdom of Italy was founded
	Şark Theatre was established		The establishment of Cemiyet-i İlmiyye-i Osmaniye	

(Continued)

Timeline

Date	Turkish Literature	World Literature and Culture	Turkish History and Politics	World History and Politics
1862	*Tasvir-i Efkar* (newspaper) was published	*Les Misérables* by Victor Hugo		Richard Gatling patented the machine gun
	Telemak'ın Serüvenleri by Yusuf Kamil Pasha	*Salambo* by Gustav Flaubert		
	Encümen-i Şuara Community was dissolved.	*The House of the Dead* by Fyodor Dostoevsky		
	Müntehabat-ı Eş'âr (*Divân-ı Şinasi*) by Şinasi	*Fathers and Sons* by Ivan Turgenyev		
	Les Misérables translated			
1863	*Durûb-ı Emsâli Osmanîyye* by Şinasi			The fourth cholera pandemic
	A Karnig, Gülünya ve Dikran'in Dehşetlü Vefatleri (*Karnig, Gülünya and Dikran's Horrible Deaths*) by Hovhannes H. Balıkçıyan			
1864	*Robinson Crusoe* was translated	*Notes from Underground* by Fyodor Dostoevsky		International Workingmen's Association was founded
		Journey to the Center of the Earth by Jules Verne		

(*Continued*)

Timeline

Date	Turkish Literature	World Literature and Culture	Turkish History and Politics	World History and Politics
1865	Tercüme Cemiyeti was founded	*Alice's Adventures in Wonderland* by Lewis Carroll		The American Civil War ended
		Our Mutual Friend by Charles Dickens		*Law of Heredity* by Gregor Mendel
		From the Earth to the Moon by Jules Verne		
		Le Moulin Rouge by Xavier de Montépin		
1866	*Muhbir* published by Ali Suavi "Lisan-i Osmaninin Edebiyatı Hakkında Bazı Mülahazatı Şamildir" (Concerning Some Views on the Literature of the Ottoman Language) by Namık Kemal	*Crime and Punishment* by Fyodor Dostoevsky	Ali Pasha became Grand Vizier	Alfred Nobel invented dynamite
1867	Ottoman Theatre was established	*Das Kapital* by Karl Marx		
	While Nâmık Kemal fled to France in May 1867, he left the responsibility of *Tasvîr-i Efkar* to Recaizade Mahmut Ekrem.	*Peer Gynt* by Henrcik Ibsen		
		The Gambler by Fyodor Dostoevsky		

(*Continued*)

Timeline

Date	Turkish Literature	World Literature and Culture	Turkish History and Politics	World History and Politics
1868	*Şiir ve İnşâ* by Ziya Pasha	*Little Women* by Louisa May Alcott	The establishment of the Mekteb-i Sultani	
	Zafernâme by Ziya Pasha			
	Güllü Agop started working at the GedikPasha Theater in 1868 and made the building the center for his works. The name of his company started to be known as "Tiyatro-i Osmani" in time. The first Turkish play was staged when the Armenian play *Sezar Borcia* was staged in Turkish on April 16, 1868.			
	Hürriyet was published by Ziya Pasha and Namık Kemal			
	Bir Sefil Zevce (A Miserable Wife) by Hovsep Maruş			
1869	*Fezleke-i Tarih-i Osmânî* by Ahmet Vefik Pasha	*The Idiot* by Fyodor Dostoevsky	Daire-i İlmiye was founded	
		War and Peace by Leo Tolstoy		
		The Man Who Laughs by Victor Hugo		
		Sentimental Education by G.Flaubert		

(Continued)

Timeline

Date	Turkish Literature	World Literature and Culture	Turkish History and Politics	World History and Politics
1870	*Afife Anjelik* by Recaizade Mahmut Ekrem The first Ottoman humor magazine *Diyojen* published by Teodor Kasap *Letaif-i Rivayat* by Ahmet Mithat *Felsefe-i Zenân* (*Women's Philosophy*) by Ahmet Mithat	*Twenty Thousand Leagues Under the Seas* by Jules Verne *The Seagull* by Anton Chekov *The Island of Doctor Moreau* by H. G. Wells *Venus in Furs* by Leopold von Sacher-Masoch		
1871	Alexandre Dumas's *Monte Kristo* was translated. *Nağme-i Seher* by Recizade Mahmut Ekrem *Müsâmeretnâme* by Emin Nihat *Yeniçeriler* (*The Janissaries*) by Ahmet Mithat *Temâşa-i Dünya ve Cefakâr u Cefakeş* (*Contemplation of the World and Tormentor and Tormented*)	*Le bateau ivre* by Arthur Rimbaud		Paris Commune German unity established
1872	*Ibret*, with Namik Kemal as its chief writer, begins publication *Atala* was translated *Terkib-i Bent and Terci-i Bent* by Ziya Pasha *Taaşşuk-ı Talat ve Fitnat* by Şemsettin Sami	*Around the World in Eighty Days* by Jules Verne *The Birth of Tragedy* by Nietzsche *Demons* by Fyodor Dostoevsky *Marxism, Freedom, and the State* by Bakunin *Middlemarch* by George Eliot	The world's first car ferry "Suhulet" was designed by Hüseyin Haki Efendi, Director of the Company-i Hayriye, İskender Bey, General Inspector and Mehmet Bey, Chief Architect of Hasköy Shipyard	

(*Continued*)

Timeline

Date	Turkish Literature	World Literature and Culture	Turkish History and Politics	World History and Politics
1873	*Vatan Yahut Silistre* (*Homeland or Silistra*) by Namık Kemal			Economic crisis in Europe
	Pol ve Virjini by Bernardin de Saint-Pierre was translated			
	Çıngıraklı Tatar by Teodor Kasap			
	Zavallı Çocuk by Namık Kemal			
1874	*Akif Bey* by Namık Kemal	*Les Diaboliques* by Barbey d'Aurevilly	Darü'l-Fünun-ı Sultani was established; the beginning of civil engineering education in the Ottoman Empire	
	İşkilli Memo by Teodor Kasap	*Far from the Madding Crowd* by Thomas Hardy		
	Dünyaya İkinci Geliş by Ahmet Mithat Efendi			
	Harabat by Ziya Pasha			
	Hasan Mellah by Ahmet Mithat			

(*Continued*)

Timeline

Date	Turkish Literature	World Literature and Culture	Turkish History and Politics	World History and Politics
1875	Sabah newspaper was launched			
	Felatun Bey ile Rakım Efendi by Ahmet Mithat Efendi (Felâtun Bey and Râkım Efendi, which was published in 1875, was also published in Turkish in Armenian letters in 1879.			
	Hüseyin Fellâh by Ahmet Mithat Efendi			
	Pinti Hamid by Teodor Kasap			
	Karı-Koca Masalı (*A Husband and Wife's Tale*) by Ahmet Midhat Efendi			
	Gülnihal and *Intibah* (*The Awakening*) by Namık Kemal			

(*Continued*)

Timeline

Date	Turkish Literature	World Literature and Culture	Turkish History and Politics	World History and Politics
1876	*Tahríb-i Harabat,* *Celalettin Harzemşah* by Namık Kemal *Lehçe-i Osmani* by Ahmet Vefik Pasha	*Daniel Deronda* by George Eliot *The Adventures of Tom Sawyer* by Mark Twain	The deposition of Abdüllaziz Murad V's accession to the throne The dethronement of Murad V Abdelhamid II's ascension to the throne The establishment of the Majlis-i Mebûsan	Alexander Graham Bell patents the telephone
1877	*Aşk-ı Vatan (Love for Homeland)* by Zafer Hanım *Çengi -Çengi yahud, Daniş Çelebi-* by Ahmet Mithat Efendi *Meşahirü'n-Nisâ* by Mehmed Zihni	*Anna Karenina* by Leo Tolstoy *L'Assommoir* by Émile Zola *Den gaadefulde* by Knut Hamsun	Russo–Turkish War Fenn-i Resim ve Mimari Mektebi was established	Edison invented the phonograph
1878	Ahmet Mithat founded the newspaper *Terceman-ı Hakikat* *Alayın Kraliçesi'ne Zeyl* by Ahmet Mithat			
1879	*Ta'lîm-i Edebiyyât* by Recaizade Mahmud Ekrem *Hilal-i Ahmer* by Ahmet Mithat *Istikbal* published by Teodor Kasap, Ali Şefkati Telif ve Tercüme Dairesi was founded	*A Doll's House* by Henrik Ibsen "Rain of Diamonds" by Emile Waldteufel		

(Continued)

Timeline

Date	Turkish Literature	World Literature and Culture	Turkish History and Politics	World History and Politics
1880	*Les Misérables* translated by Şemsettin Sami	*The Brothers Karamazov* by Fyodor Dostoevsky		
		Ben-Hur by Lew Wallace		
		Nana by Emile Zola		
		Ab-i-Hayat (*Water of Life/Elixir*) by Muhammad Husain Azad		
		A Confession by Leo Tolstoy		
		Boule de Suif by Maupassant		
1881	*Eş'ar-ı Ziyâ* by Ziya Pasha	*La Maison Tellier* by Maupassant	The birth of Mustafa Kemal Atatürk	
	Cezmi by Namık Kemal			
	Karnaval by Ahmet Mithat			
1882	*Dürdane Hanım* by Ahmet Mithat	*An Enemy of the People* by Henrik Ibsen	The establishment of the Sanayi-i Nefise Mektebi and Osman Hamdi Bey becoming its director	
1883				
		The Adventures of Pinocchio by Carlo Collodi		
		The Merry Adventures of Robin Hood by Howard Pyle		
		The Metropolitan Opera House established		
		Thus Spake Zarathustra by Friedrich Wilhelm Nietzsche		

(*Continued*)

Timeline

Date	Turkish Literature	World Literature and Culture	Turkish History and Politics	World History and Politics
1884	*Yazmış Bulundum* by Muallim Naci *Esrar-ı Cinayat, Voltaire 20 Yaşında* and *Çerkez Özdenleri* (*Circassian Nobles*) by Ahmet Mithat	*The Wild Duck* by Henrick Ibsen *The Adventures of Huckleberry Finn* by Mark Twain *With Fire and Sword* by Henryk Sienkiewicz		
1885	*Kamus-i Fransevi* by Şemsettin Sami *Makber* by Abdülhak Hamit *Zemzeme III* by Ziya Pasha *Takip* by Namık Kemal *Bahtiyarlık* (*Happiness*), *Cinli Han, Bir Tövbekar* by Ahmet Mithat *Bir Kitabın Sergüzeşti* (*The Adventure of a Book*) by Ebüzziya Tevfik	*Germinal* by Emile Zola *Bel Ami* by Guy de Maupassant		
1886	*Takdir-i Elhan* by Recaizade Mahmut Ekrem *Demdeme* by Muallim Naci Halit Ziya Uşaklıgil's novel *Sefile* published in *Hizmet*	*L'Œuvre* (*The Masterpiece*) by Émile Zola *The Death of Ivan Ilyich* by Leo Tolstoy *Dr. Jekyll and Mr. Hyde* by Robert Louis Stevenson		

(*Continued*)

Timeline

Date	Turkish Literature	World Literature and Culture	Turkish History and Politics	World History and Politics
1887	Tâmât by Cenap Şahabettin	*The Flowers of Evil* by C. Baudelarie		Emile Berliner invented the gramophone
	Çifte İntikam, Fenni Bir Roman Yahut Amerika Doktorları and Çingene by Ahmet Mithat			
1888	Bir Muhtıranın Son Yaprakları and Nemide by Halit Ziya			Nikola Tesla invented the AC motor and transformer
	Bir İzdivacın Tarih-i Muaşakası by Halit Ziya Uşaklıgil			
	Ayine – Şık by Hüseyin Rahmi			
	Sergüzeşt by Sami Pashazade Sezai			
	Tarih-i Edebiyat-ı Osmaniye (History of Ottoman Literature) by Abdülhalim Memduh			

(*Continued*)

Timeline

Date	Turkish Literature	World Literature and Culture	Turkish History and Politics	World History and Politics
1889	Şık by Hüseyin Rahmi Gürpınar	The Kreutzer Sonata by Leo Tolstoy	The establishment of the Union and Progress Party	The Eiffel Tower is built 1889–1890 influenza pandemic
	The discovery of the Kül Tigin and Bilge Kagan Inscriptions.			
	Muhsin Bey yahut Şairliğin Hazin Bir Neticesi by Recaizade Mahmut Ekrem			
	Ahbar-ı Asara Ta'mim-i Enzar by Ahmet Mithat			
	Beyoğlu Sırları (Mysteries of Beyoğlu) by Epaminondas Kiriakides			
1890	Karabibik by Nabizade Nazım	Hedda Gabler by Henrik Ibsen		
	Küçük Şeyler by Sami Pashazade Sezai	Hunger by Knut Hamsun		
		The Principles of Psychology by William James		
		Paul et Virginie (Pavlos and Virginia) by Bernardin de Saint Pierre		

(Continued)

Timeline

Date	Turkish Literature	World Literature and Culture	Turkish History and Politics	World History and Politics
1891	*Tufanda mı Yoksa Turfa mı?* by Mizancı Murat	*The Picture of Dorian Gray* by Oscar Wilde		Trans Sibirya Demiryolu inşa edilmeye başlandı.
	Nâdîde by Hüseyin Cahit Yalçın			
	Müşahedat (*Observations*) by Ahmet Mithat			
	Ahmet Mithat and Fatma Aliye Topuz's novel *Hayal ve Hakikat* (*Dream and Reality*) which was published in *Tercüman-ı Hakikat*			
	Bir Ölünün Defteri by Halit Ziya			
	Seyyie-i Tesamüh by Nabizade Nâzım			
	The first issue of the magazine Servet-i Fünun was published			
	Diplomalı Kız (*The Girl With the Diploma/Degree*) by Ahmet Midhat Efendi			
1892		*The Master Builder* by Henrick Ibsen		
		Sherlock Holmes by Arthur Conan Doyle		

(*Continued*)

Timeline

Date	Turkish Literature	World Literature and Culture	Turkish History and Politics	World History and Politics
1893	*Ahmet Metin ve Şirzat yahut Roman İçinde Roman* and *Bir Muharrire-i Osmaniyenin Neşeti* (*Emergence of an Ottoman Woman Writer*) by Ahmet Mithat *Hulasa-i Ilm-i Hesap* by Emine Semiye Önasya	*From the New World* by Dvorak		New Zealand became the first country where women can vote
1894	Mehmed Fuad, a member of the Mâliye Mektûbî Kalemi, and Artin Asaduryan published the magazine *Malumat*	*Jungle Book* by Rudyard Kipling		
1895	*Ferdi ve Şürekası* by Halit Ziya Uşaklıgil *Şemsa* by Recaizade Mahmut Ekrem *Taaffüf* by Ahmet Mithat *Muharrir Kadınlar* (*Writer Women*) by Avanzade Mehmed Süleyman *Hanımlara Mahsus Gazete* published *Muharrerat-ı Nisvan* by Mustafa Reşid	*Jude the Obscure* by Thomas Hardy *Ekmekçi Hatun* (*La Porteuse de Pain*) by Xavier de Montepin		The Lumiere Brothers produced a portable camera Wilhelm Roentgen discovered X-rays

(*Continued*)

Timeline

Date	Turkish Literature	World Literature and Culture	Turkish History and Politics	World History and Politics
1896	*Zehra* by Nabizade Nazım			The first modern Olympic Games were held in Athens
	The beginning of the Edebiyat-ı Cedide period when Tevfik Fikret took over the management of the literary pages of *Servet-i Fünun*			
	W. Thomsen's publication of Kül Tigin and Bilge Kagan Inscriptions			
	Mai ve Siyah (The Blue and the Black) by Halit Ziya			
	Fatma Fahrünnisa's novel *Dilharap*, which was published in the *Hanımlara Mahsus Gazete*			
	Mihr-i Dil by Vecihi			
	Sadme-i Şebab by Mehmet Celal			
	Araba Sevdası by Recaizade Mahmut Ekrem			

(*Continued*)

Timeline

Date	Turkish Literature	World Literature and Culture	Turkish History and Politics	World History and Politics
1897	The discovery of the Tonyukuk Inscription.	*Dracula* by Bram Stoker		
	The publication of the article titled "Dekadanlar" (Decadents) written by Ahmet Midhat in *Sabah* newspaper to criticize *Servet-i Fünun writers and poets.*			
	Bu muydu? by Halit Ziya			
	Refet by Fatma Aliye			
	İffet and *Mutallaka* by Hüseyin Rahmi Gürpınar			
	Ferda-yı Garam by Mehmed Rauf			
	Uhuvvet (Fraternity) by Selma Rıza			
	Nevsal-i Nisvan by Avanzade Mehmed Süleyman			
	Le Juif Errant by Eugène Sue translated as *Serseri Yahudi*			

(*Continued*)

Timeline

Date	Turkish Literature	World Literature and Culture	Turkish History and Politics	World History and Politics
1898	*Türkçe Şiirler* by Mehmet Emin Yurdakul	*Paris* by Émile Zola		
	Zavallı Necdet by Safvet Nezihi	*The Turn of the Screw* by Henry James		
	Hayal İçinde by Hüseyin Cahit Yalçın			
	Mürebbiye by Hüseyin Rahmi			
	Saime by Recaizade M. Ekrem			
1899	*Mürebbiye* and *Metres* by Hüseyin Rahmi *Şeytankaya Tılsımı* and *Eski Mektuplar* Ahmet Mithat *Udî* (*The Ud Player*) and *Levayih-i Hayat* (Scenes of Life) by Fatma Aliye	"The Lady with the Dog" by Anton Chekhov *Heart of Darkness* by Joseph Conrad *The Yellow Wallpaper* by Charlotte Perkins Gilman		
	Aşk-ı Memnu (*Forbidden Love*) by Halit Ziya	*The Awakening* by Kate Chopin *The Interpretation of Dreams* by Sigmund Freud		

(Continued)

Timeline

Date	Turkish Literature	World Literature and Culture	Turkish History and Politics	World History, Science and Politics
1900	*Eylül* by Mehmet Rauf *Rubab-ı Şikeste* by Tevfik Fikret Fatma Fahrünissa's novel *Küçük Hikâye* (*Small Story*), was published in the *Hanımlara Mahsus Gazete*	*Lord Jim* by Joseph Conrad *The Wonderful Wizard of Oz* by L. Frank Baum *The Knights of the Cross* by Henryk Sienkiewicz		
1901	*Kamus-i Türki* by Şemsettin Sami	*Buddenbrooks* by Thomas Mann *Three Sisters* by Anton Chekhov The first Nobel Prize in Literature was awarded in 1901 to Sully Prudhomme of France		
1902	*Sis* by Tevfik Fikret	*The Power of Darkness* by Leo Tolstoy *Heart of Darkness* by Joseph Conrad		
1903		*The Call of the Wild* by Jack London		
1904	*Üç Tarz-ı Siyaset* by Yusuf Akçuralı	*Nostromo* by Joseph Conrad *Where Angels Fear to Tread* by E. M. Forster Anton Chekhov's play *The Cherry Orchard* first performed		
1905	"Sabah Olursa" (If the Morning Comes) by Tevfik Fikret	*White Fang* by Jack London *The Return of Sherlock Holmes* by Arthur Conan Doyle		
1906		*The Mother* by Maxim Gorky *Personae* by Ezra Pound		
1907		*The Wonderful Adventures of Nils* by Selma Lagerlöf		

(*Continued*)

Timeline

Date	Turkish Literature	World Literature and Culture	Turkish History and Politics	World History, Science and Politics
1908	*Renan Müdafaanamesi* by Namık Kemal *Asabi Kız* by Ahmet Rasim *Sefalet (Poverty)* by Emine Semiye	*The Tendrils of the Vine* by Colette		
1909	*Kadınlar Arasında* and *Bir İzdivacın Tarihi* by Safvet Nezihi *Heyula* by Halide Edip Adıvar	*Martin Eden* by Jack London		
1910	*Tarih-i Osmani Encümeni Mecmuası* (later called *Belleten*)			
1911	*Safahat* by Mehmet Âkif Ersoy *Genç Kalemler Dergisi* *Bomba* and *Primo Türk Çocuğu* by Ömer Seyfettin Ziya Gökalp published *Turan* in *Genç Kalemler* *Halûk'un Defteri* by Tevfik Fikret		Italo-Turkish War	
1912	*Genç Kız Kalbi* by Mehmet Rauf *Handan* by Halide Edip Adıvar Telif ve Tercüme Heyeti was founded	*Death in Venice* by Thomas Mann	Balkan Wars	
1913	*Yeni Turan* by Halide Edip Adıvar *Türk Edebiyatı Tarihinde Usul (Method in Turkish Literary History)* by Mehmet Fuat Köprülü	*Pygmalion* by George Bernard Shaw *Sons and Lovers* by D. H. Lawrence		
1914	*Kızıl Elma* by Ziya Gökalp "Târîh-i Kadîm'e Zeyl" by Tevfik Fikret *Yeni Osmanlı Tarih-i Edebiyatı (The New History of Ottoman Literature)* by Mehmet Fuat Köprülü and Şahabettin Süleyman	*Dubliners* by James Joyce		World War I

(*Continued*)

Timeline

Date	Turkish Literature	World Literature and Culture	Turkish History and Politics	World History, Science and Politics
1915	"Türk Edebiyatının Menşei" (The Origins of Turkish Literature) by Mehmet Fuat Köprülü	*The Metamorphosis* by Franz Kafka	The deportation of Armenian Intellectuals in 24 April 1915 Great Catastrophe	
1916		*A Portrait of the Artist as a Young Man* by James Joyce		Albert Einstein's *Relativity*
1917	The first and last editions of Halide Edip's novel *Mev'ud Hüküm* published in *Yeni Mecmua* "Çakmak" (The Lighter) and "Külâh" (The Conical Hat) by Ömer Seyfettin			October Revolution
1918	*Türkleşmek, İslamlaşmak, Muasırlaşmak* by Ziya Gökalp *Diyorlar Ki* by Ruşen Eşref Unaydın		Armistice of Mudros	
1919	*Memleket Hikâyeleri* by Refik Halit Karay *Tanrı Misafiri* by Reşat Nuri Güntekin *Türk Edebiyatında İlk Mutasavvıflar* (Early Mystics in Turkish Literature) by Mehmet Fuad Köprülü		Turkish War of Independence	
1920	*Gönül Hanım* by Ahmet Hikmet Müftüoğlu	*This Side of Paradise* by F. Scott Fitzgerald *The Mysterious Affair at Styles* by Agatha Christie *Beyond the Pleasure Principle* by Sigmund Freud		
1921	*Göl Saatleri* by Ahmet Haşim *Dergâh* magazine begins publication *Nur Baba* by Yakup Kadri Karaosmanoğlu *Kara Kitap* by Suat Derviş	*Tractatus Logico Philosophicus* by Ludwig Wittgenstein	Occupation of Istanbul	

(Continued)

Timeline

Date	Turkish Literature	World Literature and Culture	Turkish History and Politics	World History, Science and Politics
1922	*Ateşten Gömlek* by Halide Edip *Sisli Geceler* by Halide Nusret Zorlutuna *Sözde Kızlar* by Peyami Safa *Kiralık Konak* by Yakup Kadri Karaosmanoğlu *Çalıkuşu* by Reşat Nuri Güntekin *Yıkık Gönüller* (*Broken Hearts*) by Hadiye Hümeyra *Tarih-i Edebiyat Dersleri* (*Lectures on Literary History*) by İbrahim Necmi Dilmen	*Ulysses* by James Joyce *Siddhartha* by Hermann Hesse *Duino Elegies* and *Sonnets to Orpheus* by Rainer Maria Rilke	Abolition of the Ottoman sultanate	
1923	*Türçülüğün Esasları* by Ziya Gökalp *Kırık Hayatlar* (*Broken Lives*) by Halit Ziya Uşaklıgil	*The Prophet* by Kahlil Gibran *The Good Soldier Švejk* by Jaroslav Hašek *The Murder on the Links* by Agatha Christie	Declaration of the republic in Turkey Ankara became the capital of Republic of Turkey	
1924	*Milliyet Nazariyeleri ve Millî Hayat* (*Theories of Nationalism and National Life*) by Mehmet İzzet	*Der Zauberberg* (*The Magic Mountain*) by Thomas Mann *A Passage to India* by E. M. Forster	Abolition of the caliphate The second political party of the Turkish Republic, the Progressive Republican Party, was founded Turkish Constitution of 1924	
1925	Start of publication of the *Resimli Ay* *Türk Teceddüt Edebiyatı Tarihi* (*History of Turkish New Literature*) by İsmail Habip Sevük	*The Great Gatsby* by F. Scott Fitzgerald *Mrs. Dalloway* by Virginia Woolf *Der Prozeß* (*The Trial*) by Franz Kafka *Heart of a Dog* by Mikhail Bulgakov	Hat Revolution The closure of dervish lodges and mausoleums The changes to calendars, clocks and measurements The School of Ankara Law opened	

(*Continued*)

Timeline

Date	Turkish Literature	World Literature and Culture	Turkish History and Politics	World History, Science and Politics
1926	*Çoban Çeşmesi* by Faruk Nafiz Çamlıbel *Yüksek Ökçeler* by Ömer Seyfettin *Vurun Kahpeye* by Halide Edip Adıvar *Bir Kadın Düşmanı* by Reşat Nuri Güntekin	Ernest Hemingway's *The Sun Also Rises; Das Schloß (The Castle)* by Franz Kafka	Turkish civil code Law on the Organization of Education	
1927	*Hüküm Gecesi* by Yakup Kadri Karaosmanoğlu Remzi Kitabevi is a publishing house founded in 1927 by Remzi Bengi in the Beyazıt district of Istanbul	*In Search of Lost Time* by Marcel Proust *To the Lighthouse* by Virginia Woolf *Being and Time* by Martin Heidegger	Industrial Incentive Law First woman lawyer Süreyya Ağaoğlu takes office	
1928	*Kaldırımlar* by Necip Fazıl Kısakürek *Sodom ve Gomore* by Yakup Kadri Karaosmanoğlu *Yeşil Gece* by Reşat Nuri Güntekin The publication of *Yedi Meşale* *Jokond ile Si-Ya-U* by Nâzım Hikmet Ran *İnkılâbın Felsefesi (The Philosophy of the Revolution)* by Halil Nimetullah Öztürk	*The Threepenny Opera* by Bertholt Brecht *Gypsy Ballads* by Federico Garcia Lorca *Orlando: A Biography* by Virginia Woolf	The alphabet revolution The sentence "Islam is the official religion of the Republic of Turkey" was removed from the Constitution	
1929	*Sağanak (Downpour)* by Yakup Kadri Karaosmanoğlu	*The Sound and the Fury* by William Faulkner *A Farewell to Arms* by Ernest Hemingway *All Quiet on the Western Front* by Erich Maria Remarque *A Room of One's Own* by Virginia Woolf *The School and Society* by John Dewey	Nation's school Land reform First Turkish woman judge was appointed Courses on using Turkish instead of Arabic and Persian opened	

(Continued)

Timeline

Date	Turkish Literature	World Literature and Culture	Turkish History and Politics	World History, Science and Politics
1930	*Dokuzuncu Hariciye Koğuşu* by Peyami Safa *Yaprak Dökümü* by Reşat Nuri Güntekin	*As I Lay Dying* by William Faulkner	Kubilay was assassinated by opponents of the Republic The Free Republican Party, the third party of the Republic, was founded	
1931			The establishment of the Turkish History and Language Association Suat Rasim, the first female surgeon, receives her diploma	
1932	*Yaban (The Stranger)* by Yakup Kadri Karaosmanoğlu *Zeytindağı* by Falih Rıfkı Atay *Benerci Kendini Niçin Öldürdü and Kafatası (Skull)* by Nâzım Hikmet Ran *Divan Edebiyatı Antolojisi (Anthology of Divan Literature)* by Mehmet Fuat Köprülü *Kahraman (Hero), Akın (Influx) and Özyurt (Homeland)* by Faruk Nafiz Çamlıbel *İnkılap Çocukları (The Revolution's Children)* by Yaşar Nabi Nayır	*Brave New World* by Aldous Huxley *Journey to the East* by Hermann Hesse *Journey to the End of The Night* by Louis-Ferdinand Céline	The language revolution Turkey becomes a member of the League of Nations Adile Ayda appointed as the first female official at the Ministry of Foreign Affairs On January 30, 1932, the first Turkish call to prayer was recited by Hafiz Rıfat Bey at Fatih Mosque	

(*Continued*)

Timeline

Date	Turkish Literature	World Literature and Culture	Turkish History and Politics	World History, Science and Politics
1933	*Vergi Hırsızı* (*Tax Thief*) by Reşat Nuri Güntekin *Gazi Çocukları İçin* (*For the Ghazi Children*) by Aka Gündüz *Gavur İmam* (*Giaour İmam*) by Burhan Cahit *Kızıl Çağlayan* (*Red Waterfall*) by Nihat Sami Banarlı *29 Birinci Teşrin* (*October 29*) by Vedat Nedim Tör *On İnkılap* (*The Ten Revolutions*) by Vasfi Mahir Kocatürk *Mavi Yıldırım* (*Blue Lightning*) by Aka Gündüz	*La Condition Humaine* (*Man's Fate*) by André Malraux	The University Reform Sümerbank and Halkbank were established Recognition of women's right to vote and be elected in Turkey	
1934	*Ayaşlı ve Kiracılar* by Memduh Şevket Esendal	*Murder on the Orient Express* by Agatha Christie	The Surname Law Hagia Sophia mosque turned into museum The law on the abolition of epithets and titles	
1935		The first paperback published by *Penguin Books*		
1936	*Sinekli Bakkal* by Halide Edip Adıvar *Semaver* by Sait Faik *Atatürk Köyünde Uçak Günü* (*A Flight Day in the Village of Atatürk*) by Vehbi Cem Aşkun	*Absalom, Absalom!* by William Faulkner *Gone with the Wind* by Margaret Mitchell		
1937	*Kuyucaklı Yusuf* by Sabahattin Ali	*Of Mice and Men* by John Steinbeck *The Hobbit, or There and Back Again* by J. R. R. Tolkien	Secularism in Turkey Dersim rebellion	

(*Continued*)

Timeline

Date	Turkish Literature	World Literature and Culture	Turkish History and Politics	World History, Science and Politics
1938	*Üç İstanbul* by Mithat Cemal Kuntay *Bir Adam Yaratmak* by Necip Fazıl Kısakürek *On Yılın Destanı (The Epic of Ten Years)* by Halit Fahri Ozansoy *Sönmeyen Ateş (The Fire That Doesn't Burn Out)* by Nahit Sırrı Örik	*La Nausée (Nausea)* by Jean-Paul Sartre	Mustafa Kemal Atatürk died and was replaced by former officer and prime minister İsmet İnönü	
1939	*Sarnıç* by Sait Faik *Ateş (Fire)* by Faruk Nafiz Çamlıbel	*The Grapes of Wrath* by John Steinbeck		World War II
1940	*Çocuk ve Allah* by Fazıl Hüsnü Dağlarca *Karagöz Stepte (Karagöz on the Steppe)* by Ercüment Lav	*For Whom the Bell Tolls* by Ernest Hemingway		
1941	*Fahim Bey ve Biz* by Abdülhak Şinasi Hisar Orhan Veli, Melih Cevdet Anday and Oktay Rifat published *Garip*			
1942		*Le Mythe de Sisyphe (The Myth of Sisyphus)* and *L'Étranger (The Stranger)* by Albert Camus *The Man Without Qualities* by Robert Musil		
1943	*Abdullah Efendi'nin Rüyaları* by Ahmet Hamdi Tanpınar *Sebil ve Güvercinler* by Ziya Osman Saba	*Anti-Semite and Jew* and *Being and Nothingness* by Jean-Paul Sartre *Four Quartets* by T. S. Eliot *The Little Prince* by Antoine de Saint-Exupéry		
1944				

(*Continued*)

Timeline

Date	Turkish Literature	World Literature and Culture	Turkish History and Politics	World History, Science and Politics
1945	*Maske ve Ruh (Mask and Soul)* by Halide Edip Adıvar	*Animal Farm* by George Orwell *A History of Western Philosophy And Its Connection with Political and Social Circumstances from the Earliest Times to the Present Day* by Bertrand Russell		United Nations was founded UNESCO was founded The atomic bombings of Hiroshima and Nagasaki
1946	*Rahatı Kaçan Ağaç* by Melih Cevdet Anday *Aganta Burina Burinata* by Halikarnas Balıkçısı *Kıskanmak* by Nahir Sırrı Örik *Otuz Beş Yaş* by Cahit Sıtkı Tarancı	*Zorba the Greek* by Nikos Kazantzakis	Democrat Party was founded	
1947		*The Diary of a Young Girl* by Anne Frank *Doctor Faustus* by Thomas Mann *La Peste (The Plague)* by Albert Camus *A Streetcar Named Desire* by Tennessee Williams	Marshall Plan	
1948	*Resimli Türk Edebiyatı Tarihi (The Illustrated History of Turkish Literature)* by Nihat Sami Banarlı *Lüzumsuz Adam* by Sait Faik			
1949	*Huzur (A Mind At Peace)* by Ahmet Hamdi Tanpınar *Matmazel Norilya'nın Koltuğu (The Armchair of Mademoiselle Noralia)* by Peyami Safa *Arz-ı Hal* by Turgut Uyar 19uncu Asır Türk Edebiyatı Tarihi (Nineteenth-Century Turkish Literary History) by Ahmet Hamdi Tanpınar	*Nineteen Eighty-Four* by George Orwell *Death of a Salesman* by Arthur Miller *The Second Sex* by Simone de Beauvoir *Confessions of a Mask* by Yukio Mishima		NATO was founded Mao Zedong, the Communist Party leader who led the Red Revolution, founded the People's Republic of China

(Continued)

Timeline

Date	Turkish Literature	World Literature and Culture	Turkish History and Politics	World History, Science and Politics
1950	*Bizim Köy* (*Our Village*) by Mahmut Makal *Mahalle Kahvesi* by Sait Faik	*The Bald Soprano* by Eugène Ionesco *I, Robot* by Isaac Asimov *Canto General* by Pablo Neruda	Democrat Party came to power Celal Bayar became the third president of the Republic of Turkey. The first Democratic Party government headed by Adnan Menderes was formed	Korean War
1951	*Yalnızız* by Peyami Safa *Türk Dili*, a monthly language and literature magazine published by the Turkish Language Association *Havada Bulut, Kumpanya* and *Havuzbaş* by Sait Faik	*The Catcher in the Rye* by J. D. Salinger	Decision to remove books by Russian authors from school libraries	
1952	*Dost* by Vüs'at O. Bener *Bozkırda Günler* by Talip Apaydın *Köyümden* by Mahmut Makal	*The Old Man and the Sea* by Ernest Hemingway *Invisible Man* by Ralph Ellison		
1953	*Om Mani Padme Hum* by Asaf Hâlet Çelebi *Evler* by Behçet Necatigil *Şişhane'ye Yağmur Yağıyordu* (Rain was Falling on Şişhane) by Haldun Taner *Bozbulanık* (*Murky Affairs*) by Nezihe Meriç	*Waiting for Godot and The Unnamable* by Samuel Beckett *Casino Royale* by Ian Fleming *Fahrenheit 451* by Ray Bradbury		The first video tape recorder, a helical scan recorder, is invented by Norikazu Sawazaki.
1954	*Sisler Bulvarı* by Attila İlhan *Bereketli Topraklar Üzerinde* by Orhan Kemal *Ayışığında Çalışkur* (*Çalışkur Under the Moonlight*) by Haldun Taner	*The Lord of the Rings* by J. R. R. Tolkien *Lord of the Flies* by William Golding *The Second World War* by Winston Churchill		

(*Continued*)

Timeline

Date	Turkish Literature	World Literature and Culture	Turkish History and Politics	World History, Science and Politics
1955	The Sait Faik Story Prize begins to be awarded. Sabahattin Kudret Aksal (*Gazoz Ağacı*) and Haldun Taner (*On İkiye Bir Var*) receive the first prize *Yağmur Kaçağı* by Attila İlhan *İnce Mehmed* by Yaşar Kemal *Haney Yaşamak* by Tahsin Yücel *Çarığımı Yitirdiğim Tarla* by Mehmet Başaran	*Lolita* by Vladimir Nabokov *The Talented Mr. Ripley* by Patricia Highsmith	Istanbul pogrom (6–7 September)	Vietnam War
1956	*Rüzgâr Saati* by Gülten Akın *Esir Şehrin İnsanları* by Kemal Tahir *Perçemli Sokak* by Oktay Rifat Türkiye İş Bankası Kültür Yayınları was founded by Hasan Âli Yücel *Topal Koşma* (*Lame Running*) by Nezihe Meriç			The hard disk drive is invented by IBM.
1957	*Yerçekimli Karanfil* (*The Gravitational Carnation*) by Edip Cansever *Hababam Sınıfı* by Rıfat Ilgaz	*On the Road* by Jack Kerouac *Doctor Zhivago* by Boris Pasternak *Homo Faber* by Max Frisch *The Birthday Party* by Harold Pinter		Sputnik 1, is built and launched by the Soviet Union

(*Continued*)

Timeline

Date	Turkish Literature	World Literature and Culture	Turkish History and Politics	World History, Science and Politics
1958	*Üvercinka* by Cemal Süreya TDK Awards begin to be awarded. In the first year, Fazıl Hüsnü Dağlarca's poem *Delice Böcek*, Oktay Akbal's novel *Suçumuz İnsan Olmak*, and Tahsn Yücel's short story *Düşlerin Ölümü* were awarded *Bunaltı* by Demir Özlü *Umutsuzlar Parkı (The Park of the Despairing)* by Edip Cansever *Galile Denizi (The Sea of Galilee)* by İlhan Berk			
1959	*Aylak Adam* by Yusuf Atılgan *Yılanların Öcü* by Fakir Baykurt *Kınar Hanımın Denizleri (Kınar Hanım's Oceans)* by Ece Ayhan *Petrol* by Edip Cansever *Soğuk Otların Altında (Under the Cold Weeds)* by Ülkü Tamer *Körfez (The Bay)* by Sezai Karakoç *Dünyanın En Güzel Arabistanı (The Most Beautiful Arabia in the World)* by Turgut Uyar	*The Tin Drum* by Günter Grass *Billiards at Half-past Nine* by Heinrich Böll *Rhinocéros (Rhinoceros)* by Eugène Ionesco *In the Labyrinth* by Alain Robbe-Grillet		
1960	*Kestim Kara Saçlarımı* by Gülten Akın *Bodur Minareden Öte* by Yusuf Atılgan *Ben Sana Mecburum* by Attila İlhan *Edebiyatımızda İsimler Sözlüğü* by Behçet Necatigil Sezai Karakoç started to publish *Diriliş* *Beş Romancı Tartışıyor (Five Novelists Debate)* by Fakir Baykurt	*To Kill a Mockingbird* by Harper Lee	1960 Turkish coup d'état (27 May)	

(Continued)

Timeline

Date	Turkish Literature	World Literature and Culture	Turkish History and Politics	World History, Science and Politics
1961	*Kendi Gök Kubbemiz* by Yahya Kemal *Yuvarlağın Köşeleri* by Özdemir Asaf *Hallaç* by Leyla Erbil *Korsan Çıkmazı* by Nezihe Meriç *Başkanın Ankara Dönüşü* by Behzat Ay	*Solaris* by Stanisław Lem *Catch-22* by Joseph Heller		
1962	*Eski Şiirin Rüzgârıyla* by Yahya Kemal *Saatleri Ayarlama Ensitütüsü* (*The Time Regulation Institute*) by Ahmet Hamdi Tanpınar *Tutkulu Perçem* (*Passionate Bangs*) by Sevgi Soysal	*A Clockwork Orange* by Anthony Burgess *Labyrinths* by Jorge Luis Borges		
1963	*Küçük Ağa* by Tarık Buğra *Kurtlar Sofrası* (*Dining with the Wolves*) by Attila İlhan *Yer Demir Gök Bakır* by Yaşar Kemal *Troya'da Ölüm Vardı* by Bilge Karasu "Şiiri Bölmek" ("To Divide Poetry") by Edip Cansever	*The Bell Jar* by Sylvia Plath *Hopscotch* by Julio Cortazar		
1964	*İbrahim Efendi Konağı* by Sâmiha Ayverdi *Tragedyalar* (*Tragedies*) by Edip Cansever			

(*Continued*)

Timeline

Date	Turkish Literature	World Literature and Culture	Turkish History and Politics	World History, Science and Politics
1965	*Bakışsız Bir Kedi Kara* by Ece Ayhan Nazım Hikmet's books, which had been banned from publication since 1936, were once again published by Yön Publishing. *Kuvayi Milliye Destanı* was published Ahmet Tevfik Küflü founded Bilgi Publishing House in Ankara *Menekşeli Bilinç (Violet Consciousness)* by Nezihe Meriç *Yanık Saraylar (Burnt Palaces)* by Sevim Burak			
1966	*Memleketimden İnsan Manzaraları* by Nâzım Hikmet Ran *Çağrılmayan Yakup (Uninvited Yakup)* by Edip Cansever	*The Master and Margarita* by Mikhail Bulgakov		
1967		*Cien años de soledad (One Hundred Years of Solitude)* by Gabriel García Márquez *Žert (The Joke)* by Milan Kundera		
1968	*Hasretinden Prangalar Eskittim* by Ahmed Arif *Tante Rosa (Aunt Rosa)* by Sevgi Soysal *Gecede* by Leyla Erbil *Fosforlu Cevriye and Ankara Mahpusu* by Suat Derviş	*Do Androids Dream of Electric Sheep?* by Philip K. Dick *A Wizard of Earthsea* by Ursula K. Le Guin		May 68

(Continued)

Timeline

Date	Turkish Literature	World Literature and Culture	Turkish History and Politics	World History, Science and Politics
1969	*Han Duvarları* by Faruk Nafiz Çamlıbel *Kurt Kanunu* by Kemal Tahir *Sancho'nun Sabah Yürüyüşü* by Haldun Taner	*The French Lieutenant's Woman* by John Fowles *The Meaning of Contemporary Realism* by Georg Lukács		
1970	*Uzun Sürmüş Bir Günün Akşamı* by Bilge Karasu *Divan* by Turgut Uyar *Yürümek* by Sevgi Soysal			
1971	*Tutunamayanlar (The Disconnected)* by Oğuz Atay *Tuhaf Bir Kadın (A Strange Woman)* by Leyla Erbil *Parasız Yatılı* by Füruzan *Edebiyatımızda Eserler Sözlüğü* by Behçet Necatigil		1971 Turkish military memorandum (12 March)	
1972	*Büyük Gözaltı (Extreme Surveillance)* by Çetin Altan			
1973	*Ölmeye Yatmak (Lying Down to Die)* by Adalet Ağaoğlu *Tehlikeli Oyunlar* by Oğuz Atay *Anayurt Oteli (Motherland Hotel)* by Yusuf Atılgan *Yedi Güzel Adam* by Cahit Zarifoğlu *Benim Sinemalarım* by Füruzan *Yenişehir'de Bir Öğle Vakti (Noontime in Yenişehir)* by Sevgi Soysal *Bıçağın Ucu (The Tip of the Knife)* by Attila İlhan	*The Gulag Archipelago* by Aleksandr Solzhenitsyn		

(Continued)

Timeline

Date	Turkish Literature	World Literature and Culture	Turkish History and Politics	World History, Science and Politics
1974	*Yaralısın* by Erdal Öz *47'liler (Generation of '47)* by Füruzan *Yeni Türk Edebiyatı Antolojisi (New Turkish Literature Anthology)* by Mehmet Kaplan *Sırtlan Payı (The Share of the Hyena)* by Attila İlhan		Turkish invasion of Cyprus	
1975	*Bir Gün Tek Başına (One Day On Your Own)* by Vedat Türkali *Korkuyu Beklerken* by Oğuz Atay *Karartma Geceleri (Blackout Nights)* by Rıfat Ilgaz *Şafak (The Dawn)* by Sevgi Soysal	*The Book of Sand* by Jorge Luis Borges *Terra Nostra* by Carlos Fuentes		
1976	*Sevgilerde* by Behçet Necatigil *Bir Hülya Adamının Romanı, Ahmet Hamdi Tanpınar (The Novel of a Dreamer, Ahmet Hamdi Tanpınar)* by Orhan Okay *Anthology of Modern Turkish Drama* by Tâlât Sait Halman *Ben Ruhi Bey Nasılım (How Am I Ruhi Bey)* by Edip Cansever			
1977	The Sedat Simavi Foundation Literature Prize begins to be awarded. The first prizes were awarded to *Horoz* by Fazıl Hüsnü Dağlarca and *Üç Yirmi Dört Saat* by Peride Celal	*The Shining* by Stephen King		
1978	*Eski Bahçe* by Tezer Özlü *Jaguar* by Peride Celal *Yaraya Tuz Basmak (Rubbing Salt into the Wound)* by Attila İlhan			

(Continued)

Timeline

Date	Turkish Literature	World Literature and Culture	Turkish History and Politics	World History, Science and Politics
1979	*Gül Yetiştiren Adam* by Rasim Özdenören *Yürekte Bukağı* by Tomris Uyar *Bir Düğün Gecesi (A Wedding Night)*	*The Hitchhiker's Guide to the Galaxy* by Douglas Adams *Se una notte d'inverno un viaggiatore (If On a Winter's Night a Traveler)* by Italo Calvino *Kniha smíchu a zapomnění (The Book of Laughter and Forgetting)* by Milan Kundera		
1980	İletişim Publishing House was founded in the period when the military government was replaced by civilian parties after the coup d'état of September 12, 1980	*Waiting for the Barbarians* by J. M. Coetzee *Il nome della rosa (The Name of the Rose)* by Umberto Eco	1980 Turkish coup d'état (12 Septermber)	
1981	*Şiir Alayı* by Can Yücel Adam Publications, publishing house founded in 1981 Can Publishing was founded in 1981 by Erdal Öz *Dersaadet'te Sabah Ezanları (Morning Prayers in Dersaadet)* by Attila İlhan	*Midnight's Children* by Salman Rushdie		
1982	*Cevdet Bey ve Oğulları* by Orhan Pamuk Metis Publications founded *Bezik Oynayan Kadınlar (Women Playing Bezique)* by Edip Cansever	*Memorial do Convento (Baltasar and Blimunda)* by José Saramago *Ham on Rye* by Charles Bukowski *The Book of Disquiet* by Fernando Pessoa		

(*Continued*)

Timeline

Date	Turkish Literature	World Literature and Culture	Turkish History and Politics	World History, Science and Politics
1983	*Sevgili Arsız Ölüm* by Latife Tekin *Kamelyasız Kadınlar* by Selim İleri *Afrika Dansı* by Sevim Burak *Sessiz Ev* by Orhan Pamuk *Türk Romanına Eleştirel Bir Bakış I (Critical Approaches to the Turkish Novel)* by Berna Moran		1983 Turkish general election Motherland Party was founded Turkish Republic of Northern Cyprus was established	
1984	*Berci Kristin Çöp Masalları* by Latife Tekin			The first commercially available cell phone is created by Motorola
1985	*Gece* by Bilge Karasu Turkish Publishers Association was founded *Karanlığın Günü* by Leyla Erbil *Beyaz Kale* by Orhan Pamuk	*The Handmaid's Tale* by Margaret Atwood *El amor en los tiempos del cólera (Love in the Time of Cholera)* by Gabriel García Márquez *Perfume* by Patrick Süskind		
1986		*The Old Gringo* by Carlos Fuentes *Extinction* by Thomas Bernhard		
1987	*Kadının Adı Yok* by Duygu Asena *Hayır . . . (No . . .)* by Adalet Ağaoğlu	*Beloved* by Toni Morrison	Turgut Özal became President	
1988	*O Karanlıkta Biz (Us in that Darkness)* by Attila İlhan	*The Satanic Verses* by Salman Rushdie *Manufacturing Consent: The Political Economy of the Mass Media* by Noam Chomsky *Il pendolo di Foucault (Foucault's Pendulum)* by Umberto Eco		

(Continued)

Timeline

Date	Turkish Literature	World Literature and Culture	Turkish History and Politics	World History, Science and Politics
1989	*Hüzün ki En Çok Yakışandır Bize* by Hilmi Yavuz *Bir Kara Derin Kuyu* by Nezihe Meriç	*The Remains of the Day* by Kazuo Ishiguro *A Prayer for Owen Meany* by John Irving		
1990	*Kara Kitap* (*The Black Book*) by Orhan Pamuk			African National Congress Leader Nelson Mandela regains his freedom after 27 years in prison The World Wide Web is first introduced to the public by English engineer and computer scientist Sir Tim Berners-Lee
1991		*O Evangelho Segundo Jesus Cristo (The Gospel According to Jesus Christ)* by José Saramago	Gulf War	The Soviet Union collapsed
1992	*Gâvur Mahallesi* by Mıgırdiç Margosyan			Bosnian War
1993				
1994				
1995	*Puslu Kıtalar Atlası* by İhsan Oktay Anar	*Ensaio sobre a cegueira (Blindness)* by José Saramago *Nejimaki-dori kuronikuru (The Wind-Up Bird Chronicle)* by Haruki Murakami		
1996		*Infinite Jest* by David Foster Wallace *Fight Club* by Chuck Palahniuk *Selected Stories* by Alice Munro		
1997	*Pinhân* by Elif Şafak	*Harry Potter* by J. K. Rowling		

(*Continued*)

Timeline

Date	Turkish Literature	World Literature and Culture	Turkish History and Politics	World History, Science and Politics
1998	*Benim Adım Kırmızı (My Name is Red)* by Orhan Pamuk			
1999	*Uzun Hikâye* by Mustafa Kutlu Romantic Communist: The *Life and Work of Nâzım Hikmet* by Saime Göksu and Edward Timms	*Disgrace* by J. M. Coetzee		

Timeline

Date	Turkish Literature	World Literature and Culture	Turkish History and Politics	World History and Politics
2000				
2001	*Kötü Çocuk Türk* by Nurdan Gürbilek			September 11 attacks
2002	*Kar (Snow)* by Orhan Pamuk *Allahın Süngüleri (The Bayonets of Allah)* by Attila İlhan			
2003				
2004	*Kör Ayna, Kayıp Şark* by Nurdan Gürbilek *Kadınlar Dile Düşünce* by Jale Parla and Sibel Irzık		The European Union (EU) agreed to begin negotiations on the eventual accession of Turkey	
2005	*Ben Buradayım…: Oğuz Atay'ın Biyografik ve Kurmaca Dünyası (I am Here…: Oğuz Atay's Universe Between Biography and Fiction)* by Yıldız Ecevit *The Age of Beloveds: Love and the Beloved in Early Modern and European Culture and Society* by Mehmet Kalpaklı and Walter G. Andrews			
2006		Announcement of the 2006 Nobel Prize in Literature to Orhan Pamuk		
2007				
2008				
2009				
2010				
2011				
2012				
2013				
2014				
2015				
2016				
2017				
2018				
2019				
2020				
2021				

INDEX

Abasıyanık, S.F. 171
'Abd al-Baķi Chelebi 120
Abdülhak Hamid 127
Abdülhalim Memduh 224
Adıvar 142, 244
Ağaoğlu, A. 140, 174, 179n1, 180n4, 327–8, 338n1, 347–8, 365n1
Ahmed, S. 179, 182n39
Aḥmedī 22
Ahmed Paşa 24, 72
Ahmedzade, H. 210
Ahmet Mithat Efendi 8, 127, 129–31, 154, 188–92, 205, 207n27, 236–7, 249, 275, 280
Akabi Hikâyesi see Vartanyan, H.
AKP (Justice and Development Party) 13, 358, 364, 365n1
Alan, R. 210–11, 218n2
Aleppo 34, 73
Alexander the Great 22–3
'Alī ibn Abī Ṭālib 106
Ali Suavi 190
allegory 7, 47, 77, 80n21; characteristics of 83–4, 89; in European literature 82; types in Ottoman literature 84–7
Alpay, N. 210
Altan, Ç. 333, 337–8; *Büyük Gözaltı* 12, 333, 336–8
Anatolia 30, 35, 41, 72, 76, 202, 229–30, 238–9, 242, 247, 263, 285, 289; Islamization of 3, 41; languages of 2–3, 30–1, 40, 66n12, 187–93, 193n2, 228; literary production 1, 5–7, 9, 29, 41, 70, 75, 77, 78n2, 226; migrants to 250–3, 258; and social class 303, 344–6, 356
Anatoli (newspaper) 9, 188; serialized novels 189–91; subscribers 191–3
Anderson, B. 247, 249

Andrews, W. xi, 5, 61–2, 64, 71, 74, 78, 118, 139, 145, 150–1, 160
Ankara 238, 263, 311, 326
Apaydın, T. 304
Arabic: alphabet 108, 187, 199, 204, 217; influence on Turkish language and literature 3, 21, 70, 117, 192, 226, 257, 259, 262; language 2, 13, 30, 53n23, 53n40, 107, 109, 120–1, 123, 153, 160, 188, 192, 211–12, 215; literary genres 4, 6, 7, 25, 31, 45, 60–2, 66n13, 72, 84–5, 117, 119, 161, 198
Arif, A. 213, 218
Armenian: Catholic-Orthodox tensions 199–201, 207n22; genocide 145, 361; involvement in theatre 236; language 2, 6, 200, 212; literature 3, 9–10, 34–5, 66n12, 145–6; novel 198–206; people 31, 130, 215, 326
Armeno-Turkish 9–10, 145, 187–8, 199, 201, 203–5, 206n15, 232
Asaf, B. 260–1
Aşık Çelebi 14n9, 23, 34, 72–3, 75, 77, 149
Aşık Garip 32, 35
aşık literature 6, 34, 36n1; in Armenian and Georgian 34; connection to literacy 31–2; marginality of 33–4; and milieu 32–3; and ozan poetry 29–30, 35; and Sufi practices 35; syllabic meter 29
Aşık Ömer 34–5
Âşıkpaşazâde 31
Āsiye Ḫātūn 24
Atatürk 91, 237–239, 242, 256, 258, 259, 291, 350, 357
Atay, O. 141, 143, 327–9, 365n1
Atılgan, Y. 327–8
'Attar, F. 47, 49

Index

Auerbach, E. 248–9, 263
'Ayşe Hubbî Hâtun 153, 155
Ayvazoğlu, B. 42
Azerbaijan 29, 31, 33–4, 41, 295, 326
Baki 73, 76, 78, 152, 155
Balıkçıyan, H. H. 9, 199, 201
Balkans 1, 6, 29, 33, 40–1, 70, 72, 139, 228, 232, 252
Banarlı, N. S. 231
Başgöz, İ. 29, 33
Baydar, O. 141
Baykurt, F. 304
Beauty and Love see Şeyh Galip
Bektaşi 41
Belge, M. xi, 145, 174–5, 351n3
Bener, V. O. 171, 327
Berman, M. 287
Bezirci, A. 170, 174–5
Bīḫ-i Çīnī 116, 119–23; *see also* translation, rewriting
biographical dictionaries *see tezkire*
biographical writing 140–1
book culture 107–9, 110n14, 127, 135
Book of Dede Korkut 31
Boratav, P. N. 34
Büchner, L. 98
Buck-Morss, S. 290
Burak, S. 143

Çalışlar, İ. 141
Çamlıbel, F. N. 238–40, 239
Cansever, E. 12, 309–10, 312–16, 319
Cappadocia 187, 195n28
Casanova, P. 211–12
Caucasus 6, 29, 31–4
Central Asia 3–6, 30, 33, 223, 227–32, 239, 261
Chagatai 84
China 85, 91n27, 288, 293–5, 322
Chodźko, A. 33–6
Cixous, H. 170, 179n2
Committee of Union and Progress (CUP) 246–7
communism 11, 141, 285–9, 292, 296n44, 321–2, 330n4, 335–6, 360
cönk (books) 24–5, 31–2, 35–6, 108
conspiracy theories 13, 355, 357; grammar of 354; as literary genre 13, 356, 361, 364, 365n1; and Turkish politics 358–60, 362
constitutional monarchy *see meşrutiyet*
Constructivism 286
coup: failed of 2016 13, 354, 364; and literature 4, 12, 175–6, 333–8; March, 12, 1971 333–4, 345, 358; May, 27 1960 334–5, 345, 349–50, 358; postmodern/soft coup 1997 336, 354, 356, 358, 364; September 12, 1980 335–6, 345, 358
Crimean War 203
Cumhuriyet Halk Partisi (Republican People's Party) 235, 237–8

Dadaloğlu 34
Damrosh, D. 1
Darwin, C. 98
de Certeau, M. 43
Deleuze, G. 211–12
dervish 86, 109, 151; orders 24, 53n13; poetry 31, 41
divan poetry xi, 145, 176, 226
dreams: in *aşık* literature 21–2; compilations 24; in heroic epics 21; interpretation of 23, 25; Islamic influence on 20–1; Joseph/Yusuf and Züleyḫa 20, 22; Prophet Muhammad's views on 20–1; Sufi influence on 21, 23; symbolic meanings 19–20; in travel accounts 24
Düssap, S. 140, 146

Ebüzziya Tevfik 127, 131–2, 135, 144
Edebiyat-ı Cedide 97, 271
Egypt 32, 301
Ekinci, Y. 211, 214, 217
Eliot, T.S. 312–13
Emine Semiye (Önasya) 133, 140
encyclopedia: as literary genre 2–4
Enlightenment 190, 272, 286, 305; Greek 189, 193
Epic of Oğuz Kağan 19, 22
Erbil, L. 12, 140–1, 143, 169, 170–5, 180n4, 180n13, 181n14, 181n15, 321, 326–8, 338n4
Erdoğan, A. 140–1, 143
Erdoğan, R. T. 365n2
Ertürk, N. 5, 294
Eurasia 6, 29, 30, 32, 35
Europe: Armenians in 200; and colonialism 11, 287–9, 293 (*see also* humanism); influence on Turkish culture 229–31, 236, 259–63, 286, 290–1, 324, 328–9, 335, 361; literary scholarship in 139, 143, 191, 223–7, 263; nationalism in 247; Ottoman encounter with 2–3, 107, 133, 202–5, 223, 230–1, 271–5, 278, 287, 293; poetics in 61; print culture 32, 188; *see also* allegory
Even-Zohar, I. 190, 264
Evliya Çelebi 5–6, 24

Fatma Aliye 133, 133n30, 140, 142, 146, 154
Fatma Fahrünnisa 127, 133–5
Fattāḫī of Nishabur 87–8
feminism 146, 361, 366n26; *see also* gender
Flaubert, G. 275
French: colonialism 289, 293; cultural influence 2, 130, 205, 230–1, 262, 272, 276, 301, 312, 321, 344; translations 132, 143, 188, 200, 337
Füruzan 339n18, 345–7
Futurism 11, 286–8, 290–1, 294
Fuzulî 30, 88–9, 155

Gandhi, Mahatma 141
Garip movement 311

Index

Gavriilidis, I. 190–2
gazel: development of 70; dissemination of 72–4; as game 75–8; and other genres 71, 160, 164; patronage 73; queerness in 74
Gellner, E. 258
gender: homosociality 7–8, 107, 150, 154, 157n9; norms 25, 171–3, 178–9, 334, 341n31, 361, 364; and the Ottoman literary public 2, 5, 7–9, 74, 107, 127, 133–5, 274; in Ottoman poetry 72, 149–54, 160; studies of 139–41, 144–6; subversion of 154–6, 169–70, 180n4
German literature 91n42, 132, 144, 243, 244n27, 258, 263, 289, 321, 324
Gezi Park protests 319
ghazal *see* gazel
Ghazzali 43–5, 150
Gibb, E.G.W. 4, 60, 63, 92n21
Goethe, J. W. 292
Gölpınarlı, A. 41
Gramsci, A. 235
Greek: classical period 83, 262; community in Ottoman Empire 29, 187, 189–90, 193, 195n28, 198–9; community in Turkish Republic 326, 350; language 2, 3, 9, 188–9, 192; literature 145–6, 189; script (*see* Karamanlidika)
Guattari, F. 211–12
Güntekin, R. N. 300
Günyol, V. 172, 189
gynocriticism 9, 169–70

Hacı Bektaş 41, 52n9
hadith 2, 4, 22, 105, 108
Hagen, G. 23
Halide Edip (Adıvar) 10, 28, 140–2, 158, 236, 242–3, 244n27, 263
Halit Ziya (Uşaklıgil) 11, 237, 249, 272, 279–81, 290–5
Halkevleri (Public Houses) 235–6
Halman, T. 4–5, 65n11, 144
Hamazkyats Ingerutyun (National Society) 203
Hâtemî 149
Havlioğlu, D. 5, 8–9, 72, 139, 160
Hayalî 75
Heath, P. 32–3, 82–3, 85, 91n17, 91nn22–3
Hegel, G.W.F. 13, 333–4
Hirschler, K. 32
Holbrook, V. 5, 157n6
humanism: European sources 256, 260; translation of classics 257–8; Turkish 261–4; use for Europeanization 260–1
Ḥüsn ü Aşk see Şeyh Galip
Ḥüsn ü Dil see Fattāḥī of Nishabur
Hutcheon, L. 226–30, 232
Ḥvāb-nāme (Book of Sleep) 22–3

Ibn Sīnā 84–5, 89
İhsan, A. 272, 274, 282n12

İkinci Yeni: critiques of 177, 181n20; dramatic poetry 309–11; fragmentation 312; urbanism 318–19
Ilgaz, R. 351
İlhan, A. 179n2, 339n13, 344, 348–50
İnalcık, H. 62–3, 67nn28–9
India 141, 262, 288, 293–4
intersectionality 139–40, 144, 160, 163
İntibah see Namık Kemal
İpekten, H. 62
Iran 6, 124n29, 158n37, 237; aşıks in 29–36
Isfahan 35
İshak Çelebi 75
Islam: allegory (*see* allegory); in Anatolia 3, 31, 41; and the city 30; cosmology 7, 71, 75, 105; importance of writing 7, 105–6, 110n4, 111n20; influence on dreams (*see* dreams); and Kurds 215; literary traditions 1, 2, 6, 61, 66n14, 95–6, 118, 150, 154, 161; mystical (*see* Sufis); pre- 6, 29; and reform 3, 190, 249, 256, 287; theology 94; Turkish 3, 42, 230
Islamism 3, 5–6, 42, 286, 294–5, 335–6, 339n11, 340n25, 354–60, 362–4, 365n11
Islamization 35, 40–1, 209
Istanbul 32, 34, 64, 72, 107, 109, 121, 130–1, 141, 155, 174, 187–92, 199–201, 203–4, 213, 216, 225, 247–9, 251, 253, 263, 272, 274, 278, 285, 289, 294, 300, 310, 313, 319, 324, 326, 339n19, 356–7
İttihat ve Terakki *see* Committee of Union and Progress (CUP)

Joyce, J. 8, 143, 210, 328

Kafadar, C. 30
Kahn, A. 13, 343
Kalpaklı, M. 5, 62, 64, 66n19, 67n29, 139, 144–5, 151, 157n9, 160
Kaplan, R. 299
Karacaoğlan 34, 37n21
Karamanlidika: community reception of literature 191; as language 187, 192, 193n2; publishing history 188–90, 193; secularization 191
Karasu, B. 327, 338n1, 340n2
Karnig, Gülünya ve Dikran'ın Dehşetlü Vefatleri see Balıkçıyan, H. H.
kaside: as interrelated texts 1, 7, 64–5; and patronage 6, 155, 634; scholarly assessments of 59–61, 71, 73–4
Kayacan, F. 181n13, 327
Kemalist: approach to literature 262–4; ideology 11, 237, 239, 258, 260, 294, 321, 358, 361; reforms and modernization 10, 235, 238, 243, 256–7, 362
Kemal, O. 300, 302, 304
Kemal, Y. 210–11, 213, 218, 300, 302, 304
Keshavarz, F. 51
Kim, S. 5, 63, 139

451

Index

Kısakürek, N. F. 286–7, 294
Kitab-ı Muḥammediyye see Yazıcıoğlu Mehmed
Kligerman, E. 12, 333
Koçak, O. 260, 309, 318
Köprülü, M.F. literary history 4, 10, 225–7, 229, 233; mystical literature 3, 29–30, 42, 229; on Ottoman literature 60, 144, 227–8; on Turkish literature 14n6, 228–31
Korean War 335, 349, 352n20
Köroğlu 32–6, 189, 239
Köse Mihal 23
Köy Enstitüleri (Village Institutes) 12, 264, 298, 302–5, 306n19
Kristeva, J. 179
Kurdish language: debates 209–11, 214; in Ottoman Empire 2–3, 145–6; publishing 10, 214–17; translations 211–19
Kurds: 1925 rebellion of 240–1; and nationalism 356, 358, 360, 365n11
Kutadgu Bilig 21, 25, 228

Lacan, J. 180n7
Lamartine, A. 96
language reform 3
Laṭīfī 23, 76–7
Lefevere, A. 8, 117–18
Le Roman de la Rose (Guillaume de Lorris) 82
Les Aventures de Télémaque 205
Lewis, C.S. 84
LGBTQI+ literatures 140–1, 144
literary historiography: consolidation 230–1; and ethnicity 224–5; nationalism 225–7, 239; Ottoman period 223–4; teleology 227–30

Maḥfī-i Gīlānī 119
mahlas (pen name) 76, 149
Mahmut Sadık 272–3, 282n9
Makal, M. 302–4
Margosyan, M. 214–15
Maruş, H. 10, 203; *Bir Sefil Zevce* 199, 203–4
masculinity 7–9, 74, 77, 140, 151–4, 156, 162, 169, 170, 173–4, 181n24, 337, 340n27, 341n31
Mayakovsky, V. 286, 296n28
meclis xi, 7–8, 63, 107, 139, 149, 158n41; women's participation in 150, 155–6
medrese 34, 41, 48, 217
Mehmet Emin Yurdakul 248
Mekhitarism 199–201, 207n22
Memleket Hikâyeleri see Refik Halit (Karay)
Menderes, A. 334–5, 339nn14–15, 352n20
Meriç, N. 169–75, 177–8, 180nn4–5, 182n37
mesnevi (mathnawi) 6–7, 41, 61, 65n10, 71, 73–4, 79n11, 157n6, 161, 165n7
meşrutiyet 109, 237, 240, 244n7, 253
Mevlevi (Mawlawī) *see* dervish
Mihrî Hatun: challenging of gender roles 139, 149, 152–5; within Ottoman literary history 5, 149–50

Millî Edebiyat 10–11, 231, 246–8, 321
minority literature: literary canon 145–6, 232–3; multilingual literatures 198
minor literature 210
Misailidis, E. 188–90
modernism: Anglo-American 312; and the individual 329; narrative strategies 321; and the novel 322–8; of underdevelopment 11, 287–8, 290–3; and urban space 309–10, 315–16
modernization: in Ottoman Empire 3, 93, 223–4, 257, 271; in Turkish Republic 7, 235–6, 256–7, 287, 298, 346, 348, 351
Mongols 30–1, 40, 229
Moralızâde Leylâ Hanım 153–4
Moran, B. 145, 299–300
Müʿeyyedzâde Abdurrahman Çelebi *see* Hâtemî
Muhammad 20–2, 24, 105, 361
Muhiddin, Nezihe 143, 146
Mungan, M. 214–18
Mustafa Kemal (Atatürk) 237–9, 242, 256, 258–9, 291, 349–50, 357, 360–1
Müteferrika, İ. 109
Mystères de Paris: translations 189

Nabizade Nazım 127, 131–2, 135, 249
Naci, F. 170, 177–8, 182n35
Namık Kemal 8, 127–9, 131, 135, 190, 207n28, 236, 249, 275
Nasreddin Hoca 161, 242–3, 244n26
nationalism: anti-colonial 289; Balkan 187; ethnic 355; and identity 252–4, 359, 362, 365n1; late Ottoman 246–8; and realism 11, 248–50; and translation 11, 256–8, 260–4; Turkish 209, 225, 259, 294, 329
National Literature *see* Millî Edebiyat
Nâzım Hikmet (Ran) 432, 433, 441: anti-imperialism 293–4; biography 141, 285, 289; as dissident 310, 321; influence by Futurism 11, 286–7, 290–92; *Jokond ile Si-Ya-U* 288–9, 322–3; *Memleketimden İnsan Manzaraları* 323; as modernist 12, 322; plays 10, 236, 241–3
Necatî 6–7, 59–60, 64, 72–3, 152
Nerval, G. 323–4, 330n10
Nezihe Muhiddin 143, 146
Nigâr Hanım 133, 155
Nigeria 301
North Africa 1
Norton, A. 252, 254
novel: 12 March (*see* coup); first in Turkish 3, 10, 199, 201, 204; intelligentsia narratives 13, 343–5, 351; Islamist 5, 336; and minorities (*see* Armeno-Turkish; Karamanlidika; Kurds); modernist (*see* modernism); Ottoman origins of 3, 10–11, 127–33, 135, 188–9, 224, 231, 271–2, 275, 305n1; place in literary criticism 141–2, 144–5; and politics 241, 298, 328–9, 333, 356, 360, 364, 365n1; postmodernist 12,

452

Index

140, 143, 175, 305, 326, 355, 357, 365n1; as
social reform 190–1, 275–6, 279, 298, 305,
321, 326, 343; storytelling techniques in the
8, 249, 254, 325, 346, 364; village (*see* village
novels); women writers (*see* women writers)
Nūr Allāh 119–20

Oğuz Kagan 19–20
Oğuzname 30–1
Oğuz Turks: origins of 19, 30–1
Oktay, A. 312
Oktay, İ. A. 365n1
Ömer Fūʾādi 86
Ömer Seyfettin: national imagination 10–11,
246–7, 250–4; realism 249–50; *see also* Millî
Edebiyat
Orkhon Inscriptions 4, 228
Osman Gazi 19–20
ozan *see* aşık literature
Özata Dirlikyapan, J. 171–2
Öz, E. 170, 172, 175
Özkırımlı, A. 170, 174, 176
Öztürk, V. 12, 176–7

Paker, S. 8, 117–18, 123
Pamuk, O.; *The Black Book* 363; as global
literature 5; and modernism 12, 327, 329,
365nn1–2 (*see also Snow* (novel)); *The New Life*
359; and Nobel Prize 1, 340n20; and politics
356, 360, 364; regionalism in 300; *Silent House*
340n22; translations 214, 216; trial against 361
panegyric *see* kaside
Parthé, K. F. 301–2
patronage 6, 8, 22, 30–1, 40, 60, 62–4, 66n24,
67n29, 73, 116, 139, 155; impact on translation
117–21, 123
peasants 31, 239, 263, 288–9, 299–304, 306n18,
347, 349
Persian: customs 2, 29; language 2–3, 13, 21,
30–1, 41, 70, 142, 151, 192, 211–12, 218n2,
226, 257, 262; literature 1–2, 4, 6, 31–2, 34–5,
47, 53n34, 60–3, 65n1, 66nn12–14, 66n21,
78n2, 83–5, 91n42, 108, 117, 119–22, 150,
158n40, 161, 229, 232, 259, 262
poetics 2, 5–8, 12, 61, 73, 77, 116–19, 122–3,
150, 157n5, 294, 309, 312, 322, 328n4
positivism 224, 280
postmodernism 12, 140, 143, 175, 305, 326, 355,
357, 365n1

qasida see kaside
Qurʾān 2, 4, 7, 19–20, 45, 53n32, 105–9,
118, 122

Recaizâde Mahmud Ekrem 95–7, 127, 156,
237, 344
Refik Halit (Karay) 11, 247–50, 254

Reşit Galip 238
Romanticism 95–6, 204–5, 329n2
Rumi 22, 41, 43, 47, 49, 51, 52n7, 53n34,
54n48, 89, 119, 151
Rum *see* Greek
Russia 13, 33, 141, 212, 243, 248, 258, 262, 287,
289, 291–5, 301–2, 343, 351n3

Safa, P. 344
Safavid Empire 2, 29, 31, 343
Şair Nigar 140
Samancı, S. 211, 213–17
Samipaşazade Sezai 142
Sarı Saltuk 41
şaṭhiyye 45, 53n27
Sayat Nova 34
Second Constitutional Period *see* meşrutiyet
Second New *see* İkinci Yeni
Selçuk Empire 30–1, 244n26
Serbest Cumhuriyet Fırkası (Liberal Republican
Party) 237
Servet-i Fünun (magazine): conception of
individual 271–2, 274; coverage 272; criticisms
280–81; and science 272–5; serial novels 277;
women's fashion 277–8
Seyahatname (travel narrative) 24
Seyhan, A. 5, 145, 305n1
Şeyh Galip 5, 14n20, 82, 85, 88–9, 92n46, 152,
157n6
Şeyhî 72, 76
Shakespeare, W. 8, 144, 201, 243, 363
Sidar, İ. 210–11
Silay, K. 5, 157n5
Şinasi 127, 136n14, 190, 236
Snow (novel): absent texts within 356–7;
conspiracy in 13, 340n26, 354–5, 361; parody
358–60; as political novel 356–9
socialist realism 9, 11–12, 169–70, 174–8,
181n20, 298, 304–5, 306n3, 321
Soviet Union 141, 232, 291, 294, 326; as the
"East" 286, 292; internationalism 289, 293;
technology 287, 290; writers in 285
Soysal, S. 140–1, 169–70, 175–7, 180n4, 181n24,
181n27, 182n34, 338n1, 339n17, 351
Spenser, E. 82, 91n16
Spitzer, L. 263
Suat Derviş 143
Sufis 6, 21, 36n1, 40, 42–4, 46, 48, 53n42,
94, 109, 151; lodges 29, 33, 35, 41;
poetry 30, 61, 65n11, 72, 229; views on
dreams 20–5
Süleyman, Ş. 227–8
Sultan Abdülmecid 203
Sultan Ahmed I 22–3
Sultan Bayezid II 59, 64, 66n19, 158n35
Sultan Mehmed II 23, 64, 188
Sultan Murad III 23–4

453

Index

Sultan Süleyman 73, 155
Surūrī Muṣliḥ al-Dīn Muṣṭafā 116, 119–23
Syria 32, 34, 112n28

Tacizade Ca'fer Çelebi 64, 66n19
Tahir, K. 179, 302, 304
Taine, H. 97
Taner, H. 12, 321, 324–5
Tanpınar, A.H. 12, 74, 91n27, 141, 143, 145, 179n2, 320–1, 323–4, 328, 365n1
Tanzimat 93, 190, 209, 231–2, 235–7, 240, 243, 261, 321, 329, 329n1, 344, 351n4
Tapduk Emre 41, 49
Tekin, L. 140, 143, 145, 146n8, 327
Temaşa-i Dünya ve Cefakâr u Cefakeş see Misailidis, E.
Tercüman-ı Hakikat (newspaper) 94, 133
Tevfik Fikret: early poems 93–5, 327; editorial work 272; melancholy 96–7; profane themes in 95–6, 282n9; and science 7, 98–9, 273, 287, 294
tezkire 4, 10, 14n9, 23, 60, 72, 223–5, 227–8
theatre: opposition in 239–40, 243; Ottoman period 127, 136n14, 161, 236–7; as propaganda tool 235–6, 243, 356, 361–3; Republican period 145–6, 237–9
Topkapı Palace 73, 149
translation: contextual impacts 117–18; into English 4, 5, 14n20; of Greek philosophy 83 (*see also* Karamanlidika; Kurdish); modern Western literature into Turkish 312, 365n1; and nationalism 10–11, 256–8, 260–5; Ottoman practices in classical period 4, 25, 85, 116–17; of religious learning 7, 40–1; as retranslation 122–3; as rewriting 88, 118, 189–90
Translation Bureau 190, 264
Turcophone Greeks *see* Karamanlidika
Türkali, V. 214, 216, 339n13, 351
Turkic: heroic epics 22; peoples in Turkish nationalism 10, 209, 225, 228–9, 232–3; post-Soviet nations 232
Turkification 31, 41, 209
Turkish Language Association (Türk Dil Kurumu) 3, 237
"Turkishness" 2–3, 42, 248, 260, 359, 361

Ünaydın, Ruşen Eşref 246
Urdu 1, 83–4, 150

Uşaklıgil 11, 249, 272, 282
Uyar, T. 12, 309–11, 315–19
Uyghur 228, 295
Uzun, M. 210–11, 213

Vâ-Nû (Ahmed Vâlâ Nûreddin) 289, 294
Vartanyan, H. 9, 188, 199–201
Veli, O. 294, 311
village novels: debates and criticism 303–5; influence on theater 239; origins and definitions 298–300; and state projects 303; in world literature 300–2
villagers *see* peasants

War of Independence 239–40, 242, 258, 285, 290, 310, 349
westernization 93, 191, 236, 256–2, 294–5, 321, 329; critiques of 343–4, 347
wiles of women narratives 9, 161–5
women, representations of 161, 277–9; *see also* gender
women writers: and the critique of patriarchy 171–7, 180n4; in the literary canon 140–1, 169–70; in the Ottoman Empire 8, 9, 133–4, 145–6, 153–4; publication of 8, 143, 146
Workers' Party of Turkey (TİP) 337
world literature 1–5, 216, 233, 257, 262–4, 300, 354–5
World War I 2, 246, 250–1, 254n11, 289–90, 310
World War II 243, 264, 310, 349

Yakup Kadri (Karaosmanoğlu) 10, 236, 240, 243, 258, 260–1, 300, 344
Yazıcıoğlu, Mehmed 7, 24, 108
Yazıcıoğlu Ali 30
Yesayan, Zabel 140, 145–6
Yücel, H. A. 257
Yunus Emre: *Divan* 41; life of 40–2; and poetry and meaning 47–50; reception in Republican period 6, 42, 229; *Risaletü'n-Nushiyye* 41–2; selfhood and language 43–7; vernacular language 31, 228
Yurdakul, Mehmet Emin 248

Zafer Hanım 133, 140
Zatî 5, 63–4, 139
Ziya Paşa 66n13, 190, 287